Britain's Pacification

MW00804357

In this complete military history of Britain's pacification of the Arab revolt in Palestine, Matthew Hughes shows how the British Army was so devastatingly effective against colonial rebellion. The Army had a long tradition of pacification to draw upon to support operations, underpinned by the creation of an emergency colonial state in Palestine. After conquering Palestine in 1917, the British established a civil Government that ruled by proclamation and, without any local legislature, the colonial authorities codified in law norms of collective punishment that the Army used in 1936. The Army used 'lawfare,' emergency legislation enabled by the colonial state, to grind out the rebellion. Soldiers with support from the RAF launched kinetic operations to search and destroy rebel bands, alongside which the villagers on whom the rebels depended were subjected to curfews, fines, detention, punitive searches, demolitions, and reprisals. Rebels were disorganised and unable to withstand the power of such pacification measures.

MATTHEW HUGHES is Chair in Military History at Brunel University.

Cambridge Military Histories

Edited by

HEW STRACHAN, Professor of International Relations, University of St Andrews and Emeritus Fellow of All Souls College, Oxford

GEOFFREY WAWRO, Professor of Military History, and Director of the Military History Center, University of North Texas

The aim of this series is to publish outstanding works of research on warfare throughout the ages and throughout the world. Books in the series take a broad approach to military history, examining war in all its military, strategic, political and economic aspects. The series complements *Studies in the Social and Cultural History of Modern Warfare* by focusing on the 'hard' military history of armies, tactics, strategy and warfare. Books in the series consist mainly of single author works – academically rigorous and groundbreaking – which are accessible to both academics and the interested general reader.

A full list of titles in the series can be found at:
www.cambridge.org/militaryhistories

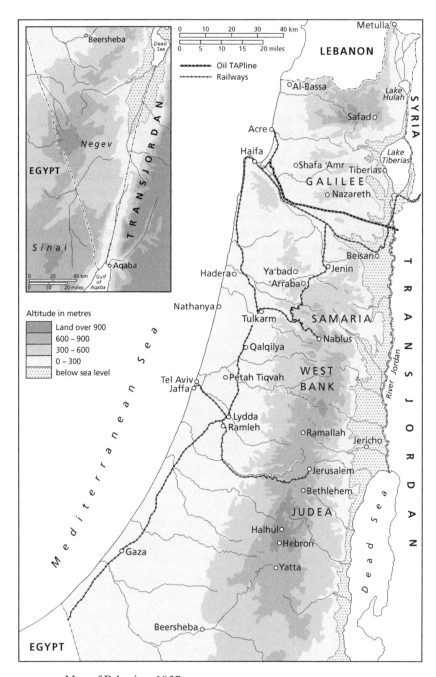

Map of Palestine, 1937

Britain's Pacification of Palestine

The British Army, the Colonial State, and the Arab Revolt, 1936–1939

Matthew Hughes

Brunel University

CAMBRIDGE
UNIVERSITY PRESS

CAMBRIDGE
UNIVERSITY PRESS

University Printing House, Cambridge CB2 8BS, United Kingdom

One Liberty Plaza, 20th Floor, New York, NY 10006, USA

477 Williamstown Road, Port Melbourne, VIC 3207, Australia

314-321, 3rd Floor, Plot 3, Splendor Forum, Jasola District Centre, New Delhi - 110025, India

79 Anson Road, #06-04/06, Singapore 079906

Cambridge University Press is part of the University of Cambridge.

It furthers the University's mission by disseminating knowledge in the pursuit of education, learning and research at the highest international levels of excellence.

www.cambridge.org
Information on this title: www.cambridge.org/9781107501492
DOI: 10.1017/9781316216026

© Matthew Hughes 2019

This publication is in copyright. Subject to statutory exception and to the provisions of relevant collective licensing agreements, no reproduction of any part may take place without the written permission of Cambridge University Press.

First published 2019
First paperback edition 2020

A catalogue record for this publication is available from the British Library

Library of Congress Cataloging in Publication data
Names: Hughes, Matthew.
Title: Britain's pacification of Palestine : the British Army,
the colonial state, and the Arab revolt, 1936–1939 / Matthew Hughes.
Description: Cambridge : Cambridge University Press, 2019. |
Series: Cambridge military histories
Identifiers: LCCN 2018039214 | ISBN 9781107103207 (hardback) |
ISBN 9781107501492 (paperback)
Subjects: LCSH: Palestine–History–1917–1948. |
Counterinsurgency–Palestine–History–20th century. |
Mandates–Palestine–History–20th century. | Palestine–Politics and
government–1917–1948. | Great Britain–Foreign relations–Palestine. |
Palestine–Foreign relations–Great Britain. |
Imperialism–History–20th century. |
BISAC: HISTORY / Military / General.
Classification: LCC DS126.H82 2019 | DDC 956.94/04–dc23
LC record available at https://lccn.loc.gov/2018039214

ISBN 978-1-107-10320-7 Hardback
ISBN 978-1-107-50149-2 Paperback

Cambridge University Press has no responsibility for the persistence or accuracy of URLs for external or third-party internet websites referred to in this publication, and does not guarantee that any content on such websites is, or will remain, accurate or appropriate.

For KH

The irregular report of the firing squad would be heard, sometime followed by a single finishing shot; a little bluish cloud of smoke would float up above the green bushes, and the Army of Pacification would move on over the savannahs, through the forests, crossing rivers, invading rural pueblos, devastating the haciendas of the horrid aristocrats, occupying the inland towns in the fulfilment of its patriotic mission, and leaving behind a united land wherein the evil taint of Federalism could no longer be detected in the smoke of burning houses and the smell of spilt blood.

Joseph Conrad, Nostromo: A Tale of the Seaboard (1904), p. 114

Contents

Figures

Acknowledgements

The author completed much of the research for this book during his tenure of the Major-General Matthew C. Horner Distinguished Chair in Military Theory held at the United States Marine Corps University, Quantico, Virginia, funded by the Marine Corps University Foundation through the gift of Mr and Mrs Thomas A. Saunders, and supported by the Gray Research Center at the Marine Corps University. The author thanks the Saunders family, and General Thomas V. Draude, Colonel John Hales, and Dr Jerre Wilson at the Marine Corps Foundation and University. The author owes debts of gratitude to the following individuals for their advice and support: Dr Amal al-Abduljaffar, Dr Nir Arielli, Shlomi Chetrit, Professor W. G. Clarence-Smith, Professor David French, Mohamed Gaballa, the late Bahjat Abu Gharbiyya (and his son, Sami), Joshua Goodman, Dr Bruce Gudmundsson, Dr Eldad Harouvi, Edward Horne, Sabri Jiryis, General Sir Frank Kitson, Dr John Knight, Professor Mark Neocleous, Professor Laila Parsons, Daniel Perry, Najat al-Rahy, Professor Matthew Seligmann, Professor Yigal Sheffy, Dr Wayne Sullivan, Debbie Usher, Dr Steven Wagner, and Dr Daniel Whittingham. The author gives special regard to Dr Itamar Radai for his advice on the text and for the transliteration of Arabic and Hebrew. Dr Simon Innes-Robbins read and commented on the manuscript. The following individuals kindly gave access to privately held papers: Christobel Ames-Lewis and Philip Keith-Roach (civil administrator Edward Keith-Roach), the late Prunella Briance (police officer John Briance), Owen Humphrys (Field Marshal Lord Wavell), and John Robertson (police officer Raymond Cafferata). Rachel Lev gave exceptional access to the American Colony Hotel archive in Jerusalem. Illustrations from the American Colony Hotel Archive used herein are from the 'Arab Revolt in Palestine Photograph Albums 1936–39' and the 'Scrapbook of Articles about the American Colony, Palestine, People and Events and Loose Enclosures, 1938–39' and credit is due photographers Eric G. Matson and John D. Whiting. Dr Dov Gavish gave freely the

RAF aerial photographs of the British Army's destruction of old Jaffa reproduced here. Michael Watson at Cambridge University Press and the three anonymous referees supported the production of this book. The author acknowledges the many British regimental museums and local archives that hosted him on research trips, sent research material, and replied to later queries. The British Academy, Brunel University, and the Marine Corps University Foundation funded research in Jordan, Israel, Lebanon, Saudi Arabia, the USA, and in UK regimental archives. The author reproduces material from the Liddell Hart Centre for Military Archives with permission of its trustees. He claims any inaccuracies.

Matthew Hughes
Quantico, Virginia
Islington, London

Abbreviations and Glossary

A/	Acting
ACHA	American Colony Hotel Archive, Jerusalem
ACM	Air Chief Marshal
ADC	Assistant District Commissioner or aide-de-camp
'Agal	See *Iqal*
AHC	Arab Higher Committee formed 25 April 1936, properly Supreme Arab Committee, *al-Lajnah al-'Arabiyyah al-'Ulya*
AL-KR	Papers of Edward Keith-Roach in possession of Christobel Ames-Lewis and Philip Keith-Roach
AOC	Air Officer Commanding, supreme British RAF military commander in Palestine
Arab Party	Palestine Arab Party, synonymous in British files with the *Majlis* (the Council, see below) but the party was not identical to the *Majlis*. The Husaynis controlled both the party and the *Majlis*
Askari	Black African soldier or police officer, from *'Askari*, the Arabic for soldier
ASP	Assistant Superintendent Police
Auxiliaries	Para-military unit of former British military officers deployed during the Irish War of Independence (1919–21)
Awqaf	See *waqf*
Bayan	Statement/declaration/report or a communiqué issued by rebel forces in this book but can refer to a Government or any other statement, plural *bayanat*
Bde	Brigade of around 3,500 men, usually comprising three to four battalions

BIO	Brigade or Battalion Intelligence Officer
BL	British Library, London
Black and Tans	Temporary constables (often former British soldiers) attached to the Royal Irish Constabulary as a special reserve force during the Irish War of Independence (1919–21), many of whom then went to Palestine to fill the police force ranks there
BLARS	Bedfordshire and Luton Archives and Record Service, Bedford
Bn	Army battalion of around 800 soldiers comprising three (sometimes four) rifle companies plus support and HQ companies
BP	Papers of John Briance (formerly) in possession of Prunella Briance
Brig	Brigadier
BRM	Border and King's Own Royal Border Regiment Museum, Carlisle
C-in-C	Commander-in-Chief
CID	Criminal Investigation Department
CIGS	Chief of the Imperial General Staff (the head of the British Army before 1964)
CO	Colonial Office/Commanding Officer
COIN	Counter-insurgency
Col	Colonel or an Army column, the latter a unit somewhere between a platoon and a company
Council, The	See *Majlis*
Coy	Army company of around 150 soldiers, usually of three platoons plus a company headquarters
CP	Papers of Raymond Cafferata in possession of John Robertson, now stored in the Middle East Centre, Oxford
Cpl	Corporal
CUP	Cambridge University Press
CWGC	Commonwealth War Graves Commission
CZA	Central Zionist Archives, Jerusalem
DC	District Commissioner
Defence Party	Nashashibi-controlled National Defence Party linked to the *al-Mua'rada* Opposition (see below)
DIG	Deputy Inspector General (Palestine Police)
DIS	Daily Intelligence Summary

DMO	Director of Military Operations
DSO	Defence Security Officer (of SIME) or Distinguished Service Order
DSP	District Superintendent Police
Effendi	Ottoman courtesy title used by the British to describe local Arab notables and merchants of high social standing or education, and used by Arabs to address middle- and upper-class gentlemen
EOKA	Cypriot insurgent organisation Ethniki Organosis Kyprion Agoniston (National Organisation of Cypriot Fighters)
ERMC	Essex Regiment Museum Chelmsford
ESRO	East Sussex Record Office, Brighton
ETA	Basque insurgent organisation Euskadi Ta Askatasuna (Basque Country and Freedom)
Etzel	From *Irgun Zvai Leumi* (National Military Organisation), revisionist Jewish military and political group, sometimes abbreviated to *Etzel*
Fasa'il	Palestinian rebel bands, platoons or units (literally 'groups' or 'sections,' sometimes 'factions') singular *fasil* whose numbers varied but could comprise up to 200 fighters
Fasa'il al-salam	Peace bands, referring in this book to anti-rebel Government- and Nashashibi-backed armed bands
Fasad	A blood feud or a long-running quarrel, literally 'corruption,' usually between two or more rival clans, akin to a 'vendetta' in English
Faz'a	Call for help in war, reinforcements or (colloquially) people called for help in a quarrel
Fellahin/fallahin	Arab rural peasants, singular fella/fallah
Fez	See *tarbush*
Field officer	Military officer of major, lieutenant-colonel or colonel rank
Fitna	Arabic for a clash or problem between two individuals or groups (plural *fitan*), or a trial, in classical Arabic from the *Quran* 'sedition,' traditionally between Sunnis and Shias but could encompass sectarian clashes between Muslims and Christians or a succession crisis in Islam, and in this book denotes clan-based

	Palestinian (usually Husayni–Nashashibi) family clashes; attractive people can cause *fitna* with their beauty
FM	Field Marshal
FO	Foreign Office
FOSH	Jewish military field companies
Ghaffir	A village or settlement guard
GHQ	British military General Headquarters based in Jerusalem
GOC	General Officer Commanding, supreme British Army military commander in Palestine
HA	Haganah Archive, Tel Aviv
Haganah	Jewish defence force (literally 'The Defence')
Hamula	Arab/Palestinian patrilineal clan or extended family, plural *hama'il* (*hamulot* in Hebrew)
al-Haram al-Sharif	The Muslim 'noble sanctuary' (or Dome of the Rock/Temple Mount) in Jerusalem's old city
Hashomer	Used to describe a Jewish guard, derived from the name of a Jewish paramilitary organisation of the late Ottoman period (literally 'the watchman')
Hatta	See *Kufiyya*, a colloquial word for traditional Palestinian headdress, plural *hittat* or *hattat*
Histadrut	Jewish Labour Federation founded in 1920, *Ha-Histadrut* in Hebrew (The Histadrut) to acknowledge its importance
HLC	Haifa Labour Council
HMA	Haifa Municipal Archive
HMSO	His/Her Majesty's Stationery Office
IED	Improvised Explosive Device (i.e., a roadside mine)
IG	Inspector-General (Palestine Police)
Inf	Infantry
IOR	India Office Records, African and Asian Library, British Library
IPC	Iraq Petroleum Company
IPS	Institute for Palestine Studies, Beirut and Washington, DC
Iqal	The cord around traditional Palestinian peasant headdress
IRA	Irish Republican Army
ISA	Israel State Archive, Jerusalem

'Isabat	Singular *'isaba*, bands or gangs in Arabic, see Oozlebarts
Istiqlal	Palestinian 'Independence' Party formed in 1932
IWMD	Imperial War Museum, London, Department of Documents
IWMFA	Imperial War Museum, London, Film Archive
IWMSA	Imperial War Museum, London, Sound Archive
J&EM	Jerusalem and the East Mission of the Christian Anglican Diocese of Jerusalem, papers held at the Middle East Centre, St Antony's Oxford
Jihad	'Struggle' or 'striving' in Arabic but in a religious context a 'holy war,' properly *al-Jihad al-Muqaddas* meaning a Muslim holy (or sacred) war
JMA	Jerusalem Municipal Archive
JRL	John Rylands Library, Manchester
KCB	Knight Commander of the Order of the Bath
Kibbutz (im)	Jewish settlement(s), those living there being kibbutzniks
KMM	The Keep Military Museum, Dorchester, Dorset
KORRM	King's Own Royal Regiment Museum, Lancaster
KOSB	King's Own Scottish Borderers
KRI	King's Royal Irish
Kufiyya	Traditional Palestinian peasant turban-style headdress (plural *kufiyyat*), also worn by some *Mizrahi* Jews. Yasir Arafat adopted the black and white chequered *kufiyya* as a Palestinian national symbol in the 1960s
L/Cpl	Lance Corporal
LAL	Lincolnshire Archives, Lincoln
Lewis gun	British portable machine gun weighing 28 pounds, widely used in Palestine by the Army and police; soldiers in Palestine also used the newer Bren gun
LHCMA	Liddell Hart Centre for Military Archives, King's College London
Lira	Can refer to the Ottoman pound currency in use in Palestine to 1917 or the Egyptian pound in use in Palestine from 1917 to 1927, and used in the 1930s in Hebrew-language files to refer to the Palestine pound

LP	Palestine pound, from *libra pondo*, Latin for a pound by weight
Lt	Lieutenant
Maj	Major
Majlis	*al-Majlis al-Islami al-A'la* (the Supreme Muslim Council or properly the Islamic Supreme Council) or 'Council' and controlled by the Husaynis who were also in charge of the Palestine Arab Party, with *majlisiyyun/majlisi* being 'people of the council.' The British used 'Majlis' synonymously with the Palestine Arab Party and the Husayni family
MC	Military Cross
MEC	Middle East Centre, St Antony's College, Oxford
MI5	British domestic security intelligence agency responsible for security in British colonies such as Mandate Palestine
MI6	See SIS
Mils	Palestine coinage, 1,000 to the Palestine Pound
Mista'arvim	Hebrew slang of the Arabic *Musta'aribun* (literally 'Arabised'), usually applied to Jews who masqueraded as Arabs for intelligence or sabotage purposes
Mizrahi	Eastern (Oriental) or 'Arab' Jew, plural *mizrahim*
al-Mua'rada	The Opposition (Nashashibi controlled) in charge of the National Defence Party, although the two were distinct. The British used Opposition and Defence Party synonymously to denote Nashashibi-led opposition to the revolt and the Husaynis
Mufti	In this book the chief Muslim cleric in Jerusalem, Hajj Amin al-Husayni. More generally, an Islamic jurist scholar and in the Ottoman era each city had its own Mufti, answerable to Istanbul; since the British conquest of Palestine the Mufti of Jerusalem became the 'Grand Mufti of Palestine,' the chief Muslim cleric in the country. Also slang for a British (uniformed) Serviceman in civilian clothes

Mujahideen	Muslims engaged in jihad, used in the 1930s to describe the Arab fighters of the struggle (or holy war) in Palestine, singular mujahid
Mukhtar	Headman/mayor/leader of a village or urban quarter (literally 'chosen one'), larger conurbations having more than one, plural properly *makhatir* not *mukhtars*, and used also by the British to denote the secretary of a Jewish kibbutz or head of a Jewish village or township. In Jewish settlements the *mukhtar* was sometimes not in overall control but was an Arabic speaker in charge of liaison with and collecting intelligence on Palestinian neighbours
NAM	National Army Museum, London
NARA II	US National Archives and Records Administration, College Park, Maryland
National Defence Party	Or Defence Party, Nashashibi-controlled political party, see *al-Mua'rada*
NCO	Non-commissioned officer (a sergeant or a corporal)
Noter	Jewish watchman or guard, plural *notrim*, sometimes used to describe a Jewish supernumerary police officer
OBE	Officer of the Order of the British Empire
OC	Officer-in-Charge/Commanding
Oozlebarts	Military slang for rebels from Arabic plural for gangs 'ursabat' wrote former British policeman, Ted Horne, so probably from the Arabic word for insurgents or guerrillas *'isabat*, singular *'isaba*, meaning gangs or bands, with men on operations talking of 'oozlebarting' or 'oozling'[1]
Opposition, The	See *al-Mua'rada*
OUP	Oxford University Press
Palestine Arab Party	See Arab Party and *Majlis*
Palestine pound	See currency details in Appendix F
Passia	Palestinian Academic Society for the Study of International Affairs
PCP	Palestine Communist Party

---

[1] Edward Horne, *A Job Well Done (Being a History of the Palestine Police Force, 1920–1948)* (Tiptree: Anchor Press, 1982), p. 228.

Piastre	Egyptian currency in use in Palestine, 1917–27, of 100 piastres to the Egyptian pound
Platoon	Military unit of around forty men commanded by an officer, usually three platoons to a company
PLL	Palestine Labour League formed in 1932 as the Arab branch of *Histadrut*. In Hebrew *Brit Poa'lei Eretz Yisrael* (League of Workers of the Land of Israel), in Arabic *Ittihad 'Ummal Filastin* (Union of the Workers of Palestine)
PLO	Palestine Liberation Organisation
POH	Papers of Lord Wavell in joint custody of Owen Humphrys
Pte/Pvt	Private
QLRM	Queen's Lancashire Regiment Museum, Fulwood Barracks, Preston (now the Lancashire Infantry Museum)
QRWS	Queen's Royal West Surrey Regiment
RAFM	RAF Museum Hendon
ROLLR	Record Office for Leicestershire, Leicester and Rutland, Leicester
RTR	Royal Tank Regiment
RUR	Royal Ulster Rifles, regimental archive at Waring Street, Belfast
RYM	The Prince of Wales's Own Regiment of Yorkshire Museum, York
Sangar	A temporary military position usually made from raised stonework (also spelt sanger)
Sarafand	Or Surafend or Sarafend, large British military base on Palestine's coastal plain three miles from Ramleh, now an Israeli military base
Section	A military unit of around eight men (in the US a squad) commanded by a corporal, usually three (sometimes four) sections to a platoon
Shai	*Sherut Yedi'ot* (Information Service), Jewish intelligence and counter-intelligence branch of Haganah founded 1940, superseded in 1948 by new Israeli intelligence services but authors and Haganah archival material mark material from before 1940 as *Shai*
SHC	Surrey History Centre, Woking

SIME	British Security Intelligence Middle East (formed after 1937) under which served Defence Security Officers, part of the international arm of MI5 with a DSO in Palestine[2]
SIS	British Secret Intelligence Service (or MI6) agency for espionage abroad outside the British Empire
Slick/slik	A hidden weapons cache in a Jewish settlement, with *slickerit* being a female hiding weapons under her clothes
SNSs	Special Night Squads (led by British officer Orde Wingate)
SSO	RAF political-intelligence Special Service Officer
SUNY	State University New York
Suq/Souk	Market place or bazaar
Sûreté	Detective (CID) branch of the (Syrian and Lebanese) police
TAMA	Tel Aviv Municipal Archive
TAP(line)	The 585-mile-long pipeline from Iraq's Kirkuk oilfields across Transjordan and then Galilee to the Haifa refinery in Palestine (with a spur to Tripoli in French-run Lebanon) with pumping stations along the route marked H1 to H5; not to be confused with the Trans-Arabian pipeline built in the 1940s from Saudi Arabia to Sidon in Lebanon
Tarbush	Headdress (properly a head covering) synonymous with what is known in the West as a fez, invariably in red
TJFF	Transjordan Frontier Force
TLSAC	Tameside Local Studies and Archive Centre, Ashton-under-Lyne
TNA	The UK National Archives, Kew, London
Tommy gun	US-made Thompson sub-machine gun but generically also used as a term for any sub-machine gun
Troopers	Signals codeword for the War Office, London

---

[2] Christopher Andrew, *The Defence of the Realm: The Authorized History of MI5* (London: Penguin, 2009), p. 138 dates this to 1937–38 while Eldad Harouvi to 1939 in his *Palestine Investigated: The Story of the CID of the Palestine Police Force, 1920–48* (Sussex: Academic Press, 2016), p. 251.

UP	University Press
Waqf	Muslim religious endowment, plural *awqaf*
WL	Weston Library, Oxford
WO	War Office
Yishuv	The Jewish community in Palestine (literally 'settlement'), with 'New' *Yishuv* often used to describe the modern Zionist society in the country that participated in the new Hebrew-speaking culture

Nomenclature

Ranks and titles for people discussed in this book are usually as they were at the time, excepting in the bibliography where they are typically those at the end of individuals' careers. The text refers to soldiers when referring to British armed forces, mindful that the RAF ran Palestine up to September 1936 and was heavily involved in intelligence work throughout the revolt; similarly, it uses at times Army and security forces interchangeably, when the latter encompassed the RAF, civil officials, the police, intelligence personnel (some from MI5, MI6 or CID), and Jewish and Palestinian supernumerary auxiliary units. Army regiments and battalions are synonymous in the text as a regiment in Palestine was a battalion of infantry as no regiment ever simultaneously deployed more than one of its battalions to the place. Regiments usually had two battalions, with one garrisoned at home and one serving abroad, so 1st Royal Ulster Rifles (or 1 RUR) in the text refers to the 1st Battalion of that regiment. Towns have more than 5,000 inhabitants, villages fewer than 5,000 people, with Jewish villages usually described as settlements, kibbutzim or colonies. Druze is both singular and plural, similarly Bedouin. The text omits diacritical marks when transliterating Arabic excepting the *ayn* (') and the *hamza* ('). The use of square or round brackets after proper nouns for spelling or location is the author's sense of the correct form; the text includes the original spelling. The book uses Arabic and Hebrew rather than Anglicised forms for plural nouns, so *kufiyyat* not *kufiyyas*, *bayanat* not *bayans*, kibbutzim as plural for kibbutz, excepting some commonly occurring words such as *mukhtars* as the plural for *mukhtar* (the plural is properly *makhatir*) where the contemporary files make the sibilant plural. It uses Bayt ('house') (literary Arabic) and Beit (colloquial) for village names interchangeably. *Mizrahi* is both singular and plural (plural properly *Mizrahim*). The text renders 'Abdallah as the ruler of Transjordan to Abdullah. The author has differentiated between Palestinians (and, say, Syrians or Jordanians) and Arabs more generally where proper (or possible) in discussing rebel operations. The British usually spoke of fighting Arabs during the revolt and not Palestinians, partly because insurgent forces included men from places such as Syria. The book describes the Jewish community in Palestine, the *Yishuv*, as Jews and Jewish or, at times, settlers, as was the case at the time – Jews in the 1930s wrote in Hebrew of the Land of Israel – avoiding the label Zionists, except in the context of Zionism as a political movement. Not all Jews in Palestine were political Zionists, as was the case with some religious Jews and *Mizrahi* (and Sephardic) Oriental 'Arab' Jews who had been living for many years in the country. Identities shifted as violence increased and people took sides. Palestinians at the time of the 1929 riots spoke of new 'Zionist Jews' in the country, 'the new breed of Jew in the land,' in contrast to the older Jewish communities who were not recent arrivals from Europe.[1] The *Oxford Dictionary for Writers and Editors* has guided word style.

---

[1] Hillel Cohen, *Year Zero of the Arab–Israeli Conflict 1929* (Waltham, MA: Brandeis University Press, 2015), pp. 107, 158.

1   Framing the Arab Revolt

The Deaths of Zvi Danenberg and Israel Chazan, 15 April 1936

The Arab revolt from 1936 to 1939 – *al-Thawra al-Kubra*, 'the Great Revolt' in Arabic – was a popular uprising by Palestinians battling British Mandate rule in Palestine and Jewish immigration to the country.[1] An intense counter-insurgency pacification campaign and an immense deployment of British troops crushed the rebellion. This is the subject of the book. The spark for the revolt came on the evening of 15 April 1936 when Arab gunmen stopped a convoy of vehicles on the Nablus–Tulkarm road and shot three Jews in one of the vehicles, two of whom died. This was another outrage in the cycle of attacks and counter-attacks between Jews and Palestinians stretching back to 1920 but these deaths ignited a three-year nationwide rebellion. *Kufiyyat* hid the faces of the gunmen at the roadblock who demanded money and stole £P.275 and so it seemed that they were bandits there to rob the convoy.[2] In the cab of one truck there were two Jews, Zvi (or Tzvi) Danenberg (or Danenburg) in the driver's seat accompanied by Israel Chazan (or Hazan). Along the row of halted vehicles the gunmen asked who was Jewish, adding for the benefit of their victims: 'Go and inform the police and the press that we are robbing this money to purchase arms and take vengeance for the murder of the Holy Sheikh, Izza Din El Kassam.'[3] The gunmen were Qassamites (*Qassamiyyun*) of the Palestinian Black Hand band (*'Isabat al-Kaff al-Aswad*) proclaiming their allegiance to the late Muslim cleric, nationalist, and insurgent leader, Shaykh 'Izz al-Din al-Qassam, shot dead by British Palestine police in a gun battle at Ya'bad village near Jenin in November 1935. The armed band seized a Jew in a car, a man called

---

[1] The Army awarded the campaign clasp 'Palestine' to the medal ribbon for the General Service Medal (1918) for service, 19 April 1936–3 September 1939.

[2] *al-Liwa'* [*The Province*] (Jerusalem) (16 April 1936).

[3] The Murder of Chazan and Danenburg, pp. 1–2, S25/22765, CZA. This record informs the account here of the killings.

1

Nafchi, who was travelling with Knoll, a German Christian, and they forced Nafchi into the cab of the truck with Danenberg and Chazan. They left Knoll behind after he protested that he was not Jewish; in other such robberies, Jews had escaped by pretending to be Arabs.[4] The gunmen then shot point-blank the three Jews in the truck, Danenberg and Chazan fatally but neither died at once.[5] There is no record of what happened to the wounded Nafchi. The two fatally wounded men were taken to local hospitals and Chazan appears to have died the next day. The Palestinian press recorded the attack not as a bandit outrage but the work of anti-Jewish Qassamite fighters who killed three Jews.[6] Chazan's funeral was set for 17 April but the day before it was held gunmen shot two Arab workers occupying a hut on the highway between Petah Tikva and Yarkona. One of the two men, Hasan Abu Ras (Hassin Abu Ruz in Jewish files), died on the spot; the assassins mortally wounded the other man, Salim al-Masri, who died on the 17th. When the two men heard knocking at the door of their abode, Hasan Abu Ras 'had a premonition of ill and was afraid to open the door,' said al-Masri before he died.[7] The Arabic press suggested that the murders were Jewish *Etzel* revenge action for the earlier murders of Danenberg and Chazan. Jews argued that al-Masri thought the attackers to be Christians as they were bareheaded and dressed in khaki shorts and European jackets, or they could have been Arabs. The 'only basis for the suggestion that the assailants were Jews was apparently the fact that they were dressed in khaki shorts and jackets. It is submitted that this form of dress is not uncommon amongst the Arab workingmen of this particular neighbourhood.'[8] Jews pursued the defence that the attack was the work of fellow Arabs, pointing to Abu Ras being a 'notorious thief' known to the police who had informed on other Arabs a few days before being shot.[9] At Chazan's funeral in Tel Aviv on the morning of 17 April, as the cortege passed the Eliyahu Hanavi synagogue on Levinsky Street,[10] tempers flared when rumours spread

---

[4] Police HQ Haifa to DC Haifa, 28 March 1938, Scrivenor Papers, MSS. Brit. Emp. S. 377, p. 136, WL.

[5] Chazan died on the spot in some accounts: Abigail Jacobson and Moshe Naor, *Oriental Neighbors: Middle Eastern Jews and Arabs in Mandatory Palestine* (Waltham, MA: Brandeis University Press, 2016), p. 151.

[6] *al-Jami'a al-Islamiyya* [*The Islamic Community*] (Jaffa) (16 April 1936).

[7] The Murder of Chazan and Danenburg, p. 3, S25/22765, CZA; Matiel Mogannam, *The Arab Woman and the Palestine Problem* (London: Herbert Joseph, 1937), p. 293.

[8] The Murder of Chazan and Danenburg, p. 3, S25/22765, CZA.

[9] Ibid.

[10] According to the current list of the Central Rabbinate there are five synagogues called Eliyahu Hanavi in Tel Aviv, one of which is at 44 Levinsky Street or at 13 Zevulun Street at the crossroads of the two roads.

that Danenberg had also died. Jewish hotheads at the funeral shouted, 'let us go to Jaffa' to attack Palestinians there, some sang the Zionist (and later Israeli national) anthem *Hatikva*, and some raised flags, at which point the police intervened forcefully to disperse the crowd, injuring fifteen in the ensuing mêlée. Official accounts detailed three Jews killed in the first ambush and three more murdered in rioting on 17 April at one of the funerals.[11] Jews attacked Palestinians and vice versa in and around Tel Aviv during and after the funeral, and by 19 April 1936 a countrywide disturbance prompted by the killings on the 15th had erupted amongst Palestinians. Curiously, Chazan's grave in Tel Aviv's Trumpeldor Old Cemetery records that he died on 19 April while Danenberg's tombstone in the same place dates his death to the 20th, suggesting that they died as the revolt started.

The revolt symbolically started on 19 April 1936. It was the moment when Palestinians escalated and sustained countrywide attacks on the British and Jews, and began a general strike, organised by local National Committees, and directed centrally from 25 April by an Arab Higher Committee (AHC) standing for the six Palestinian political parties and the Husayni and Nashashibi family blocs, and whose composition is detailed in Appendix E. The British responded rapidly and decisively, forewarned by earlier outbreaks of violence between Jews and Palestinians in 1920, 1921, and 1929, and anti-British Palestinian riots in 1933, which presaged a recrudescence of inter-communal and anti-British trouble. On the same day, 19 April 1936, the British Palestine High Commissioner, General Sir Arthur Wauchope, using the powers vested in him by Article IV of the Palestine (Defence) Order in Council of 1931 issued the Emergency Regulations 1936 that formed the repressive legal basis for British counter-rebel measures, as will be seen in the next chapter.[12] The British also flooded the country with soldiers, mobilising and moving in troops to supplement Palestine's permanent garrison of two infantry battalions and RAF-manned armoured cars, as detailed in the order-of-battle appendix (Appendix A). The British called first on their Egyptian garrison, but the scale of the fighting forced them to marshal regiments from across the empire. The revolt endured in its first phase to 12 October 1936 when a ceasefire paved the way for a British mission to Palestine headed by Lord Peel to decide the country's future,

[11] *A Survey of Palestine, Prepared in December 1945 and January 1946 for the Information of the Anglo-American Committee of Inquiry* [1946] (Washington, DC: IPS, 1991), i, p. 35.
[12] Emergency Regulations 1936 in Supplement No. 2 to the *Palestine Gazette Extraordinary* No. 584 of 19 April 1936 in *Ordinances, Regulations, Rules, Orders and Notices. Government of Palestine. Annual Volume for 1936. Volume 2* (Jerusalem: Government Printing Press, 1937), pp. 259ff.

the British Palestine Royal (or Peel) Commission of 1937. Palestinians adamantly opposed the conclusion of the Peel Commission on 22 June 1937 to partition the country into Arab and Jewish areas and this prompted renewed action from Qassamite hitmen who ignited a second phase of the revolt by shooting nine times and killing British District Commissioner Lewis Andrews on his way to church in Nazareth on 26 September 1937. The assassins killed alongside Andrews his bodyguard, British Constable Peter McEwan. Palestinians hated Andrews for his support for Jewish settlements in Galilee: 'one of the strongest enemies of the Arabs,' notes an Arab author, while a Jewish fighter interviewed in 1950 recalled how 'he wanted us to organize a Jewish defence organization quite openly.'[13]

The police assiduously tracked down the Black Hand Qassamites responsible for Andrews' death and they arrested hundreds of terrorist suspects as an immediate punishment, while others exacted unofficial reprisals for the killing of Andrews and this book devotes a closing chapter to the extra-judicial dirty war to suppress rebellion in Palestine. Andrews, an Australian, had ridden into Palestine as a soldier with the Australian Light Horse during the First World War and an Australian friend working in the Mandate Government, 'another Light Horsemen, was so distressed at Andrew's death that blind drunk and in full evening dress, he staggered about the old city of Jerusalem with a brace of revolvers shooting at every Arab he could see. The Australian was sent home and the matter hushed up.'[14] At the same time, police CID – there was no dedicated Special Branch in Palestine although CID had a political division – tortured suspects arrested after Andrews' death in an empty senior police officer's house and in police cells, what were euphemistically called 'rough measures' where police 'smartened up' prisoners until blood 'spurt' from their noses and ears, elsewhere described euphemistically as 'gentle persuasion,' 'Turkish,' 'Black and Tan,' or 'third degree' methods.[15] This included sexual violence, which

[13] Subhi Yasin, *Al-Thawra al-'Arabiyya al-Kubra (fi Filastin) 1936–1939* [*The Great Arab Revolt in Palestine, 1936–1939*] (Damascus: Shafa 'Amr Haifa, 1959), p. 92; Haganah Member, Interviewed 23 March 1950 in Haifa, Alice Hay of Seaton Papers, JRL; Ghassan Kanafani, 'Thawrat 1936–1939 fi Filastin: Khalfiyyat, tafasil wa tahlil' ['The 1936–1939 Revolt in Palestine: Background, Details and Analysis'], *Shu'un Filastinyya* [*Palestinian Matters*] 6 (January 1972), p. 67.

[14] John Bierman and Colin Smith, *Fire in the Night: Wingate of Burma, Ethiopia and Zion* (New York, NY: Random House, 1999), p. 73; Typed Memoir, Pieces of War, p. 54, Simonds Papers, 08/46/1, IWMD.

[15] High Commissioner to Shuckburgh (CO), 20 October 1938, FO 371/21865, p. 197, TNA; Letter, Burr (Inlying Piquet Haifa) to Father, n.d. [late December 1937], Burr Papers, 88/8/1, IWMD; Jack Binsley, *Palestine Police Service* (Montreux: Minerva, 1996), p. 39; David Smiley, *Irregular Regular* (Norwich: Michael Russell, 1994), pp. 15–16;

was muted, and is discussed further in Appendix C on women and violence, including stories of how some peasant women such as Fatma
Ghazzal fought and died in battle against the British.[16] Prison guards
tortured and molested one naked female detainee in Bethlehem women's
jail and threatened that they would have her raped but as she recounted,
'it seems that they had an order not to rape me.'[17] One rebel, Bahjat Abu
Gharbiyya, told this author of the rape of male prisoners by Arab guards
in British-run prisons, as also allegedly happened in Kenya in the 1950s
where askaris sodomised prisoners.[18] Such brutality vividly illustrates
the terror of imperial pacification but it was a less powerful repressive
tool than the attritional wearing down of the insurgents through legally
enforced non-violent or non-lethal punishments of the population, as
this book will argue.

The revolt symbolically ended with Britain's White Paper of 17 May
1939 – or 'Black Paper' as the Palestinian newspaper *Filastin* (*Palestine*)
put it – that once the British had crushed the rebellion largely conceded
rebel demands to halt Jewish immigration but as many Palestinians
never accepted its conclusions sporadic rebel attacks carried on into late
1939 and beyond.[19] The campaign officially ended for the British Army
on 3 September 1939. The White Paper was the end point to Britain's
adroit diplomatic track to outflank the rebels politically that ran alongside Army counter-rebel tactics that could be 'political' in that they
were population-centric and less obviously violent, such as establishing
security zones, and favouring certain villages and individuals, but which
were not concerned with understanding the political basis for the revolt.
The afterword to this book touches on the diplomatic track to isolate
rebels, notably the collaboration of Arab rulers in Transjordan, Iraq,
Yemen, and Saudi Arabia with the British. British diplomatic moves to

Martin Kolinsky, 'The Collapse and Restoration of Public Security,' in Michael J. Cohen
and Martin Kolinsky (eds), *Britain and the Middle East in the 1930s: Security Problems,
1935–39* (London: Macmillan-King's, 1992), p. 157; Letter, Burr (Central Police Billet
Box 523 Haifa) to Mother and Father, n.d. [c. May–June 1937], Burr Papers, 88/8/
1, IWMD.

[16] This is not to relegate women's role to a footnote but reflects the author's wish to concentrate exiguous source material on women and combat, a pertinent subject considering
the focus here on methods of pacification. Ellen Fleischmann's study of urban middle-
class women in *The Nation and Its 'New' Women: The Palestinian Women's Movement,
1920–1948* (Berkeley, CA: University of California Press, 2003), p. 126 for Ghazzal.

[17] Case of RL, Arrested 15 May 1936 in J&EM Papers, GB165-0161, Box 65, File 5,
pp. 7–8 (pp. 122–23 in overall file pagination), MEC.

[18] Author interview, Bahjat Abu Gharbiyya, Amman, 21 June 2009, and subsequent e-mail
correspondence; Caroline Elkins, *Britain's Gulag: The Brutal End of Empire in Kenya*
(London: Jonathan Cape, 2005), pp. 136, 157, 208.

[19] *Filastin* [*Palestine*] (Jaffa) (17 May 1939), p. 1.

defeat the rebels evolved alongside the flood of officially sanctioned violence that roiled the country after April 1936 and coerced Palestinians into submission.

The Death of Shaykh 'Izz al-Din al-Qassam, 20 November 1935

The Qassamites who ambushed the vehicle convoy and killed Danenberg and Hazan had been fighting the British and the Jews long before April 1936 and their violent history points to a different periodisation for the Arab revolt. The death of al-Qassam in November 1935 could mark the start of the revolt, or the Qassamite bomb attack on the Jewish settlement of Nahalal in 1932, as could the 'year zero' of the 1929 Palestinian–Jewish rioting, or one could go back further to the League of Nations' assignment of the British Mandate in 1922 or to the Balfour Declaration of 1917.[20] Other armed resistance groups such as 'Abd al-Qadir al-Husayni's Holy War band (*'Isabat al-Jihad al-Muqaddas*) and the anti-Jewish Green Hand fighters (*al-Kaff al-Akhdar*) were also active before April 1936. This study of the mechanics of the British pacification of Palestine starts on 19 April 1936 as this was the moment when Palestinian resistance peaked to a level demanding an unprecedented deployment of British troops, the activation of repressive legislation, and the establishment of new forms of military rule in Palestine to beat the rebels. Jewish immigration to Palestine, the social and political evolution of the Palestinians, and forms of British colonial rule, which all predate April 1936, are the backdrop to the revolt and explain why it happened; this study focuses on pacification after April 1936, not why the revolt erupted then.

Al-Qassam's tomb stands in a small walled compound in the derelict Muslim cemetery on the edge of the Israeli town of Nesher near Haifa, what in 1935 was the Palestinian town of Balad al-Shaykh. The dramatis personae appendix (Appendix E) to this book records his full epitaph. The faded inscriptions on the tomb are hard to read, made worse by the original stone having been badly vandalised and later repaired with a new headstone, the broken memorial laid flat and cemented in behind the replacement. Inscribed are Muslim (1354 so 1935–36 in the Christian calendar) and Christian dates for al-Qassam's death on the broken headstone, the latter placed incorrectly to 19 November 1935. The inscriptions record variously al-Qassam's death as a Muslim martyr

---

[20] Hillel Cohen, *Year Zero of the Arab–Israeli Conflict 1929* (Waltham, MA: Brandeis University Press, 2015).

(*shahid*), that he was the first to raise the flag of holy war (jihad) for the victory of Islam, and 'may his name be written in history ... together we will be united on al-Qassam's path'; indeed, his band had set off with the slogan 'This is jihad, victory or a martyr's death!'[21] Carved on al-Qassam's tombstone is the Arabic phrase *husn yaqin* – a clear act of grace or firm conviction. This was the resting place of someone who had led a good life and had had a fitting death. Two of the men who died with al-Qassam on 20 November 1935 are buried alongside him, Ahmad Shaykh Sa'id and Sa'id al-Masri, although one cannot easily decipher their names from the remaining inscriptions.[22] It is not clear how many men died with Qassam. The local English-language press reported four 'brigands' killed; other accounts recorded two dead in addition to al-Qassam; Arabic-language newspapers noted a six-hour battle in dense trees with the police (and not the usual cave where police purportedly killed al-Qassam) that left five of the 'jihadist' gang dead and four captured.[23] Before the British trapped al-Qassam and his eight-strong band (up to eleven men in some accounts) near the village of Ya'bad, his unit had shot dead Jewish Palestine police Sergeant Moshe Rosenfeld on 7 November 1935. Rosenfeld is buried in the Gidona Jewish cemetery near Ein Harod with a plaque marking the spot where he died.[24] Police CID chief Harold Rice hovered overhead in a light plane for the final gun battle on 20 November 1935 to make sure that his men terminated this existential threat to British power, during which al-Qassam's band fatally shot British police Constable R. C. V. Mott through the lung.[25] Mott succumbed to his wound an hour later. Mott was posthumously awarded the King's Police Medal for his bravery at Ya'bad and he is buried in the Protestant cemetery on Mount Zion in Jerusalem. Interred alongside Mott are Lewis Andrews with the epitaph 'Who gave his life for this land' and Andrews' bodyguard, Peter McEwan. The last battle with

[21] Fieldtrip visit, Nesher Muslim cemetery, 2010; Rudolph Peters, *Islam and Colonialism: The Doctrine of Jihad in Modern History* (The Hague: Mouton, 1979), p. 98; for meaning of jihad see Rudolph Peters, *Jihad in Classical and Modern Islam: A Reader* (Princeton, NJ: Wiener, 2005), pp. 1–8, 115–16.

[22] Mark Sanagan, 'Teacher, Preacher, Soldier, Martyr: Rethinking 'Izz al-Din al-Qassam,' *Welt des Islams* 53/3–4 (2013), p. 316.

[23] *Filastin* (21 November 1935); 'British Constable Killed, 1 Hurt, in battle with bandits near Jenin,' *Palestine Post* (21 November 1935); Bruce Hoffman, *Anonymous Soldiers: The Struggle for Israel, 1917–1947* (New York, NY: Vintage, 2015), p. 48.

[24] Yasin, *Al-Thawra al-'Arabiyya al-Kubra*, pp. 27–28; Yehoshua Porath, *The Palestinian Arab National Movement: From Riots to Rebellion. Volume 2, 1929–1939* (London: Cass, 1977), p. 136. *Filastin* (21 November 1935) reported twenty-two men in al-Qassam's band.

[25] 'British Constable Killed, 1 Hurt, in Battle with Bandits near Jenin,' *Palestine Post* (21 November 1935); Correspondence, Ted Horne to Author, 28 September 2016 for Rice in aeroplane.

al-Qassam's band raged from 5 am to 10 am, during which Qassamites shot Mott as he and fellow officers closed with the enemy. Mott was

endeavouring to close with the gang and in doing so came under fire at point blank range. British Constable Mott in a courageous effort to get still closer exposed himself to fire and he was mortally wounded. He died one and a half hours later ... Mott with his knowledge of the country was in advance of his companions and was actually within 15 metres of the bandits when a bullet through the lungs brought him down. He lay for fully half an hour while his comrades were engaged with the bandits before it was possible to go to his aid.[26]

Aftershocks of the battle with al-Qassam rippled through Palestine, with the surviving Qassamites captured at the battle in November 1935 getting fourteen-year jail sentences for murder when they finally came to trial in October 1936; Qassamites simultaneously targeted Arab police officers and prosecutors who had helped challenge al-Qassam's band.[27]

The life and death of al-Qassam prove that there was continuity to Palestinian resistance. His passing also makes us think about the nature of Palestinian resistance and rebel leadership and this helps us to understand the successful British counter-insurgency campaign after 1936. The death of the popular al-Qassam was a potent mobilising national symbol for the Palestinians, comparable to that of the one-armed Jewish fighter Joseph Trumpeldor who was killed in 1920 by Arabs in a battle at the Jewish settlement of Tel Hai. However, while the Jews made the most of Trumpeldor's death and mobilised it for the cause of Jewish self-defence and for the Zionist struggle for a Jewish state, the response from the Palestinian elite nationalist leadership to al-Qassam's death was 'underwhelming.'[28] Palestinians were divided between a populist rebel willing to die for their cause and an elite, notable leadership willing to ignore him and so preserve its 'black skin, white masks' comprador power base alongside the colonial authorities.[29] Al-Qassam had demanded armed struggle of the Palestinians, proclaiming from the pulpit, 'You are a people of rabbits who are afraid of death and scaffolds and engaged in prattle. You must know that nothing will save us but our arms.'[30] The Palestinian nationalist *Istiqlal* (Independence) Party founder Akram Zu'aytir excoriated the elite leadership following al-Qassam's death,

---

[26] *The Palestine Police Force. Annual Administrative Report, 1935*, p. 13; *Palestine Police Magazine* 3/12 (December 1935), p. 6.

[27] CID, Jerusalem, by Deputy IG Rice, Periodical Appreciation Summary, 18/36, 7 November 1936, p. 3, L/PS/12/3343, IOR (also in FO 371/20018, TNA).

[28] Sanagan, 'Teacher, Preacher, Soldier,' p. 347.

[29] As described by Frantz Fanon in *Black Skin, White Masks* [1952 in French] (London: Pluto, 1986) but without specific reference to Palestine.

[30] In Hoffman, *Anonymous Soldiers*, p. 47.

questioning on 22 November 1935, 'Why did the nation stand on one side regarding the death of al-Qassam' while the mainstream leadership 'stood on the other? Why did you not attend the funeral? Where were the goodwill messages from the Grand Mufti [Hajj Amin al-Husayni], from Raghib al-Nashashibi ... and Husayn al-Khalidi?'[31] Zu'aytir might not have had all the facts as other sources record that Raghib Nashashibi of the National Defence Party (connected to *al-Mua'rada*, the Nashashibi-family-backed Opposition) sent his condolences, as did Jamal al-Husayni of the Palestine Arab Party (linked to *Majlis*, the Husayni-family backed Council), and the leader of the Palestine Youth Congress Party, Ya'qub al-Ghusayn.[32] (Al-Qassam may have been a member of *Istiqlal*.[33])

The British echoed Zu'aytir and criticised Palestinian political elites as an effendi class there to control rather than represent the people and 'entirely without courage and will follow any movement that promises a material gain to themselves.'[34] Mark Sanagan reinforces this view in his recent account of al-Qassam's death where he puts sharply the case against the notable leadership:

The Palestinian leaders were frightened that al-Qassam's revolt was the beginning of a populist nationalist movement that would no longer look to the traditional leadership who derived power from membership in the notable class or an important family. This was borne out a week later, when the five heads of the Arab parties met with High Commissioner Arthur Wauchope. They made what reads like a last-ditch attempt to convince the Mandate authorities to concede something concrete that might legitimize their leadership in the eyes of a discontent population ... There was good reason for the traditional leadership and the Mandate authorities to be concerned. Al-Qassam's unique blend of a populist syncretic Islam coupled with his charismatic activities made his death a significant moment in the development of Palestinian Nationalism.[35]

Al-Qassam stood for something, not just himself. Later Palestinian activists such as the Marxist Ghassan Kanafani – killed by a car bomb in Beirut in 1972, allegedly by Israeli agents – saw al-Qassam's potential

---

[31] In Sanagan, 'Teacher, Preacher, Soldier,' p. 347. All three men cited were notable Palestinian leaders, Husayn al-Khalidi leading the Palestinian Reform Party and later sitting on the AHC.

[32] Samih Hammudah, *Al-Wa'y wa-al-thawrah: dirasah fi-hayah wa-jihad al-Shaykh 'Izz al-Din al-Qassam 1882–1935* [*Awareness and Revolution: A Study in the Life and Struggle of Shaykh 'Izz al-Din al-Qassam 1882–1935*] (Jerusalem: Arab Studies Association, 1986), p. 88.

[33] Porath, *The Palestinian Arab National Movement*, pp. 137–38.

[34] Nazareth Town, Political, Agitators, Gang Leaders and Terrorists, Palestine Police Force: Report from Tiberias: M/4212/8, ISA; Summary of Intelligence, Palestine and Transjordan, 4 November 1938, by Wing Commander Ritchie at GHQ [22/38], CO 732/81/10, TNA.

[35] Sanagan, 'Teacher, Preacher, Soldier,' pp. 348–49.

and highlighted his appeal to the masses as a charismatic populist leader who had exposed the reactionary traditional leadership, and whose slogan to 'die as martyrs' was revolutionary in a 'Guevarist' sense; he was the 'initiator of an advanced revolutionary focus,' and wanted to build rebel base areas as a precursor to revolt.[36] Al-Qassam was undoubtedly a revolutionary with 'clear political and military aims,' and his movement a 'complete novelty' in how it encompassed lower strata of Palestinian society and gave expression to their discontent.[37] But he was an Islamic revolutionary and comparable to the Latin American Marxist Che Guevara in that both men excited people for a political cause, and that security forces thus saw them as existential threats and so hunted them down and killed them. Al-Qassam had 'clearly touched a deep chord in the popular imagination, and was much more closely in tune with Palestinian sentiment than was the elite leadership,' in the words of a contemporary Palestinian academic.[38] The Palestinian notable-religious Husayni-family leader Hajj Amin al-Husayni, the 'Grand Mufti' above and uncle to 'Abd al-Qadir al-Husayni, had rejected a call from al-Qassam to coordinate resistance as conditions were 'not yet ripe,' and only the poor supported al-Qassam and attended his funeral: 'The leaders adopted an indifferent attitude, which they soon realized was a mistake. For the killing of al-Qassam was an occurrence of outstanding significance,' notes Kanafani.[39] Hajj Amin's position on the Government payroll complicated any overt support he might have had for al-Qassam. The Palestinians were split between Qassamites who wanted jihad-led armed combat and political-religious mobilisation of the peasantry, but who had lost their leader, and elite nationalist notable leaders who believed in political negotiation with the British and peaceful demonstration, and who invoked religion only when it might help the nationalist cause.[40] The Palestine Communist Party (PCP) never bridged the gap, instead preferring to link up with the left wing of the *Istiqlal* Party and to leave the fighting to others. The populist Islamism of al-Qassam tinged with rural-style socialism was more influential than communism in the 1930s. Only later in the 1960s did Palestinian nationalists in the PLO

---

[36] Ghassan Kanafani, *Palestine: The 1936–1939 Revolt* [1972 in Arabic] (London: Tricontinental, n.d., c. 1982), p. 15.

[37] Porath, *The Palestinian Arab National Movement*, p. 137; Peters, *Islam and Colonialism*, p. 97.

[38] Rashid Khalidi, *Palestinian Identity: The Construction of Modern National Consciousness* (New York, NY: Columbia University Press, 1997), p. 189. Nephew to Husayn al-Khalidi of the Palestinian Reform Party.

[39] Kanafani, *Palestine: The 1936–1939 Revolt*, pp. 15–16.

[40] Peters, *Islam and Colonialism*, pp. 98, 103.

adopt Marxist and Maoist slogans.[41] While the British were intensely watchful of communism in Palestine during the revolt, seeing it as the 'greater menace' than the 'petty quarrel' between Arabs and Jews, they made no note of communist guerrillas during the troubles and the PCP provided only a few rebel fighters, a small communist guerrilla group, and the 'Red Corporal' Fakhri Maraka, right-hand man to rebel leader Hasan Salama.[42] The communist movement never fomented or directed the revolt. It alienated its Jewish cadres when Moscow ordered the party to Arabise after 1929 at a moment when rebels were attacking Jews, the British arrested its leadership in 1937, and the PCP opposed the renewal of fighting in September 1937.[43] Palestinian elites lagged behind popular leaders such as al-Qassam and the lack of leadership fatally weakened Palestinian resistance to the well-oiled British counter-insurgency campaign that descended like a fury on Palestine after 19 April 1936. In effect, a ground swell of populist Palestinian anger sustained a leaderless insurgency.

Counter-insurgency and Pacification

This study uses the terms counter-rebel, counter-insurgency, and imperial policing interchangeably to describe British military operations in Palestine against armed bands, while pacification encompasses the wider targeting by the British of the country and includes the colonial legal and political superstructure that set up a new imperial order in British-run Palestine after 1917. As so many counter-rebel military sweeps in Palestine involved targeting (and shooting) unarmed villagers, it is not easy disentangling the two. The phrase counter-insurgency only became fashionable in the 1960s so describing operations in Palestine in the 1930s as imperial policing or pacification chimes with contemporaneous language.[44] Military anti-rebel field operations are a sub-set of pacification; in the same way, insurgents will employ a range of non-military counter-pacification methods to attack their enemy. The nomenclature and military technologies will vary, but whether it was the Normans in

---

[41] See web material at http://learnpalestine.politics.ox.ac.uk/ (accessed 3 August 2017).

[42] US Consul General Palestine to State Department, 19 September 1931, 867N.00/122 [Reel M#1037/1], NARA II. The British seem to have wounded Fakhri Maraka in 1936 and taken him prisoner.

[43] Musa Budeiri, *The Palestine Communist Party, 1919–1948* (London: Ithaca, 1979), pp. 97, 119; Tareq Ismael, *The Communist Movement in the Arab World* (London: Routledge, 2005), p. 63.

[44] Ian Beckett, 'The Study of Counter-Insurgency: A British Perspective,' *Small Wars and Insurgencies* 1/1 (April 1990), p. 50; Paul Dixon, '"Hearts and Minds"? British Counter-Insurgency from Malaya to Iraq,' *Journal of Strategic Studies* 32/3 (June 2009), p. 356.

1069 subjugating the north of England by harrying (or harrowing) and wasting the land, or the Chinese Nationalists' suppression campaigns against communists in the 1930s, the collective, punitive destruction of pacification changed very little. Pacification at an extreme was liquidation or genocide of entire communities. This never happened in Palestine under the British but did happen elsewhere, as with the French destruction of the entire Ouled Rhia tribe in Algeria in 1845 or with genocidal German operations in south-west Africa against the Herero people from 1904, to give two salient examples.[45] Nazi counter-partisan operations in occupied Europe after 1939 are an extreme case of maximal, eliminationist pacification.

British pacification in Palestine was never absolute and restraints on the use of violence are as interesting as are the abuses that one would expect to find in such operations. The British did not hang Rosenfeld's and Mott's killers, and all through the revolt they acquitted suspects, even those arraigned before supposedly draconian military courts. They commuted death sentences and they hanged just 112 men, only two of whom were Jewish: a policeman who shot a Palestinian comrade in September 1937 in the ceasefire period and an *Etzel* fighter hanged in June 1938. The British by contrast hanged a record number of 1,090 black insurgents in Kenya in the 1950s during the Mau Mau rebellion. British civil officials and senior Army officers in Palestine sanctioned forceful operations that cowed Palestinians, and then deplored, denied, or partially investigated any brutality that attracted bad publicity. They had the 'blameworthy' minds that constitute part of a crime, the *mens rea* knowledge of wrongdoing.[46] Such ambivalence contained the violence of pacification. The Foreign Office also made the case for leniency.[47] Official reticence alongside legal strictures, Arab protests, critical questions in Parliament and from the Anglican church in Jerusalem, international pressure from the German and Italian press, and the ingrained humanity of many soldiers and colonial officials constrained the security forces pacifying Palestine. The British Army never articulated doctrinally a minimum-force philosophy for colonial pacification – coercion was always the basis of operations – but cultural and operational precepts of 'compatible' force minimised the scale of potential abuse; the Chief of the Imperial General Staff even warned the Palestine commander against using the word

---

[45] Isabel Hull, *Absolute Destruction: Military Culture and the Practices of War in Imperial Germany* (Ithaca, NY: Cornell University Press, 2006), *passim*.

[46] Gary Slapper and David Kelly, *The English Legal System, 2014–15* (London: Routledge, 2014), pp. 105–06.

[47] Minute by J. Y. Mackenzie (FO) on Military Measures, 30 November 1938, FO 371/21867, p. 60, TNA.

'punitive.'[48] This was not 'minimum force' as less than maximal force. British forces in Palestine were ambivalent and ambiguous on the use of force. They curtailed improper, unmanaged violence, as when the military shut down the irregular British–Jewish Special Night Squads.[49] The stress of brutal pacification in the field strained abstract ideals on the legal use of limited force. Or as Palestine divisional commander General Bernard Montgomery put it, soldiers must be 'scrupulously fair' when dealing with Palestinian peasants – 'We want them to realise that they will always get a fair deal from the British Army' – before adding that if Palestinians 'assist the rebels in any way they must be expected to be treated as rebels' and 'anyone who takes up arms against us will certainly lose his life.'[50]

This book presents pacification in Palestine as a raft of military *and* social, political, psychological, and economic punishment of recalcitrant peoples, and not just in periods of open rebellion, executed by soldiers and colonial officials working in tandem using pre-existing and new legislation. Pacification is the use of violence to achieve a political purpose, as is the case in all wars, but the primary target is the subject, occupied population and not the destruction in open battle of similarly formatted regular armies, comparably armed, at least in the early phases of insurgency when guerrilla forces are small and irregular.[51] The British soldier-author Colonel C. E. Callwell candidly laid out the harsh, scorched-earth kinetic measures of imperial pacification whereby the Army laid waste villages and crops in rebel areas in his standard practitioners' manual of 1896 on 'small wars,' one that had the official HMSO imprimatur.[52] Rather than complicated nation-building, modernisation 'COIN' doctrines and theories so fashionable today, British forces punished recalcitrant communities whose surrender ensured their 'security' and continued colonial rule. This shifted after the First World War and the 1919 Amritsar massacre in Punjab of demonstrators by

---

[48] M. L. R. Smith and D. Jones, *The Political Impossibility of Modern Counterinsurgency* (Columbia, NY: Columbia University Press, 2015), pp. 138–39; Deverell (CIGS, London) to Dill, 22 April 1937, Dill Papers, 2/9, LHCMA. For a contra view see Thomas Mockaitis, *British Counterinsurgency, 1919–1960* (New York, NY: St Martin's, 1990).

[49] Matthew Hughes, 'Terror in Galilee: British–Jewish Collaboration and the Special Night Squads in Palestine during the Arab Revolt, 1938–39,' *Journal of Imperial and Commonwealth History* 43/4 (December 2015), pp. 590–610.

[50] 8th Division Instructions by Gen Montgomery, Haifa, 25 November 1938, O'Connor Papers, 3/4/4, LHCMA.

[51] Smith and Jones, *Political Impossibility*, pp. 4–6.

[52] C. E. Callwell, *Small Wars: Their Principles and Practices* [1896] (London: HMSO, 1906). See also Daniel Whittingham, 'The Military Thought and Professional Career of Charles E. Callwell (1859–1928)' (Doctoral Thesis: University of London, 2013).

British-led troops. Soldiers regarded their violence against rebels and their language of repression, and by 1952 General Sir Gerald Templer (who won the DSO with the Loyal Regiment in Palestine) when fighting Malayan communists spoke of 'hearts and minds' counter-insurgency strategies to win over the people, a phrase that became very popular.[53] (There was a crude hearts and minds strategy in Palestine, although the British never called it as such, soldiers sparing good villages from the destructive punishments due 'wicked' ones.[54]) Pacification after Amritsar still targeted civilians but soldiers were circumspect and primarily targeted property and livelihoods using emergency legislation. British security forces were mindful of adverse publicity in a new era of the League of Nations.

Military histories of counter-insurgency have long recognised the wider pacification element to operations if not the concomitant brutality but have examined such things in the context of particular military campaigns and their success or failure: their effectiveness, a key issue for military historians.[55] Marxist studies of pacification similarly distinguish 'pure' military action from secondary actions – psychological war, propaganda, intelligence, police measures, personal contacts, and socio-economic programmes – but from a radically different perspective, seeing pacification more broadly as the permanent combination of destructive military operations with the 'second group' of actions to reconstruct a new peace and a new, exploitative capitalist social order.[56] The idea of pacification as the wider construction of social control is useful here as this history situates the effective, destructive, military element to pacification after 1936 within the British colonial legal order established long before the outbreak of the revolt. Pacification began in December 1917 when British forces captured Jerusalem in the First World War and set up new systems of military and then colonial government in southern Palestine. This is the subject of the next chapter. Destructive military methods after 1936 followed on from the construction of an emergency colonial state in the 1920s that made possible and legal the far-reaching pacification after April 1936, and not the other way around, supported by imperial traditions and British soldiers' long-standing experiences of

[53] David French, *The British Way in Counter-Insurgency, 1945–67* (Oxford: Oxford University Press, 2011), p. 2.
[54] Edward Horne, *A Job Well Done (Being a History of the Palestine Police Force, 1920–1948)* (Tiptree: Anchor Press, 1982), p. 177.
[55] For brutality see Douglas Porch, *Counterinsurgency: Exposing the Myths of the New Way of War* (Cambridge: Cambridge University Press, 2013), *passim*.
[56] Mark Neocleous et al., 'On Pacification: Introduction to the Special Issue,' *Socialist Studies/Études Socialistes* (Special Issue, Winter 2013), p. 1.

suppressing insurrection. The British Army was not trying to construct a
new order of capitalist exploitation by its suppression of the Arab revolt;
nor were the rebels consciously trying to tear down the political economy
of the country, wanting instead an end to Jewish immigration and British
rule. Rather, by the summer of 1939, pacification had left Palestine
in ruins – the 'smoke of burning houses' after the passage of Guzmán
Bento's Army of Pacification in Joseph Conrad's fictional Republic of
Costaguana quoted at the start of this book – restored Pax Britannica
and freed up the British Army to fight Germany in September 1939.

Terrorists and Terrorism: Guerrillas and Bandits

The British and Jews described rebel bands in politically loaded terms,
as terrorists, insurrectionists, brigands, marauders, robbers, and gangs,
and with it came the political inferiority of the 'inflamed mob.'[57] The
language could be racist. British Constable Sydney Burr's sentiment
that local people, Arabs and Jews, including non-British policemen,
were 'wogs,' a 'horrible brute,' 'ugly specimens' and targets for beatings
articulated colonial bigotry.[58] Other police officers described Arabs as
'easy going' and 'cordial,' a common feeling expressed by soldiers, too,
not like the 'boorish, ill-mannered' Jews with their 'curious little eyes.'[59]
British Palestine police felt differently towards the Druze and Bedouin,
the former seen as descendants of the crusaders and who were a non-
Arab 'older "white" race,' and 'a much cleaner and better looking race.'[60]
Army slang was less obviously racist, soldiers disinterestedly battling
rebels, gangsters, terrorists, or 'oozlebarts,' a corruption of the Arabic for
gangs; many soldiers, like some policemen, expressed a condescending
fondness for the 'genuine' Arab, in contrast to the 'extremely clever'
modern Jewish settlers who as 'much as one may dislike them' at least
exhibited 'industry and progressiveness.'[61] For the Jews, the rebels were
'punks' or more usually *knufiyot*, Hebrew for gangs, and they described
rebel violence as rioting or disturbances, never a popular revolt.[62] How

---

[57] Cohen, *Year Zero*, pp. 11–12.
[58] Letters, Burr to home, Burr Papers, *passim*, 88/8/1, IWMD; Douglas Duff, *Palestine Unveiled* (London: Blackie, 1938), p. 52.
[59] Dennis Quickfall, *Shadows over Scopus: Reflections of an Ex-Palestine Policeman* (Manchester: Cromwell, 1999), p. 54.
[60] Letter, Burr (Inlying Piquet) to Mother and Father, 24 February 1938, Burr Papers, 88/8/1, IWMD; Douglas Duff, *Bailing with a Teaspoon* (London: John Long, 1953), p. 78.
[61] Gratton, 4506/03, p. 11, IWMSA; Brig G. S. Brunskill, Typed Memoir, p. 9, Brunskill Papers, PP/MCR/136, IWMD; Typed Memoir, Maj B. A. Pond, Pond Papers, 78/27/1, IWMD; Diary, 14 October 1938, Mullens Papers, LHCMA.
[62] Handwritten Entries, Information from Arab Office and Intelligence from Arab Countries, 9 February–26 July 1936: 8/GENERAL/35, HA.

did the rebels see themselves? Their insurgency was publicly a 'national revolt' for the Arab (and more rarely Palestinian) 'nation' and for justice for fellahin, articulated as religious jihad in the style of the late al-Qassam who had urged his followers as individuals to fight against the British and Jews as mujahideen – those engaged in struggle or striving but within now a sacred Muslim holy war (*al-jihad al-muqaddas*) – but privately the revolt was also an intra-communal battle.[63] Privately, mujahid status masked feuding, robbery, and intimidation amongst Palestinians. (The Vietminh fighting the French in the 1950s had the same defining notion of struggle, if much better organised, called *dau tranh*.) The religious part to the rebels' war might explain why just 1.5 per cent of rebel leaders were Christians when they formed 9 per cent of the Palestinian population, and why many Druze (and some Christians and Muslims) stayed neutral, sided with, or even fought with the British and Jews.[64] Chapter 3 and Chapter 4 of this book examine the substance of the insurgency.

How should we see the rebels? While this study focuses on British pacification, Palestinian resistance is the causal variable that explains victory and defeat against an imperial power that suppressed colonial unrest in roughly the same way across its empire. Changing geopolitics in various parts of the empire certainly affected British actions but the Arab revolt still raises the question of why the Palestinians in 1936 failed when the Irish in 1922, the Indians in 1947, and the Jews in 1948 won their anti-colonial struggles against Britain – or the Vietnamese in 1975 against US-backed South Vietnam. Framing the Palestinian rebels is problematic, not helped by counter-insurgency histories skipping over the Arab revolt, examining at times the rebellions in Ireland and India in the 1920s and 1930s before focusing on post-1945 decolonisation wars and then the current war on terror.[65] Classic radical studies on insurgencies such as Robert Taber's in the 1960s ignore the Arab revolt, although Taber discusses the Jewish rebellion against the British after 1945 as an example of a successful insurgency.[66] The British labelled rebels in 1936 as bandits, gangs, and gangsters, sometimes as bands in Army regimental war diaries, so discounting their political agency, although they conceded

---

[63] Peters, *Islam and Colonialism*, p. 99; Rebel Statement to DC Jerusalem, Attachment to CID Intelligence Summary, Jerusalem, No. 50/39, 20 July 1939, 47/89, HA.

[64] Porath, *The Palestinian Arab National Movement*, pp. 264, 269–70.

[65] Excepting Tom Bowden, *The Breakdown of Public Security: The Case of Ireland 1916–1921 and Palestine 1936–1939* (London and Beverly Hills, CA: Sage, 1977) and Porath, *The Palestinian Arab National Movement*. See also practitioner studies: Col H. J. Simson, *British Rule and Rebellion* (Edinburgh and London: Blackwood, 1937) and Maj-Gen Sir Charles Gwynn, *Imperial Policing* (London: Macmillan, 1934). See also Simon Innes-Robbins, *Dirty Wars: A Century of Counterinsurgency* (Stroud: History Press, 2016).

[66] Robert Taber, *War of the Flea* [1965] (Washington, DC: Brassey's, 2002), pp. 107–10.

that al-Qassam's group was something new that they had not encountered before, what they called 'politico-religious banditry.'[67] The Palestinian insurgents were not robber bandit gangs but they lacked the political activity, the radical drive for progressive (secular, socialist-communist) social revolution and land reform, the tight cohesion and organisation, the politically conscious leadership, and centralised political mobilisation of modern partisan, guerrilla movements, and this study side steps describing them as guerrillas for this reason.[68] This might also explain why Taber and others have overlooked the Arab revolt.

Eric Hobsbawm's 'archaic' social banditry of 'primitive rebels' is a useful tool for understanding the rebels in Palestine. Rebels represented a largely illiterate people – just 11 per cent of Muslim Palestinians could read in 1931, compared with 72 per cent of Jews and 48 per cent of Christians – adapting to modernity and acquiring some political consciousness through primitive social protest.[69] (Words such as primitive and archaic should not detract from the fact that such movements had considerable historical evolution, and that this gave them great moral if not political strength.) This approach challenges the Palestinian rebels both for *how* they resisted (as bandits or guerrillas), and *why* they resisted politically (because of British occupation, Jewish settlement, or rapid economic change) and personally (a brush with the law, religion, opportunity for theft, or for a blood feud). This study is interested in second-order military, instrumentalist questions of *how* and *who* and not the first-order political and social *why* of rebellion to understand what makes an insurgency effective, but it emphatically accepts that the nature of the rebellion will decide the outcome. Thus, it sets up the Palestinian rebels as something less than guerrillas, more in the mould of social bandits, especially later in 1938 as the rebellion consumed itself, but with elements of class struggle and who would fight the rich to help the poor, but who could equally fight with their family *hamula* groupings against another and its poor. The rebels were pre-political revolutionary traditionalists untouched by any 'potent political injection' of Leninism

---

[67] CID, Jerusalem, by Deputy IG Rice, Periodical Appreciation Summary, 18/36, 7 November 1936, p. 3, L/PS/12/3343, IOR.

[68] Discussed in full in Mao Tse-tung [Mao Zedong] (trans. Samuel B. Griffith), *On Guerrilla Warfare* [1937 in Chinese] [1961] (New York, NY: Doubleday Books, 1982); Carl Schmitt, *Theory of the Partisan* (New York, NY: Telos, 2007); John Ellis, *From the Barrel of a Gun: A History of Guerrilla, Revolutionary and Counter-Insurgency Warfare, from the Romans to the Present* (London: Greenhill, 1995).

[69] Eric Hobsbawm, *Primitive Rebels: Studies in Archaic Forms of Social Movement in the Nineteenth and Twentieth Centuries* (Manchester: Manchester University Press, 1959); Hobsbawm, *Bandits* (London: Weidenfeld and Nicolson, 1969); *Statistical Abstract of Palestine, 1937–38* (Jerusalem: Office of Statistics, 1938), p. 14.

but with a determined political cause and historical evolution.[70] Their struggle was built on traditional kinship and religious networks, with inchoate political action, parochial organisation, and hit-and-run military raids that had some characteristics of guerrilla war, all mixed up with clan-based *fasad* vendettas and feuds that blended into endemic social brigandage.[71] If rebels seeking state power fought as social bandits against an imperial power as mighty as Britain, they were bound to lose, for social banditry

is little more than endemic peasant protest against oppression and poverty: a cry for vengeance on the rich and the oppressors, a vague dream of some curb upon them, a righting of individual wrongs. Its ambitions are modest: a traditional world in which men are justly dealt with, not a new and perfect world. It becomes epidemic rather than endemic when a peasant society which knows of no better means of self-defence is in a condition of abnormal tension and disruption. Social banditry has next to no organization or ideology, and is totally inadaptable to modern social movements. Its most highly developed forms, which skirt national guerrilla warfare, are rare and, by themselves, ineffective.[72]

The revolt in Palestine was a hybrid insurgency. Rebels employed some unorthodox guerrilla war methods and they built proto-guerrilla base areas such as around the towns of Jenin–Nablus–Tulkarm, what the British called the 'triangle of terror' and the Palestinians 'fire mountain' (*Jabal al-Nar*) with their own taxes and revolutionary (Sharia) courts, but they never developed these into safe base areas such as Mao Zedong's one in Shaanxi region in China after the 1935 Long March. When the British lost control of southern Palestine in 1938 to the rebels, it was not to a new revolutionary order but to anarchy. In Mao's seminal revolutionary thinking, the fundamental issues for insurgents were political and social, and once revolutionary cadres had sufficiently mobilised local people, a temporary guerrilla area would become a permanent revolutionary base area that would spread like an oil stain.[73] The issue was organisation. Palestinian rebels eschewed sustained politicised guerrilla war to create such base areas in favour of a 'roving' style of fighting that Mao, for one, argued needed to be 'thoroughly eradicated' if guerrillas were to win.[74] In fact, Palestinian rebel forces were more parochial than roving, stuck to local clan territory and unwilling to combine to spread the rebellion. Moreover, as with Pancho Villa's revolutionaries in northern

---

[70] Mao Tse-tung, *On Guerrilla Warfare*, p. 11.
[71] Hobsbawm, *Primitive Rebels*, pp. 28, 100.
[72] Ibid., p. 5.
[73] Mao Tse-tung, *On Guerrilla Warfare*, pp. 109–10.
[74] Mao Tse-tung, *Strategic Problems in the Anti-Japanese Guerrilla War* [1938 in Chinese] (Peking: Foreign Language Press, 1954), p. 30.

Mexico after 1910, Palestine's rebels had no concrete progressive social aspirations to fire up the peasantry, so it was a 'case of every man for himself,' in contrast to Emiliano Zapata's insurgency in southern Mexico where peasants supported the rebels' fight for land reform right up to the Zapatista guerrillas in action today.[75] The Palestinians were not guerrillas in the style of their peasant contemporaries in China where guerrillas built rebel base areas and successfully matched protracted irregular warfare to 'severe' discipline, grass-roots political activism, and codified revolutionary thought attuned to rural societies before building regular armies to win set-piece battles, as with the Vietnamese victory at the battle of Dien Bien Phu in 1954 against the French.[76] China with its peasant-based insurgency is an instructive parallel case study to Palestine, even if local circumstances might vary. For example, rebels could hide in the road-less hilly terrain of the West Bank and Galilee, but they never had the secure fastness of China's vast interior spaces – Palestine's 10,434 square miles covered an area not much bigger than Wales – and the British built new roads, Tegart and frontier forts,[77] and border fences to reduce rebel zones. While regimental journals commented on the harsh tactical terrain where soldiers lost touch with comrades just five yards away and others fainted from heat stroke, rebels in Palestine had no deep strategic manoeuvre space within the country.[78]

This book frames Palestinian rebels as a movement and not an organisation, one that was parochial in form at the start of the revolt and had fragmented by late 1938, and which never reached up to be a vanguard or integrated movement with robust rather than fragile central and local command structures, to use the language of Paul Staniland.[79] Of the four ascending phases of Maoist revolutionary war, from organisation through terrorism and rural guerrilla war to full-scale mobile war, the rebels in Palestine never moved far into the third phase and arguably never beyond the second one of terrorism, and they even lacked the good organisation that was the jumping-off point for any insurrection.[80] Just four days after

[75]   Ellis, *From the Barrel of a Gun*, p. 119.
[76]   Mao Tse-tung, *On Guerrilla Warfare*, pp. 17, 45, 67.
[77]   The Tegart forts, named after the senior Indian police officer Sir Charles Tegart sent as an adviser to Palestine in December 1937, were generally sited for internal control and are still standing across Israel today.
[78]   'Notes on Palestine Operations,' *The Wasp: The Journal of the 16th Foot* 8/5 (March 1937), p. 265; *Ça Ira: The Journal of the West Yorkshire Regiment (The Prince of Wales's Own)* 9/4 (June 1939), p. 219.
[79]   Paul Staniland, *Networks of Rebellion: Explaining Insurgent Cohesion and Collapse* (Ithaca, NY and London: Cornell University Press, 2014), pp. 5–10.
[80]   John McCuen, *The Art of Counter-Revolutionary Warfare* (London: Faber and Faber, 1966), pp. 31ff.

the revolt started, some of its 'lukewarm' Palestinian leaders were already urging an end to the violence so that they could accept an official invitation to go to London to discuss a legislative council offer cleverly made by the British in December 1935 to prevent trouble after al-Qassam's death.[81] Such organisation as existed in the Arab revolt followed violence and not vice versa, as with Latin American revolutionary *foquismo* in the 1960s but without its foundational radical political ideology built on the Cuban insurgency of guerrilla action substituting for the vanguard party, and *foquismo* also failed.[82] The Palestinians never organised effectively: whether as a revolutionary communist force in the style of Mao's guerrillas, as conservative nationalists as EOKA did in Cyprus, as urban guerrillas in the mould of the IRA or ETA, as Castro–Guevara revolutionary chic, or religiously as with Islamic State today.[83] It might have been different if al-Qassam had lived. His followers furnished many of the most committed, effective rebel band commanders in the revolt. Other rebel leaders who impressively organised and mobilised, such as Fawzi al-Qawuqji, rated highly by British soldiers and supported by the fellahin, either served only intermittently in Palestine (in al-Qawuqji's case for just two months in 1936) or as with Fakhri 'Abd al-Hadi, switched sides and later fought for the British. Some Palestinians, notably Hajj Amin, argued that al-Qawuqji was a British spy, and the RAF flew in a 'payment' to al-Qawuqji when he left the country in a convoy of British vehicles that passed through Transjordan in November 1936.[84] The payment and the British trucks formed part of a deal to get al-Qawuqji and his men out of Palestine so that the 12 October 1936 ceasefire could go into effect, as readers can discover in Appendix G. The point here is that Hajj Amin's divisive gossip highlights Palestinian disunity. The third and fourth chapters to this book evaluate rebel command and combat power, and the role of popular commanders such as al-Qawuqji; another chapter examines British intelligence information-gathering systems and

[81] Disturbances of April 1936, US Consul General Palestine to State Department, 25 April 1936, 867N.00/283 [Reel M#1037/1], NARA II.

[82] For *foquismo* (or *focoism*) the classic text is Régis Debray, *Revolution in the Revolution? Armed Struggle and Political Struggle in Latin America* (London: Penguin, 1968) and discussed in John Shy and Thomas Collier, 'Revolutionary War,' in Peter Paret (ed.), *Makers of Modern Strategy: From Machiavelli to the Nuclear Age* [1986] (Oxford: Clarendon, 2000), pp. 849–50.

[83] Marxist studies make this point: Kanafani, 'Thawrat 1936–1939 fi Filastin,' with an English version ten years later: Kanafani, *Palestine: The 1936–1939 Revolt*.

[84] CID, Jerusalem, Periodical Appreciation Summary 18/36, 7 November 1936, L/PS/12/3343: Political Situation, Police Summaries, IOR; From a Diary of a Clerk at H3, 1936 November, dated 4–5 November 1936, S25/3033–124, CZA; Porath, *The Palestinian Arab National Movement*, p. 191; Laila Parsons, *The Commander: Fawzi al-Qawuqji and the Fight for Arab Independence* (New York, NY: Hill and Wang, 2016), pp. 117ff, 199.

the use of bribery, spies, and informers to divide-and-rule. The British and Jews instinctively exploited divisions in enemy ranks, and those that the British could not bribe or counter-mobilise and turn, they killed, harried, forced into exile, wounded, imprisoned, or hanged.

To counter this onslaught, effective rebel leadership united behind anti-colonial programmes of mobilisation and organisation was the key to insurgent victory, more especially for the rural populace across Palestine who were the backbone to the revolt, as was the case in Mao's China or in Mexico after the 1910 revolution, or, indeed, anywhere without an advanced industrial, urban working class. The Arab revolt was not fundamentally an urban struggle, nor could it have been. Urban areas expanded in Palestine under the Mandate and Arab Jaffa city grew from 32,524 inhabitants in 1922 to 76,900 in 1938; Jewish areas grew even more rapidly, with the Jewish city of Tel Aviv increasing its population from 15,185 in 1922 to 127,900 in 1938, and the Jewish labour union *Histadrut* heavily organised Jewish workers.[85] The 1931 Palestine census classified 37 per cent of the country's overall population as urban, rising to 45 per cent in 1938; in 1931, of a total urban population of 387,291, 33 per cent was Jewish.[86] Palestine was still fundamentally rural when the revolt started, certainly for the Palestinians, with just 30 per cent of their community living in urban areas in 1931, or 25 per cent if one excludes Christian Palestinians who were generally better educated and richer.[87] Moreover, Muslim Arab migrants to the city were often recent arrivals from the countryside and not well established, debt-ridden, and they lived in poverty in slum housing. Al-Qassam had conscripted from Haifa's city-fellahin and recruits from the urban poor had their part to play in the revolt, but the argument here is that they had negligible impact on the course of the revolt when compared with the rural masses. The urban equivalent of rural social bandits was the 'mob' of the old city streets and migrant shantytowns of Jaffa, Jerusalem, and Haifa, and when they became too unruly the British destroyed their homes, as the British did in June 1936 when they blew up Arab Jaffa's old city.[88] The British levelled parts of Jenin after the rebel assassination

[85] *Statistical Abstract of Palestine, 1939* (Jerusalem: Office of Statistics, 1939), p. 11. The British recorded overall urban–rural statistics for 1938 but for the revolt they did not break this down by religion and so the last confessional figures derive from the 1931 census.

[86] *Statistical Abstract of Palestine, 1937–38* (Jerusalem: Office of Statistics, 1938), p. 19.

[87] Ibid.

[88] Hobsbawm, *Primitive Rebels*, pp. 6–7, 110. For Jaffa see Dov Gavish, 'Mivz'a Yafo: Shipur Koloniali Shel Pnei ha-'Ir' ['The Old City of Jaffa, 1936: A Colonial Urban Renewal Project'], *Eretz Israel: Mehkarim be-Yedi'at ha-Aretz ve-Atikoteha* [*Eretz Israel: Archaeology, Historical and Geographical Studies*] 17 (1983), pp. 66–73.

of Assistant District Commissioner Walter Moffatt in October 1938. The 'Suq will "go up" again,' as soldiers described their punishment of Lydda in 1939.[89] In October 1938, the Coldstream Guards and the Royal Northumberland Fusiliers accompanied by Jewish Haganah militia men stormed Jerusalem's old city.[90] Urban bank robberies and assassinations in Palestine played second fiddle to the real war in the countryside to build rebel base areas that could raise the Palestinian struggle to a full-scale military confrontation.[91] Urban insurgents have never won a revolution on their own, not in Dublin in 1916, not in Guangzhou in 1927, not in Vienna in 1934, not in Warsaw in 1944, not in Algiers in 1957, not in Belfast in 1972, nor anywhere else and the rare exceptions such as Paris in 1830 and 1848 prove the rule.[92] This book frames the Arab revolt as a rural peasant-based insurgency.

Turning to the terror on both sides, the British legally sanctioned exemplary, draconian collective punishments with house destruction, internment, deportation, curfew, fining, travel restrictions, confiscation of livestock and crops, and corvée, alongside which there were semi-legal and illegal acts of robbery, theft, vandalism, brutality, torture, assassin-ation, and 'shot while trying to escape,' as a civil official remembered: 'I have it on the authority of Major Ashby that these men were not attempting to escape and were in fact shot in cold blood.'[93] The study here distinguishes between legal and illegal violence by Government forces, preferring generally the use of terror to describe the latter while grading the legal methods employed within imperial ideas and practices surrounding the use of force against rebellious colonial subjects.[94] This is discussed in more depth in the final chapter. While rebel violence never had the sanction or organisation of the state, this study differentiates between politically motivated versus personally driven acts of rebel vio-lence that were not legal inasmuch as the rebel Central Command in Damascus never sanctioned such things.[95] Political motives for violence

---

[89] HQ, 19th Infantry Brigade, Sarafand, to O'Connor, 10 March 1939, O'Connor Papers, 3/4/42, LHCMA.

[90] Testimony of Isaac Avrahami (Lt in Haganah), Testimonies of Haganah Officers Collected in the 1950s and 1960s, 94/29, p. 10, HA.

[91] As when Jerusalemite urban insurgent Bahjat Abu Gharbiyya shot British Servicemen in the summer of 1936: Matthew Hughes, 'A History of Violence: The Shooting of British Assistant Police Superintendent Alan Sigrist, 12 June 1936', *Journal of Contemporary History* 45/4 (October 2010), pp. 725–43; Ellis, *From the Barrel of a Gun*, p. 14.

[92] Ellis, *From the Barrel of a Gun*, p. 14.

[93] Diary, 12 November 1938, Scrivenor Papers, MSS. Brit. Emp. S. 378, WL.

[94] See Nasser Hussain, *The Jurisprudence of Emergency: Colonialism and the Rule of Law* (Ann Arbor, MI: University of Michigan Press, 2003).

[95] See David French, *Fighting EOKA: The British Counter-Insurgency Campaign on Cyprus, 1955–1959* (Oxford: Oxford University Press, 2015), pp. 10–11.

morphed into personal acts of primal terror that are harder to decipher but which the chaos and violence of the state of emergency in Palestine after April 1936 facilitated. The Government and the rebels established norms of violence that legitimated extraordinary cruelty by 'ordinary men,' and whose causes are as much psychological as they are historical.[96] Finally, this book uneasily draws a distinction between brutality and torture, between immediate, unplanned, reactive and (usually) non-lethal violence by men on the ground that intuitively seems less atrocious compared with planned assassination or abuse in dedicated, secret torture centres organised and managed by people with evil intent.[97]

Sources and Bias

This study is a military history of the Arab revolt that sees events through the lens of the mass of English-language source material left by the British soldiers and colonial officials who fought the Palestinian rebels, and through extensive Jewish source material that is often but not always in Hebrew – the inquisitor as anthropologist as Carlo Ginzburg describes it.[98] Jewish officials in Palestine working for the British copied masses of English-language files and the stolen and copied material is in the Central Zionist, Israel State, and Haganah archives, alongside captured or intercepted Arabic-language material from the 1930s stored in the Haganah and State archives, such as in the 41/104 and RG65: P3221/18 series respectively. The local British regimental archives and in-house unit journals accessed by this author have been a gold mine for understanding how the British Army carried out pacification. They offer colour and detail that is often missing in the well-used British Government files in the National Archives in Kew, London. For instance, the material from the Belfast archive of the Royal Ulster Rifles detailing the regiment's pacification of Palestinian villages by the Lebanese

---

[96] Christopher Browning, *Ordinary Men: Reserve Police Battalion 101 and the Final Solution in Poland* (New York, NY: HarperCollins, 1993), pp. 159ff. See also Stanley Milgram, *Obedience to Authority* [1974] (London: Pinter and Martin, 1997) and Philip Zimbardo, *The Lucifer Effect: Understanding How Good People Turn Evil* (New York, NY: Random, 2007).

[97] Henri Alleg, *The Question* (New York, NY: Braziller, 1958); Mika Haritos-Fatouros, *The Psychological Origins of Institutionalized Torture* (London: Routledge, 2003); Joshua Phillips, *None of Us Were Like This Before: American Soldiers and Torture* (London: Verso, 2012); Darius Rejali, *Torture and Democracy* (Princeton, NJ: Princeton University Press, 1997); Jean-Pierre Vittori, *Confessions d'un professionnel de la torture: La Guerre d'Algérie* (Paris: Ramsay, 1980). See John McGuffin, *The Guinea Pigs* (London: Penguin, 1974), p. 90 for a useful definition of brutality.

[98] In Carlo Ginzburg, *Clues, Myths and the Historical Method* (Baltimore, MD: Johns Hopkins University Press, 1990).

border – not with horrible tortures but through the daily grind of low-level punishments – exemplifies how soldiers operated, 'screwing down,' impoverishing, starving, and confining the population.[99] Privately held papers such as those of police officer (and later SIS officer) John Briance and interviews with surviving police officers such as Ted Horne have also provided new perspectives. The papers of colonial officials held in Oxford such as Sir Thomas Scrivenor's in the Weston Library that detail how the Army co-opted him to suppress dissent in urban Haifa augment our understanding of pacification, as do the oral histories stored by the Imperial War Museum in London. The interview transcripts completed for the 1977–78 television series 'Palestine: Promises and Rebellion' held in the Imperial War Museum film archive are another fine, under-used resource. These sources and many others offer fresh, fascinating insights into how the British suppressed colonial rebellion.

The weight of English- and Hebrew-language source material biases any study of the Arab revolt and overshadows the rebels – the other side of the hill – who have left no extensive, accessible archives detailing their actions. It reduces the rebels to passive subjects of pacification for us to understand through the eyes of colonial officials and Jewish settlers. The stories of the 'poor, illiterate and inaccessible rural population' are seen 'through a glass darkly, largely via records left by foreigners who did not speak their language or understand their culture, who had little sympathy for them, and who often were their enemies,' in the words of a Palestinian historian.[100] Moreover, heavy British censorship of Palestinian newspapers limits their usefulness for giving Palestinian perspectives on the revolt; the Arabic-language press in neighbouring states had fewer restrictions but the British blocked the import of foreign newspapers. Newspapers in Palestine were closed for weeks, even months at a time; the British shut *al-Difa'* (*The Defence*), for instance, from 8 December 1938 to 10 September 1939. There are ways of overcoming this archival gap. First, the British and the Jews assessed the rebels in candid secret internal reports, and they captured, stored, and translated Arabic-language rebel material, the biggest single set of which is in the Palestine section of Orde Wingate's papers held on microfilm in the British Library (the originals went to the US), many or all translated by Jewish intelligence officers such as Ezra Danin who may also have written the English-language commentary

---

[99] Karl Hack, 'Screwing Down the People: The Malayan Emergency, Decolonisation and Ethnicity,' in Hans Antlöv and Stein Tønnesson (eds), *Imperial Policy and Southeast Asian Nationalism* (Richmond: Curzon, 1995); Smith and Jones, *Political Impossibility*, pp. 40, 136.

[100] Khalidi, *Palestinian Identity*, pp. 91, 116.

at the end of the file.[101] These files replicate Danin's Hebrew-language collection of captured Arab gang documents first published in 1944.[102] The British at the time gave Danin captured documents to translate. These captured documents and assessments are a vital resource, as are the critical internal reports by the many British officials who had no 'real sympathy' for Jewish claims to Palestine and who felt 'so strongly about the injustice of it all that they are seeking transfers,' and so were candid in what they said.[103] Assistant District Commissioner Aubrey Lees' papers held at the Liddell Hart Centre exemplify these anti-Zionist (and at times anti-Semitic) sentiments. The Colonial Office transferred Lees out of Palestine for his pro-Palestinian views, after which Britain imprisoned him for being a fascist during the Second World War.[104] Second, the Palestinians and their supporters in neighbouring countries deployed lawyers, petitioned, and protested the military methods employed, and the British kept these petitions. Pro-Palestinian British residents of Palestine such as Frances Newton added their voice, so much so that the British banned her from the country, as did the Jaffa-based lawyer S. O. Richardson. Third, the Arabs opened propaganda offices in London and in Damascus that produced Arabic- and English-language pamphlets designed to influence Arab, Muslim, and British public opinion. Fourth, there is Arabic-language primary source material on the revolt, such as the collections of documents by 'Abd al-Wahhab al-Kayyali and Akram Zu'aytir, and the *bayanat* collected together at the end of the second edition of Khayriyya Qasimiyya's memoir of the Arab field commander Fawzi al-Qawuqji who served in Palestine in 1936.[105]

[101] For Danin translating see Asa Lefen, *Ha-Shai: Shorasheha Shel Kehilat ha-Modi'in ha-Yisraelit* [*The Roots of the Israeli Intelligence Community*] (Tel Aviv: Ministry of Defence, 1997), p. 44.

[102] Ezra Danin, *Te'udot u-Dmuyot me-Ginzey ha-Knufiyot ha-Arviyot, 1936–39* [*Documents and Portraits from the Arab Gangs Archives in the Arab Revolt in Palestine, 1936–39*] [1944] (Jerusalem: Magnes, 1981).

[103] Political Situation in Palestine, US Consulate General, 11 January 1930, 867N.00/77–330 [Reel M#1037/1], NARA II.

[104] Memoir, Unbeaten Track: Some Vicissitudes in Two Years of a Public Servant's Life by el-Asi, Lees Papers, 5/13, *passim* (Lees' nom de plume of al-'Asi, the Arabic name of the River Orontes, also means a rebel); T. Kushner and K. Lunn (eds), *Traditions of Intolerance: Historical Perspectives on Fascism and Race Discourse in Britain* (Manchester: Manchester University Press, 1979), p. 74.

[105] 'Abd al-Wahhab al-Kayyali, *Watha'iq al-Muqawama al-Filastiniyya al 'Arabiyya dida al-Ihtilal al-Baritani wa al-Sahyuniyya* [*Documents of the Palestinian Arab Resistance against British Occupation and Zionism*] (Beirut: IPS and Association of Palestinian Fund in Baghdad, 1968); Akram Zu'aytir, *Watha'iq al-Haraka al-Wataniyya al-Filastiniyya, 1918–39: Min Awraq Akram Zu'aytir* [*Documents of the Palestinian National Movement, 1918–39: From the Papers of Akram Zu'aytir*] (Beirut: IPS, 1979); Khayriyya Qasimiyya (ed.), *Filastin fi-Mudhakkirat Fawzi al-Qawuqji* [*Palestine in the Memories of Fawzi al-Qawuqji*] (two vols) (Beirut: PLO Research Centre and Jerusalem Publishing House,

While al-Qawuqji's family in Beirut still holds his papers for the revolt (the Institute for Palestine Studies in Beirut has material labelled as his papers but it mostly covers the 1948 war), Laila Parsons used them for her recently published assessment of him as a military commander.[106] Fifth, Palestinian activists and educators such as Bahjat Abu Gharbiyya, Khalil al-Sakakini, Akram Zu'aytir, Muhammad 'Izzat Darwaza, Khalil Totah, and Shaykh Abdul Hamid Sayih left diaries, memoirs, and documents.[107] This author interviewed Bahjat Abu Gharbiyya in 2009 and his recollection of British brutality informs the chapter on torture and extra-judicial punishment. Sixth, there are Palestinian oral histories of the revolt, as collected by Ted Swedenburg and Sonia Fathi al-Nimr, alongside some recondite (semi-fictional) accounts of the revolt that shed light on the Palestinian fight against the British, in one case as a response to soldiers raping a family member.[108] The Arabic TV drama series 'al-Taghriba al-Filastiniyya' ['The Palestinian Exile'] (Syria, 2004) shows how Palestinians have remembered the revolt and portrayed its leaders and those who collaborated, the director obscuring the names of the latter, making linkages to the next defeat in the war of 1948.[109] The contrasting

1975), with a second edition published as one volume and amended in 1995 but published a year later as Qasimiyya (ed.), *Mudhakkirat Fawzi al-Qawuqji* [*Memories of Fawzi al-Qawuqji*] (Damascus: Dar al-Namir, 1996).

[106] Parsons, *The Commander.*

[107] Bahjat Abu Gharbiyya, *Fi Khidamm al-nidal al-'arabi al-filastini: Mudhakkirat al-munadil Bahjat Abu Gharbiyya* [*In the Midst of the Struggle for the Arab Palestinian Cause: The Memoirs of Freedom-Fighter Bahjat Abu Gharbiyya* (Beirut: IPS, 1993); Khalil al-Sakakini (ed. Hala al-Sakakini), *Kadha Ana Ya Dunia* [*Such Am I, Oh World!*] [1955] (Beirut: al-Ittihad, 1982) and al-Sakakini (ed. A. Mussalam), *Yawmiyyat Khalil al-Sakakini: Yawmiyyat, Rasa'il, ta'amulat* [*Diaries of Khalil al-Sakakini: Diaries, Letters and Meditations*] (eight vols) (Jerusalem: Institute of Jerusalem Studies, 2003–10); Akram Zu'aytir, *Al-Haraka al-Wataniya al-Filastiniyya, 1935–39: Yawmiyyat Akram Zu'aytir* [*The Palestinian National Movement, 1935–39: Diaries of Akram Zu'aytir*] [1980] (Beirut: IPS, 1992); Muhammad 'Izzat Darwaza, *Mudhakkirat Muhammad 'Izzat Darwaza: Sab'a wa tis'una 'aman fil-haya* [*The Diaries of Muhammad 'Izzat Darwaza: 97 Years in a Life*] (six vols) (Beirut: Dar al Gharb al Islami, 1993); Thomas Ricks (ed.), *Turbulent Times in Palestine: The Diaries of Khalil Totah, 1886–1955* (Jerusalem: IPS and Passia, 2009); Shaykh Abdul Hamid Sayih, *Filastin; la Sala Tahta al-Hirab: Mudhakkirat al-Shaykh 'Abd al-Hamid al-Sa'ih* [*Palestine; No Prayer under Bayonets: The Memoirs of Shaykh Abdul Hamid Sayih*] (Beirut: IPS, 1994).

[108] Ted Swedenburg, *Memories of Revolt: The 1936–1939 Rebellion and the Palestinian National Past* (Minneapolis, MN: University of Minnesota Press, 1995); Sonia Fathi el-Nimr, 'The Arab Revolt in Palestine: A Study Based on Oral Sources' (Doctoral Thesis: University of Exeter, 1990); Muhammad Mustafa Ghandur, *Tha'r al-Dam* [*Blood Revenge: A Story from the Core of the Events of the Palestinian Revolt by the Pen of the Fighter Muhammad Mustafa Ghandur*] (Syria: n.p., 1939).

[109] Mustafa Kabha, 'The Palestinian Exile: Drama Shapes Memory,' in A. Sela and A. Kadish (eds), *The War of 1948: Representations of Israeli and Palestinian Memories and Narratives* (Bloomington, IN: Indiana University Press, 2016).

histories of Jewish victors and Palestinian vanquished are reflected in the Palestinians giving priority to memory over critical history; the past is simply too painful and involves too much self-criticism, and there is little accessible archival material available anyway. Weighted source bases and partisan national memories have skewed histories of the revolt, but creative methodologies and a wide reading of archival material construct a new critical history of the rising and the crushing of the Palestinians in the 1930s. New books on the revolt by authors such as Matthew Kelly and Steven Wagner do just this.[110]

Positioning the Text

This book is a military history of British pacification in Palestine but its discussion of internal Palestinian weaknesses and the Jewish use of British power to help their cause augments the polarised debates on the triangle of war between Palestinians, Jews, and British before 1948, and the Palestinian–Israeli conflict after 1948. With the Palestinians, this book details the remarkable suffering of Palestinians at the sharp end of British counter-insurgency but it establishes them as 'lions led by donkeys,' to steal Alan Clark's description of British soldiers and their commanders in the Great War, or 'sheep without a shepherd' in the words of King Abdullah of Transjordan.[111] For this reason, moderately effective rebel leaders such as al-Qassam and al-Qawuqji stand out from the crowd. Rich, elite town-based Palestinians, many of whom decamped during the revolt, looked down on the peasants who led the revolt as 'riffraff' and supported the urban-born, former Ottoman officer al-Qawuqji as he lent the revolt some 'respectability,' as would balefully happen again in 1948.[112] Palestinian elites saw peasants as metaphorical signifiers of identity rather than literal agents of revolutionary change. Peasants were 'sheep' and the rich enjoyed being photographed 'dressed in mock-village attire' alongside the poor as 'a token of authenticity.'[113]

[110] Matthew Kelly, *The Crime of Nationalism: Britain, Palestine, and Nation-Building on the Fringe of Empire* (Berkeley, CA: University of California Press, 2017); Steven Wagner, *Statecraft by Stealth: How Britain Ruled Palestine 1917–40* (Ithaca, NY: Cornell University Press, 2018).

[111] Alan Clark, *The Donkeys* (London: Random House, 1961); Yuval Arnon-Ohanna, *Herev mi-Bayit: ha-Ma'avak ha-Pnimi ba-tnu'a ha-le'umit ha-falastinit, 1929–39* [*The Internal Struggle within the Palestinian Movement, 1929–39*] (Tel Aviv: Hadar, 1989), p. 287.

[112] Parsons, *The Commander*, p. 123; Itamar Radai, *Palestinians in Two Cities, 1948* (London: Routledge, 2015), *passim*; Memorandum on Palestine Disturbances, August–September 1936, US Consul General Palestine to State Department, 9 October 1936, 867N.00/407 [Reel M#1037/2], NARA II.

[113] Ted Swedenburg, 'The Palestinian Peasant as National Signifier,' *Anthropological Quarterly* 63/1 (1990), pp. 18–30; Itamar Radai, 'The Rise and Fall of the Palestinian–Arab

Palestinians' 'networks of rebellion' were flawed. The urban bourgeoisie and higher echelons of insurgent command interacted badly with operational leadership in the field and its peasant support base. This made rebel fighting forces ineffective, with peasant-based rebel bands challenging their own leadership.[114] The leaders of the Arab revolt inside and outside of Palestine (and neighbouring Arab national rulers, at times) emerge from the violence of 1936 as disorganised, and at times as venal, naïve, and foolish. The absence of vanguard leadership was corrosive. It fed down the chain-of-command, corrupted rebels in the field, and transformed potential guerrillas backwards into socially reactionary rural bandit criminal gangs tinged with Islamic religious fundamentalism whose insurgent manifestos proscribed against townspeople listening to the radio, wearing Western headdress (as detailed in Appendix D), using (Jewish-supplied) electricity, women going unveiled, or wearing make-up or short-sleeved dresses, including Christian women. Photographs show 'Christian girls wearing "Muslim veils"' akin to a hijab while simultaneously dressed in Western dresses; Muslim urban women 'were to don the more conservative form of veiling' (see Figure 1.1)[115] A captured rural rebel tellingly complained to the British how while townsfolk may have 'controlled us for a hundred years, we will control them for one year.'[116] The rebels were rational actors with clear political goals to save Palestine from Jewish immigration but quite quickly their struggle stopped being politically instrumental. It did not have to be this way, for as Mao observed, 'it is only necessary to correct' bandits' 'political beliefs to convert them' into guerrillas.[117] Rather than forge unity with revolutionary education programmes and sculpted acts of exemplary violence to intimidate and liquidate the colonial ruling caste – excepting Andrews, the only other British civil official assassinated was Moffatt – rebels turned inwards, pursued vendettas, robbed peasants, and killed at least 1,000, perhaps 4,500, collaborators.[118] (Moffatt was

Middle Class under the British Mandate, 1920–39,' *Journal of Contemporary History* 51/ 3 (July 2016), pp. 487–506; Weldon C. Matthews, *Confronting an Empire, Constructing a Nation: Arab Nationalists and Popular Politics in Mandate Palestine* (London: Tauris, 2006), p. 251.

[114] From Staniland, *Networks of Rebellion* but without examination of Palestine.

[115] Arab Revolt in Palestine Photograph Album 1938, ACHA. The American Colony Hotel's archive in Jerusalem differs to the Vester Palestine collection at the Library of Congress in Washington, DC.

[116] Arnon-Ohanna, *Herev mi-Bayit*, p. 284.

[117] Mao Tse-tung, *On Guerrilla Warfare*, p. 76.

[118] Hillel Cohen, *Army of Shadows: Palestinian Collaboration with Zionism, 1917–1948* (Berkeley, CA: University of California Press, 2008), pp. 142–44 argues convincingly for the lower figure.

deep in intelligence work, which might explain his execution, as might the claim that he executed Palestinians who did not hand over hidden guns.[119]) Rebels tried to kill senior police officers Sir Charles Tegart and Roy Spicer. Gunmen murdered British archaeologist James Starkey in a bungled robbery in January 1938, and rebels wounded a British woman in an ambush in February 1938, but these were unplanned, unlike the provocative, proactive shootings of, say, two British sergeants' wives by EOKA in Cyprus in 1958. The answer to why the revolt failed lies within the Palestinian community as much as it does with the tough, well-established British pacification measures examined in this book. Why would Arab state leaders trust the British and encourage the rebels to call a ceasefire in October 1936, just when they were beginning successfully to organise and mobilise forms of protracted guerrilla war under al-Qawuqji, and why did Hajj Amin and the Palestinian leadership accede to this démarche? Why did rebel headquarters in Damascus run out of recruits and funds by 1938, forcing rebels to rob banks and villagers for funds, and forcibly conscript local men to fight for them? Why did so many Palestinians collaborate? Why did the Husayni and Nashashibi families prefer internecine fighting to combining against a common enemy? Having successfully with violence forced the British to scrap the Peel partition plan of 1937 with the Woodhead Commission re-negotiation of November 1938, why did Palestinian leaders not transform the diplomatic deal embodied in the consequent May 1939 White Paper into a tangible political settlement?

Jewish collaboration to support British anti-rebel operations in Palestine was the second apex of the triangle. The argument here is that British forces on the ground conspired with the Jews to defeat the rebels, a collaboration that suited both sides at the time. The British had been arming Jewish settlements since the early 1920s through the provision of sealed armouries that Jews supplemented with secret *slick* weapons caches; after 1936, the British expanded cooperation, jointly gathered intelligence with Jewish operatives, and they trained, paid for, and equipped more Jewish auxiliary police and paramilitary units that directed even more violence towards Palestinians. The hard-edged manoeuvres of the anti-rebel British–Jewish Special Night Squads in Galilee in 1938 were the most visible collaboration between the two sides but day-to-day, low-level training and joint action endured throughout Palestine, and secured the country.[120] The *Yishuv* carried over colonial methods learned from

---

[119] Morton, 12960/6, IWMSA; Author interview, Abu Gharbiyya, Amman, Jordan, 21 June 2009; Yasin, *Al-Thawra al-'Arabiyya al-Kubra*, pp. 152–53.
[120] See Matthew Hughes, 'Terror in Galilee,' pp. 590–610.

1.1 The American Colony Hotel Archive has images of Christian women covering their heads during the revolt with 'Muslim veils' (from American Colony Hotel Archive)

the British to the Israeli State after 1948. Israel's collective punishments and house demolitions of Palestinians convicted of terror offences stem from imperial Order in Council legislation from 1931 that the British codified in the 1945 Defence (Emergency) Regulations, used originally against Jewish insurgents.

Turning to Britain, this study sits between two poles of scholarship on British counter-insurgency. On the one hand, it rejects the traditional, dated view that British armed forces, 'generally more scrupulous than most,' worked within the rule of law to avoid the human rights abuses that marked out other colonial or post-colonial powers.[121] General Sir Frank Kitson, a foremost proponent of British counter-insurgency, expressed the ideal of the British 'way' in counter-insurgency, writing how 'No country which relies on the law of the land to regulate the lives of its citizens can afford to see that law flouted by its own government, even in an insurgency situation. In other words everything done by a government and its agents in combating insurgency must be legal.'[122] This book proves that British security forces simply changed the law to make considerable brutality legal, on top of which many soldiers inflicted extra-judicial violence. On the other hand, the measured use of state-sanctioned force in Palestine described in detail in this book – as awful as it now seems – falls short of recent arguments on British imperial rule of Nazi-style 'Gestapo' excesses in places such as British Kenya in the 1950s with its 'Gulag' prison archipelago of concentration camps.[123] Parts of the empirical evidence presented here support critical arguments on Kenya in the 1950s and on the structural, systemic oppression of British imperialism across the piece. But this study makes the case for British particularism in counter-insurgency, arguing that British pacification in Palestine was brutal absolutely but relatively benign when set against other colonial and neo-imperial powers, as even a cursory glance at other twentieth-century counter-insurgency campaigns proves, from the Spanish in the Rif mountains to the Germans in Africa before the Great War and during the Second World War, the Japanese in China, the Italians in Libya, the French in Algeria, the Americans in Vietnam, or the Sri Lankan Army more recently against Tamil separatists. There was never a British hearts and minds, minimum-force way in counter-insurgency but focusing on sadistic outrages and death squads detracts from the controlled use of quotidian, atomising, non-lethal oppressive collective punishments such as draconian fines, tight censorship, and extensive summary detention that cumulatively ended insurrection and sustained imperial rule.[124]

---

[121] John Pimlott, 'The British Experience,' in Ian F. W. Beckett (ed.), *The Roots of Counter-Insurgency: Armies and Guerrilla Warfare 1900–1945* (London: Blandford, 1988), p. 11.

[122] Frank Kitson, *Bunch of Five* (London: Faber and Faber, 1977), p. 289. See also Robert Thompson's classic *Defeating Communist Insurgency: The Lessons of Malaya and Vietnam* (New York, NY: Praeger, 1966).

[123] Elkins, *Britain's Gulag*, pp. xiii, 61, 171, 306; Marc Parry, 'A Reckoning: Colonial Atrocities and Academic Reputations on Trial in British Courtroom,' *Chronicle of Higher Education* (1 June 2016); David Anderson, *Histories of the Hanged: Britain's Dirty War in Kenya and the End of Empire* (London: Weidenfeld and Nicolson, 2005), pp. 311ff (and dust jacket blurb); Huw Bennett, *Fighting the Mau Mau: The British Army and Counter-Insurgency in the Kenya Emergency* (Cambridge: University Press, 2013), *passim*. See also John McGuffin, *The Guinea Pigs* (London: Penguin, 1974), pp. 131, 136.

[124] Smith and Jones, *Political Impossibility*, p. 40.

Radical 'the blood never dried' theses on British imperialism miss the point that repression in Palestine was not especially bloody and they overlook the friction that retarded applications of absolute force and the human texture of British pacification.[125] Nor did the British behave as one. Some security forces were more vicious than others. Palestinians singled out 'wicked' Scottish regiments for their harshness, policemen saying the same thing, as would Catholics in Northern Ireland in 1970.[126] It was police CID and not the Army that ran dedicated torture houses to inflict 'third degree methods' on suspects, what it called 'Arab Investigation Centres,' replicated in Kenya in the 1950s with 'Mau Mau Investigation Centres' and in Aden's (Army-run) investigation centres in the 1960s; the Army in Palestine even complained to the High Commissioner about police brutality and thought them ill disciplined, 'not very good I'm afraid.'[127]

This book concentrates on the Army's part in pacification as the Palestine police collapsed under the weight of an insurgency that targeted the local officers employed in peaceful times to police the country, with many Arab officers and clerks leaking information to rebels.[128] The British eventually disarmed Arab police officers.[129] Army intelligence officers accused senior policemen of gross corruption during the revolt, while 'unsuitable' constables sold guns to Arabs.[130] Reforms after the 1929 riots to transform the police into a civil-based force had only incrementally improved it and Indian police adviser Sir Charles Tegart in 1938 recommended re-activating its pre-1926 military-style gendarmerie incarnation.[131] The police force was neither a coercive

---

[125] John Newsinger, *The Blood Never Dried: A People's History of the British Empire* (London: Bookmarks, 2006).

[126] Addressed to British Regiments in Palestine, Arab Revolutionary Council, Southern Syria, Palestine, Signed by Aref Abdul Razik ['Arif 'Abd al-Raziq], Commander in Chief of the Arab Forces in Palestine, 19 November 1938, Report on an Arab Commander, 41/94, HA; Proud, 11109/3, IWMSA; T. P. Coogan, *On the Blanket: The Inside Story of the IRA Prisoners' 'Dirty Protest'* [1980] (Houndmills: Palgrave, 2002), pp. 54–55.

[127] Edward Keith-Roach (ed. Paul Eedle), *Pasha of Jerusalem: Memoirs of a District Commissioner under the British Mandate* (London: Radcliffe, 1994), p. 191; High Commissioner Palestine to Shuckburgh (CO), 20 October 1938 FO 371/21865, p. 197, TNA; Letter, Burr (Inlying Piquet Haifa) to Mother and Father, n.d, Burr Papers, 88/8/1, IWMD; Letter, O'Connor to Wife, n.d., O'Connor Papers, 3/1/20, LHCMA; Fuare-Walker, 6612/5, IWMSA.

[128] Letter, Brooke-Popham (HQ, RAF, Cairo) to ACM Ellington (London), 20 July 1936, Brooke-Popham Papers, 4/3/44, LHCMA.

[129] Diary/Notes, October 1938, p. 4, Edward Keith-Roach Papers, AL-KR.

[130] Typed Memoir, Pieces of War, pp. 41–48, Simonds Papers, 08/46/1, IWMD; Letter, Burr (Inlying Piquet) to Mother and Father, 24 February 1938, Burr Papers, 88/8/1, IWMD; Colin Imray, *Policeman in Palestine* (Devon: Gaskell, 1995), p. 11.

[131] For police-military differences see Hew Strachan, *The Politics of the British Army* (Oxford: Clarendon, 1997), pp. 163–94.

fighting army nor a consensual civil police force. Its job was to oversee the political economy of colonial exploitation rather than repress major political dissent in one academic's view, with the 'biggest incompetents in the world' without 'brains or energy' in the Palestine Chief Secretary's opinion, and full of fascists in the Jews' estimation who gave each other Nazi salutes and painted swastikas on their riot shields.[132] The Army took over the police in September 1938 and ran pacification its own way based on military ideas about security. Soldiers sidelined CID and gathered their own intelligence, often from Jewish Haganah sources.[133] The Army's roots to counter-insurgency were intuitive as they derived from military doctrine as embodied in the *Field Service Regulations*, last updated in 1935. Legal and illegal counter-rebel measures reflected military practices and collective memories from earlier pacification campaigns that soldiers absorbed at Sandhurst, in regimental messes, and from the pages of Service journals. Emergency legislation, the *King's Regulations, Field Service Regulations*, the *Manual of Military Law*, and War Office pamphlets guided officers, alongside reflective imperial policing texts by Callwell, Colonel H. J. Simson, General Sir John Dill, Major-General Sir Charles Gwynn, and General Sir Andrew Skeen, but experience of pacification underpinned the increasingly tough actions of the soldiers in charge in Palestine by late 1938.[134] Without the post-Vietnam War era counter-insurgency managerial jargon and modernisation methodologies so fashionable today, British forces in Palestine killed rebels

---

[132] Diary, 14 August 1937 and 29 December [1938], Battershill Papers, MSS. Brit. Emp. S. 467, Box 12, File 6, WL; Martin Thomas, *Violence and Colonial Order: Police, Workers and Protest in the European Colonial Empire, 1918–1940* (Cambridge: Cambridge University Press, 2012), pp. 2–3, 325–27; Note of a Conversation with Lord Lloyd, CO, 24 May 1940 at 16.00 hrs. Present Lord Lloyd, Sir George Gator and Chaim Weizmann, S25/7563, CZA; Letter, Burr to Jill, n.d., Burr Papers, 88/8/1, IWMD.

[133] Telegram, High Commissioner to Secretary of State Colonies, 12 September 1938, FO 371/21863, TNA; Eldad Harouvi, *Palestine Investigated: The Story of the CID of the Palestine Police Force, 1920–48* (Sussex: Academic Press 2016), *passim*. D. J. Clark, 'The Colonial Police and Anti-Terrorism: Bengal 1930–1936, Palestine 1937–1947, and Cyprus 1955–1959' (Doctoral Thesis: University of Oxford, 1978), pp. 23, 254; David Anderson and David Killingray, 'An Orderly Retreat: Policing the End of Empire,' in Anderson and Killingray (eds), *Policing and Decolonisation: Politics, Nationalism and the Police, 1917–65* (Manchester: Manchester University Press, 1991), p. 4–5; Strachan, *The Politics of the British Army*, pp. 163–94.

[134] Callwell, *Small Wars*; Simson, *British Rule and Rebellion*; Gen Sir John Dill, *War Office, Notes on the Tactical Lessons of the Palestine Rebellion 1936* (London: War Office, 1937); Gwynn, *Imperial Policing*; Gen Sir Andrew Skeen, *Passing It On: Short Talks on Tribal Fighting on the North-West Frontier of India* [1932] (Aldershot: Gale and Polden, 1943); *War Office, Issued by Command of the Army Council, Manual of Military Law* (London: War Office, 1929); *War Office, By Command of the Army Council, Notes on Imperial Policing, 1934* (London: War Office, 30 January 1934); *War Office, By Command of the Army Council, 5 August 1937, Duties in the Aid of the Civil Power* (London: War Office, 1937).

and punished civilians. Their ad hoc method of tactical flexibility, civil–military cooperation, and exemplary (i.e., brutal) force worked; crafted violence equalled political success. Pacification was an operational art *and* an instrument of politics, the former contingent on long-term governmental political will and with the Second World War looming London refused to cut and run from Palestine. This book introduces briefly the Army's experience and understanding of pacification in Chapter 5, the author not wishing to replicate in detail studies on British military traditions in suppressing colonial insurrection.[135]

---

[135] Bennett, *Fighting the Mau Mau*, pp. 83–107; Ian Beckett, 'The Study of Counter-Insurgency: A British Perspective,' *Small Wars and Insurgencies* 1/1 (April 1990), pp. 47–53; Matthew Hughes (ed.), *British Ways of Counter-Insurgency: A Historical Perspective* (Oxford: Routledge, 2013); French, *The British Way in Counter-Insurgency*.

2 The Emergency State in Mandate Palestine

The Law in These Parts[1]

Law was the bedrock of Britain's pacification of Palestine. The extra-judicial violence detailed in the later parts of this book was not fundamental to British victory. Instead, 'lawfare' pacified the country through quotidian application of a crafted, all-encompassing legal system that restrained, detained, and impoverished Palestinians, hanged and killed them, and demolished their homes. It banned newspapers, interned people, fined and exiled them, censored their mail and telephone calls, took away livestock and crops, whipped them, imposed curfews and police posts, exacted corvée, and restricted travel. It made singing, shouting, and waving flags illegal, alongside processing the wrong way down a street, buying a toy children's gun, or meeting in a cafe. People paid financial bonds to ensure their good behaviour. If they had a nice house, the authorities marked it for destruction if a stranger in the neighbour-hood broke the law. Photographs in regimental archives show soldiers painting big numbers on buildings for future destruction.[2] Whole village populations walked miles and back every day to report their presence at a police station.[3] Legality gave repression the correctness demanded by the British colonial state, the 'golden rule' being that each 'new law must be effective and must be fairly applied' rather than fair, noted a soldier-proponent of British counter-insurgency.[4] Before examining the often bewildering, always extensive, and necessarily supplemental laws

---

[1] To borrow the title of the Hebrew-language film 'The Law in These Parts' (2012) that presents comparable Israeli legal structures in the Occupied Territories.

[2] Photograph at 170A12W/P/5035, Royal Green Jackets Regimental Archive, Hampshire Local Record Office, Winchester. The photograph appears again with the caption 'Marking houses for blowing up at Beit Dajan.'

[3] Ghassan Kanafani, 'Thawrat 1936–1939 fi Filastin: Khalfiyyat, tafasil wa tahlil' ['The 1936–1939 Revolt in Palestine: Background, Details and Analysis'], *Shu'un Filastinyya* [*Palestinian Matters*] 6 (January 1972), p. 69.

[4] Robert Thompson, *Defeating Communist Insurgency: The Lessons of Malaya and Vietnam* (New York, NY: Praeger, 1966), p. 53.

that the Mandate Government effected in Palestine after 1917 and their implications for the pacification of the country, three points that were central to British control of Palestine require clarification in the first part of this chapter. First, British power in Palestine was prerogative, pre-eminent sovereign authority deriving from unilateral Orders in Council issued by London without independent scrutiny, authorising the High Commissioner in Jerusalem, Sir Arthur Wauchope in the revolt's first phase to February 1938, succeeded by Sir Harold MacMichael, to exercise power by way of subsidiary Ordinance legislation. The Government in Palestine made laws official by publication in the journal of record, the *Palestine Gazette*. Second, the Palestine Government lacked the typical democratic checks and balances between executive, judiciary, and legislature. Third, the Army's part in pacification gave it a powerful role in civil affairs as it appropriated executive functions and with forms of martial law assumed judicial authority. The Army injected into the tough civil legislation detailed here its own experience and rules on pacification, and it took command of the militarised Palestine police force.

Instead of a separation of the branches of government or a Westminster-style Walter Bagehot 'fusion of powers' model with healthy blending of executive and legislative responsibilities, in Palestine there was no legislature.[5] Instead, the law served a British-appointed, all-powerful colonial executive that without parliamentary scrutiny and with help from the Army tested the judiciary. For instance, when Sir Michael McDonnell, Palestine's Chief Justice who was seen to have 'very marked Arab sympathies,' upheld the law and found against the Army's destruction of Arab old Jaffa in June 1936, much to the delight of Palestinians who distributed his findings, the Colonial Office dismissed him.[6] When civil criminal courts were too slow or lenient in processing rebel suspects, the Army admonished them and replaced them with military courts. Government in Palestine was by fiat, by proclamation through the High Commissioner. If politics is the formal execution of power and law is the formal restraint of power, law in Palestine was synonymous with executive power, and infused with colonial ideas of the subject population's collective lives and shared guilt that demanded group punishments. Britain sought 'an empire based on laws but laws flexible enough to sanction and excuse

---

[5] Walter Bagehot, *The English Constitution* [1867] (Cambridge: Cambridge University Press, 2001), pp. 8–9, 12, 19.
[6] Charles Townshend, 'Martial Law: Legal and Administrative Problems of Civil Emergency in Britain and the Empire, 1800–1940,' *The Historical Journal* 25/1 (1982), p. 188.

the expedient use of terror,' in the words of one critic.[7] The two worlds of core and peripheral legal systems rubbed up badly, for how 'is a constitutional nation to contend with the nakedly brutal realities of empire? Can such a country rule over alien lands and peoples without corrupting its defining ideals?'[8] Just such a 'boomerang effect' shook France when military coups in Algeria in the late 1950s and 1960s threatened the overthrow of metropolitan rule in Paris and pushed Charles de Gaulle to end French rule in Algeria.[9] In the Carnation revolution in Portugal in 1975, the country's colonial wars in Africa prompted a liberal coup by the Portuguese Army that toppled the authoritarian Lisbon government and augured in democracy.

When the British conquered Palestine in 1917, they inherited an amalgam of Ottoman and French (Napoleonic Code) laws, with some English law, alongside Christian, Islamic, and Jewish religious courts for the day-to-day life of the country's different communities.[10] The 1924 Trial Upon Information Ordinance introduced English codes of procedure – so how courts conducted their business – and replaced the Ottoman Code of Criminal Procedure but the new Ordinance applied only to Palestine's superior courts, so District courts and above, while the Ottoman Magistrate's Law guided the first-tier Magistrates' courts formally established in 1922.[11] The British kept in force but updated many Ottoman Penal Code laws, sometimes cited in the Muslim calendar, and written in Ottoman Turkish that used Turkish, Arabic, and Farsi (Persian) languages. After twenty years of running with a complex, hybrid legal system, the British formalised a new Criminal Code in December 1936 based loosely around English common (and some statute) law. The new Code was 'still very much the familiar Ottoman interpretation of what constituted a criminal offence but with many English interpretations added to it,' noted police officer Ted Horne.[12] The British prosecuted suspects during the revolt using the Criminal Code, but they were mostly charged using emergency legislation that superseded civil criminal codes, even though until the establishment of military courts in late 1937 they prosecuted captured rebels in civil criminal courts.

---

[7] R. W. Kostal, *A Jurisprudence of Power: Victorian Empire and the Rule of Law* (Oxford: Oxford University Press, 2005), pp. 481–82.

[8] Ibid., p. ix.

[9] Hannah Arendt, *On Violence* (New York, NY: Harcourt Brace, 1970), p. 54.

[10] Assaf Likhovski, *Law and Identity in Mandate Palestine* (Chapel Hill, NC: University of North Carolina Press, 2006), p. 2.

[11] Henry Kantrovitch, *The Law of Criminal Procedure in Palestine* (Tel Aviv: Mizpah, 1938), pp. 3–5.

[12] Edward Horne, *A Job Well Done (Being a History of the Palestine Police Force, 1920–1948)* (Tiptree: Anchor Press, 1982), p. 220.

The British established the administrative and legal superstructure for Mandate Palestine and for the emergency legislation used during the Arab revolt through Orders in Council, issued by the King, to whom Parliament had delegated law-making powers.[13] Following the substitution of military with civil rule in 1920, Palestine's 1922 Order in Council created the country's constitution.[14] Orders in Council were historically the exercise of Royal Prerogative in consultation with the monarch's closest advisers of the Privy Council (or Ministers nowadays), and were 'simply a means through which government, in the form of a committee of ministers, can introduce legislation in the form of Orders in Council, without the need to go through the full parliamentary process.'[15] They reflected the fact that before the establishment of the modern state, the monarch in council was the 'obvious authority' available to make rules and regulations.[16] Imperial Statutes, Acts, and Royal Instructions fulfilled similar functions. Orders in Council saved time but lacked accountability and were an unusual tool for modern metropolitan democracies where parliaments and judiciaries scrutinised and agreed new laws. Government used them in wartime and in the 1830s to stop the spread of cholera. They could not alter an established rule of English Law but there was no well-established English law in Palestine to challenge Orders in Council, nor any tradition of such things, not until the Criminal Code of 1936 at which point the Emergency Regulations had taken over.[17] Parliament in London gave the Crown through statute the power to make laws through Orders in Council but unilateral Orders without any legislative scrutiny were and are an uncommon form of enacting major legislation in Britain, if not unknown in times of emergency or more recently in relation to the European Union. Thus, in 1914, Orders in Council rushed through Parliament made into law the Defence of the Realm Act that altered the state of the British constitution, 'the executive became the legislature, and parliament declined into a relatively unimportant sounding board for public opinion,' as one lawyer curtly put it.[18] The same happened in 1939 with the Emergency Powers (Defence) Act. Despite this, in the culturally 'white' metropolis the judiciary, legislature,

[13] Gary Slapper and David Kelly, *The English Legal System, Fifteenth Edition, 2014–15* (London: Routledge, 2014), p. 110.
[14] *A Survey of Palestine, Prepared in December 1945 and January 1946 for the Information of the Anglo-American Committee of Inquiry* (Jerusalem: Government Printer, 1946), i, p. 4.
[15] Slapper and Kelly, *English Legal System*, pp. 110–11.
[16] Sir William Holdsworth, *A History of English Law* [1903] (London: Methuen, 1982), xiv, p. 103.
[17] Ibid., i, p. 566, xiii, p. 680, xiv, p. 102.
[18] A. W. B. Simpson, *In the Highest Degree Odious: Detention without Trial in Wartime Britain* (Oxford: Clarendon, 1992), pp. 6–7.

and the people mitigated emergency regulations and Orders existed only at Parliament's will.[19] In Palestine, by contrast, Orders in Council were the primary form of law making and the unaccountable corner stone of colonial rule, untampered by legislative or judicial scrutiny. They suited military rule, as soldier-author Colonel H. J. Simson noted at the time, Orders in Council preventing courts from challenging regulations made by military commanders.[20] Common law, individual rights, and habeas corpus applied at home, in the white Dominions, and to British subjects abroad, but not 'in the empire of dark-skinned peoples,' where threats to the state led easily to the suspension of the 'normative universe of a rule of law.'[21] British (and local Arab and Jewish) judges in Palestine rarely used English case law in Palestine to challenge official rulings, while pre-Mandate Ottoman laws did little to resist the new body of British colonial law except to preserve local religious and communal customs, which the British had little interest in changing as they ensured local social stability. The British had washed away the Ottoman legal code by 1936 anyway. Illiteracy and poverty compounded poor access to and limited comprehension of the law, especially amongst rural Palestinian Muslim peasants who felt the rasp of pacification.

There were sixty-three Orders in Council for Palestine up to 1944 and twenty amendments thereof,[22] some repealed while others such as the 1925 citizenship Order shaped Palestine's history, but only six of these Orders (and Acts) concern us here, alongside two associated Emergency Regulations:

- 1922 Order in Council
- 1931 Palestine (Defence) Order in Council
- 1936 Emergency Regulations derived from the 1931 Order in Council
- 1936 Palestine Martial Law (Defence) Order in Council dated 26 September 1936 but not published in the *Palestine Gazette*[23]
- 1937 Palestine (Defence) Order in Council
- 1939 Emergency Powers (Colonial Defence) Order in Council

---

[19] Norman Wilding and Philip Laundy, *An Encyclopaedia of Parliament* (New York, NY: St Martin's, 1971), p. 511.

[20] Col H. J. Simson, *British Rule and Rebellion* (Edinburgh and London: Blackwood, 1937), p. 108.

[21] Kostal, *Jurisprudence of Power*, pp. 481–82; Nasser Hussain, *The Jurisprudence of Emergency: Colonialism and the Rule of Law* (Ann Arbor, MI: University of Michigan Press, 2003), pp. 16–17.

[22] *Survey of Palestine*, ii, Appendix A.

[23] Foreign Jurisdiction, 1890. Order in Council, dated 26 September 1936, entitled The Palestine Martial Law (Defence) Order in Council 1936. Presented to the House of Commons in Pursuance of Section 11 of the Act. Privy Council Office, 20 November 1936 (courtesy of Parliamentary Archives, Houses of Parliament).

- 1939 Emergency Powers (Defence) Act
- 1945 Emergency Regulations derived from the 1937 Order in Council

The 1922, 1931, and 1937 Orders in Council were pivotal to the repression of the Arab revolt as they enabled a raft of subsidiary enforcement legislation – notably Ordinances but also Emergency Regulations – that underpinned pacification. Article 17 of the 1922 Order set the paramount rule that the High Commissioner could make any law that he thought necessary for public order:

The High Commissioner shall have full power and authority, without prejudice to the powers inherent in or reserved by this Order to His Majesty and subject always to any conditions and limitations prescribed by any such instructions as may be given to him under the Sign Manual and Signet or through a Secretary of State, to promulgate such Ordinances as may be necessary for the peace, order, and good government of Palestine, provided that no Ordinance shall be promulgated which shall restrict complete freedom of conscience and the free exercise of all forms of worship save in so far as is required for the maintenance of public order and morals.[24]

After the 1929 Jewish–Palestinian disturbances, London issued the 1931 Palestine (Defence) Order in Council that made additions to the High Commissioner's powers, giving him even greater powers, and its Article IV made possible the Emergency Regulations issued on 19 April 1936:

This Order shall have effect in Palestine from time to time in case any public emergency, touching the public safety and defence of His Majesty's Empire or of Palestine on being proclaimed by the High Commissioner, and shall come into operation at such time as it shall be so proclaimed by the High Commissioner and shall continue in operation therein until the High Commissioner shall by Proclamation declare that it has ceased to be in operation ... The High Commissioner may make Regulations for securing the public safety and the defence of Palestine and as to the powers and duties for that purpose of the High Commissioner and the Officers of His Majesty's Naval, Military, or Air Forces and other persons acting in their behalf, and in particular by such Regulations, make provision with regard to all matters coming within the classes of subjects hereinafter enumerated, that is to say:- (a) Censorship, and the control and suppression of publications, writings, maps, plans, photographs, communications and means of communications; (b) Arrest ... (c) Control of harbours ... (d) Control of aerodromes ... (e) Transportation by land ... (f) Trading ... (g) Appropriation ... and may by such Regulations authorize the trial ... of persons committing offences against the Regulations.[25]

[24] *Legislation of Palestine, 1918–25, Including the Orders-in-Council etc.* (compiled by Norman Bentwich) (Alexandria: Whitehead Morris, 1926), i, pp. 6–7.
[25] Robert Drayton, *The Laws of Palestine in Force on 31 December 1933* (London: Waterlow, 1934), iii, pp. 2619–24.

The threat of disorder meant that in 1937 Britain issued a further Order in Council that referred to the Palestine (Defence) Order in Council of 1931 and to the Palestine Martial Law (Defence) Order in Council of 26 September 1936. The 1937 Order would come into effect from 'time to time on being proclaimed by the High Commissioner.' It empowered him to make 'Defence Regulations' 'as appear to him in his unfettered discretion to be necessary or expedient for securing the public safety, the defence of Palestine, the maintenance of public order and the suppression of mutiny, rebellion and riot, and for securing the essentials of life to the community.' Defence Regulations allowed for the detention and deportation of anyone if it 'appears to the High Commissioner to be expedient in the interests of the public safety of the defence of Palestine.' Defence Regulations authorised the taking of any property or undertaking, the search and entering of any premises, and for the High Commissioner to amend 'any law, suspend the operation of any law, and apply any law with or without modification.'[26] The emergency of the Second World War and the Jewish revolt against British rule after 1945 prompted new Acts and Emergency Regulations based on the 1931 and 1937 Orders in Council, against new enemies. Israel adopted elements of these British colonial-era laws to support repression of Palestinians under occupation after 1948, as did Jordan and Egypt on the West Bank and in Gaza.[27]

The Orders in Council triggered a tsunami of subsidiary legislation in the form of principal Ordinances and Emergency Regulations, to which the British added amendments, the key ones being:

- 1926 Collective Punishments Ordinance
- 1926 Police Ordinance
- 1926 Prisons Ordinance
- 1933 Press Ordinance

[26] The Palestine (Defence) Order in Council 1937 in *Ordinances, Regulations, Rules, Orders and Notices. Government of Palestine. Annual Volume for 1937. Volume 2* (Jerusalem: Government Printing Press, 1938), pp. 260–64.

[27] Raja Shehadeh, *Occupier's Law: Israel and the West Bank* (Washington, DC: IPS, 1985), p. 65; Lisa Hajjar, *Courting Conflict: The Israeli Military System in the West Bank and Gaza* (London: University of California Press, 2005), pp. 49, 52, 60; Baruch Bracha, 'Restriction of Personal Freedom without Due Process of Law According to the Defence (Emergency) Regulations, 1945,' in Y. Dinstein and F. Domb (eds), *Israel Yearbook on Human Rights. Volume 8* (Tel Aviv: Intersdar, 1978), pp. 296–323; Arie Pach, 'Human Rights in West Bank Military Courts,' in Y. Dinstein and F. Domb (eds), *Israel Yearbook on Human Rights. Volume 7* (Tel Aviv: Tel Aviv University, 1977), pp. 224–25; 1945 Defence (Emergency) Regulations in *Official Gazette of Palestine Supplement 2* (No. 1442) 855, 27 September 1945 in *Ordinances, Regulations, Rules, Orders and Notices. Government of Palestine. Annual Volume for 1945. Volumes 2 and 3* (Jerusalem: Government Printing Press, 1946), pp. 1055–95 (on microfilm in BL at SPR Mic. P1).

- 1936 Criminal Code Ordinance
- 1936 Emergency Regulations

The myriad amendments to these Ordinances and to the Emergency Regulations of April 1936 – alongside other discrete Ordinances on daggers, knives, guns, explosives, movement, fines, and curfews, all of which also had amendments – were immensely versatile, allowing the security forces to reassess Ordinances and Emergency Regulations and close loopholes considering rebel actions with suitable amendments. Tracking the multiple amendments to the regulations is not straightforward, one succeeding the next, referring to earlier principal (or main) Ordinances and Emergency Regulations that are not always the first chronologically. Alongside the Ordinances, Emergency Regulations and their amendments there were Public Notices, Rules, Proclamations, Orders, Bylaws, Rules of Court, Curfew Notices, Notices of Fines, and Ottoman legislation superseded in 1936 by the new Criminal Code. The weak spot in this system for soldiers and police was the civil criminal court system that, first, acted too slowly and, second, judges sitting without a jury, as was the case in Palestine, acquitted too many suspects, sometimes on what security forces saw as technicalities such as whether a weapon or ammunition was useable. Findings of innocence help explain the large numbers of suspects shot out-of-hand when captured, circumventing for security forces any legal due process, or '"bumpings-off" – nothing more or less,' recalled one British civil official.[28] Soldiers wanted speedy justice. 'One must arrest a man in the morning, try him in the afternoon, and shoot him at dawn the next day, if one has to go to drastic measures,' in the words of an RAF officer.[29] A model of this was when the British captured Qassamite leader Shaykh Farhan al-Sa'di on 22 November 1937 – relatives of a local man killed by his rebel band turned him in – they tried him on the 24th and executed him three days later.[30] The British hanged in Acre jail rather than shot those convicted of capital offences. The commander (GOC) of the Army in Palestine by 1937–38, who also commanded the police from September 1938 as the force fractured when rebels targeted Palestinian officers, and not the High Commissioner confirmed the sentence. (The order of battle appendix – Appendix A – details the four supreme armed

---

[28] Note, Jerusalem, 25 June 1939, Lees Papers, 5/9, LHCMA.
[29] Letter, Brooke-Popham (HQ, RAF, Cairo) to ACM Ellington (London), 29 August 1936, Brooke-Popham Papers, 4/3/48, LHCMA.
[30] Hillel Cohen, *Army of Shadows: Palestinian Collaboration with Zionism, 1917–1948* (Berkeley, CA: University of California Press, 2008), p. 135; Hugh Foot, *A Start in Freedom* (London: Hodder and Stoughton, 1964), p. 51.

forces commanders in Palestine during the revolt, the first properly an AOC and not GOC as he was an RAF airman.) The GOC commuted vast numbers of death penalties, signing off a maximum of 112. The slow-turning wheels of justice prompted the Army to demand the right to use military courts to try suspects, a request met with the Defence (Military Courts) Regulations of 1937, enabled by the principal legislation of the 1936 Emergency Regulations, itself enabled by the 1931 Order in Council, the 1937 Regulations then becoming the principal legislation for amendments. Repressive legislation snowballed one to the next. While military courts were separate to the judiciary and staffed by military personnel, they acquitted surprisingly many suspects, contra Palestinian claims of their overwhelming harshness. Army officers acted humanely while local circumstances transformed their behaviour. Some security officials 'loathed' the collapse of civil order while others 'relished' the power afforded them by the 'emergency conditions' of political disturbances.[31] The same soldiers who 'insulted' and 'robbed' villagers before the October 1936 ceasefire, behaved in a 'good manner' and paid for what they took once there was peace, rebel commander Fawzi al-Qawuqji noted.[32]

Military courts and the Army's demands to impose martial law and take charge of the executive and judiciary threatened the civil administration's autonomy. The colonial Government and the Colonial Office resisted this. The Army was ambivalent on assuming full authority as emergency legislation and 'statutory' martial law by 1937–38, a stage between semi-military rule under civil powers and full (or 'real') martial law under military powers, gave it the coercive powers that it wanted, without the opprobrium and inconvenience of running the country.[33] Acting as an aid to the civil power might have been 'disagreeable,' but martial law was freighted with danger.[34] Without an indemnity, there was the risk of post-crisis prosecutions for martial-rule excesses, as happened with Governor Edward Eyre in Jamaica following the Morant Bay rebellion in 1865 and with General Reginald Dyer after the Amritsar massacre in 1919, and the Government and the military agreed that substitution of

---

[31] David Anderson and David Killingray, 'An Orderly Retreat: Policing the End of Empire,' in David Anderson and David Killingray (eds), *Policing and Decolonisation: Politics, Nationalism and the Police, 1917–65* (Manchester: Manchester University Press, 1991), pp. 17–18.

[32] Khayriyya Qasimiyya (ed.), *Filastin fi-Mudhakkirat Fawzi al-Qawuqji* [*Palestine in the Memories of Fawzi al-Qawuqji*] (Beirut: PLO Research Centre and Jerusalem Publishing House, 1975), ii, p. 51.

[33] Simson, *British Rule*, pp. 96ff, 103; Douglas Porch, *Counterinsurgency: Exposing the Myths of the New Way of War* (Cambridge: Cambridge University Press, 2013), pp. 134–35.

[34] S. T. Banning, *Military Law (Made Easy)* (Aldershot: Gale and Polden, 1932), p. 299.

civil by military rule was a victory for terrorism.[35] Moreover, martial law, the continental notion of a 'state of siege,' sat badly with British legal and constitutional traditions that manifested a 'semi-conscious desire to avoid making formal Military rule arrangements for coping with possible internal crises.'[36] As the Duke of Wellington remarked, 'martial law means no law at all.'[37] The Army's complaint in Palestine boiled down not to the severity of legislation, with which it was generally content, but the decisiveness with which the Government executed the law. To understand pacification in Palestine is to understand the relationship between the colonial executive and the Army. The military drew on emergency laws as discussed here but also on its experience of pacification, more so as the Army gripped executive power and without a counter-balancing judiciary or legislature turned to internal texts as guides, such as the *Manual of Military Law*, first published by the War Office in 1884 and last updated in 1929. As mentioned in the last chapter, the War Office also produced handy pocket-sized pamphlets to guide soldiers in the field, and there were *The King's Regulations*, too. The *Manual of Military Law* and similar texts restrained soldiers in imperial policing operations to be an 'aid to civil power,' but civil power was built on control of the law and with the military now assuming civil functions this further diminished restraints to pacification. By October 1938, the tables had turned, the civil executive becoming an aid to military power. The growing strength of the Army in Palestine meant that discussion of colonial law moved from the Colonial Office to the War Office.

The imbalance between the executive, legislature, and judiciary in Palestine was such that checks on executive power came from within the executive branch of the Palestine Government, from the Army, occasionally from the judiciary or the Colonial Office, or from external actors. Formal legislative scrutiny came indirectly, from the High Commissioner to the Secretary of State for the Colonies, who was responsible as a Minister to Parliament in London. This depended on there being MPs in Westminster interested in arguing the case for either community in Palestine, which happened for the Jews at times, less so for the Arab side, although Palestinians opened media offices in London after 1936. The High Commissioner headed the Government of Palestine, while under

---

[35] David French, *The British Way in Counter-Insurgency, 1945–67* (Oxford: Oxford University Press, 2011), pp. 74–75.

[36] Townshend, 'Martial Law,' p. 194; Charles Townshend, *Britain's Civil Wars: Counterinsurgency in the Twentieth Century* (London: Faber and Faber, 1986), p. 15; Banning, *Military Law*, p. 304; A. V. Dicey, *Introduction to the Study of the Law of the Constitution* (London: Macmillan, 1902), pp. 284–87.

[37] Hussain, *The Jurisprudence of Emergency*, pp. 99ff.

him there was an executive council to which he had to present all legislation such as Ordinances, as well as liaising with the Colonial Office
and sending laws to a local advisory council. The High Commissioner
chaired the all-British executive council alongside his Attorney
General, Chief Secretary, and Treasurer, *ex officio*, with other personal
appointments made as needed, subject to the approval of the King. The
High Commissioner exercised some powers 'in council' with his executive, but this was with trusted, like-minded confederates. The Attorney
General and the Palestine Government legal department drafted new
laws and Ordinances that went from the High Commissioner sitting with
the executive council to the advisory council, although in certain cases
he referred laws first to the Secretary of State for the Colonies, before
sending them to the advisory council. The King gave Royal Assent for
Ordinances but not to amendments thereof, that as far as this author
can determine did not go to the advisory council either. The Emergency
Regulations of 19 April 1936 derived from King George V's assent to the
Palestine (Defence) Order in Council 1931 and appeared the same day
in a special supplement to the *Palestine Gazette Extraordinary*, but they
had not had even the nominal scrutiny of an Order in Council.[38] The
High Commissioner enacted the Emergency Regulations. They simply
came into force that evening. The local press compared the Emergency
Regulations to the more familiar Ordinances and queried their status.[39]
The day-to-day rules of the Emergency Regulations used to fight rebels
after April 1936 had no accountability and only post facto public notice
by way of the *Palestine Gazette*. Local scrutiny of new laws was phoney
and perfunctory. Bureaucrats on both the executive and advisory councils
'merely nodded the legislation through, without acting as the slightest
check on executive power.'[40] The High Commissioner appointed the
advisory council and he was the chair, so advising himself, and membership was entirely from within the Palestine Government: the Attorney
General and Treasurer again, the Chief Secretary, the Inspector General
of police, alongside nine heads of Government departments, and the
three District Commissioners, so all British.[41] The advisory council never
acted as a balancing force, with the Peel Commission noting starkly in

---

[38] Emergency Regulations 1936, in *Supplement No. 2* to the *Palestine Gazette Extraordinary*
No. 584 of 19 April 1936 in *Ordinances, Regulations, Rules, Orders and Notices. Government
of Palestine. Annual Volume for 1936. Volume 2* (Jerusalem: Government Printing Press,
1937), pp. 259ff.
[39] 'Emergency Regulations not an Ordinance,' *Palestine Post* (30 August 1936), p. 2.
[40] Martin Kolinsky, *Law, Order and Riots in Mandatory Palestine, 1928–35* (London: St
Martin's, 1993), pp. 6–7.
[41] *Palestine Civil Service List 1937* (Jerusalem: Government Printing Press, 1937), p. 5.

1937 'that it is used for formal assent to legislation [rather] than for the purposes of consultation or discussion.'[42]

Other British colonies such as India (notably Bengal) and Cyprus had local parliaments of sorts, if short-lived for Cyprus and with 'no separate existence' in India from the British-run executive but Palestine never had any legislature.[43] Local contribution to law making in Palestine was limited to what pressure Palestinians and Jews could bring to bear informally on the executive or the Attorney General, or on decision-makers in London. The High Commissioner twice proposed a legislative council, in 1922–23 and in 1935–36, but these came to nothing. The Palestinians rejected the first legislative council with its elected membership of twelve local (eight Muslims, two Jews, and two Christians) and ten appointed British members, including the Inspector General of Police, Chief Secretary, and Attorney General, plus the High Commissioner as its eleventh British member, at a time when Palestinians formed 88 per cent of the population. The proposed legislative council was effectively the executive council, with both chaired by the same person, but with some local representation, and so not a separate legislature but a revised executive. The British then tried to co-opt ten Palestinians in 1923–24 to the advisory council after the failure of the first proposed legislative council but this also foundered as Arab leaders opposed to pro-Zionist Mandate principles built on the 1917 Balfour Declaration pressurised appointees to decline, so it stayed all British. Had the legislative council come into being, the High Commissioner with his eleven British members alongside the two Jews would have had a voting majority anyway. The Jews rejected the 1935 proposal for a larger legislative council that favoured the Palestinian majority, and one in which the High Commissioner would still determine immigration quotas and 'would be empowered to legislate in certain circumstances.'[44] The judiciary had some power to challenge executive power, and the Chief Justice appointed judges and did not sit on the executive council, but McDonnell's sacking and the introduction of military courts underscore how the executive (and the Army) impinged on the judiciary. Emergency laws also granted colonial civil officers and soldiers rights to detain suspects without trial for up to a year in internment camps, with the possibility to extend this, to deport or internally exile them, or curfew them in their homes, further

---

[42] Cmd. 5479 *Report of the Palestine Royal Commission (Peel)* (London: HMSO, 1937), p. 159.

[43] Robin J. Moore, 'Imperial India, 1858–1914,' in Andrew Porter (ed.), *Oxford History of the British Empire. Volume 3, The Nineteenth Century* (Oxford: Oxford University Press, 1999), pp. 424–39.

[44] *Survey of Palestine*, i, p. 34.

marginalising the judiciary as security forces could detain anyone that they considered to be suspect without trial. This was precautionary executive detention before the crime; if the authorities believed that a suspect had committed a serious crime, they put him (more rarely her but there was a women's prison in Bethlehem[45]) before a civil or military court. Nor could Palestinians depend on the police or judiciary to tackle official wrongdoing. There was only one prosecution of British security personnel for abuse: of four British policemen in a 'special squad' who assassinated in broad daylight in October 1938 in Jaffa an arrested suspect whom police had previously tortured, for which the men involved got risibly light sentences, reduced on appeal, or were bound over to keep the peace, and a matter examined in detail later in this book.[46] That British policemen felt able to commit murder in the middle of the day in front of local witnesses speaks volumes about the rule of law in Palestine during the revolt. The Government in London trumpeted the prosecution of the four men as proof of the rule of law in Palestine. Similarly, in the Irish War of Independence in the early 1920s there was just one successful prosecution for murder, with the court finding the British Auxiliary soldier responsible guilty but also finding him insane.[47] Nor did British Major Roy Farran's special forces involvement in the death of Jewish insurgent Alexander Rubowitz in 1947 lead to successful prosecution.

The moral compass of civil (and military) officers in Palestine acted as a brake on the pacification that flowed from Emergency Regulations, but moral sensibilities did not prevent draconian legislation in the first place. Thus, the High Commissioner's private secretary wrote in his diary for June 1936 of his unhappiness at pacification, and how he should have left Palestine before 'these new emergency regulations imposing the death penalty for many offences' and 'giving the High Commissioner power to destroy villages the inhabitants of which have "aided or abetted any offence involving violence or intimidation". The Government is coming steadily nearer to making open war on the Arabs.'[48] Most civil administrators got on with their jobs and muted where they could

---

[45] For a Jewish account of the prison see Tzila Heller, *Behind Prison Walls: A Jewish Woman Freedom Fighter for Israel's Independence* (Hoboken, NJ: KTAV, 1999), pp. 43–53.

[46] Memoir, Unbeaten Track: Some Vicissitudes in Two Years of a Public Servant's Life by el-Asi, Lees Papers, 5/13, pp. 6–7, LHCMA; Matthew Hughes, 'A British "Foreign Legion"? The British Police in Mandate Palestine,' *Middle Eastern Studies* 49/5 (2013), pp. 696–711.

[47] Robert Kee, *The Green Flag: A History of Irish Nationalism* (London: Weidenfeld and Nicolson, 1972), p. 691.

[48] Diary, 12 June 1936, in E. C. Hodgkin (ed.), *Thomas Hodgkin: Letters from Palestine, 1932–36* (London: Quartet, 1986), p. 173.

security forces' violence that seemed ultra vires, or they compensated Palestinians for their losses as happened at Halhul village in May 1939, but as the law allowed for so much rough treatment it was hard to know what was beyond the law.[49] Systemic legal force blurred the line between legal and illegal punishment, encouraging the latter both by the example of extreme judicial measures and by the fact that extra-judicial punishment bypassed bothersome military and civil courts. Some intuitive sense of right and wrong as much as the law guided the British, simply what soldiers and civil officials thought was fair, a nebulous qualitative cultural metric and one calibrated differently for European or *Mizrahi* Jews, between rural peasants and townsfolk, Bedouin, Christian Palestinians, women, children, Druze, and Muslims in Palestine. It was also one made differently by a soldier on his first tour of duty in Palestine, by a long-serving police officer, an Arabic-speaking District Commissioner, an intelligence officer working closely with Jews, or by a senior commander under political pressure from London. Rank-and-file soldiers were generally disinterested and saw violence in immediate terms, as one Jewish girl noted when soldiers came to defend her in 1929 and

refused to take sides; they regarded the whole affray as just another military assignment. In vain did my sister and her friends try to expound the ideological background of the conflict and win the British army over to the cause of the *yishuv* ... The soldiers listened politely enough but whenever asked what they thought they just leered at the girls and said, 'Are you married?'[50]

At times, the British absolved themselves by outsourcing abuse to local Arab – a Lebanese Christian CID officer, for instance – and Jewish security personnel, remaining 'discreetly in the background, not wishing to have the skirts of our garments soiled,' while still using intelligence wrung from victims.[51] Soldiers talked of 'military frightfulness' and drew historical comparisons to what they saw as un-British Prussian abuses in the Great War to measure their behaviour, while their commanders simultaneously admired German thoroughness in repressing civil dissent,

---

[49] For Halhul see typed two-page document by Edward Keith-Roach, untitled or dated, at the end of which is added pencilled comment, Keith-Roach Papers, AL-KR; Matthew Hughes, 'The Practice and Theory of British Counter-Insurgency: The Histories of the Atrocities at the Palestinian Villages of al-Bassa and Halhul, 1938–39,' *Small Wars and Insurgencies* 20/3–4 (September–December 2009), pp. 528–50.

[50] Ruth Jordan, *Daughter of the Waves: Memories of Growing up in Pre-War Palestine* (New York, NY: Taplinger, 1983), pp. 94–95.

[51] Author interview, Bahjat Abu Gharbiyya, Amman, Jordan, 21 June 2009 (and subsequent correspondence); Matthew Hughes, 'A History of Violence: The Shooting of British Assistant Superintendent Alan Sigrist, 12 June 1936,' *Journal of Contemporary History* 45/4 (2010), pp. 725–43; Douglas Duff, *Bailing with a Teaspoon* (London: John Long, 1953), p. 168.

with one lamenting, 'If the Germans were in occupation in Haifa we'd not have any bloody trouble from the Arabs.'[52] Labelling of practices mattered. For District Commissioner Alec Kirkbride, his strategy was 'not to encourage frightfulness' but 'to make everything awkward for people who were not co-operating with the government.'[53] Nor did the League of Nations tamper much with British law making and execution. The British as the Mandatory power sent an annual report to the League in Geneva, but the ones for the period of the Arab revolt show that the League was only an 'element of constraint.'[54] The papers of the civil and military British officials involved in crushing the revolt express scant concern for the League's views. The League was not a friction to operations, as opposed to bothersome protests from, say, Germany or Italy, Muslims across the British Empire, from Egypt, or from the British press.

The Criminal Court System

Before setting out the legislative timeline, a description of the criminal court system and the burden of proof in Palestine introduces the Mandate Ordinances and military courts described in the second part of this chapter. It is worth reiterating, first, the point made above about the relevance of British (or English) law to the criminal courts, one that proves a fundamental absence of metropolitan standards of arrest, charging, prosecution, and burden of proof in judgement, or the presence of a jury. Article 46 of the 1922 Order in Council instructed judges to turn to the substance of English common law and the doctrine of equity. This meant that what applied in the UK applied equally in Palestine, but with a critical caveat: 'provided always that the said common law and doctrines of equity shall be in force in Palestine so far *only as the circumstances of Palestine and its inhabitants ... permit* and subject to such qualifications

---

[52] Simson, *British Rule and Rebellion*, p. 110; Anon., *Frightfulness in Retreat* (London: Hodder and Stoughton, 1917); Jon Lawrence, 'Forging a Peaceable Kingdom: War, Violence, and Fear of Brutalization in Post-First World War Britain,' *Journal of Modern History* 75/3 (2003), pp. 557–89; Conversation, Wavell to Evetts in Percy Munn, 4503, Tape 3, IWMSA; Diary, 14 May 1939, Forster Papers, GB165-0109, pp. 119–20, MEC. The French in Syria similarly ruthlessly repressed insurrection: Simon Innes-Robbins, *Dirty Wars: A Century of Counterinsurgency* (Stroud: History Press, 2016), p. 178.

[53] Alec Kirkbride quoted in Naomi Shepherd, *Ploughing Sand: British Rule in Palestine, 1917–48* (London: Murray, 1999), p. 210.

[54] *Report by His Majesty's Government in the United Kingdom of Great Britain and Northern Ireland to the Council of the League of Nations on the Administration of Palestine and Transjordan for the Year 1936* (London: HMSO, 1937); *Report by His Majesty's Government in the United Kingdom of Great Britain and Northern Ireland to the Council of the League of Nations on the Administration of Palestine and Transjordan for the Year 1937* (London: HMSO, 1938); Kolinsky, *Law, Order and Riots*, p. 6.

as local circumstances render necessary.'[55] Palestinian and Jewish judges were unfamiliar with English law, while British judges tended not to apply equity as they felt with reason that English law applied only to English customs. Judges could use English legal precedence in Palestine but as British customs seemed alien this rarely happened: 'Article 46 was thus not viewed as a pipeline for importing English law but rather as a filter for Ottoman law that the judges could utilise to screen local law and weed out those parts that seemed unworthy.'[56] With no meaningful English law, judges could rely on the Ottoman laws but these were written in a form of Turkish that no British judge could understand and so required careful translation, and the British phased them out anyway. Emergency legislation after 1936 overshadowed the new Criminal Code of that year. Thus, when it came to legal decisions, judges relied on the growing body of unilateral Ordinances and Notices that derived from colonial experience across the British Empire. The British often bypassed the legal system altogether by arbitrating through *mukhtars* and local religious leaders.

Turning to the courts, the Government in Palestine built a system using elements of what existed under the Ottomans and in Britain at the time, to which it added (or kept) special courts for local religious and social customs. The British created a modified version of the four-tiered Ottoman secular court system, from which appeals went now to the Privy Council in London. First, there were some thirty-five Magistrates' courts that sat without a jury, as a bench of one magistrate and not three as in the UK. Unlike the British system of lay justices of the peace, Palestine's Chief Justice appointed professional magistrates, although in the first years of British rule, he employed judges inherited from the Ottoman period. The British granted magistracy powers to Jewish and Arab civil District Officers to use in the field, as they did with British Assistant District and District Commissioners during the revolt when District Officers faced partisan, communal pressures. By 1948, the British had appointed five chief magistrates to sit atop the magistracy, supporting colonial control of the first tier of justice. Second, five District courts in Jerusalem, Jaffa, Haifa, Nablus, and (from 1937) Tel Aviv formed the next level of the court system. The District Court had a British judge presiding with two local Arab or Jewish judges. District courts heard appeals from the Magistrates' courts and sat as the first court in major civil and criminal cases. Third, there was the Court of Appeal, later named the Supreme Court, which heard appeals from the District courts and,

[55] Quoted in Likhovski, *Law and Identity*, p. 60.
[56] Ibid., p. 64.

sitting as a High Court of Justice, decided administrative and constitutional matters. Finally, a Criminal Assize Court composed of District and Court of Appeal/Supreme Court judges decided capital cases. The High Commissioner confirmed the death penalty, a role never fully arrogated by the GOC Army in the revolt.[57] Courts were diverse. A photograph of Supreme Court judges from 1925 shows six men: two British judges in short wigs, three sporting *tarbushes*, and one bareheaded.[58] There were also supplementary courts for land rights, Muslim, Jewish, and Christian religious affairs, Bedouin tribal business, and the Jewish *Histadrut* had Comrade Courts.[59] Municipal courts with lay 'honorary' magistrates dealt with municipal law and government regulations. The need to translate testimonies into Arabic, English, and Hebrew slowed proceedings, as did the need to translate Ottoman laws into English and make sense of them. One judge heard eight languages in his court in a single day: Arabic for Palestinians; Turkish for Greeks and Armenians; Hebrew, Yiddish, and Judeo-Spanish for Jews; and German and French for priests. Some Jewish lawyers did not know Hebrew and so pleaded in Arabic before a Jewish judge, while one Arab lawyer pleaded in Hebrew.[60] The need to balance benches with reliable Jewish, Christian, and Muslim judges further encumbered courts. This was grist to the mill for the Army that demanded speedy, exemplary justice, ideally through its in-house all-British military courts. In November 1937, the Army's military courts annulled the criminal court system and appeal to the Privy Council, but for three sets of offences only relating to weapons, explosives, and sabotage. Criminal courts sat throughout the revolt to try lesser offences.

Guilt and the Burden of Proof

The British agreed a perverse form of 'joint venture' (or 'joint enterprise') for Palestine's population, the idea (in UK law) that if someone is part of a group committing a crime then that person is equally guilty even if someone else in the group pulled the trigger or threw the punch. This was common colonial practice; indeed, the Bolsheviks adopted the same 'collective responsibility' strategy in their suppression campaigns in the 1920s and 1930s, followed by mass deportation.[61] In Palestine, the British chose the village, tribe (if nomadic), or urban quarter as a

---

[57] Secretary of State for Colonies to High Commissioner Palestine, 19 December 1938, FO 371/21868, p. 415, TNA.
[58] Likhovski, *Law and Identity*, p. 51.
[59] Ibid., pp. 29–51.
[60] Ibid., p. 30.
[61] Innes-Robbins, *Dirty Wars*, pp. 92–99.

collective entity to which they would apply joint venture punishment, through *mukhtars*, sheikhs or mayors, assuming without proof that such bodies had collective knowledge of any crime committed by another part of itself. This assumed that everyone in a quarter was the same. A civil official wondered what would happen with punitive action against a neighbourhood whose inhabitants were a mixture of German, Arab, and Jewish.[62] General Bernard Montgomery in December 1938 queried explicitly if he could not simply punish a 'community' rather than an urban 'quarter' of Haifa in 1939, and his civil adviser said that the law allowed this.[63] Colonial ideas on subalterns' collective lives deepened after 1936 when the British saw any rebel attack as a joint undertaking by all Palestinians and discriminated only in that those punished needed to be reasonably close to the crime, or just the nearest. The occasional use of tracker dogs imported from South Africa could prove the link between crime and punishment – the rebels, say, passing through a local village after an attack – and connected deed and guilt; the British even flew in dogs by aeroplane.[64] In later campaigns in Malaya and Borneo, the British replaced animals with humans and used aboriginal Iban trackers or as in Rhodesia after 1965 security forces trained white soldiers as trackers.[65] Tracking and hunting replaced judicial process to secure guilty individuals to punish. In Palestine, once given a spoor, dogs did the police work and identified suspects in line ups, achieving results 'quite beyond the highest human intelligence,' in the words of policeman Sir Charles Tegart.[66] The breed of dog mattered, it seems, Alsatians drawing the fire of a suspect while the 'Boxer ran straight in to knock down and hold his man'; security forces mostly used Dobermans, the South African handlers speaking to them in Afrikaans, their dogs tending 'to go for the throat.'[67] Photographs show the dogs with their handlers

---

[62] Diary, 25–26 November 1938, Scrivenor Papers, MSS. Brit. Emp. S. 378,WL.

[63] Diary, 12 December 1938, Scrivenor Papers, MSS. Brit. Emp. S. 378,WL.

[64] Palestine Press Cuttings, 11 March 1937–23 June 1938, *The Observer* (14 March 1937), Briance Papers, BP.

[65] Jonathan Pittaway (ed.), *Selous Scouts: The Men Speak* (Durban: Dandy Agencies, 2013), pp. 95ff. The Iban headhunted insurgents: Peter Dickens, *SAS: The Jungle Frontier. 22 Special Air Service Regiment in the Borneo Campaign, 1963–66* (London: Fontana, 1984), p. 202; Simon Harrison, *Dark Trophies: Hunting and the Enemy Body in Modern War* (New York, NY: Berghahn, 2012), p. 157.

[66] Quoted in Gad Krozier, 'From Dowiggin to Tegart: Revolutionary Change in the Colonial Police in Palestine during the 1930s,' *Journal of Imperial and Commonwealth History* 32/2 (2004), p. 126.

[67] Norman Phillips, *Guns, Drugs and Deserters: The Special Investigation Branch in the Middle East* (London: Werner Laurie, 1954), p. 156; Kitson, 10688/6, IWMSA; Notes of Interviews, Ted Horne (London), 21 October and 9 November 1976, Palestine Research Lever Arch File, Thames TV Material on 'Palestine: Promises, Rebellion and Abdication' (1977–78), IWMFA.

2.1 An armed security force dog handler in a slouch hat
(from American Colony Hotel Archive)

in mufti standing alongside soldiers and sporting South African-style slouch hats and armed with pistols (Figure 2.1).[68] The dogs did such 'wonderful work' but 'unfortunately they can't give evidence in a court of law,' grumbled General Archibald Wavell.[69] Policeman Douglas Duff, who was with dogs 'hounding' rebels after they had killed an RAF officer and wounded a British female passenger in a road ambush spotted that 'the foxes had gone to ground just ahead' near 'bad' Ijzim village that security forces then 'put to the question' and wrecked.[70] 'I had read of

[68] Arab Revolt in Palestine Photograph Album 1937, ACHA; *Daily Telegraph*, 19 January 1938 in Scrapbook of Articles about the American Colony, Palestine, People and Events and Loose Enclosures 1938, ACHA.
[69] Wavell to Haining (DMO, WO), 27 November 1937, Palestine, 1937–38 Volume, Wavell Papers, POH. For dogs see *The Palestine Police: Annual Administrative Report, 1936* (Jerusalem: Government Printing Press, 1936), pp. 30–31.
[70] Douglas Duff, *Palestine Unveiled* (London: Blackie, 1938), pp. 58–59; Col W. V. Palmer, 'The Second Battalion in Palestine,' in H. D. Chaplin (ed.), *The Queen's Own Royal West Kent Regiment* (London: Michael Joseph, 1954), p. 85.

a Roman Peace – of making a desolation and calling it peace; I now saw what it meant,' wrote Duff, who then had a discerning exchange with a senior police officer on the burden of proof:

'But there's no proof that these people had anything to do with that ambush of yesterday,' I persisted. He looked amazed. 'Good Lord, man' he objected, 'didn't the dogs lead us here?' 'But, hang it, that's not evidence,' I objected. 'At best it is only proof that the murderers passed this way. It doesn't prove that they came from this place. Your people and the soldiers have turned the village upside down, but you haven't found anything to connect Ijzim with the murder.' 'Of course we have,' he said, stubbornness in his voice; 'didn't the trail lead here?' 'Then if it had led to your own front door because the criminals may have come to your house, you would have been guilty of the murder of the British officer, I suppose?' I asked sarcastically. He was looking at me with narrowed eyes. 'Looks to me as though you were on the side of these wogs,' he said, suspiciously.[71]

Tracker dogs required years of training and there were very few available, so the British discriminated a priori by triaging rural Palestine into good, moderate, and bad villages, as they did with Ijzim, or by labelling someone as a 'known bad character,' and delivered matching punishment after any outrage.[72] 'Good' villages could expect 'friendly' treatment, the Army kept 'moderate' ones under 'strict control,' while 'bad' villages could expect to be 'rigorously and punitively searched.'[73] The British summarily pre-assigned guilt, or passed judgement based on community, religion, proximity to a crime, or the scent of a dog. This was not the burden of proof standard for criminal cases in the UK of 'beyond reasonable doubt' or 'convinced so that you are sure.'[74] A legal system that wilfully targeted innocent people had baleful effects on the enforcers, too, as an Assistant District Commissioner's secret correspondence shows:

We can also do much, I think, by refusing to consider any case brought by the Police under the Prevention of Crimes Ordinance or the Emergency Regulations unless the balance of probabilities is strongly against the accused. Instruments

---

[71] Duff, *Palestine Unveiled*, pp. 59–61.

[72] 2nd Battalion The West Yorkshire Regiment, Battalion Intelligence Summary No. 2, Ramallah, 26 October 1938, RYM; 8th Division Operation Instruction No. 10 by Gen Montgomery, 21 January 1939, Queen's Royal West Surrey Regiment, QRWS/3/6/7, SHC; Lecture No. 2: Operational Cordon: Check and Search Village, n.d., Diary of Events, 1939, Queen's Royal West Surrey Regiment, QRWS/3/8/8, SHC; Letter, Lt H. J. Darlington to Wife, 6 October 1938, KO1333/01, KORRM; Druze Activities File in S25/22793, CZA; Testimony of Tuvia Omani, 18 February 1971, 95/23, HA; *The Hampshire Regimental Journal* 32/12 (December 1937), p. 383.

[73] Minutes of a Conference held at HQ 14th Inf Bde, 26 January 1939, Queen's Royal West Surrey Regiment, QRWS3/6/7, SHC.

[74] Personal knowledge, the author is a magistrate.

like the Emergency Regulations have a demoralising effect upon Police work and the tendency is to punish the easiest instead of the real culprit. Mr Shaw, when I hesitated to sign a warrant for detention the other day, complained that in other districts the District Commissioner or Assistant District Commissioner would sign 100 blank warrants to be filled in by the Police with names and periods ... Wherever we are not satisfied that a village or an individual is involved in any particular crime then we should, I submit, refuse to take any punitive action.[75]

The issue was not burden of proof or guilt but punishment. Proof was unnecessary or impossible to determine in fast-moving military operations or a dog would supply it. Everyone was guilty. British notions of collective Palestinian and Jewish identities meant group punishment, although effective, united Jewish resistance blunted this form of imperial control. Shared pre-assigned criminality ran counter to British legal traditions of individual rights and innocence before guilt and marked a fundamental difference between metropolitan and colonial legal systems, with collective corporate guilt in the UK being the only (contemporary) exception that this author can discern where a defendant is not directly involved in the offence. The British saw Palestinian village life as a collective 'social system based on mutual protection rather than justice,' a view in some measure endorsed by local arrangements such as the collective rural *faz'a* (alarm) security system whereby certain villages would help one another in times of crisis.[76] Groups of villages on the West Bank also had traditions of uniting together, at the head of which stood a family recognised as regional leader.[77] Seeing Palestinians collectively and punishing them accordingly facilitated imperial rule in Palestine on a limited budget without a permanent military garrison before the 1929 riots, after which the Army stationed two battalions there. The British were not alone in this: the French did the same in Algeria, as did European colonial powers across Africa and Asia, and Nazi Germany in occupied Europe where German forces inflicted horrific, unprecedented collective punishments.[78]

---

[75] Secret, Letter, Bailey to/from Scrivenor, Haifa and Samaria, 7 April 1938, Scrivenor Papers, MSS. Brit. Emp. S. 377, pp. 153–55, WL.

[76] Ylana Miller, 'Administrative Policy in Rural Palestine: The Impact of British Norms on Arab Community Life, 1920–1948,' in Joel Migdal (ed.), *Palestinian Society and Politics* (Princeton, NJ: Princeton University Press, 1980), p. 132; Sonia Fathi el-Nimri, 'The Arab Revolt in Palestine: A Study Based on Oral Sources' (Exeter: Doctoral Dissertation, 1990), pp. 128–30.

[77] Cohen, *Army of Shadows*, p. 77.

[78] J. House and N. MacMaster, *Paris, 1961: Algerians, State Terror and Memory* (Oxford: Oxford University Press, 2006), p. 54; Douglas Porch, *The French Foreign Legion: A Complete History of the Legendary Fighting Force* (New York, NY: HarperCollins, 1991), p. 576.

2.2 Contemporaneous cartoon. The Arabic text reads: 'This is a picture that shows the justice of the English with their Arab allies in the past. Oh! Nations take this lesson into your consideration [learn this lesson] and history mark this down. Widely distributed in the market places.' (from Central Zionist Archives, Jerusalem S25/22510–34)

The Legislative Timeline, 1917–1935

A forensic inspection of the year-on-year accretion of enabling repressive legislation shows empirically the legal track for British pacification that paralleled colonial and Army practices in pacification, dealt with later in this book. The British designed the legal system as a cost-effective substitute for the lack of a strong military garrison in Palestine, there to intimidate the local population and make it internalise the maintenance of order and so pacify itself. The Army ruled Palestine from its conquest in 1917 to 1920, when Sir Herbert Samuel arrived as the first civil High Commissioner, two years prior to the 1922 Order in Council that set up the country's Government. Before then, in 1921, the British had issued the Collective Responsibility for Crime Ordinance, repealed and updated in 1926.[79] This established that if anyone caused damage or destruction in a village, then the owner of the damaged property could petition the whole village to pay, or if it was common land then the nearest village was the target. The District Commissioner was to collect monetary compensation or collect saleable goods.[80] This meant that the Palestine Government did not have to pay compensation but targeted instead the 'assessable inhabitants' for any damages to pay.[81] When rebels attacked Government property after 1936, the Government transferred intra-communal fines to the state, so compensating itself. This blurred the distinction between intra-communal conflict and anti-Government actions, both of which received the same punishment.[82] In 1921, the High Commissioner issued a Prisons Ordinance, amended and updated with a principal Ordinance in 1926 and another in 1936, with Acre and Jerusalem jails as execution sites. The Firearms Ordinance of 1922 became the principal ordinance for limiting small arms, with amendments in 1926, 1933, 1934, 1935, 1936, and 1938, and security forces obsessively disarmed Palestinians during the Arab revolt, while simultaneously arming Jews and loyalist Palestinians – *divide et impera*. In July 1936, an amendment increased the penalty for illegally importing or exporting firearms from three to seven years in prison.[83] There was a Police Ordinance in 1921, updated with a principal Ordinance in 1926 that still guides serving Israeli police officers today. The emergency laws of the security state were taking root.

Between 1924 and 1928, the Palestine Government secured itself and solidified the collective punishment laws first codified in 1921 by marrying the idea of 'prevention' to that of collective, joint endeavour in the 1924 Prevention of Crime (Tribal and Village Areas) Ordinance. This allowed the (British) District Commissioner to 'sanction' under the power of the High Commissioner 'that a fine be levied collectively' from tribal groups.[84] The British issued the Prevention of Crime (Continuance) Ordinance in 1925 and the principal Collective Punishments Ordinance (No. 22) in 1926 that partially repealed the 1924 Prevention Ordinance

[79] *Legislation of Palestine, 1918–25*, i, p. 246.
[80] Ibid., p. 249; Max Laserson, *On the Mandate: Documents, Statements, Laws and Judgments Relating to and Arising from the Mandate for Palestine* (Tel Aviv: Igereth, 1937), pp. 75–76.
[81] Collective Punishments Ordinance 1926 in Moses Doukhan (ed.), *Laws of Palestine, 1926–1931* (Tel Aviv: Rotenberg, 1932), pp. 286–92; also in Drayton, *Laws of Palestine*, i, pp. 147–56.
[82] Ylana Miller, *Government and Society in Rural Palestine, 1920–48* (Austin, TX: University of Texas Press, 1985), p. 126.
[83] *The Palestine Police: Annual Administrative Report, 1936* (Jerusalem: Government Printing Press, 1936), p. 71.
[84] *Legislation of Palestine, 1918–25*, i, pp. 386–87.

and repealed the 1921 Collective Ordinance. The Collective Punishments Ordinance of 1926 was the legal foundation for much of the pacification during the Arab revolt, and it established a group penalty norm embodied in later Ordinances such as the Collective Fines one of August 1936 that gave District Commissioner the right to take payment in cash or cattle.[85] Police posts could be quartered in any town or quarter and failing to render assistance was a crime.[86] The 1926 Ordinance had established schedules of targeted areas and villages, ones made public in the English-language *Palestine Gazette*. If a place on the schedule was in a 'dangerous and disturbed condition' the High Commissioner could increase the force of police and make the assessable inhabitants pay for a punitive police post, so keeping down Government costs.[87] The Government also expected villagers to feed the police stationed in their village. Point 5 of the 1926 Ordinance made scheduled areas collectively complicit in any crime and introduced the nebulous notion of conniving in a crime. If an offence or damage had been committed and the District Commissioner had 'reason to believe' that inhabitants committed it or 'connived' or 'failed to render all their assistance in their power' or they 'connived at the escape of, or harboured, any offender' or they 'combined to suppress material evidence,' he could fine them.[88] The average villager was poor, 'born in debt, lives in debt, and dies in debt' with peasant families subsisting on £P.25–30 per annum – British soldiers often remarked on rural poverty – and Government fines were substantial, running to hundreds and for larger towns thousands of pounds.[89] The right of appeal gave the semblance of fairness and those charged could do this within fifteen days of notification of the order but 'No petition for rectification shall be heard unless the petitioner has paid into Court the amount chargeable against him under the order of apportionment.'[90]

[85] Collective Fines Ordinance No. 57 of 1936 in *Supplement No. 1* to the *Palestine Gazette Extraordinary No. 618*, 4 August 1936 in *Ordinances, Regulations, Rules, Orders and Notices. Government of Palestine. Annual Volume for 1936. Volume 1* (Jerusalem: Government Printing Press, 1937), pp. 241–42.

[86] Collective Fines Ordinance No. 57 of 1936 in *Supplement No. 1* to the *Palestine Gazette Extraordinary No. 618*, 4 August 1936 in *Ordinances, Regulations, Rules, Orders and Notices. Government of Palestine. Annual Volume for 1936. Volume 1* (Jerusalem: Government Printing Press, 1937), pp. 243–44.

[87] Collective Punishments Ordinance 1926 in Doukhan, *Laws of Palestine, 1926–1931*, i, pp. 286–92; Drayton, *Laws of Palestine*, i, pp. 147–56.

[88] Collective Punishments Ordinance 1926 in Doukhan, *Laws of Palestine, 1926–1931*, i, pp. 286–92.

[89] J. B. Hobman (ed.), *Palestine's Economic Future* (London: Percy Lund, 1946), p. 57; Col J. S. S. Gratton, 4506/03, p. 25, IWMSA; Rosemary Sayigh, *The Palestinians: From Peasants to Revolutionaries* [1979] (London: Zed, 2007), p. 25.

[90] Collective Punishments Ordinance 1926 in Doukhan, *Laws of Palestine, 1926–1931*, i, pp. 286–92.

Thus, petitioners paid their share of the fine before the appeal. One or more person could make an appeal but if there were more than one petitioner then the courts joined the petitions collectively in one appeal. If one petitioner successfully appealed, then 'the sum total of the fine or compensation shall be reduced by the like sum. No alteration in the amounts chargeable against any other person other than the petitioner shall be made.'[91] This meant that villagers could not easily combine to fight levied fines. Appeals also meant hiring an advocate, whose numbers boomed under the Mandate, adding cost to the fine already paid to the court before making the petition.

The High Commissioner gave magisterial warrants to his regional officers – (Arab and Jewish) District Officers, (British) Assistant District Commissioners, and (British) District Commissioners – and to Government officers who had passed an 'elementary law examination' to enforce unilaterally collective punishment.[92] The stresses of the Arab revolt led to two changes. First, the power to inflict collective punishment devolved to reliable British Commissioner-level officers. This created a second problem in that during a period of mass unrest there were not enough of these officials as there were in 1938 only three District Commissioners and twelve Assistant District Commissioners to administer a population of 1,435,285 comprised of 900,250 Muslims, 411,222 Jews, 111,974 Christians, and 11,643 'others,' mostly Druze (that add up to 1,435,089 not 1,435,285).[93] In the first stages of the revolt, a British civil official or a police officer usually accompanied the Army but there were too few civil officers for large-scale operations and such people (police included) were not fit enough to keep up with fast-moving soldiers, so the Army instituted collective punishment as sanctioned by the executive. As the Army seized executive functions through statutory military law in October 1938, civil officials no longer even rubber-stamped punishments. Instead, they advised the Army and did its bidding. The papers of Sir Thomas Scrivenor's lodged in Oxford's Weston Library, who was then an Assistant District Commissioner in Galilee, chart this change in power, 1938–39. There was a further Collective Punishments (Amendment) Ordinance (No. 5) in 1928 with

---

91 Ibid.
92 Norman Bentwich, *England in Palestine* (London: Kegan Paul, 1932), pp. 281–82.
93 *Statistical Abstract of Palestine, 1939* (Jerusalem: Office of Statistics, 1939), p. 11; *Survey of Palestine*, i, pp. 140–41. *Government of Palestine: Civil Service List 1938* (Jerusalem: Government Printing Press, 1938) lists three District Commissioners for Galilee–Acre, Jerusalem, and Southern districts but leaves vacant the DC post for Haifa–Samaria District so an acting DC must have been in charge. The same source lists nine Assistant DCs with one extra British official, suggesting that some ADCs were in acting roles.

a new schedule of villages and areas, and more amendments thereafter.[94] The Collective Punishments Ordinance (No. 32) of 1929 empowered the High Commissioner to appoint a 'public officer' with the powers of a District Commissioner, allowing the Government to extend the number of its officers able to apply collective punishment under the 1926 Ordinance.[95] The Collective Punishments (Amendment) Ordinance (No. 35) of 1929 allowed for the punishment of villages and areas even if they were not on existing schedules of such places. The legal materials of this period have long appended lists (or 'schedules') of villages with amendments of more villages; this amendment made all of Palestine eligible for collective punishment as it added villages to existing schedules post facto.[96]

A principal Police Ordinance in 1926 dissolved the British Gendarmerie force in Palestine and established a new police force, so reducing the need to deploy military force.[97] The Police Ordinance allowed the police to enlist 'suitable persons' as supernumerary constables on 'special service.'[98] This opened the way during periods of major disturbance for a police officer of Inspector rank or above to 'apply to the nearest District Commissioner or Magistrate to appoint so many of the residents of the neighbourhood as may be required to act as Special Police Officers' and who would have the same powers and privileges as regular police officers.[99] The police could close liquor stores and referencing Ottoman law on assemblies, arrest people singing songs or using words or gestures likely to breach the peace.[100] Police could outlaw processions, ban flags, emblems, and music, and change the route of any march.[101] Jews complained about the blanket music ban for cafes in Tel Aviv, the Mayor's office insisting that playing classical music was acceptable.[102] Such restrictions were common across the British Empire but the option to raise supernumerary police is significant as it allowed in times of emergency for the employment of masses of Jewish auxiliary police, especially as the British civilian population of Palestine was tiny. The Government made amendments to the Police Ordinance, notably in 1929, 1934, and

[94] Doukhan, *Laws of Palestine, 1926–1931*, i, pp. 286–92.
[95] Ibid.
[96] Ibid.
[97] Police Ordinance 1926 in Doukhan, *Laws of Palestine, 1926–1931*, iii, p. 1170.
[98] Doukhan, *Laws of Palestine, 1926–1931*, iii, p. 1171.
[99] Ibid., p. 1172.
[100] Ibid., pp. 1173–74.
[101] Ibid., p. 1174.
[102] Letter, Dr Shalom Hildeshemier to Mayor's Office, 25 June 1936, and reply from the Mayor's Office in the next file dated 2 July 1936, File 04-161-B/621: Riots, May–July 1936 [one bundle of papers], TAMA.

1936. The 1934 Police (Amendment) Ordinance 1934, for instance, amended sections of the 1926 Ordinance, tightened up rules on meeting and processions, and licences thereof, and it penalised further people for unlawful assemblies and refusals to obey police orders.[103]

In 1931, London issued the second of the Orders in Council that directly affected pacification: the Palestine (Defence) Order in Council, as detailed above, with its Article IV making possible the tranche of emergency legislation in 1936.[104] The Order was an enabling one. It allowed the High Commissioner to take prompt action in the future and it followed on from the bloody riots of 1929 that left hundreds dead and necessitated for the first time the imposition in lieu of an effective police force of a permanent garrison of two infantry battalions. Article V of the 1931 Order recognised the right to demolish houses, a central plank to pacification after 1936, further codified in June 1936. It gave the High Commissioner swingeing powers to 'take and retain' any 'land or building' and he 'may, if he thinks necessary for the purpose of the defence of Palestine, cause any buildings to be pulled down and removed, and any property to be removed from one place to another to be destroyed.'[105] This was a significant addition to emergency powers, widely and indiscriminately used during the Arab revolt, targeting the nicest or biggest houses in a village, and done to effect a big explosion to satisfy watching soldiers, as Assistant District Commissioner Aubrey Lees complained:

Major Chirnside, of the 8th K.R.I. [King's Royal Irish] Hussars, then began to protest and complain, first asking me why I had brought out a squadron of Hussars to demolish so small a house … announcing loudly that it was 'all balls' and proceeding to explain as he has frequently done before, that his men were 'fed up' and couldn't stand much more, the implication being that the 8th K.R.I. Hussars could only be kept in hand by the repeated spectacle of large houses being demolished.[106]

A Press Ordinance of 1933 gave the High Commissioner extensive powers to control domestic newspapers, censor reporting, and ban the import of foreign newspapers.[107] The Press (Amendment) Ordinance of March 1936 gave the High Commissioner rights to warn newspaper

---

[103] Police Amendment Ordinance No. 2 of 1934 in *Supplement No. 1* to the *Palestine Gazette Extraordinary No. 415*, 13 January 1934, pp. 113–14.

[104] Drayton, *Laws of Palestine*, iii, pp. 2619–24.

[105] Ibid.

[106] ADC Lees (Gaza) to DC (Jaffa), 29 September 1936, Lees Papers, 5/6/6, LHCMA.

[107] Press Ordinance 1933, Order-in-Council under Section 20(1), 17 January 1935 by Clerk to the Executive Council in *Proclamations, Regulations, Rules, Orders and Notices. Annual Volume for 1935* (Jerusalem, Government of Palestine: Greek Convent Press, 1936), p. 96.

owners and 'by Orders in Council suspend the publication of the newspaper for such period as he may think fit,' and the Government closed Arabic-language newspapers for months on end during the revolt.[108] As a coda, some amendments to legislation in this period were repetitions of forms of words of a previous Ordinance or Order but this obviously mattered to the Attorney General's lawyers who busily copper bottomed regulations. Thus, in 1935, another Collective Punishments (Amendment) Ordinance repeated key parts of the 1926 principal Ordinance and a 1929 amendment, and a 1937 Ordinance on collective punishment repeated parts of the 1935 Ordinance verbatim.[109]

Emergency Regulations, 1936

When mass disturbances erupted after the deaths of Zvi Danenberg and Israel Chazan on 15 April 1936, the emergency state was primed for action. The High Commissioner proclaimed the 1931 Order in Council and declared Emergency Regulations at 9 pm on the 19 April 1936 as 'a precautionary measure,' with a simultaneous curfew order for Jaffa and Tel Aviv to run from 7 pm to 5 am, the first of many such town curfews, alongside others attached to the borders of railways and roads.[110] The Emergency Regulations appeared the same day in a supplement to an extraordinary edition of the *Palestine Gazette.*[111] Over the course of 1936, from 19 May to 14 September, the Government made eleven amendments to the Emergency Regulations.[112] The principal regulations on 19 April gave security forces the following key powers:

[108] Press (Amendment) Ordinance No. 14 of 1936 (18 March 1936) in *Supplement No. 1* to the *Palestine Gazette No. 577*, 19 March 1936 in *Ordinances, Regulations, Rules, Orders and Notices. Government of Palestine. Annual Volume for 1936. Volume 1* (Jerusalem: Government Printing Press, 1937), p. 128. See also *The Palestine Police: Annual Administrative Report, 1936* (Jerusalem: Government Printing Press, 1936), p. 71.

[109] Collective Punishments (Amendment) Ordinance No. 39 of 1935 in *Supplement No. 1* to the *Palestine Gazette Extraordinary No. 542*, 10 October 1935, pp. 161–62; *Government of Palestine. Revised Edition of the Laws (Revision) Ordinance, No. 1 of 1937. Supplement No. 1 to the Palestine Gazette Extraordinary No. 660 of 22 January 1937* (Jerusalem: Government Printing Press, 1937), p. 8.

[110] Jordan, *Daughter of the Waves*, p. 188.

[111] Emergency Regulations 1936 in *Supplement No. 2* to the *Palestine Gazette Extraordinary No. 584*, 19 April 1936 in *Ordinances, Regulations, Rules, Orders and Notices. Government of Palestine. Annual Volume for 1936. Volume 2* (Jerusalem: Government Printing Press, 1937), pp. 259ff.

[112] Emergency (Amendment) Regulations 1936 in *Ordinances, Regulations, Rules, Orders and Notices. Government of Palestine. Annual Volume for 1936. Volumes 2 and 3* (Jerusalem: Government Printing Press, 1937), pp. 354, 361, 577, 609, 629, 641, 680, 775, 777, 1031, 1093.

- The Government would determine all offences in accordance with the established court system and associated Ordinances.
- It will be lawful to seize any buildings needed for the life of the community, such as gas works or electricity stations.
- It will be lawful to seize food, fuel, material, or stores needed for public life.
- The Government can regulate trade and fix prices.
- The Inspector General Police, a District Commissioner or Assistant District Commissioner, or superior police officer may: regulate road transport, use of traffic, fares; take possession of cars and vehicles for government use; prescribe and restrict routes.
- The High Commissioner may prohibit and regulate the sale, supply, and delivery of motor fuels and oils.
- The High Commissioner can prohibit arms sales.
- Anyone who injures or who prevents the proper working of the country's infrastructure is committing an offence.
- A District Commissioner (p. 262) 'or some person duly authorised by him' may by order impose a curfew.
- The censor shall have the authority (p. 262) 'to detain, open and examine' all mail and he can withhold from delivery anything that (p. 263) 'he shall consider ... to contain anything the publication of which is in his opinion prejudicial ... to the public safety or to the defence of Palestine.'
- The censor by written authority can prohibit the publication or printing of newspapers.
- The censor can demand that newspaper proprietors send to the censor any material prior to publication.
- The censor can ban import of newspapers and he can ban publication inside Palestine of newspapers either with a notice in the *Gazette* or via an order to any person concerned.
- Anyone who has a banned newspaper, posts one, or carries one is committing an offence.
- Premises can be searched for banned publications or printing presses.
- The High Commissioner can restrict the use of telephone services (p. 265) 'to such persons as he may think fit.'
- No ship shall leave a port without official permission.
- 'No person shall, without lawful excuse, loiter in any public place, and every person shall, when so ordered by a Police Officer in uniform, move on' (p. 265).
- The High Commissioner can deport anyone from Palestine with a Deportation Order.

- Anyone obstructing, misleading or interfering with, or withholding information from an officer acting under these regulations will be committing an offence.
- Any police office or *mukhtar* can arrest anyone without warrant (p. 266) 'who so acts as to endanger the public safety.'
- Police officers can enter, by force if necessary, premises (p. 267) 'suspected of being used for purposes endangering the public safety.'
- Police officers can search vehicles and anyone they suspect of carrying an illegal article.[113]

Some Emergency Regulations amendments tweaked the principal text, merely changing a verb or (25 August) adding 'indecent gestures' and 'shouts' as offences while others solidified substantial restrictions. Three amendments affecting travel (22 May), detention (22 May and 1 June), the death penalty (12 June), and house demolition (12 June) merit further scrutiny.[114] Amendment 2 to the Emergency Regulations on 22 May instituted permits for travel and empowered District Commissioners to place people under police supervision, make them live in a designated place, notify police of their whereabouts, and/or keep a curfew. As these amendments were to Section 15 of the principal Emergency Regulations, they became Regulation 15A. Amendment 3 on 1 June amended detention Regulation 15A to become 15B and said that a District Commissioner had imprisonment powers of one year and he could detain 'in such place of detention as may be specified by the District Commissioner in the order.'[115] This was detention without trial, or internment in 'concentration' camps. This solved for the Army the issue of detaining suspects who had not committed any chargeable offence, but it did not provide the desired exemplary deterrence or punishment as soldiers had to hand those found with a weapon to the police, and the arrested person then passed through the criminal courts. Some rebel suspects never got to the courts as security forces shot them in situ, or executed them or beat them

---

[113] Emergency Regulations 1936 in *Supplement No. 2* to the *Palestine Gazette Extraordinary No. 584*, 19 April 1936 in *Ordinances, Regulations, Rules, Orders and Notices. Government of Palestine. Annual Volume for 1936. Volume 2* (Jerusalem: Government Printing Press, 1937), pp. 259ff.

[114] Emergency (Amendment) Regulations 1936 in *Ordinances, Regulations, Rules, Orders and Notices. Government of Palestine. Annual Volume for 1936. Volumes 2 and 3* (Jerusalem: Government Printing Press, 1937), pp. 354, 361, 577, 609, 629, 641, 680, 775, 777, 1031, 1093.

[115] Emergency (Amendment) Regulations 1936 in *Ordinances, Regulations, Rules, Orders and Notices. Government of Palestine. Annual Volume for 1936. Volumes 2 and 3* (Jerusalem: Government Printing Press, 1937), p. 578.

to death at Army camps or in police cells.[116] 'Take him for a ride,' as a
police CID sergeant euphemistically put it when he instructed his men
to assassinate a suspect.[117] Amendment 4 on 12 June referred back to
the 1931 Order and instituted a new sub-section to Regulation 8 of the
Emergency Regulations (so Regulation 8A) confirming the death penalty for any person firing a weapon, throwing a bomb, or interfering with
Palestine's infrastructure. Anyone found 'guilty of an offence against
this regulation' would 'upon conviction by a Court of Criminal Assize
be punished with death or with imprisonment for life.'[118] These three
offences became the ones processed by military courts in 1937, but
without any right of appeal to a higher court. In 1936, those charged with
capital offences still passed slowly through the court system to the Assize
Court, after which the High Commissioner or GOC considered the political value of commuting or executing the death sentence. The British
caveated this regulation in 1936 by saying that if an attack on infrastructure such as railways or roads did not endanger life, then life imprisonment was the maximum sentence, to be decided by a District Court. The
amended regulations were political, a way to ratchet up harsh legislation
to intimidate rebels and convince their leadership to accept a ceasefire.
The 12 June amendment with Regulation 19B confirmed the demolition
powers embodied in the 1931 Order in Council. District Commissioners
could mark houses seen as rebel firing points and any building 'situated
in any town, quarter, village or other area the inhabitants of which he is
satisfied have committed, aided or abetted any offence involving violence
or intimidation, the actual offenders being unknown to him; and where
any house, building or construction is appropriated as aforesaid it shall
be forfeited to the High Commissioner without compensation and may
be demolished.'[119] This power to demolish devolved over the course of
the revolt to Assistant District Commissioners, the Army, and the police.

An amended and suitably updated legal system considering events on
the ground was in place by June 1936, the month in which reinforcing
infantry battalions arrived in Palestine. A battery of parallel subsidiary

---

[116] For deaths in Army camps, see oral testimony of Manchester Regiment soldier Arthur
Lane, 10295, pp. 23ff, IWMSA, repeated in Arthur Lane, *Lesser Gods, Greater Devils*
(Stockport: Lane, 1993).
[117] Memoir, Unbeaten Track: Some Vicissitudes in Two Years of a Public Servant's Life by
el-Asi, Lees Papers, 5/13, pp. 6–7, LHCMA.
[118] Emergency (Amendment) Regulations 1936 in *Ordinances, Regulations, Rules,
Orders and Notices. Government of Palestine. Annual Volume for 1936. Volumes 2 and 3*
(Jerusalem: Government Printing Press, 1937), p. 610.
[119] Emergency (Amendment) Regulations 1936 in *Ordinances, Regulations, Rules,
Orders and Notices. Government of Palestine. Annual Volume for 1936. Volumes 2 and 3*
(Jerusalem: Government Printing Press, 1937), pp. 612–13.

Ordinances and Notices further screwed down the country, tackling movement, weaponry, assembly, and explosives. Various parts of the security apparatus issued new instructions. The Police (Amendment) Ordinance on 18 May 1936 targeted persons carrying 'any knife, stick, bludgeon, iron bar, stone, or weapon of any sort' and those 'inciting others to assemble by either word or writing, or by any other means, and any person singing a song or making use of words or gestures' who police could now arrest without warrant.[120] Security forces spun a bewildering web of overlapping and intertwining laws, with different pedigrees, as when the District Commissioner Order on 8 August 1936 replicated the text of the Police Amendment Ordinance from 18 May 1936 but referred back to the Police Ordinance of 1926.[121] The Knives and Daggers Ordinance 1936 on 18 May 1936 applied 'anywhere' that the High Commissioner saw 'fit' and prescribed a £P.300 fine and/or three years in jail for anyone making or selling daggers. Those carrying a knife were liable to the suitably 'severe' penalty of a year in jail.[122] The Inspector General of Police, Roy Spicer, issued a Mechanically Propelled Vehicles Order on 23 May 1936 banning road travel across most of Palestine except for those holding a police permit. There were Collective Punishments (Amendment) Ordinances on 23 and 28 May 1936.[123] The Emergency Regulations (Manufacture of Explosives) Order on 1 June 1936 prohibited explosives manufacture and banned a detailed range of chemicals.[124] The Police (Amendment) Ordinance on 1 June 1936

[120] Police (Amendment) Ordinance (No. 2) of 1936, 18 May 1936, signed by Wauchope in *Ordinances, Regulations, Rules, Orders and Notices. Government of Palestine. Annual Volume for 1936. Volume 1* (Jerusalem: Government Printing Press, 1937), p. 201 that repeated forms of words from the 1926 Police Ordinance in Doukhan, *Laws of Palestine, 1926–1931*, iii, p. 1174.

[121] Order by the DC, Jerusalem District, 8 August 1936 in *Ordinances, Regulations, Rules, Orders and Notices. Government of Palestine. Annual Volume for 1936. Volume 3* (Jerusalem: Government Printing Press, 1937), p. 1034.

[122] Knives and Daggers Ordinance 1936, 18 May 1936, signed by Wauchope in *Supplement No. 1* to the *Palestine Gazette Extraordinary No. 594*, 18 May 1936 in *Ordinances, Regulations, Rules, Orders and Notices. Government of Palestine. Annual Volume for 1936. Volume 1* (Jerusalem: Government Printing Press, 1937), pp. 199–200; *The Palestine Police: Annual Administrative Report, 1936* (Jerusalem: Government Printing Press, 1936), p. 71; Knives and Daggers Ordinance 1936, 9 June 1936 in *Supplement No. 2* to the *Palestine Gazette Extraordinary No. 602*, 11 June 1936 in *Ordinances, Regulations, Rules, Orders and Notices. Government of Palestine. Annual Volume for 1936. Volume 2* (Jerusalem: Government Printing Press, 1937), p. 608.

[123] Collective Punishments (Amendment) Ordinance No. 36 of 1936 in *Supplement No. 1* to the *Palestine Gazette Extraordinary No. 598*, 28 May 1936 in *Ordinances, Regulations, Rules, Orders and Notices. Government of Palestine. Annual Volume for 1936. Volume 1* (Jerusalem: Government Printing Press, 1937), p. 207.

[124] Emergency Regulations (Manufacture of Explosives) Order 1 June 1936 in *Ordinances, Regulations, Rules, Orders and Notices. Government of Palestine. Annual Volume for 1936. Volumes 2 and 3* (Jerusalem: Government Printing Press, 1937), pp. 579–80.

tackled the issue of people congregating, closing cafes and bars on pain of fines or six months in jail for the patron.[125] There were also orders for shops to open to help break the general strike.[126] Police could arrest without a warrant, search suspects on a whim, detain without trial, search premises without a warrant, prohibit arms, disarm anyone, and soldiers had similar powers.[127]

On 25 June 1936, the first Palestinian to be tried under amended Emergency Regulations that made the use of arms against soldiers a capital offence went before a Magistrates' Court, for aiming a rifle at troops, with a British officer and two soldiers bringing the charge.[128] For such a serious offence, the magistrate sent the defendant to the higher District Court for trial. Soldiers handed suspects over to the police after taking their names, some of whom they had arrested for curfew breaking, intimidation, and 'attempting to buy rifles and signalling,' but also for the 'illegal sale of meat.'[129] A South Wales Borderers 'anti-intimidation patrol' in Jaffa arrested and handed over to police four Palestinians.[130] Dorsetshire Regiment soldiers passed on to police curfew breakers and some men arrested for possession of empty ammunition cases.[131] This was an impossible process for the Army and for successful pacification: slow, cumbersome and burdened with disclosure and evidence gathering, finding legal counsel, and it required soldiers back on operations in the field to return and attend court at some date hence, but it was fair. This system could not survive prolonged rebellion. The desire to keep to the law versus the need to defeat the rebels tensed the Government. In July 1936, the courts challenged the Emergency Regulations in two cases of persons charged with having ammunition, acquitting them because the prosecution had not proved that a bullet (or round) was an explosive article within the meaning of the Regulations. This meant that in all 'cases

---

[125] Police (Amendment) Ordinance (No. 3) of 1936 (made on 1 June 1936) in *Supplement No. 1* to the *Palestine Gazette Extraordinary No. 600*, 1 June 1936 in *Ordinances, Regulations, Rules, Orders and Notices. Government of Palestine. Annual Volume for 1936. Volume 1* (Jerusalem: Government Printing Press, 1937), p. 209.

[126] Amendment 3 of 1 June 1936 to the Emergency Regulations on Emergency (Amendment) Regulations 1936 in *Ordinances, Regulations, Rules, Orders and Notices. Government of Palestine. Annual Volume for 1936. Volumes 2 and 3* (Jerusalem: Government Printing Press, 1937), pp. 577–78.

[127] Henry Baker, 'Emergency Regulations: A Survey of the Recent Amendments,' *Palestine Post* (7 June 1936), p. 2.

[128] 'Political Notes,' *Palestine Post* (25 June 1936), p. 5.

[129] Dorsetshire Regiment, Intelligence Reports, Prisoners Captured File, 88/352, Shelf C4, Box 3, KMM.

[130] Dorsetshire Regiment, Narrative of Events, Jaffa, 15 August 1936 and Jerusalem, 30 August 1936, 87/89, Shelf C4, Box 3, KMM.

[131] Dorsetshire Regiment, War Diary, 2–3 July 1936, 88/453, Shelf C4, Box 3, KMM.

of prosecution on a similar charge in future, at least one round of the confiscated ammunition will be fired before the case goes to court and the empty cartridge case produced in evidence by the officer who fired it.'[132] Then there was the issue of whether a rifle was a firearm if it was not serviceable, the Army having captured an old man at Yatta on 10 July 1936 running away with a fifty-year-old Greek rifle without ammunition:

> At the trial, in examination-in-chief, an officer stated that the rifle was serviceable, but that it would not take any modern kind of ammunition. On cross examination, he further stated that he could not say whether it was serviceable or not as without ammunition it could not be tried. There was no evidence that the rifle was of any military value. The accused pleaded 'Not Guilty' but did not deny that he was in possession of the rifle. The court's decision was that the prosecution had failed to show that the exhibit came within the definition of a firearm and the accused was acquitted.[133]

The police appealed this judgement. A British magistrate acquitted a Palestinian charged with possession of a kilo of gunpowder because it was an explosive 'substance' and not 'article' as defined in the Emergency Regulations.[134] In August 1936, the chief magistrate of Jerusalem acquitted a Jew, Asher Friedman, of breaking curfew and obstructing a police officer on the procedural issue that the prosecution had not proved that the authorities had issued the relevant curfew even though the court accepted that such curfews were intra vires and legal under the Emergency Regulations. An Inspector 'Abd al-Samad appeared for the prosecution, pulling a senior officer away from his daily police work.[135] As late as October 1938, a court acquitted four Arabs caught with explosives in a car on the grounds that a fifth man who had run away was the culprit.[136] There were also limited numbers of magistrates: thirty-four and five British chief magistrates for the whole country by 1947.[137] The Army was unwilling to tolerate such legal process and evidentiary requirements, and took the law into its own hands, arguing for its own courts, as it could not realistically process captured rebels through civil courts, or soldiers just ignored the law. The other option was to declare captured rebels as prisoners-of-war, but this conferred a raft of internationally agreed rights on (non-state) insurgents, as

---

[132] Miscellaneous Notice, Important, by DIG Rice, n.d. [July 1936], Arab Office and Intelligence: 8/GENERAL/39, HA; 'Law Reports,' *Palestine Post* (12 August 1936), p. 2.

[133] Case of a Rifle being held not to be a Firearm, Brooke-Popham Papers, 4/5/33, LHCMA.

[134] Ephraim Kluk, *A Special Constable in Palestine* (Johannesburg: Kluk, 1939), p. 12.

[135] 'Validity of Curfew Regulation Upheld,' *Palestine Post* (12 August 1936), p. 12.

[136] *Haaretz* [*The Land*] (Tel Aviv) (18 October 1938).

[137] Likhovski, *Law and Identity in Mandate Palestine*, p. 29.

well as unfavourably changing the basis of British operations away from internal British imperial policing. Paradoxically, the desire to keep to the law made summary military justice inevitable.

Before the first ceasefire on 12 October 1936, the British drew up a final Order: the Palestine Martial Law (Defence) Order in Council 1936 on 26 September 1936, not published in the *Palestine Gazette* but signed by the Privy Council in London on 20 November.[138] The US Consul General wrote to the State Department on 30 September 1936 that the Order 'does not proclaim martial law but sets the stage for its proclamation.'[139] It introduced military courts and military rule, allowing the High Commissioner to

authorise the trial by Civil Courts (including Courts of Summary Jurisdiction) or such military courts as may be established by the Regulations, of persons committing offences against the Regulations or any other offences under the law for the time being in force in Palestine, and the infliction by any civil courts or by any military courts established as aforesaid of such punishments as may be prescribed ... The procedure and practice of military courts established by Regulations made under this Article may be determined by Regulations under this Article or by such authority and in such manner as the Regulations may prescribe ... The following Articles are hereby inserted in the Principal [1931] Order immediately after Article V thereof ... The High Commissioner may, if he thinks fit, by Proclamation delegate to the General Officer Commanding the Forces in Palestine all or any of his powers under Articles IV and V of this Order.[140]

The October 1936 ceasefire, agreed in some measure because rebels feared the heavy punishment of the mooted martial law, nullified this Martial Law Order whose subject, the exercise of power and the delegation of full power to the GOC, re-emerged with a vengeance in September 1937 when the second phase of the revolt erupted with the assassination of Lewis Andrews. But the British never enacted the full martial law embodied by the September 1936 Order, unwilling right to the end of the revolt to give the Army complete governmental executive and judicial functions.

---

[138] Foreign Jurisdiction, 1890. Order in Council, dated 26 September 1936, entitled The Palestine Martial Law (Defence) Order in Council 1936. Presented to the House of Commons in Pursuance of Section 11 of the Act. Privy Council Office, 20 November 1936 (courtesy of Parliamentary Archives, Houses of Parliament).

[139] US Consul General Palestine to State Department, 9 October 1936, 867N.00/407 [Reel M#1037/2], NARA II.

[140] Foreign Jurisdiction, 1890. Order in Council, dated 26 September 1936, entitled The Palestine Martial Law (Defence) Order in Council 1936. Presented to the House of Commons in Pursuance of Section 11 of the Act. Privy Council Office, 20 November 1936 (courtesy of Parliamentary Archives, Houses of Parliament).

The Legislative Timeline, 1937–1939

The suspension of the revolt in October 1936 did not slow the accumulation of new regulations that eventually transitioned into the 1939 Emergency Powers (Colonial Defence) Order in Council and the 1939 Emergency Powers (Defence) Act, there to meet the menace of another world war. The Criminal Code of December 1936 streamlined and codified criminal law. In January 1937, a new amendment further tackled newspaper censorship.[141] In a notice in the same *Palestine Gazette Extraordinary*, amendments to both the Collective Punishments (Amendment) Ordinance, 1935 and Collective Punishments (Amendment) Ordinance, 1936 conclude with a six-page list of villages on the schedule.[142] Significantly, London issued the Palestine (Defence) Order in Council in March 1937, while the Peel Commission was deliberating, the authorities preparing for renewed violence. The Order allowed the High Commissioner 'unfettered discretion' to introduce as required Defence Regulations.[143] The Order succeeded the Palestine Martial Law Order in Council of September 1936 and opened the way for forms of military rule and justice, without any right of appeal. The Order permitted civil and military courts to work in combination – difficult, as they had different codes of procedure – and allowed using a form of words from the 1936 Martial Law Order,

the infliction of fines upon bodies of persons or upon corporations and the forfeiture and destruction of property as punitive measures, whether the actual offenders can or cannot be identified … that judgements, orders and proceedings of such military courts shall not be called in question, whether by writ or otherwise, or challenged in any manner whatever by or before any court … any provision of a law which may be inconsistent with any Defence Regulation shall, whether that provision shall or shall not have been amended, modified or suspended in its operations under this section, to the extent of such inconsistency have no effect so long as such Regulations shall remain in force … The High Commissioner may, if he thinks fit, by Proclamation delegate to the General

---

[141] Changes to Section 19 of the Press (Amendment) Ordinance 1936 in *Supplement No. 1* to the *Palestine Gazette Extraordinary No. 660*, 22 January 1937 in *Ordinances. Government of Palestine. Annual Volume for 1937. Volume 1* (Jerusalem: Government Printing Press, 1938), p. 113.

[142] *Supplement No. 1* to the *Palestine Gazette Extraordinary No. 660*, 22 January 1937 in *Ordinances. Government of Palestine. Annual Volume for 1937. Volume 1* (Jerusalem: Government Printing Press, 1938), pp. 7–14.

[143] The Palestine (Defence) Order in Council 1937 in *Ordinances, Regulations, Rules, Orders and Notices. Government of Palestine. Annual Volume for 1937. Volume 2* (Jerusalem: Government Printing Press, 1938), pp. 260–64. See also Simson, *British Rule and Rebellion*, pp. 96–98.

Officer Commanding the Forces in Palestine all or any of his powers ... on such condition (if any) as he may specify.[144]

The acceptance of group punishment without evidence and military rule was explicit recognition of what was already happening. The statement that new defence regulations would supersede all other laws, even if defence regulations were inconsistent with those laws, recognised the real foundation of colonial power. The military with the High Commissioner's agreement could manage the criminal courts with its own judges and codes of procedure, and it could set the laws with which security forces arrested, charged, tried, and sentenced suspects. New regulations made some civil offences criminal and they transformed civil business like making a telephone call into a crime, too. The Defence (Military Courts) Regulations of 11 November 1937, discussed below separately, operationalised the new system, although it did not do away with criminal courts.

As with the 1936 Emergency Regulations, revisions in the form of Defence (Amendment) Regulations, of which there were eleven in 1937, followed the 1937 Order, some referring back to the 1936 Emergency Regulations as the principal legislation and reiterating elements of earlier regulations. One (No. 8) allowed Bedouin in the south of Palestine to carry guns but not grenades.[145] The British favoured in some measure minority communities such as the Bedouin (of which there were 66,553 in 1931, classified as 'nomads') and Druze (of which there were some 12,000 in 1936), also the Christians, who when all combined with the Jews comprised 42 per cent of Palestine's population.[146] (Israel does the same today, conscripting Druze and Circassian men into its armed forces, forming special units for Bedouin, and encouraging Christians to join up.[147]) The Government made twenty-seven amendments in 1938, with Defence (Amendment) Regulations (No. 1) removing another safeguard from the justice system by permitting coroners to dispense with an inquest if a death resulted from

---

[144] The Palestine (Defence) Order in Council 1937 in *Ordinances, Regulations, Rules, Orders and Notices. Government of Palestine. Annual Volume for 1937. Volume 2* (Jerusalem: Government Printing Press, 1938), pp. 260–64.

[145] Defence (Amendment) Regulations 1937 Nos. 1–11 in *Ordinances, Regulations, Rules, Orders and Notices. Government of Palestine. Annual Volume for 1937. Volumes 2–3* (Jerusalem: Government Printing Press, 1938), pp. 293–94, 673–74, 753, 911–12, 955, 971, 1135–38, 1311.

[146] *Survey of Palestine*, i, pp. 140, 159, ii, p. 925.

[147] Gili Cohen, 'Bedouin and Christian Arabs, the Israeli Army Wants You,' *Haaretz* (2 January 2017); Rhoda Kanaaneh, *Surrounded: Palestinian Soldiers in the Israeli Military* (Stanford, CA: Stanford University Press, 2008), pp. 9–25.

military operations, a significant alteration to standard procedures in the case of a death.[148] The Government had forbidden its officers to hold inquests on persons killed by security forces as far back as 1929, and when civil official Aubrey Lees pushed for them in 1936 'both the suggestion and the offer were declined.'[149] Coroners noted that they would be noting nothing, as one did for a body with a skull fracture from a soldier's bullet: 'and in pursuance of Section 19c of the Emergency Regulations I dispense with inquest.'[150] Other amendments covered the press, placards, border fences, forfeiture of contraband, the marking of buildings to denote the race of the inhabitants, limits to ammunition for licensed firearms, taking photographs, closure of post offices, and permits to travel.[151] The text of the October 1938 Defence (Military Commanders) Regulations marked emphatically the incremental move from civil to military rule, shifting the balance between military field commanders and civil officials by transforming the latter into advisers for the former, but without proclaiming full martial law:

The General Officer Commanding may, with the consent of the High Commissioner, appoint for any area or place a military commander who shall be responsible in such area or place for public security and in any area or place in which a military commander is appointed the District Commissioner shall in all matters relating to public security become and act as a political adviser to the military commander. Where a military commander has been appointed all the powers and duties vested in the District Commissioner by the Defence Regulations in respect of that area or place shall become vested in the military commander ... and upon such vesting the District Commissioner shall cease to exercise within the area or place for which the military commander has been appointed any of the powers or duties vested in him by the Defence Regulations.[152]

---

[148] Defence (Amendment) Regulations (No. 1) 1938, signed by Battershill, 19 January 1938 in *Ordinances, Regulations, Rules, Orders and Notices. Government of Palestine. Annual Volume for 1938. Volumes 2 and 3* (Jerusalem: Government Printing Press, 1939), p. 90 (on microfilm in BL at SPR Mic. P1).

[149] Letter, Lees to MacDonald (Secretary of State for Colonies), 8 January 1939, Lees Papers, 5/8, LHCMA.

[150] Coroner's Report, Haifa and Samaria District, 3 May 1939, Death of Abdul Khalik Masud Salami of Saida, M/4826/49, ISA.

[151] Defence (Amendment) Regulations (Nos. 1–24) 1938 in *Ordinances, Regulations, Rules, Orders and Notices. Government of Palestine. Annual Volume for 1938. Volumes 2 and 3* (Jerusalem: Government Printing Press, 1939), pp. 90ff (on microfilm in BL at SPR Mic. P1).

[152] Defence (Military Commanders) Regulations 1938, 18 October 1938, signed by Battershill in *Ordinances, Regulations, Rules, Orders and Notices. Government of Palestine. Annual Volume for 1938. Volumes 2 and 3* (Jerusalem: Government Printing Press, 1939), p. 1361 (on microfilm in BL at SPR Mic. P1). See also Summary of Intelligence, Palestine and Transjordan, 21 October 1938, by Wing Commander Ritchie at GHQ [21/38], CO 732/81/10, TNA.

Low-level notices tackled day-to-day opposition. A Proclamation on 8 December 1938 from area commander Brigadier H. C. Harrison warned inhabitants against making 'deliberately false accusations' against soldiers: 'the public are hereby warned that any person deliberately circulating such false information is liable to be dealt with by me under Emergency Regulations.'[153] Dissent was now illegal. The security forces issued masses of curfew orders alongside principal legislation amendments that allowed military courts to sentence minors to whipping 'with a light rod or cane or birch' not exceeding twenty-four strokes.[154] Amendments banned toy pistols, closed shops indefinitely – rather than force them to stay open as happened in 1936 – and post offices could refuse to send packages.[155] When London issued the Emergency Powers (Defence) Act in August 1939 to prepare Britain for a war with Germany, which prompted more Defence Regulations in Palestine, the revolt was over.[156] The British had won. The legal-administrative force of the colonial state, or its violence – the 'restriction on or alteration of natural action, behaviour, or inclination ... undue or enforced constraint ... the abuse of power or authority to persecute or oppress' – had overwhelmed the rebels.[157] To put this differently, rebels had found no good counter measures to the power of the emergency state. Britain's colonial legal architecture in Palestine was flexible and exemplary, and so effective that the British had no need to torture, kill, and hang masses of rebels. While the *Manual of Military Law* instructed soldiers that 'no one is allowed to use more force than is necessary' and when 'called to the aid of the civil power soldiers in no way differ in the eyes of the law from other

---

[153] Proclamation, 8 December 1938, by Brig H. C. Harrison (Military Commander, Central Area) in *Ordinances, Regulations, Rules, Orders and Notices. Government of Palestine. Annual Volume for 1938. Volumes 2 and 3* (Jerusalem: Government Printing Press, 1939), p. 1575 (on microfilm in BL at SPR Mic. P1).

[154] Defence (Amendment) Regulations (No. 4) 1939, 17 February 1939, signed by Battershill in *Ordinances, Regulations, Rules, Orders and Notices. Government of Palestine. Annual Volume for 1939. Volumes 2 and 3* (Jerusalem: Government Printing Press, 1940), p. 131 (on microfilm in BL at SPR Mic. P1).

[155] Defence (Amendment) Regulations (No. 5) 1939, 4 March 1939, signed by Battershill in *Ordinances, Regulations, Rules, Orders and Notices. Government of Palestine. Annual Volume for 1939. Volumes 2 and 3* (Jerusalem: Government Printing Press, 1940), pp. 165–66, 497 (on microfilm in BL at SPR Mic. P1).

[156] Emergency Powers (Defence) Act 1939, 26 August 1939 in *Ordinances, Regulations, Rules, Orders and Notices. Government of Palestine. Annual Volume for 1939. Volumes 2 and 3* (Jerusalem: Government Printing Press, 1940), pp. 649–56 (on microfilm in BL at SPR Mic. P1); Defence Regulations 1939, 26 August 1939, signed by MacMichael in *Ordinances, Regulations, Rules, Orders and Notices. Government of Palestine. Annual Volume for 1939. Volumes 2 and 3* (Jerusalem: Government Printing Press, 1940), pp. 659–708 (on microfilm in BL at SPR Mic. P1).

[157] Violence, *n.* in *Oxford English Dictionary* at www.oed.com (accessed 24 May 2017).

citizens,' transformations of the law and recalibration of what constituted citizenship made acceptable and so enabled the force necessary for pacification.[158] The Army's mission in Palestine was not just to hunt down rebel bands but to be the Government's 'bailiff's men' and administer the colonial state's emergency law in lieu of a functioning police force and this it did admirably.[159]

Military Courts

The Defence (Military Courts) Regulations on 11 November 1937, to be 'read as one' with the Emergency Regulations of 1936, established that there

shall be courts in Palestine which shall be called Military Courts ... A Military Court shall consist of a President who shall be an officer of or above the rank of Field Officer, and two other officers ... No person shall be found guilty by a Military Court on any charge except by the unanimous verdict of its members ... The Courts shall have jurisdiction throughout Palestine to try and determine all offences ... Every sentence of death shall direct that the person condemned shall be hanged by the neck until he is dead ... If the accused does not employ an advocate the Court shall, at the close of the examination of each witness for the Prosecution, ask the accused whether he wishes to put any questions to that witness.[160]

The regulations came into force on 18 November. Military courts tried capital offences of discharge of firearms and the carrying of arms and bombs, as well as sabotage and intimidation that were not necessarily hanging crimes.[161] The accused paid for legal counsel. The GOC confirmed capital sentences; there was no right of appeal to the Privy Council. Soldiers could arrest anyone without warrant if they thought that the offender had done something to merit going before a military court. There were amendments to the Defence (Military Courts) Regulations in 1937 and 1938.[162]

Military courts ran parallel to criminal courts and never fully replaced the civil judiciary for two reasons. First, civil courts still dealt with criminal offences except firing a gun, carrying a weapon or explosives, or

---

[158] *Manual of Military Law 1929* (London: HMSO, 1940), p. 246.
[159] Roger Courtney, *Palestine Policeman* (London: Herbert Jenkins, 1939), p. 83.
[160] Defence (Military Courts) Regulations 1937, 11 November 1937 in *Ordinances, Regulations, Rules, Orders and Notices. Government of Palestine. Annual Volume for 1937. Volume 3* (Jerusalem: Government Printing Press, 1938), pp. 1138–43.
[161] *Survey of Palestine*, i, p. 43.
[162] Defence (Military Courts) (Amendment) Regulations 1937 in *Ordinances, Regulations, Rules, Orders and Notices. Government of Palestine. Annual Volume for 1937. Volume 3* (Jerusalem: Government Printing Press, 1938), pp. 1175–77.

intimidation and sabotage.[163] Soldiers in the field had to decide on charging and thus allocation of civil or military court. Without legal training, soldiers sent defendants into the court system on different tracks depending on their lay assessment of the offence. This was usually the task of the police, but the force had collapsed. A clear act of firing on soldiers in a battle, with comrades killed or injured, could lead to execution on the spot. Soldiers had options. They could legally detain suspects under internment rules or punish them on the spot by taking away crops and livestock, destroying villagers' personal possessions, fining villagers, imposing a curfew, or blowing up houses. Internment, examined in Chapter 6, allowed security forces to imprison anyone, comparable to the 'pipeline' detention camps in Kenya in the 1950s.[164] Security forces could also avoid the court system altogether – or, put another way, establish a new layer of justice – and inflict illegal punishments in the field, waterboarding or bastinado whipping villagers 'near the scene' of an incident.[165] Second, while the military had its own courts, it did not have administrative control over Palestine, at least not before October 1938, and even then not full power. Civil administrators working alongside the Army softened the military courts system, depending on the strength of character of local British Assistant and District Commissioners, and the attitude of local military area commanders. Brigadier John Evetts in the north of Palestine was a hard-charging regional commander, for instance, as was his northern area divisional commander Montgomery.[166] While Evetts encouraged Wingate's Special Night Squads and 'consistently urged tough action,' southern Palestine divisional Commander (and Jerusalem military governor) Major-General Richard O'Connor was of the view that 'harshness and unnecessary violence' by soldiers was 'un-British.'[167] The High Commissioner's attitude also determined force levels, with the military complaining that Wauchope was too lenient and held back on exemplary force, while police officers called him 'washout' for the same reason.[168] As GOC Dill wrote in late 1936, Wauchope 'hated' martial law.[169] Wauchope was guilty of 'extreme moderation' in

[163] Note in Scrivenor Papers, MSS. Brit. Emp. S. 377, p. 20, WL.

[164] Caroline Elkins, *Britain's Gulag: The Brutal End of Empire in Kenya* (London: Jonathan Cape, 2005), p. 471.

[165] Duff, *Bailing with a Teaspoon*, p. 168.

[166] Diary, 13 November [1938], Battershill Papers, MSS. Brit. Emp. S. 467, Box 12, File 6, WL.

[167] Quoted in Charles Townshend, 'In Aid of the Civil Power: Britain, Ireland and Palestine, 1916–1948,' in Daniel Marston and Carter Malkasian (eds), *Counterinsurgency in Modern Warfare* (Oxford: Osprey, 2008), p. 32.

[168] Letter, Burr (Inlying Piquet) to Mother and Father, 24 February 1938, Burr Papers, 88/8/1, IWMD.

[169] Letter, Dill to Wavell, 31 October 1936, Palestine, 1937–38 Volume, Wavell Papers, POH.

the words of a former pro-Zionist Palestine Attorney General.[170] Nor was his successor MacMichael always willing to bend to the Army's will. Governmental standing orders reminded soldiers that 'All Arabs are not your enemies'; the 'motive of the Administration – a most laudable one, was to avoid causing unnecessary hardship and suffering among the innocent Arabs, and to avoid leaving memories of British "cruelty",' noted a British military journal.[171] Without complete control of the civil executive, the military could fully regulate neither the passage of suspects into the court system, civil or military, nor the management of the complete judicial system, and it all required thoughtful use of arrest and charging by soldiers without legal training, and their sending some form of evidence to the military court.

Britain attached 'real' martial law to great upheavals like the 1857 Indian mutiny. It was outdated by 1936. The Army worked with the civil executive under statutory martial law in 'sub-wars' as in Palestine. Martial law was never a 'feasible proposition within the British Empire,' in the words of Simson.[172] Nonetheless, many field officers still demanded absolute powers. Simson saw the 1936 Palestine Martial Law (Defence) Order in Council as statutory martial law and not the streamlined real martial law of 'three or four general paragraphs,' as 'statutory martial law regulations have to be drawn up article by article, like a long code of rules' and this meant equivocation.[173] The issue at hand was control of the Palestine executive. At a meeting at the Colonial Office in February 1937, the military representative queried civilian interpretations on the 'absolute power of control of the High Commissioner,' concluding that 'it is quite impracticable and visionary to believe that the High Commissioner can act side by side with the General Officer Commanding.'[174] Nevertheless, this is what happened in Palestine. The two sides fudged control of the country, the Colonial Secretary producing a note 'to retain the *substance* of the amending Order of 1936 by making full provision for the delegation of powers by the High Commissioner to the General Officer Commanding the Forces in Palestine, while eliminating any reference to "Martial Law" as a description of that procedure.'[175] The Defence (Military Commanders) Regulations in October 1938 solved the problem

---

[170] Norman and Helen Bentwich, *Mandate Memories, 1918–1948* (London: Hogarth, 1965), p. 156.
[171] Anon., 'Service Problems in Palestine: From a Correspondent in Jerusalem,' *Journal of the Royal United Service Institution* 81 (November 1936), p. 809.
[172] Simson, *British Rule and Rebellion*, pp. 101, 108–09.
[173] Ibid., pp. 257–59.
[174] Quoted in Townshend, 'Martial Law,' p. 192.
[175] Quoted in ibid., p. 193.

by retaining the Palestine executive but switching roles and subordinating it to the Army in an advisory role, but without disposing of civil government altogether or giving it wholesale to the Army. Tensions between the civil executive and the armed forces mollified actions by soldiers keen to pacify Palestine with a show of force and then return for the war looming in Europe. This they did, crushing the revolt with the powerful legal structure described here. Protracted struggle and disciplined opposition might have overcome Britain's all-encompassing colonial emergency state, but the rebels were disorganised, badly led, and lacked funds, and they self-immolated with an unfocused terror campaign and a disastrous call to strike. A successful revolt in Palestine demanded dynamic leaders willing to embody self-sacrifice and to articulate self-reliance, with matching propaganda slogans – such as Irish rebels' 'ourselves alone,' the Zapatista leaders' 'for everyone, everything, for us nothing,' EOKA's oath that 'I shall work with all my power for the liberation of Cyprus from the British yoke, sacrificing for this even my life,' or the Jews' 'there is no alternative' – and this never happened.[176]

---

[176] *Sinn Féin; para todos todo, para nosotros nada; ein breira.*

3   Rebels and Revolt

A Farmers' Revolt

In the beginning of the Arab revolt was its end.[1] Popular anger sparked an uprising without method and such organisation as appeared chased rather than led events on the ground. It may be that the *Istiqlal* Party embodied politically conscious Palestinians striving to break notable politics to effect real change and that its network of younger activists influenced by recent strikes in Egypt and Syria shaped protests before and during the revolt, but the argument here is that the revolt wanted leadership once the violence escalated.[2] Rebels were trapped between a moribund communist movement, a self-regarding urban bourgeoisie, and an inchoate *Istiqlal* founded only in 1932, and so dragged to defeat by 'feudal' notable leaders fearful of armed rural resistance and articulate politico-religious 'public apostle' figures like 'Izz al-Din al-Qassam.[3] The British acknowledged al-Qassam's threat and killed him, possibly after his men attempted a white flag parley, just as the Bolivian Army executed Che Guevara in 1967 and US Special Forces shot dead Osama bin Laden in 2011 in better dead than alive operations.[4] The revolt had no good strategy on how to use force. The creation of National Committees and an Arab Higher Committee (AHC) to guide the revolt occurred four to eleven days *after* Qassamite gunmen shot Zvi Danenberg and Israel Chazan on 15 April 1936. The regional National Committees predated

---

[1] Paraphrasing T. S Eliot's 'East Coker' from his *Collected Poems, 1909–1962* (London: Faber and Faber, 2002), p. 184.

[2] Weldon C. Matthews, *Confronting an Empire, Constructing a Nation: Arab Nationalists and Popular Politics in Mandate Palestine* (London: Tauris, 2006), pp. 233–35.

[3] Ghassan Kanafani, 'Thawrat 1936–1939 fi Filastin: Khalfiyyat, tafasil wa tahlil' ['The 1936–1939 Revolt in Palestine: Background, Details and Analysis'], *Shu'un Filastinyya* [*Palestinian Matters*] 6 (January 1972), pp. 62–63; Rashid Khalidi, *Palestinian Identity: The Construction of Modern National Consciousness* (New York, NY: Columbia University Press, 2010), p. 115.

[4] Mark Sanagan, 'Teacher, Preacher, Soldier, Martyr: Rethinking 'Izz al-Din al-Qassam,' *Welt des Islams* 53/3–4 (2013), pp. 346–47.

the AHC. There were also village committees. This was a bottom-up revolt. No field commander or ideological-political leader appeared to fill the hole left by the dynamic al-Qassam, neither from the Palestinians nor from neighbouring Arab states, not before Fawzi al-Qawuqji's short spell in Palestine from late August to October 1936 just as the AHC sued for a ceasefire that most of its members had wanted all along. Fellahin supported al-Qawuqji and came out to fight for him but he never reappeared as Palestinian leaders of rebel *fasa'il* units ('groups,' 'factions,' or 'sections,' military Arabic for a platoon) resented his foreign presence – al-Qawuqji was born in what became Lebanon – compounded by unhelpful politicking at rebel headquarters in Damascus in 1937–38.[5] The leader of the AHC, Hajj Amin al-Husayni (the Mufti), vacillated. He maintained British patronage and did 'his best to convince the Government that he had nothing to do with the rebels and that he was a moderate factor' while being the rebellion's figurehead.[6] These were incompatible roles. The AHC functioned as a semi-official executive and not a guerrilla high command, until October 1937 when the British abolished it. Instead of its leaders going underground, power shifted to headquarters in Damascus that ran out of money and lost touch with field units, after which no one was in charge. Once Hajj Amin escaped to Lebanon in October 1937, he pursued internecine fighting with other Palestinians such as elements within the Nashashibi family rather than unite against a common enemy. This is not to damn the Palestinians. Factional infighting bedevils all insurgent movements but successful ones keep it in-house or leave their civil wars until after victory, whether it was the Irish over the British, the Chinese over the Japanese (the 1936 Xi'an incident is instructive here), or the Angolans against the Portuguese in the 1970s.[7] The actions of the Qassamite gunmen on 15 April 1936 forced on Palestinian notable leaders unwanted burdens of command that they were unable or unwilling to shoulder, obligations that they tried to escape or foist on others. The regional National Committees only partially filled the gap. Palestinians struggled with themselves as they did with the British, but more exactly they struggled with the notion of struggle itself. Without central planning, nationwide terror attacks lacked focus, generated no strategic momentum, and dissipated rebel combat power. Shaky top-down command structures explain the misplaced decision to

---

[5] Yehoshua Porath, *The Palestinian Arab National Movement: From Riots to Rebellion. Volume 2, 1929–1939* (London: Cass, 1977), p. 244.

[6] Ibid., p. 193.

[7] Ethnic communities divided Angolan resistance before the Portuguese withdrew: W. G. Clarence-Smith, 'Class Structure and Class Struggles in Angola in the 1970s,' *Journal of Southern African Studies* 7/1 (1980), pp. 109–26.

sustain a general strike. Instead of an expanding torrent of anti-colonial terror, rebel violence plateaued at a level that inconvenienced but never threatened Britain.

While the revolt started in towns, the violence quickly spread to the country where the rural poor became the 'primary face' of the national movement.[8] The countryside was the 'womb' of a three-year rural 'farmers' revolt,' attached to which was a discrete secondary urban-based general strike in 1936.[9] The revolt and strike were not coterminous. Violence neither forged a new social order in the countryside, nor strengthened old ways of doing things.[10] Rather, prolonged insurgency melded with rural social matrices and the 'fatalism' of village life to channel violence inwards.[11] Peasants revolted because traditional social relations had failed to protect them from adverse Mandate-induced economic and political changes that they attempted to tackle organically through a peasants' revolt, like Wat Tyler's in 1381 against the poll tax and serfdom.[12] Villagers felt the 'disdain' of the urban leaders who did not see peasants 'as equal partners but rather as tools to be used in the achievement of their goals' and so went it alone.[13] This gave the revolt grassroots grit – sufficient to challenge the British Army for three years but also to exhaust Palestinians for the next war in 1948 with Israel – but no means to energise reactionary strength and stop peasant-rebel anti-state violence morphing into supercharged forms of traditional intra-communal violence and robbery, exacerbated by the social dislocation wreaked by British punishment of the countryside.[14] British and Jewish collective punishments and intelligence gathering encouraged *fitan* clashes between parties that many Palestinians instinctively preferred over (or along with) fighting a common enemy and a primitive urge that disciplined guerrilla organisations eradicate. As the mother of

---

[8] Yuval Arnon-Ohanna, *Falahim ba-Mered ha-'Aravi be-eretz Yisrael, 1936–39* [*Fellahin during the Arab Revolt in the Land of Israel*] (Tel Aviv: Shiloh Institute, Tel Aviv University, 1978), p. 26; Laura Robson, *Colonialism and Christianity in Mandate Palestine* (Austin, TX: University of Texas Press, 2012), p. 151.

[9] Kanafani, 'Thawrat 1936–1939 fi Filastin,' pp. 67–69; Baruch Kimmerling and Joel S. Migdal, *The Palestinian People: A History* (Cambridge, MA: Harvard University Press, 2003), pp. 106–08.

[10] Ylana Miller, *Government and Society in Rural Palestine, 1920–48* (Austin TX: University of Texas Press, 1985), p. 125.

[11] Ibid., p. 122.

[12] Ibid., pp. 121–38.

[13] Hillel Cohen, *Army of Shadows: Palestinian Collaboration with Zionism, 1917–1948* (Berkeley, CA: University of California Press, 2008), p. 79.

[14] Khalidi, *Palestinian Identity*, pp. 26–27; Rashid Khalidi, 'The Palestinians and 1948: The Underlying Causes of Failure,' in E. Rogan and A. Shlaim (eds), *The War for Palestine* (Cambridge: Cambridge University Press, 2007).

a Palestinian girl exclaimed, '"Why don't they fight the Jews instead of each other?"'[15] Rebels ran out of funds and ammunition, lacked medical services, fought one another, and irregular troops reverted to banditry and instinctively exploited the peasants that they were supposed to be helping.[16] Mao Zedong wrote in 1937 that the 'moment' that a 'war of resistance dissociates itself from the masses of the people is the precise moment that it dissociates itself from the hope of victory' but what damned the resistance war in Palestine was precisely that it was synonymous with the lumpen mass.[17] The rebels in Palestine were the people, and the people were the peasants. The British had a clear target and they punished and executed rural villagers. Indeed, the absence of tangible rebel command structures aggravated Britain's counter-insurgency campaign, as security forces could not easily win the war by decapitating a non-existent insurgent leadership, even after banning the AHC and deporting many of its leaders to the Seychelles in October 1937. They targeted entire communities.[18] As Palestine GOC General Sir Robert Haining complained, the rebels had no central organisation whose 'destruction would cause the rebellion to collapse.'[19] All that the British could do once they had abolished the AHC was energetically to hunt down minor field commanders. The British also successfully targeted rebel access routes to the Syrian safe base area and rebel headquarters in Damascus, ably supported by the British Consul there, Colonel Gilbert MacKereth, in conjunction with Jewish agents and the Sûreté when the French were in the mood to cooperate. Without the October 1936 ceasefire and the 1938 Munich crisis slowing military operations, the British would have won sooner. It is to the 1936 general strike that this chapter turns before assessing the leadership of rebel forces and their funding. This chapter focuses on the politics and economics of the revolt, while the next chapter examines the military shock action of rebel forces, the role of rebel headquarters in Damascus, and rebel depredations against Palestinians. Taken together, they give a summary of the military effectiveness of rebel actions and begin the analysis of British counter-rebel measures. The impact of British counter-rebel operations on Palestinians – battles, punishments, fines,

[15] Ghada Karmi, *In Search of Fatima* (London: Verso, 2009), p. 10.
[16] Mao Tse-tung [Mao Zedong] (trans. Samuel B. Griffith), *On Guerrilla Warfare* [1937 in Chinese] [1961] (New York, NY: Doubleday Books, 1982), pp. 17, 45, 67.
[17] Ibid., p. 44.
[18] Martin Thomas, *Empires of Intelligence: Security Services and Colonial Disorders after 1914* (Berkeley, CA: University of California Press, 2008), p. 249.
[19] Report by Gen Haining, Hostile Propaganda in Palestine, 1 December 1938, FO 371/21869, p. 169, TNA.

demolition, detention, curfews, hunger, and homelessness – is the subject of Chapter 5 and Chapter 6.

General Strike

The revolt erupted at a moment when Britain was set to hold on to the Middle East against rising German and Italian power, and when it had the troops to do so. On 7 March 1936, German forces reoccupied the Rhineland, setting Europe on the road to a war in which Britain demanded Palestine as a strategic base area. On 5 May 1936, the Abyssinia crisis that had preoccupied Britain since 1934 ended with the Italian capture of Addis Ababa. Britain could now redeploy troops in Egypt and elsewhere from a possible conflict in the Horn of Africa to imperial hot spots such as Palestine. It was an inauspicious time for rebellion as Britain refused to surrender its position in Palestine and it had the troops and time to pacify the country. The contest of wills between the British Empire and the Palestinians was also an organisational battle for funds and equipment in which London would bankroll the Palestine Government and pay for the troops needed for pacification. Money for the rebels bought weapons and food, provided doctors, gave insurgent fighters salaries, paid wages for striking workers, printed propaganda leaflets, kept newspapers open, paid off informers, turned enemies into friends, and it meant that rebel forces would not prey on peasant villagers for sustenance. In principle, a general strike and boycott of British and Jewish goods in Palestine threatened Britain with crippling loss of revenue for local Government coffers and collapse of the country's infrastructure, especially if coordinated with terror attacks on transport and commercial nodes. Arab labour filled Palestine's citrus groves, the lower echelons of the colonial civil service, the railways and ports, and the rank-and-file of the police. In practice, the general strike hurt Palestinians much more than it did the British who were willing and able to weather the storm of strike with help from Palestine's 411,222 Jewish inhabitants – 29 per cent of the overall population – who seized the opportunity to fill gaps left by the withdrawal of Arab labour while Royal Navy engineers ran trains.[20] This was when workers did strike. Some Palestinians pretended to strike, or in vital jobs such as citrus fruit, the civil service, and the deep-water Haifa port complex they never went on strike. Shops secretly stayed open.

---

[20] *Statistical Abstract of Palestine, 1939* (Jerusalem: Office of Statistics, 1939), p. 11; *A Survey of Palestine, Prepared in December 1945 and January 1946 for the Information of the Anglo-American Committee of Inquiry* (Jerusalem: Government Printer, 1946), i, pp. 140–41.

To understand the strike of 1936 is to understand Government taxation and revenue streams. Before 1940, there was no income tax in Palestine. Palestine Government revenues came from taxes on land and property, on crops with a 10 per cent agricultural tithe (including a small share as *waqf*), on animals, and from customs duties levied on goods that transited via the country's three ports of Jaffa, Haifa, and Tel Aviv.[21] There were stamp duties on certain business transactions, bringing in £P.98,347 in 1937–38, and the Government collected excise on goods manufactured in Palestine such as cement, salt, tobacco, matches, and liquor.[22] There was no purchase or sales tax on goods in Palestine, nor did Britain have one before 1940. Rural debt was so bad that the Government remitted a sizeable proportion of the tithe on crops and collections fell from £P.286,521 in 1921–22 to £P.109,000 in 1934–35 despite a growing population. Between 1933 and 1935, the Government remitted as much as £P.345,000 of tithes.[23] Wheat was the staple tithe peasant crop and it is worth reiterating here the point made briefly in the last chapter that many peasants lived with terrible debt, subjected to crippling levels of interest of up to 50 per cent for short-term loans.[24] Peasants did not have the financial reserves to pay Government fines, nor the money to subsidise rebels, and any diminution of their personal wealth threatened rapid impoverishment. Indeed, when the British could not get fines paid in coin, they took away crops and animals, and smashed up (and soldiers stole) villagers' personal effects. Theft and robbery were so bad that security forces even robbed the Anglican Archdeacon of Jerusalem, maltreating in the process the Arab boy that the cleric had left to look after his affairs.[25] Peasants had little advantage over Government by withholding agricultural taxes. While the tithe constituted 12.4 per cent of Government revenue in 1922, twelve years later in 1934–35 the figure was just 2 per cent, the Government making up the shortfall from customs revenues, for one, as international trade improved.[26] The fall in tithes is significant as any agricultural strike in 1936 would have little effect on government income, unless it was the citrus industry, 'the backbone of Palestine's export trade,' whose volume exported increased from 931,000 cases in 1920–21 to 15,310,000 cases in 1938–39 and whose value went from £P.206,000 in 1921 to £P.3,808,000 in 1939.

---

[21] Ibid., i, pp. 246–54.
[22] Ibid., ii, p. 549.
[23] J. B. Hobman (ed.), *Palestine's Economic Future* (London: Percy Lund, 1946), p. 58.
[24] Ibid., p. 57.
[25] Diary, Forster Papers, GB165-0109, p. 74, MEC.
[26] Hobman, *Palestine's Economic Future*, p. 58.

Palestinians produced 45 per cent of the citrus fruit.[27] Citriculture was booming. Jaffa port could export 4,500,000 cases of citrus, while Haifa's new harbour would shortly be exporting 15,000,000 cases noted a report in 1935.[28] But the AHC was keen to end the strike before the late autumn 1936 citrus fruit harvest – buyers also bought fruit 'on the tree' several months beforehand based on predicted harvest yields – precisely so that rich landowners were not adversely affected by withdrawal of labour and loss of exports.[29] A CID file from August 1936 made note of this: only Hajj Amin's Palestine Arab Party opposed a ceasefire, while the Nashashibi-backed National Defence Party and *Istiqlal* wanted an end to the trouble as both parties 'consist mostly of orange exporters who wish the strike to stop before the season starts.'[30]

Import duties were the most important source of tax revenue, and customs and excise during the revolt period totalled £P.2,958,521 in 1934–35, £P.2,338,381 in 1937–38, and £P.2,515,160 in 1940–41.[31] The revolt did not stop imports of goods to Palestine and customs thereof. The value of imports shows that the economy functioned throughout the rebellion: in 1935 £P.17,853,493, in 1936 £P.13,979,023, in 1937 £P.15,903,666, in 1938 £P.11,356,963, and in 1939 £P.14,632,822. Turning to the value of exports (excluding re-exports), this totalled in 1935 £P.4,215,486, in 1936 £P.3,625,233, in 1937 £P.5,813,536, in 1938 £P.5,020,368, and in 1939 £P.5,117,769.[32] There was a steady upward trend to 1944, with a slight dip in revenue and trade in 1936–37. Elsewhere, figures suggest that the value of exports had almost doubled from 1934–35 to 1937–38.[33] The rebels never seriously threatened revenue or trade. Nor did the revolt have a significant impact on tax gathering that before income tax was straightforward to assess on fixed objects, excepting animals. The tax take for urban and rural property and land in 1934–35 was £P.477,670, falling in 1937–38 to £P.424,218. The rebellion did not stop citizens paying the bulk of their tax.[34] Moreover, Jews contributed a large share of the land tax, 58 per cent or £P.664,000 of the aggregate of the taxes on land by 1944, and they were not in revolt, not until 1945 anyway.[35]

[27] Ibid., p. 59.
[28] C. M. Jenkin-Jones, *Report on the Traffic Organisation, Facilities and Rates of the Palestine Railways 1935* (London: Crown Agents, 1935), p. 7.
[29] Nahum Karlinsky, *California Dreaming: Ideology, Society, and Technology in the Citrus Industry of Palestine, 1890–1939* (Albany, NY: SUNY Press, 2005), p. 191.
[30] CID dated 25 August 1936, Shai Intelligence Reports: 8/GENERAL/40, p. 253, HA.
[31] *Survey of Palestine*, ii, pp. 544, 549.
[32] Ibid., i, p. 462.
[33] Ibid., ii, p. 536.
[34] Ibid., ii, p. 544.
[35] Ibid., ii, p. 573.

Nor were grants from London large, just £P.152,946 in 1937–38, while public debt remained constant through the revolt.[36] In 1929, internal revenues supported the entire civil administration of Palestine.[37] That said, there were overall budget deficits, but only in 1936–37 and 1937–38, the latter to the tune of £P.2,400,332, and it is not clear who paid for the Tegart fence and forts – probably the Palestine Government but the Jewish Agency and London funded projects, too – or what was the total figure for secret service payments.[38] The Jewish Agency paid some of the cost of soldiers protecting the IPC TAPline, for instance.[39] Costs for security related infrastructure projects carried over into annual budgets for the early 1940s. Palestinian corvée labour during the revolt built many roads for free, while Jewish funding covered much of the Jewish supernumerary police expenditure and *Histadrut*-led road construction; Tegart gave a Jewish company led by David Hacohen the contract for fortress building.[40] Certainly, the economy kept functioning during the revolt.

Before further examining the relationship between economy and rebellion, some brief comment on Palestine's transport infrastructure and citrus industry is necessary to understand the failure of the general strike. The Arab-run port of Jaffa had long been Palestine's main entrepôt, from where lighters shuttled goods to and from bigger boats in the roadstead. The opening of the 185-acre deep-water port at Haifa in 1933 with mixed Arab–Jewish workers gave ships direct docking access and connection to the railway system. There was renovation of dockside buildings at Jaffa port in 1935 but the authorities never connected it to Palestine's railways.[41] There was also a small Jewish-run port at Tel Aviv by the Yarkon River estuary.[42] Haifa port transformed Palestine, out-performing the lighter basins at Jaffa and Tel Aviv by getting rid of tran-shipment by lighters and by having direct access to the railway.[43] Jaffa port was the traditional export route for citriculture but the presence of the standard-gauge line that went from Lydda to Haifa offered an

---

[36] Ibid., ii, pp. 536, 549.
[37] Israel Cohen, *Palestine and the British Tax Payer* (London: Jewish Agency, 1929), pp. 5–6.
[38] *Survey of Palestine*, i, pp. 124–25, ii, p. 536.
[39] Meeting with Moshe Sharett and Reuven Shiloah, p. 24, Alice Hay of Seaton Papers, JRL.
[40] Charles Tegart, Memoir of an Indian Policeman, by K. F. Tegart (wife), pp. 247ff, Mss Eur C.235/2, IOR; Kevin Connolly, 'Charles Tegart and the Forts That Tower over Israel,' *BBC News* (10 September 2012).
[41] There was a light railway spur to Jaffa harbour but it could not tranship heavy loads and was eventually dismantled. Images on the internet of a light railway at Jaffa port are of a temporary one from the 1890s used for constructing the Jaffa–Jerusalem line.
[42] Tamir Goren, 'Developing Jaffa's Port, 1920–1936,' *Israel Affairs* 22/1 (2016), p. 182.
[43] *Survey of Palestine*, ii, pp. 856ff.

alternative route for sending out fruit once Haifa was fully open in 1933. Indeed, Jewish fruit growers in the *Pardess* (literally 'orange grove') citrus marketing cooperative had been using parts of Haifa port since 1928 and Jewish growers easily switched to Haifa port once it was fully open. Direct loading onto ships avoided the rough handling in small boats as happened at Jaffa, as did the direct standard-gauge rail link to Haifa harbour. Some Jewish growers near Jaffa stuck with their local port and until the 1935 season the proportion of citrus shipped through Haifa did not exceed 40 per cent of total exports. By the spring of 1936, it had risen to 60 per cent. The revolt hastened the move of citrus exports to the mixed-labour Haifa port, it disengaged Jews from Palestinian citriculture, and it encouraged the growth of the completely Jewish-run Tel Aviv port that increased its citrus exports from 3 per cent in 1936–37 to 10 per cent a year later.[44]

Palestine's 520-kilometre railway system imported 96,893 tons and exported 47,055 tons of goods in 1936–37. In 1939, the ports of Palestine discharged 929,231 tons and loaded 545,384 general tonnage as well as 1,811,916 tons of oil from the TAPline.[45] Imports and exports came predominantly through Palestine's ports, the railways mostly moving domestic freight, with 1,162,992 tons conveyed in 1936–37.[46] Railway staff was mostly non-Jewish: of 5,450 railway workers in Palestine during the Second World War, only 600 or 11 per cent were Jewish, mainly in salaried and 'monthly grades.'[47] Keeping the railways open during the revolt was vital for the economy and the British built small armoured wagons for the railway with 'pony truck' extensions, on which they put local hostages to deter trackside attacks, some on the chassis of Ford V8 motor cars; Royal Navy personnel ran armoured trains.[48] The point here is that the British kept the railways functioning during the disturbances and this helped to destroy Jaffa port as insurgent violence drove passengers from trains but not freight that now transhipped via Haifa.[49] Britain could tolerate the closure of Arab-run Jaffa port now that the more efficient Haifa facility was open and the Army could keep open roads and railways to the port.

To damage the Palestine Government, select parts of the labour force needed to strike in conjunction with terror attacks to interdict transport and build rebel base areas. Crafted and coordinated targeting of labour

[44] Karlinsky, *California Dreaming*, pp. 199–200.
[45] *Survey of Palestine*, ii, pp. 854–57.
[46] Ibid., ii, p. 857.
[47] Ibid., ii, p. 856.
[48] P. Cotterell, *Railways of Palestine and Israel* (Abingdon: Tourret, 1984), p. 64.
[49] Ibid., p. 66.

and transport would have had an impact on British administration. Instead of closing their shops, Palestinians had to strike vulnerable parts of the colonial economic architecture: the IPC oil pipeline, Haifa and Jaffa harbours, Haifa oil refinery, the civil service, citriculture, railways and roads, the police, tax collection on property, and shops that sold cheap produce like vegetables to Jews. Indeed, rebels assembled villagers and gave them speeches instructing them not to sell Jews vegetables or 'mix up with them.'[50] Rebel action in the end managed only to close Jaffa harbour and reduce the police force; it was not enough. Crucially, rebels needed a counter to Britain's punitive financial counter-measures, so would need good access to funds to pay fighters and those not working, and these could not come from poor peasants who would get much poorer as the Army pacified rural areas. Nor could money easily come from urban merchants and the middle class whose businesses were closed and who when pushed could (and did) decamp to neighbouring Arab states. Italy gave some limited funding, it seems, but insufficient to sustain an entire community. The British seized back lost revenues through draconian fining of the people and they had the emergency apparatus in place to do it, as the last chapter has proved.[51] Chapter 6 on 'screwing down the population' suggests that Britain extracted more in fines than it lost in revenue during the revolt, excepting the cost of military deployment but London had to pay for its Army anyway so fighting the rebels was not excessive additional expense, notwithstanding the added security infrastructure costs, with roads often built with free forced labour. The Army had to be somewhere. Rebels also needed a strategy to deal with Palestine's Jews who would readily fill gaps made by striking labour, sell produce to Jews who previously had bought more cheaply from Palestinians, and supply British forces.

There had been short precursor strikes in late 1935 and early 1936 prior to the general strike. The 'network of activists' driving this was an alternative node to the notable leaders and their five main political parties (excluding *Istiqlal* and the communists).[52] The notable leaders were based in Jerusalem alongside British Government – and Jerusalem was consequently the last place to form a National Committee as it was arguably the least committed – and they vied with decentralised leadership based in hill towns like Nablus around figures such as Akram Zu'aytir, a founding member of *Istiqlal*.[53] National Committees spread out across

[50] Arnon-Ohanna, *Falahim ba-Mered ha-'Aravi*, p. 35.
[51] Miller, *Government and Society in Rural Palestine*, p. 128 argues that Palestinians only paid about a third of fines.
[52] Matthews, *Confronting an Empire*, p. 248.
[53] Ibid., pp. 251–52.

Palestine after 19 April 1936 and their activists 'planned to try and turn the strike into an armed uprising' but crucially 'in the earliest stage of the revolt, there was little contact between the armed groups and minimal preparation for military action.'[54] It augured badly that the strike was leading the armed resistance, that there was little preparation, and that armed groups had minimal contact with one another. If the elite leadership could not check the violence, its usefulness to colonial Government faded.[55] The British helped to save the mainstream leaders by arresting National Committee members and *Istiqlalists* on the AHC, some of whom had formed guerrilla cells, including Bahjat Abu Gharbiyya who had met with al-Qassam and who went on to fight Israel in 1948.[56] It was only when the British were unable to work with the AHC that they abolished it. The Palestinians had by then four resistance networks, none of which effectively coordinated terror or the withdrawal of labour: notables and the mainstream parties, local activists and National Committees, armed peasant-based rural bands led locally, and foreign-led armed bands like al-Qawuqji's. These parochial and fragmented networks prompted local factional initiatives rather than a national strategy. For example, urban fighter Abu Gharbiyya shot British police officer Alan Sigrist in June 1936 in reaction to Sigrist's rough handling of Jerusalemites and two months later he shot two RAF aircraftsmen in retaliation for Britain's supposed aerial bombing of rural areas.[57] These were self-generated, reactive attacks, not planned urban assassination campaigns. The AHC never resurrected itself within Palestine during the revolt after its abolition, nor when extant did it give unity to the strike action that it half-heartedly supported and that continued nominally for six months. The National Committees could fill the gap, but they were regional in scope. The strike's success depended on coordinated terror action by armed insurgents against roads, railways, and ports to halt imports, exports, and domestic freight, and against Arabs and Jews willing to carry on with commerce, and those paying taxes.

Palestinians closed their enterprises in an impressive show of unity. This achieved little except to deny merchants business, cut revenues,

---

[54] Ibid., p. 253.
[55] Ibid., p. 254.
[56] Ibid., p. 255; Bahjat Abu Gharbiyya, *Fi Khidamm al-nidal al-'arabi al-filastini: Mudhakkirat al-munadil Bahjat Abu Gharbiyya* [*In the Midst of the Struggle for the Arab Palestinian Cause: The Memoirs of Freedom-Fighter Bahjat Abu Gharbiyya* (Beirut: IPS, 1993).
[57] Author interview, Bahjat Abu Gharbiyya, Amman, Jordan, 21 June 2009 (and subsequent email correspondence); Matthew Hughes, 'A History of Violence: The Shooting of British Assistant Superintendent Alan Sigrist, 12 June 1936,' *Journal of Contemporary History* 45/4 (2010), pp. 725–43.

encouraged some to sell produce secretly, alienated the middle class, and it imbued the revolt with an unhelpful aimlessness. It transformed Palestinian urban quarters into noticeably quiet places to visit and dirty, too, as street cleaners stopped working. The US Consul General went into Jerusalem's old city in July 1936, to find troops everywhere and everything shuttered and areas out-of-bounds with barbed wire and police barricades. With a police escort, he heard his 'footsteps echoing from roofs of empty covered bazaars, abandoned construction projects, a silent unattended Wailing Wall, gave one the effect of an all but deserted city.'[58] There were curfews at night. This was imprisonment, with the entire guilty population of urban Palestinians locked up. It was an opportunity for Jewish merchants to feed and supply the thousands of British soldiers pouring into Palestine. The British did not raise sales or income tax, so shop closures did not directly affect Government income. A strike and boycott only affected revenues from services such as road transport and forestry licences, post office business, land registry, and minor matters like fishing licences that in 1944–45 combined to produce £P.261,892, mostly from road transport.[59] But without these licences, Palestinians could not legally fish, collect wood, drive their vehicles, manufacture tobacco or liquor, or buy land.

The strike crippled the Palestinians, made worse by British punishments. In Nablus, the Dorsetshire Regiment noted in September 1936 how 'many of the townspeople are feeling the effect of the prolonged strike, in some cases even well-to-do citizens having to sell their household goods. They appear to be depressed by the recent strong action by the government.'[60] The report added how 'notables' could not agree on whether to support 'the policy of violence. After the recent punishments imposed on the town, nearly all are agreed that peace and quiet in the town itself is highly desirable, but there is still a feeling that the armed gangs in the hills should be strongly supported.'[61] The poverty of striking eroded the people's passion, and Nablus was a rebel heartland. Elsewhere, merchants and traders ignored the strike, or it was localised to city areas such as Jaffa, while 'the lukewarm attitude of the Arab leaders in general and of Nashashibi in particular appears to have prevented the spread of the disturbances.'[62] Shops opened secretly. Traders in Haifa in July 1936 worked from private

---

[58] US Consul General Palestine to State Department, 13 July 1936, 867N.00/338 [Reel M#1037/2], NARA II.
[59] *Survey of Palestine*, ii, p. 547.
[60] Dorsetshire Regiment, Narrative of Events, Nablus, 15–18 September 1936, 88/367, Shelf C4, Box 3, KMM.
[61] Ibid.
[62] Disturbances of April 1936, US Consul General Palestine to State Department, 25 April 1936, 867N.00/283 [Reel M#1037/1], NARA II.

houses while coffee houses also re-located to people's homes. Workers honoured the strike in the breach, with guilty shopkeepers shouting at each other, while villagers brought sheep to Haifa to sell as they were worried (rightly) that collective fines would mean loss of livestock.[63] In the same month, traders complained bitterly, saying that they would break the strike and start trading in private homes.[64] The police in Jaffa reported that 'hawkers have been plying freely in the streets and the small shopkeepers are selling usually from their back doors, but in several cases from partly opened shops ... There is a feeling of confidence springing up and if we keep these measures [of counter-intimidation] going, probably some shops will be encouraged to open.'[65] Many Christians were half-hearted in their commitment to strike action and just a week after the revolt started, Christian traders wanted to open their shops and break the strike.[66] Jewish files in August 1936 noted that the majority of Arabs wanted an end to the strike and had the 'same opinion' as the Nashashibis. Some Christian stores in Haifa had opened.[67] The Christian bourgeoisie was a 'marginal player' to the national struggle and preferring British rule but without the Balfour Declaration 'only a few of them could wholeheartedly support the Muslim opposition to the West.'[68] The revolt reduced the incidence of Jews buying cheaper Palestinian produce, although some Jews still clandestinely bought vegetables despite calls for Jewish solidarity in the face of the revolt.[69] Here was the dilemma: without Jews buying produce, Palestinians had reduced income just as the British fined them and rebels demanded donations, while if Jews bought produce then the strike was not working and Palestinian sellers risked assassination as traitors. One Palestinian trading with 'the boycotted Jews' to make a 'handsome profit' argued that he had to as the Jewish merchants supplied information for a spy ring.[70]

[63] Dated 3 July 1936, Information from the Arab Office, Reports of the Situations and Gangs, Communist Activity, Polish and Italians, 22 April–31 July 1936: 8/GENERAL/ 39, p. 36, HA.

[64] Dated 16 July 1936, Information from the Arab Office, Reports of the Situations and Gangs, Communist Activity, Polish and Italians, 22 April–31 July 1936: 8/GENERAL/ 39, p. 74, HA.

[65] Counter Intimidation in Jaffa, DSP Foley (Southern Division) to IG, n.d. [June– July 1936], Arab Office and Intelligence: 8/GENERAL/39, HA.

[66] Daily Intelligence, 27 April 1936, Arab Office and Intelligence: 8/GENERAL/35, HA.

[67] Haganah Report, 30 August 1936, Shai Intelligence Reports: 8/GENERAL/40, p. 137, HA.

[68] Itamar Radai, 'The Rise and Fall of the Palestinian–Arab Middle Class under the British Mandate, 1920–39,' Journal of Contemporary History 51/3 (July 2016), p. 498.

[69] Ephraim Kluk, A Special Constable in Palestine (Johannesburg: Kluk, 1939), p. 11.

[70] Appendix: Explanatory Notes, Captured and Translated Arabic Material with Commentary, pp. 63, 141, Wingate Papers, Microfilm M2313, BL.

The Arab workforce at Jaffa port went on strike and ended contacts with Jewish trade unions. Arab motor transport shut down. What did not close down was Haifa port whose moderate (or for his critics pro-Zionist, pro-British) Arab mayor, Hasan Shukri, opposed the general strike and so became the target of rebel assassination attempts.[71] Jews had been working with Arabs in Haifa for many years and Arab merchants ignored the boycott and strike: 'Numerous reports told of the limited participation of most Arab merchants in Haifa in the boycott, and of the many ways developed to bypass it.'[72] This was business: the Jews had finance and foreign contacts, while Arabs had labour. But the labour force was changing. Jewish trade unions like the *Histadrut* had made 'patient and persistent' efforts to put Jews 'into economically and politically strategic workplaces which had once been almost exclusively Arab' and the footholds that the *Histadrut* had made in these places of work greatly helped Britain's 'ability to block Arab nationalist efforts to spread the strike and fully paralyze the country's economy.'[73] The *Histadrut* had formed in 1932 the (known in English as) Palestine Labour League (PLL) for Arab workers as a non-Jewish auxiliary branch of *Histadrut*, there to stop Arabs joining and transforming the Zionist *Histadrut* and which was now a potential strike-breaking force.[74] There was a short, ineffectual strike by a hundred porters in Haifa port in April 1936 but Arab workers and contractors stayed at their posts despite pleas from the National Committees. Hajj Amin headed an AHC delegation that travelled to Haifa on 13 May 1936 to meet with the heads of the port workers and persuade them to down tools but Arab stevedores argued that the port authorities could easily substitute them, so the port remained open.[75] Only in August 1936 after assassinations and threats was there a brief ten-day strike that spread to railways and the Public Works Department, at which point the British sent in security forces to protect strike breakers and run trains. The Jews contributed with labour from their kibbutzim settlements while the PLL played its part by readying Arab strike breakers.[76] Strikers fearful of losing their jobs to Jews all returned to work and the strike did not disrupt the port again. By the end of the summer of 1936, and with Jaffa port closed,

---

[71] Zachary Lockman, *Comrades and Enemies: Arab and Jewish Workers in Palestine, 1906–1948* (Berkeley, CA: University of California Press, 1996), p. 241.

[72] Deborah Bernstein, *Constructing Boundaries: Jewish and Arab Workers in Mandatory Palestine* (Albany, NY: SUNY Press, 2000), p. 68.

[73] Lockman, *Comrades and Enemies*, p. 241.

[74] Ibid., p. 197. In Hebrew *Brit Poa'lei Eretz Yisrael* (League of Workers of the Land of Israel) and in Arabic *Ittihad 'Ummal Filastin* (Union of the Workers of Palestine).

[75] Bernstein, *Constructing Boundaries*, p. 152.

[76] Lockman, *Comrades and Enemies*, p. 242.

Haifa harbour was handling more cargo than ever. Emboldened, Jewish businesses hired additional Jewish workers.[77] The main Arab contractor, 'Abdallah Abu Zayd, had long-standing personal and business links with the Jews, and the Jewish Agency 'was secretly disbursing considerable sums to him (and presumably to others as well)' to keep open Haifa harbour.[78] Many Arab workers left Haifa for their home villages.[79] The Jewish workforce expanded as Jewish citrus fruit flowed through Haifa harbour and by the revolt's end Jewish porterage carried Jewish citrus fruit to the boats at Haifa.[80]

The Government had been reticent before the revolt to use *Histadrut* labour for fear of antagonising Palestinians. This all changed in April 1936. The Government now had strong political and security reasons to support the *Histadrut*'s drive for Jewish labour.[81] The Army supplied the muscle and the Jews the motivated workers. When Arabs at the Jewish-run *Nesher* cement quarry went on strike, the quarry moved its contract from an Arab contractor – who had fled to Lebanon after nationalists made threats against him – to the *Histadrut*.[82] The British then despatched police to help the *Histadrut* bring Jewish workers into the quarry and the Jews convinced the remaining Arab workers to join the PLL. Jews gained control of the Majdal Yaba quarry during the revolt by introducing Jewish labour, after which the quarry authorities sacked the Arab workers. Arabs stayed away from Jewish-run citrus groves, Jewish workers taking their place. The Zionist-linked PLL died a death during the revolt, except in Haifa where its Jewish liaison officer recorded 'numerous instances in which Arab workers from Haifa and from villages near and far' approached him, asking to join the PLL 'in the conviction that membership brought with it secure and well-paid employment at some Jewish enterprise.'[83] The PLL was an employment bureau supplying reliable workers for the British and Jews. The Jewish Agency passed money through the PLL to Arab workers to keep them working and it paid taxi drivers. The Jews bought their first boats for Tel Aviv port from Arabs in Haifa through PLL contacts. The PLL was also a useful source of intelligence for the Jews.[84] The PLL even issued anti-revolt propaganda.[85]

---

[77] Ibid.
[78] Ibid.
[79] Bernstein, *Constructing Boundaries*, p. 62.
[80] Ibid., p. 154.
[81] Lockman, *Comrades and Enemies*, p. 243.
[82] Ibid., p. 244.
[83] Ibid., pp. 246–47.
[84] Ibid., p. 248.
[85] Ibid., pp. 242ff.

The rebels did not bring out on strike the Palestinian civil servants running the Government. They preferred to tax their wages – so an early form of income tax – to supply funds for the revolt. Such funds supported other striking workers such as the Jaffa dockworkers, or monies disappeared. Civil servants' striking was an issue in the second phase of the revolt, too, there being a call to strike in December 1938, by which stage the Army was running the country. The opposition to strike action in 1938 was the same as in 1936:

Strong protests were made against this proposal [to strike] both by the officials themselves and by the general populace who pointed out that the officials were the only people earning and spending any money and that the strike would only add to the prevailing economic distress. The proposal was therefore abandoned and instead a levy varying from 20% to 5% on officials' salaries suggested. It is reported that the officials have refused to submit to this imposition and, perhaps as a result, a notice by the local rebel committee has appeared in JERUSALEM deploring the unauthorised demands for subscriptions which, it is alleged, are being made on Arab officials.[86]

The strike successfully cleaved Palestinian officers from the police and it broke the force. The Army then took charge of it. The police functioned in peaceful times by getting Palestinian and Jewish officers to do the policing, using whatever violence was necessary. With mass revolt and consequent pressure on Palestinian officers, morale and discipline collapsed as British police officers could not keep order alone, and failure manifested itself in violence, drunkenness, and looting, as it had done in Ireland before.[87] London rushed out hastily trained British police replacements to replace lost Palestinian officers.[88] The Army feared that collapsing police morale would infect soldiers who saw policemen 'running amok a bit in the bazaar and breaking things up in a most wanton manner. No doubt they have an awful lot of provocation for behaving like that but the whole proceeding was rather revolting and a very bad example to the troops.'[89] No better than 'second class' was how a brigade commander described the police in a letter to his

---

[86] Summary of Intelligence, Palestine and Transjordan, 16 December 1938, by Wing Commander Ritchie at GHQ [25/38], CO 732/81/10, TNA.
[87] Police Incident on Nablus Road, 1 March 1939 in Letter, Haining to O'Connor, 14 March 1939, O'Connor Papers, 3/4/43, LHCMA; Letter, O'Connor to Wife, 22 October 1938, O'Connor Papers, 3/1/16, LHCMA; Letter, O'Connor to Wife, n.d., O'Connor Papers, 3/1/20, LHCMA; Matthew Hughes, 'A British "Foreign Legion"? The British Police in Mandate Palestine', *Middle Eastern Studies* 49/5 (2013), pp. 696–711.
[88] 8th Division Instructions by Montgomery, Haifa, 25 November 1938, O'Connor Papers, 3/4/4, LHCMA.
[89] Diary, 15 October 1938, Mullens Papers, Vol. 1, p. 33, LHCMA.

wife.[90] This was a mixed success for rebels. London sent out extra police recruits while the Army easily assumed police functions and worst of all the collapse of the Arab part of the police encouraged the British to recruit, equip, and train extra Jewish police officers in supernumerary units. As with shop closures and the strike action in Haifa, the collapse of the police helped the Jews.

Leadership and Command

Successful revolt needed leadership *and* command (and control), the former inspirational and motivational, the latter a coordinating, managerial function.[91] The politico-military process-systems of command and control need comprehension and personal intelligence, while leadership is a moral quality and can exist without any intellectual capacity at all. Al-Qassam and al-Qawuqji had all these qualities but they operated operationally and not strategically. Al-Qawuqji attempted to grow his operation with a proto field staff system of officers who could act as the commander's 'collective brain' and ensure common action, supplies, discipline, and run branches like intelligence and planning.[92] Command can exist in some form without inspirational leadership but fighters will expect charismatic moral qualities (such as bravery) in their military commanders or insurgent political leaders. Al-Qassam and al-Qawuqji were brave, magnetic operational leaders but the first died before the revolt while the other spent only a brief time in Palestine. They lacked coordinated field command with higher political leadership that, say, Colonel Grivas in Cyprus had with Archbishop Makarios. There was none of the political direction of insurgent commanders such as Jomo Kenyatta or Gerry Adams. Instead, Hajj Amin was the supreme political commander of the Palestine revolt – indeed, the 'Mufti's Revolt in Palestine' was a British regimental battle honour – but he had no military experience, while politically he fought internal enemies as much as (or more than) he did the British, notably the Abdullah–British–Jewish backed Nashashibi-family Opposition.[93] A Palestinian nationalist later noted that Abdullah 'would sooner have seen' Jerusalem 'become Jewish

---

[90] Brig Carr (Jaffa) to Wife, 25 October 1936, Carr Papers, Letter 247, LHCMA.
[91] G. D. Sheffield, 'Introduction: Command, Leadership and the Anglo-American Experience,' in G. D. Sheffield (ed.), *Leadership and Command: The Anglo-American Experience since 1861* (London: Brassey's, 2002), pp. 1, 117.
[92] Russell Weigley, *The American Way of War: A History of United States Military Strategy and Policy* (Bloomington, IN: Indiana University Press, 1977), p. 200.
[93] Arthur Swinson (ed.), *A Register of the Regiments and Corps of the British Army* (London: Archive Press, 1972), p. 212.

than under the Mufti,' ignoring how in 1948 Abdullah resisted his powerful British patrons and intervened militarily to stop the Israelis capturing all of Jerusalem.[94] Al-Qawuqji archly commented on Hajj Amin's inexperience and duplicity, remarking that he 'never fought on the battlefield of any country. He lays claim to leadership whenever he feels that his life is threatened, then he steals the money and retreats in defeat.'[95] A British office recalled many years later how al-Qawuqji's picture was 'in all the cafes. Not the Mufti, it was Fawzi who was the hero with the Arabs,' although later, after the defeat of 1948, this changed.[96] This is not to rehearse the baleful effects of intra-Palestinian clashes between Hajj Amin's Husayni family bloc and others such as the Nashashibis on the Palestinian national cause, but two points need stating. First, counter-insurgencies instinctively drive wedges in insurgent ranks, searching for fissures and disunity, threatening and buying off people, seeking collaborators, blackmailing, spreading tales, and gathering intelligence. British security forces in Northern Ireland during the Troubles even launched psychological operations that included rumours that paramilitary terror had unleashed devil-worshipping forces of evil.[97] Second, the Nashashibis and Husaynis were fundamentally the same. Both parties managed violence for patronage not national politics, the Nashashibis just less effectively. The Palestinians fought without united national, strategic-political command and once al-Qawuqji had gone they had no effective operational military leaders in the field either. The middle class never filled the political space. The Government bought off bourgeois Palestinians (and Christians) with jobs and the Christian and Muslim middle class saw the uprising as a threat to their status and so avoided anti-British action.[98] Neither rebels nor notables won over minority communities. Instead, they extorted them. Christians paid protection money to Hajj Amin in exile in Beirut to the tune of £P.2,000, it being 'unhappily all too reasonable an assumption' that Christian Haifan building contractor 'Aziz Khayat[99] and other Christian Palestinians were 'paying heavily for immunity of attack.'[100] The revolt was a 'Holy War against a

---

[94] Notes of Interviews, Izzat Tannous (Beirut), 22 September 1977, Palestine Research Lever Arch File, Thames TV Material on 'Palestine: Promises, Rebellion and Abdication' (1977–78), IWMFA.

[95] Quoted in Laila Parsons, 'Soldiering for Arab Nationalism: Fawzi al-Qawuqji in Palestine,' *Journal of Palestine Studies* 36/4 (Summer 2007), p. 44.

[96] Gratton, 4506/03, p. 19, IWMSA.

[97] Richard Jenkins, *Black Magic and Bogeymen: Fear, Rumour and Popular Belief in the North of Ireland 1972–74* (Cork: Cork University Press, 2014).

[98] Radai, 'The Rise and Fall of the Palestinian–Arab Middle Class,' pp. 487–506.

[99] 'Cherished Tailor,' the name can be Christian or Muslim (or even Jewish). Family members still live in Haifa.

[100] Diary, 17 May 1938, Scrivenor Papers, MSS. Brit. Emp. S. 378, WL.

Christian Mandate and against Christian people' in the words of a local British churchman.[101] The growing Islamic content to the rebellion and to the *Majlis* further estranged Christians and drew them to collaborationist *al-Mua'rada* forces. Palestinian notable leaders' attitude to violence was peculiar, not so much in how they saw internal enemies everywhere but in how they valorised force. As with South Vietnam's Ngo Dinh Diem in the early 1960s who delegated authority with a 'miser's hand,' always worried that subordinates would turn and use official authority against him, Palestinian elites mobilised force to make money and stabilise power bases against internal enemies.[102] Violence for Palestinian elites was personal and not political, reactionary not revolutionary; violence for the middle-class was anathema; for peasants, violence was personal, social, and premeditated, but not political; for many rebel bands, violence was a way of making money.

Without political guidance or any guiding ideology, violence was pointless, but without violence, politics was pointless, certainly in Palestine where only kinetic action would change pro-Zionist British policies. Well-mobilised guerrilla forces tie violence to long-term political effect while operationally they control battle space. Consider the Vietnamese insurgent victory at the battle for Ap Bac in 1963 at the beginning of the insurgency in South Vietnam – and in the start of the Vietnam war was its end, too – that led twelve years later to complete victory over the US global superpower:

The 350 guerrillas had stood their ground and humbled a modern army four times their number equipped with armor and artillery and supported by helicopters and fighter-bombers. Their heaviest weapon was the little 60mm mortar that had proved useless to them. They suffered eighteen killed and thirty-nine wounded, light casualties considering that the Americans and their Vietnamese protégés subjected them to thousands of rifle and machine-gun bullets, the blast and shrapnel of 600 artillery shells, and the napalm, bombs and other assorted ordnance of thirteen warplanes and five Huey [helicopter] gunships. The Hueys alone expended 8,400 rounds of machine-gun fire and 100 rockets on the tree lines at Bac. With the weapons they held in their hands the guerrillas killed or wounded roughly four of their enemies for every man they lost ... They had done more than win a battle. They had achieved a Vietnamese victory in the way of their ancestors. They had overcome the odds.[103]

[101] Yuval Arnon-Ohanna, *Herev mi-Bayit: ha-Ma'avak ha-Pnimi ba-tnu'a ha-le'umit ha-falastinit, 1929–39* [*The Internal Struggle within the Palestinian Movement, 1929–39*] (Tel Aviv: Hadar, 1989), pp. 64–65; Robson, *Colonialism and Christianity*, p. 151.
[102] Mark Moyer, *Triumph Forsaken: The Vietnam War, 1954–1965* (New York, NY: Cambridge University Press, 2006), p. 34.
[103] Neil Sheehan, *A Bright Shining Lie* (London: Pan, 1990), pp. 262–64.

Vietnamese peasants were no more or less brave than their Palestinian counterparts. The notion that 'Arab culture' negatively affects military effectiveness must be set against hard-fighting, successful Arab warriors from Saladin to Hizbollah.[104] Typically, political organisation transforms peasants into guerrilla warriors and it gives them the required physical and mental strength: guns, food, and uniforms, but also mental steadfastness. The remarkable tactical-operational triumph at Ap Bac demanded organisation, commitment, coordination, and good leadership and command at the strategic level, and clear policy goals. Palestinian bands lacked such structures and so never fought positional battles like Ap Bac where the Vietcong left the battlefield on their own terms. Palestinian rebels adopted 'shoot and scoot' tactics that left British soldiers exhausted chasing the heels of bands but never even remotely threatened them with tactical or operational defeat, as one officer remembered: 'we could see them silhouetted on the skyline of the ridge opposite and they were raising their rifles and sort of shaking them at us as if to say "Well we'll be back another day." This was quite a long way away ... they were too far for us to shoot with small arms ... but it gave us a sort of slight chivalrous feeling.'[105] British picquets exchanged shots with the rear parts of retreating bands and never the advancing van.[106] Insurgents never left the field of combat on their terms; the British chased them away. The Army remained master of the battlefield throughout. British military files recount endless, repetitive small-scale tactical skirmishes and sniping that exhilarated rather than intimidated troops. There were no set-piece manoeuvre battles and no culminating point to rebel violence. 'Quite honestly we found it fun,' one soldier recounted in a later oral history, and very different to the war against the Jews after 1945 that he fought in, too: 'And I hope the Jews if they ever hear this programme will forgive me for saying that they played a dirty game ... One understood the Arabs in a way. He wasn't as merciless as the Jew could be.'[107] That the Jews 'ran rings around us' and 'pulled off the most fantastic coups' talks to another insurgency after 1945 that had excellent organisation and political velocity.[108] British security forces thought Palestinian rebels to be 'gentlemen and sportsmen' – 'give me the Arab every time, said Tommy Atkins' – compared with the organised ruthlessness of the 'bloody Yid'

---

[104] Kenneth Pollack, *Arabs at War: Military Effectiveness 1948–1991* (Lincoln, NE: University of Nebraska Press 2002), pp. 3–4.
[105] Bredin, 4550/05, p. 17, IWMSA.
[106] C. T. Atkinson, *The Dorsetshire Regiment. Volume 2* (Oxford: Oxford University Press, 1947), p. 186.
[107] Gratton, 4506/03, pp. 20–21, 32, IWMSA.
[108] Grove, 4510/03, p. 11, IWMSA.

after 1945 who 'kills at night, without a fight, which Jerry [the Germans] never did.'[109] The British assessed Palestinian rebels as lowly opponents set against other insurgents, excepting al-Qawuqji who impressed them. If soldiers 'fired back at them, they ran, they didn't stand and fight,' with shooting 'at very extreme range.'[110] 'They all used to run away in disarray, once we caught their leader. Because they didn't know what to do'; 'they scarpered away as soon as we got near them'; 'not very brave'; and 'they have neither the courage nor the natural aptitude for war possessed by the Pathans.'[111] As GOC Palestine General Sir John Dill put it, 'there is always the comforting fact that the Palestinian Arab is not really a fighting man. The troops out here have been taking risks which would spell disaster on the N.W. Frontier' of India.[112] An Army report at the close of the first phase of the revolt was equally critical:

A remarkable feature of the rebellion has been the lack of enterprise shown by the rebels even with the help of that reputed soldier Fawzi [al-Qawuqji], and the apparent complete lack of appreciation of the trouble they were in a position to cause. It is only necessary to compare the half-hearted measures adopted in this country with what the Arabs of Mesopotamia did during the rebellion in 1920 to realise what the problem might have been. Another feature was the lack of training and the poor equipment of the rebels. Further they proved very bad shots.[113]

British battle casualties tell the same story of a weak insurgency, one told in more detail in Appendices A and B. The tally of Army, RAF, (one) Royal Navy, and (one) Arab Legion dead in Ramleh British military cemetery for April 1936 to December 1939 is 244, omitting the period from December 1936 to August 1937; some infantry battalions served whole tours without fatalities while the largest infantry regiment loss was up to sixteen dead from the Royal Scots spanning its year's deployment.[114] (The RAF lost the most men during the revolt with at

[109] Douglas Duff, *Bailing with a Teaspoon* (London: John Long, 1953), p. 30; John Bierman and Colin Smith, *Fire in the Night: Wingate of Burma, Ethiopia and Zion* (New York, NY: Random House, 1999), p. 63; Alwyn Holmes in Philip Ziegler, *Fighting Men's Lives, 1901–2001* (New York, NY: Knopf, 2002), p. 288; Crookenden, 16395/7, IWMSA.
[110] Norman, 4629/02, pp. 8–9, IWMSA.
[111] Edwards, 10317/5, p. 13, IWMSA; Crookenden, 16395/7, IWMSA; Letter, Brig R. Montagu-Jones to Tom Steel (Thames TV), 12 October 1976, Lever Arch File Letters, Thames TV Material on 'Palestine: Promises, Rebellion and Abdication' (1977–78), IWMFA; Gen Sir N. M. Ritchie, Palestine Retrospective, p. 1, KO LIB 285, KORRM.
[112] Dill to Deverell (CIGS, London), 10 November 1936, Dill Papers, 2/9, LHCMA.
[113] Printed Security Pamphlet, Notes on Tactical Lessons of the Palestine Rebellion 1936 (Jerusalem HQ, 1937), Wheeler Papers, LHCMA.
[114] The naval loss was a Royal Marine from HMS *Malaya*. The CWGC web material for Ramleh at www.cwgc.org/find-a-cemetery/cemetery/72001/RAMLEH%20WAR%20 CEMETERY does not include inter-war 'non-war burials' so the figure of 244 comes

least thirty-one dead but this was over the whole length of the revolt.) The figure of 244 excludes headstones obviously marking deaths from accidents or illness, as some do, recording, say, death by drowning or accidental death, but as the wording on some is ambiguous it is certain that some of the 244 deaths are from non-combat causes. Similarly, regimental histories remark that a battalion had no combat fatalities, while there is a death recorded in Ramleh, so the loss was obviously an accident or illness-related.[115] (That non-combat losses outnumber combat ones is typical, with more British soldiers, for example, dying from accidents and suicides than in battle in the recent wars in Afghanistan and Iraq.[116]) The Ramleh headstones are not uniform, in that some say died in battle, while others do not but mark deaths that one can tell from the date relate to a battle that a particular regiment had with rebel forces. As some sixty infantry battalions and armoured units rotated through Palestine, excluding extensive support corps deployment, airmen, and land-based naval units, the figure of 244 dead is tiny, just 0.49 per cent of troop numbers assuming conservatively a total troop throughput plus policemen of 50,000, or 0.24 per cent combat fatalities if we assume that half the number was non-combat deaths. In thirty-six months of active operations, April 1936–December 1939, excluding December 1936–August 1937, seven soldiers per month died on average, many from non-combat causes. By contrast, Vietnamese guerrillas killed over 1,000 American soldiers per month by 1968. Police deaths recorded in Ramleh, Jerusalem, and Haifa cemeteries for the same timeframe total fifty-four.[117] Meanwhile, according to official British figures, security forces killed more than 2,000 Arabs in combat and they hanged 112, while 961 died because of 'gang and terrorist activities.'[118] Building on the British statistics, Walid Khalidi presents figures of 19,792 casualties

from the author's recording of headstone details at Ramleh cemetery. There are 3,502 casualties in total from 1917 through to the end of the Mandate in Ramleh cemetery. Even assuming an error in calculation by the author of 10 per cent, the figure of dead from the revolt does not exceed 270 and this is to the end of 1939, after the official end date of the revolt of 3 September 1939. The Ramleh burials are of sixteen dead from the Royal Scots; see Royal Scots entry in Appendix A here for figure of fifteen.

[115] Such as W. L. Vale, *The History of the South Staffordshire Regiment* (Aldershot: Gale and Polden, 1969), p. 399, contradicted by the presence of a dead soldier from the regiment in Ramleh cemetery.

[116] There are mandatory on-base road tests at the US Marine base at Quantico, Virginia as more young male Marines were dying in motorbike crashes than in combat.

[117] Haifa Khayat Beach war cemetery and adjoining Haifa (Sharon) British civil cemetery; Haifa Jaffa Road cemetery; Jerusalem Protestant cemetery (Mount Zion, via Jerusalem University College); Jerusalem Latin (Catholic) cemetery (Mount Zion).

[118] Derived from *A Survey of Palestine*, i, ch. 2 and cited in Walid Khalidi (ed.), *From Haven to Conquest* (Beirut: IPS, 1971), pp. 846–49.

for the Arabs including 5,032 dead (so 14,760 wounded), broken down further into 3,832 killed by the British and 1,200 dead because of intra-communal 'terrorism.'[119] Hebrew sources record between 900 and 4,500 Palestinians deaths from intra-communal violence, with Hillel Cohen's more recent work making the case for the lower figure, so if half of British Service deaths were non-combat related – 122 soldiers and twenty-seven policemen totalling 149 – rebels killed between six and thirty Palestinians for every Serviceman that they killed.[120] Put differently, for every British policeman or soldier that the rebels killed, security forces killed twenty-six rebels, accepting Khalidi's figure of 3,832 divided by 149. The author challenges this and posits a figure of at least 5,748 rebel dead at the hands of security forces in Appendix B. The British harried, exiled, imprisoned, hanged and killed the entire rebel field and higher command leadership, while rebels killed just two British Government officials, Lewis Andrews and Walter Moffatt, captured no one, and never assassinated any senior military personnel above the rank of major (two killed) or equivalent in the RAF with two squadron leaders.

Without a higher command to decide Palestinian military strategy, untrained field commanders with experience only of banditry and skirmishing made poor ad hoc tactical and operational decisions, or at times mobs of leaderless peasants came out to fight the British. Rebels did not sever the link between violence and politics; they never set up the link in the first place. The largest military encounter that Palestinian insurgents had with the Army was at Bal'a village north-east of Tulkarm in early September 1936 where al-Qawuqji's men impressively shot down several RAF warplanes and escalated the violence, five weeks before the AHC leaders deescalated and finalised the ceasefire that they had been urging throughout and had al-Qawuqji removed from the country.[121] This made neither political nor military sense unless one accepts that Palestinian leaders had never wanted a revolt in the first place, excepting possibly Hajj Amin whose commitment to rebellion

---

[119] Khalidi, *From Haven to Conquest*, pp. 846–49; Ted Swedenburg, *Memories of Revolt: The 1936–1939 Rebellion and the Palestinian National Past* (Minneapolis, MN: University of Minnesota Press, 1995), p. xxi; Walid Khalidi and Yasin Suweyd, *Al-Qadiyya al-Filastiniyya wa al-Khatar al-Sahyuni* [*The Palestinian Problem and the Zionist Danger*] (Beirut: IPS, Lebanese General Staff Fifth Branch and Ministry of Defence, 1973), pp. 239–40.

[120] Arnon-Ohanna, *Herev mi-Bayit*, pp. 286–87; Arnon-Ohanna, *Falahim ba-Mered ha-'Aravi, passim*; Hillel Cohen, *Tzva ha-Tzlalim: Mashtapim Falestinim be-Sherut ha-Ziyonut, 1917–48* [*An Army of Shadows: Palestinian Collaborators in the Service of Zionism, 1917–48*] (Jerusalem: 'Ivrit, 2004), pp. 142–45.

[121] Ghassan el-Khazen, *La Grande Révolte Arabe de 1936 en Palestine* (Beirut: Éditions Dar An-Nahar, 2005), p. 283.

must be weighed against his self-serving fight to maintain power. By 23 April 1936, just four days into the unrest, the US Consul wrote home how the Nashashibis had 'urged' that the AHC 'leaders make a statement disavowing the present unrest,' favouring instead a British call to come to London to discuss a proposed legislative assembly.[122] The Nashashibis again urged colleagues to abandon the strike on 25 April, against Hajj Amin's call for strike action and unanimity, but Raghib Nashashibi 'saw that he was outnumbered and consented, for the sake of solidarity, to lend his support to the strike.'[123] The US Consul reported that

no two leaders reacted in the same way. The Mufti called a general strike which had but the scantiest support, Nashashibi suggested that the delegation deplore the killing and go to London on schedule, Dr [Husayn] Khalidi [of the Reform Party] was at first apparently quite uninspired to become the patriot he now claims to be ... It was after it became known that there would be no money worries that all leaders enthusiastically supported the strike ... Throughout it all Ragheb [Raghib Nashashibi] has been, like Caesar's wife, far above suspicion. He has proved himself a master politician, but no great selfless patriot.[124]

Fractious leadership was a gift to the British, not least as it meant intelligence leaks. Thus, Fakhri Nashashibi gave CID chief Harry Rice reports of key meetings prior to the call to end the strike and violence in October 1936.[125] The arrest of *Istiqlalist* AHC secretary 'Awni 'Abd al-Hadi divided rather than united the committee. Raghib Nashashibi 'declared that the Mufti was using his present situation to further his own ends and that it was entirely due to his influence with the High Committee that the present banishments were taking place' and pointed out that the British had not banished any of Hajj Amin's supporters.[126] Palestinian leaders within the AHC worked together with the British to take back control from the 'golem' released by the revolt before it destroyed the Palestinian ruling class.[127] The British targeted middle-rank cadres, arresting sixty-one of them in May 1936 while leaving the compliant AHC fundamentally intact. For Marxist Ghassan Kanafani, the end of first stage of the revolt was a rightist triumph by the effendi class that

---

[122] Disturbances of April 1936, US Consul General Palestine to State Department, 25 April 1936, 867N.00/283 [Reel M#1037/1], NARA II.

[123] Disturbances of 1936, Further Developments, US Consul General Palestine to State Department, 6 May 1936, 867N.00/287 [Reel M#1037/1], NARA II.

[124] Disturbances of 1936, Cause and Effect, US Consul General Palestine to State Department, 6 June 1936, 867N.00/311 [Reel M#1037/1], NARA II.

[125] Eldad Harouvi, *Palestine Investigated: The Story of the CID of the Palestine Police Force, 1920–48* (Sussex: Academic Press, 2016), p. 62.

[126] Disturbances of 1936, 5–12 June, US Consul General Palestine to State Department, 13 June 1936, 867N.00/315 [Reel M#1037/1], NARA II.

[127] Arnon-Ohanna, *Falahim ba-Mered ha-'Aravi*, p. 73.

wanted a return to making money.[128] The Jewish Agency pitched in by meeting with both Raghib Nashashibi and Husayn al-Khalidi to push opposition to Hajj Amin, and with 'Awni 'Abd al-Hadi.[129] British intelligence summaries recorded more AHC disagreements in July 1936, again between the Nashashibis and Hajj Amin, predicting that although differences were 'very strong' to date 'no splits have as yet occurred.'[130] The police expected the AHC to call off the strike by the end of July 1936 after leaders quarrelled at Hajj Amin's residence.[131] Jaffa seamen joined AHC meetings to demand money, a matter referred to a committee of needs and an issue examined below.[132] The AHC never channelled the energy of the armed bands, meeting on 20 August 'to stop the wild situation but they still don't know the position of the extremists.'[133] Violent action outpaced any command authority. One British judge wagered a bet with a Palestinian colleague 'that even after the strike is called off the activities of the terrorist gangs will continue because the Arab Higher Committee has no influence over them.'[134] He was right. Qassamites restarted the violence by assassinating Lewis Andrews on 26 September 1937. The AHC considered calling off the strike on 1 August, a move championed by Nashashibi, but the 'Mufti however was adamant in his opposition to such a course and the Committee, bound by an oath to act only on motions carried by unanimity, was therefore constrained to carry on *in status ante quo.*'[135] Once the British forced Hajj Amin into exile in October 1937, he continued targeting opponents 'through violence and intimidation,' telling the proprietor of an Arab news agency in October 1938 that he could sustain a five-year revolt but his 'first step, however, was to remove all the leaders of the opposition,' by which he meant the Nashashibi-backed *al-Mua'rada* Opposition.[136] Hajj Amin

---

[128] Ghassan Kanafani, *Palestine: The 1936–1939 Revolt* (London: Tricontinental, n.d., c. 1982), pp. 18–21.

[129] Abigail Jacobson and Moshe Naor, *Oriental Neighbors: Middle Eastern Jews and Arabs in Mandatory Palestine* (Waltham, MA: Brandeis University Press, 2016), pp. 63–64.

[130] Summary of DIS from 5 July 1936, Jerusalem, dated 7 July 1936, Arab Office and Intelligence: 8/GENERAL/39, HA.

[131] Police/DIS Report entitled Jerusalem Information, dated 21 July 1936, Arab Office and Intelligence: 8/GENERAL/39, HA.

[132] Minutes of the AHC, 21 July 1936, RG65: P3221/18, ISA.

[133] 15 August 1936, Shai Intelligence Reports: 8/GENERAL/40, p. 36, HA.

[134] Haganah Report, n.d. [August 1936], Shai Intelligence Reports: 8/GENERAL/40, p. 253, HA.

[135] Memorandum on Palestine Disturbances, August–September 1936, US Consul General Palestine to State Department, 9 October 1936, 867N.00/407 [Reel M#1037/2], NARA II.

[136] Mustafa Kabha, *The Palestinian People: Seeking Sovereignty and State* (Boulder, CO and London: Lynne Rienner, 2014), p. 15; CID, Jerusalem, Periodical Appreciation

was determined that no-one would fill 'the void' created by his exile to Lebanon.[137]

Funding

Money was a poor substitute for good political organisation, but it sustained workers on strike, paid fighters in the field, kept newspapers open, and funded propaganda. Rebel fighters' salaries were the biggest outlay, anything from 30 shillings (£P.1.500 mils, see Appendix F on currency) to £P.4 per month for an active mujahid, while some wounded rebels received the large sum of £P.5 a month when convalescing.[138] Financial patronage gave political leaders influence over armed bands whose motivations were pecuniary as they were ideological. Without money to disburse, both the AHC and Damascus headquarters lost control of rebel units. Without funds, armed bands robbed peasants. Meanwhile, bands were suspicious that leaders stole funds. The British called this a case of the 'pot calling the kettle black,' adding:

There are, however, clear signs that the gang leaders are becoming daily more independent of political control. This is due in large measure to the drying up of supplies, both of money and material from abroad which has led to the growing belief among the active rebels that too great a proportion of the funds contributed from outside PALESTINE are being misapplied by the exiled leaders for their own benefit.[139]

A nationwide strike and uprising demanded consistent and substantial funding. It never materialised. It is impossible to give an exact figure for the cost of strike pay, for instance, but in 1939 there were 18,000 salaried workers in transport and communication in Palestine that with a pro rata adjustment for population, gives a figure of around 12,000 Palestinian workers in that sector.[140] Assuming a pay rate for an experienced steve-dore in Haifa port of £P.13.500 per month (500–550 mils per day) this equals around £P.6,000 per day strike pay for transport and communica-tion workers if all these people were on strike with full pay, although this is too high a figure considering that such work was erratic and that Jewish

Summary 73/38, 18 October 1938, L/PS/12/3343: Political Situation – Police Summaries, IOR.
[137] Kabha, The Palestinian People, p. 15.
[138] CID, Jerusalem, Periodical Appreciation Summary 73/38, 18 October 1938, L/PS/12/3343: Political Situation – Police Summaries, IOR.
[139] Summary of Intelligence, Palestine and Transjordan, 7 October 1938, by Wing Commander Ritchie at GHQ [20/38], CO 732/81/9, TNA.
[140] Survey of Palestine, ii p. 731.

labourers earned a maximum of £P.7.500 per month.[141] Construction employed 25,000 workers in 1939 and even assuming that only half were Arab and on strike this would add another £P.1,250 per day in strike pay on the basis of Arab workers' daily rate of 100–125 mils per day with *Nesher* cement company.[142] Did no one do the maths? The sums involved were immense. There were some 300,000 Palestinians in urban areas and so possibly on strike, and with Palestinians out of work or the Army subjecting them to punitive action, internal funding would be hard to extract, or it would be a case of income extraction from a population on strike and so not generating any revenue.[143] An alternative strategy would have allowed people to work while honest rebel tax collectors gathered funds. Even if the AHC only paid some key strikers such as the Jaffa dockworkers, and at a reduced rate, strike pay could not sustain all those nominally unemployed for months on end. Palestinians were surviving at their own expense, eating up capital, moving abroad, or ignoring the call to strike.

The Jews made play of Italy and Germany funnelling money and weapons to rebels. Some monies and arms did arrive via this route, but as RAF intelligence noted, the sums involved were 'comparatively small' and 'all this talk about Italians supplying money to the Arabs has been purposely fomented by the Jews in order to discredit the Arabs in the eyes of the British.'[144] Jews saw the hand of Italian diplomats in Cairo and Damascus who channelled money to rebels through Egypt's Bank Misr, while the US Consul in Palestine reported that the Italian Consulate there passed 2,000 gold sovereigns and on another occasion £P.5,000 to an 'Arab leader.'[145] Haganah detailed 'outside' support for rebels of £P.3,000 to £P.30,000.[146] Italian banks or ships were the usual

---

[141] Bernstein, *Constructing Boundaries*, p. 154; Lilach Rosenberg-Friedman, *Birthrate Politics in Zion: Judaism, Nationalism, and Modernity under the British Mandate* (Bloomington, IN: Indiana University Press, 2017), p. 106.

[142] Bernstein, *Constructing Boundaries*, p. 122; *Survey of Palestine*, ii, p. 731.

[143] A figure of 257,325 in 1931 so with undocumented shanty-town dwellers and urban growth over the interim seven years from 1931, we can assume at least 300,000 city dwellers. *Statistical Abstract of Palestine, 1937–38* (Jerusalem: Office of Statistics, 1938), p. 19.

[144] Letter, Brooke-Popham (HQ, RAF, Cairo) to ACM Ellington (London), 8 July 1936, Brooke-Popham Papers, 4/3/41, LHCMA.

[145] Undated note [first page is missing], Sasson (in Damascus) to Shertok, n.d. [7 January 1938], S25/3639-98/99, CZA; Disturbances of 1936, Further Developments, US Consul General Palestine to State Department, 6 May 1936, 867N.00/287 [Reel M#1037/1], NARA II.

[146] Minutes of an Interview [Moshe Shertok?] with the High Commissioner, 31 May 1936, Reports from 1937 on Abdullah, National Commission, January–July 1936, 80/153P/9, HA.

conduit, Jewish spies noting two Italians and an Arab, one of whom was the vice-manager of Rome Bank, entering a banking establishment through the back door, staying for thirty minutes, after which a car came from the AHC strike committee to remove money.[147] Italian ship captains reportedly brought in money, passed to Arab dockworkers, while German ships smuggled in money and weapons to rebels via the Jaffa 'Helping Committee.'[148] Italian ships smuggled in guns from the Red Sea through Beersheba.[149] Jewish intelligence from January 1938 noted that Hajj Amin's 'Committee of the Jihad' had sent men to Germany and Italy to purchase modern weapons and ammunition, and that these were smuggled in via the Syrian and Lebanese coast to Palestine.[150] The Jewish driver of pro-Palestinian British resident Frances Newton went further and claimed that German and Italian 'experts' instructed the Palestinians in modern weaponry.[151] There is no evidence of foreign European instructors, nor did British soldiers capture modern German or Italian equipment. There is a reference to German manufactured mines planted in a Jewish cemetery but rebels mostly fought with anti-quated rifles ('ropey old things') that used different ammunition and they pilfered Great War-era shell dumps for explosives.[152] 'They used to use half petrol cans full of scraps of iron' for mines, noted a soldier.[153] 'Awfully primitive' bombs made of jam jars and old food cans recorded the York and Lancaster Regiment.[154] The lack of good weapons 'and the constant lack of rounds' were the problem, compounded by rebel supply couriers 'looting' their own cargoes.[155] That said, Syrian Jewish Member of Parliament Joseph Laniado told Jewish agents Reuven Zaslani (codenamed 'Shiloah' and later Mossad's first director) and Eliyahu

[147] Information from the Arab Office, 12 May 1936: 8/GENERAL/37, HA.
[148] 12 July 1936, Information from the Arab Office, Reports of the Situations and Gangs, Communist Activity, Polish and Italians, 22 April–31 July 1936: 8/GENERAL/39, p. 149, HA.
[149] What happened in Tulkarm, Report of the National Committee in Tulkarm, 11–12 August 1936, Shai Intelligence Reports: 8/GENERAL/40, p. 184, HA; Report of Meeting between Zaslani, Sasson with Jewish MP in Syrian Parliament and sent to Shertok, 3 February 1938, File: Letters from Syria, 1937–38 and 1946, S25/3639-23/106/107/108/109, CZA.
[150] Sasson (Damascus) to Shertok, 7 January 1938, S25/3639-137, CZA.
[151] Benjamin 'Adin (Edelman), *Adventures at the Wheel: Memoirs of a Native-born Jerusalemite* (Jerusalem: Alfa, 1965), pp. 74–75.
[152] File 1836/00090/14: Commission of the Current Situation, 1939, HMA; Grove, 4510/03, p. 21, IWMSA.
[153] Packer, 4493/02, p. 9, IWMSA.
[154] *The Tiger and Rose: A Monthly Journal of the York and Lancaster Regiment* 11/16 (August 1936), p. 320.
[155] Appendix: Explanatory Notes, Captured and Translated Arabic Material with Commentary, p. 160, Wingate Papers, Microfilm M2313, BL.

(Elias) Sasson that Germany and Italy had channelled 'large amounts of money' to foment rebellion in Palestine:

In the case of the foreign funding, we can't provide overwhelming evidence but we have some examples of foreign sources. These cases shed light. We know for example in the days of the 1936 revolt the German bank in Jerusalem transferred large amounts of funds and the Syrian Orphanage in Jerusalem [a German one] is now serving as the centre for terrorist attacks.[156]

Italy was vying for influence with Britain in the eastern Mediterranean and was keen, as was Germany, to support anti-British Arab nationalists and some Axis funding arrived for rebels but not sufficient to turn the course of the revolt, while the analysis below proves that rebels were short of basic equipment like bullets, rifles, and medicine.[157] The British successfully blocked Italians arms shipments via Saudi Arabia and the Italians achieved very little in the long run, ending their financial support to Palestinians by about late 1938.[158]

Funding came mostly from within Palestine and from the Arab and Muslim world – 'Egypt, Syria, Iraq and Moslem India are said to be the chief contributors' – the British intercepting the transfers of foreign monies when they could.[159] The sums were not vast and to be measured against the financial history detailed above and the material in later chapters on British collective punishment fines. Hajj Amin started a £P.100,000 'ticket system' campaign across Muslim communities in June 1936 and CID wrote to the Chief Secretary that £12,000 (sterling) was in Egypt and that it could not block Syrian funds from this source, but only £P.200 had arrived from Iraq and Syria, £P.91 from Transjordan, and £P.20 from the Jerusalem women's committee.[160] In July 1936, Egypt collected £P.500, while AHC treasurer Ahmad Hilmi 'Abd al-Baqi was said to have floated a £P.10,000 loan in India to ensure the arrival of relief funds from Muslims there.[161] Palestinian Government officials contributed £P.1,000

[156] Report by Zaslani and Sasson to Shertok (plus transcript of meeting with Joseph Laniado), 2 February 1938, S25/3639-106/107/108, CZA.
[157] Nir Arielli, 'Italian Involvement in the Arab Revolt in Palestine, 1936–39,' *British Journal of Middle Eastern Studies* 35/2 (2008) pp. 187–204; Nir Arielli, *Fascist Italy and the Middle East, 1933–40* (Houndmills: Palgrave, 2010); Steven Wagner, *Statecraft by Stealth: How Britain Ruled Palestine 1917–40* (Ithaca, NY: Cornell University Press, 2018), ch. 7.
[158] Massimiliano Fiore, *Anglo-Italian Relations in the Middle East, 1922–1940* (Farnham: Ashgate, 2010), pp. 89, 102–05.
[159] Disturbances of 1936, 30 May–5 June, US Consul General Palestine to State Department, 6 June 1936, 867N.00/310 [Reel M#1037/1], NARA II.
[160] H. P. Rice (CID) Deputy IG to Chief Secretary, 8 June 1936, FO 371/20021, TNA.
[161] Summary of DIS from 14 July 1936, Jerusalem, dated 16 July 1936, Arab Office and Intelligence: 8/GENERAL/39, HA; Summary of DIS from 21 July 1936, Arab Office and Intelligence: 8/GENERAL/39, HA.

in June 1936, and £P.700 the following month.[162] Another report said that Egypt gave £P.2,000 in July 1936, 'enough money to carry on for 2 more months,' which cannot be true as this equalled a paltry £P.33 a day.[163] Women formed fund-raising committees and donated jewellery, there were flag days in Jaffa, contributions came from America, and Government officials contributed up to 50 per cent of their salaries.[164] Arab and Muslim countries held Palestine support days, 'the Women's Society of Jerusalem' that year approaching the 'Distress Fund' in Beirut 'for financial assistance on behalf of the dependants of detainees.'[165] The rebels attempted to tackle dishonesty by issuing 'jihad coupons' and anyone who did not give such coupons when gathering money 'must be punished for his treason.'[166] The Central Committee for Jihad in Palestine detailed exacting financial auditing. Money collected went to a local town chairman and he gave the people who had been gathering money a receipt. The chairman sent the money to the supreme commander who also gave a receipt. The supreme commander passed the money to the central committee, which also gave a receipt. 'Everyone must keep their receipts for accounts. Money collectors must be honest, loyal and have a good measurement so they will treat the public nicely.'[167] Every money collector received £P.35 per month for his expenses, if he did his job loyally. If the person approached for money was out of the country in, say, Syria, Lebanon, or Egypt, then his relatives or representatives must send him the money demand by registered mail and keep the receipt for the registered letter.[168] Collectors could give a week's grace on payment and accept partial payments. It was paramount that money collectors behaved well and had a 'smooth tongue.' There was a jihad tax on citrus groves. National and foreign companies 'will take part in the donation effort because their profits are taken from the nation fighting for its existence.'[169] If someone who could pay refused, then 'severe measures must be taken against him to teach the others a lesson.'[170] Rebels also attempted to control the collection of funds by giving their money collectors official seals,

[162] Summary of CID from 18–20 July 1936, Arab Office and Intelligence: 8/GENERAL/ 39, HA.
[163] Summary of DIS from 13 July 1936, Arab Office and Intelligence: 8/GENERAL/ 39, HA.
[164] CID, Jerusalem, Periodical Appreciation Summary 14/36, 18 August 1936, L/PS/12/ 3343: Political Situation – Police Summaries, IOR.
[165] CID, Jerusalem, Periodical Appreciation Summary 52/39, 26 July 1939, 47/89, HA.
[166] The Central Committee for Jihad in Palestine, signed/sealed, National Jihad in Palestine, To Abu Bakr, n.d., Intelligence on Arab Leaders: 41/104, HA.
[167] Ibid. 'Measurement' is the literal translation of the Arabic.
[168] Ibid.
[169] Ibid.
[170] Ibid.

police retrieving a typewritten letter in March 1938, 'signed by Sheikh Attieh [Shaykh 'Atiyya Muhammad 'Awad, killed in battle the same month] asking to render the bearer assistance.'[171] Honest enforcement vied with evasion, dishonesty, and poverty.

In the first fifty days of the revolt, the AHC strike committee received £P.4,000 that was 'sufficient for two days only' noted one source.[172] There were twenty payment centres throughout Palestine, while in Jerusalem alone 17,000 people received income from the strike committee according to the Arab press; the AHC promised full wages and a special bonus to Arab dockers in Haifa and to drivers.[173] Haganah noted in July 1936 that funds from Egypt had 'proved very disappointing,' adding that there were 'indications that funds particularly among the National (District) Committees are running short. There were signs of a shortage towards the end of last month but there are a number of subscriptions due towards the end of the month notably from officials who give a portion of their salaries.'[174] That rebels applied 'heavy pressure' to villagers near Jerusalem to strike proves that local communities were avoiding their national duty; at the same time, 'bus drivers and chauffeurs in Jaffa have not been paid recently. This is attributed to lack of funds in the Strike Committee Fund.'[175] Jerusalem's al-Liwa' (The Province) newspaper asked for and received £P.100 from the strike committee in July 1936, 'with the remark that this would be the last sum they would get.'[176] British intelligence was 'puzzled' in December 1937 about the 'amount and source of the funds at the disposal of the Damascus gang. But their general impression is that they have just enough to carry on the present efforts in Palestine, but not very much more.'[177] In March 1938, Hajj Amin had £2,000 from Iraq to spend in a secret budget in Syria for weapons but there was a 'bitter spirit' among the rebels who 'lack solidarity.'[178] By July 1938, money in Syria had dried up, compounded by the British blockade of the Syria–Palestine

---

[171] Daily Situation report, Divisional Police HQ, Haifa Rural Division, 27 March 1938, Scrivenor Papers, MSS. Brit. Emp. S. 377, p. 132, WL.

[172] Disturbances of 1936, 30 May–5 June, US Consul General Palestine to State Department, 6 June 1936, 867N.00/310 [Reel M#1037/1], NARA II.

[173] Ibid.

[174] Report of the Air HQ Jerusalem dated 24 July 1936, Arab Office and Intelligence: 8/GENERAL/39, HA.

[175] Summary of DIS from 5 July 1936, Jerusalem, dated 7 July 1936, Arab Office and Intelligence: 8/GENERAL/39, HA.

[176] Intelligence Summary, 8 July 1936, Arab Office and Intelligence: 8/GENERAL/39, HA.

[177] Wavell to Haining (DMO, WO), 8 December 1937, Palestine, 1937–38 Volume, Wavell Papers, POH.

[178] Report by Reuven Zaslani, 6 March 1938, Letters from Syria, 1937–38 and 1946, S25/3639-1/7, CZA.

border: 'People are growing tired of the continual calls on their pockets for subscriptions … Reports indicate that the leaders in SYRIA are short of money and are finding growing difficulty in purchasing arms and ammunition getting them into PALESTINE.'[179] Recruiting depended on funding and as the latter dried up, 'greater efforts are being made to obtain both in PALESTINE itself,' next to which a British intelligence officer has pencilled, 'This was before the bank robberies.'[180] If money was short in 1936, by 1938 it was critical. Hajj Amin was unable to raise funds 'and that is why he is making every effort to pull off something spectacular that will give his fund-raising campaign a boost.'[181] Rebel headquarters in Syria by the summer of 1938 told local commanders that they could not

expect any further payments for their upkeep and that they should see to their own needs. This has led to renewed attempts to take money from people by force, and that explains the escalation in internal Arab terror activity. Relations between the various gangs are not good. They operate independently of each other, with each one of the separate leaders claiming to be the supreme commander.[182]

The revolt was 'ever more like an Arab civil war.'[183]

Hajj Amin despatched Palestinian Christian, English-speaking lawyer Emile Ghoury (or Ghuri) to London in 1936 on a propaganda mission to spread news of the Palestinian struggle, while also setting up a London-based Palestine Information Centre, later called the Arab Centre and 'dominated by English Arabists.'[184] Having a London-based Palestinian media office was an exciting development but Ghoury ran out of money, and his story encapsulates the financial mismanagement afflicting the revolt. Hajj Amin told him to expect £150 from Midland Bank along with Palestinian newspapers but nothing arrived.[185] In a candid letter in September 1936 to Jamal al-Husayni of the Palestine Arab Party, Ghoury wrote how by 26 July,

I then possessed sufficient money to cover my and my wife's passages home. It is about 45 days now, and I have spent the last pound of what I had this morning. It is true that I received from the Delegation before you left £.41 and few shillings

---

[179] Summary of Intelligence, Palestine and Transjordan, 29 July 1938, by Wing Commander Ritchie at GHQ [15/38], CO 732/81/9, TNA.
[180] Ibid.
[181] Quoting a report from Shertok's diaries in Haggai Eshed, *Reuven Shiloah: The Man behind the Mossad* (London: Cass, 1997), p. 33.
[182] Reuven Zaslani in Eshed, *Reuven Shiloah*, p. 33.
[183] Eshed, *Reuven Shiloah*, p. 33.
[184] Rory Miller, *Divided against Zion: Anti-Zionist Opposition in Britain to a Jewish State in Palestine, 1945–49* (London: Cass, 2000), pp. 10–13.
[185] Letter, Hajj Amin (Mufti, Jerusalem), Headed SMC (Supreme Muslim Council) Paper, to Emil Ghoury (London), 17 September 1936, Arab Office in London, RG65: P351/37, ISA.

but I have actually spent more than that amount, as I purchased the typewriter, paid rent for two months in advance, purchased stationery, and so forth as well as postage, telephones, and newspapers. Ever since I submitted a proposed statement of accounts necessary for the propaganda mission in London (I sent that on August 7th) I have been waiting for some money. As I could not wait any longer (seeing that not one pound was left with me) I telegraphed you today ... NO MONEY LEFT PLEASE DESPATCH IMMEDIATELY. GHORY. ... hope that you have received same and made immediate arrangements to send me some money. If the money will not be here by the end of this week, I really do not know what I am going to do. So I really hope that you have obtained some money from His Eminence [Hajj Amin] and despatched it to me.[186]

Nor did Ghoury know how to style himself, whether as Hajj Amin's party representative or a Palestinian national leader, with the added worry that Ghoury's pregnant wife needed money for her medical bills, too:

What name shall I give to myself? At times I refer to myself as 'Palestine Arab Delegate,' and at other times 'Secretary, Palestine Arab Party.' It is necessary to have a definite name. To whom shall I send my letters, and press cuttings ... For 40 days I received nothing from Jerusalem as to news ... As several times there were important events in Palestine, such as the Nuri Pasha negotiations, I received several questions from our friends here, but was unable to give any answer besides what appeared in the papers here ... Do you not think it is advisable, therefore, to let me know exactly what is the situation at times? Furthermore there certainly are several instructions or information that I should be receiving from Jerusalem. Unfortunately nothing was heard.[187]

Richer Arabs evaded payment for the revolt by escaping abroad. One estimate at the end of June 1936 was that the strike cost £P.50,000 per day, surely an exaggeration, adding that notables were leaving Haifa for Syria because they were unable to meet strike fund demands.[188] British intelligence detailed in July 1936 that rich Jaffans had made a third contribution to the fund for distressed people and how new collections were imminent 'before the rich Arabs leave for Cyprus and Lebanon.'[189] 'Many rich Arabs from Syria have returned to Palestine. It is said that they have finally paid their contributions to the Strike Fund,' noted another intelligence file in the same month.[190] Poorer Palestinians pleaded poverty, too,

---

[186] Letter, Emil Ghoury (London) to Jamal Husayni (Palestine), 7 September 1936, Arab Delegation to London: RG65: P3220/17, ISA.

[187] Ibid.

[188] *Filastin* quoted in Disturbances of 1936, 13–25 June, US Consul General Palestine to State Department, 27 June 1936, 867N.00/322 [Reel M#1037/1], NARA II.

[189] Summary of DIS from 14 July 1936, Arab Office and Intelligence: 8/GENERAL/39, HA.

[190] Summary of DIS from 9 July 1936, Jerusalem, dated 10 July 1936, Arab Office and Intelligence: 8/GENERAL/39, HA.

as when rebels fined a villager £P.40 who pointed out that he had already donated £P.18 and given £P.2 to each rebel band that came to his village. Rebel field commander 'Arif 'Abd al-Raziq agreed to reduce his payment by £P.10.[191] Meanwhile, strike committee members accused each other of using funds for private purposes.[192] Rebels 'drained' villagers of their 'ready cash,' without which peasants paid Government fines in livestock and grain.[193] Corruption spread from the strike committees and the rural bands to couriers who took money into Palestine and frequently misappropriated funds, so much so that rebel command in Damascus only trusted 'Abd al-Qadir al-Husayni to act as an honest go-between and distribute monies with no profit to himself.[194] Rebels whipped fund distributors for stealing money that did survive the journey to Palestine:

Since Abed el-Rakhman Awira [Aweidah in another file] was found guilty of irregularities when collecting money on behalf of the Arab Revolt, the office of the Chief Headquarters of the Arab revolt has decided that he should be flogged in public, 25 lashes, and a fine should be taken off him of £P.4.220 mils. That is the sum he received earlier from the headquarters for the warriors, but he didn't deliver the money. He will stay in custody until he pays this sum. He must stay in his village and not go to Jaffa.[195]

Even without good financial auditing, insurgents could still have had moral effect, seizing weapons from Government forces in hit-and-run raids, methodically building the struggle while mobilising the peasantry for sustenance and recruits. This demanded organisation, protracted insurgency, internal discipline, good behaviour towards local people, secure peasant-based rebel base areas, and signal military successes to light the path to victory, but these never materialised.

---

[191] Document/Petition, n.d., Intelligence on Arab Leaders: 41/104, HA.
[192] Summary of DIS from 9 July 1936, Jerusalem, dated 10 July 1936, Arab Office and Intelligence: 8/GENERAL/39, HA.
[193] Summary of Intelligence, Palestine and Transjordan, 29 July 1938, by Wing Commander Ritchie at GHQ [15/38], CO 732/81/9, TNA.
[194] Ibid.
[195] Chief HQ, Arab Revolt in Palestine, in the Name of the Merciful God, n.d., signed Aref Abd el-Razek, the Slave of God, Intelligence on Arab Leaders: 41/104, HA. This seems to be the same incident as mentioned in Aref Abd el Razek, The High Command, Arab Rebellion in Palestine, n.d., Captured and Translated Arabic Material with Commentary, p. 73, Wingate Papers, Microfilm M2313, BL.

4　From Insurgency to Banditry

Shock Action

Excepting Fawzi al-Qawuqji's two-month tour in Palestine in 1936, rebels in the revolt neither evolved militarily nor pulled off spectacular terror strikes like the IRA's assassination of the British 'Cairo Gang' intelligence unit in Dublin in 1920, the Vietcong's 1968 Tet Offensive, *Etzel*'s destruction of the King David Hotel in 1946, or the 9/11 airplane attacks. Instead, insurgent forces regressed into bandit gangs that robbed villagers. The zenith of the fighting in Palestine came in the autumn of 1938 when insurgents seized Jerusalem's old city, assassinated Assistant District Commissioner Walter Moffatt in Jenin, held Beersheba for many months, and attacked the Jewish quarter of Tiberias. The Government lost control of much of southern Palestine. Rebel bands had pushed into other towns prior to taking the old city, such as Nazareth for a few hours on 6–7 July 1938 or Hebron on 20 August 1938 – where they burnt out the post office and tried to blow the Barclay's Bank safe, after which they burnt down the bank, too – but they raided as outlaws robbing banks and never consolidated as guerrillas, preferring to run than fight when soldiers arrived.[1] While Vietnamese insurgents held Hue for five weeks in 1968 against a full-scale US assault, and Islamists fought for two weeks in Fallujah against US–Coalition forces in 2004, two British battalions recaptured the urban tangle of the old city in an easy half-day operation with just one British soldier and up to four Jerusalemites killed.[2] Britain

[1] Monthly Administrative report for July 1938, Galilee and Acre District, 2 August 1938, by A/DC K. W. Blackburne, Blackburne Papers, MSS. Brit. Emp. S. 460, Box 3, File 2, WL; *Haaretz* [*The Land*] (Tel Aviv) (21 August 1938); Arab Revolt in Palestine Photograph Album 1938 and Scrapbook of Articles about the American Colony, Palestine, People and Events and Loose Enclosures 1938, ACHA.

[2] Yosef Eshkol, *A Common Soldier: The Story of Zwi Brenner* (Tel Aviv: Ministry of Defence Books, 1993), p. 168; John Baynes, *The Forgotten Victor: General Sir Richard O'Connor* (London: Brassey's, 1989), p. 54; Anon., 'Troops in Control at Jerusalem,' *Yorkshire Post* (24 October 1938); Translation of letter in Arabic dated 24 October 1938 received by Musa Husseini [al-Husayni] on 28 October in Creech Jones Papers, MSS. Brit. Emp. S. 332, Box 30, File 2, WL; Julian Paget, *Second to None: The Coldstream Guards*,

inflicted prompt legal and illegal reprisals for the Moffatt and Tiberias outrages, and 'disgusted by the dismal performance' of the troops at Tiberias, dismissed the local South Staffordshire Regiment battalion commander for his alleged inaction, while Beersheba was geographically peripheral to the revolt and retaken when the Army had the men and inclination to do so in 1939.[3] Instead of guerrilla concentration to a culminating battle as at Dien Bien Phu in 1954, at Saigon in 1975, or with Castro's triumphal march down from the Sierra Maestra to Havana in 1959, British counter-insurgency diluted the violence of the peasant 'poor farmers,' the 'urban and rural poor and not the rich' who spearheaded the Arab revolt.[4] When rebels abducted a fourteen-year-old boy, he was initially terrified but 'soon saw they were only a group of peasants, like our own peasants in Tulkarm, and I didn't feel afraid anymore.'[5] Rebel labelling of units as *fasa'il* (bands or platoons) speaks to a rebellion that never stretched beyond small-scale action.[6] A platoon is the smallest military unit commanded by a commissioned officer but in the Arab revolt this was the largest rebel unit. Even when Fawzi al-Qawuqji in September 1936 organised his force into four companies of Iraqis, Syrians, Druze, and Palestinians, totalling 200 men, with an attached intelligence unit, each nominal company was a reinforced platoon of around fifty men.[7] British counter-insurgency was so effective that the Army quickly spotted, attacked, and smashed larger formations such as Fakhri 'Abd al-Hadi's 200-strong one in 1936 and 'the ease with which its movements could be detected soon persuaded him to adopt the *fasa'il* system.'[8] Good leadership and command for rural-based bands could have broken the military stasis and grown rebel base areas and forces – platoons into companies into battalions and so on – but local *fasa'il* commanders instead bickered

1650–2000 (London: Leo Cooper, 2000), p. 83. The British dead was Guardsman E. J. Patfield who died on 21 October and was buried in Ramleh cemetery.

[3] John Bierman and Colin Smith, *Fire in the Night: Wingate of Burma, Ethiopia and Zion* (New York, NY: Random House, 1999), p. 118; Eshkol, *Common Soldier*, p. 168.

[4] Ghassan Kanafani, 'Thawrat 1936–1939 fi Filastin: Khalfiyyat, tafasil wa tahlil' ['The 1936–1939 Revolt in Palestine: Background, Details and Analysis'], *Shu'un Filastinyya* [*Palestinian Matters*] 6 (January 1972), p. 69; Ted Swedenburg, *Memories of Revolt: The 1936–1939 Rebellion and the Palestinian National Past* (Minneapolis, MN: University of Minnesota Press, 1995), p. 26.

[5] Ghada Karmi, *In Search of Fatima* (London: Verso, 2009), pp. 9–10.

[6] For force structures see Eliezer Tauber, 'The Army of Sacred Jihad: An Army or Bands?,' in Efraim Karsh and Rory Miller (eds), *Israel at Sixty: Rethinking the Birth of the Jewish State* (London: Routledge, 2009).

[7] Laila Parsons, 'Soldiering for Arab Nationalism: Fawzi al-Qawuqji in Palestine,' *Journal of Palestine Studies* 36/4 (Summer 2007), pp. 39–40.

[8] Martin Thomas, *Empires of Intelligence: Security Services and Colonial Disorders after 1914* (Berkeley, CA: University of California Press, 2008), p. 247.

among themselves and they resented al-Qawuqji and his purported pan-Arab Iraqi and Syrian backers. Instead of combining, they generated a multiplicity of contending, separate commands without hierarchy and with dramatic names like 'the destruction,' 'the attack,' 'the struggle,' the 'black' and 'red' hand, but which crumbled when the British killed their local leaders.[9] Rebel high command gave direction by articulating Islamic concepts and declaring a jihad in 1937, the British fighting back by persuading the rector of Cairo's al-Azhar University to deny the call to holy war.[10] Moreover, while bands reflected socially conservative Islamic rural life, urbane Palestinian resistance at the higher levels was not fundamentally religious but secular and invoked Islam only when it would 'result in popular support for nationalist issues.'[11] Al-Qassam's organisation is interesting because it resembled earlier jihad movements, articulating protracted struggle in religious terms and forming over a ten-year period a network of secret cells, like 'lightning through the clouds.'[12] Without effective forms of politico-religious leadership, military operations failed.

Lacking leadership and funds, rebels were ill-prepared and short of doctors, ammunition, explosives, military organisation, and recruits. The relatively well-prepared al-Qawuqji, a former Ottoman Army officer, still only had a pharmacist with him in the field and for wounded fighters the 'pain was so bad that men wanted to die.'[13] In September 1936, rebel leaders called on Arab doctors to contribute by helping wounded fighters in the field, but this was at the *end* of the first phase of fighting.[14] Rebels had insufficient ammunition. In May 1936, they tried to buy ammunition but without funding they could not afford to buy any; later in the revolt rebels used bullets that had 'a large proportion of wood and

---

[9] Yuval Arnon-Ohanna, *Falahim ba-Mered ha-'Aravi be-eretz Yisrael, 1936–39* [*Felahin during the Arab Revolt in the Land of Israel*] (Tel Aviv: Shiloh Institute, Tel Aviv University, 1978), pp. 90–91, 109.

[10] Rudolph Peters, *Islam and Colonialism: The Doctrine of Jihad in Modern History* (The Hague: Mouton, 1979), pp. 99, 102.

[11] Ibid., p. 103.

[12] Ibid., p. 103; Weldon C. Matthews, *Confronting an Empire, Constructing a Nation: Arab Nationalists and Popular Politics in Mandate Palestine* (London: Tauris, 2006), p. 245; Muhammad Muhammad Hasan Shurrab, '*Izz ad-Din al-Qassam: Shaykh al-Mujahidin fi Filastin* [*Izz ad-Din al-Qassam: Noble Fighters in Palestine*] (Damascus: Dar al-Qalam, 2000), pp. 267–68; Mark Sanagan, 'Lightning through the Clouds: Islam, Community, and Anti-colonial Rebellion in the Life and Death of 'Izz al-Din al-Qassam, 1883–1935' (Doctoral Thesis: McGill University, 2016).

[13] Khayriyya Qasimiyya (ed.), *Filastin fi-Mudhakkirat Fawzi al-Qawuqji* [*Palestine in the Memories of Fawzi al-Qawuqji*] (Beirut: PLO Research Centre and Jerusalem Publishing House, 1975), ii, p. 46.

[14] Walid Khalidi and Yasin Suweyd, *Al-Qadiyya al-Filastiniyya wa al-Khatar al-Sahyuni* [*The Palestinian Problem and the Zionist Danger*] (Beirut: IPS, Lebanese General Staff Fifth Branch and Ministry of Defence, 1973), p. 235.

soil,' with rebels 'complaining that bad ammunition has caused them to withdraw from a number of engagements' and how this had caused rebel leaders 'great anxiety.'[15] The rebels fought with 50–60 per cent 'dud' rounds in many battles, while 'practically' rounds 'never were less than 20% useless.'[16] As rebels ran out of ammunition, the price of bullets went up.[17] A Syrian supporter informed rebels in Nablus in August 1936 that there was no more ammunition in Syria: 'He suggests that Palestine gets supplies from Europe. It is thought that the ammunition at present in the hands of gangs will not suffice for more than two more weeks. There is also a lack of gelignite for explosives.'[18] Rebel explosives for roadside bombs came mainly from thefts of dynamite from Palestine's quarries, from abandoned First World War-era British artillery shell dumps, mostly around Gaza and Rafah, and from old Turkish shells. Men from the 1st Seaforths ran over one such mine three times before they detected it: 'The bursting charges, consisting of old Turkish shells, were exploded on the spot, and the working parts removed to Nablus … It is obvious that they were constructed and adjusted by someone of experience in such work,' noted the battalion report.[19] The British countered mines by abducting and carrying local people ('mascots') on lead vehicles in convoys, handcuffing them to the driving wheel of taxis driven in front of military convoys, placing them on trolley cars in front of train locomotives, and by tying civilians to bonnets of trucks; the British also blew up local villagers over British-laid mines to discourage mine laying, as happened at al-Bassa;[20] and they counter-bombed, as GOC Wavell noted: 'We put a booby trap at a bridge on the JAFFA rd which we thought might be attacked by saboteurs. A loud explosion has just been reported from there. I wonder if it was the booby trap and if so who the poor booby was.'[21] The Army later discovered that it was a

---

[15] Information from Arab Office, 11 May 1936, Arab Office and Intelligence: 8/GENERAL/ 37, p. 150, HA; CID, Jerusalem, Periodical Appreciation Summary 73/38, 18 October 1938, L/PS/12/3343: Political Situation – Police Summaries, IOR.

[16] Appendix: Explanatory Notes, Captured and Translated Arabic Material with Commentary, p. 160, Wingate Papers, Microfilm M2313, BL; Arnon-Ohanna, *Falahim ba-Mered ha-'Aravi*, p. 56.

[17] Summary of Intelligence, Palestine and Transjordan, 16 December 1938, by Wing Commander Ritchie at GHQ [25/38], CO 732/81/10, TNA.

[18] CID of 4 August 1936, Shai Intelligence Reports: 8/GENERAL/40, p. 164, HA.

[19] Dorsetshire Regiment, Narrative of Events, Nablus, 18 August 1936, 88/367, Shelf C4, Box 3, KMM.

[20] Close to the Lebanese border and destroyed in 1948, now Moshav Betzet.

[21] Shepperd, 4597/06, p. 64, IWMSA; Dill to Deverell (CIGS, London), 18 September 1936, Dill Papers, 2/9, LHCMA; Matthew Hughes, 'The Practice and Theory of British Counter-Insurgency: The Histories of the Atrocities at the Palestinian Villages of al-Bassa and Halhul, 1938–39,' *Small Wars and Insurgencies* 20/3–4 (September–December 2009), pp. 528–50; Wavell to Haining (DMO, WO), 12 and 16 November 1937,

hawk that had set off the booby trap. The rebels electronically fired mines to counter minesweeping cars or those containing Palestinian civilians, but most Army accounts are of men hitting an unsophisticated mine composed of an old shell with a protruding nail: 'there is a bang and flash in the dark and the car rears up on its hind legs. When a rear wheel touches off the mine it is more serious.'[22] Thefts from shell dumps were so bad that the British in 1937 sent in Royal Engineers and Royal Army Ordnance Corps men to destroy decaying ordnance, forcing rebels to look elsewhere.[23] The British responded to the simple rebel anti-vehicle device of strewing nails across the road by tying brooms to the fenders of their cars (see Figure 4.1).[24] Rebel training was rudimentary, one local band commander bizarrely showing his men 'American movies with episodes of gang fights in order to give them an example of how to attack by deception,' if Jewish files are correct.[25] Foreign fighters from Syria did not know the local terrain or people.[26]

The bands inducted recruits from local villagers as willing part-time fighters, press-ganged villagers at other times, or they paid (usually foreign) insurgents. Rebel bands relied throughout the troubles on local villagers to augment numbers as needed but the struggle for recruits worsened as the revolt progressed and pacification hit hard, and with too many foreign volunteers fighting for pay, and short of funds, rebels mobilised or coerced villagers, or rebels were villagers performing as hybrid rebel-bandits. Villagers supplied men more-or-less voluntarily. British intelligence noted that rebels 'forced' villages 'to supply not less than 10 men or 10 rifles to the gangs under threat of death.'[27] The bands were a motley crew, some more political or religious than others, some local and some foreign, some criminal. The police observed 'religious fanatics and extreme nationalists' backed up by 'reservists' from villages when needed in the armed bands, along-side 'a comparatively small number of hired mercenaries from Syria,

Palestine, 1937–38 Volume, Wavell Papers, POH; O'Connor, 12/8, p. 32, IWMSA; Lane, 10295/11, pp. 17–18, IWMSA.

[22] Summary of Intelligence, Palestine and Transjordan, 23 September 1938, by Wing Commander Ritchie at GHQ [19/38], CO 732/81/9, pp. 9–10, TNA; Dill to Deverell (CIGS, London), 18 September 1936, Dill Papers, 2/9, LHCMA.

[23] Capt E. C. W. Myers, 'An Arab "Mouse Trap" and Other Booby Traps, Palestine 1936,' *Royal Engineers Journal* 51 (December 1937), p. 555.

[24] Arab Revolt in Palestine Photograph Album 1937, ACHA.

[25] File 04/-163-A/621: Riots, April 1936 [but June–September 1938, one bundle of papers], TAMA.

[26] Sasson (Damascus) to Shertok, 7 January 1938, S25/3639-136, CZA.

[27] Daily Intelligence Summary 5/38, Divisional Police HQ, Haifa Rural Division, 10 February 1938, Scrivenor Papers, MSS. Brit. Emp. S. 377, p. 80, WL.

4.1 British counter-rebel measures: brooms attached to a car bumper
to sweep away nails
(from American Colony Hotel Archive)

Lebanon, Iraq and Transjordan' and 'Persons who joined the gangs,
either by force or circumstances, e.g. fugitives from justice, or those
attracted by the prospect of loot.'[28] As the British screwed down the
country, 'Gangsters' demanded more pay. The Chief Secretary 'received
thoroughly reliable information from Syria that the price for gangsters
has risen 100 per cent and that these men also demand that their lives
shall be insured to provide for their families should they be killed.'[29]
Overall rebel numbers were never great and fluctuated as many were
temporary warriors. Subhi Yasin gives a figure for the rebels at the zenith
of their power at 9,000–10,000, comprising 3,000 full-time fighters,
1,000 urban rebels, and 6,000 part-time villagers, some of whom were

---

[28] *The Palestine Police: Annual Administrative Report, 1938* (Jerusalem: Government Printing
Press, 1938), p. 29.
[29] Letter, Battershill to Sir John Shuckburgh, 21 November 1937, Battershill Papers, MSS.
Brit. Emp. S. 467, Box 10, File 3, WL.

raised with *faz'a* calls for local help.[30] When al-Qawuqji left Palestine in October 1936, a call to arms to help him raised an impressive 5,000 villagers including women and children who brought what weapons that they had to hand.[31] Naji 'Allush gives a total for rebels of 6,000–10,000.[32] The High Commissioner assessed full-time rebel numbers in December 1938 at 2,000, while a Hebrew-language source gives totals of between 1,000 and 3,000 alongside 6,000–15,000 ad hoc rebels.[33] A British General Staff report in 1939 detailed the 'active insurgents' as never exceeding 1,500.[34] The Staff figure is interesting as if correct it means that across an area not much bigger than Wales the Army faced by the end of the revolt just twenty-one larger seventy-strong armed bands, or thirty smaller fifty-strong ones. Taking Arab source figures at, say, 5,000 full-time fighters, this equalled seventy-one larger bands, or about one rebel every two square miles, or with a non-Jewish population of 1,024,063, just 0.48 percent of people were in armed bands falling to 0.14 percent by 1939, taking the General Staff estimate.[35] The permanent cadre of rebels was small and scattered in penny packets that fought locally and never combined nationally. Instead, they degenerated. The British commander in Palestine in April 1939 assessed that rebel bands of more than a dozen men were by then a 'rarity.'[36] Al-Qawuqji's unit of some 200 men deployed in September–October 1936 was the largest single band. Permanent bands of fifty to seventy full-time insurgents whose members devoted all their time and energy to the insurgency began appearing in the summer of 1936 and fought all through the revolt, but discrete full-time rebel bands never exceeded this figure. Numbers for bands and for local recruitment drives were typically in

[30] Subhi Yasin, *Al-Thawra al-'Arabiyya al-Kubra (fi Filastin) 1936–1939* [*The Great Arab Revolt in Palestine, 1936–1939*] (Damascus: Shafa 'Amr Haifa, 1959), pp. 41–42.

[31] Akram Zu'aytir, *Al-Haraka al-Wataniya al-Filastiniyya, 1935–39: Yawmiyyat Akram Zu'aytir* [*The Palestinian National Movement, 1935–39: Diaries of Akram Zu'aytir*] [1980] (Beirut: IPS, 1992), pp. 221ff.

[32] Naji 'Allush, *Al-Muqawama al-'Arabiyya fi Filastin, 1917–48* [*The Arab Resistance in Palestine, 1917–1948*] (Beirut: Attaliya, 1969), p. 127.

[33] Yehoshua Porath, *The Palestinian Arab National Movement: From Riots to Rebellion. Volume 2, 1929–1939* (London: Cass, 1977), p. 248; Arnon-Ohanna, *Falahim ba-Mered ha-'Aravi*, pp. 88–90.

[34] A. R. B. Linderman, *Rediscovering Irregular Warfare: Colin Gubbins and the Origins of Britain's Special Operations Executive* (Norman, OK: University of Oklahoma Press, 2016), p. 77.

[35] *Statistical Abstract of Palestine, 1939* (Jerusalem: Office of Statistics, 1939), p. 11; *A Survey of Palestine, Prepared in December 1945 and January 1946 for the Information of the Anglo-American Committee of Inquiry* (Jerusalem: Government Printer, 1946), i, pp. 140–41.

[36] Despatch on the Operations carried out by the British Forces in Palestine and Transjordan, 1 November 1938–31 March 1939, GOC Palestine to WO London, 24 April 1939, Evetts Papers, File 1, LHCMA.

the low tens. The 'majority' of Arab villages in 'less frequented districts' in northern Palestine turned out thirty to forty armed men to support a 'gang when called upon.'[37] Al-Qawuqji visited three villages in October 1936 just before the ceasefire and asked them to be prepared to provide fifty men 'each armed with rifles at a date to be notified later.'[38] Rebels called on young men, with police removing notices 'calling upon the youth to take up arms and join the "Arab Army" in the hills.'[39] Recruits lacked weapons. Ordinances criminalised the carrying of weapons and the Army obsessively disarmed villagers through the revolt. It constantly demanded hidden weapons on its searches, as happened at Halhul village near Hebron in 1939 with men left to die in open cages in the sun as the village collectively would not hand over weapons or did not have any.[40] British punitive pacification reduced the pool of willing recruits and the stock of rifles, as did the Army's ability to track down and kill rebels using tactics such as the 'XX' system whereby soldiers rapidly and exactly radioed in RAF warplanes to firefights, while the chaos wrought by British forces encouraged willing recruits to express rebellion through banditry. Brigandage was so bad that villagers saw the immediate problem in non-political terms, asking the authorities to leave them alone to deal with the chronic stress of rebel banditry and military counter-measures. Counter-rebel Palestinian 'peace bands' – *fasa'il al-salam*, examined in the later chapter on collaboration – developed initially from local forces raised to protect villages from 'brothers of Jehad terrorists.' They were similar in form and function to the peasant 'green' armies of the Russian civil war that fought both red and white exactions.[41] Thus, 'Fighter Hassan' wrote: 'Do you think we can consider ourselves safe in our village?,' adding that 'I say that the inhabitants of Bala'a want to become neutral, and this has been our feeling for a long time.'[42]

---

[37] Summary of Intelligence, Palestine and Transjordan, 29 July 1938, by Wing Commander Ritchie at GHQ [15/38], CO 732/81/9, TNA.

[38] 1st Battalion Seaforth Highlanders, Narrative of Events No. 135, Acre, 5 October 1936, 88/353, Shelf C4, Box 3, KMM.

[39] Dorsetshire Regiment, Narrative of Events, Ramleh, 6 September 1936, 88/367, Shelf C4, Box 3, KMM.

[40] Hughes, 'The Practice and Theory of British Counter-Insurgency,' pp. 528–50.

[41] Appendix, Captured and Translated Arabic Material with Commentary, p. 114 Wingate Papers, Microfilm M2313, BL; Orlando Figes, *Peasant Russia, Civil War: The Volga Countryside in Revolution* (Oxford: Clarendon, 1989), pp. 321–56; Eric Hobsbawm, *Primitive Rebels: Studies in Archaic Forms of Social Movement in the 19th and 20th Centuries* (Manchester: Manchester University Press, 1959), p. 27.

[42] Fighter Hassan [Hasan] ('Abdallah al-Khair) to the Fighting Brothers, 9 January 1938 [1939?], Captured and Translated Arabic Material with Commentary, p. 62, Wingate Papers, Microfilm M2313, BL.

Rural Palestinians supported the revolt ideologically and they might or might not give practical help. Villagers were wounded rushing out to pick up a wounded fighter in a battle near Silat but their ardour must be set against British punishments and increasingly criminal rebel demands.[43] One villager well expressed their dilemma:

> We think on the whole that the activities of the gangs a mistake and we strongly object to the trouble their presence inevitably leads to. But if anyone has been telling you that either I or anybody else do not sympathise with the gangs, they are lying. We consider that the gangs represent a good cause and that it is Government's policy that is the root of all the trouble in the country.[44]

Rebel successes could boost recruitment. Nablus-based British intelligence concluded that al-Qawuqji would struggle with recruitment unless he gained an immediate major success and how certain villages favoured the insurgency: 'FAWZI feels that his gang is much better received in villages like YA'BAD, KAFR RA'I [Ra'i], MEITHALUN [Maythalun] and SANUR [four villages south of Jenin], and he may use any of these villages in forthcoming activities.'[45] British intelligence noted variations in local commitment and to detach the people from the insurgents the Army favoured villages seen as pro-Government. Shortages of men pushed up pay rates, as discussed above. By January 1938, recruits in Syria were demanding £P.8 per month pay rather than the usual £P.5.[46] With Syrian recruits demanding more money and the British blockade of Palestine's borders, the revolt ran out of men so bands resorted to abduction and murder, such as in the Nablus–Jenin–Tulkarm area where without large parties arriving from outside Palestine the increase in numbers was almost entirely from local villagers.[47] Foreign fighters often lacked equipment and good discipline, one half of an Iraqi contingent leaving for home as the men did not like the food or the weather, al-Qawuqji having to train Palestinians to fill the gap; Syrians also left, while some Druze arrived, so disrupting a planned attack.[48] Villagers came out willingly to fight for al-Qawuqji but willing support depended on the charisma and character of

---

[43] Dorsetshire Regiment, Narrative of Events, Silat, 30 August 1936 in 88/367, Shelf C4, Box 3, KMM. This is probably a reference to Silat al-Harithiya north-west of Jenin.

[44] Note, Typed, n.d., Security Matters, 1938–39, S25/22762, CZA.

[45] Dorsetshire Regiment, Military, Armed Bands I – Effect of the Jaba' Engagement on Nablus District, Stamped Orderly Room and dated 30 September 1936 but from the SSO in Nablus originally and dated 27 September 1936, 88/352, Shelf C4, Box 3, KMM.

[46] Summary of Intelligence, Palestine and Transjordan, 14 January 1938, by Wing Commander Ritchie at GHQ [1/38], CO 732/81/9, TNA.

[47] Summary of Intelligence, Palestine and Transjordan, 6 May 1938, by Wing Commander Ritchie at GHQ [9/38], CO 732/81/9, TNA.

[48] Qasimiyya, *Filastin fi-Mudhakkirat al-Qawuqji*, ii, p. 48.

the local leader, the behaviour of his men, and the threat of British counter-measures. Some village men might not have been as brave as their women-folk would have liked, as when women in Ara village ('Ara south-east of Haifa) encouraged their 'menfolk to go to the assistance of the gang, but this, it is thought, they refused to do.'[49] To 'encourage' villagers to 'turn out' in support of the revolt, bands told them that Jewish settlers were attacking Palestinian villages.[50] Villages responded differently. As early as July 1936, a British intelligence summary noted that 'Many villagers are joining the gangs' but also that 'Pressure is being brought to bear upon Mukhtars in villages forcing them to send men to join the gangs.'[51] Coercive methods got tougher. The *mukhtar* of Kufr Kara'a (Kafr Qara' south-east of Haifa) told police in 1938 that fifty armed men – 'strangers,' some dressed in khaki and some in peasant dress – came to the village at sunset and collected the *mukhtar* and village elders and 'demanded from them 3 young men from every family to join the armed gangs.'[52] By the end of 1938, British intelligence noted that if 'enthusiasm wanes locally amongst the villagers,' then more 'outside' volunteers were to be expected but that such men needed to be paid.[53]

Fawzi al-Qawuqji

Al-Qawuqji gave the revolt military momentum but his force was small, and he battled in his brief time in Palestine not just with poor recruit-ment, equipment shortages, and the British Army, but with resentful local commanders and with Hajj Amin. Al-Qawuqji arrived in late August 1936, visited villages, built morale, and established base areas around Nablus.[54] He infiltrated men into Government and started a rebel media department under a former Syrian journalist to spread misinforma-tion and to print fake official communiqués.[55] Al-Qawuqji consolidated

[49] Daily Police Report, 9 April 1938, Scrivenor Papers, MSS. Brit. Emp. S. 377, p. 160, WL.
[50] Summary of Intelligence, Palestine and Transjordan, 21 October 1938, by Wing Commander Ritchie at GHQ [21/38], CO 732/81/10, TNA.
[51] Intelligence Summary, n.d. [1 July 1936], Arab Office and Intelligence: 8/GENERAL/ 39, HA.
[52] Subject: Armed Gangs, Divisional Police HQ, Haifa Rural Division, 16 March 1938, Scrivenor Papers, MSS. Brit. Emp. S. 377, p. 114, WL.
[53] Summary of Intelligence, Palestine and Transjordan, 4 November 1938, by Wing Commander Ritchie at GHQ [22/38], CO 732/81/10, TNA.
[54] Dorsetshire Regiment, Narrative of Events, Nablus, 10–11 September 1936 in 88/367, Shelf C4, Box 3, KMM.
[55] Internal Document from the PM's Office from the Class of Stateworkers who deal with Minorities, Documents from Arab Gangs, 1936–39, report dated 4 September 1938, Printed in Jerusalem in 1958, 80/58P/14, pp. 10–11, HA; Captured and Translated Arabic Material with Commentary, p. 12, Wingate Papers, Microfilm M2313, BL.

local bands with their 'different leaderships' by rationalising rebel forces into three zones around Nablus–Tulkarm–Jenin, under which he fixed smaller local commands.[56] These vied with rebel areas around Jerusalem that were 'very much pro-Mufti.'[57] There were special courts 'to punish, judge and try the enemies of the revolt.'[58] Convinced that the British had infiltrated spies into rebel areas, al-Qawuqji gave revolutionary tribunals powers to deal with spying.[59] The British press took note of rebel autonomy, the *Yorkshire Post* two years after al-Qawuqji's departure from Palestine telling its readers how in the 'sub-war' there,

These leaders, ensconced in the tortuous hills of Palestine, have succeeded in largely imposing their will on the Arab countryside. They have set up their own courts of justice. They have decreed what headdress Arab men and women, both Moslem and Christian shall wear in Palestine. They have, in short, created the rudiments of a government independent of, and antagonistic to, the Palestine Government.[60]

Rebel courts under al-Qawuqji could hit suspects up to fifty times and were thus able to 'purify' the region of the spies; the tribunals frequently passed and 'many times' carried out the death sentence.[61] Al-Qawuqji had special groups all over Palestine to gather the information that he needed for bigger battles like Jaba' and Bal'a in September 1936.[62] Using Iraqi officers, he trained the rebels how to shoot at warplanes and counter armoured vehicles. One fighter crudely attacked a broken-down tank in October 1936 by trying to gain entry to the turret with a rock. The crew removed him by rotating the turret.[63] A Seaforth Highlander's photograph of a downed RAF aeroplane on an Army lorry flatbed was one of several shot down by al-Qawuqji's men.[64] Intelligence was vital and in al-Qawuqji's Beirut papers there is mention of how 'our secret formations of intelligence inside Palestine did their job very well' by supplying the information needed for operational planning.[65] The organisation,

[56] Qasimiyya, *Filastin fi-Mudhakkirat al-Qawuqji*, ii, pp. 21–22, 27–30.
[57] Letter, Battershill to Sir John Shuckburgh, 21 November 1937, Battershill Papers, MSS. Brit. Emp. S. 467, Box 10, File 3, WL.
[58] Khalidi and Suweyd, *Al-Qadiyya al-Filastiniyya*, p. 235.
[59] Qasimiyya, *Filastin fi-Mudhakkirat al-Qawuqji*, ii, pp. 21–22, 27–30.
[60] Anon., '"Sub-War" in Palestine,' *Yorkshire Post* (24 October 1938).
[61] Qasimiyya, *Filastin fi-Mudhakkirat al-Qawuqji*, ii, pp. 21–22, 27–30.
[62] Ibid.
[63] Ibid., ii, p. 36; Col H. J. Simson, *British Rule and Rebellion* (Edinburgh and London: Blackwood, 1937), p. 279.
[64] An Aeroplane Brought Down by the Arabs, Photograph Album, Tulloch Papers, MSS. Brit. Emp. S. 477, Files 7 and 8, Box 2, WL.
[65] Notebook [photocopied] of Handwritten Pages [of a daily journal], pp. 1–89, n.d. [1936–37], p. 80, Qawuqji Papers, IPS, Beirut.

psychological warfare, general staff work, operations room planning, recruiting, training, and use of intelligence and counter-intelligence mark out al-Qawuqji, like al-Qassam before him, and the British took note, too. 'A very good man,' noted one soldier, while Captain E. C. W. Myers of the Royal Engineers wrote how al-Qawuqji, a 'soldier of no mean ability,' must have been to the French military academy at St Cyr as he was so good; the Arabs learned 'to realise the value of preliminary reconnaissance and of detailed plans before their attacks.'[66] 'Head and shoulders above all others was the Arab Overall Field Commander Fawzi ed Din Kauwakji,' in the words of a Palestine policeman, who added in conversation with this author how al-Qawuqji was 'a born leader, led from the front.'[67] Al-Qawuqji combined military acumen with popular appeal. Schoolchildren turned out in support of him in October 1936, with a 'noisy collection' of small children assembling outside Army headquarters in Nablus, obviously aware that al-Qawuqji had shot down RAF warplanes. 'One of the urchins carried a toy aeroplane on the end of a long pole while another brandished what appeared to be an imitation Lewis gun. They seemed to be repeating some set piece in which the words "FAWZI BEY" and "mabsut" [Arabic for 'happy,' Arabic and Hebrew slang for 'pleased with' or 'happy with'] were all that could be distinguished.'[68] Al-Qawuqji's political character and popular appeal impressed the Army. The following extract from 2 Dorset Narrative serves to illustrate the influence which FAWZI must have exercised over his followers:

It has now come to light that when they heard FAWZI was in danger from the troops between 23 and 25 Oct his supporters came to his aid in cars from as far afield as HEBRON and KHANYUNIS [Khan Yunis near Gaza]. There is NO doubt that the Palestinians look upon FAWZI EL KAWAKJI much more as a national hero than as a brigand chieftain who goes round terrorising villagers. Before he left RABA [south-east of Jenin] during the night 25/26 Oct he is reported to have congratulated the Palestinians on putting up a stout fight for 'The Cause' and to have promised to return to Palestine to help them once more should the need arise.[69]

Al-Qawuqji made exaggerated claims of enemy defeats in his battles with the British in September 1936, with convoys of vehicles carrying

---

[66] Packer, 4493/02, p. 16, IWMSA; Myers, 'An Arab "Mouse Trap",' p. 552.
[67] Edward Horne, *A Job Well Done (Being a History of the Palestine Police Force, 1920–1948)* (Tiptree: Anchor Press, 1982), p. 223; Author interview, Ted Horne, 9 September 2006 (and subsequent correspondence).
[68] Dorsetshire Regiment, Situation Report 32, 16th Infantry Brigade, Nablus, 31 October 1936, 88/353, Shelf C4, Box 3, KMM. *Mabsut* also means 'flat surface.'
[69] Dorsetshire Regiment, Situation Report 30 by BIO, 16th Infantry Brigade, Nablus, 28 October 1936, 88/353, Shelf C4, Box 3, KMM.

British dead back to base and 'a number of officers and three planes and around 200 injured and dead.'[70] This was not true but al-Qawuqji effectively planned battles against the British and he fought set-piece engagements, prior to extending operations to a guerrilla-style campaign, all done in just six weeks. The numbers of British military dead were small but they spiked between September and November 1936, coincident with the battles with al-Qawuqji: twenty-eight dead from 244 across the revolt, equalling 11 per cent of all Army deaths, but the figure is likely to be around 20 per cent of combat fatalities as most of the twenty-eight seem to be in battle.[71] Al-Qawuqji's struggle genuflected to organised, protracted people's war, and the order-of-battle appendix (Appendix A) to this book detailing the multiple regiments hunting him in October 1936 proves how big a threat he was. The Bedfordshire Regiment soldiers who carved the following tribute to al-Qawuqji on the walls of their field emplacement obviously thought him a worthy opponent:

> It was in Palestine in 36,
> A guy named Fawzi was up to his tricks.
> For this occasion the troops were called out,
> But this guy Fawzi was never about.
> They sought him over hill, valley and dale,
> But it was always said with the same old tale
> As oft heard in the days of yore,
> Fawzi didn't live there anymore.
> Upon the top of this hill we made
> A sanger of Gold, Silver and Jade.
> If dear old Fawzi we do but see
> Upon this earth he'll no more be.
> Is he in Nablus, Tulkarm or Lenin [Jenin]?
> That fellow Fawzi is the fellow we mean.
> If dear old Fawzi comes near this sanger
> His life will not be worth a tanner [a six-pence coin].[72]

---

[70] Qasimiyya, *Filastin fi-Mudhakkirat al-Qawuqji*, ii, pp. 23–34; Document entitled memorandum number 7 issued by General Command of Arab Revolt in Southern Syria (signed Qawuqji as GOC) regarding the victory at the battle of Jabaʻ, 23–24 September 1936 in Khayriyya Qasimiyya (ed.), *Mudhakkirat Fawzi al-Qawuqji* [*Memories of Fawzi al-Qawuqji*] (Damascus: Dar al-Namir, 1996), pp. 575–76; Supplement document to memorandum number 7 issued by General Command of Arab Revolt in Southern Syria (signed Qawuqji as GOC) regarding the victory at the battle of Jabaʻ, 23–24 September 1936, dated 27 September 1936 in Qasimiyya, *Mudhakkirat Fawzi al-Qawuqji*, p 577.

[71] As recorded at Ramleh war cemetery; see the discussion in the previous chapter and in Appendix B on casualties.

[72] 'Dedicated to Fawzi,' *The Wasp: The Journal of the 16th Foot* 8/4 (December 1936), p. 199.

Al-Qawuqji fought the British while contending with local operational and AHC-level disputes. His standing and successes piqued band commanders and threatened Hajj Amin. Al-Qawuqji never asserted full control over Palestinians and the local bands opposed his return to Palestine in 1938. Before his arrival, rebel coordination was almost non-existent. Rebels had tried to form a 'unified framework' but neither 'Abd al-Qadir al-Husayni nor other southern region commanders took part.[73] Rebels at the end of July 1936 attempted to coordinate bands and they held a second meeting to arrange coordination on 7 August 1936, where 'Abd al-Hadi was regarded as commander-in-chief of bands around Jenin and Tulkarm, but local commanders through the revolt squabbled over their honorific titles and which of them should be supreme commander in Palestine. This was more symbolic than real as none ever held sway beyond the immediate locality. Al-Qawuqji tried to change this. On 2 September 1936, he had met six commanders of bands – Fakhri 'Abd al-Hadi, 'Abd al-Rahim al-Hajj Muhammad, 'Arif 'Abd al-Raziq, Shaykh Farhan al-Sa'di, Shaykh 'Atiyya Muhammad 'Awad, and Muhammad al-Salih (the last three were Qassamites) – and they gave him a written assurance of his position as overall commander.[74] His departure in late October 1936 meant the collapse of rebel hierarchical military structures.

Palestinian band commanders were suspicious of al-Qawuqji's external pan-Arab connection, as the head of an Iraqi delegation, Sa'id Thabit, had promoted his mission to Palestine. Meanwhile, al-Qawuqji's deputy, Fakhri 'Abd al-Hadi, had ties to the Nashashibis, while Hajj Amin and the Husaynis had power in the AHC, creating further friction within higher command echelons.[75] In the middle of the September–October 1936 battles with the Army, al-Qawuqji received a letter from a messenger from Transjordan's Amir Abdullah, opponent of Hajj Amin, supporter of the Nashashibis, and friendly with the Jews, complaining about the AHC and asking for information on his forces. 'I was astonished to hear such an idea which aimed at dividing the country in two parts and would sow sedition and corruption among us ... As if the revolt was moving from a dispute between Arabs and English to one between Arabs. So, I answered him with anger.'[76] Al-Qawuqji read the letter many times

---

[73] Porath, *The Palestinian Arab National Movement*, p. 186.

[74] Ibid., p. 189.

[75] Joseph Nevo, 'Palestinian–Arab Violent Activity during the 1930s,' in Michael J. Cohen and Martin Kolinsky (eds), *Britain and the Middle East in the 1930s: Security Problems, 1935–39* (London: Macmillan/King's, 1992), p. 177; Swedenburg, *Memories of Revolt*, pp. 85–86; Joseph Nevo, *King Abdallah and Palestine: A Territorial Ambition* (Houndmills: Macmillan, 1996), pp. 32, 38–39.

[76] Qasimiyya, *Filastin fi-Mudhakkirat al-Qawuqji*, ii, pp. 38–39; Nevo, *King Abdallah and Palestine*, pp. 32, 38–39.

to check the signature and his amazement increased with each reading. Abdullah wanted him to give up: 'They want us to surrender ... They want us to give him [the English] the enemy the secrets of the revolt ... This can't be expected from an Arab prince.'[77] Al-Qawuqji was caught between Abdullah's pro-British interference and Hajj Amin's enmity, the latter symbolising for al-Qawuqji 'all that was wrong with politics.'[78] Al-Qawuqji may not be the hero here as he was quick on 12 October 1936 to tell his men to stop fighting to prevent any 'spark' that might harm ceasefire talks.[79] Certainly, there was no unity of command, not even with common enemies, or more exactly the common enemy was each other. Laila Parsons, who had access to the bulk of al-Qawuqji's privately held papers, includes a frank note detailing al-Qawuqji's view of Hajj Amin that is emblematic of rebel leadership problems:

He never fought on the battlefield of any country [the Ottomans had conscripted Hajj Amin during the Great War but he did not go to the front, it seems]. He lays claim to leadership whenever he feels that his life is threatened, then he steals the money and retreats in defeat. He is an ignorant man. He is not a graduate of either a religious school or a secular one. He claims absolute knowledge and authority. He restricts all work in all fields to his person only and he exerts every effort to destroy any name that starts to shine among the Arabs. He is a conceited man. He believes that each individual must be at his disposal and if it happens that he disagrees with him, he accuses him of betrayal. His motto is either you agree with me or you will play the role of hypocrite and traitor. He is a devious man. Whenever he hears that an influential name has surfaced, he is gripped by a fit of rage and desperation so he gives orders to annihilate him or assassinate him.[80]

Divisive rumours spread that al-Qawuqji was a British spy sent by the British commander in Transjordan, John Bagot Glubb, or that he had links to RAF intelligence officers in Iraq such as Flight-Lieutenant J. P. Domvile (sometimes Domville), who worked closely with the Jews and had their agent Reuven Zaslani as his secretary-translator.[81] Parsons'

---

[77] Qasimiyya, *Filastin fi-Mudhakkirat al-Qawuqji*, ii, p. 39.
[78] Parsons, 'Soldiering for Arab Nationalism,' p. 42.
[79] Muhammad 'Izzat Darwaza, *Mudhakkirat Muhammad 'Izzat Darwaza: Sab'a wa tis'una 'aman fil-haya* [*The Diaries of Muhammad 'Izzat Darwaza: 97 Years in a Life*] (Beirut: Dar al Gharb al Islami, 1993), ii, p. 245.
[80] Quoted in Parsons, 'Soldiering for Arab Nationalism,' p. 44.
[81] Porath, *The Palestinian Arab National Movement*, p. 191; Laila Parsons, *The Commander: Fawzi al-Qawuqji and the Fight for Arab Independence* (New York, NY: Hill and Wang, 2016), p. 117; Haggai Eshed, *Reuven Shiloah: The Man behind the Mossad* (London: Cass, 1997), pp. 23–24; Zaslani in Who's Who of Palestine Jewish Politicians and Personalities, Jerusalem 1944, CID HQ Political Reference Library, Catling Papers, MSS. Medit. S. 20, File 4, WL. The *Air Force List* for December 1937 details Domvile (sometimes Domville) as posted to Iraq from 9 September 1937.

conclusion on Hajj Amin is damning: 'Scholars writing about the Mufti have shown that accusing people of treachery was part of his standard repertoire and served as one of the many weapons he used to silence his opponents. There is no evidence in any of the hundreds of original sources used for this book [*The Commander*] to indicate that Qawuqji was a spy for the British.'[82] If he were a British spy, it was a temporary fix as in 1941 British warplanes targeted and machine-gunned al-Qawuqji near Palmyra during Rashid Ali's Iraq revolt, leaving al-Qawuqji so badly wounded that a bullet lodged permanently in his head forced him to wear a hat indoors in cold weather thereafter as the metal of the bullet cooled down. Hajj Amin would later claim that al-Qawuqji was an Israeli spy. Al-Qawuqji was a nationalist and not a traitor. He offered Hajj Amin and Palestinians effective leadership, but they were unable to subsume their differences and they preferred internecine fighting and so hobbled al-Qawuqji. Local politicians would support al-Qawuqji in public but then 'withhold real resources from him in private, out of fear that those resources might eventually be turned against them.'[83] The issue was securing and consolidating safe rebel base areas without antagonising local people, as Mao knew, but without unified command – for 'divided commands have plagued guerrilla leaders through the centuries and are probably more responsible for failed insurgencies than any other factor' – this was impossible, and so the British atomised the population and inexorably destroyed *fasa'il* piecemeal, what in military terms is a defeat in detail.[84]

As al-Qawuqji left Palestine and funds dried up, control of bands shifted from 'foreign volunteers and mercenaries' to 'nationalistic' Palestinians.[85] British identification of post-battle bodies confirmed to them that by the summer of 1938 there were 'few, if any, foreign gangsters in the country and that the disturbances are now being carried out entirely by local villagers under the leadership of a few professional gang leaders.'[86] The rebellion deflated and sank back on itself, with selfish motives moving armed men: 'In addition the central funds have proved insufficient to

[82] Parsons, *The Commander*, pp. 117, 173.
[83] Ibid., p. 192.
[84] Mao Tse-tung [Mao Zedong], *Strategic Problems in the Anti-Japanese Guerrilla War* [1938 in Chinese] (Peking: Foreign Language Press, 1954), pp. 7–8, 29–30, 36–39; Robert Asprey, 'Guerrilla Warfare' in 'The Theory and Conduct of War,' in *Encyclopaedia Britannica: Macropaedia* (Fifteenth Edition, 1997), xxix, pp. 689–93.
[85] Summary of Intelligence, Palestine and Transjordan, 9 September 1938, by Wing Commander Ritchie at GHQ [18/38], CO 732/81/9, TNA.
[86] Monthly Administrative report for July 1938, Galilee and Acre District, 2 August 1938, by A/DC K. W. Blackburne, Blackburne Papers, MSS. Brit. Emp. S. 460, Box 3, File 2, WL.

finance the bands and local leaders have been driven to fend for themselves, by employing every means of extortion they have been fairly
successful.'[87] Effective rebel organisation and co-ordination disappeared,
'Even in SAMARIA, where the organisation is probably most complete, the various leaders have been quarrelling violently ... In southern
PALESTINE there is even less control and the various gangs are at times
in almost open conflict, and it is apparent that some of them are engaged
in pure banditry.'[88] Parochial, fragmented band structure made simultaneous, concerted action 'practically out of the question.'[89] As wild violence from below led the insurrection, the British moved in to 'acquire
information, play leaders off against followers, and make taking on
command responsibilities a dangerous affair,' as they always did in such
situation: 'how essential it is for vanguard insurgents to build social links
to local communities, lest they be isolated and targeted.'[90] By December
1938, rival rebel commands in Jaffa were approaching open warfare, the
'attention' of both factions 'largely focussed' on each other's activities.[91]
Intra-communal clashes forced rebels into exile, from where they path-
etically pleaded for the British to allow them back into Palestine while
admitting their past sins against both the British and fellow Palestinians:

District Commissioner, Jerusalem. We, the undersigned, beg to submit to
Your Excellency the following:- You know that we took share in our national
revolt, such as did every member of the Palestinian nation, from purely national
motives, which you will appreciate, in your capacity as belonging to Great
Britain, the mother of democracies and the real type of nationalism. However,
when we saw that the revolt was being used for personal motives and fearing to
shed the blood of the innocent we took refuge in Syria, condemning all what is
happening in Palestine. Our economic situation is, however, bad and we beg you
to facilitate our return to Palestine as true patriots. Signatures: Yousef Ibrahim
Ijneid of Hebron (Secretary of rebel leader in the South and member of the War
Committee). Mohd. Ismail Murib of Halhul [north of Hebron], i/c [in charge]
Hebron hills rebels and second member of the War Committee. Badawi Ahmad
Ijneid of Hebron. Officer of the rebel guard. Hussein Ismail Murib of Halhul.
Rebel.[92]

[87] Summary of Intelligence, Palestine and Transjordan, 9 September 1938, by Wing
    Commander Ritchie at GHQ [18/38], CO 732/81/9, TNA.
[88] Summary of Intelligence, Palestine and Transjordan, 23 September 1938, by Wing
    Commander Ritchie at GHQ [19/38], CO 732/81/9, TNA.
[89] Ibid.
[90] Paul Staniland, *Networks of Rebellion: Explaining Insurgent Cohesion and Collapse* (Ithaca,
    NY and London: Cornell University Press, 2014), pp. 47–48.
[91] Summary of Intelligence, Palestine and Transjordan, 16 December 1938, by Wing
    Commander Ritchie at GHQ [25/38], CO 732/81/10, TNA.
[92] Rebel Statement to DC Jerusalem, Attachment to CID Intelligence Summary, Jerusalem,
    No. 50/39, 20 July 1939, 47/89, HA.

Rebel Depredations

The Arab revolt opened Pandora's box. Instead of the support for and of the people that underpins any successful insurgency, Palestinians fought one another. While the evidence that follows on intra-communal Palestinian violence is mostly from British and Jewish sources, neither party had any interest in lying about such things. It suited the British and Jews publicly to portray the rebels as bandits and criminals, but their in-house reports were honest assessments and captured Arabic-language material makes the same point. Moreover, Jewish information often derived from Palestinian contacts. The litany of bandit thuggery detailed below dominated the violence of the revolt and overshadowed the politics of rebellion and the actions of true rebels, not just al-Qawuqji but so many others whose political aim to rid Palestine of the British and Jews vanished in a miasma of criminality and recrimination. 'Virtual anarchy reigns,' in the words of British intelligence in 1938, encouraged by those such as Hajj Amin who from '1936 to the end of 1937, to my certain knowledge,' remembered intelligence officer Tony Simonds, 'personally organised the murder of over 4,000 pro-British Arabs.'[93] 'Everyone does what he sees fit,' in the *Yishuv*'s view.[94] Palestinians claimed that British officials encouraged *fitan* between Muslims by leaving revealing papers on their desks for cleaners to find that rebels mistakenly used to kill innocent *muhktars* in 'false liquidations,' and that people in 1948 remembered this internecine war and were fearful to mobilise because of it. Such claims detract from the self-generated internecine violence of the revolt that had little to do with British subversive operations, while such operations if true confirm how subversion so easily opened up internal Palestinian fissures.[95] If violence by soldiers against Palestinians was warp and weft of the imperial battle to pacify an alien colonial population in revolt, the personally motivated abuses of mujahideen insurgents – if indeed that is what they were – make no political sense as they alienated ordinary Palestinians and so supported that part of British pacification that detached insurgents from the people. Soldiers noted that villagers were 'delighted' to see the Army as this meant that the 'bandits' 'wouldn't go anywhere near them.'[96] Palestinians reserved

---

[93] Summary of Intelligence, Palestine and Transjordan, 23 September 1938, by Wing Commander Ritchie at GHQ [19/38], CO 732/81/9, TNA; Typed Memoir, Pieces of War, pp. 43–44, Simonds Papers, 08/46/1, IWMD.
[94] Sasson to Caplan (Jerusalem), 23 January 1939, S25/3639-151, CZA.
[95] 'Khaled al-Fahoum Yatadhakkar' ['Khaled al-Fahoum Remembers'], *al-Quds* (2 September 1998), p. 17.
[96] Shepperd, 4597/06, p. 47, IWMSA.

the worst horrors for themselves. Hitmen chopped to pieces a butcher in Haifa who allegedly had 'Jewish sympathies' and had bought flour from a Jew, a British policeman writing to his parents how afterwards 'it was a difficult thing to find which was Arab and which was mutton.'[97] To 'make certain that they had got every last pound from him,' rebels lowered a terrified richer villager down into a cistern.[98] British violence was political and targeted, while Palestinian violence was personal and politically indiscriminate, or personally political in the case of Hajj Amin's battle with the Nashashibis. In short, the culture of violence was superior to its political value.[99] Rebels morphed into bandits and attacked their own people because the revolt prompted brigandage by armed men who were simultaneously social-political rebels *and* criminal opportunists, the latter triumphing over the former in the absence of disciplined guerrilla organisation. Eric Hobsbawm's 'social banditry' of 'primitive rebels' is as good a description as any of this phenomenon.[100] As political content faded, pejorative 'gang' and 'bandit' labels fit. There were four spheres of violence, the last two growing in importance as the revolt dragged on: insurgent attacks on the British and Jews, British counter-insurgency supported by Jewish forces, bandit gang attacks on villagers, and intra-Palestinian political assassinations. Rebels inadvertently worked with the British spreading terror, with only one quarter of the violence directed at the real targets – Government and the Jews – as disparate armed Arab–Palestinian groups more-or-less fighting for the national cause took over the rebellion.

While the British legally fined, punished, and detained villagers by day, gangs illegally robbed, assaulted, and abducted them by night. The language and time of day differed but the effects were the same: countrywide social and economic dislocation, poverty, and hunger. By July 1936, reports were coming in of 'lawless elements' bringing pressure to bear on villagers who had not 'fully assisted' with men and money: 'The Mukhtar (Arab) of Um el Faham [Umm al-Fahm], Northern District, received a demand from eight armed men to provide LP.100 to assist the gangs.'[101] £P.100 was the yearly salary of four rural households. The

---

[97] Letter, Burr to Mother and Father, 17 September 1937, Burr Papers, 88/8/1, IWMD.

[98] Bertha Stafford Vester, *Our Jerusalem: An American Family in the Holy City, 1881–1949* (Lebanon: Middle East Export, 1950), pp. 343–44.

[99] See the broad discussion in John Keegan, *A History of Warfare* (London: Pimlico, 1993), pp. 3–60.

[100] Hobsbawm, *Primitive Rebels*; Eric Hobsbawm, *Bandits* (London: Weidenfeld and Nicolson, 1969).

[101] CID Periodical Appreciation Summary No. 12/36, 12 July 1936, Deputy IG to Chief Secretary, FO 371/20018 TNA.

following month, forty gang members went to Dalia and Osfia villages (the mostly Druze villages of Daliyat al-Carmil and 'Isfiya) at night and demanded money and men for the revolt. During an argument, they hit the *mukhtar*'s wife, agreeing finally to return in the morning for their demands. Someone then told the authorities and in the morning British soldiers were waiting for the gang.[102] Some Druze retaliated by fighting for the Jews and the British, while a Jewish–Druze delegation went to Syria in October 1937 to make sure that Druze there did not join the revolt, starting a 'de facto alliance' with the Jews that weakened the revolt.[103] A British–Jewish intelligence report noted that all the Druze considered 'themselves wronged and insulted by the rebels,' after rebel leader Yusuf Sa'id Abu Durra killed Druze and destroyed their holy books, adding how disaffected Druze in Lebanon and Transjordan could thus seriously disturb rebels' arms transport, mail, care of wounded, and escape routes for fighters.[104] The Druze sect may not have been big but 'her sons are scattered in the police and in such government positions that they could be most damaging,' noted a commentary from what seems to be a Jewish intelligence officer.[105] Gangs behaved as the Army did, with one taxing Tira village[106] 100 sacks of wheat.[107] In August 1938, brigands fined each household in the Christian village of Bayt Jala south of Jerusalem £P.10–100 apiece and sentenced a man to death for not supporting the 'warriors.'[108] Gangs turned popular revolt into an extortion racket and made real the endemic social banditry of the people. They targeted relatives of those who could not pay, blackmailed whole towns and organisations, stopped the movement of cattle, and picked on *al-Mua'rada* supporters and so further divided the country.[109] They

---

[102] Haganah Report, 20 August 1936, Shai Intelligence Reports: 8/GENERAL/40, p. 100, HA.

[103] Zachary Lockman, *Comrades and Enemies: Arab and Jewish Workers in Palestine, 1906–1948* (Berkeley, CA: University of California Press, 1996), p. 251; Report attached to Letter from Haifa Labour Council, sent to Shertok, 1 November 1937, S25/5570-158/159 CZA.

[104] Appendix: Explanatory Notes, Captured and Translated Arabic Material with Commentary, p. 109, Wingate Papers, Microfilm M2313, BL. Swedenburg, *Memories of Revolt*, pp. 92–93 dates the attack to 27 November 1938.

[105] Appendix: Explanatory Notes, Captured and Translated Arabic Material with Commentary, p. 109, Wingate Papers, Microfilm M2313, BL.

[106] Probably a reference to al-Tira (or at-Tira) south of Haifa but there are several Palestinian villages with this name.

[107] Haganah Report, 20 August 1936, Shai Intelligence Reports: 8/GENERAL/40, p. 100, HA.

[108] *Haaretz* (18 August 1938).

[109] Yuval Arnon-Ohanna, *Herev mi-Bayit: ha-Ma'avak ha-Pnimi ba-tnu'a ha-le'umit ha-falastinit, 1929–39* [*The Internal Struggle within the Palestinian Movement, 1929–39*] (Tel Aviv: Hadar, 1989), pp. 285–86.

abducted bank managers. One paid £P.600 ransom for his release.[110] Villagers complained to the revolt leadership that they were 'so poor that they could barely support their families, or the fighters billeted on them.'[111] Like the soldiers, gangs demanded money and guns, so stripping away villagers' exiguous wealth and protection: 'During the night 7 armed Arabs entered a house near here owned by an Arab and demanded money. They obtained none, but stole a licenced shot gun and some ammunition.'[112] Gangs wanted recruits, too. One twelve-strong one went to Jeba (Jaba') village[113] and demanded £P.50 and twenty men for forced conscription. At Ain Jzal ('Ayn Ghazal south of Haifa), the same gang demanded £P.150 and twenty men. The gang told both villages that they wanted this the same evening.[114] Such actions drew villagers to the Jews, whose agents were watching and waiting, exploiting the fear that Arab police officers leaked intelligence on Palestinians who talked to the authorities: 'The Arabs are afraid to submit this information to the police so they ask the Jews to do it for them.'[115] Villagers were victims twice over. In August 1936, the British collected wheat in lieu of a fine from Tira, added to the 100 sacks of wheat mentioned above demanded by the rebels, if it were the same village, and they assaulted people – badly injuring many villagers, Jewish intelligence reported – and then the next day soldiers demanded money for an immediate fine.[116] A day later, Arabs including an 'officer' (from a gang or the police, it is hard to tell from the transliteration) came to the village and rebuked villagers for paying the fine. A 'Khlaid Effendi' (possibly Khalid) with this group fined them again, this time the sum of £P.400.[117] Thus, soldiers and gangs working in tandem had assaulted and levied the same villagers twice over in the space of three days, 19–21 August 1936. Arab villagers (probably near Haifa) complained – 'crying' in Hebrew – about payments to the gangs and addressed their concerns to the revolt's strike committee in Haifa that called a meeting with the band leaders and decided that bands would task

---

[110] Summary of Intelligence, Palestine and Transjordan [26/38], 30 December 1938, by Wing Commander Ritchie, CO 732/81/10, p. 3, TNA.

[111] 4 Members of Council and 7 Elders to His Excellency the Commander of the Rebellion in Palestine, 30 September 1938, Captured and Translated Arabic Material with Commentary, p. 69, Wingate Papers, Microfilm M2313, BL.

[112] Dorsetshire Regiment, Narrative of Events, Safad, 31 August 1936, 88/367, Shelf C4, Box 3, KMM.

[113] There are villages with this name near Jenin, Haifa, and Bethlehem but this is probably a reference to the one south of Haifa.

[114] 4 August 1936, Shai Intelligence Reports: 8/GENERAL/40, p. 15, HA.

[115] Ibid.

[116] Haganah report, 23 August 1936, Shai Intelligence Reports: 8/GENERAL/40, pp. 104–05, HA.

[117] Ibid.

two to three men to collect money.[118] A day later, on 29 August 1936, a band came to Balad al-Shaykh, al-Qassam's burial place, and demanded money from the *mukhtar*'s son. He refused, so the robbers attacked and injured him.[119] Rebel command in Damascus challenged a rebel fine of £P.14,000 on Nablus. Damascus talked of 'intimidation methods' for this 'enormous sum' with individual merchants paying £P.500–1,000 and of the need for a local leader to 'content himself with smaller sums'; there was also a whopping £P.60,000 rebel fine on Jaffa that the British were sure to exploit for propaganda.[120] Rebel fines were larger than those levied by security forces and a way of local band leaders 'to line their pockets,' in the view of military intelligence.[121] (The Arabic material in Wingate's papers in the British Library damningly details rebel exploitation, intimidation, corruption, and robbery.) When rebels fined villages, villagers resisted, so gangs applied more force to what 'had changed into a debt. Henceforth moneys are claimed as debts, the collection of which had to be fought,' so encouraging *fasad* and a 'thousand blood feuds' engendered by intra-communal terrorism.[122] If one *hamula* had a gang then other clans needed one.[123] In the words of Jewish intelligence, those employing terror knew what they 'started with but did not imagine how far they would reach and what facts and results they would have to face' as the 'mass realised what the real practical power of the "new rulers" was' and so 'repulsed them as something disgusting and handed them over to the authorities.'[124]

Some incidents were straightforward robberies. Six armed men, one of whom was dressed in 'European clothes,' broke into a Palestinian's house one evening in September 1936, 'beat up' the man and his wife, and 'stole money and clothes to the value of £P.60.'[125] The same file marks another

[118] Haganah Report, 28 August 1936, Shai Intelligence Reports: 8/GENERAL/40, p. 131, HA.
[119] Haganah Report, 29 August 1936, Shai Intelligence Reports: 8/GENERAL/40, p. 134, HA.
[120] Rebellion Command Letter to the Brother [Jaffa?] Secretary of the Office, Signed Central Committee for the National Jihad, 26 December 1938, Captured and Translated Arabic Material with Commentary, pp. 19–21, Wingate Papers, Microfilm M2313, BL.
[121] Summary of Intelligence, Palestine and Transjordan [26/38], 30 December 1938, by Wing Commander Ritchie, CO 732/81/10, p. 3, TNA.
[122] Appendix: Explanatory Notes, Captured and Translated Arabic Material with Commentary, p. 155, Wingate Papers, Microfilm M2313, BL; Arnon-Ohanna, *Herev mi-Bayit*, p. 279.
[123] Arnon-Ohanna, *Falahim ba-Mered ha-'Aravi*, pp. 37–38.
[124] Appendix: Explanatory Notes, Captured and Translated Arabic Material with Commentary, p. 157, Wingate Papers, Microfilm M2313, BL.
[125] Dorsetshire Regiment, Narrative of Events, Ramallah, 18 September 1936, 88/367, Shelf C4, Box 3, KMM.

similar robbery in Ramleh. Soldiers came across villagers with black eyes after having been beaten up by rebels: 'Oh yes, they were harsh to their own cousins. They were very harsh indeed, putting the fear of God into them.'[126] As one *mukhtar* put it, villagers feared the rebels 'more than they fear God and the Government, because the rebels know no mercy.'[127] Recalcitrant villages responded to rebel demands for 'a number of lads' with guns by paying money to get their young men back.[128] Rebels even charged villagers up to £P.10 to put cases before rebel courts, while gang commanders acting as judges issued biased judgements in favour 'of the one important in their eyes.'[129] Rebel courts were 'an inquisition for the draining of money in diverse and involved ways' in a Jewish appreciation.[130] When 'Abd al-Rahim al-Hajj Muhammad clashed with the Irsheid family, he sent men who not only killed and robbed family members but also 'violated the honour of the women and did other unpleasant things'; family members fled the country 'with a burning desire to take revenge.'[131] Rising gang extortions swamped fading rebel violence. One genuine rebel warned another, 'Do not take money from the inhabitants, because such an act will blemish our war.'[132] 'Everyone is acting independently. I fear our work has changed into an instrument for private interests, and the quarrels are a sure sign of this,' noted another; 'no national enthusiasm anywhere and all heads dipped in quarrels and badness.'[133]

Police CID noted that chronic lawlessness worsened in the second phase of the revolt after September 1937:

A great deal of robbery and extortion has gone on in the country districts, both with the authority of the National and Supreme Committees, and by unauthorised

---

[126] Hose, p. 8, 4501/03, IWMSA.
[127] Diary/notes, May 1938, p. 12, Keith-Roach Papers, AL-KR.
[128] Appendix: Explanatory Notes, Captured and Translated Arabic Material with Commentary, p. 115, Wingate Papers, Microfilm M2313, BL.
[129] Rebellion Courts, as told by a Magistrate, Captured and Translated Arabic Material with Commentary, p. 28, Wingate Papers, Microfilm M2313, BL.
[130] Appendix: Explanatory Notes, Captured and Translated Arabic Material with Commentary, p. 160, Wingate Papers, Microfilm M2313, BL.
[131] Abd el Rahim el Haj Mahmad ('Abd al-Rahim al-Hajj Muhammad), Captured and Translated Arabic Material with Commentary, p. 33, Wingate Papers, Microfilm M2313, BL.
[132] Abu Abdallah to Abu Khaled (Khalid), 17 July 1938, Captured and Translated Arabic Material with Commentary, p. 34, Wingate Papers, Microfilm M2313, BL.
[133] Council of High Command of Rebellion Army in Palestine, Abd el Rahim el Haj Mahmad to Abu Khaled, 23 August 1938 and Abd el Rahim el Haj Mahmad, Council of High Command of Rebellion, to Abu Khaled, 11 September 1938, Captured and Translated Arabic Material with Commentary, pp. 37, 42, Wingate Papers, Microfilm M2313, BL.

robbers and wealthier Arabs have been mulcted [money taken by fraudulent means] of large sums towards the distress funds, which are doubtless used inter alia for maintenance of bandits. Many villagers have been molested and some shot in this connection, while a large number who have been found proceeding townwards with produce have been interfered with, their goods destroyed, and in many cases their animals killed.[134]

Rebel intimidation alienated swathes of the population who were 'thoroughly tired of the continual exactions and violence of the rebels' and were 'only waiting until they are assured that the Government disposes of sufficient forces to afford them protection, for the opportunity to come forward on the side of law and order.'[135] Rebels assassinated Jews to intimidate wealthy Haifan Arabs into paying up.[136] The Government needed only to exert its control and counter the 'open intimidation' by men travelling in cars from village to village demanding recruits and rifles, spreading terror amongst their own people, reported British civil officials.[137] Villagers paid rebel fines in guns.[138] In the words of Acting District Commissioner Kenneth Blackburne, the 'visits of these gang organisers are seldom disclosed by the villagers as they realise that the smallest suspicion against them will result in their murder by gangsters … I have been told by one man however that a gang organiser visits his village more frequently than the police.'[139] The British were short of troops to show the flag and fight bands as many soldiers were guarding the border fence or inflicting punishments on villagers, at least before October 1938.[140]

Villagers (and townsfolk) had tough choices. They could refuse rebel demands, get beaten up, robbed, and see their menfolk press ganged; accede to the rebels and become targets as a 'bad' village for brutal Army punitive raids; or fight the British, have troops destroy their village, be assaulted more systematically, and watch their men disappear into

---

[134] CID Periodical Appreciation Summary No. 16/36, 28 September 1936, Deputy Inspector General to Chief Secretary, FO 371/20018, TNA.

[135] Summary of Intelligence, Palestine and Transjordan, 7 October 1938, by Wing Commander Ritchie at GHQ [20/38], CO 732/81/9, TNA.

[136] Diary, 17 December 1938, Scrivenor Papers, MSS. Brit. Emp. S. 378, WL.

[137] Monthly Administrative Report for June 1938, Galilee and Acre District, 1 July 1938, by A/DC K. W. Blackburne, Blackburne Papers, MSS. Brit. Emp. S. 460, Box 3, File 2, WL.

[138] Abd el Rahim el Haj Mahmad, Council of General Command of Head of the Rebellion in Palestine, to Abu Khaled, 6 September 1938, Captured and Translated Arabic Material with Commentary, p. 41, Wingate Papers, Microfilm M2313, BL.

[139] Monthly Administrative Report for June 1938, Galilee and Acre District, 1 July 1938, by A/DC K. W. Blackburne, Blackburne Papers, MSS. Brit. Emp. S. 460, Box 3, File 2, WL.

[140] Monthly Administrative Report for August 1938, Galilee and Acre District, 2 September 1938, by A/DC K. W. Blackburne, Blackburne Papers, MSS. Brit. Emp. S. 460, Box 3, File 2, WL.

detention camps. Gangs attacked villagers for not giving money and men, while the Army targeted villages for giving them. Survival for villagers meant supporting the revolt ideologically, while resisting the gangs in the hope that rebels and soldiers would not molest them. As General Wavell put it, 'The chief hope lies in the villagers themselves dealing with the gangs and keeping them out' as 'villagers are all for peace, but not for helping the Government.'[141] As villagers knew from harsh experience, the Army was far better at articulating violence. Backed up by the colonial state's legal ordinances, the Army was more systematic and efficient than rebels in inflicting punishments. Later, in 1938, the Army saw the opportunity afforded by villagers' ambivalence and it began arming them in pro-Government peace bands – or best described as anti-gang, or not anti-Government – while turning and paying erstwhile rebels such as 'Abd al-Hadi to fight for the British. 'Abd al-Hadi's motives for working with the British are interesting and speak to a wider discourse on collaboration as in occupied France after 1940.[142] He saw himself not as a collaborator but as a nationalist, settling vendettas rooted in his social, rural life with some help now from the British. When talking to a British colonial officer in December 1938, 'Abd al-Hadi espoused the nationalist cause, dismissed with 'indifference' a British offer of money, and made it clear that he was fighting for 'wounded pride,' concluding how, 'he has his pride and his duty towards his own country, Jenin, and his people, who have been murdered and robbed by rebels. He must revenge himself on these rebels. He must kill them. He reiterated this desire to kill several times and emphasized it by laying hands on his revolver and dagger. For these reasons he was helping the Government.'[143]

Villagers resisted as best they could the rapacious small platoon-sized gangs of ten or twenty men that preyed on them. This was impossible against an 800-strong battalion of heavily armed British infantry with machine guns, limitless bullets, and reinforced with warplanes and artillery. Thus, when four armed men visited Si'ir (Sa'ir) in the Hebron sub-district and demanded food in September 1936, 'The villagers who recognised them as having come to the village some time ago when they robbed some houses and killed some donkeys, chased them away, whereupon the four men fired, killing one villager and wounding another.'[144]

[141] Wavell to Haining (DMO, WO), 6 January 1938, Palestine, 1937–38 Volume, Wavell Papers, POH.
[142] See Christopher Lloyd, *Collaboration and Resistance in Occupied France: Representing Treason and Sacrifice* (Houndmills: Palgrave, 2003).
[143] Subject: Fakhri Abdul Hadi, from Robert Newton, ADC, Jenin, 17 December 1938, S25/22793-39/43, CZA.
[144] Official Communique 261/36, 19 September 1936, Official Communiques, M/567/4, ISA.

Later in the same month, near 'Ajjur village north-west of Hebron, three armed men shot and wounded an Arab and robbed him, after which a larger party 'entered a house in Al Khadr village in the Bethlehem sub-district demanding money. They stabbed the house owner killing him and left firing some shots at the villagers who pursued them.'[145] Food procurement in lean times was hard. Rebel bands tasked certain tribes and villages 'to collect rice, oil, flour, cigarettes etc. and to store these provisions.'[146] This meant that bands 'drained' local villages 'of all food' to the extent that such places could not welcome visitors.[147] Meanwhile, the British armed the victims of bandit raids, as with one Bedouin tribe that was 'extremely angry' at gang attacks so Scrivenor promised them more shotguns for protection.[148] Villagers chased gangs, as did the Army. The British had the rebels working for them punishing villagers, while villagers worked with soldiers hunting down gangs, and all at no cost beyond that of supplying some shotguns. One 'terrorist,' Jamil Abu Hanfer, was 'murdered in his own home by the representatives of the peace gangs in partnership with the military,' while the residents of Tulkarm asked the Army if they could carry weapons for use against gangs.[149]

The ceasefire of 12 October 1936 and the Peel Commission inter-regnum to September 1937 did not mean an end to violence. Banditry and feuding rumbled on. An Army laundry van picked up a badly wounded Palestinian whose injury was 'probably the result of some pri-vate feud as there have been no recent military encounters in the area south of Nablus. Now that peace has been restored it is quite probable that there will be more cases of this description as there exist numerous "fassad" [feuding] between families and villagers in this area.'[150] There were 'enough blood feuds in this country to keep the inhabitants shooting each other for the next quarter of a century at least,' in the words of one civil administrator.[151] Those who had not resisted fully or had informed to

---

[145] Official Communique 269/36, 27 September 1936, Official Communiques, M/567/4, ISA.
[146] Daily Intelligence Summary 5/38, Divisional Police HQ, Haifa Rural Division, 10 February 1938, Scrivenor Papers, MSS. Brit. Emp. S. 377, p. 80, WL.
[147] Bertha Stafford Vester, *Our Jerusalem: An American Family in the Holy City, 1881–1949* (Lebanon: Middle East Export, 1950), p. 345.
[148] Diary, 23 May 1938, Scrivenor Papers, MSS. Brit. Emp. S. 378, WL.
[149] Note on Letter, HQ, Arab Revolt Office, 20 November 1938, Signed Abu Omar, Intelligence on Arab Leaders: 41/104, HA; Arnon-Ohanna, *Falahim ba-Mered ha-'Aravi*, p. 84.
[150] Dorsetshire Regiment, Situation Report 17 by BIO, 16th Infantry Brigade, Nablus, 15 October 1936, 88/353, Shelf C4, Box 3, KMM.
[151] Diary, 16 November 1938, Scrivenor Papers, MSS. Brit. Emp. S. 378, WL.

the authorities in the first phase of the revolt were now targets and people in Nablus feared a secret society established to attack collaborators.[152] Gunmen shot Arab police officers and civilians. On other occasions, as in December 1936, 'bandits' robbed passengers in road convoys, but at least they did not, as they had done before, 'strip them of all their clothes and let them go on their way naked.'[153] Hajj Amin's gunmen attacked the Nashashibis, narrowly missing Fakhri Nashashibi in Jaffa in June 1937. Fakhri produced a leaflet in late 1938 complaining about attacks on opponents.[154] Fakhri Nashashibi referred to Hajj Amin's terrorism and misuse of monies as a 'voice from the graves,' these being those of the people he had had killed.[155] While Palestinian political elites killed each other, mercenaries in gangs levied villages. Thus, in December 1937, Wavell reckoned that rebel bands in the north, 'I fancy consist mainly of out-of-work Syrians, trying to earn with as little risk to their skins as possible the £5 or so a month that the gun-man receives from Damascus, and to supplement it by levies on the villages.'[156] Balah (Bal'a near Tulkarm) villagers fought back and fired on a gang, leaving the gang leader angry; they also ejected commanders of gangs: 'If they do it what is our worth? How dare they do it? What will be our position against them? I leave it for you to decide.'[157] Bands planned a revenge attack on Balah: 'For these reasons, I ask you [to other gang leaders] to forgive me, because I'm going to act with the village of Balah with cruelty.'[158] Villagers hoped to fragment gangs into smaller units so that they could rob or kill them, before gangs did the same to them.[159] Insurgent-criminals met with Balah's villagers who accused them of not protecting them and then tried unsuccessfully to take the gang's weapons, after which the villagers ejected the men. Balah's villagers then told those of Dir el-Gusun (Dayr al-Ghusun north-west of Bal'a) that if the gang came again, they would

---

[152] Dorsetshire Regiment, Situation Reports 34 and 35, 16th Infantry Brigade, Nablus, 3–4 November 1936, 88/353, Shelf C4, Box 3, KMM.

[153] Letter 252, Carr to Wife, 2 December 1936, Carr Papers, Letters 239–288, LHCMA.

[154] Zu'aytir, *Al-Haraka al-Wataniya al-Filastiniyya, 1935–39*, pp. 293, 521, 530. See also Hillel Cohen, *Army of Shadows: Palestinian Collaboration with Zionism, 1917–1948* (Berkeley, CA: University of California Press, 2008).

[155] Fakhri Nashashibi, *Sawt Min Qubur Filastin al-'Arabiyya* [*A Voice from the Graves of Arab Palestine*] (Jerusalem: n.p., 1938); Extract from the *Yorkshire Post* of 24 October 1938 in Creech Jones Papers, MSS. Brit. Emp. S. 332, Box 30, File 2, WL.

[156] Wavell to Haining (DMO, WO), 8 December 1937, Palestine, 1937–38 Volume, Wavell Papers, POH.

[157] Official Letter from the Commander of a Gang to Other Gang Leaders, 9 January 1939, Signed Hassan, Intelligence on Arab Leaders: 41/104, HA.

[158] Ibid.

[159] Ibid.

call on the Army to 'annihilate' the rebels.[160] The Army was now a better possibility than rebel forces. One *mukhtar* told soldiers that he was hoping for a return of the 'good old days.'[161] Villagers hit and insulted a rebel messenger, forcing the gang to retaliate: 'we decided to kill some of the notables from Balah ... if we do not decide to kill some of the notable villagers the revolt is doomed because they [the villagers] have claimed that the leaders have escaped to Syria, leaving us [the rebels] to destroy the country.'[162] As targeted military sweeps by debussed lorry-borne soldiers supported by the RAF scattered bands, Damascus high command lost control of directionless section-sized units that went it alone, as British intelligence noted:

The removal by death or flight of a number of the principal leaders has left these small bands leaderless, disorganised, without money to pay for supplies, or the prestige to obtain them peacefully from the villages. As the majority of them are either foreigners or absconded offenders who dare not return to their homes, they have been forced to resort to banditry ... these activities are making the bands increasingly unpopular which may lead to information being given more freely ... there is a considerable dearth of gang leaders and that those at present in the country are lacking in military training.[163]

The police in Haifa intimated the presence of uniformed Iraqis in a gang that robbed Palestinians, an external contribution that diminished as the revolt progressed and rebel command in Damascus was unable to pay foreign fighters:

At 0710 hours this morning ABDULLA STAMBOULI, Tax Collector of Haifa reported to the Shefa Amr [Shafa 'Amr east of Haifa] Police Station and stated that at 1945 hours last night while he was sleeping in the house of Tewfik Nasser [Tawfiq al-Nasir] in Ebbellin village [I'billin near Shafa 'Amr] it was surrounded by a large armed band. Three of the band entered the house and took from him LP23: 960 mils Government money and LP2: 400 mils his own property, a watch, 2 receipt books and a note book. The men were dressed in khaki uniforms with Iraqi Hattas [presumably coloured red and white as Palestinian *hattat* were likely to be white or later black and white].[164]

---

[160] Letter in the Name of God the Merciful to Warrior Brothers, 8 January 1939, Signed Hassan, Intelligence on Arab Leaders: 41/104, HA; Arnon-Ohanna, *Falahim ba-Mered ha-'Aravi*, p. 84.
[161] 'Notes on Palestine Operations,' *The Wasp: The Journal of the 16th Foot* 8/5 (March 1937), p. 268.
[162] Letter in the Name of God the Merciful to Warrior Brothers, 8 January 1939, Signed Hassan, Intelligence on Arab Leaders: 41/104, HA.
[163] Summary of Intelligence, Palestine and Transjordan, 25 March 1938, by Wing Commander Ritchie at GHQ [6/38], CO 732/81/9, TNA.
[164] District Police HQ Haifa to DC Office Haifa, 19 March 1938, Scrivenor Papers, MSS. Brit. Emp. S. 377, p. 117, WL.

Gangs slaughtered livestock at Kaffrein village[165] in an attack on 'Shaker Assad El Khader' (Shakir Asa'd al-Khadr), who returned fire with his licensed shotgun, then hid, and on returning later to his house found his mare, donkey, and six goats dead.[166] (The Army by contrast confiscated rather than killed livestock.) Such outrages gelled with Government policies to turn villagers away from the national cause. The British captured documents that bore 'witness to the distress caused to rebel supporters by the marauding propensity of certain gangs.'[167] When rebels came to Tireh village (probably al-Tira south of Haifa) to kill the *mukhtar*, he was not in, so they abducted several of his relatives.[168] Disfigured bodies were a grisly reminder of the endemic chaos, with the body of an Arab taxi driver found hanging in Haifa bound, gagged, and mutilated.[169] In August 1938, assailants stoned to death a Jew near Jerusalem.[170] Two months later, on 12 October 1938, assassins shot dead an Arab bus driver in broad daylight in Jaffa and cut off both of his ears.[171] Many Palestinians killed at this time had notes pinned to their bodies. The 'usual note was pinned to the body' in British intelligence files.[172] Intelligence flooded in on the spreading anarchy and the insurgent legal system that punished Palestinians with 'a large number of persons, 35 in the last fortnight' abducted and put before alternative rebel courts.[173] Gangs of men robbed banks, with two successful robberies in Nablus, one of the post office messenger carrying the mail bag that included £P.2,000 from Barclay's Bank. A gang entered Hebron post office but was unable to force the safe. Men stole *awqaf* Muslim endowments in raids on offices in Hebron and Nablus, while three armed men held up the post office in Qalqilya, stole

---

[165] Either the existing West Bank Palestinian village of Kafr Ein (Kafrayn) five miles south-west of the Israeli settlement of Ariel, or al-Kafrayn ('the two villages' archaically) twenty miles south-east of Haifa near Mishmar Ha'emek and demolished in 1948.

[166] Daily Situation report, Divisional Police HQ, Haifa Rural Division, 20 March 1938, Scrivenor Papers, MSS. Brit. Emp. S. 377, p. 119, WL.

[167] Summary of Intelligence, Palestine and Transjordan, 22 April 1938, by Wing Commander Ritchie at GHQ [8/38], CO 732/81/9, TNA.

[168] Reports, April 1938, Scrivenor Papers, MSS. Brit. Emp. S. 377, pp. 142–46, WL.

[169] Summary of Intelligence, Palestine and Transjordan, 15 July 1938, by Wing Commander Ritchie at GHQ [14/38], CO 732/81/9, TNA.

[170] Summary of Intelligence, Palestine and Transjordan, 26 August 1938, by Wing Commander Ritchie at GHQ [17/38], CO 732/81/9, TNA.

[171] Summary of Intelligence, Palestine and Transjordan, 21 October 1938, by Wing Commander Ritchie at GHQ [21/38], CO 732/81/10, TNA.

[172] Summary of Intelligence, Palestine and Transjordan, 26 August 1938, by Wing Commander Ritchie at GHQ [17/38], CO 732/81/9, TNA; Summary of Intelligence, Palestine and Transjordan [26/38], 30 December 1938, by Wing Commander Ritchie, CO 732/81/10, p. 2, TNA.

[173] Ibid. Rebel courts appear in the Arabic TV drama series 'al-Taghriba al-Filastiniyya' ['The Palestinian Exile'] (Syria, 2004), episode 8.

£P.40, and the postmaster's watch. When a train struck a landmine near Deir Esh Sheikh (Dayr al-Shaykh west of Jerusalem), an armed gang boarded the train and robbed passengers. Two armed men tried to force their way into Barclay's Bank in Nazareth.[174] Raids netted armed gangs £P.5,020 from Barclay's in Nablus and from a security van at the same place – fabulous sums of money.[175] As a coda, it is interesting that classic American films such as 'Bonnie and Clyde' (1967) and 'Butch Cassidy and the Sundance Kid' (1969) transformed such bank-robbing, train-ambushing outlaws into Wild West cultural legends and so positively reimagined crime, fame, justice, popular heroes, and American history. There is no comparable cultural understanding of men such as 'Abd al-Hadi.[176] While Hollywood established the assassination of cowboy outlaw Jesse James by 'the coward' Robert Ford in American folklore, and the Italian–Algerian film 'Battle for Algiers' (1966) reworked former pimp and 'illiterate drifter' Ali la Pointe into a hero of the Algerian revolution, 'Abd al-Hadi's murder at a wedding in 1943 is dismissed as another Arab 'blood feud' by vendetta-driven bandit-criminals.[177]

Bands led by a field commander such as Yusuf Sa'id Abu Durra – later chased down by a joint Haganah–Druze unit and subsequently hanged by the British – made themselves immensely unpopular with their 'brutality' and 'high handed manner' towards prominent notable families.[178] Even gangs dressed in uniforms, so suggesting more disciplined control, extorted villagers.[179] Rebels targeted town dwellers, too, such as Palestinian Quaker–Christian teacher Khalil Totah who in September 1938 recorded how three men had come in the night when he was away 'and left an anonymous note demanded £50 from school or I would be

[174] Summary of Intelligence, Palestine and Transjordan, 26 August 1938, by Wing Commander Ritchie at GHQ [17/38], CO 732/81/9, TNA.
[175] *Haaretz* (11 and 17 August 1938).
[176] See Parsons, *The Commander*, pp. 146–47 for popular imaginings of al-Qawuqji.
[177] 'The Assassination of Jesse James by the Coward Robert Ford' (Warner Bros, 2007); Patrick Harries, 'The Battle of Algiers: Between Fiction, Memory and History,' in Vivian Bickford-Smith and Richard Mendelsohn (eds), *Black and White in Colour: African History on Screen* (Oxford: Currey, 2007); Alistair Horne, *Savage War of Peace: Algeria, 1954–62* (London: Pan, 2002), pp. 216–17; Philip French, 'Battle of Algiers,' *The Guardian* (5 February 2006); Ezra Danin, *Te'udot u-Dmuyot me-Ginzey ha-Knufiyot ha-Arviyot, 1936–39 [Documents and Portraits from the Arab Gangs Archives in the Arab Revolt in Palestine, 1936–39]* [1944] (Jerusalem: Magnes, 1981), p. 24; Letter, Ted Horne to Author, 23 April 2013.
[178] Cohen, *Army of Shadows*, p. 167; Summary of Intelligence, Palestine and Transjordan, 12 August 1938, by Wing Commander Ritchie at GHQ [16/38], CO 732/81/9, TNA.
[179] Summary of Intelligence, Palestine and Transjordan, 12 August 1938, by Wing Commander Ritchie at GHQ [16/38], CO 732/81/9, TNA.

kidnapped. Surely, it is as not from rebels.'[180] In the same month, Totah witnessed a large rebel band enter (largely Christian) Ramallah and it 'marched through it, shouting and singing. Fired a lot into the air. The same night men came to house of our servants and demanded £10. The owner would not open the door. Armed men kept worrying the household from 8:30–12 midnight.'[181] The foreign press took note, with Beirut's *L'Orient* informing its readers how rebels 'sacked' a moderate Nashashibi-supporting village, ripping up trees and destroying farm equipment.[182] The brutality extended to families of enemies, including women and children, as when in September 1938, armed men went to Deir esh Sheikh and shot and killed the wife of the *mukhtar*, his three sons, aged from ten to fourteen, and a shepherd in his employ, alongside shooting a horse, a donkey and fourteen sheep.[183] Political rebels recognised the harmful impact of such attacks and so killed those suspected of committing such robberies, leaving behind as a reminder the bodies of their victims: '24/9/38: The bodies of two Arabs, both of whom had been shot, were found near MUZEIRI'A (146163) [al-Muzayri'a north-east of Ramleh]. A note pinned to one of the bodies indicated that they and two others had been killed by the rebels for robbing villages.'[184] In the chaos of inter-gang rivalry in the Hebron area, rebel groups received orders to arrest minor gang leaders who were robbing villagers.[185] Meanwhile, high-level political assassinations continued apace, hitmen from Hajj Amin's camp targeting supporters of Transjordan's Abdullah, such as Hasan Sidqi Dajani, who was also a good friend of Fakhri Nashashibi, murdered on 13 October 1938.[186] Totah noted the same killing, ascribing it to 'Arif 'Abd al-Raziq who killed Dajani after taking him from a car that they were all travelling in near Ramallah: 'It is said he was a spy to the British. Anyway, he was a supporter of Emir Abdullah.'[187] The Jews described 'Abd al-Raziq as a bully, cruel, and a thief, and someone forever fighting

---

[180] Diary, 2 September 1938, in Thomas Ricks (ed.), *Turbulent Times in Palestine: The Diaries of Khalil Totah, 1886–1955* (Jerusalem: IPS and Passia, 2009), p. 231. Totah was born into the Friends' Society but was also baptised Greek Orthodox, it seems.

[181] Diary, 9 September 1938, in Ricks, *Turbulent Times in Palestine*, p. 232.

[182] *L'Orient* [*The Orient*] (Beirut) (8 September 1938), p. 2.

[183] Incident on 20 September 1938 in Summary of Intelligence, Palestine and Transjordan, 23 September 1938, by Wing Commander Ritchie at GHQ [19/38], CO 732/81/9, TNA.

[184] Summary of Intelligence, Palestine and Transjordan, 7 October 1938, by Wing Commander Ritchie at GHQ [20/38], CO 732/81/9, TNA.

[185] Summary of Intelligence, Palestine and Transjordan, 18 November 1938, by Wing Commander Ritchie at GHQ [23/38], CO 732/81/10, TNA.

[186] Summary of Intelligence, Palestine and Transjordan, 21 October 1938, by Wing Commander Ritchie at GHQ [21/38], CO 732/81/10, TNA.

[187] Diary, 13 October 1938, in Ricks, *Turbulent Times in Palestine*, p. 236.

fellow rebel leader 'Abd al-Rahim al-Hajj Muhammad and his associated villages.[188] Anti-gang peace bands helped the British to track down and kill al-Hajj Muhammad in March 1939.[189]

As the revolt deepened, insurgent justice hardened. The authorities found the body of an Army interpreter in a cave near Nazareth with his head and hands severed from his body, the British having issued a communiqué in 1936 inviting English-speaking Arabs to act as interpreters for troop reinforcements.[190] Rebels held court in Kafr Manda in lower Galilee 'at the hands of which a considerable number of persons met an untimely death. Three members of the Khoury family were sentenced to death by this court and the sentence was executed some distance from the village.'[191] Police death squads – examined in Chapter 8 – added to the terror by dumping their victims near villages.[192] In October 1938 when villagers captured an 'Abu Njaim' (Najm or Nujaym meaning star or a little star), who formerly led a gang in the Qalqilya area, they sent him under guard to 'Aref' ('Arif 'Abd al-Raziq) who tried him on a charge of robbery and general brutality, and had him stoned to death. 'He was found guilty and condemned, but according to reports was found unworthy of shooting and condemned to be stoned to death. This sentence was duly carried out.'[193] 'Abd al-Raziq later became the target for rough justice, wrapped up in claims of collaborationist betrayal. CID noted that he fled to Syria from where,

He is believed to have proceeded to Iraq. His disappearance has given rise to considerable speculation in Arab circles. A report from Syria states that he fled to escape the vengeance of the relatives of his victims in Palestine. In an article printed in the Cairo newspaper 'Al Riyada,' Muhammad Ali Taher of the Arab Propaganda Bureau describes Aref Abdul Razzik as a traitor, and alleges that he, Aref, received the sum of LP 10,000 from the British government as a bribe to

---

[188] Court Houses of the Revolt, Internal Document from the PM's Office from the Class of Stateworkers who deal with Minorities, Documents from Arab Gangs, 1936–39, Report dated 4 September 1938, Printed in Jerusalem in 1958, Letters and Files Relating to Ezra Danin, 80/58P/14, p. 21, HA.

[189] Cohen, *Army of Shadows*, p. 152.

[190] Summary of Intelligence, Palestine and Transjordan, 18 November 1938, by Wing Commander Ritchie at GHQ [23/38], CO 732/81/10, TNA; Anon., 'Service Problems in Palestine: From a Correspondent in Jerusalem,' *Journal of the Royal United Service Institution* 81 (November 1936), p. 810.

[191] Kafr Manda, Political Activities, Villages Collective Punishment and Punitive Reports, Police Station Diary, Nazareth, M/4212/8, ISA.

[192] Matthew Hughes, 'A British "Foreign Legion"? The British Police in Mandate Palestine,' *Middle Eastern Studies* 49/5 (2013), pp. 696–711.

[193] Summary of Intelligence, Palestine and Transjordan, 21 October 1938, by Wing Commander Ritchie at GHQ [21/38], CO 732/81/10, TNA.

leave Palestine. The 'Oppositionist' refugees in Cairo are convinced that Aref left Palestine with the connivance of the British Government.[194]

Meanwhile, Abu Durra insulted the leader of the Nazareth rebels and the Zoabi family who then demanded 'that he be brought to court' or 'I hope you will forgive me if I teach him a thorough lesson.'[195] In a report in May 1939, Damascus command noted how the 'behaviour of the fighters towards the villagers is very despotic and terrible' with so much looting, murder, and cruelty that fellahin 'have applied to God for help against this treatment.'[196] Palestinians fled the violence. The Damascus press noted how the 40,000 Palestinians who emigrated to Syria and Lebanon 'in order to save their skins' were 'neither for nor against the rebels.'[197] Apartment rents in Beirut soared as wealthy Palestinians arrived looking for accommodation.[198] Government forces seized the moment to coax villagers and ask for loyalty notices, while rewarding them with licensed shotguns, travel permits, cuts in curfews, payments, remission of fines, and the promise to end damaging Army raids, to which rebels replied with threats:

WARNING. To the Mukhtars and Elders of Hebron town and its Sub-districts and to the Mukhtar of Halhoul [north of Hebron]. We send you this notice having heard that [the] Government has requested you to sign Loyalty Notices sent to you. We inform you that if you concurred with Government wishes you will run the risk of being shot with bullets made of the year 1939; and from the mouths of very recently manufactured machine guns. We are determined to enforce every order we issue in case you sign the Government declaration. The only alternative if you are afraid from the Government is that you should leave the country before signing it. 'Abdul Halim Julani ['Abd al-Halim al-Jawlani, colloquially Julani, band commander Hebron district[199]] on behalf of the GENERAL HEADQUARTERS OF THE ARAB FORCES. 30.4.39[200]

[194] Police CID Jerusalem, Intelligence Summary 33/39, 11 May 1939, p. 2, 47/82, HA; Porath, *The Palestinian Arab National Movement*, p. 259.
[195] From Leader of Nazareth District, Naif Diab Said el Zoabi, 31 August 1938, Captured and Translated Arabic Material with Commentary, p. 77, Wingate Papers, Microfilm M2313, BL.
[196] Memorandum by Abu Baker to the Command in Syria [after visit to Palestine], May 1939, Captured and Translated Arabic Material with Commentary, pp. 88–89, Wingate Papers, Microfilm M2313, BL.
[197] Extract (translated from the Arabic) from the Damascus Newspaper 'Alef Ba,' Issue No. 5363, 17 December 1938, FO 371/21869, TNA.
[198] Arnon-Ohanna, *Herev mi-Bayit*, p. 285.
[199] Listed as a guerrilla commander for Hebron District in Walid Khalidi (ed.), *Before Their Diaspora: A Photographic History of the Palestinians, 1876–1948* (Washington, DC: IPS, 2004), p. 209; Kabha, *The Palestinian People*, p. 13.
[200] Attachment dated 30 April 1939 in Police CID Jerusalem, Intelligence Summary 32/39, 6 May 1939, 47/82, HA.

When rebels abducted two men from Ramallah, the town was 'bewildered' and unsure how to reply, prompting the Army to despatch sixteen armed men to defend the place. 'Insufficient,' noted Totah the headteacher.[201] Rebel outrages drew Palestinians to the British and the Jews. Unable to find an older relative, Hajj Amin's men abducted the fourteen-year-old son of an opponent's family, while assassins targeted other family relatives in Lebanon, forcing them to seek help from the Jews, as Palestinian woman Ghada Karmi remembered. 'Another of my uncles, Abdul-Ghani, also a journalist and also opposed to Hajj Amin, whom he openly accused of being a British agent, had barely escaped an assassination attempt a few months before. Another man had been killed by mistake for him and he had taken to living in [Jewish] Tel Aviv where the Mufti's men could not reach him.'[202] Palestinian leaders 'turned on each other and ordinary people like my parents paid the price' wrote Karmi.[203] That the uncle, 'Abd al-Ghani al-Karmi, was allegedly informing to *Shai* who gave him the codename 'farmer' or 'vineyard owner'[204] might explain why he was a target.[205] On other occasions, villagers sought sanctuary from gangs in neighbouring Jewish settlements.[206]

Obscurantist rural bandit-gangs transformed a potential political rebellion into a socially conservative, anti-urban, criminal-Islamic one. They issued anti-Christian, anti-bourgeois leaflets and demanded that people's headdress change to rural-style *kufiyyat*; they ordered people to stop using Jewish-supplied electricity and forbade men from wearing shorts;[207] they told women to adopt the veil.[208] Battery-powered radios were acceptable as they did not use Jewish mains electricity but for listening to the news and the Koran only.[209] Insurgents put an Armenian Christian before a rebel court for refusing to wear peasant Arab headdress.[210] Rebel leaflets that encouraged young city people to join the bands also told women to march after their village 'sisters' and to stop

---

[201] Diary, 14 March 1939, in Ricks, *Turbulent Times in Palestine*, p. 257.

[202] Karmi, *In Search of Fatima*, p. 10.

[203] Karmi, *In Search of Fatima*, p. 11.

[204] The codeword was *yogev* in Hebrew, an archaic word that probably meant 'farmer' but became associated with the cultivation of vineyards, hence al-Karmi's other codename as the Arabic for vineyard is *karm* (*kerem* in Hebrew).

[205] Cohen, *Army of Shadows*, pp. 171, 218, 238, 297n2, 311n27. Misspelt al-Karami.

[206] Arnon-Ohanna, *Falahim ba-Mered ha-'Aravi*, p. 118.

[207] Muslim men should cover themselves from the knees to the stomach and some pious ones extend this rule to below the knees.

[208] Itamar Radai, 'The Rise and Fall of the Palestinian–Arab Middle Class under the British Mandate, 1920–39,' *Journal of Contemporary History* 51/3 (July 2016), p. 502; Cohen, *Army of Shadows*, p. 291n74.

[209] Arnon-Ohanna, *Falahim ba-Mered ha-'Aravi*, p. 133.

[210] Radai, 'The Rise and Fall of the Palestinian–Arab Middle Class,' p. 503.

wearing make-up, to visit cinemas 'and other forms of entertainment,' instead rising to the level of peasant women who 'carry jars of water on their heads' and make the 'death of the fighters easier.'[211] 'Terror-stricken' richer Christians viewed rebels as their 'despised enemies.'[212] The middle class yearned for an end to the revolt. Instead of adopting Mao's precept of building base areas to convert the enemy's rear into his front and make the enemy fight ceaselessly, Palestinians fought ceaselessly against themselves: poor against rich, Muslims against Christians and Druze, gangs against villagers, country versus town, Husaynis opposing Nashashibis, and patriots killing traitors.[213] By June 1939, the Army was holding 'reconciliation' ceremonies to stop villages fighting one another.[214] With the British having exiled the AHC in October 1937 (urged on by the Nashashibis), the revolt demanded central command from rebel headquarters in Damascus to give political purpose, recruits, and guns, and stop its descent into myriad small gangs fighting each other while preying on the people, the subject of the final part to this chapter.[215]

Damascus Rebel Command

The infighting that bedevilled the armed bands in Palestine continued apace among the Palestinian nationalist rebels and their supporters based in French-Mandate Syria and Lebanon, from where Jewish agents and the British Consul in Damascus, Colonel Gilbert MacKereth, busily exploited the enemy's disunity. (The Foreign Office covered relations with Syria, while the Colonial Office ran Palestine.) MacKereth developed an extensive intelligence and covert action network to subvert Syrian-based rebels, so much so that he wired London for a bulletproof waistcoat as protection against Black Hand rebel assassination threats.[216] Palestinian-centred scholars are right to say that the British with their 'vast experience of dividing colonized societies in order to rule them more effectively' manipulated subject peoples, but such divide and

---

[211] Quoted in Arnon-Ohanna, *Falahim ba-Mered ha-'Aravi*, p. 45.
[212] Appendix: Explanatory Notes, Captured and Translated Arabic Material with Commentary, p. 115, Wingate Papers, Microfilm M2313, BL.
[213] Mao Tse-tung, *Strategic Problems*, p. 29.
[214] A. H. K. to Moshe Sharett, 28 June 1939, reporting a Meeting between High Commissioner and Chief Secretary, and Fakhri and Raghib Nashashibi, S25/7644, CZA.
[215] Nasser Eddin Nashashibi, *Jerusalem's Other Voice: Ragheb Nashashibi and Moderation in Palestinian Politics, 1920–1948* (Exeter: Ithaca, 1990), pp. 55–56.
[216] Minute by G. W. Rendel, 12 November 1937, in Michael Fry and Itamar Rabinovich, *Despatches from Damascus: Gilbert MacKereth and British Policy in the Levant, 1933–39* (Tel Aviv: Dayan Center, 1985), p. 178.

rule strategies only worked against already divided communities.[217] The British never split the Jews after 1945 during their revolt in Palestine, just as Israel failed more recently to infiltrate and divide Lebanon's Shia-dominated Hizbollah resistance. 'Dissatisfaction and disagreement continue to be the keynote of relations between the Palestinian rebels in Damascus,' noted the Foreign Office.[218] Instead of forming a new node of authority, rebel headquarters in Damascus mimicked the personal clashes in Palestine, partly because field leaders periodically decamped to Syria, and partly because no strong alternative leader emerged in Damascus to stamp his authority, in lieu of which Hajj Amin in exile in Lebanon remained nominally in overall charge. The same accusations of corruption emerged as they had in Palestine, with rebels in Damascus complaining about AHC favouritism and its alleged misappropriation of money.[219] Meanwhile, Yusuf Sa'id Abu Durra and 'Abd al-Rahim al-Hajj Muhammad both found excuses for not returning to Palestine, not least as by 1938 effective British Army counter-rebel sweeps made Palestine a very dangerous place for insurgents.[220] Damascus was never a depot and safe base area for the revolt. There were shortages of ammunition, uniforms, and recruits, while the British made smuggling into Palestine what was available very difficult with added patrols on both side of the border – convincing the French to cover their side of the frontier – in addition to building a border 'Tegart' fence and forts across northern Palestine by August 1938 alongside internal road building programmes.[221] MacKereth wrote to the Colonial Office in October 1937 about the issue of border control and he observed that Syrian gendarmes were now arresting rebels trying to cross the border, while the Sûreté was warning rebel leaders in the country and that this 'has had a chilling effect on their ardour' to go to Palestine.[222] Wavell noted that the French had 'played up very well' during operations near the border in late 1937 and 'turned out quite a small army the other day to act as "stops" for a drive we were making.'[223] Jews noted that the Lebanese had increased

---

[217] Rashid Khalidi, *Palestinian Identity: The Construction of Modern National Consciousness* (New York, NY: Columbia University Press, 1997), p. 189.

[218] Political Report Syria No. 11, Damascus, 11 February 1939, FO371/23276, p. 250, TNA.

[219] Ibid.

[220] Ibid.

[221] Charles Tegart: Memoir of an Indian Policeman, by K. F. Tegart (wife), pp. 247ff, Mss Eur C.235/2, IOR.

[222] MacKereth to Secretary of State for Foreign Affairs (Eden), 25 October 1937, L/PS/12/3346: Disturbances and Anti-Jewish Riots, IOR.

[223] Wavell to Deverell (CIGS), 24 November 1937, Palestine, 1937–38 Volume, Wavell Papers, POH.

their gendarmes on the border by June 1938, while by the spring of 1939, the French were putting smugglers before military courts.[224] As the Damascus Consulate informed the Foreign Office in September 1938, 'MacKereth's efforts here during the past two years have been successful in greatly limiting active Syrian participation.'[225] MacKereth worked behind the scenes to pressure the French to limit rebel activities, setting up for himself a branch of the intelligence service that became 'one of the most successful [or "informed"] assets of the authorities in the Land of Israel,' noted Jewish files, and with 'extraordinary' sources of information, emphasising joint British–Jewish action.[226] The French in Syria arrested key rebel leaders in Syria such as Muhammad 'Izzat Darwaza at the behest of the British, the two parties coming together over the impending war in Europe.[227] MacKereth worked with the French as with the Jews. His independent, 'forceful style' that called for 'direct action' forged British strategy, someone described by General Wavell as a 'live wire' but who 'produces very good information,' and worthy of a lengthy study.[228] He 'bombarded' the Chief Secretary in Palestine, William Battershill, with telegrams offering 'gratuitous advice on how the situation in Palestine should be properly dealt with. He overstepped all limits … He is working hard for us in Damascus but should stick to his own business and not intervene via the Foreign Office.'[229] MacKereth had attached to him in Damascus Palestine police liaison and he also met with senior police officer advisers such as Sir Charles Tegart and future MI5 Director General Sir David Petrie.[230] MacKereth wrote to the Palestine High Commissioner after the revolt about his 'intimate cooperation' with Palestine CID that was now at a 'natural end,

---

[224] Sasson to Shertok (Jerusalem), 28 June 1938, S25/3639-18, File: Letters from Syria, 1937–38 and 1946, CZA; Report of Visit to Beirut and Damascus, Epstein to Dr Joseph, 1 March 1939, S25/5570–91, CZA.

[225] Ogden (British Consulate Damascus) to L. Baggallay (FO), 8 September 1938, FO 371/21881, p. 235, TNA.

[226] Report titled Visit to Damascus and Beirut between 1–5 April 1938, by Reuven Zaslani and Elias Sasson to Moshe Shertok, S25/3639-8/9, File: Letters from Syria, 1937–38 and 1946, CZA; overview see Martin Thomas, *Empires of Intelligence: Security Services and Colonial Disorders after 1914* (Berkeley, CA: University of California Press, 2008), pp. 254–55.

[227] Darwaza, *Mudhakkirat Muhammad 'Izzat Darwaza*, iii, pp. 840–47.

[228] J. S. Bennett, Handwritten Minute, 28 February 1938, CO733/368/4, p. 4. Wavell to Haining (DMO), 5 November 1937, Palestine, 1937–38 Volume, Wavell Papers, POH. Fry and Rabinovich cover MacKereth's role in their *Despatches from Damascus*.

[229] Letter, Battershill to Wauchope, 6 November 1937, Battershill Papers, MSS. Brit. Emp. S. 467, Box 10, File 4, WL.

[230] Memorandum summarising the talks on the 11 and 12 January [1938] in Jerusalem between Sir C. Tegart, Sir D. Petrie and Lt-Colonel G. MacKereth on terrorist activities in Palestine organised from Syria, by G. MacKereth (British Consulate, Damascus), 31 January 1938, FO 371/21872, TNA.

I shall wind up this branch of my work and then instruct Mr Harris, who was lent to this Consulate by the Inspector-General of the Palestine Police in May 1938, to return to Jerusalem.'[231] MacKereth talked also of the 'unusual nature' of his work, 'necessitated in the first place by the unusual nature of the relations existing between the French mandatory authorities and the Syrian administration,' a reference to the (unratified by France) 1936 Franco-Syrian treaty that curtailed French intervention in Syrian domestic affairs, at least until September 1939 when France instituted military rule.[232]

MacKereth paid or bribed Syrian Government officials to clamp down on or dissuade dissident Palestinian forces and for information that he could use to fight the rebels. The Colonial Office noted how one of MacKereth's suggestions for Syria would be 'difficult to contemplate' as it would be 'authorizing what would amount to wholesale bribery of the principal ministers of a neighbouring state,' with the added problem that said ministers 'would more likely pocket their retaining fees and allow things to go on as before.'[233] The Foreign Office faintly ignored MacKereth's clandestine activities while also faintly admonishing him: 'we have, as you know, always felt uneasy about your special work on behalf of the Palestine Government.'[234] The Foreign Office caveated MacKereth's work, warning him about the 'inconvenience' to which he would 'be personally put' if his clandestine work became public: 'the disclosure of certain unusual methods forced upon us by the inability, or unwillingness, of the French to keep adequate check on the Syrian authorities in the pay of, and sympathy with, the Palestinian insurrectionists.'[235] A Foreign Office note on one of MacKereth's letters recorded 'the monthly subvention which was paid by the Palestine Government through Colonel MacKereth to Jamil Mardam [Bey],' the Syrian Prime Minister during the revolt, payments that 'ceased with the disappearance of the latter from the scene' in 1939.[236] The Palestine High Commissioner wrote to MacKereth after the revolt asking for the return of £P.747 left over from the latter's counter-propaganda campaign, to be remitted via police CID in Jerusalem.[237] The Foreign Office shilly-shallied through all of this, worried that it 'should be assuming

---

[231] Letter, Mackereth (Damascus) to MacMichael (High Commissioner, Palestine) [Report 112], 5 September 1939, FO 371/23251, TNA.

[232] Ibid.

[233] Handwritten minute by J. S. Bennett, 28 February 1938, CO 733/368/4, p. 4, TNA.

[234] Letter, Baggallay (FO) to MacKereth (Damascus), 30 November 1939, FO 371/23251, TNA.

[235] Letter, MacKereth (Damascus) to Baxter (FO), 3 October 1939, FO 371/23251, TNA.

[236] Minute, 2 November 1939 to MacKereth (Damascus) to Baxter (FO), 3 October 1939, FO 371/23251, TNA.

[237] MacMichael to MacKereth, 15 November 1939, FO371/23281, TNA.

a grave responsibility' if it 'did not instruct MacKereth to abandon his practice of paying a monthly subvention to the Syrian Prime Minister.'[238] That the Palestine Government was paying Syrian political leaders proves the extent of British secret operations. Afterwards, the Palestine High Commissioner thanked MacKereth for 'the special duties which you have been so good as to undertake[, which] have been of the highest value to this Government, and it is doubtful whether the promised cooperation of the French civil and military authorities ... could entirely replace the special assistance which you have been giving to the administration.'[239] MacKereth's spies supplied useful information, as when Adil al Arslan (Syrian Druze notable leader Amir 'Adil Arslan) came to Damascus to see Palestinians there, one of whom, Muin al Madi (Syrian-based Palestinian nationalist Mu'in al-Madi), 'complained of the increasing difficulty of getting recruits and other effective action against the Palestine Government, owing to the terrifying effect of the Military Courts.'[240] MacKereth made representations to the French about stories of British atrocities emanating from rebel propaganda offices in Beirut.[241] MacKereth's drive impressed Jewish agents in Syria and he and the Jews moved in lockstep, the latter worried about any repercussions for Syria's Jews if the enemy learnt of the link.[242] The two groups combined to block rebel attempts to purchase uniforms. When Jewish agents Reuven Zaslani and Elias Sasson went to Damascus, 3–4 April 1938, MacKereth told them that there was a 'crisis' among the bands, including with ammunition supply, and that they were struggling to smuggle weapons into Palestine.[243] Jewish agents went to Lebanon to complain to the head of the French Army's department for political espionage about Hajj Amin and to liaise with the first secretary to the French High Commissioner.[244] Operatives from

---

[238] Letter, Baggallay (FO) to Shuckburgh (FO), 10 November 1939, FO 371/23251, TNA.
[239] Letter, MacMichael (High Commissioner, Jerusalem) to MacKereth (Damascus), 26 September 1939, FO 371/23251, TNA.
[240] MacKereth (Syria) to Kingsley-Heath (Jerusalem), 30 December 1937, FO 371/21872, p. 86, TNA.
[241] Eileen Byrne, 'Palestine as a News-Story: Axis Initiatives and the British Response, 1936–39' (MLitt Thesis: University of Oxford, 1985), pp. 108–16.
[242] Report titled Visit to Damascus and Beirut between 1–5 April 1938, by Reuven Zaslani and Elias Sasson to Moshe Shertok, S25/3639-8/9, File: Letters from Syria, 1937–38 and 1946, CZA.
[243] Report titled Visit to Damascus and Beirut between 1–5 April 1938, by Reuven Zaslani and Elias Sasson to Moshe Shertok, S25/3639-9/10, File: Letters from Syria, 1937–38 and 1946, CZA.
[244] Visit to Lebanon, 12–15 March 1938, Epstein to Shertok, 29 March 1938, S25/5570-124, CZA; Report by Epstein of Visit to Syria and Lebanon, 10–17 December 1937, S25/5570-125/134, CZA.

the Jewish Agency's Political Department made numerous visits to Syria and Lebanon during the revolt to see Arabs, Druze, the French, and MacKereth. These were mostly Sasson, Eliyahu Epstein, and Zaslani, and whose multiple hotel receipts from Damascus and Beirut in the first half of 1938 show how busy they were in this regard, including a trip to Egypt in late 1938; none was a heavy drinker as they submitted only one receipt for a bottle of wine.[245] Sasson made payments on these trips to an 'AA,' a Mohamed Faris (£15), and to Arabic newspapers (£23).[246] The Jews sent 'AA' into Galilee from Syria with an insurgent band where he took pictures and reported back, and talked elsewhere about 'our sources' in the rebel movement.[247] The Jews had an agent in Amman, too, an 'MA' who worked with an 'AI,' who seemed to be a high official in the Transjordan Government.[248] As British intelligence widened and improved 'as of late,' the British authorities persuaded the French to keep a watch for smuggling and under French pressure Aleppo-based lawyer and smuggler Shafiq Suleymen fled to Iraq.[249] The British-led Transjordanian Arab Legion blocked smuggling routes through Transjordan and intercepted an arms convoy of 8,000 rounds and 200 explosive shells, one that bands in Palestine deemed to be a 'great loss.'[250]

With field bands unable to put pressure on Hajj Amin, coordination of operations and strategy was poor. Hajj Amin had formed the Central Committee of the Jihad shortly after he escaped Palestine in October 1937. The Central Committee tried to organise the revolt, but local peasant-based commanders were reluctant to follow orders from abroad. In late 1938, commanders in Palestine formed the Bureau of the Arab Revolt in Palestine. This organisation included local leaders such as 'Abd al-Rahim al-Hajj Muhammad, 'Arif 'Abd al-Raziq, Yusuf Sa'id Abu Durra, and Hasan Salama.[251] Neither the Central Committee nor the Bureau was much good. The Bureau was 'stillborn from the outset,' not least as it did not represent the Jerusalem–Hebron bands, while

---

[245] Hotel receipts in S1/284, CZA.
[246] Ibid.
[247] Report from Damascus to Sasson [from AA], 25 May 1938, S25/3639-14/15, CZA; File: Letters from Syria, 1937–38 and 1946, S25/3639, CZA; Sasson to Shertok, 18 January 1938, S25/3639-124, CZA.
[248] Information from the Arab Office, Reports of the Situations and Gangs, Communist Activity, Polish and Italians, 22 April–31 July 1936: 8/GENERAL/39, HA.
[249] Report titled Visit to Damascus and Beirut between 1–5 April 1938, by Reuven Zaslani and Elias Sasson to Moshe Shertok, S25/3639-9/10, File: Letters from Syria, 1937–38 and 1946, CZA.
[250] Ibid.
[251] Nevo, 'Palestinian–Arab Violent Activity,' pp. 180–82.

'Abd al-Qadir al-Husayni (of the Husayni family) resisted his subordination to peasant commanders, as he had done before in 1936.[252] 'At best the Bureau served as a limited coordination body,' notes Yehoshua Porath.[253] The head of the Bureau should have changed in rotation but two commanders competed for the role, al-Hajj Muhammad and 'Abd al-Raziq, the British relentlessly hunting both men. 'Each believed that the crown belonged to him.'[254] Recruitment fell as battle casualties from December 1937 to March 1938 caused a 'crisis of enlistment' in Syria, not least as many of those wounded and killed (some 30 per cent) were Syrian.[255] Hajj Amin anticipated weapons shipment from Saudi Arabia and officers from Iraq to come via Transjordan.[256] It is not clear that such supplies arrived. As the numbers of Syrian recruits tapered off, Hajj Amin looked further afield and sent special emissaries including Akram Zu'aytir to Iraq to recruit Iraqis for the rebellion, intending to widen the conflict.[257] Without strong external support, Hajj Amin gradually reduced the materiel that he sent to Palestine and he urged bands to be much more sparing of resources and to save money and be financially prudent prior to the big effort that never materialised. Financial parsimony translated into bands in Palestine extorting villagers. Perhaps because of MacKereth's entreaties, the Syrian opposition put pressure on Muhammad al-Ashmar, a Syrian military leader who had fought with al-Qawuqji as his Syrian company commander in 1936, not to go back to Palestine, even though Hajj Amin had offered him up to £P.3,600.[258] The Government in Palestine sent men to Cairo to see a Syrian opposition leader there to persuade him to convince his followers in Syria not to join the revolt.[259] Other Syrian leaders refused requests for help from Hajj Amin. Interestingly, rebel high command in Damascus appointed better-educated political commissar-style deputy commanders in December 1938 to tackle the problems of criminality and control of operational

[252] Porath, *The Palestinian Arab National Movement*, pp. 244–45.
[253] Ibid.
[254] Appendix: Explanatory Notes, Captured and Translated Arabic Material with Commentary, pp. 144–45, Wingate Papers, Microfilm M2313, BL.
[255] Report titled Visit to Damascus and Beirut between 1–5 April 1938, by Reuven Zaslani and Elias Sasson to Moshe Shertok, S25/3639-10, File: Letters from Syria, 1937–38 and 1946, CZA.
[256] Ibid.
[257] Report titled Visit to Damascus and Beirut between 1–5 April 1938, by Reuven Zaslani and Elias Sasson to Moshe Shertok, S25/3639-10-11, File: Letters from Syria, 1937–38 and 1946, CZA.
[258] Report titled Visit to Damascus and Beirut between 1–5 April 1938, by Reuven Zaslani and Elias Sasson to Moshe Shertok, S25/3639-10, File: Letters from Syria, 1937–38 and 1946, CZA.
[259] Ibid.

field leaders. Thus, Wasif Kamal and Mamduh al-Sukhn from Nablus served as deputies for 'Abd al-Rahim al-Hajj Muhammad; Farid Ya'ish of Nablus and Mustafa Tahir from Jaffa (both teachers) were deputies for 'Arif 'Abd al-Raziq; while al-Hajj Khalid al-Farid (a journalist) from Jaffa and Amin al-Sharqawi of Haifa were the commissars for Abu Durra.[260] The British arrested Farid Ya'ish a week after starting in post, while the other *politruks* arrived too late to stem the tide of British military success. The rebels needed to have deployed such cadres back in April 1936.

The key variable for both sides was the reaction of the French-dominated administrations in Syria and Lebanon. The Lebanese Government told Hajj Amin that it wanted him to stay in Lebanon to prove that it offered sanctuary to nationalists such as him, despite Hajj Amin wanting to move to Damascus. Rebels sought support from Iraq and looked to Transjordan as a base for operations, moves that Britain countered as it controlled both countries.[261] The French arrested Fakhri 'Abd al-Hadi in November 1937 for smuggling, after which the Syrian 'security department' got him to sign a written declaration 'that he will not continue to work in these types of matters [weapons smuggling] and the security department informed him that if he were to break this agreement they would expel him from Syria. The security department sent this written consent to the Lebanese security department,' after which 'Abd al-Hadi complained to Syrian politicians.[262] MacKereth obviously had his eye on 'Abd al-Hadi and called on a Syrian 'delegate' to have 'Abd al-Hadi 'closely watched' in October 1937; MacKereth later helped turn 'Abd al-Hadi to work for the British.[263] The British sent spies from Palestine into the rebel camp in Damascus, with one Jaffan, a Salah al-Din al-Mukhtar, doing so under the cover of renewing his passport, although the rebels knew of this as they had a source inside the Syrian secret service.[264] The British worked with the *Yishuv* and Jewish agents who tracked the movements of 'Abd al-Hadi between Beirut and Damascus. *Mizrahi* (or 'Arabised' *Mista'arvim*) Jews moved easily in Arab countries, with Eliyahu Sasson welcomed with 'warmth and affection' in Beirut: 'No door there was locked for him.'[265] Meanwhile, the AHC in

---

[260] Porath, *The Palestinian Arab National Movement*, p. 258.

[261] Note, Despatch from Syria' by Sasson, 28 October 1937, S25/3639-61, CZA.

[262] Note, Despatch from Syria' by Sasson, 24 November 1937, S25/3639-83, CZA.

[263] MacKereth to Secretary of State for Foreign Affairs (Eden), 25 October 1937, L/PS/12/3346: Disturbances and Anti-Jewish Riots, IOR.

[264] Note, Despatch from Syria by Sasson, 24 November 1937, S25/3639-83, CZA.

[265] Sasson to Shertok, 18 January 1938, S25/3639-124, CZA; Abigail Jacobson and Moshe Naor, *Oriental Neighbors: Middle Eastern Jews and Arabs in Mandatory Palestine* (Waltham, MA: Brandeis University Press, 2016), pp. 64, 178ff.

exile made little attempt to resolve inter-band disputes, absurdly concluding 'that its absolute authority over the individual guerrilla leaders
would be greatly weakened if they were united under one leadership. They
are also believed to be of the opinion that the unification of the bands
under one supreme commander would be of no advantage in the sporadic fighting taking place in Palestine.'[266] Elements of the Nashashibi-led
National Defence Party based in Syria intervened, 'taking every opportunity of discrediting the Majlis [the Council, Husayni-led] leaders, and
are now reported to have the support of some of the Abdel Hadis.'[267]
The Husayni camp made counter claims of treachery, while someone
accused 'Abd al-Hadi of being 'an agent for the Government and the
Amir Abdullah.'[268] Fakhri Nashashibi attempted to establish an alternative AHC in Beirut.[269] Other opponents of Hajj Amin threatened an
armed campaign against him.[270] At the same time, in October 1938 at the
high point of insurgency, the Husayni-led *Majlis* tried to replace *Istiqlalist*
'Abd al-Rahim al-Hajj Muhammad with the pro-Hajj Amin rebel field
commander 'Arif 'Abd al-Raziq, worried that al-Hajj Muhammad might
throw in his lot with 'Abd al-Hadi who by this point was working with
the British.[271] Rebels kept money donated by villagers, while band leader
al-Hajj Muhammad 'ceased' sending money to Damascus.[272] Splits
between those doing the grunt work against British forces and those
safely ensconced in Damascus widened in the second phase of the revolt.
Thus, al-Hajj Muhammad told Damascus command how the 'shoe of the
most insignificant mujahid is nobler than all the members of the Society,
who have indulged in pleasure while their brethren suffer in the mountains.'[273] Instead of uniting mujahideen to their commanders, the fragile,
corrupted command and force structures described here cleaved motley
bands of fighters in the field from their leaders and from the people, and
as the revolt unwittingly devolved violence to the people it could not halt
the endemic banditry that consumed the revolt and further alienated
the masses. Rebels were without a central command, had no cadre of
effective field leaders such as Vo Nguyen Giap in Vietnam, and were
without a commander-in-chief, excepting Hajj Amin who was no Ho

---

[266] Political Report Syria No. 8, Damascus, 10 January 1939, FO371/23276, p. 183, TNA.
[267] CID, Jerusalem, by Deputy IG A. J. Kingsley-Heath, Intelligence Summary, 73/38, 18
October 1938, L/PS/12/3343, IOR.
[268] Ibid.
[269] Entry, 7 January 1938, Darwaza, *Mudhakkirat Muhammad 'Izzat Darwaza*, iii, p. 179.
[270] CID, Jerusalem, by Deputy IG A. J. Kingsley-Heath, Intelligence Summary, 73/38, 18
October 1938, L/PS/12/3343, IOR.
[271] Ibid.
[272] Ibid.
[273] Ibid.

Chi Minh or Le Duan. Jewish intelligence concluded that 'one cannot talk of an Arab Military Organisation' but instead there was one in the 'oriental style which cannot be compared with occidental conceptions, because they are of two separate worlds, that cannot be joined,' but the precise issue was Palestinian military effectiveness.[274] When set alongside the flawed rebel decision-making and strategies outlined in the previous chapter, it is surprising that the revolt lasted as long as it did, and is partly explained by Britain's willingness initially to push for a political ceasefire in October 1936 and then the distraction of the Czechoslovakia crisis up to September 1938. The revolt's fury is testament to Palestinians' profound anger at British rule and Jewish immigration but without effective networks of rebellion, their passion stood no chance against Britain's eight powerful, overlapping coercive-violence spheres, the subject matter for the rest of this book:

(1) The **colonial legal machinery** of the emergency state, as examined in Chapter 2 and which informs the analysis of military operations and pacification in Chapter 5 and Chapter 6, and is the legal use of violence that is the obverse to the illegal violence examined in Chapter 8;

(2) The **military power of the security forces**, notably the Army but also the police, the focus of Chapter 5 and Chapter 6;

(3) **Population-centric pacification** driven by the emergency state, built on the ordinances and laws as discussed in Chapter 2, and enforced by the Army, the subject of Chapter 6;

(4) The **information-intelligence gathering systems** of the British colonial state and military forces, supported by the Jews and Palestinian agents, examined in Chapter 7;

(5) The **collaboration and cooperation** of local Palestinians and Jews, and the creation of pro-Government anti-rebel auxiliary forces to fight and confuse insurgents, the topic for Chapter 7;

(6) The **terror of dirty wars** of torture and assassination, the focus of Chapter 8;

(7) The **prison system** and the use of indefinite detention, assessed in Chapter 6;

(8) Britain's **political-diplomatic war** against the rebels and its co-option of other Arab leaders to collaborate and help suppress the Arab revolt briefly discussed in the Afterword on the relationship of policy to violence.

---

[274] Appendix: Explanatory Notes, Captured and Translated Arabic Material with Commentary, p. 157, Wingate Papers, Microfilm M2313, BL.

5 The Regiments Arrive

Military Traditions

This chapter on Army operations against rebel bands should be read as one with the next on the impact of legal-civil pacification measures. British counter-insurgency yoked military operations and civil pacification. The Army enforced pacification with punitive measures against civilians while its hard-edged 'enemy-centric' operations against insurgents simultaneously targeted complicit Palestinians and so reinforced civil-based population-centric pacification.[1] Military operations and civil pacification were two sides of the same coin, it being impossible to pacify the population without the presence of soldiers who enforced the fines, curfews, corvée, detentions, and house destructions, while military operations on their own would fail without the emergency state's supportive civil-legal superstructure. The Army worked with the colonial civil service to ensure victory, if uneasily at times as the military demanded rapid and forceful action. Counter-insurgency was an administrative war as it was a shooting one, and it demanded civil–military partnership.[2] Army operations in Palestine re-established order for civil administration and the threat of punishment visibly showed the populace who was in charge. The Army and colonial state made terror and poverty rather than resistance the primary issues for Palestinians. By the creation of insecurity, security forces ensured imperial security. Predatory bandit gangs did the same, turning Palestinians from resistors towards passivity, what has been called *attentisme* ('wait and see') in occupied France after 1940 where people survived violence and hunger by adopting a passive acceptance of the changing social and political order; others

---

[1] Julian Paget, *Counter-Insurgency Operations: Techniques of Guerrilla Warfare* (New York, NY: Walker, 1967), p. 169; David Kilcullen, *Counterinsurgency* (London: Hurst, 2010), p. 10.
[2] See Robert Thompson *Make for the Hills: Memories of Far Eastern Wars* (London: Leo Cooper, 1989), p. 127 for discussion of this issue during the US war in Vietnam.

collaborated.[3] Re-establishing order in Palestine was mostly through punishment. The Army's reward for accepting official order was moderation of military punitive raids and provision of licensed shotguns to *mukhtars* for use against rebels. Disarming and rearming so that villagers could protect themselves rumbled on into the 1940s.[4] The Army gripped executive functions in late 1938 just when it had the men after the Munich settlement to swamp Palestine with troops. The Army executed directly some parts of pacification such as house demolitions, effected by its sappers, and discussed in this chapter as a kinetic operation. Moreover, as the Army assumed civil authority, its soldiers ordered and enforced measures such as fining and sentencing where they had previously aided the civil powers with such things. This chapter thus returns to matters of civil–military relations during counter-insurgency through its study of the establishment of military courts and military rule, introduced in Chapter 2, and of how the military supported the civil authorities in times of imperial civil unrest, as an 'aid to the civil power' in the language of the time, and vice versa.[5] What made the British so effective in counter-insurgency, more especially against as badly organised a foe as the Palestinians, was the Army's application of measured force in combination with the civil-legal foundations of the colonial state. The consequent friction between colonial administrators and soldiers retarded excessive violence and this strengthened counter-insurgency as it kept open politico-diplomatic negotiating tracks, it elicited collaborators, it made rebels and their violence less attractive, it supported intelligence gathering, and it allowed villagers escaping the destruction to proclaim forms of neutrality.

The Palestinian and British relationship to violence was fundamentally different. Palestinian force lacked central structure, with men on the ground setting its limits. The British by contrast shaped their violence and they agreed permitted levels of force that met policy goals. British security forces inflicted horrible abuses – beating men to death, leaving them to die in wired cages in the sun, illegally executing people, blowing up villagers trapped in vehicles on mines, torturing and whipping people,

[3] C. Lloyd, *Collaboration and Resistance in Occupied France: Representing Treason and Sacrifice* (Houndmills: Palgrave, 2001), pp. viii–ix.
[4] Personal Diary, 1940–April 1941, 16 and 26 November 1940, Briance Papers, BP.
[5] *War Office, Issued by Command of the Army Council, Manual of Military Law* (London, 1929); *War Office, By Command of the Army Council, Notes on Imperial Policing, 1934* (London: War Office, 30 January 1934); *War Office, By Command of the Army Council, 5 August 1937, Duties in the Aid of the Civil Power* (London: War Office, 1937); Simeon Shoul, 'Soldiers, Riots, and Aid to the Civil Power in India, Egypt and Palestine, 1919–39' (Doctoral Thesis: University of London, 2006).

demolishing houses, stealing and destroying effects – but the British high command controlled excessive violence and de-escalated, if imperfectly, and it reined in its men as needed. Security forces hard wired the link between politics and violence by grading their use of violence to have moral effect. Good intelligence helped to target operations. The Army used necessary force, and this could be minimal or maximal, legal or illegal, but it was always exemplary as it sent a message to, say, a village by favouring or punishing it. Counter-insurgency blurred the line between legal and illegal violence. The draconian legal parts of the system alongside rank-and-file anger at rebel attacks that killed comrades encouraged wilder illegal violence but military sensibilities, regimental differences, and civil pressures constrained such rough-and-ready reprisals that anyway reinforced the exemplary 'counter-terror' element to heavier uses of legal force.[6] Soldiers on the ground saw their job in Palestine as 'to bash anybody on the head who broke the law, and if he didn't want to be bashed on the head then he had to be shot. It may sound brutal but in fact it was a reasonably nice, simple objective and the soldiers understood it,' and such things were usually legal.[7] The high command tolerated to a point or ignored semi-legal or illegal abuse that seemed justified or inevitable and was limited to one operation, as when tracker dogs sealed the fate of Silwan village near Jerusalem by leading police and Black Watch troops there after the assassination of two of the regiment's men by the Jaffa Gate. Soldiers killed some twenty villagers at al-Bassa, after a rebel mine nearby killed four soldiers, a reactive attack to a rebel one as at Silwan but this time at a distant location by the Lebanese border. The area's divisional commander, Montgomery, protected the 2nd Royal Ulster Rifles battalion involved from later criticism (Montgomery arrived in Palestine to take command shortly after the al-Bassa incident). Civil officials made extensive compensation payments to Halhul villagers after Black Watch operations to punish and gather weapons there left up to fifteen men to die in open cages in the summer sun.[8] At Ijzim, as in so many other places, complaints on brutality fizzled out. Senior officers

---

[6] Charles Townshend, 'In Aid of the Civil Power: Britain, Ireland and Palestine, 1916–1948,' in Daniel Marston and Carter Malkasian (eds), *Counterinsurgency in Modern Warfare* (Oxford: Osprey, 2008), p. 32.

[7] Bredin, 4550, p. 10, IWMSA.

[8] 'Palestine: The First Intifada' (BBC: Timewatch, 27 March 1991); Allegations of Ill-treatment of Arabs by British Crown Forces in Palestine (translated from the Arabic by Frances Newton, 19 June 1939), J&EM Papers, GB165-0161, Box 65, File 5, p. 145, MEC; 'Palestine: Promises and Rebellion' (Thames TV, 1977–78); Matthew Hughes, 'The Practice and Theory of British Counter-Insurgency: The Histories of the Atrocities at the Palestinian Villages of al-Bassa and Halhul, 1938–39,' *Small Wars and Insurgencies* 20/3–4 (September–December 2009), pp. 528–50.

objected to the excessive and irregular violence of Orde Wingate's British–Jewish Special Night Squads from the summer of 1938, ensuring Wingate's removal six months later.[9] There are two stories to tell, both true in varying measure: the official one of restraint and legality, and a darker tale glimpsed through deep archival mining. For instance, returning to Silwan, GOC Wavell remarked on the restraint shown by the Black Watch there – his own regiment, after all – while admitting that a suspect died 'falling over a cliff.'[10] The 'prompt measures against Silwan will have done good' as it was a 'bad village which has given trouble before,' he informed London in his official report.[11] Yet, the private diary of a North Staffordshire Regiment officer tells a different tale, recording how the Black Watch beat to death twelve Palestinians in Silwan with rifle butts after the deaths of their two comrades, left with their kilts raised and buttocks exposed, and 'an insult the local Arabs suffered for.'[12] Or as another officer put it, high command gave the 'Jocks' eight hours to 'search' Silwan without rifles: 'a lot of Arabs were very sorry that it had happened.'[13]

The story of what really happened in villages and towns across Palestine during the revolt is opaque, but the argument here is that the British directed the bulk of their violence at property not people, and they restrained illegal physical abuse.[14] The British use of force was political, discriminate, and built on law, so they needed less of it and the 'awfulness was less awful.'[15] For other colonial powers force was political only through disproportionate application of extreme force. Discrimination meant that violence in Palestine was proportional,[16] measured crudely in comparative ratios of dead soldiers to civilians, and geographically to victims near an insurgent attack. Thus, German forces legally killed over

---

[9] Matthew Hughes, 'Terror in Galilee: British–Jewish Collaboration and the Special Night Squads in Palestine during the Arab Revolt, 1938–39', *Journal of Imperial and Commonwealth History* 43/4 (December 2015), pp. 590–610.

[10] John Connell, *Wavell: Scholar and Soldier. To June 1941* (London: Collins, 1964), p. 194; E. and A. Linklater, *The Black Watch* (London: Barrie and Jenkins, 1977), p. 175; *Haaretz* [*The Land*] (Tel Aviv) (7–8 November 1937).

[11] Wavell to Haining (DMO), 6 November 1937, Palestine, 1937–38 Volume, Wavell Papers, POH.

[12] Diary, 7 November 1937, Maj White, Relating to Service in Palestine, 1974-04-24-8 [now 7404/24], NAM; Letter, Ted Horne to Author, 5 September 2009.

[13] Typed Memoir, Pieces of War, Simonds Papers, 08/46/1, p. 148, IWMD.

[14] Charles Townshend, *Britain's Civil Wars: Counterinsurgency in the Twentieth Century* (London: Faber and Faber, 1986), p. 19.

[15] Matthew Hughes, 'The Banality of Brutality: British Armed Forces and the Repression of the Arab Revolt in Palestine, 1936–39,' *English Historical Review* 124/507 (April 2009), p. 354.

[16] Or 'proportionate' but this has unhelpful connotations of being somehow justified.

a period of several months some 1,300 Czechs in 1942 in retaliation for the death of SS commander Reinhard Heydrich, 340 from the distant village of Lidice that not even a tracker dog had marked as guilty, and they sent many more to concentration camps; at Oradour-sur-Glane in France in 1944, German troops killed 642 villagers as retaliation for unrelated acts of resistance elsewhere. The French Army's *ratissage* ('raking over') search and sweep operation following the Sétif massacre in Algeria in 1945 killed between ten and 450 Algerians for every dead French settler. American soldiers killed over 400 Vietnamese civilians at My Lai village in 1969, scalping and gang raping victims, as a reprisal for booby traps or more likely because such outrages were common across Vietnam at the time.[17] By contrast, British soldiers illegally killed over a period of one or two days between five and six Palestinians for each soldier killed at Silwan and al-Bassa. British police in civilian clothes kept to the ratio of about six-to-one when they killed seven villagers at Miska on 27 May 1938 for the death of a comrade, as well as torturing ('Turkish' method) and executing the day before four captured rebels 'when "interrogation" had been completed,' it was alleged.[18] The British-run Special Night Squads claimed to decimate villages but they more usually killed three or four people in a single village raid.[19] Sexual violence by Servicemen was limited or non-existent.

British soldiers after the death of a comrade sometimes did nothing or they might smash up a village without killing anyone, their violence immediate and mechanistic, sometimes personal but *pace* the underlying racism of empire not viscerally ideological, or this at least was how they saw themselves: 'British soldiery were very bad at brutality; we used it half-heartedly or even not at all.'[20] Soldiers went home and they had no skin in the game; they were not settlers. When rebels wounded two soldiers, the Army took 'drastic steps, not according to their custom' at a local village noted the Jews, such things being aberrations.[21] When local Arab women came to see Ms Hulbert, a British female teacher in Bir

---

[17] For the latest word on the brutality at My Lai and elsewhere, see Howard Jones, *My Lai, Vietnam, 1968, and the Descent into Darkness* (New York, NY: Oxford University Press, 2017), *passim* and Max Hastings, 'Wrath of the Centurions,' *London Review of Books* 40/2 (25 January 2018), pp. 19–22.

[18] Conduct of Police, Miska [spelt Miske in some of the file] Case, 1938, CO 733/371/3, TNA; PS to Letter, Richardson (Solicitor, Jaffa) to Lees, 6 April 1939, Lees Papers, 5/9, LHCMA; Letter, Street to Father, 29 May 1938, Street Papers, File: Letters Home, LHCMA.

[19] Hughes, 'Terror in Galilee,' pp. 590–610.

[20] Bredin, 4550, p. 11, IWMSA; Hackett, 4527, p. 50, IWMSA.

[21] Appendix: Explanatory Notes, Captured and Translated Arabic Material with Commentary, p. 161, Wingate Papers, Microfilm M2313, BL.

Zayt, crying and complaining about the Army detaining their menfolk for road repairs:

'They are beating them! The soldiers are beating our men!' 'Beating!' exclaimed Miss Hulbert. 'How do you mean – like this?' giving an energetic pantomime of two-handed whacking with a stick. 'Oh no no!' replied the women. 'Only like this' – demonstrating the mildest of pats and pushes; obviously no more than would be necessary to show the men where to go or what to do – not surprising when soldiers and villagers cannot speak each other's language.[22]

Soldiers and junior officers in Palestine were disinterested in the Palestinian–Zionist conflict ('at that time, in the Army at least there was almost total indifference in and ignorance of political affairs') while many had pity for the Palestinians ('a gentlemanly easy-going community ... the average soldier rather liked the Arab, preferring him generally to the Jew'), unlike French officer Paul Aussaresses' chilling comment in Algeria that 'I think I really forgot what having any pity meant,' amidst systemic mass abuse of local people.[23] 'What the devil is wrong with these Jews and Arabs that they can't live decent peaceful lives, and allow us to go on soldiering nice and quietly in Aldershot? Why?' asked an Army lecturer disinterestedly.[24] Such attitudes influenced (or reflected) soldiers' behaviour. While the British high command, genuinely or otherwise, deplored and curtailed illegal violence, punitive massacres were the norm with German pacification, as gross torture was with the French Army in Algeria in the 1950s, for one. Britain's systemic emergency state legally suppressed subject populations, and this achieved the desired political effect with relatively low casualty rates on both sides and without the use of systematic unsightly deadly force. Individual illegal military measures by soldiers killed handfuls and not hundreds of Palestinians, with al-Bassa's twenty dead the worst single atrocity that this author can uncover of unarmed civilians. That said, the cumulative number of Palestinian dead at the hands of the British could be as high as 7,727, as Appendix B proves. What is certain is that security forces in Palestine made violence politically purposeful, turning it on and off depending on troop numbers and local needs, without leaving the tap fully open. The Army had been pacifying subject peoples for hundreds of years and the

---

[22] Diary, Wilson Papers, GB165-0302, p. 27, MEC.
[23] Rex King-Clark, *Free for a Blast* (London: Grenville, 1988), pp. 146, 152; Haigh, p. 5, 44/50/05, IWMSA. *Je crois que j'ai oublié ce que c'était que la pitié* in Paul Aussaresses, *Service Spéciaux: Algérie, 1955–57* (Paris: Perrin, 2001), p. 64.
[24] Lecture on Palestine to 5th Inf Bde Aldershot, 25 August 1938, Functions of the British in Palestine, Palestine Box, RUR.

first part of this chapter introduces the traditions and regulations that guided soldiers on operations in Palestine.

The Army had always targeted non-combatants during military campaigns, especially where it had also to suppress the local populace. After the Scottish highlanders' uprising of 1745, the campaign ended 'as a victorious campaign against mountaineers must always end, in the hunting of fugitives, the burning of villages, and the destruction of crops. To this work, the troops were now let loose.'[25] In the American revolutionary war after 1776, British troops burned churches, executed surrendered rebels, and inflicted 'savage reprisals against all those suspected of supporting or merely being related to any of the rebels.'[26] Soldiers attacked civilians caught up in regular battles, too, with enemy resistance and dead comrades supercharging their anger, as would happen in Palestine, although never with the savagery of the men who sacked Badajoz in 1812 after storming the town during the Peninsular War, as witnessed by one of their officers:

> What scenes of horror did I witness there! They can never be effaced from my memory. There was no safety for the women even in the churches; and any who interfered or offered resistance were sure to get shot. Every house presented a scene of plunder, debauchery and bloodshed, committed with wanton cruelty on the persons of the defenceless inhabitants by our soldiery; and in many instances I beheld the savages tear the rings from the ears of beautiful women who were their victims, and when the rings could not be immediately removed from their fingers with the hand, they tore them off with their teeth … The infuriated soldiery resembled rather a pack of hell-hounds vomited up from the infernal regions for the extirpation of mankind than what they were but twelve short hours previously – a well-organised, brave, disciplined and obedient British army, and burning only with impatience for what is called glory.[27]

Soldiers burned down Kachin villages and destroyed paddy fields in Burma in the 1880s, after which they tried to starve out the Chins with blockade and when that failed 'the standard policy of the punitive expedition was taken up.'[28] In South Africa during the Boer War, the British intensified their 'scorched-earth' operations, 'scouring areas

---

[25] J. W. Fortescue, *A History of the British Army. First Part. Volume 2* (London: Macmillan, 1899), pp. 142, 146.

[26] Anthony James Joes, *Guerrilla Warfare: A Historical, Biographical, and Bibliographical Sourcebook* (Westport, CT: Greenwood, 1996), p. 14; John Ellis, *From the Barrel of a Gun: A History of Guerrilla, Revolutionary and Counter-Insurgency, from the Romans to the Present* (London: Greenhill, 1995), p. 65.

[27] Julian Sturgis (ed.), *A Boy in the Peninsular War: The Services, Adventures, and Experiences of Robert Blakeney, Subaltern in the 28th Regiment* (London: John Murray, 1899), pp. 273–74.

[28] Ellis, *From the Barrel of a Gun*, p. 126.

clean, indiscriminately destroying crops, livestock, and wagons, and firing farmhouses. A punitive scouring to chill the spines of those in the field.'[29] Alongside farm burning and the slaughter of livestock, the British controlled the population with a pass system, as they would in Palestine, and by 'herding non-combatants into concentration camps,' as they would later intern Palestinians.[30] 'Our course through the country is marked as in prehistoric ages by pillars of smoke by day and fire by night,' wrote one soldier with a column in South Africa.[31] 'The country is now almost entirely laid waste. You can go for miles and miles – in fact you might march for weeks and weeks and see no sign of a living thing or a cultivated patch of land – nothing but burnt farms and desolation,' remarked another.[32] The British laid waste fertile valleys in the Tirah campaign in India 'with fire and sword from end to end ... unearthed and consumed the grain and fodder supply of the country, uprooted and ringed the walnut groves, prevented the autumn tillage of the soil, and ... caused the inhabitants to live the lives of fugitives, upon the exposed ... and bitterly cold hill tops.'[33] British and empire troops destroyed Egyptian villages and whipped people in Egypt in 1919. In 1920 during the Arab revolt in Iraq, one infantryman described the 'Modus Operandi' as

artillery 'strafes' the nearest village where most probably the marauders came from. Sometimes they get the wrong village which matters little! and [sic] after an hour or two's bombardment a 'strafing' party of infantry, the exact number depends on the size of the village go and proceed to 'wipe out' all who are foolish enough to wait for us. Gurkhas, in particular, like these jobs and can be relied on to scientifically 'despatch' all inhabitants mostly per the 'kukri' [a curved knife] methods, bury them and burn down the village *and* have everything tidied up before we arrive.[34]

Even the official history of the Iraq campaign admitted that 'punitive measures' had 'an immediate effect in cooling the ardour of the disaffected inhabitants of Mosul'; soldiers dealt with one village 'in so thorough a manner that there was no question of its harbouring any living things.'[35] The British instituted tough measures in Ireland after the First World War, if not to the extreme possible with distant non-white

[29] Bill Nasson, *The South African War, 1899–1902* (London: Arnold, 1999), p. 199.
[30] Byron Farwell, *The Great Anglo-Boer War* (New York, NY: Norton, 1976), p. 350.
[31] Ibid., p. 353.
[32] Quoted in ibid.
[33] Maj-Gen J. G. Elliott, *The Frontier, 1839–1947: The Story of the North-West Frontier of India* (London: Cassell, 1968), p. 204.
[34] Quoted in Charles Townshend, *Desert Hell: The British Invasion of Mesopotamia* (Cambridge, MA: Harvard University Press, 2010), p. 285.
[35] Lt-Gen Aylmer Haldane, *The Insurrection in Mesopotamia, 1920* [1922] (Nashville, TN: Battery Press, 2005), pp. 43, 50, 76, 199.

colonies, as British soldier Frank Crozier who served there candidly recalled: torture, murder, heavy drinking, looting, perjury, robbery, and arson were the order of the day, as they would be in Palestine (with 'prodigious' alcohol consumption by policemen), often committed by the same Servicemen who decamped from Ireland to Palestine after Irish independence in 1921–22.[36]

Major (later Major-General Sir) C. E. Callwell condensed the 'small wars' pacification practices of the Army in his classic 1896 book *Small Wars: Their Principles and Practice* that detailed the methods that would later be employed in Palestine, and were derived from operations in India:

> The adoption of guerrilla methods by the enemy almost necessarily forces the regular troops to resort to punitive measures directed against the possessions of their antagonists. It must be remembered that one way to get the enemy to fight is to make raids on his property – only the most cowardly of savages and irregulars will allow their cattle to be carried off or their houses to be destroyed without making some show of resistance ... it has generally been found very useful to send raiding parties consisting of mounted men great distances to carry off the enemy flocks and herds or to destroy encampments and villages.[37]

In Callwell's view, 'uncivilised races' attributed 'leniency to timidity' and so 'must be thoroughly brought to book and cowed or they will rise again.'[38] The Army's *Field Service Regulations* of 1909 repeated Callwell's prognosis and in the 1930s Major-General Sir Charles Gwynn and Colonel H. J. Simson, the latter serving in Palestine during the revolt, developed Callwell's lessons, applying them to imperial hot spots such as Palestine and arguing that such situations demanded firm military rule.[39]

How does this savage history square up to the argument at the start of this chapter that British forces moderated their violence in Palestine? There are three points that help here, beyond the obvious one that other powers' pacification methods were visibly worse, from the French in the Vendée in the 1790s to the Americans in Vietnam to the Sri Lankan Army's slaughter of Tamils in 2009. First, Callwell's text reflected the late Victorian 'high renaissance' of British imperialism, one infused with

---

[36] F. P. Crozier, *Ireland for Ever* (London: Jonathan Cape, 1932), pp. 91, 97–99, 101ff; F. P. Crozier, *Impressions and Recollections* (London: Werner Laurie, 1930), pp. 256ff; Douglas Duff, *A Sword for Hire* (London: Murray, 1934), p. 111.
[37] Brian Bond (ed.), *Victorian Military Campaigns* (New York, NY: Praeger, 1967), p. 17; C. E. Callwell, *Small Wars: Their Principles and Practices* [1896] (London: HMSO, 1906), p. 145.
[38] Callwell, *Small Wars*, p. 148.
[39] Maj-Gen C. Gwynn, *Imperial Policing* (London: Macmillan, 1934); Col H. Simson, *British Rule and Rebellion* (Edinburgh: Blackwood, 1937); *Field Service Regulations 1909. Part I. Operations* (London: HMSO, 1912), pp. 191ff.

racism and Army-led brutality.[40] Callwell was truly 'the founding father of modern counter-insurgency' as he recognised that the civilian population sustaining rebellion was the central target, but the nineteenth-century methods that he summarised in 1896 were not proper in 1936, not for Britain anyway.[41] The political aim stayed the same, the military method was changing. Soldiers in Palestine in 1936 had the conundrum of how to coerce civilians without being too coercive. History had moved on, mores had changed, and draconian military methods against civilians in the context of the League of Nations and emerging national movements after the Great War were harder to sustain. German abuses in Belgium in 1914 had also strongly influenced the British sense of what was right and wrong (or, more exactly, the British did not want to be like the Germans). Second, the 1919 Amritsar massacre in India by British-led troops changed the rules of the game, soldiers wary thereafter of employing excessive force. The British did not moderate their violence in Palestine as they measured it, and this meant avoiding politically disastrous outrages like Amritsar. Third, official guides issued to soldiers on operations in Palestine instructed them that ordinary civil law bound them, that they were there as an aid to the civil power only, and that excessive force was wrong. Before moving on to examine military operations, demolition, and civil–military relations, brief discussion here of Amritsar and military regulations helps explain the motivations of Servicemen in Palestine.

In 1919, British-led troops commanded by Brigadier-General Reginald Dyer fired on unarmed Indian demonstrators in Amritsar. In a short, decisive exchange, soldiers shot dead some 400 people, wounding many more, after which the military withdrew without offering succour to the wounded. The resulting furore led London to set up a committee chaired by Lord Hunter to examine the massacre. When questioned by the Hunter Committee, Dyer was remarkably candid, both on the use of force and of the role of the legal system in colonial control. Dyer's admissions to Hunter betrayed both himself and the colonial state. Dyer's aim was not just to disperse the Amritsar crowd but to produce a 'moral effect.' When asked by the Indian lawyer, Sir Chimanlal Setalvad, whether

---

[40] Quoting Douglas Porch in unpublished MS from Daniel Whittingham, 'The Military Thought and Professional Career of Charles E. Callwell (1859–1928)' (Doctoral Thesis: University of London, 2013), p. 8 of the revised MS. For racism and brutality with a focus on Dum-Dum bullets see Kim Wagner, 'Savage Warfare: Violence and the Rule of Colonial Difference in Early British Counterinsurgency,' *History Workshop Journal* (January 2018) (doi.org/10.1093/hwj/dbx053).

[41] Charles Callwell in H. C. G. Matthew and Brian Harrison, *Revised Oxford Dictionary of National Biography* (Oxford: Oxford University Press, 2004), ix, p. 559.

what he meant by this was 'to strike terror,' Dyer replied: 'You can call it what you like. I was going to punish them.'[42] Dyer's candour and the Commission's findings meant that he was relieved of his command, sent home and retired. Popular subscription raised a huge £26,000 purse for Dyer.[43] Dyer's mistake was to tell the truth. Minimum force was necessary force, there to have moral effect, to strike (or threaten) terror to sustain imperial control. But necessary force was not always acceptable force. Here was the 'friction' that retarded the maximal tendency of the violence inherent in the colonial project. British officers learned the lesson from Amritsar and Dyer's fate at courses at Sandhurst and the Staff College, and in conversations in the officers' mess everywhere. They faced a dilemma: damned if they used too much force and they ended up in the dock for killing civilians, damned if they used too little and an unlawful assembly escalated to a riot and full-scale insurrection: 'shall I be *shot* for my forbearance by a court martial, or *hanged* for over zeal by a jury?'[44] The Army 'bitterly resented' Dyer's treatment but it learned the lesson of his case: 'In the future they would leave the finer points of law to the solicitors and apply the principle of minimum force to all forms of civil unrest.'[45] Victorian suppression campaigns such as during the Indian Mutiny of 1857 were not acceptable sixty years later and Amritsar was a hinge event marking the shift from racist-eliminationist small wars to the managed brutality of sub-war imperial policing.

Soldiers operated in the space between the norms and laws of British counter-insurgency. While colonial governors and military commanders through the legal framework detailed in Chapter 2 could use limitless violence to suppress insurrection, military regulations for soldiers on the use of force were ambiguous. Soldiers' actions depended heavily on whether they were fighting riot or insurrection, at home or in the colonies. Maximum force was permissible against insurrection in the colonies. The *King's Regulations* and the 1929 *Manual of Military Law* bound soldiers of all rank in Palestine, the latter a bulky hard-back volume updating the Army Discipline and Regulation Act (1879) and Army Act (1881). The key points from these volumes appeared in abridged form in post-Great War pocket-sized paperback pamphlets such as *Notes on Imperial Policing,*

---

[42] Quoted in Arthur Swinson, *Six Minutes to Sunset: The Story of General Dyer and the Amritsar Affair* (London: Peter Davies, 1964), p. 115; Hew Strachan, *The Politics of the British Army* (Oxford: Clarendon, 1997), p. 167.
[43] Nigel Collett, *The Butcher of Amritsar: General Reginald Dyer* (London: Hambledon, 2005), p. 405.
[44] General Napier in 1837 quoted in Townshend, *Britain's Civil Wars*, p. 20.
[45] Thomas Mockaitis, 'The British Experience in Counterinsurgency, 1919–1960' (Doctoral Thesis: University of Wisconsin-Madison, 1988), p. 53.

1934 and the 1937 *Duties in the Aid of the Civil Power* that officers could take with them on operations.[46] The 1929 manual was precise on how soldiers should conduct themselves, forbidding, for instance, stealing from and maltreatment of civilians. The 1929 regulations stated that a soldier was also a citizen and subject to civil as well as military law, and that an 'act which constitutes an offence if committed by a civilian is none the less an offence if committed by a soldier,' but it also provided a legal framework for shooting rioters and allowed for 'collective punishments' and 'retribution,' both loosely defined terms in the 1929 volume and both of which affected what happened in Palestine.[47] Neither the 1929 volume nor the subsequent 1934 and 1937 pamphlets provided any concrete definition for what constituted collective punishment and reprisals, thereby giving commanders considerable leeway when it came to interpreting the rules. The law for soldiers was clear: they should use collective punishment and retribution as a last resort and, if possible, they should avoid needless civilian suffering and any offence towards religion, race or class, but the 1929 volume clearly stated that where coercion was required or where terrorism needed to be checked collective punishment and reprisals, which will 'inflict suffering upon innocent individuals,' were 'indispensable as a last resource.'[48] As the law stated, 'The existence of an armed insurrection would justify the use of any degree of force necessary effectually to meet and cope with the insurrection.'[49] As these rules applied in British colonies in ways that they never did in the UK, this meant more savagery, but confirmation of soldiers as citizens as embodied in military regulations, the fear of prosecution (as had happened in colonial crises), and the change in mood on colonial violence after 1918 shifted the balance in counter-insurgency away from untrammelled forms of maximal force.

Kinetic Operations

Excepting al-Qawuqji's extended battles in early September 1936 around Tulkarm and Jenin, rebel forces throughout the revolt raided, skirmished and ambushed. They neither sought nor fought set-piece battles. Numerous small-scale, brief firefights characterised field operations for

---

[46] *War Office, Issued by Command of the Army Council, Manual of Military Law* (London, 1929); *War Office, By Command of the Army Council, Notes on Imperial Policing, 1934* (War Office, 30 January 1934); *War Office, By Command of the Army Council, 5 August 1937, Duties in the Aid of the Civil Power* (London: War Office, 1937).

[47] *Manual of Military Law, 1929*, p. 103.

[48] Ibid., pp. 331ff, 343; *Notes on Imperial Policing, 1934*, pp. 12, 39–41.

[49] *Manual of Military Law, 1929*, p. 255.

security forces. 'I personally saw them on one occasion running like hell over a hill. But they disappeared ... gangs of somewhere around twelve, fifteen,' noted a field officer.[50] The Army reacted with operational-tactical systems to hunt down and fragment rebel bands, never affording them space to expand and holding them to platoon-sized units, reduced even further by 1939; the Army rapidly smashed units of company strength; it punished villages that gave support. The Army found and fixed the enemy, despatched mobile columns to the scene, and coordinated operations with the (up to four) RAF fighter squadrons in Palestine via an 'XX' system that radioed in air support to an exact spot.[51] Troops also taught local Jewish and Arab collaborators to use military signals equipment to call in support.[52] Troops and warplanes relentlessly harried fleeing bands 'from pillar to post,' keeping them on the move and unable to rest among villagers who under military pressure were 'not anxious to assist them,' while troops blocked the escape route to Syria.[53] Road building, border fences, and demolitions supported operations, as did intelligence and collaboration with friendly Jewish and Palestinian auxiliary forces. The RAF also had a 'GG' system whereby it located rebel bands from the air and called in troops, and not the other way around, as well as instituting an 'airpin' arrangement whereby warplanes surrounded and cordoned urban areas prior to ground troops arriving, usually following intelligence tip-offs that rebel bands or suspects were in a certain village.[54] That the rebels moved amongst the people blurred the line in military operations between those directed at armed bands and those targeting villages or city quarters in which rebels hid.

Infantry battalion bases grouped under a brigade headquarters despatched 'flying' columns to locations that the RAF, military or Jewish intelligence, or SSO information identified, or as reactions to rebel ambushes or to an unfolding battle sparked by another unit. Troops rushed in to block escape routes and trap rebels: 'Our object is to catch these bands NOT merely drive them off.'[55] Battalions broke off sub-units

[50] Gratton, 4506/03, p. 25, IWMSA.
[51] Discussed in full in Arthur Harris, Lecture on RAF Operations in Palestine during the Arab Rebellion 1936–39, 1 July 1939, HQ RAF Jerusalem, Harris Papers, RAFM.
[52] Information courtesy of Dr Steven Wagner.
[53] Letter, Battershill to Wauchope, 6 November 1937, Battershill Papers, MSS. Brit. Emp. S. 467, Box 10, File 4, WL.
[54] Use of the GG Call, Functions of the British in Palestine, Palestine Box, RUR; Tinson, 15255/5, IWMSA noted a YY system, while there were suggestions for a TT tank call out system: C Coy 6th Bn RTR, Daily Report, Tulkarm, 24 August 1936 in War Diary, 2nd Bn Lincolnshire Regiment, REGI/376/DOCU, Box 1, LAL.
[55] Rounding up Armed Gangs, Functions of the British in Palestine, Palestine Box, RUR; Dorsetshire Regiment, War Diary, 14–20 August 1936, 88/453, Shelf C4, Box 3, KMM.

to area posts or picquets of anything from a section to a company, often based in existing stone buildings and tasked with improving local infrastructure such as roads with village labour. These smaller army units were based across the country and ready for immediate action. Police stations used telephone landlines to call for help. Army columns went in lorries with vehicle-borne donkeys in 'donk vans' from which soldiers bodily lifted them to the ground to give mobility once the road ran out, at which point rough, hilly terrain in Samaria and Galilee favoured the rebels and slowed pursuing soldiers.[56] Lorry-borne soldiers usually went out in 'columns' with two to three platoons plus a headquarters, along with around eight donkeys, 3-inch mortars, and wireless sets that were still bulky – so twelve to fifteen vehicles and 100 men.[57] This was a subaltern's war of fleeting firefights over rocky ground with caves for concealment: 'the country is too involved and they [rebels] slip through or hide in caves or disperse,' wrote Wavell to London.[58] Security forces used gas when searching caves – 'All caves gassed and bombed' – with what appears to have been lachrymose gas, with one police officer noting that 'gas squad' training was 'very warm work' in November 1936.[59] When the authorities refused permission in 1941 to use gas, the police complained that 'if we can't use, why keep? We used it in Hebron in 1937' to evict besieged 'bandits with women and children' in a house.[60] British use of tear gas was limited.[61] The XX system meant that troops could radio in RAF close air support. Warplanes also dropped pouches with information for troops telling them the direction of flight of rebels or smoke and flares coordinated Army–RAF action, and this 'brought aircraft usually to the spot within minutes.'[62] The RAF played a vital role. Troops relied on air power 'almost entirely' for

every ambush. We had a system where all the roads were marked and each kilometre had a key attached to it – a key marking on the scheme. And the Air Force were held in a position of readiness ... and when a column was held up all it had to do was to radio XXY the road, the code for the road, 73, milestone. And they

[56] M. J. P. M. Corbally, *The Royal Ulster Rifles, 1793–1960* (London: Paramount, 1960), p. 142.
[57] Dove, 4463/03, p. 32, IWMSA; Rounding up Armed Gangs, Functions of the British in Palestine, Palestine Box, RUR.
[58] Wavell to Haining (DMO, WO), 31 October 1937, Palestine, 1937–38 Volume, Wavell Papers, POH.
[59] Police Notebook, Palestine Police Force, 13 March 1938 and Letter, Briance to Father, 5 November 1936, Unnamed Loose Folder of Letters from Briance, Briance Papers, BP.
[60] Personal Diary, 1940–April 1941, 14 January 1941, Briance Papers, BP.
[61] RAF Palestine to Air Ministry [PA249], 21 June 1936, AIR 2/1761, p. 173, TNA and Military Lessons of the Arab Rebellion in Palestine 1938, p. 84, AIR 5/1244, TNA.
[62] Dove, 4463/03, p. 28, IWMSA.

came straight, absolutely straight within minutes, over the target. It was simply magnificent the way they did it ... Yes, I would say the cooperation was superb, absolutely superb.[63]

Other officers made the same tribute, emphasising how Army–RAF cooperation transformed the search for rebels: 'Oh, awfully well. Each battalion headquarters had a set called a No. 1 set. And you had a thing I think called an XX call. And that would get you – and Palestine's pretty small as you know – an aeroplane or if it was thought worthwhile more than one, usually one, in about a quarter of an hour.'[64] Aeroplanes spotted rebel bands, machine gunned and harried them, and later maintained contact for follow-up ground troops. Gloucester Gladiators arrived to strafe a band distantly seen by soldiers and out of rifle range following a battle, 'my first experience of army and RAF cooperation.'[65] The RAF 'bombed-up' cooperating warplanes and instructed its pilots to machine gun and bomb armed parties.[66] Warplanes could kill scores of rebels as well as monitoring them and this was why al-Qawuqji formed riflemen into anti-aircraft squads, with his men using metal grids correctly to pattern rifles skywards for greatest effect.

The RAF contributed further with an 'airpin' system that cordoned towns and villages, as when RAF commander Arthur Harris (who would lead Bomber Command in the Second World War) sent warplanes to fly a mile outside Bethlehem on continuous patrol with loudhailers attached proclaiming in Arabic that anyone leaving the town would be shot, before the Army went in and captured an armed band.[67] By flying in the RAF to cordon areas, soldiers were 'able to have breakfast before they started, and travel by daylight in buses in a civilized fashion.'[68] The Army had tried before to sneak up quietly on villages at night to catch suspects unawares with a dawn raid, but villagers would hear the soldiers or barking dogs gave them away, or running suspects broke the cordon and were lost. While soldiers were reluctant to fire on fleeing children, they fired on running Palestinians as a rule.[69] Police officers also dressed in Arab headdress to get closer to villages for a quick rush in with weapons ready but getting closer than 400 yards was a problem: 'Some villagers

---

[63] Dove, 4463/03, p. 30, IWMSA.
[64] Grove, 4510/03, p. 7, IWMSA.
[65] Bredin, 4550/05, p. 17, IWMSA.
[66] *Essex Regiment Gazette* 6/46 (March 1938), p. 282.
[67] Typed Memoir, Pieces of War, p. 146, Simonds Papers, 08/46/1, IWMD.
[68] Douglas Saward, *Bomber Harris* (New York, NY: Doubleday, 1985), pp. 63–64; Harris, 3765/4, Reel 4, IWMSA.
[69] Dorsetshire Regiment, Narrative of Events, Mazraa Ash Sharqiya [al-Mazra'a al-Sharqiyya], 17 August 1936, 88/367, Shelf C4, Box 3, KMM.

and most Bedouin could tell from the dog bark whether it was an animal as opposed to a man.'[70] What the RAF did not do in Palestine, as it did elsewhere, was to bomb villages, despite discussions about doing so. The British saw the Palestine 'problem' as 'essentially a police task.'[71] The Air Ministry in June 1936 had permitted aerial bombing but it forbade any action within 1,000 yards of urban limits.[72] Wauchope opposed aerial bombing and wrote to the Secretary of State for the Colonies on 1 September 1936 to underline the civil authority's reticence about using such levels of force:

> It is true that Air Officer Commanding has suggested that bombing from the air will soon cow the country. I see no reason to allow me to share this view. It is mainly based on results of air action in Iraq. The analogy is far from exact. The unweakened determination of the Arabs of Palestine during the past four months of resistance to our troops despite loss of one thousand killed and wounded and economic distress is an earnest of what we must expect if we start on ruthless measures when necessarily the innocent cannot be separated from the guilty.[73]

The proscription against bombing urban areas left house demolitions to ground forces that could be more discriminate in what they destroyed. In 1938, the Cabinet in London again discussed aerial bombing, referring back to the 'careful instructions' issued in 1936 on use of aircraft against bands, and concluded how, 'Special care had been taken to avoid the destruction of villages with the possible exception of the bombing of refractory villages after due warning … The present position was that the General Officer Commanding had authority to use his Air Forces in the same way as in the rebellion of 1936.'[74] Insurgent Bahjat Abu Gharbiyya emphasised in interview to this author in 2009 that the RAF did bomb rural villages but this author has found no evidence to support such a charge; in an interview in 1977, Abu Gharbiyya again claimed that the British used Wellington bombers, a warplane only coming into commercial production in 1937.[75] AHC files from August 1936 spoke of the British using 'incendiary bombs' and 'burnt bodies' at Bab al-Wad west

---

[70] Letter, Ted Horne to Author, 1 November 2009.
[71] Saward, *Bomber Harris*, p. 63; David Omissi, *Air Power and Colonial Control: The Royal Air Force, 1919–39* (Manchester: Manchester University Press, 1990), p. 46.
[72] Air Ministry to AOC in Palestine and Transjordan, 20 June 1936, Brooke-Popham Papers, 4/6/7, LHCMA.
[73] High Commissioner Palestine to Secretary of State for Colonies, 1 September 1936, FO 371/20024, TNA.
[74] Extract from Cabinet Conclusions 5(38), 16 February 1938, FO 371/21870, p. 37, TNA.
[75] Notes of Interviews, Bahjat Abu Gharbiyya (Amman), 18 September 1977, Palestine Research Lever Arch File, Thames TV Material on 'Palestine: Promises, Rebellion and Abdication' (1977–78), IWMFA.

of Jerusalem.[76] The Secretary of State for the Colonies in the summer of 1938 wrote to the Palestine High Commissioner about the 'delicacy' of aerial bombardment, and that the 'View of Air Ministry is that so long as operations of Royal Air Force in Palestine are as now "operations in aid of the civil power" bombardment without prior notice and evacuation of civil populations of areas concerned is not permissible.'[77] The international context weighed heavily. As Anthony Eden, the Foreign Secretary, put it in February 1938:

I confess that from an international point of view I contemplate any extension of the use of bombing in British-controlled territory with the utmost misgiving. Even the recent very mild and wholly legitimate use of bombs for police purposes against evacuated villages in the Hadramaut [in Yemen] has started a series of accusations against us in the press of several foreign countries. The international effects of these bombings can thus prove most unfortunate, and incidentally, greatly weaken our hands in protesting against the bombings which have been taking place in Spain and China.[78]

Air power for reconnaissance, location, strafing, and pursuit was a vital weapon in the British armoury, but any culminating battle demanded ground troops. Here, the mundane business of road construction opened rural areas to military ingress and administrative control, the two parts to pacification. When GOC Haining assumed charge from Wavell in early 1938, he made plans to occupy hilly Galilee and Samaria to 'provide security for a road-building programme to improve access to the villages and consequently deny bases to the bands. This would encourage loyalist elements, and protect them from retribution, and would facilitate the reintroduction of civil control.'[79] Haining was right. Road building discouraged rebel troop build-up and transformed inaccessible mountainous areas whose value to rebels was now 'lost because the authorities built a tarmac road and the trip takes only a few minutes'; new roads were 'one of the most effective' methods transferred from counter-insurgency on the north-west frontier of India.[80] Steven Wagner's recent monograph

---

[76] Minutes of the AHC, 28 July and 1 August 1936, RG65: P3221/18, ISA.
[77] Secretary of State for Colonies to High Commissioner, 7 June 1938, FO 371/21870, p. 105, TNA.
[78] Memo by Eden for W. Ormsby Gore (Secretary of State for Colonies), 7 February 1938, FO 371/21870, p. 18, TNA.
[79] Martin Kolinsky, 'The Collapse and Restoration of Public Security,' in Michael J. Cohen and Martin Kolinsky (eds), *Britain and the Middle East in the 1930s: Security Problems, 1935–39* (London: Macmillan-King's, 1992), p. 156.
[80] Appendix: Explanatory Notes, Captured and Translated Arabic Material with Commentary, p. 141, Wingate Papers, Microfilm M2313, BL. For road building programmes see also the online files (information courtesy of Steven Wagner) at www.archives.gov.il/en/archives/#/Archive/0b0717068003223c/File/0b07170680b978da.

details the security state's expanding network of new roads and forts that gripped and reduced rural Palestine.[81] Indian police adviser Sir Charles Tegart argued within the coordinating Public Security Committee on which he sat with the Army commander, the Inspector General of Police, and the Chief Secretary that the British needed a presence in the countryside. Road building was not just about getting troops into areas for operations but concerned administrative control and showing the flag. Population control cut rebels off from food, intelligence, recruits, and weapons, and so enabled successful rebel-centric military sweeps. Tegart took the idea of control of movement, access, and blockade to a new level by instructing the building of a fence along the northern border with Lebanon and Syria. The British already used Bedouin spies beyond the northern border to give notice of any parties coming in from the north and north-east; the new fence would be a formidable new fixed barrier.[82] The British contracted Jewish building firms like *Solel Boneh* to build the border fence using Palestinian labour but they also resurrected a lapsed ordinance concerning road building to permit forced village labour. They completed it by August 1938.[83] The cost was substantial. The fence ran along the Palestine–Lebanon border before curving down to friendly Jewish kibbutzim around Lake Huleh, leaving the Metullah panhandle north of the barrier, after which the fence continued south to Lake Tiberias where motor launches patrolled the lake. Plans were in place to block the fords across the River Jordan south of Tiberias, the Transjordan Frontier Force (TJFF) supporting operations there alongside Jericho-based policeman Assistant Superintendent Hassan Faiz Idrissi (formerly of the Turkish Army and awarded the OBE in 1937) who ran a rough-and-ready border patrol force covering Jordan valley crossings.[84] The Transjordan administration blocked rebel access to Palestine from the east, so turning the country into a buffer zone to limit the revolt in Palestine. Bahjat Abu Gharbiyya recalled how the British arrested close family members of Transjordan-based fighters who went to Palestine,

[81] Steven Wagner, *Statecraft by Stealth: How Britain Ruled Palestine 1917–40* (Ithaca, NY: Cornell University Press, 2018), *passim*.

[82] Letter, Battershill to Wauchope, 21 October 1937, Battershill Papers, MSS. Brit. Emp. S. 467, Box 10, File 4, WL; 'Tegart's Wall,' Cutting from *The Times*, 28 May 1938, Chief Secretary's Office: M/5088/10, ISA.

[83] Charles Tegart: Memoir of an Indian Policeman, by K. F. Tegart (wife), pp. 247ff, Mss Eur C.235/2, IOR.

[84] The author is grateful to Dr Steven Wagner for this information, derived from his research in Diaries, 4 January and 29 January 1938, Tegart Papers, 4/6, MEC; material in RG65: P3056/37, ISA; Eastern Frontier, S25/22737-14, CZA; and material in S25/22768 and S25/22753, CZA. Idrissi held the King's Police Medal from 1932: *Palestine Civil Service List 1939* (Jerusalem: Government Printing Press, 1939), pp. 224, 312, 314.

before encouraging tribal leaders to make the fighters return, at which point the authorities released the family members: 'These measures had a tangible impact.'[85] With British cordoning of Lebanon, Syria, and Transjordan, rebels had no functioning routes into and out of Palestine, and they lacked safe base areas inside the country.

Tegart's fence varied from two to three parallel lines six feet in height and five feet apart with wire-mesh rabbit fence at the bottom and masses of loose wire in between plus mines, police posts, pill boxes, and searchlights along the cordon.[86] Army Engineers in the UK offered to provide tear gas bombs for the fence at 3/3d each but only if 'higher authority' agreed this as gas was 'strictly against British policy at the moment.'[87] The British recruited a new frontier force of British personnel for the maintenance of the fence, observed by a local policeman as a tough bunch:

To day there arrived 60 ex army men who will be the start of the frontier force. I think they will need some policemen here to keep order. They were only in Port Said 8 hours and they had to call the troops out. The general impression at home is that the Englishman abroad is a quite [sic] chap. I have found out differently most of the trouble out here is caused by the police and the army.[88]

Local villagers tore down Tegart's barrier as it was being built, with three big raids by 'large bands' hitting the fence at the end of June 1938.[89] As bands and local Palestinians attacked the fence, so soldiers detained the menfolk of villages along the border as punishment: 'These measures have proved efficient and no attempts have been made on the fence or the road during the past three weeks.'[90] The British in July 1938 detained some 1,000 men aged between sixteen and sixty from villages near the frontier until they had finished the fence, such prisoners 'being fed and watered by their villages' while detained and used by the British for labour

---

[85] Bahjat Abu Gharbiyya, *Fi Khidamm al-nidal al-'arabi al-filastini: Mudhakkirat al-munadil Bahjat Abu Gharbiyya* [*In the Midst of the Struggle for the Arab Palestinian Cause: The Memoirs of Freedom-Fighter Bahjat Abu Gharbiyya* (Beirut: IPS, 1993), p. 61.

[86] 'Tegart's Wall,' Cutting from *The Times*, 28 May 1938, Chief Secretary's Office: M/5088/10, ISA.

[87] Watkinson (School of Military Engineering Chatham) to Maj Artus (HQ Jerusalem), 28 April 1938, Tegart Papers, GB165-0281, Box 3, File 2, p. 92, MEC.

[88] Letter, Burr to Mother and Father, 27 May 1937 [but date then crossed out], Burr Papers, 88/8/1, IWMD.

[89] Monthly Administrative report for June 1938, Galilee and Acre District, 1 July 1938, by A/DC K. W. Blackburne, Blackburne Papers, MSS. Brit. Emp. S. 460, Box 3, File 2, WL.

[90] Monthly Administrative report for July 1938, Galilee and Acre District, 2 August 1938, by A/DC K. W. Blackburne, Blackburne Papers, MSS. Brit. Emp. S. 460, Box 3, File 2, WL.

details: 'work is being found for them.'[91] The fence worked. It became a barrier on which British and French forces fixed and destroyed rebel bands escaping from or entering Palestine. French forces by 1938 were calling in British mobile columns and RAF support for their operations in southern Lebanon around Bint Jbeil.[92] When 16th Brigade chased a band to the Syrian border in November 1937, it set up a combined operation to 'shift them' with the French who 'turned out quite an army on their side of the frontier to assist us.'[93] The Royal Ulster Rifles in July 1938 acted on information from the French whose forces cooperated during the operation on the Syrian side of the border.[94]

Alongside conventional operations, the British dropped 'divide and rule' propaganda leaflets asking the populace: 'Who is suffering due to the outlaw operations that are taking place now? The rich men living happily in the city. The rich man does not put his source of living in danger. But he demands of the poor man to do so ... He who suffers is the small merchant forced to close his shop ... Isn't it true that the poor man always suffers?'[95] Security forces instituted unconventional operations, too, such as 'Q' vehicles that appeared unarmed but when ambushed revealed soldiers within, replicating the Q ships of the Great War.[96] The 'biggest toughs from each regiment' in Q platoons slept by day and lay in ambush by night, as would Wingate's Special Night Squads.[97] In the Queen's Own Royal West Kents a Q platoon under a Lieutenant Rooke 'quickly proved its worth,' while on another occasion the same Q unit hid in the cellar of the anti-rebel *mukhtar* of Sindyana village (al-Sindiyana south of Haifa) to try and capture a band leader; men went on ambushes disguised as Arabs.[98] Nor did military preparations let up in the interim of the Peel Commission. The Army was sure that fighting

---

[91] Summary of Intelligence, Palestine and Transjordan, 29 July 1938, by Wing Commander Ritchie at GHQ [15/38], CO 732/81/9, TNA; 2nd RUR (Safad) Report on Operations to 16th Inf Bde, 6 July 1938, Report on Occupation Northern Area, Night 2/3 July, December 1937–March 1939 File, Palestine Box, RUR.

[92] Summary of Intelligence, Palestine and Transjordan, 26 August 1938, by Wing Commander Ritchie at GHQ [17/38], CO 732/81/9, TNA.

[93] Wavell to Haining (DMO, WO), 21 and 23 November 1937, Palestine, 1937–38 Volume, Wavell Papers, POH.

[94] Col Whitfeld (OC 2nd RUR, Safad) to HQ 16th Inf Bde, 29 July 1938, December 1937–March 1939 File, Palestine Box, RUR.

[95] Subhi Yasin, *Al-Thawra al-'Arabiyya al-Kubra (fi Filastin) 1936–1939 [The Great Arab Revolt in Palestine, 1936–1939]* (Damascus: Shafa 'Amr Haifa, 1959), pp. 128–29.

[96] Letter, Brooke-Popham (HQ, RAF, Cairo) to ACM Ellington (London), 20 July 1936, Brooke-Popham Papers, 4/3/44, LHCMA.

[97] Letter, Street to Father, 12 June 1933 [properly 1938], Street Papers, File: Letters Home, LHCMA.

[98] H. D. Chaplin, *The Queen's Own Royal West Kent Regiment* (London: Michael Joseph, 1954), pp. 92, 105–06.

would start again and so it utilised 'the truce in order to prepare a wide operational infrastructure for a comprehensive struggle against the guerrilla and terror tactics.'[99] This included arming Jewish supernumerary police and auxiliary forces, discussed later in the book, and training Jewish soldiers, many of whom became 'later cadres' of Israel's armed forces.[100] More gradually, the British armed local Palestinian anti-gang forces known as peace bands but they were cautious about equipping local Arab forces (less so Jews), unlike the Americans in Vietnam who transferred masses of weapons to client forces that went straight into the insurgents' armoury.[101] The British also got tough with rebel sanctuaries in mosques. General O'Connor told Muslim clerics during the recapture of the old city in October 1938 that his men would counter shooting from the *Haram al-Sharif* with heavy return fire.[102] Changes to the emergency laws allowed troops to follow suspect rebels into mosques in 'Hot Pursuit,' a ruling used very occasionally.[103] The use of Arab hostages in front of or with military convoys to deter rebel sniping and roadside mines supported operations and extended to Brigadier Evetts placing the mayor of Nablus on the roof of his headquarters to deter incoming fire.[104]

Then there was the question of numbers of men, discussed in more detail below. Before the Munch settlement in September 1938, London held back troops. After Munich, Britain flooded Palestine with fresh infantry battalions and the tempo and scale of operations picked up, as did military control of civil pacification, as we will see shortly. Royal Ulster Rifles and sometime SNS officer H. E. N. 'Bala' Bredin (who won the MC and Bar in Palestine) dated the change in tone to the summer of 1938, with the departure of Wauchope and the arrival of the new High Commissioner, MacMichael: 'By about mid-1938 all the various restrictions I think had been done away with. And I think it had a lot to do with the fact that the high commissioner changed and a chap called Sir Harold MacMichael arrived who, in my humble opinion, was a much more realistic man than his predecessor.'[105] Such comments about civil

---

[99] Yigal Eyal, 'The Arab Revolt, 1936–1939: A Turning Point in the Struggle over Palestine,' in Mordechai Bar-On (ed.), *A Never-Ending Conflict: A Guide to Israeli Military History* (Westport, CT and London: Praeger, 2004), p. 27.

[100] Ibid., pp. 27–28.

[101] Neil Sheehan, *A Bright Shining Lie* (London: Cape, 1989), pp. 373–74.

[102] O'Connor, 12/8, p. 31, IWMSA; John Baynes, *The Forgotten Victor: General Sir Richard O'Connor* (London: Brassey's, 1989), p. 54.

[103] Baynes, *The Forgotten Victor*, pp. 53–54.

[104] Notes of Conversation with E. V. [Emmanuel Vilensky?], 10 February 1950, Alice Ivy Hay of Seaton Papers, JRL.

[105] Bredin, 4550/05, p. 24, IWMSA.

restrictions from field officers were not unusual. Police officer Burr saw the reinforcements arrive in Haifa docks in the autumn of 1938, now 'full of troops and daily ships are arriving with tanks, cars and field guns.'[106] Civil official C. E. Buxton based in Gaza felt the wind of change in late 1938 in southern Palestine, as local Palestinian leaders saw that the Government did not intend to withdraw and came

to the conclusion that it would be best to get out of the rebellion and stand well with Govt ... The committee gradually resisted the activities of armed men and rebel agents, not by refusing to take part in the rebellion, but by insisting on conducting it their own way, and in reality opposing it ... Much money has been collected by armed men for the rebellion between September and December [1938], but thereafter payment was refused ... there is in this area a counter revolutionary movement led by the same people who at one period organised the local rebel activities ... The better situation is probably due to the councils of these leaders who have changed their tune since December ... It would also serve our interests to adopt new methods in the application of force to the present situation.[107]

Demolition

As well as shooting rebels, the Army impoverished people and pacified the country by demolishing property. This was as a rule a non-lethal method but 'Sometimes we did demolish houses etc etc where there must have been people inside.'[108] The Army's demolition of houses was both a rebel- and population-centric pacification tool. It cleared buildings in urban areas that hid fighters, while more broadly being a punishment against civilians considered by the British to have helped rebels (so detaching them from supporting rebels), and this included simply being the closest point to a rebel attack: the 'joint venture' rule discussed in Chapter 2. Demolition was the kinetic side of civil pacification that gelled with fining, curfews, passes, and detention. Security forces used it in conjunction with these other punishments. Demolition came in two forms, internal and external. Internal demolition meant sending soldiers on punitive raids to destroy Palestinian households, furniture, clothing, and personal effects, alongside which soldiers stole things. External demolition meant removing the whole building, village or town quarter, usually with explosive charges, sometimes carried in by the house owner,

---

[106] Letter, Burr (Bury Billet Haifa) to Mother and Father, 22 September and 21 October 1938, Burr Papers, 88/8/1, IWMD.
[107] Letter, C. E. Buxton (DC, Gaza-Beersheba) to Battershill, 16 February 1939, Buxton Papers, MSS. Brit. Emp. S. 390, Box 1, Palestine File, WL.
[108] Watton, 14750/3, IWMSA.

but soldiers also made Palestinians take apart their own houses brick-by-brick.[109] Internal and external demolitions were not mutually exclusive and in conjunction left whole villages derelict, some houses in complete ruins, the insides of all sacked, and the population in penury. The 'burn scars' of West Yorkshire Regiment operations at the village of Bayt Rima north-west of Ramallah were still visible three years afterwards, 'a disgrace to the British name' in the words of a senior CID officer.[110] 'The procedure now when a soldier is killed is to blow up the nearest village' and for this purpose the British supplied sea mines from HMS *Malaya* noted police officer Burr who had spoken to a soldier back from the Syrian border area where there were now 'no traces of the villages he once knew.'[111] Military restraint here was that some regiments and local brigade commanders effected demolition less often or less completely, that soldiers rarely killed anyone directly through demolition, local and international protests slowed the pace of such punishment, and 'good' villages (ones that supplied intelligence and resisted rebel bands) might escape destruction.

The most spectacular single act of demolition was that of old Jaffa in June 1936 in what the Jews called Operation 'Anchor' (*Ogen*) as the destruction was anchor shaped to give access from three points (see Figure 5.3). The bars of the anchor stretch today up Mifrats Shlomo Promenade to Kedumim Square and then along Segev Street, with the stem running from Kedumim Square through Abrasha Park to HaPninim Street. Each of the three bars was up to 100 feet (10–30 metres) wide and extended in length for some 650 feet (200 metres). Artisanal craft shops and Israeli gentrification now fill the remains of the housing. The British described the demolished area as in the shape of a bow.[112] The operation blurred punishment and military necessity, as old Jaffa's alleys restricted access and were a refuge for insurgents. As Haussmann's wide boulevards did for Paris in the nineteenth century, the demolition (or town planning as the Army euphemistically put it) of Jaffa's casbah facilitated ingress and state control. This was the obverse to Tegart's

[109] *The Hampshire Regiment Journal* 32/12 (December 1937), p. 383; Monthly News Letter No. 2, 2nd Battalion, Lincolnshire Regiment, 1–30 September 1936 in Abdul-Latifa Tibawi Papers, GB165-1284, MEC.
[110] Personal Diary, 1940–April 1941, 13 December 1940, Briance Papers, BP; see also Diary, 14 May 1939, Forster Papers, GB165-0109, pp. 119–20, MEC.
[111] Letter, Burr (Bury Billet Haifa) to Mother and Father, 9 September 1938, Burr Papers, 88/8/1, IWMD.
[112] Dov Gavish, 'Mivz'a Yafo: Shipur Koloniali Shel Pnei ha-'Ir' ['The Old City of Jaffa, 1936: A Colonial Urban Renewal Project'], *Eretz Israel: Mehkarim be-Yedi'at ha-Aretz ve-Atikoteha* [*Eretz-Israel: Archaeology, Historical and Geographical Studies*] 17 (1983), p. 68.

fence: instead of containment, the Army destroyed. The operation began early on 18 June 1936. Soldiers completed much of the destruction by midday but it carried on fitfully to the end of the month. Clearing the blown masonry after 200–300 lbs gelignite charges brought down buildings was a big problem.[113] RAF aerial photographs captured great plumes of smoke over Jaffa (see Figure 5.2) and the progress of the three pathways carved through the old town.[114] Arab sources claim that the British destroyed 220 (multiple-occupancy) homes and left 6,000 people homeless. The last is an inflated figure considering Jaffa's population and the extent of the damage but might be correct as the British levelled adjacent *bidonvilles*, too.[115] Looking at the aerial images one would say that the British directly destroyed around 15 per cent of old Jaffa. The AOC in charge at the time, Richard Peirse, detailed 6,000–7,000 people in old Jaffa, but not all were made homeless, and later maps delimit urban housing alongside the roads cut in 1936.[116] British sensibilities extended to evacuating homes beforehand, genuflecting to planning regulations, avoiding religious buildings, and providing some relief and compensation for the homeless. It was a devastatingly effective military and social measure. It struck terror into and impoverished Palestinians' lives. It was an economic tool, too, as access to Jaffa allowed the passage of Egyptian and Jewish strike-breaking stevedores to the port.

The origins of the operation illustrate British concern for legality. From late May 1936, the British had warned Jaffans to stop firing from the old city, prior to pinpointing and returning fire with machine-guns on sniper points.[117] Then, on 16 June, the British informed residents by air-dropped leaflets in Arabic that they had to clear out 'so that the city can be improved.'[118] The leaflets told residents:

The Government intends to execute a programme for opening the roads and undertaking improvements in the Old City of Jaffa. This programme involves demolishing a number of buildings for which appropriate compensations will be given. In each case a fair solution will be discussed. The demolition will be done

---

[113] 'Notes on Palestine Operations,' *The Wasp: The Journal of the 16th Foot* 8/5 (March 1937), p. 267.

[114] Aerial Photographs in Gavish, 'Mivz'aYafo,' pp. 66–73.

[115] Ghassan Kanafani, 'Thawrat 1936–1939 fi Filastin: Khalfiyyat, tafasil wa tahlil' ['The 1936–1939 Revolt in Palestine: Background, Details and Analysis'], *Shu'un Filastinyya* [*Palestinian Matters*] 6 (January 1972), p. 65; Abu Gharbiyya, *Fi Khidamm al-nidal al-'arabi al-filastini*, pp. 60–61.

[116] Peirse (Palestine) to ACM Ellington (London), 24 June 1936, Brooke-Popham Papers, 4/6/19, LHCMA; Map of Jaffa (1944) in Salman H. Abu-Sitta, *Atlas of Palestine, 1917–1966* (London: Palestine Land Society, 2010), p. 71.

[117] Gavish, 'Mivz'aYafo,' p. 67.

[118] Ibid., p. 68.

by the military forces. Law-abiding citizens of the Old City of Jaffa will not be hurt in any way but if there is resistance the army will employ force to complete the mission.[119]

The official notice given, also on 16 June, talked of 'opening' the old city 'for the benefit of the community and the entire city.'[120] The original plan was to start demolition a day later, the 17th, but a mosque in the way of the clearance changed the plan and led to a delay to the 18th. The Army targeted initially forty-six homes, increased by seventy more buildings; Arab sources detail the loss of 200 homes; a British report to the League totalled 237 destroyed homes.[121] Royal Engineers entered a deserted city on the 18th escorted by two infantry battalions from the Bedfordshire and Hertfordshire Regiment and the Royal Scots Fusiliers and they blew pathways, often badly damaging adjoining buildings. Soldiers blew trumpets to announce each successive blast: 'Here it comes!' in photograph captions alongside a soldier at attention with a trumpet to his mouth standing by building rubble (Figure 5.1).[122] There was no resistance. Watching the demolition, one British officer remarked that 'there was the most enormous bang and about 10% of Jaffa went up in the air. I said enthusiastically, "That will fucking well teach them," and was promptly put under arrest by Major Perrott [a devout Christian], on the charge of "using obscene language whilst on active service"!!'[123] Blowing up a city was legal, uttering a profanity was illegal. Military satisfaction at Jaffa's demise was palpable: 'When this was finished, the troops withdrew from Jaffa, which never gave even another squeak of trouble … After this notable military success it was most unfortunate that the civil administration should have made a pathetic attempt to announce that the demolitions were carried out as part of a new town planning scheme! … The Arabs laughed.'[124] The local press reverted to sarcasm about the 'beautification' of Jaffa, 'carried out through boxes of dynamite.'[125] One Christian Palestinian family evacuated their home without even being able to take personal belongings, just the clothes that they had on their backs.[126] Another newspaper lamented, 'Goodbye, goodbye, old Jaffa, the Army has exploded you,' a phrase stolen from the British

[119] Ibid.
[120] Ibid.
[121] Ibid., pp. 68–70.
[122] Arab Revolt in Palestine Photograph Album 1937, ACHA. Misdated to June 1937.
[123] Typed Memoir, Pieces of War, p. 149, Simonds Papers, 08/46/1, IWMD.
[124] A Quarter of My Century by Dudley Clarke, p. 563, Clarke Papers, 99/2/1–3: DW/8, IWMD.
[125] Filastin [Palestine] (Jaffa) (19 June 1936).
[126] Ibid.

5.1 Soldiers blew trumpets to announce each successive blast of house
demolition
(from American Colony Hotel Archive)

press to get around the censor.[127] Residents had attempted to resist the
destruction legally but with only two days' notification this was impossible. Arab Government officials had brought personal warnings to the
old city that families must leave on the evening of 16 June, after which
those whose homes were slated for destruction went to a special session
of the Jaffa branch of the National Committee. Representatives then
went to the British District Commissioner by way of an Arab District
Officer, but the British official refused to meet him. The local committee
sent translated petitions higher up to the High Commissioner and the
House of Commons. There was no time for preparations or to find alternative shelter. The Government warned houses a quarter of a mile away
to leave their windows open to prevent the glass shattering from explosive blast waves.[128] Once demolition started, residents could leave via one

---

[127] *al-Difa'* [*The Defence*] (Jaffa) (23 July 1936).
[128] *al-Difa'* (17 June 1936).

5.2 RAF aerial photograph of smoke from the destruction of old Jaffa
in June 1936
(from Dov Gavish)

exit only, and searchers checked them, with women searchers in a special
building assigned to the task. The British bricked up the doors of some
buildings.[129]

Destitute families found temporary accommodation in local schools
and received the tiny sum for one week as 'a special compensatory
allowance of 20 mils per head.'[130] The US Consulate noted fifty-six

[129] *al-Difaʻ* (19 June 1936).
[130] Telegram, High Commissioner Palestine to Secretary of State for Colonies, 18 June
1936, L/PS/12/3344–45: Palestine Situation, IOR.

families totalling 400 people in Government shelters, with 2,000 more receiving a housing allowance of 20 mils per day, adding that with more demolitions the figure of 2,400 would increase.[131] In September 1936 after much wrangling, the Government told homeless families that they could claim for compensation based on property values under the provisions of the Urban Property Tax Ordinances. Claims had to be made within a month of the notice and no demands could be made for moveable assets such as jewellery.[132] The Chief Justice in Palestine, Sir Michael McDonnell, could do nothing about the demolition as it was technically legal under the Emergency Regulations but he put out a legal ruling criticising the claim that the operation was done to improve town planning: 'the singularly disingenuous lack of moral courage displayed by the Administration ... It would be a negation of justice if in a glaring case of evasion such as that before us, this high Court did not speak its mind freely.'[133] McDonnell's rebuke was a 'stinging, open-handed slap' to Wauchope and other senior judges felt the same, in the view of the US Consul in Palestine.[134] It was the reason why the Government dismissed McDonnell and contributed to the Army's eagerness to appropriate the legal system. Interestingly, when the British levelled parts of Jenin in October 1938 as punishment for the assassination of civil official Walter Moffatt, they again introduced the idea, as with Jaffa, of town planning, this time with an 'outline road scheme,' to mask the destruction.[135] The Jews were amazed at McDonnell's criticisms, as Moshe Shertok noted after meeting Wauchope in July 1936:

I referred to the talk which his Excellency had had with Joshua Gordon [of the Jewish Agency] on Friday last on the subject of the judgement delivered by the Chief Justice and by Judge Manning in the Jaffa demolition case. H. E. [His Excellency, so the High Commissioner] had expressed in very strong terms his indignation with the censure which the judges passed on the Government and asked Gordon whether I had sent a copy of the judgement to Weizmann.

[131] Disturbances of 1936, 13–25 June, US Consul General Palestine to State Department, 27 June 1936, 867N.00/322 [Reel M#1037/1], NARA II.
[132] Emergency Regulations (Compensation for Jaffa Demolitions) 4 September 1936 in *Ordinances, Regulations, Rules, Orders and Notices. Government of Palestine. Annual Volume for 1936. Volumes 2 and 3* (Jerusalem: Government Printing Press, 1937), pp. 1077–79.
[133] Gavish, 'Mivz'a Yafo,' p. 69; Walid Khalidi and Yasin Suweyd, *Al-Qadiyya al-Filastiniyya wa al-Khatar al-Sahyuni* [*The Palestinian Problem and the Zionist Danger*] (Beirut: IPS, Lebanese General Staff Fifth Branch and Ministry of Defence, 1973), p. 234; R. Bridgeman (Colonial Information Bureau) to John Parker MP, 10 November 1938 in Creech Jones Papers, MSS. Brit. Emp. S. 332, Box 30, File 2, WL; Frances Newton, *Fifty Years in Palestine* (London: Coldharbour, 1948), p. 288.
[134] US Consul General Palestine to State Department, 25 July 1936, 867N.00/341 [Reel M#1037/2], NARA II.
[135] Gavish, 'Mivz'a Yafo,' pp. 66–73.

5.3 RAF aerial photograph of the aftermath of the destruction of old
Jaffa in June 1936
(from Dov Gavish)

He referred to the Chief Justice as a Jew-hater ... I said that this was the most
astonishing instance of one arm of the Government letting down the other ...
The High Commissioner shrugged his shoulders.[136]

When later questioned in Parliament about demolitions, the Secretary of
State for the Colonies referred back to the 1936 Emergency Regulations
and the 1931 Order in Council: 'Demolitions of houses are carried
out by virtue of the powers conferred by Regulation 19 B (1) of the
Regulations made by the High Commissioner under Article IV (4) of
the Palestine Defence Order-in-Council 1931.'[137] The Foreign Office,
for one, queried demolition policy in November 1938 and the justice of

---

[136] Minutes of an Interview by Moshe Shertok with His Excellency the High Commissioner,
6 July 1936, Reports from 1937 on Abdullah, National Commission, 80/153P/9, HA.
[137] Extract from Parliament, written reply, Malcom MacDonald to John Parker, 16
November 1938 in Creech Jones Papers, MSS. Brit. Emp. S. 332, Box 30, File2, WL.

collective punishment, quoting a letter by GOC Haining, but this did not stop such things, not least as the Army was now in charge:

General Haining evidently thinks that the blowing-up of Arab houses is 'necessary as a warning' and deterrent amongst inhabitants 'the vast majority of which ... are potential rebels,' and, secondly, as a collective punishment where villages are concerned. It is difficult to believe that demolitions act as deterrents in any circumstances. Where the sympathies of a people are concerned and isolated personal action is probably not usual, the blowing-up of one or two homes must surely embitter the hostility of persons whose houses are selected, while if the house of some merely passive agent be chosen, it would, I should have thought, be sufficient to turn any 'potential rebel' into something far more active. I think too the GOC exaggerates when speaking of 'collective punishment.' Such punishment must by its very nature be essentially unfair – and I doubt very much if it is understood by inhabitants. Has, too, demolition proved so 'usually effective' as the GOC would have us believe? Does not the need of continual repetition of the practice rather give lie to his argument of 'effectiveness'?[138]

British diplomats in Cairo made similar points and requested that the Army stop house demolition as the practice savoured of 'Prussianism' and 'was doing us untold harm.'[139] The Army ignored such entreaties. The High Commissioner wrote to the Secretary of State for the Colonies about how the GOC told him that any relaxation of demolition 'would be seriously prejudicial to military operations: and might leave H. M. Government open to the charge that we have been using excessive force in the past ... I would point out that our two most effective sanctions are searches and demolitions, for which no alternative can be found.'[140] The Lord Chancellor in London fancifully wondered whether closing houses without destroying them might work.[141] The Arab Centre in London, probably based on information from pro-Palestinian British resident Frances Newton, pressed the Foreign Secretary and pointed to how the Army had 'savaged' Jenin after Moffatt's assassination 'by blowing it – (or a large part of it) – to smithereens. Certain persons were "shot down while attempting to escape," in true Nazi fashion. Some of the means resorted to to obtain information from the population will not bear repetition.'[142]

---

[138] Minute by J. Y. Mackenzie (FO) on Military Measures, 30 November 1938, FO 371/21867, p. 60, TNA.
[139] Secretary of State for Colonies to High Commissioner, 17 November 1938, FO 371/21866, p. 171, TNA.
[140] High Commissioner to Secretary of State for Colonies, 20 November 1938, FO 371/21866, p. 218, TNA.
[141] Extract from Cabinet Conclusions 56(38), 22 November 1938, FO 371/21866, p. 246, TNA.
[142] Arab Centre London to Foreign Secretary, 1 October 1938, enclosing Extract from a Letter Received from an English friend in Palestine Dated 16 September 1938, FO 371/21881, p. 69, TNA.

Meanwhile, the Palestine administration paid compensation to a pro-Government Palestinian adviser who had property in Jenin: 'the production of a cheque book for compensation purposes calmed him down.'[143] When policeman Robert Martin visited Jenin a year later, it still showed the signs of 'the Government's wrath. It was in a shocking state, having the appearance of a front-line town in a modern war. Huge gaps were visible between the blocks of buildings and houses, while piles of rubble lay across the street.'[144] The Arab propaganda bureau in Damascus assessed the damage in Jenin at twenty-one buildings and all the houses along a stretch of the main street.[145]

Jaffa was the biggest single house demolition but pro rata other demolitions were bigger in that while the number of buildings destroyed was smaller, those destroyed represented most or all of an urban conglomeration, such as forty houses in the small village of Irtah south of Tulkarm in November 1938 after a band was found in the village.[146] The average village size at this time was over 800 people but some were very small with fewer than 100 inhabitants and sappers levelled whole villages, dynamiting 135 houses in Sha'ab east of Acre.[147] Hebronites caused the Dorsetshire Regiment so much trouble that eventually half a local village 'had to be blown up.'[148] Soldiers photographed demolitions as vast distant plumes of smoke over town centres with sub-titles like 'Blowing up the Sook,' as at Nablus.[149] An article in the Royal Engineers' journal gives details of demolition including diagrams and it comments usefully on how the Army viewed judicial process. A village north of Lydda had been 'naughty' but as legal proceedings took too long, 'before the evidence was completed, it was possible to get a fair idea of what the court's decision was likely to be, and a reconnaissance was carried out, and a tentative plan made.'[150] This was in 1936 when civil District

[143] Ibid.
[144] Robert Martin, *Palestine Betrayed: A British Palestine Policeman's Memoir (1936–48)* (Ringwood: Seglawi, 2007), p. 89.
[145] Bulletin issued by Bureau Nationale, Damascus [summer 1938] in Creech Jones Papers, MSS. Brit. Emp. S. 332, Box 30, File 2, WL.
[146] Summary of Intelligence, Palestine and Transjordan, 18 November 1938, by Wing Commander Ritchie at GHQ [23/38], CO 732/81/10, TNA.
[147] Walid Khalidi (ed.), *All that Remains: The Palestinian Villages Occupied and Depopulated by Israel in 1948* (Washington, DC: IPS, 1992), p. xviii; Bulletin issued by Bureau Nationale, Damascus [summer 1938] in Creech Jones Papers, MSS. Brit. Emp. S. 332, Box 30, File2, WL.
[148] Letter, Burr (Depot Mt Scopus) to Mother and Father, n.d. [late 1937], Burr Papers, 88/8/1, IWMD.
[149] Blowing up the Sook, Tulloch Photograph Album, MSS. Brit. Emp. S. 477, Files 7 and 8, Box 2, WL.
[150] Capt A. J. H. Dove, 'House Demolitions in Palestine,' *Royal Engineers Journal* 50 (December 1936), p. 515.

Commissioners still held sway. One such official told soldiers not to damage a next-door house during demolition, which the Army managed to do: 'The four charges went up in succession quite successfully, and were greeted by faint cheers from the assembled villagers. Perhaps some of the snipers were not too popular.'[151] By late 1938, the Army had demolition powers over the more discerning civil administration, as when civil officers agreed to the demolition of four houses in a village after a local gun battle: 'but this was not done till after Military Control was introduced' so the (Queen's Own) Royal West Kent Regiment 'went down to Breika [Burayka south of Haifa] which has, I understand, been almost entirely demolished.'[152] 'And they blew the lot, Got the people out and they just flattened it,' sometimes on the basis of intelligence from an informer, noted a soldier.[153] Soldiers' memories of flattening villages and parts of towns are consistent, if not always on the exact location. When rebels sabotaged the Jaffa–Jerusalem railway in March 1939, the Army determined Lydda town was responsible 'for a radius of five miles,' warned the populace and marked houses for demolition in case of future sabotage, 'two belonging to the mayor's party: two to the opposition,' before cautioning that any trouble would mean that the town's 'Suq will "go up" again' if residents broke their word.[154] As GOC Wavell put it, 'guilty' villages 'have had, I think, a fairly severe lesson.'[155] Jews suggested that the British confiscate all the property of 'assassins' and of Hajj Amin and give it all to orphaned families: 'Demolishing their homes won't be as effective as taking all their money and fields and giving it to the victims.'[156] One suggestion was to scale demolition against rifles surrendered by villages, thereby 'combining disarmament with punishment.'[157] Flying debris in some demolitions injured local people and soldiers alike.[158] As sometimes only parts of gelignite charges in buildings exploded, rebels extracted the remains for use in IEDs (ten cases in one incident), while also recovering 'scattered fingers' of unignited gelignite

---

[151] Ibid., p. 517.
[152] Diary, 12 November 1938, Scrivenor Papers, MSS. Brit. Emp. S. 378, WL.
[153] Tinson, 15255/5, IWMSA.
[154] HQ, 19th Infantry Brigade (Sarafend), to O'Connor, 10 March 1939, O'Connor Papers, 3/4/42, LHCMA.
[155] Wavell to Deverell (CIGS), 20 October 1937, Palestine, 1937–38 Volume, Wavell Papers, POH.
[156] Letter, City of Bnei Brak to Weizmann, 17 July 1938, File 04/-163-A/621: Riots, April 1936 [but actually June–September 1938, one bundle of papers], TAMA.
[157] Appreciation by AOC Peirse of the Political Situation, 31 July 1936, Peirse Papers, AC71/13/47, RAFM.
[158] Telegram, High Commissioner Palestine to Secretary of State for Colonies, 30 June 1936, L/PS/12/3344–45: Palestine Situation, IOR.

left by Army sappers in haystacks.[159] The Royal Hampshire Regiment museum in Winchester has one of these IEDs on display: made mostly of wood with a battery in the centre core and two wooden contact levers. Demolition kept open the transport routes that sustained Palestine's economy and Jewish settlements, with Tel Aviv's Jewish mayor asking the British to cut down orange groves and demolish walls alongside roads out of Tel Aviv and to Jewish conurbations.[160] Soldiers had earlier demolished walls from 'which it had been observed some shots had been fired' and they issued wayside curfews to roads and railways to support demolition of hiding places.[161] After rebels shot at trains near Lydda, the British imposed a £P.5,000 collective fine and 'the house of a notorious agitator was demolished.'[162] The size of a structure or random accusations of guilt could determine the choice of buildings for demolition. At Hamama village north-east of Gaza, civil official Lees had to choose a house for demolition after sniping and sabotage of the railway line nearby, adding that local *mukhtars* would suffer personally if they did not help: 'I asked them, accordingly, to give me within ten minutes the names of ten bad characters in the village from whom I would select at random one person whose house would be demolished and told them that if they failed to produce the list within the specified time I would demolish one of their own houses.'[163] In the interim, a policeman told Lees the name of the 'worst Mukhtar' so when after deliberation the *mukhtars* returned to say that they could not find ten bad men, 'I said that in that case I would carry out my ultimatum to the letter and that the house of Mukhtar so-and-so was expropriated and would be demolished,' this being the man picked out by the police.[164] Lees gave the victim ten minutes to clear the house of his effects, after which he handed over the operation to the Army. There then ensued a discussion about which building was the man's home. The more sympathetic Lees accepted that what looked like a barn was his home, while the Army was keen to blow up a bigger building nearby. The soldiers were unhappy at Lees calling them out to blow up a small building, while Lees was angry that soldiers could only be 'kept in hand

---

[159] Appendix: Explanatory Notes, Captured and Translated Arabic Material with Commentary, p. 134, Wingate Papers, Microfilm M2313, BL.

[160] Letter, Councils of Jewish Neighbourhoods to DC Southern District, 30 September 1938, File 04/-165-B/622: The Riots: Negotiations with the Government, July 1936–June 1940, TAMA.

[161] Telegram, High Commissioner Palestine to Secretary of State for Colonies, 15 July 1936, L/PS/12/3344–45: Palestine Situation, IOR.

[162] Telegram, High Commissioner Palestine to Secretary of State for Colonies, 27 June 1936, L/PS/12/3344–45: Palestine Situation, IOR.

[163] ADC Lees (Gaza) to DC (Jaffa), 29 September 1936, Lees Papers, 5/6/6, LHCMA.

[164] Ibid.

by the repeated spectacle of large houses being demolished.'[165] Obviously annoyed, the Army laid excessively large charges that badly damaged two bigger buildings nearby. The Army could be exact with demolitions, so when Colonel Thornton in charge expressed 'mild regret' at this to Lees and said that it was due to the thickness of the walls of the house:

This explanation was greeted by a burst of quickly-controlled giggles from a certain Captain who was standing by. This Captain and I had both witnessed two days ago, a demolition in Isdud village [north-east of Gaza] where I had ordered a dwelling-house to be demolished without injuring an irrigation pump-house which practically formed part of the dwelling-house – an operation which had been carried out with perfect success, but at which Col. Thornton had not been present.[166]

Palestinians were furious at the destruction and one wrote defiantly to the Army in 1939 that the 'kings [sic] houses are being stolen by thieves. If you believe that this will do us any harm, you are mistaken ... we will die for the sake of our country.'[167] But such punishment had the desired effect of pacifying the people. Deaths of soldiers fortified demolition as an alternative punishment to, say, illegally executing local villagers and a way of calming other ranks and deterring future rebel attacks. For example, when rebels killed two men from the Royal Scots and wounded four in 1938, an Army officer wrote home how

they are trying out a new policy in the country. It will be interesting to hear what the effects of this will be and what people in England will say about it – I suppose they'll talk a lot of nonsense in the House of Commons. Today just over half of this village was blown up and completely flattened, tomorrow some more of the village is being blown up. Up to now they've never blown up more than an odd house or two in a village – today they blew up fifty-three and tomorrow another ten will be blown up. They are broadcasting tonight that this village is being made an example of and if anyone else cares to shoot up the army from their village again exactly the same thing will happen to them. We are all delighted about it, our only regrets are that we have not been allowed to flatten the whole village ... I am sure it's the only way to deal with these people and it's all nonsense condemning the Italians for using the same methods in Abyssinia.[168]

The method of rebel attack had some impact on security force reprisals, with soldiers angry at hidden bombs: 'We didn't mind being shot at but

[165] Ibid.
[166] Ibid.
[167] Palestine Press Cuttings, 17 November 1938–26 January 1944, Letter, Sa'id Abdul Kada Eshker, Leader of Jerah Party in Jerusalem and Ramallah Area to District Military Officer Ramallah, 1 February 1939, Briance Papers, BP.
[168] Letter, Street to Father, 21 July 1938, Street Papers, File: Letters Home, LHCMA.

land mines were hardly fair play.'[169] Elsewhere, the Army over-rode civil objections to making *mukhtars* personally responsible for safe passage on nearby roads, 'usually in a personal interview.'[170]

Internal building searches paralleled demolitions and when these were punitive the destruction could be immense; even when they were not, soldiers stole effects and damaged things. As the German press put it, 'Searching is destroying ... inhabitants are torn from their beds; neither men nor women are given a chance to dress; and then the searching begins.'[171] 'Occasionally we were ordered to rough the place up a bit,' as one officer put it; 'we did certainly mess villages up,' in the words of a policeman.[172] 'I'm very sorry. Looking back now,' an officer recalled many years later, 'we must have caused a lot of nuisance in those houses, having to tidy up the place afterwards.'[173] When police failed to catch an alleged sniper at his house, they at least had the pleasure of turning over his home: 'It will take him about a month to put things straight[;] this might be a lesson to him in future.'[174] Soldiers usually divided the men and women and contained them on village threshing room floors or in wired 'cages' on prolonged searches, while soldiers searched and destroyed effects, burnt grain, and poured olive oil over household food and effects.[175] The British meanwhile screened the village men in front of hooded or hidden Arab informers who would nod when a 'suspect' was found, or by British officials checking their papers against lists of suspects. If the Army was not on a reprisal operation but was following up an intelligence lead and looking for suspects or hidden weapons, destruction was incidental to the searching of properties. Troops also used primitive metal detectors on such operations.[176] However, on such operations, brutality against villagers could occur as the Army tried to extract from them intelligence on the whereabouts of hidden weapons caches or suspects, as happened at the village of Halhul in 1939. In some cases, the brutality would then extend to the vandalism of property as a means of gaining information. The level of destruction varied. The Army used the excuse of weapons searches to justify any damage if there were

[169] King Clark, *Free for a Blast*, p. 158; King Clark, p. 34, 448607, IWMSA.
[170] Baynes, *The Forgotten Victor*, pp. 54–55.
[171] In anon., 'British Methods in Palestine,' *Yorkshire Post* (23 November 1938).
[172] Shepperd, 4597/06, p. 47, IWMSA; Kitson, 10688/6, IWMSA.
[173] Hose, p. 7, 4501/03, IWMSA.
[174] Letter, Burr to Mother and Father, n.d., Burr Papers, 88/8/1, IWMD.
[175] Diary of School Year in Palestine, 1938–39, by H. M. Wilson, Wilson Papers, GB165-0302, pp. 36ff, MEC; correspondence and pictures in J&EM Papers, GB165-0161, Box 61, File 3, MEC.
[176] D. S. Daniell, *The Royal Hampshire Regiment. Volume 3* (Aldershot: Gale and Polden, 1955), p. 34.

complaints. The destruction of property was alien behaviour for soldiers but they did the job with gusto, once prompted. The officer tasked with checking on destruction in one village reprimanded a corporal who had left intact a beautiful cabinet full of glasses; the officer then destroyed the cabinet and its contents.[177] The British designated some searches as 'punitive,' as one private recalled, 'Oh yes, punitive. You smashed wardrobes with plates, glass mirrors in and furniture, anything you could see you smashed.'[178] The local civil official told Colonel J. S. S. Gratton, then a subaltern with the Hampshire Regiment, that the unit's search of Safad was a punitive raid, and so they could

knock the place about. And it's very alien to a chap like you or me to go in and break the chair and kick chatty in with all the oil in and mixed it in with the bedclothes and break all the windows and everything. You don't feel like doing it. And I remember the adjutant coming in and saying, 'You are not doing your stuff. They're perfectly intact all those houses you've just searched. This is what you've got to do.' And he picked up a pick helve and sort of burst everything. I said, 'Right OK,' so I got hold of the soldiers and said, 'this is what you've got to do,' you know. And I don't think they liked it much but once they'd started on it you couldn't stop them. And you'd never seen such devastation.[179]

Photographs of 'searches' show the tremendous vandalism: rooms torn apart, bedding, books and clothing in great heaps (Figure 5.4).[180] The Essex Regiment acting 'on info that a house had ammo' found two 'poor old dames (blonde)' in the house: 'we shooed them out (gently) and then pulled the house apart. Results Nil.'[181] In such operations, away from officers' view, looting or the taking of 'souvenirs' was inevitable, and periodic personal searches of men by NCOs under officers' orders failed to stop the problem of endemic petty thieving. While the security forces could legally loot citizens' goods and take away livestock and crops, the Army genuinely frowned on soldiers' illegal looting, as a special order to the two battalions tasked with re-taking the old city of Jerusalem in October 1938 shows: 'Any attempts, even the most minor, at looting, scrounging or souveniring by individual troops or police will be rigorously suppressed.'[182] Troops had to 'turn out their pockets in the presence of the master or mistress of the house' on other occasions, and

[177] 'Palestine: The First Intifada' (BBC: Timewatch, 27 March 1991).
[178] Howbrook, 4619, p. 2, IWMSA.
[179] Gratton, 4506, pp. 14–15, IWMSA.
[180] Arab Revolt in Palestine Photograph Album 1937, ACHA.
[181] Letter, Passfield to Bet[ty], 24 December 1937, Passfield Papers, ERMC.
[182] Special Order by Brig I. C. Grant, CO, 20th Infantry Brigade, October 1938 in J&EM Papers, GB165-0161, Box 61, File 4, MEC.

5.4 The wreckage from an Army house search
(from American Colony Hotel Archive)

householders signed certificates to confirm that nothing was missing or damaged, 'turn out every man's kit,' proof of the care that troops might take on searches.[183] That said, when a policeman returned £P.4.800 found on a suspect to his wife, villagers delighted in 'the Government's justice,' the officer concluding how they 'would never have seen it again had troops carried out the capture.'[184] Men in military uniform even broke into a household, robbed two Palestinians and pressed a revolver to the stomach of one man and pressed the trigger, but the weapon failed to fire.[185] There is extensive archival material on petty thieving during searching, even of policemen in cars holding up and robbing people, but

---

[183] Capt E. P. A. Des Graz, 'Military Control of Disturbed Areas,' *Journal of the Royal United Service Institution* 81 (November 1936), pp. 813–14; Hose, p. 4, 4501/03, IWMSA.

[184] Personal Diary, 1940–April 1941, 21 January 1941, Briance Papers, BP.

[185] Daily Situation Report, Divisional Police HQ, Haifa Rural District, 9 January 1938, Scrivenor Papers, MSS. Brit. Emp. S. 377, p. 51, WL.

such files also detail Army officers trying to stop such things.[186] British Dr Elliot Forster, typically very critical of the Army, also commented on positive changes in troops' behaviour in Hebron – 'military thieving has stopped' – showing that patterns of theft depended on unit military discipline and local circumstances, even if soldiers' propensity to steal was chronic.[187] Senior Army officers passed on the blame and claimed that soldiers only looted when they went on searches with the police whose morale had collapsed.[188] Jews complained that Arab policemen beat and robbed them.[189]

Civil–Military Relations: From Military Courts to Military Rule

In 1937, the Palestine Government's Chief Secretary, William Battershill, made the following diary entry on High Commissioner Arthur Wauchope and his administration:

And now we have the picture not overdrawn. A service in certain respects below the standard of the usual Colonial administration in ability, a terribly difficult task to carry out owing to the terms of the mandate and the warring sects, no esprit de corps, no clear cut policy, administration run on opera bouffe lines, the whole service terrified of its chief and hating him. The chief brilliant but unstable and always about to be rude to his officials ... It is all tight rope walking with a vengeance. Palestine has been described to me by a man who knows it well as a ship sailing on an angry sea rudderless and without a pilot.[190]

The Colonial Office replaced Wauchope, effectively from late 1937 and formally on 1 March 1938, but under his successor, Harold MacMichael, Government rule disappeared from swathes of Palestine during the zenith of the insurgency in the summer of 1938. The problem was not Wauchope but the depth of the insurgency, the numbers of soldiers available for suppression, and the civil–military balance supporting pacification. Good administration was not going to beat the rebels on its own. Certainly, effective counter-insurgency demanded good politico-military coordination, as in Malaya in the 1950s where chains-of-command and interleaved layers of military and civil hierarchies alongside a central

---

[186] Letter, Burr (Depot Mt Scopus) to Mother and Father, n.d. [late 1937], Burr Papers, 88/8/1, IWMD; ADC Lees (Gaza) to DC (Southern District, Jaffa), 7 June 1936, Lees Papers, 5/6/1, LHCMA.
[187] Diary, 14 November 1938, Forster Papers, GB165-0109, p. 95, MEC.
[188] Letter, O'Connor to Wife, 22 October 1938, O'Connor Papers, 3/1/16, LHCMA.
[189] Avraham Mizrahi to Municipal Office, 4 May 1936, File 04-161-B/621: Riots, May–July 1936 [one bundle of papers], TAMA.
[190] Diary, 14 August 1937, Battershill Papers, MSS. Brit. Emp. S. 467, Box 12, File 6, WL.

Federal War Council, regional War Executive Committees and district-level Executive Committees managed pacification.[191] Coordination was vital in lots of ways, as with giving soldiers access to pre-existing systems of legal-civil controls, so boosting the number, scale and type of punishments and controls available to them, but only through the heavy use of force was Britain going to prevail against determined (if disorganised) resistance. The argument here is that when the Army made the effort it swamped the country with troops and beat the rebels. The emphasis is on military action and authority, even if much of that 'action' was against civilians and not armed insurgents, as with demolition. The Army won by taking charge, the civil administration helping them in the job with its District and Assistant District Commissioners advising Army area commanders. The limit was martial law. Without full martial law and with an extant civil infrastructure, there was restraint and this kept open diplomatic channels and made possible, firstly, the October 1936 ceasefire and the Peel Commission of 1937 (that introduced the idea of partition of Palestine into Arab and Jewish areas) and, secondly, the Woodhead Commission of 1938 (that started the process of doing away with partition[192]) and the London St James' Palace negotiations of February 1939 prior to the May 1939 White Paper (that formally reversed Peel's partition plan). This was classic British strategy that moved from exemplary military force to political conciliation. The issue was whether the Army would make a peace by creating a desert of Palestine by smashing, stealing, and demolition, and by detaining, impoverishing, and beating everyone, without effecting a follow-up political settlement with Arab political elites, as actually happened. Or as a cartoon at the time put it, the 'Zionist' says to British soldiers as they leave behind them wretched Palestinian women and children amidst the ruins of their homes: 'Congratulations, my dear Sir, on the conscientious way in which you are fulfilling your order as the Mandatory Power' (Figure 5.5).[193] Britain wanted a long-term political solution and managed military force could make this happen, cowing the Palestinians before any political settlement, but this was impossible as the Zionist project and Palestinian resistance were irreconcilable and so dashed British hopes of a long-term solution and in 1945 there was a Jewish insurgency, after which Palestinians and Jews went to war in 1948 and

---

[191] John McCuen, *The Art of Counter-Revolutionary Warfare* (London: Faber and Faber, 1966), p. 184.

[192] See the correspondence in FO 371/21864–21865, TNA.

[193] Anon., Cartoon from c. July 1938 in Scrapbook of Articles about the American Colony, Palestine, People and Events and Loose Enclosures 1938, ACHA.

The Zionist: Congratulations, my dear Sir, on the conscientious way in which you are fulfilling your orders as the Mandatory Power.
(*The Palestine Government demolishes the property of Arabs suspected of possessing arms.*)

5.5 Contemporaneous Palestinian cartoon
(from American Colony Hotel Archive)

the British left. Successful pacification demanded a political peace and any faint hope of this disappeared with Palestinian rejection of the May 1939 White Paper and then global war in September 1939. Palestinians rejected the White Paper's conclusion that future Jewish immigration would be subject to 'Arab acquiescence,' a subject beyond the remit of this study but elite politics had its part to play here, 'another sign of the curious, uncompromising appearance of the politics of the notables; compromise was always sought but could not be sought visibly.'[194]

The order-of-battle appendix (Appendix A) to this book is the starting point to understanding the impact that masses of similarly well-trained, motivated troops with emergency state powers can have on suppressing rebellion. Only superbly organised, united, and ruthless guerrilla resistance

[194] Walid Khalidi (ed.), *Before Their Diaspora: A Photographic History of the Palestinians, 1876–1948* (Washington, DC: IPS, 2004), p. 191; M. E. Yapp, *The Near East since the First World War* (London: Longman, 1991), pp. 132–33.

could undercut such powerful civil–military structures, and Palestinians fought with determination and little else, and often against each other. Army deployment came in three waves (or 'surges' to use a more recent term) that washed over Palestine: in June 1936, September 1936, and September 1938. These surges ended rebellion. Of the twenty-seven infantry battalions and armoured units in Palestine in the first phase of the revolt in 1936, only two were there on 19 April 1936. Twelve more arrived between May and July and thirteen after 30 August 1936. There was then a ceasefire on 12 October 1936 before the twenty-five formations could grip the country. In the second phase of the revolt, thirty-seven units went to Palestine, with sixteen arriving in or embarking for Palestine by or soon after the Munich settlement (September–December 1938) and four more prior to the White Paper (January–May 1939). Thus, 54 per cent of units deployed from September 1937 to December 1939 arrived between September 1938 and May 1939. In the first phase, before the troops could institute martial law and have 'moral effect' there was a ceasefire; in phase two, the Army with forms of martial law and supported by the troop surge after Munich defeated the rebellion in about four months. New supportive legislation in October 1938 gave the Army control of the country. Irregular units such as the Special Night Squads in the summer of 1938 reflected the lack of boots on the ground and military weakness not strength. Murky abuses substituted for what the Army preferred: legal suppression without illegal action, and was why it terminated the squads after Munich when conventional forces arrived in numbers, notwithstanding that the SNSs killed large numbers of Palestinians.

These troops operated within an enabling (and evolving) civil–military framework and the final part of this chapter examines the balance of civil–military relations and the forms of military rule that enabled pacification. The Army instinctively argued for forms of military rule from the start and it opposed the first ceasefire that Wauchope forced through as it anticipated a recrudescence of insurgency from an undefeated enemy. The Army found Wauchope's hopes for a political solution 'difficult to understand,' the Government having 'no desire to stop sub-war and re-establish British authority in the country.'[195] In the second phase of the revolt after September 1937, the Army decisively clamped down, referring back to 1936 and what it saw as the 'remarkably free run' given to rebels and the 'conciliation policy' whereby the 'rebellion had been given a six-months' run without the imposition of any intensive measures of repression.'[196] The issue was the strength of civil authority over the Army

---

[195] Simson, *British Rule and Rebellion*, p. 77.
[196] Ibid., p. 286.

in the first phase of the revolt, maintained on 12 October 1936 by the ceasefire cancelling out the Palestine Martial Law (Defence) Order in Council of 26 September 1936 that never came into effect then.[197] GOC Dill arrived in Palestine as the first Army commander to replace RAF AOC Peirse on 9 September 1936[198] and wrote how Wauchope 'hated' martial law and was

delighted that peace has come without having to resort to stern measures. But the peace is only an armed truce. The whole Arab organisation, under that arch-scoundrel the Mufti, remains to re-new rebellion when the result of the Royal [Peel] Commission's labours proves distasteful to the Arab population … Moreover they [Arab rulers] prevented the declaration of Martial Law, because we obviously could not act while the conversations, which we had encouraged, were going on. And so the Arab leaders skipped out with honour and renown instead by [sic] being scattered to the four winds.[199]

With renewed fighting in September 1937, the Army took charge of the judiciary and then the executive (there being no legislature) but both branches survived in attenuated form. There were four types of military rule available for what the military deemed 'sub-war,' all of which required the Army (or militarised police) to varying degrees: 'real' martial law, 'statu-tory' martial law, semi-military rule by the civil power, and emergency rule by the civil power.[200] Government in Palestine after 1920 was emergency rule by the civil power, with police Gendarmes up to 1926 and a garrison of two infantry battalions from 1929; by the summer of 1936 and with amended Emergency Regulations, Government was semi-military rule by civil powers; by October 1938, Government was 'statutory' martial law but with regulations 'drawn up article by article, like a long code of rules' along-side some civil authority, so stopping short of full 'real' martial law.[201]

Martial law was 'an almost mystical remedy' for the Army and Dill told Wauchope that he had it ready for 4 October 1936, returning to his headquarters convinced that the High Commissioner agreed with him.[202] Martial law depended on Wauchope's agreement, after which

---

[197] Foreign Jurisdiction, 1890. Order in Council, dated 26 September 1936, entitled The Palestine Martial Law (Defence) Order in Council 1936. Presented to the House of Commons in Pursuance of Section 11 of the Act. Privy Council Office, 20 November 1936 (courtesy of Parliamentary Archives, Houses of Parliament).

[198] The *Air Force List* for October 1936 gives a date of 15 September 1936 for the change in command; the *Army List* for December 1936 gives a date of 9 September for the start of Dill's command.

[199] Letter, Dill to Wavell, 31 October 1936, Palestine, 1937–38 Volume, Wavell Papers, POH.

[200] Simson, *British Rule and Rebellion*, p. 103.

[201] Ibid., pp. 257–59.

[202] Charles Townshend, 'Martial Law: Legal and Administrative Problems of Civil Emergency in Britain and the Empire, 1800–1940,' *The Historical Journal* 25/1 (1982),

the Army would take over. Wauchope prevaricated, using the text of the September 1936 martial law order 'by which the High Commissioner was authorised to delegate to the G.O.C. at his discretion all *or any* of his powers' to delay: 'It was these last words that gave Sir Arthur the one outlet for which he was so desperate.'[203] Wauchope repeatedly put back the date for martial law while working the diplomatic track so that Arab rulers could convince Hajj Amin to call off armed action and by the time that martial law had been pushed back once again to 14 October a ceasefire was in force. While Wauchope resisted martial law, he used it as leverage to warn the AHC before the ceasefire that 'he would be unable to continue his efforts for a settlement as the reins of government would then pass into other hands. This is taken to indicate that General Dill will take control of the country.'[204] Instead of holding their nerve, the rebels yielded to the promise of the Peel Commission, pressure from Arab potentates in Transjordan, Iraq, Yemen, and Saudi Arabia, and the threat of draconian martial law.[205] Power at this stage of the revolt lay with Wauchope and the Colonial Office; nor did the War Office necessarily want the encumbrance of colonial administration, despite the Army constantly demanding it. The CIGS in London had told Dill on 29 September 1936 that the Secretary of State for the Colonies 'insisted that to hand over complete control to you would mean handing over the whole of Palestine lock, stock and barrel, to the War Office. He explained the difficulties in doing this: and it is a commitment we here would be sorry to add to those already with us.'[206] Interestingly, while Dill and al-Qawuqji arrived in Palestine at the same time wanting to intensify military action, for both men their political masters chose de-escalation. Dill never sought a ceasefire. He wanted to finish the business quickly. He wrote to the CIGS how Wauchope was negotiating with the AHC 'and that body is thinking hard what martial law may mean. Most if not all of them are, I understand, very anxious to find a way out. What I fear is that they may call the strike off. That would make it very difficult for H.M.G. to declare martial law … I am beginning to feel that the best thing that can happen is for negotiations to fail and for us to get busy

p. 189; A Quarter of My Century by Dudley Clarke, p. 572, Clarke Papers, 99/2/1–3: DW/8, IWMD.

[203] A Quarter of My Century by Dudley Clarke, p. 572, Clarke Papers, 99/2/1–3: DW/8, IWMD. Text is from Section V(1) of the 1936 Palestine Martial Law (Defence) Order in Council: 'The High Commissioner may, if he thinks fit, by Proclamation delegate to the General Officer Commanding the Forces in Palestine all or any of his powers.'

[204] Note, 14 September 1936, 867N.00/395 [Reel M#1037/2], NARA II.

[205] US Consul General Palestine to State Department, 9 October 1936, 867N.00/407 [Reel M#1037/2], NARA II.

[206] Deverell (CIGS, London) to Dill, 29 September 1936, Dill Papers, 2/9, LHCMA.

under martial law.'[207] Dill wanted 'full-blooded' martial law as without it the Arabs would go 'bleating' to the civil authorities.[208] Had Dill had his way in 1936, the British may well have ended the revolt two years earlier than was the case, and using the same methods. Significantly, when London issued the Palestine (Defence) Order in Council in March 1937, in anticipation of renewed violence, it allowed the High Commissioner by 'Proclamation' to delegate all his powers to the GOC but the power to give power still lay with the High Commissioner.[209]

The High Commissioner (more exactly Chief Secretary Battershill as Wauchope was away at the time) agreed in November 1937 to military courts but not military rule, for certain offences, and with his holding the Royal prerogative of clemency; nor did the GOC at the time, Wavell, want military rule.[210] The clemency point reappeared in December 1938 regarding an Egyptian sentenced to hang for having a revolver, and confirmed by the GOC. Sir Miles Lampson in charge in Egypt petitioned for clemency. The Secretary of State for the Colonies was of the opinion that MacMichael 'should make use of the power conferred upon' him 'by Article 16 Order in Council which, I am advised, remains unimpaired by regulation 14A of Defence (Military Courts) Regulation, 1937' to commute the sentence; this proves that the GOC never had the final word on capital sentences.[211] Military courts came into force on the 18 November 1937. Each was chaired by an officer of field rank alongside two other officers to try those charged with '(1) the discharge of firearms at any persons; (2) the carrying of arms, bombs etc. and (3) causing sabotage and intimidation. Offences in the first two categories will be punishable by death,' with no right of appeal after the GOC's (or High Commissioner's) confirmation.[212] This was a graded judicial measure. Civil courts still tried offences excepting firearms, sabotage and intimidation, as we saw in Chapter 2.[213] Wavell, as Dill's successor as GOC,

---

[207] Dill to Deverell (CIGS, London), 22 September 1936, Dill Papers, 2/9, LHCMA.
[208] Ibid.
[209] The Palestine (Defence) Order in Council 1937 in *Ordinances, Regulations, Rules, Orders and Notices. Government of Palestine. Annual Volume for 1937. Volume 2* (Jerusalem: Government Printing Press, 1938), pp. 260–64. See also Simson, *British Rule and Rebellion*, pp. 96–98.
[210] 'Death Sentence in Palestine, Palestine Sheikh Executed,' Cuttings from *The Times*, 25 and 29 November 1937, Chief Secretary's Office: M/5088/10, ISA.
[211] Secretary of State for Colonies to High Commissioner Palestine, 19 December 1938, FO 371/21868, p. 415, TNA.
[212] 'Terrorism in Palestine: Military Courts,' Cutting from *The Times*, 11 November 1937, Chief Secretary's Office: M/5088/10, ISA; 'Death Sentence in Palestine, Palestine Sheikh Executed,' Cuttings from *The Times*, 25 and 29 November 1937, Chief Secretary's Office: M/5088/10, ISA; Note in Scrivenor Papers, MSS. Brit. Emp. S. 377, p. 20, WL.
[213] Note in Scrivenor Papers, MSS. Brit. Emp. S. 377, p. 20, WL.

in August 1937 had seen military courts while 'retaining civil control' as a 'suitable middle course between the present unsatisfactory situation as regards punishment of crime and full military control, for which I feel the time has not yet come.'[214] After the assassination of Andrews in September 1937, Wavell still hesitated to use 'the big gun of martial law' but pressure was such that he would 'probably be called on to take over and am making preparations accordingly.'[215] Instead, Wavell negotiated the establishment of military courts with the Colonial Office, with the Palestine Government's executive council, and with Battershill as Officer Administering the Government. Military judicial process would overcome the problem that with the 'present Judiciary' it was 'unlikely' that capital changes to the law for firearms 'would be enforced.'[216] Moreover, Wavell did not have sufficient troops to enforce martial law in full and so, as he put it, 'If I took over with my present force, I should not be in a position to jump on trouble wherever it occurred, and might be thrown largely on the defensive, which would soon ruin the moral effect, and might in the end mean more troops still.'[217] Rather than ruthless military control, the Army in Palestine was short of men and reluctant to assume power. Wavell's aim was to try to get through to the colder winter months without military rule or courts, hoping also for another post-Peel Commission.[218] That the 'Arab hates the wet and cold more than most people, and is inclined to be dormant from December onwards,' in Wavell's view, encouraged such delay.[219] Military courts for terror-related offences were a graded judicial measure short of military executive control and the practicable option in the autumn of 1937. The view of the CIGS in London on 2 November 1937 was that military rule was 'our last and strongest card' and while Government and police were in charge he was against this measure, but he supported Wavell's proposals for military courts for certain offences.[220] Wavell then wired London for a supply of suitable officers for military courts, and the War Office

---

[214] Letter from Wavell [to Haining, DMO, London?], 6 October 1937, Palestine, 1937–38 Volume, Wavell Papers, POH.

[215] Appreciation, 30 September–1 October 1937, Wavell to Haining (DMO, London), Palestine, 1937–38 Volume, Wavell Papers, POH.

[216] Cypher Message, Wavell to Troopers (WO) London, 7 October 1937, Palestine, 1937–38 Volume, Wavell Papers, POH; Wavell to Field Marshal Deverell, 1 October 1937, Palestine, 1937–38 Volume, Wavell Papers, POH.

[217] Wavell to Deverell (CIGS), 20 October 1937, Palestine, 1937–38 Volume, Wavell Papers, POH.

[218] Ibid.

[219] Ibid.

[220] Deverell (CIGS) to Wavell, 2 November 1937, Palestine, 1937–38 Volume, Wavell Papers, POH.

sent four 'good' officers.[221] The military wanted extension of powers to include death sentences for those who worked for the revolt but did not carry arms – 'superior officers' rather than the 'private soldiers' – but this was politically undesirable and so never implemented.[222] The Jewish Agency, meanwhile, worried about Jews caught with illegal arms, so Shertok went to see Wavell, who reassured him about the real target: 'I explained to him that it would be applied with common sense and the death penalty was not intended to be inflicted on those who carried arms in genuine self-defence.'[223] According to one policeman, only in January 1938 did courts first sentence a Jew (to five years) for carrying arms.[224]

The British were sure that Palestinians were 'very frightened' of the new courts.[225] The power of military law impressed Bahjat Abu Gharbiyya who had a press job at the time. The process took less than an hour and the court passed the death sentence. Wavell confirmed it that evening and the accused was hanged the next day: 'We cheered for British justice!'[226] This is an exaggeration. The speediest processing of a capital offence suspect usually given was that of rebel band leader Shaykh Farhan al-Sa'di, turned in to British authorities on 22 November 1937, tried on 24 November and hanged on 27 November 1937.[227] Civil officer Hugh Foot recalled pleading not with the GOC but with the High Commissioner for the old man's life, to no avail, and the British hanged al-Sa'di 'within the week.'[228] Hanged after a military trial despite being eighty years old, noted an Arab source.[229] Wavell put al-Sa'di's age at between fifty-five and sixty and as the hanging was

---

[221] Wavell to Haining (DMO, WO), 8 November 1937, Palestine, 1937–38 Volume, Wavell Papers, POH; Deverell (CIGS) to Wavell, 19 November 1937, Palestine, 1937–38 Volume, Wavell Papers, POH.

[222] Section IX, Draft Military report, n.d., O'Connor Papers, 3/4/55, LHCMA.

[223] Wavell to Haining (DMO, WO), 12 November 1937, Palestine, 1937–38 Volume, Wavell Papers, POH; Wavell to Haining (DMO, WO), 16 November 1937, Palestine, 1937–38 Volume, Wavell Papers, POH. See also 'Terrorism in Palestine: Military Courts,' Cutting from *The Times*, 11 November 1937, Chief Secretary's Office: M/5088/10, ISA.

[224] Palestine Press Cuttings, 11 March 1937–23 June 1938, n.d. but c. 24 January 1938, Briance Papers, BP.

[225] Subject DIS, No. 23/37, Divisional Police HQ, Haifa Rural Division, by ASP I, 15 November 1937 in Scrivenor Papers, MSS. Brit. Emp. S. 377, p. 24, WL.

[226] Abu Gharbiyya, *Fi Khidamm al-nidal al-'arabi al-filastini*, pp. 114–17.

[227] Hillel Cohen, *Army of Shadows: Palestinian Collaboration with Zionism, 1917–1948* (Berkeley, CA: University of California Press, 2008), p. 135.

[228] Hugh Foot, *A Start in Freedom* (London: Hodder and Stoughton, 1964), p. 51; Cohen, *Army of Shadows*, p. 135; 'Death Sentence in Palestine, Palestine Sheikh Executed,' cuttings from *The Times*, 25 and 29 November 1937, Chief Secretary's Office: M/5088/10, ISA.

[229] Izzat Tanus, *Al-Falastiniyun [The Palestinians]* (Beirut: PLO Research Centre, 1982), p. 194.

taking place during Ramadan, he referred back to the Ottoman legal code under which executions during the Muslim holy month were 'perfectly legal.'[230] That said, the British had postponed the execution of two men for firing on troops in 1936 because it was Ramadan.[231] The Jewish press reported a man tried on 16 February 1938 and sentenced to death on the 18th. The military court found him guilty after deliberating for fifteen minutes.[232] Abu Gharbiyya complained that Jews received prison sentences for capital offences such as discharging firearms, rather than be hanged as was the case for Arabs, one of whom was executed for carrying four bullets.[233] Regimental journals talked of courts working at 'high pressure' as the 'Arab is slow to learn.'[234] Did military courts disproportionately find guilt, prefer Jews, and hang the convicted? Some basic quantitative analysis suggests otherwise, supporting points made above on limits to British violence, and this was for courts sitting in the high period of insurgency in 1938:

- Cases tried by military courts 29/12/37–13/1/38: 17 cases (several being juveniles 14–15 years old): 2 death sentences (1 executed and 1 got life), 4 acquitted, and 11 imprisoned.[235]
- Cases tried by military courts 14/1/38–27/1/38: 13 cases tried and 1 man listed as 110 years old: 3 executed, 2 acquitted and 1 prosecutor withdrew case, and 7 imprisoned of which 2 bound over.[236]
- Cases tried by military courts 7/3/38–21/3/38: 9 cases (1 an 85-year-old): 3 to hang and all executed, 3 acquitted, and 3 imprisoned.[237]
- Cases tried by military courts 21/4/38–4/5/38: 12 cases (from a 14-year-old to a man aged 75): 2 hanged, 4 acquitted, 6 imprisoned (including the 14-year-old to a borstal), but of the 6 sent to jail 1 reduced to binding over and 1 'finding reversed accused released.'[238]

[230] Cypher Message, Wavell to Troopers (WO, London), 25 November 1937, Palestine, 1937–38 Volume, Wavell Papers, POH.
[231] Dorsetshire Regiment, Situation Reports, 16th Infantry Brigade, Nablus, 16 November 1936, 88/353, Shelf C4, Box 3, KMM.
[232] *Haaretz* (20 February 1938).
[233] Author interview, Abu Gharbiyya, Amman, Jordan, 21 June 2009 (and subsequent correspondence).
[234] 'Extracts from the CO's Quarterly Letter to 31 December 1937,' *The Essex Regiment Gazette* 6/46 (March 1938), p. 280.
[235] Summary of Intelligence, Palestine and Transjordan, 14 January 1938, by Wing Commander Ritchie at GHQ [1/38], CO 732/81/9, TNA.
[236] Summary of Intelligence, Palestine and Transjordan, 28 January 1938, by Wing Commander Ritchie at GHQ [2/38], CO 732/81/9, TNA.
[237] Summary of Intelligence, Palestine and Transjordan, 25 March 1938, by Wing Commander Ritchie at GHQ [6/38], CO 732/81/9, TNA.
[238] Summary of Intelligence, Palestine and Transjordan, 6 May 1938, by Wing Commander Ritchie at GHQ [9/38], CO 732/81/9, TNA.

- Cases tried by military courts 3/5/38–16/5/38: 10 cases (1 a boy aged 12–14 and another a man aged 90): 6 imprisoned of which 2 reduced to binding over (including the boy), 1 hanged, and 3 acquitted.[239]
- Cases tried by military courts 14/6/38–25/7/38: 31 cases tried (aged from 16–88): 8 sentenced to death (4 hanged, the rest reduced to prison terms), 12 imprisoned (but 4 reduced to 'binding over' including the 88-year-old), and 11 acquitted.[240]
- Cases tried by military courts 12/7/38–10/8/38: 13 cases with 5 sentenced to death (3 reduced to prison sentences and 2 hanged), 4 acquitted, and 4 imprisoned.[241]
- Cases tried by military courts 1/8/38–23/8/38: 15 people tried (2 of whom have Jewish names) and 10 acquitted (including both Jews, one of whom was 13 years old), 4 were imprisoned and 1 sentenced to death and hanged 'for carrying a firearm and ammunition' but others with this charge were acquitted.[242]
- Cases tried by military courts 17/8/38–14/9/38: 21 Arabs tried, 5 acquitted, 13 imprisoned, 3 executed. Many sentences reduced under the column 'confirmation.'[243]
- Cases tried by military courts 18/8/38–2/9/38: 12 Arabs tried, 7 sentenced to death (2 reduced to imprisonment), 1 imprisoned, and 4 acquitted.[244]
- Cases tried by military courts 13/9/38–4/10/38: 9 Arabs tried, 5 acquitted, 3 sentenced to death (and executed), and 1 imprisoned. One of the 'discharging a firearm at a person' acquitted.[245]
- Cases tried by military courts 26/9/38–19/10/38: 29 Arabs tried before military courts and 6 executed and 18 acquitted and 5 imprisoned.[246]

Carrying a weapon or ammunition in November 1938 did not necessarily mean a death sentence.[247] A military court sentenced one man with

[239] Summary of Intelligence, Palestine and Transjordan, 20 May 1938, by Wing Commander Ritchie at GHQ [10/38], CO 732/81/9, TNA.
[240] Summary of Intelligence, Palestine and Transjordan, 29 July 1938, by Wing Commander Ritchie at GHQ [15/38], CO 732/81/9, TNA.
[241] Summary of Intelligence, Palestine and Transjordan, 12 August 1938, by Wing Commander Ritchie at GHQ [16/38], CO 732/81/9, TNA.
[242] Summary of Intelligence, Palestine and Transjordan, 26 August 1938, by Wing Commander Ritchie at GHQ [17/38], CO 732/81/9, TNA.
[243] Summary of Intelligence, Palestine and Transjordan, 23 September 1938, by Wing Commander Ritchie at GHQ [19/38], CO 732/81/9, TNA.
[244] Summary of Intelligence, Palestine and Transjordan, 9 September 1938, by Wing Commander Ritchie at GHQ [18/38], CO 732/81/9, TNA.
[245] Summary of Intelligence, Palestine and Transjordan, 7 October 1938, by Wing Commander Ritchie at GHQ [20/38], CO 732/81/9, TNA.
[246] Summary of Intelligence, Palestine and Transjordan, 21 October 1938, by Wing Commander Ritchie at GHQ [21/38], CO 732/81/10, TNA.
[247] See court details in appendices to Summaries of Intelligence, Palestine and Transjordan, 1938, by Wing Commander Ritchie at GHQ, CO 732/81/9–10, TNA.

ammunition, primers, rifle parts, cartridge cases, percussion caps, and some gunpowder to seven years.[248] Courts supplied interpreters and they exercised judgement, as when security forces arrested a Transjordanian Bedouin with eighty rounds of ammunition in Jerusalem: 'He did not seem in any way to be concerned with terrorist activities and was probably taking the ammunition to TRANSJORDAN where the carrying of arms is not illegal.'[249] A military court dismissed the case against a thirteen-year-old girl (a *Mizrahi* Jew judging by the name) accused of throwing a bomb due to inconsistent evidence.[250] A military prosecutor recalled how a court president told him that his 'court will never convict an Arab solely on Jewish evidence or vice versa,' adding that the Arab Bar appreciated the military prosecutors' 'impartiality.'[251] One issue was the variation between initial sentence and sentence after confirmation by the GOC, the former being the window through which the world looked at British harshness:

I have seen the report in today's 'Times' of the sentence of 10 years imprisonment on a widowed peasant woman because, during a search for a terrorist leader, a revolver was found hidden in a cave used as her dwelling. We shall almost certainly hear that this sentence has been reduced by the G.O.C., but meanwhile the original sentence has been published in the newspapers ... and we incur the opprobrium of 'neo-Herodian' severity.[252]

Regimental journals noted correctly that military courts were designed for speedy rather than draconian justice.[253] As always, security force personnel moaned about the burden of proof and weight of evidence: 'I was giving evidence at the military court against 3 oozlebarts caught with rifles in my division. We lost the case over the fact that the Ulster Rifles had cleaned and polished the weapons like new.'[254]

The military control introduced in October 1938 like the military courts of November 1937 also stopped short of extreme measures. This was thrashed out during nine meetings at the Colonial Office during

[248] Palestine Press Cuttings, 11 March 1937–23 June 1938, Cutting from 2 December 1937, Briance Papers, BP.
[249] Summary of Intelligence, Palestine and Transjordan, 28 January 1938, by Wing Commander Ritchie at GHQ [2/38], CO 732/81/9, TNA.
[250] *Davar* [*Issue*] (Tel Aviv) (23–24 August 1938).
[251] Notes of Interviews, Col A. Ingham-Brooke, 13 October 1976, Palestine Research Lever Arch File, Thames TV Material on 'Palestine: Promises, Rebellion and Abdication' (1977–78), IWMFA.
[252] Memorandum by Martin (CO), 17 February 1938 in Intelligence Summaries for January 1938, CO 732/81/9, TNA.
[253] *The Hampshire Regimental Journal* 33/2 (February 1938), pp. 58–59.
[254] Letter, Burr (Acre Police Station, Caesar's Camp) to Mother and Father, n.d. [March 1939?], Burr Papers, 88/8/1, IWMD.

a visit by the new High Commissioner, MacMichael, 7–12 October 1938, with War Office representatives present, and with a new GOC, Haining, in charge in Palestine.[255] The two sides simply reversed who advised whom and established formally who had the ultimate say in the field on operations. The Army was now in charge of both but the High Commissioner still had ultimate control as the GOC was only able to appoint military officers as area commanders to assume the role of District Commissioners (who would now advise the Army) 'subject to the approval of the High Commissioner.'[256] The change in command solved the problem that while in some areas civil officials 'would sign 100 blank warrants to be filled in by the Police with names and periods,' elsewhere, District and Assistant District Commissioners held the line: 'we are not satisfied that a village or an individual is involved in any particular crime then we should, I submit, refuse to take any punitive action … it is still nominally a principle of English justice that a man is innocent until he is found guilty, and that the burden of proof rests with the prosecution.'[257] As Haining told O'Connor on 20 October 1938, military control was a hybrid solution:

My delegation of powers to Military Commanders in areas does not derogate from my overriding responsibility to the High Commissioner, from whom the powers devolve. What I do is to delegate operational action in an area, or for a particular area, while remaining the policy controller. For example, you, as commander of military and police, with the District Commissioner as adviser, come to the conclusion that passes in the Old City – or identity cards – are necessary; this needs authorisation or legislation. The procedure is *not* that the District Commissioner should submit to the Chief Secretary, who takes it to the High Commissioner, who is told the General Officer Commanding wants it … The procedure is that the considered proposition is put up to me: I consult Attorney General and others as necessary: and the finished article, as agreed, is put up to the High Commissioner as my request backed by the legal definition and laid out in proper form … But the High Commissioner is H.M.G's representative and it is under him that I operate. The action of the military is my responsibility under him.[258]

The High Commissioner stayed in overall charge, only acquiescing to military control:

[I]t was unanimously decided to delegate to the General Officer Commanding the administration of all emergency regulations he requires and further to give

---

255 Details in FO 371/21864–21865, TNA.
256 Summary of Intelligence, Palestine and Transjordan, 21 October 1938, by Wing Commander Ritchie at GHQ [21/38], CO 732/81/10, TNA.
257 Secret, Letter, Scrivenor to/from Bailey [probably Scrivenor to Bailey], Haifa and Samaria, 7 April 1938, Scrivenor Papers, MSS. Brit. Emp. S. 377, pp. 153–55, WL.
258 Letter, Haining to O'Connor, 20 October 1938, O'Connor Papers, 3/2/3, LHCMA.

him power to appoint with my consent military commanders over districts who will be responsible for all mechanical, transport, security and defence measures and who will take over from district administration all the powers vested at present in the district commissioners by defence regulations. In such districts commissioners will cease to exercise such powers and will become political advisers to the local military commander.[259]

This fell short of martial law. The executive still administered Palestine. The Government 'funked it but it was almost martial law,' in Brigadier Evetts' view.[260] Haining did not like the arrangement, criticising Battershill and complaining that dual military–civil control was a 'Soviet' that would not work, to which Battershill complained: 'I am not accustomed to being cursed by people who have no right to do this.'[261] Field officers wondered at the new compromise and one, after learning who Battershill was at a cocktail party,

pitched into [him] with expressions such as that we civil people gave him all the trouble, that if one man having reasonable common sense could be left in charge they would settle it. He then went on to say that 50 per cent of the officials here were pro Arab ... What a thing to say ... I regret to say that in my opinion relations between the army and the civil power are getting worse.[262]

It was at this moment, with the post-Munich troop surge that the Army screwed down Palestine and crushed the revolt for good. Military courts and rule were pieces of the pacification jigsaw, alongside kinetic operations and demolition, and matching population-based repression: curfews, passes, controls, fines, searches, indefinite detention, confiscation, forced labour, police posts, and censorship. These are the subject of the next chapter.

---

[259] High Commissioner Palestine to Secretary of State for Colonies, 18 October 1938, FO 371/21864, p. 164, TNA.

[260] Notes of Interviews, Evetts (Cheltenham), 2 December 1976, Palestine Research Lever Arch File, Thames TV Material on 'Palestine: Promises, Rebellion and Abdication' (1977–78), IWMFA.

[261] Diary, 10–30 October [1938], Battershill Papers, MSS. Brit. Emp. S. 467, Box 12, File 6, WL.

[262] Diary, 18–29 November [1938], Battershill Papers, MSS. Brit. Emp. S. 467, Box 12, File 6, WL.

6 Screwing Down the Population

The Royal Ulster Rifles

The actions of the Royal Ulster Rifles (RUR) in Galilee in the high period of insurgency in 1938 are a case study of the military pacification method and neatly introduce the population-centric pacification theme of this chapter. The RUR massacred villagers at al-Bassa in September 1938, discussed in Chapter 8, but this was exceptional. Rather than inflicting gruesome atrocities, the RUR exhausted Palestinians through a daily grind of fining, searching, mass detention, forced labour, whipping, and shooting of running suspects. This split the rebels from their supporters, turned the people against rebellion, it controlled and surveilled Palestinians, it gathered intelligence, it disarmed the populace, and it transferred wealth from people to the state. Palestinians escaped the Army at their peril. When 'one old Arab tried to run away,' the officer present 'shot his kneecap off. That was it,' as 'anything that moved in those days you just shot it.'[1] Most if not all of this was legal, including shooting people after soldiers had shouted a challenge. Since October 1937, troops had powers to shoot any man ignoring a challenge, and to use grenades in cave and well searches.[2] The warning was *waqaf* (Arabic for halt, pronounced 'wakeef'), so perhaps as in Aden in 1967 soldiers called out rhyming phrases like 'corned beef' three times before firing on fleeing people, or they might shout 'fuck off.'[3] As soldiers often shot running suspects breaking a cordon and at a distance, it is unclear that they shouted any warning at all or that it was heard. That deafness was

---

[1] Soldier Packer (with KOSB not RUR), 4493/02, pp. 9, 17, IWMSA.
[2] 'Extracts from the CO's Quarterly Letter to 31 December 1937,' *The Essex Regiment Gazette* 6/46 (March 1938), p. 282.
[3] Gavin Goodwin and Gerry Burke, 'I Accuse the Argylls,' (Scottish) *Sunday Mail* (26 April 1981), p. 2; 'Murder in Aden' at http://blackwatchforums.co.uk/showthread.php?11583-The-%91Pitchfork-Murders%92 (accessed 15 February 2018 and originally placed on the defunct 'Troops Out' movement website). The author was told of Israeli troops more recently taught the phrase 'stop *or* we will shoot' in Arabic and genuinely mispronouncing it and unwittingly shouting 'stop *and* we will shoot.'

a common affliction in Palestine's hill lands did not help.[4] A Palestinian was 'foolish enough to run' on seeing policemen so 'we bumped him off.'[5] British-led Jewish troops killed lone Palestinians that they suspected of carrying rifles, and four running men without any warning in another incident.[6] British–Jewish soldiers 'killed on the spot' a man they caught after shouting at him to stop as they suspected that he had a weapon, despite the man begging for his life.[7] General Montgomery in Haifa commanding the larger divisional zone of operations in which the RUR operated even wondered to his civil adviser if an order would help cover men who shot someone 'acting suspiciously with his hands in his pockets.'[8] ' "Shoot first and then challenge" was common both to robbers and the British,' remarked an escaped German prisoner-of-war in the 1940s.[9] Challenge people or shoot them, 'one of the two,' in the words of a soldier protecting the IPC pipeline.[10] A policeman on patrol with Royal Marines (who in photographs wear white and not khaki uniforms when on operations in Haifa) off HMS *Malaya* had orders to shoot 'anybody I find out,' adding that this was 'good fun' as it meant getting in some 'target practice' (Figure 6.1)[11] Through such methods, the Army targeted the people, and the people targeted the rebels. The RUR screwed down the people, leaving villagers 'in such abject terror' of soldiers that it was 'almost impossible' to get near villages 'without the whole population bolting into the surrounding countryside before the cordon is formed.'[12] The Army's collection of fines and searching for suspects gelled with intelligence gathering, counter-rebel band operations, and generic collective punishment. Indeed, a punishment for not giving information was house demolition plus a fine.[13] Jewish intelligence assessed the ordinary

---

[4] E. Mills, *Census of Palestine 1931* (London: HMSO, 1933), i, pp. 252–55.
[5] Letter, Burr (Inlying Piquet) to Mother and Father, 24 February 1938, Burr Papers, 88/8/1, IWMD.
[6] Testimonies from SNS Fighters, Chaim Levkov and Yosef Assa, S25/10685, pp. 93–94, 112–13, CZA.
[7] Operations of Patrols of Englishmen and Jews, 13 June 1938, 26/6: Reports on Fosh Actions, HA.
[8] Note on Conversation with Montgomery, [12] January 1939, by Scrivenor, Scrivenor Papers, MSS. Brit. Emp. S. 377, pp. 298–304, WL.
[9] Herbert Pritzke (trans. Richard Graves), *Bedouin Doctor: The Adventures of a German in the Middle East* (London: Weidenfeld and Nicolson, 1957), p. 38.
[10] Packer, 4493/02, p. 8, IWMSA.
[11] Letter, Burr (Bury Billet Haifa) to Mother and Father, 9 September 1938, Burr Papers, 88/8/1, IWMD; Arab Revolt in Palestine Photograph Album 1938, ACHA.
[12] CO 2nd RUR to HQ 16th Infantry Brigade, 3 October 1938, Report on Operations in Palestine, December 1937–March 1939, Operation Reports, Palestine Box, RUR.
[13] 'Punitive Demolitions, 24 October 1937,' *The Hampshire Regimental Journal* 32/12 (December 1937), p. 383.

9738

British Marines and police in streets of Haifa trying to keep order during a fire.

6.1 Britain drew on all branches of its armed forces: Royal Navy personnel in white uniforms from HMS *Malaya* on patrol in Haifa (from American Colony Hotel Archive)

village wage at 80 mils per diem for a 'slaving' working day up to fourteen hours, while £P.3–4 per month was a 'large sum,' with another source estimating the yearly wage of a rural peasant family at £P.25–30, so the cumulative impact of the fining detailed below was considerable.[14] Passive Palestinian resistance had little effect against coercive military debt collection by heavily armed bailiffs. RUR riflemen went to collect £P.58 and £P.11.500 from Ein al-Zeitun (north of Safad) and Jaunai (al-Ja'una east of Safad) respectively, accompanied by a civil ADC, the first village surrounded by 4.30 am, and by 8.30 am the soldiers had collected £P.46 'by means of some furniture, bedding etc., being piled for burning. By 09.30 hrs LP53 was collected with a little more pressure, a few petrol tins being placed beside a house and finally at 10.30 hrs

---

[14] Appendix: Explanatory Notes, Captured and Translated Arabic Material with Commentary, p. 158, Wingate Papers, Microfilm M2313, BL; Rosemary Sayigh, *The Palestinians: From Peasants to Revolutionaries* (London: Zed, 2007), p. 25.

the total amount was handed over, only after the male population was lined up for beating.'[15] At Sasa, the officer commanding 'Qadcol' warned the *mukhtar* that he had come to collect fines and 'that if they were not paid furniture might become damaged. Six petrol tins were nicely placed outside his house and some petrol was given to the elders for their cigarette lighters, to show there was no deception. £11 was paid at once,' after which the Assistant District Commissioner arrived at midday and villagers paid an extra £P.19.[16] At this point, the village 'elders seemed to think that was enough,' so the Army demanded that they 'select the first house on which we could apply petrol to the furniture. A buzzing, as of angry bees, took place and not long after four five-pound notes were produced, borrowed from a woman's dowry for her daughter. Mr Gibbs decided that £50 was good enough and we left accordingly at 13.30 hrs.'[17] The dowry donated equalled 250 days' labouring for a villager. Similarly, at a Bedouin encampment the Army demanded a fine of £P.20 in twenty minutes. As less than a quarter of the sum was forthcoming, the officer commanding had 'some bedding cut up with Sword Bayonets, with the result that the remainder of the money was produced within ten minutes.'[18] When villagers from Fir'im (north-east of Safad) were slow paying fines, a Lieutenant Boyd forced village men to remove cactus hedges with their hands, at which point local women started 'weeping and wailing' but the punishment 'sped up' the fine collection.[19] The RUR concluded with satisfaction how 'local Arabs have undoubtedly already begun to realise that there is a new regime.'[20] Palestinians voted with their feet. When sent to collect fines from Tuliel (Tuleil on Lake Huleh), soldiers found the place deserted. The inhabitants had left months ago as 'when last fined they stated they were leaving the country, as they could no longer afford to live in it any longer.'[21] In another village following a £P.2,000 fine, the residents left the place with what property that they could carry; the *mukhtar* of one village tried to drop off the village keys

[15] Maj Reid, CO Tarcol, 2nd RUR, Report on Operations by Tarcol, 20 August 1938 but dated 21 August 1938, Palestine Box, RUR.
[16] Maj Davies, 2nd RUR, Report by Qadcol, 18 August 1938, Palestine Box, RUR.
[17] Ibid.
[18] CO 2nd RUR (Safad) to 16th Inf Bde, 24 August 1938, Report on Operations, December 1937–March 1939 File, Palestine Box, RUR.
[19] Lt Boyd, C Coy 2nd RUR, Report on Operations by Tarcol on 22 August 1938, Palestine Box, RUR.
[20] 2nd RUR (Safad) Report on Operations to 16th Inf Bde, 6 July 1938, Report on Occupation Northern Area, 5 July, December 1937–March 1939 File, Palestine Box, RUR.
[21] Maj Reid, CO Tarcol, 2nd RUR, Report on Operations, Collection of Fines, 18 August 1938, Palestine Box, RUR.

to a government official before all its inhabitants left.[22] Many villagers escaped to the towns, from where the British banished them back to the country.

Searching (or screening) for suspects and intelligence gathering accompanied fining and was a frightening experience, akin to the US-led Phoenix intelligence programme in Vietnam after 1965 but without the mass killings of tens of thousands of suspected insurgents as British soldiers managed comparable population-centric violence far more cost effectively and successfully than their more violent American counterparts thirty years later. Soldiers and attached police were to 'bluff' their way into a village, quickly debus, and surround the village:

Go to the most open space in the village. Send for the Mukhtar (headman). Order *all* inhabitants out of their houses within a stipulated time (e.g. half an hour). Men to be assembled in one place. Women and children to be assembled separately. When all the men are assembled they are checked one by one. Two tables are set out at some distance apart. Chairs for the checkers. The man comes to the first table and gives his name and village (if he doesn't belong to the one being searched)[.] [T]his is written down on a slip of paper and taken across to the second table, with the man. Close by the second table sit the Mukhtar and one or two selected elders. When the man comes to the table the Mukhtar has to give his name. It is the duty of the Mukhtar to know the names of everyone in his charge. Some large villages have several Mukhtars. If the name given by the M. [*mukhtar*] is the same as that given by the man himself, and if he is not on the police black list, he [is] allowed to go and sit down in a selected place. If *not* and he is suspect, he is segregated and later taken away to the police station.[23]

The RUR escalated to a more exacting three-table check at other times.[24] The RUR dominated its zone of operations, making sure to place soldiers in the highest buildings in a village as 'You must dominate the village' because Palestinians 'hate being "topped".'[25] The puns, jokes, sporting metaphors, similes, irony, and euphemisms in military papers made harsh measures palatable, as with the 'sack' of Sakhnin on Christmas Day 1937.[26] When villagers at Mallaha north-east of Safad fired at Jews near Lake Huleh, RUR battalion headquarters instructed a column 'as strong as possible' to make a 'very thorough' search of the

[22] *Haaretz* [*The Land*] (Tel Aviv) (22 December 1937, evening issue); Yuval Arnon-Ohanna, *Falahim ba-Mered ha-'Aravi be-eretz Yisrael, 1936–39* [*Fellahin during the Arab Revolt in the Land of Israel*] (Tel Aviv: Shiloh Institute, Tel Aviv University, 1978), p. 66.
[23] Searching Villages for Members of Gangs, Arms, Ammunition etc., Functions of the British in Palestine, Palestine Box, RUR.
[24] 2nd RUR (Nathanya) to 16th Inf Bde, 7 May 1938, December 1937–March 1939 File, Palestine Box, RUR.
[25] Occupation of a Village, Functions of the British in Palestine, Palestine Box, RUR.
[26] *Essex Regiment Gazette* 6/46 (March 1938), pp. 292–95.

village, with the men to go into the detention 'cage': 'Use very strong action in the village.'[27] Soldiers created fantastical stories to cover up abuse, as when the RUR gathered so much information that intelligence officer Simonds was sent north to check that its men were not torturing suspects. Simonds discovered that the colonel had instructed his regimental sergeant major to capture two men and 'take one man over to a wall and give him a "wee tap on the head" and fire a shot into the ground and then cut the throat of a cockerel over the man's face and the other man always talks.'[28] Searching and fining invariably meant detention, too, as when three columns surrounded five villages for searching and then detained in cages all males capable of bearing arms, to remain there pending further instructions.[29] Caging the men had the added benefit that village women had to walk the distance to Army camps to feed their menfolk. 'Now after a few days the women were so fed up with this that the men would probably come to an agreement you see and the whole area would be quiet.'[30] Other regiments built cages on their bases by the guard room that could hold fifty 'of the worst thugs,' as well as employing detained menfolk on road building.[31] Local Army company bases ran mini 'oozle' prisons capable of holding up to 300 suspects at their walled or wired-in picquet posts.[32] Villagers equalled free labour, too, whether detained or not, and were used extensively by the Army for wiring in camps and road making: 'many sticks were broken on unwilling backs but the road was eventually finished,' in the words of the Leicestershire Regiment.[33] 'Sergeant Duffy and his famous convicts from Athlit' removed the rocks for the swimming area for another unit, replacing them with sand.[34] Palestinians built and paid for much of the nationwide security structure that contained them, including soldiers' defensive sangars and for this 'willing help' villagers cooked a chicken supper for men of the Hampshire Regiment.[35] Policemen on other

[27] 2nd RUR Maj and Adjutant (Bn HQ) to OC Qadcol, 24 October 1938, Operations on Villages, File: 2nd Battalion Operations Orders, Palestine Box, RUR.

[28] Typed Memoir, Pieces of War, p. 146, Simonds Papers, 08/46/1, IWMD.

[29] 2nd RUR Maj and Adjutant (Bn HQ) to OCs Qad/Rit/Tarcols, 22 July 1938, Operations on Villages, File: 2nd Battalion Operations Orders, Palestine Box, RUR.

[30] Shepperd, 4597/06, p. 64, IWMSA.

[31] H. D. Chaplin, *The Queen's Own Royal West Kent Regiment* (London: Michael Joseph, 1954), p. 93.

[32] *FIRM: The Worcestershire Regiment (29th Foot)* 11/1 (April 1939), p. 59.

[33] *The Essex Regiment Gazette* 6/49 (December 1938), p. 467; *FIRM: The Worcestershire Regiment (29th Foot)* 10/4 (January 1939), p. 559; 'D Company Notes,' *The Green Tiger: The Records of the Leicestershire Regiment* 20/1 (February 1939), p. 26, ROLLR.

[34] *The Lancashire Lad: Journal of the Loyal Regiment (North Lancashire)* 57 (August 1936), p. 113, QLRM.

[35] *The Hampshire Regimental Journal* 33/2 (February 1938), p. 51.

occasions after 'eating as much as they could' at a village returned to base 'laden with chickens for our supper.'[36]

Fining went with detention, as when RUR men sped to villages after rebel military action where they collided with endemic rural poverty and fatigued villagers' willingness to accede to Army demands. The Army directly coerced villagers to coerce indirectly insurgents and anyone causing trouble, and if this did not work then soldiers piled on the pressure against villagers. At Salha (Saliha north-east of Safad), the officer-in-charge summoned the village *mukhtar* and collected all the men: 'I told him that 6 shots had been fired from his village at our patrol the night before.'[37] The *mukhtar* said that he knew who had done this, a Syrian and that he would

produce his name in a day or two. I said that A.D.C. SAFAD had fined him LP 30 because of it. There was also an outstanding fine of LP 30. I gave him half an hour to explain the situation to the Elders, he then came and said they could not pay. I fell in a party with picks and shovels and advanced on the village, looking determined. This bluff immediately produced results and the Mukhtar begged for another hour to collect the cash. He then held a Durbar and small coins of every description were showered on him, most of the cash being borrowed from a fat woman money lender. The total came to LP 20. Mils 460. The Mukhtar has promised to produce the balance of LP 30 in five days (i.e. LP 9 odd). I brought 22 men back to the cage and will free them on Wednesday evening. As regards the outstanding fine of LP 30, I doubt the easy collection of it at present, but the village owns a big doyra [sorghum or millet] crop which will be ready in 10–15 days['] time.[38]

The Army punished villagers who had done nothing. An RUR column cordoned Ein al-Zeitun early in the morning and removed all the villagers and carried out an intensive search, after which it conveyed fifty men to the cage at Malikiyya by the Lebanese frontier but 'Nothing of a suspicious nature was found in the village or environments.'[39] The Army commandeered buses to bring in all the prisoners.[40] Pacification was permanent punishment. The Hampshire Regiment searched 'Arraba village as a band was active nearby and while it found nothing the search was 'drastic enough to shake the villagers.'[41] The cost of Army reprisal raids

[36] Letter, Burr (Inlying Piquet) to Mother and Father, 24 February 1938, Burr Papers, 88/8/1, IWMD.
[37] Capt Davies, OC QADCOL, al-Malikiyya, 9 August 1938, December 1937–March 1939 File, Palestine Box, RUR.
[38] Ibid.
[39] Lt-Col [Whitfeld] OC 2nd RUR (Safad) to HQ 16th Inf Bde, 2 August 1938, December 1937–March 1939 File, Palestine Box, RUR.
[40] Packer, 4493/02, p. 10, IWMSA.
[41] *The Hampshire Regimental Journal* 33/1 (January 1938), p. 22.

after local rebel action was huge, £P.7,000 in one case, including seventeen houses totally destroyed.[42] Serious insurgent action meant harsher methods, as at al-Bassa where a rebel mine killed four RUR soldiers but even when the Army dodged an IED it enacted reprisals, as at Ras al-Ahmar (north of Safad) where vehicles narrowly avoided destruction. Afterwards at the local village, soldiers came across a large body of men walking and running from the village. Three shots rang out and soldiers saw two men with rifles, at which point the Army opened fire and 'a number of men were seen to fall.'[43] Soldiers collected village men and carried out a search. Villagers seemed to know of the ambush as Khalil, the company interpreter, overheard village women warning others to be careful not to

give away a certain man. Later the schoolmaster was overheard using this man's name, but when asked to point him out said he was not in the village. Khalil eventually discovered which man it was and it turned out that he had made a determined effort to escape but had been wounded in the arm and captured. He is now in SAFAD being detained by the Police.[44]

At Suruh village on the Lebanese border, inhabitants decamped after a local shooting incident, obviously aware of what was about to happen. The RUR commanding officer decreed that anyone remaining was to be rounded up, taken to the cage, and three men 'be flogged in the presence of the villagers after the inhabitants had been informed of the reason.'[45] Authorities readied a heavy fine for when the bulk of the villagers returned and the Army laid on a 'special Howitzer programme' with artillery fire on tracks north of the village by the border.[46] A Palestinian woman recalled how the British used whips in such searches, while a police officer used a wooden club with such force on suspects that he 'thought that the wood would snap under the impact,' alongside fellow policemen who wielded hammers and tyre levers.[47]

A British doctor in Hebron in the south, Elliot Forster, recalled the effect of living under sustained British military occupation there.

---

[42] Arnon-Ohanna, *Falahim ba-Mered ha-'Aravi*, pp. 64–65.
[43] Report by Lt Davis, CO QADCOL, 19 November 1938, December 1937–March 1939 File, Palestine Box, RUR.
[44] Ibid.
[45] 2nd RUR (Safad) CO Col Whitfeld to 16th Inf Bde, 4 September 1938, Report on Operations, December 1937–March 1939 File, Palestine Box, RUR.
[46] Ibid.
[47] Notes of Interviews, Mrs Ambara Salaam Khalidi (Beirut), 1977, Palestine Research Lever Arch File, Thames TV Material on 'Palestine: Promises, Rebellion and Abdication' (1977–78), IWMFA; Douglas Duff, *A Sword for Hire* (London: Murray, 1934), pp. 171, 229–30.

Accustomed to local life, Forster worked in Hebron's St Luke's Hospital, held surgeries in outlying villages, and he lived through periods of intense military operations. Law and order collapsed as troops in and around Hebron ran amok, shooting Arabs at random simply because they were in a free-fire zone. While some officers tried to restrain the men, Palestinians moved about Hebron and the surrounding countryside in fear of their lives, not from rebel actions but because of the violence meted out by marauding troops and police. 'Anyone who sees the army nowadays runs like a hare – I do myself!' wrote Forster.[48] Policeman Raymond Cafferata wrote to his wife how it was all 'just kill, kill, kill innocent and guilty alike' and a mirror of Britain's war in Ireland in the early 1920s.[49] Soldiers shot Arabs near battle zones, even when these were old men or boys tending flocks. Forster daily treated local people brought in to the hospital with gunshot wounds. Candid as to when he was treating a real rebel, most of the time he was tending to high-velocity rifle injuries inflicted by trigger-happy British troops. Not all regiments behaved the same. Forster noted the change in the Hebron garrison from the Queen's Own Cameron Highlanders to the Cameronians (Scottish Rifles),

a far less aristocratic affair [and disbanded in the 1960s] but worth about six times their predecessors. Soon after their arrival a village patrol was ambushed and a truck blown up by a land mine ... The Cameronians bore no malice and for the rest of their stay became very popular with the people. Gilmour [Captain G. H. Gilmour, the officer at the ambush] encouraged his men to go, in properly conducted parties, to look at the suq and the mosque.[50]

'Searching'

As the foreign press described it, Palestine was undergoing a 'searching.'[51] Security forces searched for suspects, for houses to destroy, for labour, for money, for people to contain and detain, for rifles, for people to beat, for information, for identification, for objects to smash, and for collaborators. Searching 'was intended to be a "punishment".'[52] Searching meant theft and highway robbery by security forces, of a £P.12 watch, of £P.108 in another incident, of household carpets and trinkets, the

---

[48] Diary, Forster Papers, GB 165-0109, p. 74, MEC.
[49] Letter, Cafferata to Peggy (wife), 2 December 1938, File 6: Letters to Roz and Peggy 1929–38, Cafferata Papers, CP.
[50] Diary, October 1936, Forster Papers, GB 165-0109, pp. 1–2, MEC.
[51] Quoted in anon., 'British Methods in Palestine,' *Yorkshire Post* (23 November 1938).
[52] Extract from a Letter from an English Friend in Palestine, Addressed Dear Miss Newton [possibly from S. O. Richardson, Lawyer, Jaffa], 11 January 1939, Lees Papers, 5/9, LHCMA.

three soldiers involved in the last incident caught and arrested by their visibly distressed commanding officer.[53] Jewish supernumerary police robbed villagers on searching operations and they hit prisoners, while British-led Jewish troops shot an Arab and took £P.105 as accompanying British soldiers went house-to-house looking for 'booty.'[54] Searching meant identification. As the revolt hardened, Palestinian 'identifiers' helped with identification during searches, provided that the British kept secret their identities.[55] The British triaged men from women for hidden informers in armoured cars who graded male suspects as oranges, lemons, or grapefruits for police interrogation, as with the black, grey, and white taxonomy of the Mau Mau counter-insurgency.[56] Of course, if identifiers' identity became known, this encouraged internecine fighting among Palestinians that supported pacification. Troops searched for days on end, 2,000 men for thirteen days at Bayt Rima in 1939 where they killed three villagers 'by torture' and found a hundred rifles.[57] Searching meant containment of villagers in compounds, denying them water until they gave information, rifles, or money: 'On the tenth day we started to die.'[58] With the Army in charge, civil officials arrived at villages to find the women contained in the mosque and the able-bodied men assembled in the open, all house doors unlocked, ready for searching. Soldiers may have found nothing – 'All of this only goes to show that a search is quite useless unless it is really a surprise' – but searching was attrition as it was discovery.[59] Searching could mean molestation. A Jew complained of an Arab policeman (*shawish*) who subjected him to a 'thorough' search that would have been 'perfectly proper' but for 'the obvious and disgusting zeal with which he carried out his co-called "duty" by satisfying his

[53] Petitions in Connections with Goods Thefts, Box 848, Security, Jerusalem Municipality, Historical Archive, Department of Jewish Community, JMA; Extract from a Letter from an English Friend in Palestine, Addressed Dear Miss Newton [possibly from S. O. Richardson, Lawyer, Jaffa], 11 January 1939, Lees Papers, 5/9, LHCMA; Letter, Burr (Depot Mt Scopus) to Mother and Father, n.d. [late 1937], Burr Papers, 88/8/1, IWMD; ADC Lees (Gaza) to DC (Southern District, Jaffa), 7 June 1936, Lees Papers, 5/6/1, LHCMA.

[54] Office of Supernumerary Police Afule, Report on Mixed Squads, 9 September 1938, S25/8768, pp. 64–65, CZA; Testimonies from SNS Fighters, Chaim Levkov, S25/10685, p. 103, CZA.

[55] Report by Gen Haining on Hostile Propaganda in Palestine, 1 December 1938, FO 371/21869, p. 169, TNA.

[56] Parrot, p. 25, 4514/04, IWMSA; Caroline Elkins, *Britain's Gulag: The Brutal End of Empire in Kenya* (London: Jonathan Cape, 2005), p. 136.

[57] Notes of Interviews, Dr Qassam Rimawi (Amman), 19 September 1977, Palestine Research Lever Arch File, Thames TV Material on 'Palestine: Promises, Rebellion and Abdication' (1977–78), IWMFA.

[58] 'Palestine: Promises, Rebellion and Abdication' (Thames TV, 1977–78).

[59] Diary, 7 May 1938, Scrivenor Papers, MSS. Brit. Emp. S. 378, WL.

low homosexual passion.'[60] Searches left Palestinians with the 'bitterest memories of that time.'[61] One female target of searching quoted the Palestinian poet 'Abd al-Karim Karmi (Abu Salma) to say that 'If my God was English, I would deny him.'[62] Troops used new technologies such as donkey-portable metal detectors.[63] Palestinians protested in myriad petitions, especially at purported attacks on holy books ('put them on the floor, and they were stamped on') but remained generally hospitable to visitors: 'even after searching an Arab house or Bedouin encampment, tearing them out of their beds at 5 a.m. just before sunrise, they would offer us coffee, water, melons and figs.'[64]

The searching was immense. 14th Brigade in August 1938 conducted a 'thorough' search of Nablus. Soldiers searched every house from 'top to bottom,' found a bomb factory and brought 6,000 men into a central cage for 'checking,' detaining seventy-eight, with no one allowed to enter or leave the town.[65] The Army passed 5,000 men in and around Hebron though 'identification centres' on two days, 15–16 December 1938.[66] Palestinians hid valuables outside villages to escape searches. If searching failed to secure suspects, it might become punitive seizure, as when dogs took security forces to a village after the death of a Jewish watchman. They found no murderer after a search, at which point the commanding officer and a District Commissioner appeared and levied a fine 'there and then.'[67] Soldiers removed villagers' grain onto a lorry and tried to take a laden camel whose owner, an old woman, 'begged to be spared her precious animal,' much to the amusement of the watching soldiers but probably not the elderly woman:

[60] Letter, Moshe Dweik to DC Jerusalem, 19 June 1938, Municipality Security Searching Operations, Box 848 Security, Jerusalem Municipality, Historical Archive, Department of Jewish Community, JMA.

[61] Ghada Karmi, *In Search of Fatima* (London: Verso, 2009), pp. 12–13.

[62] Mustafa Kabha, *Thawrat 1936 al-Kubra* [*The Great Revolt of 1936*] (Nazareth: Maktabat al-Kabs, 1988), p. 65.

[63] Wavell to Haining (DMO, WO), 3 December 1937, Palestine, 1937–38 Volume, Wavell Papers, POH; Haining (WO) to Wavell, 26 January 1938, Palestine, 1937–38 Volume, Wavell Papers, POH.

[64] Memorandum of Protest from the Religious Scholars to the High Commissioner about the Police Aggression against Mosques and Houses, 1 June 1936 in Akram Zu'aytir, *Watha'iq al-Haraka al-Wataniyya al-Filastiniyya, 1918–39: Min Awraq Akram Zu'aytir* [*Documents of the Palestinian National Movement, 1918–39: From the Papers of Akram Zu'aytir*] (Beirut: IPS, 1979), pp. 436–38; *China Dragon: The Regimental Magazine of the North Staffordshire Regiment* 22/2 (December 1936), p. 108.

[65] Summary of Intelligence, Palestine and Transjordan, 26 August 1938, by Wing Commander Ritchie at GHQ [17/38], CO 732/81/9, TNA.

[66] Summary of Intelligence, Palestine and Transjordan, 30 December 1938, by Wing Commander Ritchie [26/38], CO 732/81/10, p. 5, TNA.

[67] Brig J. V Faviell, Typed Memoir, Fifty Days with a Company in Palestine, pp. 13–14, Faviell Papers, 82/24/1, IWMD.

A long altercation took place, in which all the villagers took part, and at length her request was granted. At once the whole concourse was delighted. The Colonel and the D.C. were embraced and acclaimed as protectors of the poor, benevolent dispensers of justice etc etc and in their delight at the retention of this one camel the villagers appear to have completely forgotten that their entire food supply had been removed. We looked with apprehension at the bulging sacks, additional weight for already fully loaded vehicles ... These duties, tiresome and unpleasant as they sometimes were, seldom lacked a touch of humour.[68]

The value of goods taken could be more than the value of the fine, eleven truckloads of grain for a £P.100 fine in another incident.[69] The British made everything legal. Soldiers carried search certificates for *mukhtars* to sign to confirm that the Army had not damaged mosques or holy books.[70] Soldiers who had misgivings about 'bullying' civilians would 'soon grow out of being too sentimental over a job like this' wrote an officer in his diary.[71] Searching might mean disorder. Soldiers watched police running amok during a mass search of Ramleh, before some sniping occurred so the Army re-established order by shooting seven Arabs.[72] Searching was hunting, with associated metaphors and similes, as when the 'foxes' had 'gone to ground,' or when Palestinians broke the Ramleh cordon it was 'like a badly stopped pheasant drive!!,' while 'Oozle-bart hunting' was the 'great sport' in Galilee.[73] Searching meant taking souvenirs. While a policeman took grisly prize photographs of mutilated Palestinian civilian bodies following an Army reprisal at al-Bassa, there is no evidence in Palestine of the 'dark trophies' of severed hands, heads or skinned bodies from other wars, but one soldier recalled gold teeth removed from the dead 'with a delicate jab of a rifle butt.'[74] Soldiers eyed local mosques during searches but behaved properly and left them untouched, 'quite certain that the bulk of the miscreants and their arms would be hidden there.'[75] How people comported themselves affected searching, as would

---

[68] Ibid.

[69] Arnon-Ohanna, *Falahim ba-Mered ha-'Aravi*, pp. 65–66.

[70] Search Certificate, Mullens Papers, LHCMA.

[71] Diary, 15 October 1938, Mullens Papers, LHCMA.

[72] Ibid.

[73] Douglas Duff, *Palestine Unveiled* (London: Blackie, 1938), pp. 58–59; Col W. V. Palmer, 'The Second Battalion in Palestine,' in Chaplin, *The Queen's Own Royal West Kent Regiment*, p. 85; Diary, 15 October 1938, Mullens Papers, LHCMA; 'A Gunner's Impression of the Frontier,' *Quis Separabit: The Regimental Journal of the Royal Ulster Rifles* 10/1 (May 1939), p. 45.

[74] Harry Arrigonie, *British Colonialism: 30 Years Serving Democracy or Hypocrisy* (Bideford: Gaskell, 1998), pp. 35–36; Simon Harrison, *Dark Trophies: Hunting and the Enemy Body in Modern War* (New York, NY: Berghahn, 2012), *passim*; Arthur Lane, *Lesser Gods, Greater Devils* (Stockport: Lane, 1993), pp. 50–52.

[75] Diary, 15 October 1938, Mullens Papers, LHCMA.

their ethnicity or religion. When a Mr Khal wandered into Thomas
Scrivenor's office in Haifa needing a gun licence for his loaded pistol
and showed Scrivenor the weapon, Scrivenor confiscated it and sent the
man on his way unarmed. Scrivenor then wondered why his guard at the
door had not searched the man but 'he may have been wearing a hat, in
which case it is probable that the Constable mistook him for a Jew ... He
looked perfectly respectable and would no doubt be allowed in without
a search.'[76] When an English female teacher opened the door to five
soldiers wanting to search her school, the corporal said simply on seeing
her: '"Very good, Miss. Goodnight." Off they went.'[77] The British did
not much like searching fellahin as it was 'a highly unpleasant business
having to run one's hands over scores of hot, unwashed and stuffily clad
bodies.'[78]

Fining

The British fined Jewish neighbourhoods for, say, shooting incidents.
Targeted Jewish areas coordinated their response and rabbis protested
to local officials their innocence and to ensure that Jews avoided the
schedules ('black list') of places due collective punishment.[79] Security
forces directed the bulk of fining at Palestinians. The British treated the
two communities differently. Their 'attitude toward the Jews was more
quiescent and accepting,' remembered a policeman who sympathet-
ically compared the Palestinians to his home village, ignoring that the
Jews were not in revolt and so not prime targets.[80] Rebels also targeted
Palestinians for extensive fining, often comprising huge sums: £P.30,000
from Jerusalem and £P.40,000 from Jaffa.[81] 'It is believed that this levy
is an effort on the part of the leaders to cash in from the rebellion and
line their pockets while there is still time for them to do so, and that the
money is intended for their own use and that of their immediate followers
in the event of their being forced to leave PALESTINE.'[82] The British

[76] Diary, 15 November 1938, Scrivenor Papers, MSS. Brit. Emp. S. 378, WL.
[77] Diary of School Year in Palestine, 1938–39, Spring Term 1939, by H. M. Wilson, Wilson
Papers, GB165-0302, p. 35, MEC.
[78] Roger Courtney, *Palestine Policeman* (London: Herbert Jenkins, 1939), p. 87.
[79] Letters, 25 May 1938, 28–29 June 1936, 6–8 August 1938, File 3: Jewish Community in
Jerusalem, 1936–38, Box 4625, Jerusalem Municipality, Historical Archive, Department
of Jewish Community, JMA.
[80] Dennis Quickfall, *Shadows over Scopus: Reflections of an Ex-Palestine Policeman*
(Manchester: Cromwell, 1999), pp. 31–32.
[81] Summary of Intelligence, Palestine and Transjordan, 30 December 1938, by Wing
Commander Ritchie [26/38], CO 732/81/10, TNA.
[82] Ibid.

collected fines in coin or in kind. The Dorsetshire Regiment seized furniture and goods in Nablus as payment of a fine.[83] As well as imposing fines of hundreds of pounds, security forces individually levied *mukhtars* and mayors to ensure compliance, £P.9 apiece in one case.[84] The fining was endless, and the total sums and percentage collected impossible to calculate quantitatively. The totals depended on the size of the conglomeration, tens to hundreds of pounds for villages and thousands of pounds for towns and cities. A fine invariably followed every shooting or sabotage incident. The British worked hard to collect fines, too, levied against a poor rural population heavily in debt. Soldiers saw the poverty first hand but with a job to do they pressed on:

> But they were so poor there's not much they could have done anyhow except give the gangs water and a little bit of food. Most of the villages (it was) unbelievable. I remember seeing the ordinary wooden plough, which probably hadn't changed since the time of Christ, with a camel and a donkey pulling it. And this wretched Arab scratching up his bit of ground in the [sic] exactly same way; nothing had changed for a thousand years. When one talks of poverty I mean they lived all right, they didn't die of starvation, but they were poor.[85]

The following indicative list introduces qualitative aspects of the fining regime and illustrates the scale and varied forms of financial punishments of Palestinians:

- Lydda £P.5,000 (for a train derailment), Hebron £P.2,000, Yazur £P.200, Gaza £P.1,000.[86]
- An attack on troops on the Yatta–Hebron road on 9 October 1936 led to a collective fine of £P.1,000 imposed on 11 October, presumably on Hebron. But before security forces secured this fine, they had the balance of a prior £P.2,000 fine to collect. In addition, the British imposed a night curfew (9 pm–4 am) for four nights and houses would be demolished in all cases where there was evidence of 'complicity' in the earlier attack.[87]
- In September 1936, the British imposed a collective fine of £P.25 on Sajara (possibly al-Shajara 'the tree' in lower eastern Galilee) village in

[83] Dorsetshire Regiment, Narrative of Events, Nablus, 10–11 September 1936, 88/367, Shelf C4, Box 3, KMM.
[84] *L'Orient* (Beirut) (29 January 1938), p. 5.
[85] Gratton, 4506/03, p. 24, IWMSA.
[86] CID Periodical Appreciation Summary No. 12/36, 12 July 1936, Deputy Inspector General to Chief Secretary, FO 371/20018, TNA.
[87] Telegram, High Commissioner Palestine to Secretary of State for Colonies, 12 October 1936, L/PS/12/3344–45: Palestine Situation, IOR.

Tiberias sub-district in response to shooting at a neighbouring Jewish settlement.[88]

- District Commissioners imposed fines on the spot in July 1936 after rebels shot a Jewish watchman near Telmond (Tel Mond, a Jewish settlement north east of Tel Aviv). Police dogs took a search party to Miska where it arrested two men and detained sixteen as 'accessories' and it collected a fine in grain, imposed by the District Commissioner who accompanied the military force.[89]

- In June 1936 a fine of '25 bags of wheat' was collected from Taybe village (Beisan sub-district) for the cutting of telephone wires.[90]

- In June 1936, forces at Belah (Bal'a) village near Anebta ('Anabta, east of Tulkarm) searched and found both used and unused ammunition in 'three houses which were demolished. A quantity of grain was taken in part payment for a fine and nine villagers were arrested and twelve others detained for interrogation.'[91]

- Security forces took grain as security for fines to be paid, as well as payment of actual fines.[92]

- Cumulative punishments at the village of Iksal (near Nazareth) totalling: a collective fine in 1936, crops confiscated in 1936, houses demolished in 1938 for sabotage, and in 1939 a £P.400 fine for an attack on Nazareth and on the IPC pipeline.[93]

- At Mujeidal (al-Mujaydil near Nazareth, population 1,241): fined £P.10 for stealing Jewish cement in 1937, £P.275 for burning the village flour mill in 1937, £P.100 for setting fire to a Jewish forest in 1937, and then (with no dates): £P.200 and then £P.10 for IPC sabotage, and a house demolished for the same offence, and a final fine of £P.500 'for repeated offences against Public Security.'[94]

- The British fined Ailut ('Illut west of Nazareth) £P.100 in 1939 for anti-Government activities, £P.50 in 1940 for theft of wire fencing, and

---

[88] Telegram, High Commissioner Palestine to Secretary of State for Colonies, 28 September 1936, L/PS/12/3344–45: Palestine Situation, IOR.

[89] Telegram, High Commissioner Palestine to Secretary of State for Colonies, 31 July 1936, L/PS/12/3344–45: Palestine Situation, IOR.

[90] Telegram, High Commissioner Palestine to Secretary of State for Colonies, 30 June 1936, L/PS/12/3344–45: Palestine Situation, IOR.

[91] Telegram, High Commissioner Palestine to Secretary of State for Colonies, 24 June 1936, L/PS/12/3344–45: Palestine Situation, IOR.

[92] Telegram, High Commissioner Palestine to Secretary of State for Colonies, 19 June 1936, L/PS/12/3344–45: Palestine Situation, IOR.

[93] Village of Iksal, Punitive Measures, Palestine Police Force: Report from Tiberias: M/4212/8, ISA.

[94] Mujeidal, Punitive Measures, Palestine Police Force: Report from Tiberias: M/4212/8, ISA; Walid Khalidi (ed.), *All That Remains: The Palestinian Villages Occupied and Depopulated by Israel in 1948* (Washington, DC: IPS, 1992), p. 348.

also imposed on the place a punitive police post of seven policemen for a period of six months for breaking 'public tranquillity.' Listed in police files are the names of seventy-nine men sentenced to detention under the 1936 Emergency Regulations, most for at least three months.[95] (There are long lists of names of such men detained in the police logs held in the Israel State Archive.)

- In 1937, a District Officer signed an order on the basis of the 1926–29 Collective Punishments Ordinance inflicting a fine of £P.10 on the town of Qalqilya, of which £P.7.100 was to go in compensation to two Palestinians for having their wheat burned, the order stating: 'Under the provisions of Section 8 of the Collective Fines Ordinance I hereby exempt the Mukhtars of Qalqilya and Yusef Saddhe, Mohd Ahmed Odehm and Mohd Abi Aleh [the ones whose wheat was burnt] from liability to bear any portion of the above mentioned fine.'[96] There are more files detailing complainants exempt fining, such measures encouraging *fitna*.

- When four Arabs entered a house near Beit Dajan (south east of Jaffa) and shot two Jews, police searched the village and arrested five men, two of whom answered the description of the assassins, so they imposed a £P.500 fine and seized the produce on the village threshing-floor.[97]

- When rebels bombed a Jewish bus near Yazur, the British noted previous such attacks, searched the village, imposed a fine of £P.200, and removed livestock and grain as 'security' for the payment of the fine.[98]

- 'Corn and grain to the value of LP.150 was sequestered at Quabatiya [Qabatiya near Jenin] village in payment of unpaid Collective fines.'[99] How the British monetarised crops for payment of fines in kind is not clear; they usually seized whatever was available.

- 'Today a fine of LP60, of which LP20 was at once collected, was imposed on Majdal Kurum on the Acre–Safad road, near which some stones were thrown and two shots fired.'[100]

- 'This morning a fine of LP200 was imposed on Halhul village near Hebron from which shooting had been directed at the troops. The fine was collected in money in full.'[101]

---

[95] Ailut, Villages Collective Punishment and Punitive Reports, Police Station Diary, Nazareth, M/4212/8, ISA.
[96] Order Issued under the Collective Punishments Ordinance 1926–29, District Officer, 27 May 1937, Collective Punishment Ordinance, M/4826/2, ISA.
[97] Official Communique 89/36, 3 June 1936, Official Communiques, M/567/3, ISA.
[98] Official Communique 124/36, 19 June 1936, Official Communiques, M/567/3, ISA.
[99] Official Communique 134/36, 23 June 1936, Official Communiques, M/567/3, ISA.
[100] Official Communique 180/36, 15 July 1936, Official Communiques, M/567/4, ISA.
[101] Official Communique 186/36, 18 July 1936, Official Communiques, M/567/4, ISA.

- Forces imposed a £P.100 fine and one of £P.200 'in labour' on Indur village near Nazareth, close to which shots were fired, and they demolished three houses.[102] The population of Indur in 1931 was 445, living in seventy-five houses, so even a small £P.100 fine meant a payment of £1.333 per household, or the equivalent of seventeen days of work at 80 mils per day per household.[103]
- Security forces imposed a £P.300 collective fine on Samakh for the burning of a Jewish flour mill.[104]
- When three armed men robbed a tax collector, police followed tracks that passed within 150 metres of Ibellin village (I'billin near Shafa 'Amr) before the trail veered off: 'The Police are satisfied that the men who committed this robbery are mainly from Ibellin village, and in view of this I recommend that the inhabitants of the village be ordered to refund the amount of money stolen and value of the watch viz LP31.360 and that a fine of LP25 under Articles 1, 2, 3, 4 of the Collective Fines Ordinance be imposed.'[105]
- After attacks and robberies on the Haifa–Jaffa road, dogs took security forces to Igzem (Ijzim) village where they lost the scent. The British called the *mukhtar* of the village and five elders and informed them of the crime and that the tracks of the culprits had led to Igzem village and that they were required to help the police 'to detect the crime, which was of no avail,' so the officer present imposed a fine of £P.300 and issued a curfew order 500 metres either side of the Haifa–Tel Aviv road.[106]
- The police fined nomadic Arabs near the scene of a shooting £P.300 'for not passing information about the armed gang' while also fining another local village £P.500 and delivering a punitive search for firing on security forces.[107]
- The British held Palestinians close to Jewish settlements in the Roshpina area responsible for arson to Jewish crops: 'Half of the amount due has been collected and the remainder can now be collected with the aid of the military.' Simultaneously, the British fined six villages for complicity in destruction to the Tegart fence and when rebels twice blocked

---

[102] Official Communique 240/36, 31 August 1936, Official Communiques, M/567/4, ISA.
[103] Khalidi *All That Remains*, pp. 344–46.
[104] Official Communique 261/36, 19 September 1936, Official Communiques, M/567/4, ISA.
[105] Divisional Police HQ Haifa Rural Division to ADC Haifa Rural Area, 22 March 1938, Scrivenor Papers, MSS. Brit. Emp. S. 377, p. 124, WL.
[106] Divisional Police HQ Haifa Rural Division to ADC Haifa 'Murder and Firing on Cars', 29 March 1938, Scrivenor Papers, MSS. Brit. Emp. S. 377, p. 138, WL.
[107] Divisional Police HQ Haifa Rural Division to ADC Haifa Rural Area, 9 April 1938, Scrivenor Papers, MSS. Brit. Emp. S. 377, p. 163, WL.

the Acre–Safad road, a 'fine was immediately collected from the four neighbouring villages and no further damage has occurred.'[108]

- When vandals destroyed up to 300 trees, a tracker dog took troops through a number of nearby villages and due 'to the seriousness of this crime which appears to have been committed by a large party who were daring to go through the lands of the villages mentioned above' the police fined the villages £P.300, to be collected immediately under the 1936 Collective Fines Ordinance.[109]

Security forces used fines creatively and they persevered with collection. Thus, after murders on the edge of the Arab market in Haifa in December 1938, Montgomery suggested fines of £P.500 per murder, with escalatory rates thereafter. His civil adviser, Scrivenor, replied by saying this was too high and he agreed £P.200 per murder, the local senior police officer adding that they should also hold people for ransom, to which Scrivenor pointed out that the Ordinance did not allow this.[110] The collection of this fine via assessable taxable property was sporadic as tax collectors feared for their lives so Montgomery told Scrivenor that security forces could seize residents and hold them for ransom, to which Scrivenor again objected. Policemen then tried to gather the fines but with shops shut they only collected £P.20. When rebels shot another Jew, Montgomery demanded another collective fine but in the market area collection went 'very badly ... at a standstill' as tax collectors refused to go out after being terrorised.[111] Thus, the police went in to support them and collected £P.44 but several days later the 'mess over the collection in the Suq has still not yet been settled.'[112] Elsewhere, the Army seized stock and effects in lieu of monetary fines. The numbers of animals taken as fines were phenomenal, up to 2,700 goats and sheep from three villages in one incident.[113] Soldiers photographed themselves surrounded by sheep with captions such as 'collecting a fine in kind.'[114] Villagers paid to get their animals back or the authorities sold the stock: 'we didn't lose

---

[108] Monthly Administrative report for June 1938, Galilee and Acre District, 1 July 1938, by Acting DC K. W. Blackburne, Blackburne Papers, MSS. Brit. Emp. S. 460, Box 3, File 2, WL.

[109] Divisional Police HQ, Haifa Rural Division to DC Haifa, 11 December 1937 in Scrivenor Papers, MSS. Brit. Emp. S. 377, p. 45, WL.

[110] Diary, 12 December 1938, Scrivenor Papers, MSS. Brit. Emp. S. 378, WL.

[111] Diary, 15 December 1938, Scrivenor Papers, MSS. Brit. Emp. S. 378, WL.

[112] Diary, 19 December 1938, Scrivenor Papers, MSS. Brit. Emp. S. 378, WL.

[113] Palmer, 'The Second Battalion in Palestine,' p. 85; Summary of Intelligence, Palestine and Transjordan, 25 February 1938, by Wing Commander Ritchie at GHQ [4/38], CO 732/81/9, TNA.

[114] *The Lancashire Lad: Journal of the Loyal Regiment (North Lancashire)* 57 (August 1936), pp. 120–21, QLRM.

any sleep over these things.'[115] The Army inflicted collective pre-emptive punishment by telling villagers that soldiers would destroy their crops if they helped rebels.[116] Gangs compelled villagers to build road blocks; the Army made them take them down, and in one case fined them £P.700 despite villagers' protestations that rebels had coerced them.[117] Fining was so bad that as early as July 1936 Wauchope told his Chief Secretary to limit the scale of fining so that villages could realistically pay them.[118] Some civil officials took more care than others. Edward Keith-Roach delayed fining Nazarenes after Andrews' death in September 1937 as he lacked evidence of collective guilt and insisting that he must await the final CID report.[119]

Punitive Posts and Passes

The financial punishment of Palestinians came in different forms. Villagers sustained punitive police posts and hosted patrolling units. An Arab officer with Jack Binsley expected every village to provide 'a feast' as fellahin were 'noted for their hospitality and gave us better food than they themselves could afford to eat.'[120] Palestinians paid for their gaolers, fed them, and gave their homes as gratis accommodation. Villagers paid for policemen's clothes, travel, and even their salaries.[121] The British billeted troops in homes evacuated of their residents in larger towns like Lydda. One soldier when asked where they had gone reflected laconically, 'I honestly don't know.'[122] Punitive police posts of even four men could last for several months, fed and hosted at villagers' expense: 'You know, that would cost them or at least they'd be having to use eggs and milk and yoghurt that otherwise they would have brought into the towns to sell or utilise for their own purposes. I think punitive forces like that probably had more effect than did the general searches.'[123] During trouble in Haifa in February 1938, the police asked the District Commissioner for four

[115] Kitson, 10688/6, IWMSA.

[116] Yehuda Slutsky (and Ben-Zion Dinur) (eds), *Sefer Toldot ha-Haganah* [*Book of the History of the Haganah*]. Volume 3, Part 1, *Me'ma'avak le'Milhama* [*From Struggle to War*] (Tel Aviv: 'Am Oved, 1972), p. 16.

[117] Chaplin, *The Queen's Own Royal West Kent Regiment*, p. 100.

[118] Moody (Acting Chief Secretary) to District Commissioners, 23 July 1936, Shai Intelligence Reports: 8/GENERAL/40, pp. 176–77, HA.

[119] Report, Assassination of Mr L. Y. Andrews, 9 October 1938 by District Commissioner Keith-Roach, sent to Chief Secretary, Blackburne Papers, MSS. Brit. Emp. S. 460, Box 3, File 4, WL.

[120] Jack Binsley, *Palestine Police Service* (Montreux: Minerva, 1996), p. 21.

[121] Arnon-Ohanna, *Falahim ba-Mered ha-'Aravi*, p. 66.

[122] Fuare-Walker, 6612/5, IWMSA.

[123] Newman, 11577/4, p. 17, IWMSA.

urban quarters to pay for an additional thirty-two men for three months, as well as supplying a suitable house for a police office, such things tied to tax payers in the area; the area was also due an 'intensive search.'[124] In September 1938, the British fined the eastern part of Haifa and made it pay for two sergeants and sixteen supernumerary policemen for a period of two months, as well as destroying houses that had hosted wounded rebels.[125] Security forces confiscated the entire grain stock of a village near Haifa that refused to pay for a punitive police post.[126] After the revolt, policeman John Briance was sure that punitive police posts were the 'only solution for peace everlasting.'[127] Posts in or near villages had the added advantage that the men could observe the locale. Argyll and Sutherland Highlanders logged everyone who entered their local village and if anything looked suspicious troops cordoned and searched it.[128]

The British controlled all movements, whether of people, information, mail, or telephone calls, although telephone lines were rare, especially among Palestinians, and in 1937 in Jerusalem there were only 350 lines owned by Arabs, out of 2,300 non-governmental lines that were otherwise in Jewish hands.[129] The High Commissioner had instituted police permits for road travel as early as May 1936.[130] The Army ramped up this measure in late 1938. Passes for travel became standard. Personal ID cards for men were a new control and when Montgomery introduced them in Haifa in January 1939 after long discussions with Scrivenor there was chaos as fights erupted among the 2,000 people queuing at the relevant office.[131] While ID cards were voluntary, the British cleverly tied them to new travel passes when the latter came into force in November 1938 as the Army took charge, it being impossible to get a travel permit without first taking out an ID card, and a measure that expressed Government power.[132] Travel passes in English

---

[124] Attack on Supernumerary Police Patrol in Abbassiya Quarter, ASP Haifa Urban Division to ADC Haifa, 4 February 1938 Scrivenor Papers, MSS. Brit. Emp. S. 377, p. 72, WL.

[125] *Haaretz* (8 September 1938).

[126] Disturbances of 1936, 13–25 June, US Consul General Palestine to State Department, 27 June 1936, 867N.00/322 [Reel M#1037/1], NARA II.

[127] Personal Diary, 1940–April 1941, 29 November 1940, Briance Papers, BP.

[128] Proctor, 16801/5, IWMSA.

[129] Itamar Radai, 'The Rise and Fall of the Palestinian–Arab Middle Class under the British Mandate, 1920–39,' *Journal of Contemporary History* 51/3 (July 2016), p. 496.

[130] Telegram, High Commissioner Palestine to Secretary of State for Colonies, 22 May 1936, L/PS/12/3344–45: Palestine Situation, IOR.

[131] Diary, 16 November 1938 and 28 January 1939, Scrivenor Papers, MSS. Brit. Emp. S. 378, WL; Note on Conversation with Montgomery, [12] January 1939, by Scrivenor, Scrivenor Papers, MSS. Brit. Emp. S. 377, pp. 298–304, WL.

[132] Summary of Intelligence, Palestine and Transjordan, 4 November 1938, by Wing Commander Ritchie at GHQ [22/38], CO 732/81/10, TNA.

allowed travel to and from certain districts for favoured individuals and were necessary after November 1938.[133] As with the battle over *kufiyyat* headdress, rebels responded by forbidding the taking up of official passes as 'treason,' on pain of death: 'the criminal will be shot.'[134] 'Arif 'Abd al-Raziq forbade the use of travel permits, including by Government employees, but exempted the citrus industry.[135] In December 1938, a month after the introduction of the nationwide travel permits, the rebels called off their ban and travel strike. One local man noted that it was a 'blunder. It did not serve interest of rebels and decidedly hurt the economic constitution.'[136] Rebel counter-coercion failed to match the power of the emergency state, while the British observed that rebels were willing to 'wink at' the running of food lorries, not least as rebels were unable to enforce their threats of retaliation on Arabs who carried travel passes.[137] Area military commanders threatened that any more sabotage on the Jaffa–Jerusalem railway by 'evilly disposed persons' would mean a ban on all Arab traffic and passengers 'for such period as I deem necessary' between Jerusalem and Jaffa southern district.[138] The British assessed their restrictions on road travel as having great effect, hampering rebel courts, reducing abductions, and helping with information gathering.[139]

Censorship

As well as restricting movement, the Mandate Government controlled information and the press. It had been doing so for many years and after April 1936 the Army weighed in with its own direct strategies. Thus, Montgomery banned journalists from Haifa.[140] He told assembled pressmen that they were ' "encouraging the terrorists, if the terrorists didn't

[133] File 04-161-A/621: Riots, April 1936 [one bundle of papers], TAMA.

[134] Anon., 'Troops in Control at Jerusalem,' *Yorkshire Post* (24 October 1938); In the Name of the Merciful God, The Supreme HQ, Arab Revolt in Palestine, signed The Slave of God Aref Abd el-Razek, n.d., Intelligence on Arab Leaders: 41/104, HA.

[135] Diary, 30 October 1938, in Thomas Ricks (ed.), *Turbulent Times in Palestine: The Diaries of Khalil Totah, 1886–1955* (Jerusalem: Institute for Palestine Studies and Passia, 2009), p. 240.

[136] Diary, 14 December 1938, in Ricks, *Turbulent Times*, p. 245.

[137] Summary of Intelligence, Palestine and Transjordan, 4 November 1938, by Wing Commander Ritchie at GHQ [22/38], CO 732/81/10, TNA.

[138] Sabotage on Roads and Railways, 7 February 1939 in *Ordinances, Regulations, Rules, Orders and Notices. Government of Palestine. Annual Volume for 1939. Volumes 2 and 3* (Jerusalem: Government Printing Press, 1940), p. 121 (on micro film in BL at SPR Mic. P1).

[139] Summary of Intelligence, Palestine and Transjordan, 18 November 1938, by Wing Commander Ritchie at GHQ [23/38], CO 732/81/10, TNA.

[140] Film Reels with Sound, PAL 104, Maj-Gen H. E. N. Bredin, IWMFA.

read in their papers every day that they're going very well, which they're not" then "they would lose heart in their endeavours. I have warned you several times about this before so outside you'll find several 3-ton lorries standing and they are going to take you down to Jerusalem and you're not coming back into my area."'[141] Such measures helped to keep hidden the brutal edge of military operations, but even if reporters wrote critical copy they had great difficulty despatching it from the country. The Postmaster General on 8 June 1936 restricted international trunk calls to officially designated persons, so stopping foreign correspondents circumnavigating the censor by telephoning out their reports.[142] The British coordinated with Cairo to exclude or seize Egyptian newspapers with atrocity stories from coming into Palestine.[143] The Mandate Government had readied itself by establishing a pro-active Press Bureau in 1931, led and advised by Robin Furness and Owen Tweedy.[144] The British expelled German journalists who reported on atrocities; a dedicated Foreign Office-run bureau in New York tackled damaging press reports in the US, especially those relating to Jews in Palestine.[145] The authorities also approached individual journalists who wrote hostile articles.[146] Press Ordinances allowed for the suspension with or without warning of any newspaper that was likely 'to endanger peace.'[147] Pre-existing Ordinances gave the High Commissioner the power to exclude foreign newspapers, with an exclusion order in 1935 banning a Swiss newspaper for a year, and supercharged after April 1936 with new Emergency Regulations.[148] The authorities prohibited the printing of any images 'depicting scenes of acts of violence,' of anyone carrying arms against the Government, and of military operations; the authorities could open packages and

---

[141] Bredin, 4550/05, p. 24, IWMSA.
[142] Disturbances of 1936, 5–12 June, US Consul General Palestine to State Department, 13 June 1936, 867N.00/315 [Reel M#1037/1], NARA II; Official Communique 99/36, 8 June 1936, Official Communiques, M/567/3, ISA.
[143] Police CID Jerusalem, Intelligence Summary 33/39, 11 May 1939, p. 3, 47/82, HA.
[144] Memorandum No. 37: Organization and Functions of the Chief Secretary's Office in *Palestine Royal Commission: Memoranda Prepared by the Government of Palestine* (London: HMSO, 1937), p. 137.
[145] Eileen Byrne, 'Palestine as a News-Story: Axis Initiatives and the British Response, 1936–39' (MLitt Thesis: University of Oxford, 1985), pp. 115–16, 123ff.
[146] Ibid., p. 132.
[147] Cmd. 5479 *Report of the Palestine Royal Commission (Peel)* (London: HMSO, 1937), p. 83.
[148] Press Ordinance 1933, Order-in-Council under Section 20(1), 17 January 1935 by Clerk to the Executive Council in *Proclamations, Regulations, Rules, Orders and Notices. Annual Volume for 1935* (Jerusalem, Government of Palestine: Greek Convent Press, 1936), p. 96.

confiscate critical printed matter and refuse to deliver packages.[149] The British restricted tourist visas to control journalists and unwelcome visitors. They had done the same after the 1929 rioting.[150] The Government could suspend newspapers, prohibit their publication for up to three years, imprison editors for six months, and impose fines. The 1933 Press Ordinance had introduced 'a new and extraordinary provision for government propaganda,' by obliging newspapers to print for free all official communications and denials.[151] Once the revolt started, Khalil al-Sakakini sent his son to buy the English-language, Jewish-run *Palestine Post* as the British had closed (or redacted) all the Arabic-language newspapers for reasons unknown 'except by God.'[152] During the revolt, police banned newspapers from publishing or importing any materials (including photographs) relating to certain topics, such as Hajj Amin.[153] Nor could newspapers let their readers know about censorship, so when a Hebrew-language one included redacted pages, the authorities prosecuted the editor.[154] The police put newspapers under surveillance, including the blind editor of *al-Jami'a al-Islamiyya* (*The Islamic Community*).[155] If such covert measures failed, policemen physically smashed up newspaper offices, as happened at *al-Sirat al-Mustaqim* (*The Right Path*) in Jaffa.[156] Foreign correspondents complained that it was harder reporting from Palestine than from the crises in Spain, China, and Czechoslovakia.[157] The Government cleverly assigned press officers to the Army to ensure that no reports of demolitions emerged till after the fact.[158] The Jews, meanwhile, encouraged the High Commissioner to close newspapers, such as ones that made supposedly false accusations

[149] Censor's Orders, 17 January 1939 and 19 March 1939 in *Ordinances, Regulations, Rules, Orders and Notices. Government of Palestine. Annual Volume for 1939. Volumes 2 and 3* (Jerusalem: Government Printing Press, 1940), pp. 92, 237–38 (on micro film in BL at SPR Mic. P1).
[150] Giora Goodman, 'British Press Control in Palestine during the Arab Revolt, 1936–39,' *Journal of Imperial and Commonwealth History* 43/4 (December 2015), p. 701.
[151] Ibid., p. 702.
[152] Entry, 23 May 1936, Khalil al-Sakakini (ed. A. Mussalam), *Yawmiyyat Khalil al-Sakakini: Yawmiyyat, Rasa'il, ta'amulat* [*Diaries of Khalil al-Sakakini: Diaries, Letters and Meditations*] (Jerusalem: Institute of Jerusalem Studies, 2003–10), vi, p. 254.
[153] Notice, 6 October 1937 in *Ordinances, Regulations, Rules, Orders and Notices. Government of Palestine. Annual Volume for 1937. Volume 3* (Jerusalem: Government Printing Press, 1938), p. 947.
[154] Goodman, 'British Press Control in Palestine,' p. 704.
[155] Disturbances of 1936, 16–30 May, US Consul General Palestine to State Department, 30 May 1936, 867N.00/302 [Reel M#1037/1], NARA II.
[156] *al-Sirat al-Mustaqim* [*The Right Path*] (Jaffa) (1 June 1936).
[157] Goodman, 'British Press Control in Palestine,' p. 710.
[158] Ibid., p. 711.

that Jews had thrown watermelons from buses at Palestinian passers-by.[159] One journalist at Jerusalem's *al-Liwa'* (*The Province*) newspaper wrote to Emile Ghoury in London in August 1936 to say that because of 'new orders' he could not publish anything

about soldiers making searches [the Arabic verb means the rounding up of people] in villages, and we can't publish their violent attitudes towards women. And they do so [are violent towards women] during searches. And we can't publish the violent acts against the mosques and the Koran. And we can't publish any incident if it is denied by Government sources. We can't publish anything about Transjordan. We can't publish anything about the conspiracies of the Jewish Agency.[160]

Supplements and amendments to Ordinances and laws augmented censorship as needed.[161] The Government also clamped down on printing presses and banned them from printing anything without an official permit.[162] The cumulative effect of such restriction was considerable. To give a flavour of daily life under military rule, consider Brigadier Evetts' order of 1 November 1938: all people coming into Haifa came on one of five designated routes; every male had to have an ID card; all male drivers had to have an ID card and a military permit to drive outside Haifa; no one could leave by railway without an ID card and a military permit; a central pass office issued ID cards and permits daily; it was forbidden to sell petrol to someone without a military permit; and every petrol retailer had to keep a record of sales on pain of closure.[163] Military zone commanders in and around Haifa signed the same month an Order that forbade all driving in rural areas without a permit, adding that military travel permits were either good for one journey or were permanent,

---

[159] Letter, Shertok to Chief Secretary, 12 July 1936, Reports from 1937 on Abdullah, National Commission, 80/153P/9, HA.

[160] Letter, Khalid (*al-Liwa'* newspaper) to Emil Ghoury (Arab Office, London), 23 August 1936, RG65: P351/37, ISA.

[161] Defence Amendment No. 7 Regulations 1937 by Acting Chief Secretary, 30 September 1937, *Supplement No. 2* to the *Palestine Gazette Extraordinary* No. 723 of 30 September 1937 in *Ordinances, Regulations, Rules, Orders and Notices. Government of Palestine. Annual Volume for 1937. Volume 3* (Jerusalem: Government Printing Press, 1938), p. 912; *Supplement No. 1* to the *Palestine Gazette Extraordinary* No. 660 of 22 January 1937 in *Ordinances, Regulations, Rules, Orders and Notices. Government of Palestine. Annual Volume for 1937. Volume 1* (Jerusalem: Government Printing Press, 1938), p. 113.

[162] Defence (Amendment) Regulations (No. 3) 1938, signed by Shaw, 2 March 1938 in *Ordinances, Regulations, Rules, Orders and Notices. Government of Palestine. Annual Volume for 1938. Volumes 2 and 3* (Jerusalem: Government Printing Press, 1939), p. 346 (on micro film in BL at SPR Mic. P1).

[163] Orders by Brig Evetts and Maj Clay (sub-commander of Haifa Town), 1 November 1938 in *Ordinances, Regulations, Rules, Orders and Notices. Government of Palestine. Annual Volume for 1938. Volumes 2 and 3* (Jerusalem: Government Printing Press, 1939), pp. 1437–38 (on micro film in BL at SPR Mic. P1).

so favouring those who kept to the rules.[164] On 19 November 1938, the Government appointed a Controller of Food Supplies to manage food distribution.[165] Security forces controlled everything of substance in Palestine by late 1938. This was the punishment of a country.

Curfews

Curfews were ubiquitous after April 1936 and the archives are full of extensive lists of night-time curfews, and all-day ones, too. Curfew was the 'weapon' against rebellion.[166] It contained and pacified, it detained and punished. Curfews had the advantage that they imprisoned the population at no official expense for half of every day, and during the dark hours that were harder to police. Palestinians imprisoned themselves for the daylight hours with strike action. Curfews kept open vital transport routes as the authorities attached many curfews to the sides of roads and tracks, the River Jordan, the TAPline, and railways, up to three kilometres either side of the passageway.[167] Soldiers, arrested, shot, and beat those breaking curfew, including Jews who complained about soldiers flogging them for being out during curfew without a pass.[168] The authorities varied curfews to reward good behaviour. A notice on 24 April 1936 informed residents that they would have more freedom as the curfew restrictions of 7 pm to 7 am were moving to 9 pm to 5 am.[169] The authorities might lift a curfew for half an hour to let worshippers get home late from a place of worship.[170] Jerusalem's children sneaked out to shops during curfew, lookouts checking for Army patrols, proving also that shopkeepers were ignoring the rebel strike demand to close shops.[171] Army area commanders from lieutenant-colonel upwards decreed

---

[164] Order under Regulation 6A, effective 1 November 1938, signed by Evetts, O'Connor, Harrison, Wetherall and Chrystall in *Ordinances, Regulations, Rules, Orders and Notices. Government of Palestine. Annual Volume for 1938. Volumes 2 and 3* (Jerusalem: Government Printing Press, 1939), p. 1497 (on micro film in BL at SPR Mic. P1).

[165] Order of 19 November 1938 in *Ordinances, Regulations, Rules, Orders and Notices. Government of Palestine. Annual Volume for 1938. Volumes 2 and 3* (Jerusalem: Government Printing Press, 1939), p. 1447 (on micro film in BL at SPR Mic. P1).

[166] Yosef Eshkol, *A Common Soldier: The Story of Zwi Brenner* (Tel Aviv: Ministry of Defence, 1993), p. 64.

[167] Summary of Intelligence, Palestine and Transjordan, 28 January 1938, by Wing Commander Ritchie at GHQ [2/38], CO 732/81/9, TNA.

[168] Letter, Lawyer to President of the Jewish Community, Ben Zvi, 5 July 1938, File 3: Jewish Community in Jerusalem, 1936–38, Box 4625, Jerusalem Municipality, Historical Archive, Department of Jewish Community, JMA.

[169] File 04-161-A/621: Riots, April 1936 [one bundle of papers], TAMA.

[170] File 11: Licence to Walk during the Curfew, May 1936–November 1937, Box 4625, Jerusalem Municipality, Historical Archive, Department of Jewish Community, JMA.

[171] Ghada Karmi, *In Search of Fatima* (London: Verso, 2009), p. 47.

'permanent curfews' on specified areas, curfews from 5 pm to 5 am 'until further notice' or for inhabitants to remain indoors indefinitely, all-day ones, and they blocked off roads, often in response to local outrages such as a shooting.[172] Jewish companies resisted and requested permission to work during the night.[173] Jews protested and the Tel Aviv mayor asked in petitions for curfews to be lifted, sometimes for named streets; Jews successfully engaged with the British to mitigate punitive action. Wauchope wrote to Ben Zvi (presumably Yitzhak Ben-Zvi, the future Israeli president) in May 1936 to let him know how well counter-terror measures were working.[174] Remarkably, just as rebels joined the Army in beating, fining and robbing villagers, they aped security forces and instituted their own curfews, too, to make everyone emulate the austere life of the country. Thus, the Jaffa town crier proclaimed in September 1938 a 6 pm curfew and in an anti-bourgeois measure whereby Jaffans refrained from using electric lights and avoided 'any form of entertainment.'[175] Rebels were especially resentful of mains electricity that outside Jerusalem came from a Jewish company; villages had no electricity, even those next to towns on the electricity grid. Everyone targeted the people, the British to make them politically passive, the rebels to make them austere and socially passive.

Curfew hung as a threat over Palestinians' heads – the 'Damocles' sword method' – with soldiers successfully demanding from Ramleh the production of the person responsible for shooting an RAF aircraftsman on pain of curfew.[176] Curfews in February 1938 of twenty-two hours encouraged villagers to pay one 'gang leader' £P.80 to curb 'night-time prowlers' causing trouble for the Army.[177] The British granulated curfews. Most curfews were night-time ones, but in September 1936,

[172] *Ordinances, Regulations, Rules, Orders and Notices. Government of Palestine. Annual Volume for 1939. Volumes 2 and 3* (Jerusalem: Government Printing Press, 1940), pp. 3, 14, 48, 99, 374 (on microfilm in BL at SPR Mic. P1).

[173] File 04-161-A/621: Riots, April 1936 [one bundle of papers], TAMA.

[174] Letters from Rokach (Jewish mayor of Tel Aviv from November 1936 to 1953) asking Southern DC to Lift Curfews and Letter, Rokach to Southern DC, 2 August 1938, all in File 04/-163-A/621: Riots, April 1936 [but actually June–September 1938] [one bundle of papers], TAMA; Arthur Wauchope to Ben Zvi, 26 May 1936, File 04/-165-B [sic]/622: The Riots: Negotiations with the Government, February 1936– June 1936 (August 1938), TAMA.

[175] Summary of Intelligence, Palestine and Transjordan, 9 September 1938, by Wing Commander Ritchie at GHQ [18/38], CO 732/81/9, TNA.

[176] Decisions by the High Commissioner arising out of a conference held on 12 August 1938 [possibly 1936 and not 1938 as it mentions AOC and not GOC in command] regarding the situation in Nablus, S25/22764, CZA; Dorsetshire Regiment, Narrative of Events, Ramleh, 17 September 1936, 88/367, Shelf C4, Box 3, KMM.

[177] Typed Memoir, Maj B. A. Pond, Pond Papers, 78/27/1, IWMD; Chaplin, *The Queen's Own Royal West Kent Regiment*, p. 84.

CURFEW ORDER

In virtue of the powers vested in me by the Regulation made by the Officer Administering the Government under Article IV of the Palestine Orders-in-Council, 1931 and 1936, I, *E. KEITH-ROACH*, District Commissioner of Jerusalem District, do hereby order all persons within the Area of Jerusalem District described hereunder to remain within doors between the hours specified below as from the date of this Order and until further notice.

If any person within the said area is or remains out between the hours specified below without a permit in writing from the District Commissioner or some person duly authorised by him, he shall be guilty of an offence against the said Regulation and shall be liable on summary conviction to imprisonment for a term not exceeding six months or to a fine not exceeding LP. 100 or to both such penalties.

THE AREA WITHIN THE OLD CITY WALLS OF JERUSALEM

A complete night and day curfew from 7 p.m. the 16th October, 1938, and until further order.

16th October, 1938.

E. KEITH-ROACH,
District Commissioner, Jerusalem District.

أمر بمنع التجول ليـلا

استنادا إلى الصلاحية المخولة لي بموجب النظام الموضوع من قبل القائم بإعمال الحكومة بمقتضى المادة الرابعة من مرسوم دستور فلسطين لسنة ١٩٣١-١٩٣٦، أنا إ. كيث روش، حاكم لواء القدس، آمر كل شخص ضمن منطقة قضاء القدس المذكورة أدناه بأن يبقى داخل بيته ما بين الساعات المذكورة أدناه اعتبارا من تاريخ هذا الأمر وإلى إشعار آخر.

وكل شخص ضمن المنطقة الآنفة الذكر يبقى خارجا بين الساعات المذكورة أدناه دون أن يحصل على إذن خطي من حاكم اللواء أو من أي شخص مفوض من قبله يكون علميا وكالذلك للنظام المذكور ويعرض من نفسه بعد إدانته جزئيا للسجن مدة لا تتجاوز ستة أشهر أو لغرامة لا تزيد على مائة جنيه أو بكلا العقوبتين معا.

المنطقة الداخلة ضمن أسوار مدينة القدس القديمة

مع تجول تام ليلا ونهارا

من الساعة السابعة من مساء اليوم السادس عشر من شهر تشرين الأول سنة ١٩٣٨ وإلى إشعار آخر.

حاكم لواء القدس
إ. كيث روش

تاريخ ١٦ تشرين الأول ١٩٣٨

צו מצב מיוחד.

בתוקף הסמכויות המסורות לי בתקנות שהתקין מנהל עניני הממשלה עפ״י סעיף ד׳ מסעיפי דבר המלך במועצתו על ארץ-ישראל לשנת (א״י) (תננם) 1931 ו־1936 אני א. קיטרוטש מושל פלך ירושלים מצוה בזה על כל האנשים שבתוך שטחו של פלך ירושלים כמתואר להלן לבל יצאו מפתח ביתם בין השעות המפורשות להלן החל מיום פרסומו זה ועד הודעה חדשה.

כל איש או אשה בתוך השטח הנזכר, הנמצא או נשאר בחוץ בין השעות הנזכרות להלן בלי רשיון בכתב מאת מושל הפלך או איש מוסמך לכך מאת כזה, יהא אשם בעברה על התקנות הנ״ל, ולאחר שאיש כזה יורשע בזה בוא דין הקלה לישב במאסר לתקופה שלא תעלה על ששה חדשים או לקנס שלא יעלה על מאה לא״י (פ״מ), או לשני העונשים באחד.

האזור הכלול בתוך חומת ירושלים

עוצר לכל הלילה ולכל היום,
משעה 7 בערב, 16 אוקטובר 1938, ועד להודעה חדשה.

א. קיטרוטש
מושל פלך ירושלים.

16 באוקטובר, 1938.

6.2 Poster-sized Government curfew notice
(from American Colony Hotel Archive)

forces instituted an additional curfew until further notice from 6.30 am to 4.30 pm on the western quarter of Nablus until inhabitants paid a collective fine imposed the month before.[178] This might refer to a £P.5,000 fine on Nablus from August 1936, alongside which the British instituted curfews for 200 metres either side of the TAPline.[179] Government files record the long, long lists of these curfews, their places and extent.[180] Being caught out during curfew without a pass might mean being fined up to £P.100 and/or six months' imprisonment; the more usual fine was five shillings (250 mils), a not inconsiderable sum.[181] Miscreants might be beaten or shot, depending on who detained them, which regiment or set of policemen. Security forces applied curfews to tracks and roads leading to and from villages, 200 metres either side of the thoroughfare; they curfewed the whole of Jerusalem's old city; they attached fines or jail time to curfews; and they curfewed the Arab quarter of Safad (Zefat in Hebrew) but not the Jewish part of the town.[182] Regimental 'strong men' 'suitably dealt' with curfew breakers.[183] Poster-sized curfew notices signed by the District Commissioner in English, Arabic, and Hebrew told inhabitants of Jerusalem's old city of the 'complete day and night curfew from 7 p.m. the 16th October, 1938, and until further notice' (Figure 6.2).[184] The British in December 1937 put in iron gates topped with barbed wire across the 'lesser' Herod, New, and Dung gates into Jerusalem's old city; a 'needle's eye' in the gates let school children through in the daytime (Figure 6.3).[185] Palestine was a nationwide prison, with people's homes as the jail cells, while searchlights probed the night sky and lit up the hills around Jerusalem searching for wrongdoers.[186]

---

[178] Telegram, High Commissioner Palestine to Secretary of State for Colonies, 7 September 1936, L/PS/12/3344–45: Palestine Situation, IOR.

[179] Telegrams, High Commissioner Palestine to Secretary of State for Colonies, 1 and 14 August 1936, L/PS/12/3344–45: Palestine Situation, IOR.

[180] *Ordinances, Regulations, Rules, Orders and Notices. Government of Palestine. Annual Volume for 1938. Volumes 2 and 3* (Jerusalem: Government Printing Press, 1939) (on micro film in BL at SPR Mic. P1).

[181] Curfew Order, 16 February 1938, by Grimwood, Assistant District Commissioner Tulkarm District in *Ordinances, Regulations, Rules, Orders and Notices. Government of Palestine. Annual Volume for 1938. Volumes 2 and 3* (Jerusalem: Government Printing Press, 1939), p. 320 (on micro film in BL at SPR Mic. P1); Letter Darlington to Wife, 15 November 1938, September 1938–December 1939 Volume, KO 1333/01, KORRM.

[182] Curfew Order, 21 October 1938, by Reeves (ADC Safad) in *Ordinances, Regulations, Rules, Orders and Notices. Government of Palestine. Annual Volume for 1938. Volumes 2 and 3* (Jerusalem: Government Printing Press, 1939), p. 1405 (on micro film in BL at SPR Mic. P1).

[183] *FIRM: The Worcestershire Regiment (29th Foot)* 11/1 (April 1939), p. 56.

[184] In Scrapbook of Articles about the American Colony, Palestine, People and Events and Loose Enclosures 1938–39, ACHA.

[185] Arab Revolt in Palestine Photograph Album 1938, ACHA.

[186] Arab Revolt in Palestine Photograph Album 1937, ACHA.

6.3 Iron gates (later topped with barbed wire) on Jerusalem's old city
gates with a 'needle's eye' to control entry of people
(from American Colony Hotel Archive)

Detention

Detention with or without trial supplemented curfew. Confinement came in ten forms excluding curfews, only the first of which involved due process: (1) security forces arrested and processed suspects through courts, civil or military; (2) they interned people by concentrating them in detention or internment camps (also called concentration camps at the time) under Emergency Regulations for defined periods of several months up to a year, unilaterally renewable indefinitely thereafter; (3) the Army informally detained people on its bases, usually for shorter periods of weeks in 'oozle' cages; (4) soldiers in the field detained villagers for forced labour such as road building; (5) security forces banished suspects to distant parts of Palestine; (6) the British exiled abroad troublesome Palestinians (and Jews who were perhaps suspected communists) using the 1936 Emergency Regulations and they deported AHC leaders to the Seychelles, while others banished themselves to neighbouring Arab states to escape such action, as with Hajj Amin to Lebanon; (7) authorities banished non-Arab troublemakers from the country, such as Frances Newton, Aubrey Lees, and bothersome journalists; (8) security forces detained villagers in cages in their villages for periods of days; (9) people reported daily to police stations; (10) the Government placed suspects under house arrest at their own homes under police surveillance, often after jail time. Arab propaganda sources added an eleventh detention network: troops took Palestinians to barbed-wire compounds in Jewish settlements where Jewish settlers 'humiliated' them, gave them poor food, and drove them into a 'frenzy.'[187] The Army made prisoners run behind armoured cars to concentration camps prior to interrogation, to save on petrol and as a punishment.[188] This was a hard-edged detention 'pipeline' system similar to the one that Elkins outlines for Kenya in the 1950s, with two caveats: the network was not as brutal – not with the full trappings of extreme abuse outlined for Kenya, anyway – and the two systems are comparable only if one accepts that security forces detained many Palestinians informally, so boosting official figures of those detained officially under Emergency Regulations.[189] This seems to have been the case. In the winter of 1938, police commented on the harsh conditions for detainees, adding that security forces were running out of people to detain as soldiers 'pick up anyone they see and clap

---

[187] Bulletin, Bureau Nationale, Damascus [summer 1938], Creech Jones Papers, MSS. Brit. Emp. S. 332, Box 30, File 2, WL.

[188] Extract from a Letter from an English Friend in Palestine, Addressed Dear Miss Newton [possibly from S. O. Richardson, Lawyer, Jaffa], 11 January 1939, Lees Papers, 5/9, LHCMA.

[189] Elkins, *Britain's Gulag*, p. 471.

them in a concentration camp. Their relatives have no idea where they are and thousands of reports about missing persons are pouring into the police.'[190] Random detention in places unknown was common and complicated by supplemental extensions to imprisonment, sometimes in formally constituted detention centres. The Army 'very extensively used' internment of six months to a year for organisers and educated persons, although 'when the time for release comes round re-detention is ordered,' and it inflicted short periods of three months' detention for villagers known to have acted with rebels, even if under 'duress,' in what it called 'examination' camps.[191] Poor intelligence meant that 'all the time it has been most difficult to be sure we were interning the right people' so the Army pulled in all able-bodied Palestinian men.[192] GOC Haining wrote to O'Connor in 1939 how reprisals against villages meant that soldiers took 'hostages' from the nearest village and kept them 'in cages at work – say 6–20 per village depending on size. Changed over, as required. If sabotage continues, do the same for each village on the line: and warn beforehand.'[193] It is highly doubtful that these flexible, imprecise Army detentions fed into Government statistics. This proves that official totals of those detained as detailed below were far too low. Personal stories of casual detention support this thesis, including of children. A British solicitor in Jaffa wrote to Lees about the detention of his 'boy':

it is *impossible*! Nothing whatsoever can be done! My own chauffeur KAZIM – without the least knowledge of what was against him was four months in a concentration [camp] during which the British soldiery relieved him of his gold ring and silver wrist watch. The trouble is you see that not only is there no trial, but there is not charge even. If the authorities indicated that a man was imprisoned for something specific, e.g. acting as a messenger for the rebels, one might do something but they say not a word … Poor old Reynolds of St. George's [Anglican Cathedral and attached school] – some of his best boys of whom he and St G's were proudest are in indefinite confinement in like manner.[194]

Rolling detention and movement of prisoners within the prison network made (and make) tracking numbers problematic, as with Subhi al-Khadra in September 1937 who was

sentenced to be detained at Acre under defence Regulation 15B for period of 3 months. The order was renewed from time to time the total sentence amounting to 16 months. The case of this internee was reviewed before the expiration of each order the last review being made in September 1938 when owing to his being a

---

[190] Letter, Burr (Central Police Billet, Khayat House, Kingsway) to Mother and Father, n.d. [October–November 1938?], Burr Papers, 88/8/1, IWMD.
[191] Section IX, Draft Military Report, n.d., O'Connor Papers, 3/4/55, LHCMA.
[192] Ibid.
[193] Haining to O'Connor, 23 January 1939, O'Connor Papers, 3/4/22, LHCMA.
[194] Letter, Richardson (Solicitor, Jaffa) to Lees, 6 April 1939, Lees Papers, 5/9, LHCMA.

Military Camp.

6.4 Army searchlights probing the night sky around Jerusalem
(from American Colony Hotel Archive)

leading Arab Nationalist and a dangerous agitator the order was renewed for a
further period of 3 months with effect from 30th October 1938. On the representation of the Officer in Charge of the Detention camp that Subhi El Khadra was
at the back of all the intrigues and plots in the camp and as a menace to security
and fearing that he would escape Subhi El Khadra was removed from the Acre
Detention Camp on 6th November by the Order of the Area Commander and
placed in military custody in the Peninsular Barracks at Haifa.[195]

The British arrested Sadhij Nassar, a journalist at *al-Karmil* newspaper (and wife of the editor Najib Nassar) and a leader of the Palestine
women's movement, on 23 March 1939 for organising demonstrations
and they sent her to Bethlehem women's prison, and by renewing her
initial three-month detention kept her there until 23 February 1940.[196]

---

[195] High Commissioner Palestine to Secretary of State Colonies, 7 December 1938, FO
371/21868 p. 344, TNA.
[196] Ellen Fleischmann, *The Nation and Its 'New' Women: The Palestinian Women's Movement,
1920–1948* (Berkeley, CA: University of California Press, 2003), p. 132; Mustafa Kabha,
The Palestinian People: Seeking Sovereignty and State (Boulder, CO and London: Lynne
Rienner, 2014), pp. 63–64.

Much of the detention was temporary or done off the books, vague agglomerations of suspects in custody at some place or on road-building chain gangs kept for the period of corvée, as with seventy men working on a mountain road.[197] Press reports detailed a 'large number' of village men in a concentration camp.[198] As British intelligence reported in November 1938, during recent 'round-ups' and village searches, security forces now had a 'large number of Arabs of fighting age' in detention, 'some as suspects for interrogation, and the majority for work on the roads. It is certain that the greater part are at least part-time gangsters and their temporary removal from their village will still further reduce the potential rebel strength.'[199] The British interned local political leaders and imams around Nazareth for preaching jihad, but most of those in custody were peasants and ordinary townsfolk caught up in search-and-sweep operations.[200] The detail below of 'local interrogation' speaks to regional and centralised prison networks, making definitive quantitative assessment impossible but it lifts official figures to something much higher. It made sense for the British to detain informally for shorter periods as this removed any judicial scrutiny. Security forces used the April 1936 Emergency Regulations when they needed longer periods in detention, with legal process simply being that security force officers signed a renewable order sending someone to a detention camp for up to a year. Moreover, any measure of detention is also a story about release: when, how, who, and why. A District Commissioner recommended in August 1936 the release of Sarafand camp detainees whose internment period had expired, but only after a further period of detention, so they

should be released when things are once more quiet, in batches spreading out over a period of 4–6 weeks. The D.C. recommended that they should be let out on Friday afternoons to give a week's respite before the next Friday's prayers; and that they should be transported to police headquarters in their respective towns, and released from there, so as to avoid any public demonstration.[201]

The colonial state recorded detention chits in some fashion, but less so the release dates, if at all. Detention deepened in terms of length of time of incarceration, as when detainees' first period in custody expired but authorities then extended it and aggregate numbers in prison camps

---

[197] *Haaretz* (29 December 1937, evening issue).
[198] *Haaretz* (15 August 1938).
[199] Summary of Intelligence, Palestine and Transjordan, 18 November 1938, by Wing Commander Ritchie at GHQ [23/38], CO 732/81/10, TNA.
[200] Files in Nazareth Police Station Diary, M/4212/8, ISA.
[201] CID, 11 August 1936, Shai Intelligence Reports: 8/GENERAL/40, p. 181, HA.

rose. It raises the methodological question of whether we should count someone detained on multiple orders as one or more detentions. Are twenty people detained for two years more of a prison 'pipeline' than one hundred people detained for three months apiece, with twenty of these orders, say, extended for a further three months? What of village women who had to walk miles to feed their detained menfolk – did they not suffer from detention even though the Government did not directly imprison them? Detention in some form touched the lives of most Muslim Palestinians, including women, many Christians, and some Jews.

Detention in Palestine was a capricious system of inexact measure, with 'cages' full of fellahin, 'many, I am sure, quite innocent,' recalled a policeman: 'At intervals officers of HM [His Majesty's] Forces reviewed the cases of inmates and set a proportion free. Any old man with an open honest face was the first to be allowed out, but woe betide the unfortunate who was ugly and had a squint for he was regarded as being the worst type.'[202] Troops detained all males of 'gangster age' and those on police 'black lists.'[203] Intelligence reports noted simply that 'a large number of Arabs' passed through cages for interrogation in Jaffa; even the Army did not know how many men it detained for screening or who 'passed through the various cages.'[204] An officer with the Black Watch went with six arrested men from a village to the local District Commissioner's officer to 'administer justice (so called)' and was 'amazed' at the processing under emergency laws:

All that happened was that a clerk brought in a list of those arrested – the DC looked it through and said to me 'So and so is worth a year in prison, two others six months as I know that they have been assisting the gangs.' With that he signed the forms sending them to prison and off they went without another word.[205]

Arab propaganda documents from Cairo reported that 'there were always some leaders and young men interned' from two to twelve months at the District Commissioner's 'discretion.'[206] The prison architecture tells some of the story, with masses of more-or-less temporary camps alongside stone-built central prisons in Jerusalem and Acre, and a permanent

---

[202] Robert Martin, *Palestine Betrayed: A British Palestine Policeman's Memoir (1936–48)* (Ringwood: Seglawi, 2007), p. 90.

[203] War Diary, 1 September 1938 and 10 October 1938, 1st Bn Border Regiment, BRM.

[204] Summary of Intelligence, Palestine and Transjordan, 4 November 1938, by Wing Commander Ritchie [22/38], CO 732/81/10, p. 9, TNA; Summary of Intelligence, Palestine and Transjordan, 18 November 1938, by Wing Commander Ritchie [23/38], CO 732/81/10, p. 9, TNA.

[205] Letter, Street to Father, 29 May 1938, Street Papers, File: Letters Home, LHCMA.

[206] The Arab Internees in Palestine Prisons, by the Syro-Palestine Executive Committee (Cairo), 29 November 1937, FO 371/21872, TNA.

women's prison in Bethlehem, some of the temporary sites being work stations for building projects (like road making) or quarrying. The British turned old Ottoman barracks at Auja al-Hafir deep in the Negev desert into a detention camp for 'undesirable characters.'[207] The authorities appear to have transferred the Negev camp of some 450 men to Sarafand military base near Ramleh, according to a Palestinian Protestant feminist at the time.[208] Sarafand military camp held many detainees, as did the large al-Mazra'a detention centre north of Acre that lodged the most people according to Arabic-language accounts, including such luminaries as future PLO leader Ahmad Shuqeiri.[209] More than sixty of the men held at Sarafand went on hunger strike in June 1936, 'the less prominent and less well to do exiles,' US diplomats reported home.[210] There were two official jail labour camps at Nur esh Shems (Nur Shams near Tulkarm) and Athlit ('Atlit south of Haifa), fifteen district lock ups, and a boys' remand home. Police veterans' files note a prison at Latrun and one just north of Tulkarm that might be the Nur Shams one (that lies east of Tulkarm).[211] Police Tegart forts were also sites of incarceration, many still used today as jails. The Army ran a basement lock-up in Ramallah, for one. The police ran the established prison system, while the Army supplemented this with its own camps as required and run by its own personnel.

The detention system was multi-layered, some levels deeply embedded and secret, as with torture centres that the British euphemistically called 'Arab Investigation Centres,' where suspects got the 'third degree' until they 'spilled the beans,' the British only closing a major one in a Jewish quarter of West Jerusalem after officials such as Edward Keith-Roach complained to the High Commissioner.[212] (There was imperial memory

---

[207] Disturbances of 1936, 30 May–5 June, US Consul General Palestine to State Department, 6 June 1936, 867N.00/310 [Reel M#1037/1], NARA II.

[208] Matiel Mogannam, *The Arab Woman and the Palestine Problem* (London: Herbert Joseph, 1937), pp. 305–06.

[209] The Arab Internees in Palestine Prisons, by the Syro-Palestine Executive Committee (Cairo), 29 November 1937, FO 371/21872, TNA; Disturbances of 1936, 13–25 June, US Consul General Palestine to State Department, 27 June 1936, 867N.00/322 [Reel M#1037/1], NARA II; Author interview, Abu Gharbiyya, Amman, Jordan, 21 June 2009 (and subsequent correspondence); Shaykh Abdul Hamid Sayih, *Filastin; la Sala Tahta al-Hirab: Mudhakkirat al-Shaykh 'Abd al-Hamid al-Sa'ih* [*Palestine; No Prayer Under Bayonets: The Memoirs of Shaykh Abdul Hamid Sayih*] (Beirut: IPS, 1994), pp. 44–48.

[210] Disturbances of 1936, 26 June–2 July, US Consul General Palestine to State Department, 6 July 1936, 867N.00/330 [Reel M#1037/1], NARA II.

[211] *Palestine Police Old Comrades' Association Newsletter* 5–6 (March–June 1951) and 56 (June 1964).

[212] Edward Keith-Roach (ed. Paul Eedle), *Pasha of Jerusalem: Memoirs of a District Commissioner under the British Mandate* (London: Radcliffe, 1994), p. 191; Tinker,

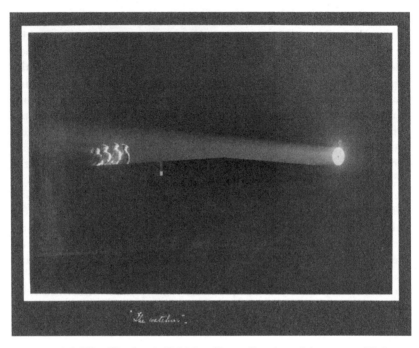

6.5 'The Watchers': British officers illuminated by a searchlight on Jerusalem's old city walls
(from American Colony Hotel Archive)

here as in Kenya in the 1950s security forces ran Mau Mau Investigation Centres or 'cruelty camps' for screening.[213]) There was a separate police-run house for torture of detainees at the Talavera military camp in the Allenby barracks in south Jerusalem, now covered by residential housing; another torture site was in Acre Citadel prison, now a museum; there was one within the main police headquarters at the Russian compound in west Jerusalem, a place where Israel tortured Palestinians in the 1970s.[214] There were hidden work-punishment camps in the country,

4492, pp. 34–35, IWMSA; Charles Smith, 'Two Revolts in Palestine: An Examination of the British Response to Arab and Jewish Rebellion, 1936–48' (Cambridge: Doctoral Thesis, 1989), pp. 114–19; Interview, Anwar Nusseibeh, 28 March 1977, Lever Arch File: Nigel Maslin, Thames TV Material on 'Palestine: Promises, Rebellion and Abdication' (1977–78), IWMFA.

[213] Elkins, *Britain's Gulag*, pp. 63, 87.

[214] Author interview, Abu Gharbiyya, Amman, Jordan, 21 June 2009 (and subsequent correspondence); Sunday Times Insight Team, *Israel and Torture* (London: Arab Dawn, 1977), p. 11; Matthew Hughes, 'A History of Violence: The Shooting of British

as at a Christian site close to Kfar Etzion south of Jerusalem, where prisoners would daily dig holes of 2 × 1 × 1 metres dimension, and then fill them in, endlessly repeating the labour.[215] This is probably a reference to the Russian monastery built on a Byzantine site close to Kfar Etzion – in Arabic, Dayr al-Shi'ar. Troops 'abducted' detainees 'after release from concentration camp,' while another released man 'as soon as he put his foot outside his prison, hands were laid on him once again and he was carried to an unknown destination. None of his people know where he is now.'[216] Detention was not just about judicial process, extent, length of time, and location, but the perpetual prison regime and the depth of incarceration.

There was internal exile, too, not to a prison but banishment to a remote locale, and not straightforward to measure for myriad minor suspects and for peasants ordered 'home' from urban shanty towns. Internal banishment could mean removing political leaders to far-away villages where they would be under police surveillance, as happened to ten 'secondary' leaders from Tulkarm and Jaffa in May 1936; at the same time, eight Jerusalemites 'were ostracised'; other leaders went from Jerusalem to Jaffa and had to report to the police three times a day for a year.[217] By the end of May 1936, the British had banished forty National Committee activists to different parts of the country, 'forced to reside in places selected for them for periods ranging between three months to one year under police supervision,' as Mussolini's fascists banished Carlo Levi in 1935 to rural southern Italy.[218] These men radicalised the local population, so the Government transferred them to detention camps.[219] The British also ordered itinerant peasants residing in cities back to their home villages. When police officer Cafferata called civil official Scrivenor in January 1939 asking if he would agree to exile 'any strangers' in Haifa to their villages, Scrivenor expressed his willingness but said that under the military control then in force the 'General' (so presumably

Assistant Superintendent Alan Sigrist, 12 June 1936,' *Journal of Contemporary History* 45/4 (2010), pp. 725–43.

[215] Correspondence, Sami Abu Gharbiyya (son of Bahjat Abu Gharbiyya, present at the author interview on 21 June 2009) to Author, 29 July 2009.

[216] Sir M. Petersen (Baghdad) to Jerusalem, 24 November 1938 [or 21 November or 3 December 1938], FO 371/21867, p. 221, TNA; Hoda Charaoui (Arab Women's Society) to HMG Ambassador Cairo (forwarded to High Commissioner Palestine), 4 December 1938, FO 371/21868, p. 301, TNA.

[217] Disturbances of 1936, 16–30 May, US Consul General Palestine to State Department, 30 May 1936, 867N.00/302 [Reel M#1037/1], NARA II.

[218] Mogannam, *The Arab Woman*, p. 305; Carlo Levi, *Christ Stopped at Eboli* (London: Farrar, 1947).

[219] Yehoshua Porath, *The Palestinian Arab National Movement: From Riots to Rebellion. Volume 2, 1929–1939* (London: Cass, 1977), p. 182.

Montgomery) had to sign the orders. Cafferata replied that he would
have 400–500 to sign, to which Scrivenor said that Montgomery would
not sign that many but might agree a few hundred.[220] The casual exile of
several hundred people by one policeman liaising with one civil official
speaks to a state-controlled detention system of indefinite, indiscriminate imprisonment, and labour camps. Was this a Gulag? The Soviet
Gulag was a permanent 'country within a country' of industrial-work
complexes underpinning the economic-social life of a totalitarian state
and not an emergency measure as in Palestine where the British detained
innocent people for the period of the revolt only, while subjecting many
to Gulag-style labour detail such as road building to support pacification.[221] They mistreated others. Once the crisis was over, the Mandate
state released detainees and closed detention camps. The Gulag was integral to the Soviet state from its inception, and even after Stalin's death in
1953 the Gulag continued in attenuated forms to the end of the USSR.
If Palestine were a Gulag, it was short lived. The colonial emergency state
only invoked its latent ability to imprison the people in times of extreme
crisis, preferring consensual indirect comprador rule and the threat of
force to the perpetual prison archipelago of coercive direct rule. Gulag
was integral to Government and economy in the USSR; in Palestine, the
Government temporarily set up a 'Gulag' that by its very transient nature
undermines its claim to be one.

This should not detract from the extent and harshness of the Palestine
detention system surrounding the revolt. The prison network after 1936
was militarised and brutalised as the Army assumed police functions,
and it did its work in police stations as well as its own camps. Security
force personnel went about their work as they wished. The insouciance
of policemen was such that they 'smartened-up' in jail a prisoner with
rubber truncheons, not caring that a British clergyman who was waiting
in the police station to report his car stolen witnessed this action.[222]
This 'smartening-up' might be the same instance in which a clergyman
witnessed the beating of a suspect whose teeth were already knocked out
before he was brought in for a sustained assault by policemen and a man
in civilian clothes who might have been a military intelligence officer
working within the prison system:

A second man came in who was in plain clothes, but whom I took to be one of
the British Police, and I saw him put a severe double arm lock on the man from

---

[220] Diary, 24 January 1939, Scrivenor Papers, MSS. Brit. Emp. S. 378, WL.
[221] Anne Applebaum, *GULAG: A History of the Soviet Camps* (London: Allen Lane,
2003), p. 4.
[222] Letter, Burr to Father, n.d. [December 1937], Burr Papers, 88/8/1, IWMD. See also
correspondence on police abuses in J&EM Papers, GB 165-0161, Box 61, File 3, MEC.

behind, and then beat him about the head and body in what I can only describe as a brutal and callous way. Once or twice he stopped and turned to the other people in the station, and in an irresponsible and gloating manner said 'I'm so sorry' – 'I'm awfully sorry.' And then proceeded to punch the prisoner round the station again. A third man came in. He was in plain clothes, and was wearing a soft felt hat. He was, I think, British, and may have been a member of the Police Force, but I thought at the time that he was a soldier in civilian clothes ... But this man also made a vicious and violent attack on the prisoner, and punched him about the head and body ... I am gravely disturbed at the possibility that one of the men who was in the station, and who beat up the first person who was brought in was not a member of the police force, but a soldier – this was the man who was wearing a soft felt trilby hat ... I was for two years Chaplain to a prison in England, and in the course of my duties not infrequently witnessed the methods which police and prison warders were compelled to use with men detained or serving long terms of imprisonment, and can only say what I saw on this occasion sickened me and filled me with the gravest misgivings.[223]

The presence of British authority figures did nothing to blunt security force violence. The Anglican Bishop in Jerusalem had to remonstrate with one police sergeant – 'under the influence of drink or mentally disturbed' – who threatened a school boy travelling in the clergyman's car.[224]

Detention as internment (or concentration) was preferable to arrest for security forces as the latter involved an encounter with the courts. The emergency state moved from arrest to detention, more especially with military control of the country in the second phase of the revolt. The numbers may seem small at first sight but with some basic data analysis a darker story emerges, considering a total Palestine population of 1,435,285 in 1938 (900,250 Muslims, 411,222 Jews, 111,974 Christians, and 11,643 others, these figures adding up to 1,435,089).[225] On 9 June 1936, the British recorded the following arrests made since 19 April, excluding those held under curfew legislation: 1,313 Arabs of whom they convicted 754, acquitted 226, and 333 were awaiting trial, alongside 182 Jews, of whom 104 were convicted and 61 were awaiting trial.[226] A CID appreciation in November 1936 of the men held at Sarafand for their 'extremist' views was that the greatest number of internees in the camp

[223] David Irving (Anglican Chaplain, Haifa) to the Lord Bishop in Jerusalem (Graham Brown), 29 December 1937 in J&EM Papers, GB 165-0161, Box 65, File 5, pp. 21–23, 29ff, MEC.

[224] Note by George Francis Graham Brown, Bishop in Jerusalem, 19 April 1939 in J&EM Papers, GB 165-0161, Box 62, File 1, MEC.

[225] Statistical Abstract of Palestine, 1939 (Jerusalem: Office of Statistics, 1939), p. 11.

[226] Telegram, High Commissioner Palestine to Secretary of State for Colonies, 9 June 1936, L/PS/12/3344–45: Palestine Situation, IOR; Official Communique 101/36, 9 June 1936, Official Communiques, M/567/3, ISA.

at any one time was 421 on 9 October 1936, down to 34 by November 1936.[227] The *Survey of Palestine* recorded how in 1937 security forces interned 903 people of whom 816 were Arabs; in 1938, they interned 2,543 people of whom 2,463 were Arabs; in 1939, they 'kept in detention' 5,933 persons, of whom 254 were Jewish, the last figure accepted in Palestinian texts as exact.[228] It may be that in the first phase of the trouble detention (as arrest or internment) was less pronounced, with an official figure of some 750 Arab captives a month in May 1936, a maximum of 421 in a major detention camp, and a rate of 500 per month interned in 1939. But these numbers are extremely low considering the qualitative examination above and quantitative figures from in-house Army reports. Thus, a fortnightly secret military intelligence report covering the two weeks before 30 December 1938, when Army operations were at their zenith, stated that 1,402 Arabs were detained for interrogation and 236 arrested but it excluded villagers interrogated 'in their own villages.'[229] In the two-week period up to 16 December 1938 security forces detained 1,197 for interrogation and arrested 694, again excluding village interrogations.[230] In the two-week period up to 2 December 1938, the British detained 3,895 suspects for interrogation and arrested 359, excluding local interrogation.[231] These fortnightly intelligence reports were a snap shot of events over the preceding two weeks, not cumulative aggregates of men being constantly rearrested. The total from 2 December 1938 of 4,254 detainees equalled 0.3 per cent of the population detained in fourteen days. Extrapolating from this, over 8,000 Palestinians – and some Jews, their community bitterly complaining about the dangers of their being locked up with Arabs and there being no prison kosher food[232] – went

[227] CID Periodical Appreciation Summary No. 18/36, 7 November 1936, Deputy Inspector General to Chief Secretary, FO 371/20018 TNA; Arnon-Ohanna, *Falahim ba-Mered ha-'Aravi*, p. 33.

[228] *A Survey of Palestine. Prepared in December 1945 and December 1946 for the Information of the Anglo-American Committee of Inquiry* [1946–47] (Washington, DC: IPS, 1991), i, pp. 38–49. Walid Khalidi (ed.), *Before Their Diaspora: A Photographic History of the Palestinians, 1876–1948* (Washington, DC: IPS, 2004), p. 226.

[229] Summary of Intelligence, Palestine and Transjordan, 30 December 1938, by Wing Commander Ritchie [26/38], CO 732/81/10, TNA.

[230] Summary of Intelligence, Palestine and Transjordan, 16 December 1938, by Wing Commander Ritchie at GHQ [25/38], CO 732/81/10, TNA.

[231] Summary of Intelligence, Palestine and Transjordan, 2 December 1938, by Wing Commander Ritchie at GHQ [24/38], CO 732/81/10, TNA.

[232] Correspondence in File 04-161-B/621: Riots, May–July 1936 [one bundle of papers] and in File 04/-163-A/621: Riots, April 1936 [but actually June–September 1938] [one bundle of papers], TAMA; Correspondence in File 04/-165-B/622: The Riots: Negotiations with the Government, July 1936–June 1940, TAMA; Correspondence in File 13: Social Help to Jewish Prisoners, June 1938–March 1939, Box 4625, Jerusalem Municipality, Historical Archive, Department of Jewish Community, JMA.

into the detention system every month in late 1938 and this gives a conservative estimate of 96,000 Palestinians in 1938 passing through the formal part of the detention system. With 900,250 Muslims in Palestine in 1938 this was 11 per cent of the Muslim population or some 22 per cent if one excludes women – although, of course, the British also detained some non-Muslim Palestinians and Palestinian women.[233] If one accepts 8,000 officially detained in some fashion each month this means that for an insurgency lasting thirty-three months from April 1936 to September 1939 – the period of the Palestine clasp to the 1918 General Service Medal but excluding the hiatus from December 1936 to August 1937 – security forces detained 264,000 people. This, however, excludes the very extensive unofficial incarcerations by security forces as detailed above, so if one (inexactly) doubles the figure to take account of this, soldiers and police detained 528,000 people, for varying periods of time from days to years, some imprisoned more than once, in varying places, and this total – that exceeds the entire Muslim male population of Palestine in 1938 – omits any detentions from December 1936 to August 1937. It equals 37 per cent of the entire population of Palestine in 1938. One issue is that the figures from late 1938 might be a spike in detentions as military operations increased with Army control of the country after the Munich settlement, set against which is the fact that unofficial, unrecorded imprisonment was high throughout the revolt. The Army pulled in whole villages for periods of incarceration and labour, hundreds of people each time. Village files of detentions and arrests reflect the system of mass detention at the micro level, with thirty-seven men from Mujeidal (al-Mujaydil near Nazareth) sentenced to periods from one to six months under Emergency Regulation 15B, or about 6 per cent of the male population of the village (with a total population of 1,241 in 1931).[234] The police sent twenty-five men into the detention system from Touran village (Tur'an with a population of 961 in 1931) for three to nine months, with another six villagers listed as 'suspected terrorists.'[235] These are officially recorded detentions, set against which are the masses of unofficial holdings of villagers, usually for shorter periods of time. The authorities imprisoned other men who failed to produce bonds and sureties, as with a Tewfiq Abu Sa' (perhaps Tawfiq Abu Sa'd) of Dier el Ghassoun (Dayr al-Ghusun north-west of

[233] *Statistical Abstract of Palestine, 1939* (Jerusalem: Office of Statistics, 1939), p. 11.
[234] Mujeidal, Persons Sentenced under Emergency Regulations 1936, Palestine Police Force, Report from Tiberias, M/4212/8, ISA; Khalidi, *All That Remains*, p. 348.
[235] Touran, Persons Sentenced under Emergency Regulations 1936, Palestine Police Force, Report from Tiberias, M/4212/8, ISA.

Bal'a) in January 1938, whose failure to produce these totalling £P.150 under emergency Ordinances led to a year's sentence; when he produced the bond and surety, they released him.[236] The British even detained pro-British Nashashibi-associated Palestinians in Acre camp for their own protection from Husayni-led attacks.[237] The higher incarceration rates in Palestine within a loosely arranged detention network as detailed here genuflect to the Gulag-Gestapo thesis on Kenya in the 1950s and they emphasise continuities in British colonial security state imprisonment regimes during revolt crises, from Egypt, Iraq, and Ireland after 1918 to Kenya and Malaya in the 1950s.

British handling of prisoners in Palestine was mixed. Abuse as detailed above sat alongside proper (or at least not brutal) care of prisoners and some remarkably nice treatment, so raising the methodological problem of the evidence being a series of varied experiences without any coherent story or quantitative structure. Inmates of 'social standing' complained that they were treated as fellahin; all detainees sleeping in wooden huts at al-Mazra'a suffered in inclement weather; food was bad; there were curfews from 5 pm to 6 am, restricting prayer times as Muslim inmates could not access water for washing.[238] Policeman Burr wrote euphemistically of having to go to the Acre labour camp to 'instil some sense into the inmates who are getting out of hand.'[239] Palestinians made complaints to the authorities about poor treatment. One young man wrote to the British detailing the treatment that his father, 'Abd al-Hamid Shuman, a bank director (and founder of the main Palestinian bank under the Mandate, the Arab Bank that is based today in Jordan), had received at the hands of the police. Arrested on 20 February 1938 in Jerusalem, the British moved the father to Acre jail and then to al-Mazra'a detention camp before he went back to Acre prison hospital after what he claimed were severe beatings by prison guards that left him unable to walk.[240] There are other accounts from arrested insurgents of detainees being left in open cages in the sun without sustenance, of men being beaten with wet ropes, 'boxed' and having their teeth smashed, and men having their

---

[236] Tewfiq Abu Sa', Release Order, Divisional Police HQ, Tulkarm, 26 March 1938 signed Acting ASP Tulkarm, M/4826/26, ISA.

[237] Letter, Burr (Central Police Station, Acre) to Mother and Father, n.d. [December 1938 or January 1939, after Christmas 1938], Burr Papers, 88/8/1, IWMD.

[238] The Arab Internees in Palestine Prisons, by the Syro-Palestine Executive Committee (Cairo), 29 November 1937, FO 371/21872, TNA.

[239] Letter, Burr (Inlying Piquet) to Mother and Father, 22 April 1938, Burr Papers, 88/8/1, IWMD.

[240] Letters of Protest to the British Government about the Torture of Abd al-Hamid Shuman and the Detainees in Acre Prison, 29 April and 23 June 1938 in Zu'aytir, *Watha'iq al-Haraka*, p. 478.

feet burnt with oil.[241] Those who were 'boxed' were beaten until they were
knocked out, 'needles' were used on suspects, dogs were set upon Arab
detainees, and British and Jewish auxiliary forces maltreated prisoners
by having them hold heavy stones and then beating them when they
dropped them. Guards also used bayonets on sleep-deprived men and
made them wear bells around their necks and dance.[242] That said, one of
Shuman's fellow detainees at al-Mazra'a, Abdul Hamid Sayih ('Abd al-
Hamid al-Sai'h) wrote of take-away food, jogging, sun-beds, educational
classes, and a prison governor's 'humane gesture ... worthy of praise
and I thank him for this,' while an Irish guard called Mr Ackley treated
detainees 'very well' and respected their 'habits,' letting them wear their
own headdress.[243] A Palestinian who took books to the men in Acre jail in
late 1938 found a 'very cordial and helpful' Quaker guard and prisoners
who 'were not gracious' and who deliberated before accepting the books,
rejecting one written by a communist.[244] Treatment at the local level for
detainees could also be reasonable, as when soldiers detained local men
and took them to a lock-up in Ramallah. They did little to them beyond
making them mend some buildings. The main complaint was that the
better-educated ones resented their gaolers leaving them in a cell with
peasants, itself an emblematic complaint. The extent of military violence
towards the suspects was to manhandle them through the door into the
basement cell. Once released, the soldier-gaolers gave the local men
cigarettes and a lift home.[245] The villagers were 'not specially indignant,
taking it rather as part of life's general unpleasantness. "Turkish soldiers
before 1918," they said, "English soldiers now. All soldiers are alike."'[246]

Hunger and Homelessness

What is certain is that population-centric pacification impoverished
Palestinians and turned them from rebellion. By November 1938, an
intelligence report noted the social dislocation wrought by military
operations, with 'Poverty, amounting almost to famine' among the peasantry to a 'greater degree than in previous years,' alongside considerable

---

[241] A Letter from the Fighter Arrested, Subhi al-Khadra, 20 September 1938 in Zu'aytir,
    Watha'iq al-Haraka, pp. 505–06, 548.
[242] Statement about the Torture of Arabs Arrested in Military Camps and Prisons, 1938–
    39 in Zu'aytir, *Watha'iq al-Haraka*, pp. 548, 579, 594, 601; Subhi Yasin, *Al-Thawra
    al-'Arabiyya al-Kubra (fi Filastin) 1936–1939* [*The Great Arab Revolt in Palestine, 1936–
    1939*] (Damascus: Shafa 'Amr Haifa, 1959), p. 47.
[243] Sayih, *Filastin*, pp. 44–48.
[244] Diary, 8 October 1938, in Ricks, *Turbulent Times*, p. 236.
[245] Diary, Wilson Papers, GB 165-0302, pp. 27–31, MEC.
[246] Ibid., p. 32, MEC.

unemployment.[247] A drought in December 1937 to early 1938 worsened the lot of ordinary Palestinians.[248] Prompted by reports from the Arab Women's Committee of Jerusalem, the communist MP William Gallacher asked questions in Parliament to the Secretary of State for the Colonies about the plight of Palestinian women and children 'left destitute in villages wrecked by punitive operations; whether he has any information concerning the lack of provision made for the families of Arab deportees,' to which the Minister replied: 'I have seen the appeal in question. I assume that when the petitioners speak of "villages wrecked on punitive operations," what they have in mind is the punitive demolition of individual homes,' before referring Gallacher to the fact that those deported to the Seychelles were maintained at Government expense and to previous statements on the matter.[249] Police officers at the sharp end dealt with orphaned children, estimated at 'over fifteen thousand who have had the bread winner shot down within the last three years.'[250] The countryside suffered the most as protracted military violence in remote rural areas away from prying eyes was easier to sustain than in towns. Police CID by July 1939 reported on the 'gradual deterioration' in the economy, widespread urban and rural poverty, and protests against tax collection; in villages the situation was 'more acute' and it was rumoured that the Government was considering the distribution of agricultural loans as a 'measure of relief.'[251] A British school teacher in Palestine wrote in her diary how by 1938 economic life was at a standstill for peasants 'who at the best of times scraped only the barest living' and now 'hundreds were starving' surrounded by the rubble of Army demolitions.[252] District Commissioners officials worried about harvest failure and the 'very grave danger of famine.'[253] The American Colony Aid Association distributed bread and milk in October 1938 to hungry Jerusalemites after the Army retook the old city (Figure 6.6).[254] Army commanders wondered at the

[247] Summary of Intelligence, Palestine and Transjordan, 4 November 1938, by Wing Commander Ritchie at GHQ [22/38], CO 732/81/10, TNA.

[248] Kenneth Stein, 'Palestine's Rural Economy, 1917–1939,' *Studies in Zionism* 8/1 (1987), pp. 43–44.

[249] Parliamentary Questions, 7 March 1938 in FO 371/21870, p. 268, TNA. From *Hansard*, HC Deb, 7 March 1938, Vol. 332, c1552W.

[250] Letter, Burr (Acre Police Station, Caesar's Camp) to Mother and Father, 14 April 1939, Burr Papers, 88/8/1, IWMD.

[251] CID Police, Intelligence Summary 50/39, 20 July 1939, 47/89, HA.

[252] School Year Diary, 1938–39, Wilson Papers, GB 165-0302, p. 2, MEC.

[253] Monthly Report for September 1938, dated 5 October 1938, by R. E. H. Crosbie (DC Southern District), Phillips Papers, GB 165-0183, File 1, p. 11, MEC.

[254] Arab Revolt in Palestine Photograph Album 1938, ACHA; 'Acts of Mercy in the Holy City,' *The Daily Sketch* (27 October 1938) in Scrapbook of Articles about the American Colony, Palestine, People and Events and Loose Enclosures 1938, ACHA.

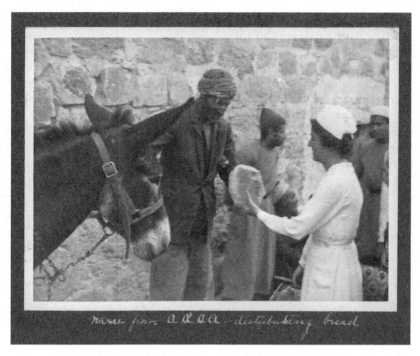

nurse from A.C.A.A. distributing bread

6.6 American Colony Aid Association distributing bread and milk in
October 1938 to hungry Jerusalemites
(from American Colony Hotel Archive)

effects of the punitive operations and their reprisals for rebel attacks,
talking about the 'evacuation' of villages that left soldiers open to the
charge of 'putting women and children homeless in the winter; lands
us with liability for their houses, furniture and flocks, with consequent
compensation and inevitable blame for what occurs: and intensifies the
feeding, poverty and unemployment problem – for what?'[255] The answer
was clear, as military commanders knew well from their experience of
imperial policing operations: such actions crushed the popular base of
insurgency. Security forces did this without vast numbers killed – up to
4,000 dead, many rebel fighters or criminals, although the number may
have approached 6,000, excluding intra-communal deaths[256] – or the systematic exceptional abuses of castrations, tortures and (legal and illegal)

[255] Haining to O'Connor, 23 January 1939, O'Connor Papers, 3/4/22, LHCMA.
[256] See Appendix B on casualties.

executions of Kenya in the 1950s, while inflicting sufficient managed systemic attritional punishment through fining, non-lethal violence, and forms of emergency detention as discussed here to turn fellahin from insurgency to passive acceptance of the status quo ante or to switch sides and provide information. The Army rewarded those who collaborated with money, travel permits, and weapons; it paid villagers near Ramallah for surrendered rifles.[257] The security forces had won, supported by collaborators and intelligence gathering, and by an extra-judicial dirty war that further pacified the populace, the subjects of the final chapters of this book.

---

[257] *Davar* [*Issue*] (Tel Aviv) (23 May 1939).

7   Collaboration and Intelligence

Jewish and Palestinian collaboration with British forces and security force intelligence gathering were force multipliers for pacification. Neither collaboration nor intelligence information was a decisive counter-insurgency tool but combined with fractured Palestinian resistance and the weight of kinetic and population-centric pacification operations they hastened the revolt's end. Irregular auxiliary collaborator units expanded the scale and scope of the security forces, while the infiltration of the rebel front through collaboration and intelligence gathering made clear the power of the colonial state to articulate new forms of persuasion and the weakness of the insurgency in equal measure. The 'lifeblood' of intelligence that flowed in to security forces from 'increasing numbers' of informants by 1939 signalled that the revolt was over.[1] This was the covert side to pacification, some of which merged with extra-judicial dirty wars examined in the next chapter. Intelligence was vital for effective counter-rebel band military operations and used heavily for village interrogation screening that produced more intelligence, but the Army's broad targeting of Palestinians as described in the last chapter did not demand the same information networks. Village-based punitive operations did, however, prompt collaboration that encouraged intelligence gathering that in turn supported powerful search-and-sweep operations that won the day and so stimulated more collaboration and information giving from Palestinians looking to survive tough times, end interrogation, escape detention, make money, or settle old scores. Collaboration and intelligence were two sides of the same coin. Security force intelligence came mostly from 'humint' (human intelligence) human informers often via collaborating Jewish forces with links to Palestinians and increasingly from captured rebel documents (some 600 papers in the biggest haul to

---

[1] Charles Tegart, Memoir of an Indian Policeman, by K. F. Tegart (wife), p. 290, Mss Eur C.235/2, IOR; Summary of Intelligence, Palestine and Transjordan, 16 December 1938, by Wing Commander Ritchie at GHQ [25/38], CO 732/81/10, TNA.

date in December 1938, usually translated by Jews for the Army[2]), less so from 'sigint' signals intercepts but security forces and Jewish agents tapped telephones and meetings; the Jews bugged verbatim conversations in Hajj Amin's residence.[3] Jewish operatives bugged the plate of a ceiling lamp in Jerusalem's Palace Hotel that hosted the Peel Commission and listened to proceedings.[4] The British even uncovered a Jewish operation tapping the central telephone switchboard.[5] The Army used reconnaissance and air photography imagery, or 'imint' intelligence.[6] The RAF had good intelligence sources in Amman.[7] District Commissioners supplied information, too, as did Arab and Jewish District Officers.[8] Central military Combined Force Staff intelligence in Jerusalem headquarters used this field information to coordinate the Army's powerful anti-band combined-arms operational sweeps down to brigade and then battalion level, and to support nationwide road, fort, and fencing construction projects that gripped the country.[9] Regimental archives detail how RAF Special Service Officers (SSOs) who coordinated much of the intelligence work fed information directly to battalions for their daily counter-rebel operations.[10] Jerusalem headquarters found funding for informers. Such people saved lives and communities, as they saw it, with Palestinian Christian Hanna Helou (al-Hilu) writing to Tel Aviv's Jewish mayor as early as 28 April 1936 telling him how while 'Some people say I am helping the Zionist but all I am doing is trying to bring peace to my people.'[11] Unsurprisingly, rebels rejected such excuses, seeing clearly the baleful effects of large-scale collaboration: 'God curse the traitors

[2] Summary of Intelligence, Palestine and Transjordan, 30 December 1938, by Wing Commander Ritchie [26/38], CO 732/81/10, pp. 3–4, TNA; Yoav Gelber, *Shorshey ha-Havatzelet: ha-Modi'in ba-Yishuv, 1918–1947* [*A Budding Fleur-de-Lis: The Intelligence Services of the Jewish Yishuv (in Palestine), 1918–47*] (Tel Aviv: Ministry of Defence, 1992), p. 150.

[3] Intelligence Transcripts of Mufti's Conversations with Sheikh Fuad, April 1937 (and other people), Yitzhak Ben-Zvi, Reports 1937, 80/153/9, HA.

[4] Testimony, Eliyahu Sochever, 19 February 1950, 161.00020, p. 2, HA.

[5] Asa Lefen, *Ha-Shai: Shorasheha Shel Kehilat ha-Modi'in ha-Yisraelit* [*The Roots of the Israeli Intelligence Community*] (Tel Aviv: Ministry of Defence, 1997), pp. 46–47.

[6] Gelber, *Shorshey ha-Havatzelet*, p. 150.

[7] Letter, Brooke-Popham (HQ, RAF, Cairo) to ACM Ellington (London), 12 August 1936, Brooke-Popham Papers, 4/3/47, LHCMA.

[8] Martin Thomas, *Empires of Intelligence: Security Services and Colonial Disorders after 1914* (Berkeley, CA: University of California Press, 2008), p. 239.

[9] A subject covered in Steven Wagner, *Statecraft by Stealth: How Britain Ruled Palestine 1917–40* (Ithaca, NY: Cornell, University Press, 2018).

[10] Dorsetshire Regiment, SSO reports from Nablus to 2nd Dorsets, 88/352, Shelf C4, Box 3, KMM.

[11] Letter, Helou to Tel Aviv Mayor, 28 April 1936, File 04-161-A/621: Riots, April 1936 [one bundle of papers], TAMA.

who degrade themselves before the imperialist forces, who act against their own people for small profits or because of private reasons.'[12] Giving information to security forces became so widespread that Palestinian newspapers reported on the 'snitches' and how 'they look like people but from the inside they are animals, like sinful women selling their bodies, like insects, like poisonous snakes.'[13] Rebels fought back and villagers 'anxious to help the Government' told the Army 'it was too dangerous to do so' but notwithstanding the counter-terror more and more information came in to security forces over the course of the revolt.[14]

There were 'two different ideologies' on how best to tackle Zionism, whether by Hajj Amin-led resistance or Nashashibi-led cooperation with the Jews, and while most Palestinians emphatically preferred the former they still informed to Jews and security forces for personally contingent, parochial reasons; strong guerrilla resistance predicts and eliminates this threat through national political education and focused terror campaigns.[15] It may be that Palestinian informers did not see themselves as collaborators – after all, the Arabic verb for collaborate, *ta'awana*, also means to cooperate – but in the face of the existential Zionist threat there was here a lack of connection between mental functions that is incongruous to the outside observer, akin to some form of collective schizophrenia that as with any delusion is hard to rationalise. Money bought informers. Jews paid one Arab prison guard nicknamed 'Abu Shilling' two shillings a day (so 100 mils, a tenth of a Palestine pound) to pass on prison lists to their intelligence service, noting that 'he did not look upon himself as an informer or a traitor, but merely as a man doing a paid job.'[16] Another collaborator remarked that he would stop informing once he had paid off his debts.[17] Such informers helped scupper Palestinian resistance. By contrast, Jewish collaboration with the British and Palestinians made good strategic sense at this time as it strengthened the *Yishuv* militarily and divided Palestinians politically.

---

[12] Rebellion Command Letter to the Brother [Jaffa?] Secretary of the Office, Signed Central Committee for the National Jihad, 26 December 1938, Captured and Translated Arabic Material with Commentary, p. 18, Wingate Papers, Microfilm M2313, BL.

[13] *al-Jami'a al-Islamiyya* [*The Islamic Community*], 14 January 1938, in Yuval Arnon-Ohanna, *Falahim ba-Mered ha-'Aravi be-eretz Yisrael, 1936–39* [*Fellahin during the Arab Revolt in the Land of Israel*] (Tel Aviv: Shiloh Institute, Tel Aviv University, 1978), p. 84.

[14] Lt-Col (CO 2nd Bn Queen's Royal West Surrey Regiment) to HQ 14th Inf Bde, 25 January 1939, QRWS3/6/7, SHC.

[15] Hillel Cohen, *Army of Shadows: Palestinian Collaboration with Zionism, 1917–1948* (Berkeley, CA: University of California Press, 2008), p. 84.

[16] Efraim Dekel, *Shai: The Exploits of Hagana Intelligence* (New York, NY: Yoseloff, 1959), p. 207.

[17] Ibid., p. 223.

Jewish collaboration was politically purposeful and not fundamentally personal. The US Consul noted how 'no Jew will inform against another Jew' after a police seizure of a Jewish weapons shipment: 'if the Arabs had been the importer our task would have been very much simplified for it would only have been a matter of a few days before the Criminal Investigation Department would have received a clue.'[18]

There were five collaborative links with British forces after 1936 that amplified pacification and supported intelligence gathering: (1) Palestinians within the country collaborated with the British against armed gangs in *al-Mua'rada* Opposition Nashashibi-backed peace bands for which the Army sponsored a meeting at Yatta near Hebron in December 1938, what one critic has called 'contras'; (2) the British armed and trained Jewish settlers, recruited supernumerary Jewish police, and fought alongside Jews in special military formations such as the Special Night Squads; (3) minority Palestinian communities such as the Druze, Christians, and Bedouin collaborated with security forces, notably armed Druze who fought rebel gangs; (4) neighbouring Arab state leaders such as King Abdullah of Transjordan collaborated with the British diplomatically to end the violence; (5) the Nashashibi-family bloc and other Palestinians combined with the *Yishuv* to obtain weapons, money, and support to fight armed gangs, the Husayni family or for personal gain.[19] This chapter details and assesses the impact of collaboration within the first three areas, leaving aside diplomatic collaboration between Britain and the rulers of Transjordan, Iraq, Saudi Arabia, and Yemen to bring peace, a subject touched on in the Afterword's assessment of policy and force during the revolt. Moreover, other authors have examined the diplomacy surrounding the revolt.[20] Diplomatic collaboration was the only area in which the Palestinian national cause potentially stood to gain from working with the British, a joint venture ruined by the machinations of Arab leaders, by Palestinian rejection of the 1939 White Paper, and by the changed geopolitics wrought by the Second World War and post-Holocaust migration of Jews to Palestine. Hillel Cohen has most recently

---

[18] Report dated 25 November 1935 on Arms and the Mandate, US Consul General Palestine to State Department, 867N.00/263 [Reel M#1037/1], NARA II.

[19] Ted Swedenburg, *Memories of Revolt: The 1936–1939 Rebellion and the Palestinian National Past* (Minneapolis, MN: University of Minnesota Press, 1995), p. 86.

[20] Norman Rose, 'The Arab Rulers and Palestine, 1936: The British Reaction,' *Journal of Modern History* 44/2 (June 1972), pp. 213–31; Joseph Nevo, *King Abdallah and Palestine: A Territorial Ambition* (Houndmills: Macmillan, 1996); Yoav Gelber, *Jewish–Transjordanian Relations, 1921–48* (London: Cass, 1997); Avi Shlaim, *Collusion across the Jordan: King Abdullah, the Zionist Movement, and the Partition of Palestine* (Oxford: Clarendon, 1988); Mary Wilson, *King Abdullah, Britain and the Making of Jordan* (Cambridge: Cambridge University Press, 1987).

examined the fifth area of collaboration between Jews and Palestinians, showing how Jews exploited divisions within the Palestinian community and how groups such as the Nashashibis looked to the Jews for help, some of which came from the Army via the *Yishuv* with RAF intelligence being the first contact point between the two sides.[21] British–Jewish collaboration encouraged pre-existing Jewish–Palestinian cooperation. Palestinians were right that the British 'capitalised' on the Nashashibi (Opposition) versus Husayni (Council) family split, keeping 'it alive in order to weaken the national movement' but the British–Jewish–Nashashibi–Abdullah anti-rebel (and anti-Hajj Amin) front was never going to win the war.[22] It still demanded, however, a disciplined rebel riposte to stamp out internal dissent that gifted the colonial state intelligence, auxiliary pro-Government Palestinian units, psychological and material disorder amongst insurgents and the populace, supportive diplomatic channels through Anglophile rulers such as Abdullah, and the passive-active help of minority communities.

The Government-backed Palestinian and Jewish irregular or semiregular auxiliary units discussed below appear in different guises in other counter-insurgency campaigns, often committing the worst atrocities and often with the 'special' moniker, with names such as Home Guard Police, Police Reserve, B Specials, Auxiliaries, Mobile Force, Black and Tans, Toads, X Squads, Kenya Cowboys, CID, Freds, Mobile Strike Force, special force, Special Reconnaissance Unit, and Native Authority Police.[23] They engaged in private wars that terrorised civilians, as peace bands, Jewish supernumerary police, and the British–Jewish Special Night Squads would do during the revolt, the subject also of the next chapter.[24] They gave tactical flexibility by pushing the limits of permissible force. The West Yorkshire Regiment formed 'special' covert units of white soldiers that operated at night, while there are photographs in regimental archives of soldiers dressed as Arabs such as Sergeant Jim Sweeney of the Loyals who on intelligence work dressed as 'El Arab' 'with the view

[21] Cohen, *Army of Shadows*; Yehoshua Porath, *The Palestinian Arab National Movement: From Riots to Rebellion. Volume 2, 1929–1939* (London: Cass, 1977), p. 256.
[22] Notes of Interviews, Hikmat Masri (Nablus), 24 March 1977, Palestine Research Lever Arch File, Thames TV Material on 'Palestine: Promises, Rebellion and Abdication' (1977–78), IWMFA; Notes of Interviews, 'Izzat Darwaza (Damascus), 1 November 1977, Palestine Research Lever Arch File, Thames TV Material on 'Palestine: Promises, Rebellion and Abdication' (1977–78), IWMFA.
[23] Douglas Porch, *Counterinsurgency: Exposing the Myths of the New Way of War* (Cambridge: Cambridge University Press, 2013), p. 128.
[24] Matthew Hughes, 'Terror in Galilee: British–Jewish Collaboration and the Special Night Squads in Palestine during the Arab Revolt, 1938–39,' *Journal of Imperial and Commonwealth History* 43/4 (December 2015), pp. 590–610.

to obtaining information.'[25] Many images of soldiers dressed as Arabs are obviously pantomime. A curious Haganah file discussed how the British commander in Transjordan J. B. Glubb (or 'Globe') sent armed counter-gangs to join the rebels.[26] Autochthonous units offered security forces unique ways of dividing insurgents and subject peoples by sowing fear and confusion through disguise, imitation, replication, psychological discombobulation, and misinformation, what was known after 1945 as pseudo warfare. Pseudo units are interesting contributory but not decisive military forces. White Kenyan settlers 'blacked up' to fight alongside loyalist black soldiers as 'pseudo gangsters' to fight Mau Mau insurgents, in the words of critics of Britain's Kenyan counter-insurgency.[27] Such units also gathered intelligence. The white Rhodesian Government in 1973 set up the discrete Selous Scouts Regiment comprised of loyalist black soldiers and white ones pretending to be black to conduct subversive war, a unit built on earlier operational experience in Kenya but not Palestine, it seems.[28] Pseudo war in Palestine supplied irregular auxiliary military units and sources for intelligence gathering, and it offered new ways to terrorise the people into submission, but the British Army as a whole was averse to irregular special units that undermined its monopoly on violence and so limited its support or closed them down.[29] The Army was institutionally conservative and uneasy about the unmanaged violence of irregular war. It utilised Jewish and some Palestinian auxiliary units, but the lure of hush-hush covert operations must not detract from the overt business of quotidian pacification by line infantry regiments as discussed in the last two chapters. Moreover, Palestinian collaboration with the Army was half-hearted, most of the population preferring Hajj Amin's resistance to the Nashashibis' collaboration, as the Army knew, not that this stopped Palestinians from temporarily working with the authorities. Similarly, Chief Secretary Battershill had little faith in

[25] 2nd Battalion, West Yorkshire Regiment, Battalion Intelligence Summaries, Nos. 5–7, Ramallah, 17 November–1 December 1938, RYM; *The Lancashire Lad: Journal of the Loyal Regiment (North Lancashire)* 57 (August 1936), p. 114, QLRM.

[26] Haganah Report, 24 August 1936, Shai Intelligence Reports: 8/GENERAL/40, p. 113, HA.

[27] David Anderson, *Histories of the Hanged: Britain's Dirty War in Kenya and the End of Empire* (London: Weidenfeld and Nicolson, 2005), pp. 284–85; Caroline Elkins, *Britain's Gulag: The Brutal End of Empire in Kenya* (London: Jonathan Cape, 2005), pp. 54, 67.

[28] Jake Harper-Ronald, *Sunday, Bloody Sunday: A Soldier's War in Northern Ireland, Rhodesia, Mozambique and Iraq* (Alberton: Galago, 2009), p. 176; R. F. Reid-Daly, *Pamwe Chete: The Legend of the Selous Scouts* (Weltevreden: Covos, 1999), pp. 15–16, 22, 33, 475; Jonathan Pittaway (ed.), *Selous Scouts: The Men Speak* (Durban: Dandy Agencies, 2013), *passim*; correspondence, Gen Sir Frank Kitson to Author, June 2013.

[29] 2nd Battalion, West Yorkshire Regiment, Battalion Intelligence Summaries, Nos. 5–7, Ramallah, 17 November–1 December 1938, RYM.

Raghib Nashashibi, seeing him as 'unstable,' 'mercenary,' and 'lacking what Kipling called "essential guts".'[30] Battershill's criticisms replicated British assessments of the ephemeral value of Palestinian collaborators and show how little long-term British commitment collaborators could expect:

> I am most disappointed in him. I saw him this week and he did not even have the courage to issue a simple statement on behalf of his part [sic] that he deplored assassinations. His influence in the country is slight. He chatters too much, gloats in public over the discomfiture of the Mufti, and thinks that he will come out on top in the end. He is such a fool that he expects the Government to pull his nuts out of the fire by allowing him to publish proclamations and manifestoes blackguarding the Government so that he can regain his prestige with the Arabs. He has no moral character or backbone. It is a great pity especially as he is such a charming rascal and exceedingly good company and popular socially with many Englishmen.[31]

Battershill added that Raghib's nephew Fakhri was a 'low fellow of the baser sort commanding no influence here,' opposed by most Palestinians who had sent masses of telegrams 'protesting' his statements and 'calling him a hireling.'[32] Battershill was right in how high-level Nashashibi Opposition collaborators had both limited popular appeal and how they mirrored rebel-bandit forces in that they, too, preferred personal polit-ical gain to shared communal national political goals. Meanwhile, rural villagers temporarily collaborated for parochial family-clan reasons or to survive the banditry of soldiers and gangs. Collaboration did not fracture the Palestinians as it reflected their pre-existing fissures. Jews lamented that Opposition collaborators encouraged the slide into 'embarrass-ment and anarchy' rather than be the alternative anti-Hajj Amin power node that favoured Zionism.[33] The Jews in Palestine were by far the better collaborators for the British military, more especially in lieu of a functioning police force, supplying motivated auxiliary units and excel-lent sources of translated intelligence via *Shai*[34] agent networks run by a united Haganah–Jewish Agency–*Histadrut* front. British officer Orde Wingate had Jews translate for him on the spot in battle.[35] The British responded by arming and training Jewish supernumerary police and

---

[30] Letter, Battershill to Sir John Shuckburgh, 21 November 1937, Battershill Papers, MSS. Brit. Emp. S. 467, Box 10, File 3, WL.

[31] Ibid.

[32] Diary, 18 November [1938], Battershill Papers, MSS. Brit. Emp. S. 467, Box 12, File 6, WL.

[33] Sasson to Caplan (Jerusalem), 23 January 1939, S25/3639-151, CZA.

[34] The *Yishuv*'s intelligence branch, formally constituted in 1940.

[35] Report 5 September 1938, Joint Operations with the Friend, Searching the Village of Lidd, S25/8768, pp. 71–72, CZA.

kibbutzniks across Palestine who had a visceral stake in the unfolding counter-insurgency and who unlike the soldiers were not going 'home' after the fighting was over.

Palestinian Collaboration: Peace Bands

The British recruited some Arab supernumerary police, one being attacked in Tel Aviv, but the visible part of Palestinian cooperation was *fasa'il al-salam* 'peace bands' and the less visible part was intelligence gathering.[36] Some peace bands grew organically from village defence units to protect local people from 'brothers of Jihad terrorists,' while others were tied to the Nashashibis and associated local families.[37] Intelligence files noted how the Irsheid family in the Jenin area hosted al-Qawuqji in 1936 and was very active thereafter in fighting the Husayni-backed Council with family members accompanying Army units to 'detect their previous friend, today's enemies.'[38] Farid Irsheid informed to *Shai* who codenamed him the 'gardener.'[39] Whether the peace bands were a spontaneous, self-generated grass-roots defence movement against Hajj Amin's 'terrorist gangs'[40] or colonial creations paid huge sums to 'weaken the revolution'[41] is not the fundamental issue here (in a sense they were both). The point is that while peace bands would never have grown as they did without British help, they never would have happened in the first place had the Palestinians been united. Moreover, unprompted low-level organic village defence units appeared in response to gang banditry without any encouragement from the British or the Nashashibis. In either incarnation, they sowed division and exacerbated Palestinian disunity that in turn supported pacification. Peace bands were British-made in some cases, but the raw material was Palestinian, as when Damascus

---

[36] Dorsetshire Regiment, Narrative of Events, Jaffa, 24 August 1936, 88/367, Shelf C4, Box 3, KMM.

[37] Appendix: Explanatory Notes, Captured and Translated Arabic Material with Commentary, p. 114, Wingate Papers, Microfilm M2313, BL.

[38] Appendix: Explanatory Notes, Captured and Translated Arabic Material with Commentary, p. 112, Wingate Papers, Microfilm M2313, BL.

[39] Porath, *Palestinian Arab National Movement*, pp. 253, 257; Cohen, *Army of Shadows*, pp. 152, 154, 235.

[40] Haggai Eshed, *Reuven Shiloah: The Man behind the Mossad* (London: Cass, 1997), p. 31.

[41] Diary, 7 January 1938, in Muhammad 'Izzat Darwaza, *Mudhakkirat Muhammad 'Izzat Darwaza: Sab'a wa tis'una 'aman fil-haya* [*The Diaries of Muhammad 'Izzat Darwaza: 97 Years in a Life*] (Beirut: Dar al Gharb al Islami, 1993), iii, p. 179; Subhi Yasin, *Al-Thawra al-'Arabiyya al-Kubra (fi Filastin) 1936–1939* [*The Great Arab Revolt in Palestine, 1936–1939*] (Damascus: Shafa 'Amr Haifa, 1959), p. 37; Yusuf Rajab, *Thawrat 1936–1939 fi-Filastin: Dirasa Askariyya* [*Revolt of 1936–1939 in Palestine: A Military Study*] (Beirut: Institute of Arab Research, 1982), pp. 99–100.

British Consul Gilbert MacKereth accelerated peace band operations by paying and convincing 1936 rebel band leader Fakhri 'Abd al-Hadi to return in 1938 on the British side.[42] Indeed, a Jewish file noted a British connection to 'Abd al-Hadi as early as July 1936 when a British officer (whose name sounds like 'Poot' from the Hebrew) met him and said he would not be arrested, only exiled, if he stopped his band's activities.[43] British support shaped the form of the peace bands but they were rooted in Palestinian societal-family structures and the brigandage of the revolt that encouraged Palestinians to protect themselves with counter-violence units that inadvertently helped the British Army. These came in three inter-connected forms: peace bands led by ex-rebel leader 'Abd al-Hadi and prompted by MacKereth; local peace gangs with Nashashibi support that held a pro-Government rally at Yatta in December 1938; and locally generated village defence units that might or might not have broader family connections.

While MacKereth in Damascus facilitated the peace band led by former rebel 'Abd al-Hadi who had sought sanctuary in Syria, the Palestinian Nashashibi family was involved throughout the operation, as were the Jews. MacKereth fixed on 'Abd al-Hadi who had fought in Palestine in 1936 against the British and was now living in exile in Syria but was short of funds. As Jewish intelligence noted, 'Abd al-Hadi 'roamed the Damascus streets, pennyless [sic] and bitter. The British consul then in Damascus knew a thing or two about oriental customs, got friendly with him and came to understandings. Later Fakhri came to Palestine in 1938 and started acting against the official line of Arab conduct and revived – together with the late Fakhri Nashashibi – the Opposition "peace gangs".'[44] MacKereth stimulated relations between 'Abd al-Hadi and the Nashashibi family; the Nashashibis already had good military and intelligence connections with the Jews.[45] Palestinians knew of Fakhri Nashashibi's work in setting up peace bands in Lebanon and his attempts to establish an alternative leadership in Beirut to counter Hajj Amin and in March 1938 Fakhri Nashashibi had met 'Abd al-Hadi in Beirut at the St George Hotel.[46] The Jews were keen to deepen the rift between the insurgents and 'Abd al-Hadi, and agents such as Zaslani,

---

[42] Eshed, *Reuven Shiloah*, p. 32.

[43] 10 July 1936, Information from the Arab Office, Reports of the Situations and Gangs, Communist Activity, Polish and Italians, 22 April–31 July 1936: 8/GENERAL/39, p. 58, HA.

[44] Appendix: Explanatory Notes, Captured and Translated Arabic Material with Commentary, pp. 112–13, Wingate Papers, Microfilm M2313, BL.

[45] Cohen, *Army of Shadows*, 95ff.

[46] Darwaza, *Mudhakkirat Muhammad 'Izzat Darwaza*, iii, p. 179.

Sasson, and Epstein travelled to Syria where MacKereth, who thought that the British authorities in Palestine were too hesitant, asked them to maintain direct contact with him to exchange information on Arab leaders.[47] British–Jewish, diplomatic–military intelligence collaboration in Palestine in this period was strong.[48]

MacKereth arranged a monthly payment for 'Abd al-Hadi, he raised funds to facilitate the rebel leader's return to Palestine to organise peace bands, and he offered 'Abd al-Hadi an amnesty if he would switch sides to the Nashashibi-backed Opposition movement.[49] The approach worked and on 21 September 1938 a British-sponsored Druze force escorted 'Abd al-Hadi back to Palestine.[50] Thereafter, Britain subsidised 'Abd al-Hadi and paid each man in his peace band £P.6 per month as opposed to the insurgents' usual pay of 30 shillings to £P.4, some of which came from levies and extortion of Palestinian villages.[51] The willingness to pay a good wage shows how seriously the British authorities took the peace bands. 'Abd al-Hadi in late September 1938 settled with official approval in his home village of 'Arraba, near Jenin, the base of his pro-Nashashibi family from where he revived *fasad*-based feuds and defended his village, helped by British personnel. 'Abd al-Hadi was ideally located in the centre of rebel 'triangle of terror' resistance with apexes at Nablus, Jenin, and Tulkarm. When he arrived at 'Arraba, 'Abd al-Hadi had some thirty followers (it is not apparent where these men came from), a British intelligence report commenting that, 'it is as yet too early to forecast the probable reactions to Fakhri Abdul Hadi's arrival but it is certain that his intrusion into the recognised "ring" of the three main gang leaders' – 'Abd al-Rahim al-Hajj Muhammad, 'Arif 'Abd al-Raziq, and Yusuf Sa'id Abu Durra – would cause 'further inter gang troubles between them.'[52]

---

[47] Eshed, *Reuven Shiloah*, p. 32; Yoav Gelber, 'Reuven Shiloah's Contribution to the Development of Israeli Intelligence' and Eldad Harouvi, 'Reuven Zaslany (Shiloah) and the Covert Cooperation with British Intelligence during the Second World War,' in Hesi Carmel (ed.), *Intelligence for Peace: The Role of Intelligence in Times of Peace* (London: Cass, 1999), pp. 16–48.

[48] Gelber, *Shorshey ha-Havatzelet*, pp. 149–64; Lefen, *Ha-Shai*, pp. 45–51; Typed Memoir, Pieces of War, pp. 42, 55, Simonds Papers, 08/46/1, IWMD; Steven Wagner, 'British Intelligence and Policy in the Palestine Mandate, 1919–39' (Doctoral Thesis: University of Oxford, 2014), *passim*.

[49] Eshed, *Reuven Shiloah*, p. 32.

[50] Porath, *Palestinian Arab National Movement*, p. 253; Intelligence Report, 29 September 1938: 8/GENERAL/2, p. 102, HA; Ezra Danin, *Te'udot u-Dmuyot me-Ginzey ha-Knufiyot ha-Arviyot, 1936–39* [*Documents and Portraits from the Arab Gangs Archives in the Arab Revolt in Palestine, 1936–39*] [1944] (Jerusalem: Magnes, 1981), p. 24, ft 56.

[51] Arnon-Ohanna, *Falahim ba-Mered*, pp. 157–60; 2nd Battalion, West Yorkshire Regiment, Battalion Intelligence Summary No. 19, Ramallah, 22 February 1939, RYM.

[52] Summary of Intelligence, Palestine and Transjordan, Wing-Commander Ritchie, 7 October 1938, CO 732/81/9, TNA.

Assistant District Commissioner Robert Newton met secretly with 'Abd al-Hadi in December 1938 'to take stock of him.'[53] Newton told 'Abd al-Hadi that the government would 'overlook his sins of the past' and hinted at 'limited funds' for his operations.[54] 'Abd al-Hadi got on well with the British, visiting the police mess in Jenin for Wild West-style pistol-drawing competitions with British officers, where he was not only 'quick on the draw' but had a 'look' in his eye that he was actually going to shoot, remembered one British officer present, who also signed for 'Abd al-Hadi's official gun permit.[55]

'Abd al-Hadi's operations paralleled the rise of peace band-type units that defended villages from gang attacks. British soldiers labelled and favoured peace band-associated villages as good or pro-Government and did not search them.[56] The British also armed friendly villages and encouraged informers, helped by the Jews who had an effective network of Arab spies. In March 1939, one villager from Ar Rumana (in written form, al-Rumana) that was 'mostly pro-government' came in to see the commander of the Border Regiment about the Army's 'supply of arms and assistance for village against gangs.'[57] Soldiers went on operations 'with the cooperation of the friendly Arabs' from one village as late as September 1939.[58] There were other tangible results. Peace bands helped British track down and kill the rebel al-Hajj Muhammad in March 1939.[59] The West Yorkshire Regiment called in village headmen who failed to inform on rebel activities – such as those of Jifna and Bir Zayt – where they were 'solemnly warned' against 'the repetition of such an omission,' after which headmen 'made amends by hastening to RAMALLAH to inform the Assistant District Commissioner that MOHAMMED OMAR NUBANI dropped into supper the previous evening, 26th December, with some sixteen followers.'[60] Army intelligence improved after the autumn of 1938 as information came in directly from Arab collaborators. The *mukhtar* of Kafr Malik in January 1939 gave intelligence to the Army

---

[53] Cohen, *Army of Shadows*, p. 150; S25/22793, p. 39, CZA.

[54] Subject: Fakhri Abdul Hadi, from Robert Newton, Assistant District Commissioner, Jenin, 17 December 1938, S25/22793-39/43, CZA.

[55] Author interview, Ted Horne, Barton-on-Sea, 26 February 2013.

[56] Recommendation of Sir Charles Tegart, Village Registers for Bad Villages, accompanying Letter, Chief Secretary to District Commissioners, 28 January 1938, S25/22762, CZA; Regimental War Diary, 1st Battalion, Border Regiment, 21 January and 1 February 1939, BRM.

[57] Regimental War Diary, 1st Battalion, Border Regiment, 2 March 1939, BRM.

[58] *Green Tiger: The Records of the Leicestershire Regiment* 20/4 (November 1939), p. 122, ROLLR.

[59] Arnon-Ohanna, *Falahim ba-Mered*, pp. 157–60.

[60] 2nd Battalion, West Yorkshire Regiment, Battalion Intelligence Summary No. 11, Ramallah, 29 December 1938, RYM.

and reported to the Assistant District Commissioner that a rebel gang had spent the night in his village; the headmen of Burham and Kobar were also forthcoming on rebel movements.[61] 'There is some improvement in the production of information, and certain mukhtars are sending in regular and reliable, if unfortunately rather historical, supplies,' noted the battalion intelligence officer for the West Yorkshire Regiment in January 1939.[62] At the same time, Nashashibi fighters hunted down rebels. 'A very severe blow was suffered by the Rebels when ABDUL FATTAH was murdered in a cave between MAZRA'A ASH SHARQIYA and KH ABU FALAH [al-Mazra'a al-Sharqiyya and Khirbat Abu Falah] last Sunday morning by one of NASHASHIBI'S followers,' noted one Army unit war diary.[63] Hunger and stress rather than any real ideological commitment to the Government or the Nashashibis prompted a flow of information from Palestinians, as the Army knew: 'The amount of war weariness throughout the country is considerable, and the whole population realizes that the longer hostilities continue, the more they stand to lose. This fact is brought out by the increasingly large numbers of people who are ready to give information.'[64] Nor could rebels always hide among villagers to escape the Army, villagers turning in to the Army rebel fighters who took refuge in one village after attempting to hide their weapons down a well.[65]

Fakhri Nashashibi mobilised peace bands in the south of Palestine and his political network supported 'Abd al-Hadi operating in the north of the country. Members of local families took sides, Jenin families supportive of the Nashashibis such as the Irsheid family joining 'Abd al-Hadi as he fought rebels in the Jenin and then Nablus–Tulkarm areas, as did the Nimer family of Nablus. The 'Amr family of Hebron – also traditionally pro-Nashashibi – joined the movement in the south, as did other smaller pro-Nashashibis families. The Army modified operations to give peace bands the freedom to work without any military interference and it allowed friendly villages to keep weapons, strictly against the law at the time. Fakhri Nashashibi requested rifles from the authorities

---

[61] 2nd Battalion, West Yorkshire Regiment, Battalion Intelligence Summary Nos. 12, 14, Ramallah, 5 and 20 January 1939, RYM.

[62] 2nd Battalion, West Yorkshire Regiment, Battalion Intelligence Summary No. 13, Ramallah, 12 January 1939, RYM.

[63] 2nd Battalion, West Yorkshire Regiment, Battalion Intelligence Summary No. 16, Ramallah, 2 February 1939, RYM.

[64] 2nd Battalion, West Yorkshire Regiment, Battalion Intelligence Summary No. 17, Ramallah, 9 February 1939, RYM.

[65] Letter from Abdel Halim Julani, Abdel Kader Husseini and Ahmed Jaber, 19 December 1938 quoted in Police CID, Jerusalem, Intelligence Report 68/38, 21 December 1938, S25/22732, CZA.

and then distributed these weapons to his men fighting rebel bands in the field, seven peace-band members killed by rebels on 18 December 1938 having Government-issued weapons.[66] The Army coordinated this in the field, the battalion commander of the Border Regiment arranging an 'interview' with 'Abd al-Hadi's emissary in December 1938 to discuss the newly formed peace bands that were now 'opposed to all the other anti-Government gang leaders.'[67] Not just battalion but also brigade commanders were involved directly in the running of the peace bands, the commander of 14th Brigade travelling to Jenin 'to talk re the FAKHRI ABDUL HADI family' in January 1939.[68] The British unit war diaries reveal the extent of the collusion between the Army and 'Abd al-Hadi's peace units, in cooperation with colonial officials who worked with the Army to, for instance, transport members of the Irsheid family to Jerusalem and who interviewed 'Abd al-Hadi in 'Arraba under Army protection.[69] RAF Special Service Officers responsible for political matters at this time intervened in these meetings, including a Flight-Lieutenant Lash who liaised with the Irsheid family and who escorted Farid Irsheid to 'Arraba village.[70] Lash's career as detailed in Appendix E here shows how the British easily moved around key intelligence officers.

Security forces paid and gave Arabs in Acre weapons and the collaborators started searching houses and handing over suspects to the British.[71] Peace band actions 'purged' Haifa of terrorists, according to a captured Arab report.[72] The authorities despatched a platoon of the Border Regiment to 'Arraba, 'Abd al-Hadi's village, to support him: 'So successful were they, that it was decided that a full company of the regiment would be posted to the village.'[73] The wife of a minor gang leader had given useful information on a rebel leader and took refuge in an Army camp, after which the Army transported her to sanctuary in 'Arraba village with 'Abd al-Hadi. As a police sergeant concluded, she would otherwise 'probably get her throat cut.'[74] Peace

---

[66] Police CID, Intelligence Summary No. 92/38, 31 December 1938, p. 3, S25/22732, CZA.

[67] Regimental War Diary, 1st Battalion, Border Regiment, 9 December 1938, BRM.

[68] Regimental War Diary, 1st Battalion, Border Regiment, 27 January 1939, BRM.

[69] Regimental War Diary, 1st Battalion, Border Regiment, 16 December 1938, BRM.

[70] Regimental War Diary, 1st Battalion, Border Regiment, 17 December 1938, BRM.

[71] Yehuda Slutsky (and Ben-Zion Dinur) (eds), *Sefer Toldot ha-Haganah* [*Book of the History of the Haganah*]. Volume 3, Part 1, *Me'ma'avak le'Milhama* [*From Struggle to War*] (Tel Aviv: 'Am Oved, 1972), p. 16.

[72] Appendix: Explanatory Notes, Captured and Translated Arabic Material with Commentary, p. 113, Wingate Papers, Microfilm M2313, BL.

[73] 'Honi Soit Qui Mal Y Pense,' *Palestine Police Old Comrades' Association Newsletter* 100 (September 1975), p. 46.

[74] Ibid.

bands deployed alongside British troops, the former indistinguishable from Nashashibi fighters. Thus, Hilda Wilson, a British schoolteacher in the largely Christian town of Bir Zayt in 1938, recorded in her diary how British soldiers used Nashashibi informers from the village of Abu Ghosh to help identify villagers suspected of being rebels – the Jews had good relations with Abu Ghosh, a village that survived the war of 1948 – the Army hiding the informers in the backs of trucks.[75] Wilson went on to record in her diary how British troops fought alongside peace units, such as when a Nashashibi band had attacked the village of Abu Shnedim (presumably Abu Shkheidim). 'British soldiers had been with them,' she wrote.[76] The system of hidden informers – widely used by troops – provoked the settling of feuds, 'working off some old score,' as the British recognised, but as the aim of the counter-insurgency was to force Palestinians to choose official authority, social dislocation suited the British, or at least the Army, keen to pacify Palestine before redeploying for the coming war in Europe.[77] The Army positioned units in villages to support local bands that were criminal as much as they wanted 'peace' and that also supplied intelligence, as when a platoon of the Leicestershire Regiment went to Umm al-Faraj ('Faraj detachment' so 'Fardet') just north of Acre where

under the auspices of the battalion lived a friendly gang of ex-rebels, led by a roguish character named Sheikh Rabah. The gang, no other term fitted them, were now in government pay as informers and allowed to carry arms for self-protection. Naturally, the authorities were very much against the formation of this party, as inevitably they took the opportunity on occasion to enforce cash levies on unfriendly villages and even to pay off old scores. They did however produce 'red hot' information on which roving platoon FARDET could act. This alone outweighed their disadvantages.[78]

Peace bands were flexible and rapid, using the tactics of the rebels, fighting violence with violence in a way that Government forces could not easily or visibly do, with 'Abd al-Hadi nicknamed 'the butcher' because of his toughness.[79] The impact of the peace bands was felt back in Damascus with the rebel high command and on 5 December 1938 a British military report concluded that negotiations were now taking place

[75] School Year Diary, Spring Term 1939, Wilson Papers, GB165-0302, p. 36, MEC.
[76] School Year Diary, Summer Term 1939, Wilson Papers, GB165-0302, p. 73, MEC.
[77] Memoir (typed in 1985), Palestine 1938, by Capt P. H. Graves-Morris, Worcestershire Regiment Museum Trust.
[78] Typed Official MS, Leicestershire Regiment, 2nd Battalion, Palestine, 1939–40, p. 1, 22D63/10/1–3, ROLLR.
[79] Arnon-Ohanna, *Falahim ba-Mered*, pp. 147–52.

between Rebel Headquarters in Damascus and Palestine with a view to making peace with Fakhri Abdul Hadi or on the other hand crushing him altogether ... Fakhri has under his command a permanent force of 60 men and that for the past week he has been a thorn in the side of the Rebel Forces ... in the meantime they will do all in their power to crush him.[80]

The peace units irked the insurgents – or the 'professional rebels' as the British put it – with one European captive of theirs observing how the rebel gang leader spat on the ground every time anyone mentioned the Nashashibis.[81] The rebel high command in Damascus sent two assassins to kill Fakhri Nashashibi, noted a British CID intelligence report in December 1938.[82] Meanwhile, 'Abd al-Hadi played both sides – 'ran with the hare and hunted with the hounds,' as one British police officer put it – and, fighting in undeveloped rural areas with parochial loyalties and traditions of brigandage, he used the Arab rebellion for his own ends.[83] As he fought the rebels and enjoyed British support, his family was negotiating with the insurgent high command in Damascus for him to re-join the rebel side, if it paid him £P.12,000 and made him a senior rebel leader.[84] 'Abd al-Hadi made the most of his special protected status, raiding neighbouring villages, whipping villagers to extort names of rebels and stealing cattle, the violence escalating to such a level that in March 1939 the Army curtailed 'Abd al-Hadi by imposing a curfew on 'Arraba.[85] The assessment from Jewish files was that 'Abd al-Hadi formed peace bands to make money and because the rebel command in Damascus had cut his subsidy.[86] Ted Horne, a policeman who knew 'Abd al-Hadi personally, noted later how 'Fakhri was negotiating with the British authorities to swap sides and leave his Arab contemporaries to stew in their own juice, while in exchange for money he would be the mantle of "truthful Informer and friend of King George".'[87] For the British, not just 'Abd al-Hadi but also the urban, urbane Nashashibis sought personal gain. Edward Keith-Roach, a District Commissioner, remarked to Major-General Richard O'Connor, the commander in

---

[80] British Report, Armed Gangs 60/38, 5 December 1938, S25/22732, CZA.
[81] MacMichael (High Commissioner) to Malcolm MacDonald (Secretary of State for Colonies), 16 January 1939, S25/22761, CZA.
[82] Police CID, Jerusalem, Intelligence Summary 92/38, 31 December 1938, p. 3, S25/22732, CZA.
[83] Author interview, Ted Horne, Barton-on-Sea, 21 April 2013.
[84] British Report, Armed Gangs 61/38, 6 December 1938, S25/22732, CZA.
[85] Regimental War Diary, 1st Battalion, Border Regiment, 18 March 1939, BRM; Ezra Danin, *Tsiyoni be-Kol Tnay* [*Zionist under Any Condition*] (Jerusalem: Kidum, 1987), 140.
[86] Danin, *Te'udot u-Dmuyot me-Ginzey*, p. 24, ft 56.
[87] 'The Royal Bee Lady,' *Palestine Police Old Comrades' Association Newsletter* 124 (September 1981), p. 52.

Jerusalem, that, in 'the 18 years I have known Fakhri [Nashashibi] he personally is only after the main chance, and the main chance, as far as he is concerned, is "Fakhri".'[88] Talking about the Arabs in the Ramallah area, the West Yorkshire Regiment intelligence summary summed up local opinion as follows: 'That FAKRI NAHISHIBI [sic] is out for his own ends, and for no other reason, is universally agreed.'[89] The assessment was even harsher elsewhere: 'The Hebronites do not take the Nashashibi supporters in their area too seriously. They claim that the latter and their satellites thrive on material benefit and pecuniary emolument as well as food etc. and that they are venal minions who will present no problem in the proper time and at the right moment they shall be eliminated without difficulty.'[90]

Peace bands meant more violence and disorder, mixing up the attacks of the real rebels and bandit gangs with counter-gangs. Peace bands became brigands, too, and with official support, seized on by elements within the Nashashibi family and by 'Abd al-Hadi to make money, settle old scores, and play out long-standing feuds, 'an ideal opportunity for the waging of private or semi-public feuds, and the opportunity has not been allowed to slip. Murder, abduction, robbery, attack and counter-attack have been the order of the day.'[91] Palestinians could no longer distinguish between government, rebel and bandit forces; pseudo war and peace bands had destroyed identifying markers. The British Army was complicit in subversive action, issuing travel passes and driving the Nashashibis in military vehicles when on operations:

Only yesterday ... a piece of paper was shown to me by one of these men bearing on one side (in English) the name of Fakhri Nashashibi and on the paper the name of a British officer. These men appear to imagine (wrongly of course) that if they whisper 'Fakhri' to a British official they will be granted a dispensation from all restrictions (e.g. travel permits) which apply to others.[92]

There are other, cryptic, comments from soldiers about their work with the Nashashibis, 'all roads lead to the Nashashibi Bridge,' proving how engagement with peace bands was significant enough to find its way into in-house regimental journals.[93]

---

[88] Keith-Roach to O'Connor, 25 January 1939, O'Connor Papers, 3/4/10, LHCMA.
[89] 2nd Battalion, West Yorkshire Regiment, Battalion Intelligence Summary No. 9, Ramallah, 15 December 1938, RYM.
[90] Jewish Report, Hebron 29 February 1939, p. 140, S25/22269, CZA.
[91] Memorandum on Hebron Sub-District, by Assistant District Commissioner Stewart, 25 January 1939, O'Connor Papers, 3/4/10–11, LHCMA.
[92] Ibid.
[93] FIRM: Worcestershire Regiment Journal 11/2 (July 1939), p. 226.

Spurred on by support from the British and the Jews, Fakhri Nashashibi in October 1938 published a letter to the High Commissioner in which he asked for 'reasonable moderation' and attacked the Mufti, accusing him of 'terrorism' and 'diverting' the 'noble ends' of the Arab revolt for 'his own selfish ends.'[94] Local rebels replied by issuing communiqués calling Fakhri Nashashibi a 'microbe' for his actions in approaching the British, threatening him with murder: 'it is the duty of every rebel to try and bring about his death.'[95] Rebels also passed a death sentence on 'Abd al-Hadi.[96] Hajj Amin's gunmen attempted to assassinate a member of the Nashashibi clan.[97] The Nashashibis then published a more provocative letter, after which they sent a deputation to O'Connor, the military second-in-command in Palestine, to thank him for the actions of the British Army, after which the British sponsored the most visible expression of the peace bands: a large public meeting at the village of Yatta on 18 December 1938, attended by some 3,000 Palestinians and by General Richard O'Connor.[98] (The photograph here of the Yatta meeting – Figure 7.1 – shows O'Connor addressing the crowd from the back of an Army vehicle, the Union Jack flying behind him, Fakhri Nashashibi standing to one side wearing a Western-style suit and *tarbush*.[99])

The British and Nashashibis stage-managed the pro-Government rally at Yatta near Hebron.[100] It was not a success. Palestinians saw it for what it was: a contrived, official attempt to bribe them into changing sides, peasants encouraged to attend with promises of loans, seeds and animals, and given transport to get there. They went along only to encounter Fakhri Nashashibi arriving with armoured cars, British troops, and a prepared speech. No one present would read the speech, until the authorities intimidated a Khalil esh Sharif (al-Sharif) into reading it, introduced as an influential sheikh but a 'simple farmer' according to the British; other village elders at Yatta claimed they had been tricked into

[94] Quoted in 'Arab Leader and Former Mufti,' *Yorkshire Post* (24 October 1938).
[95] Mansour, HQ Arab Army in the South 28th Ramadan 1357 [21 November 1938] quoted in *FIRM: Worcestershire Regiment Journal* 10/4 (January 1939), p. 560.
[96] Cohen, *Army of Shadows*, p. 133.
[97] Joseph B. Schechtman, *The Mufti and the Fuehrer: The Rise and Fall of Haj Amin el-Husseini* (New York, NY: Yoseloff, 1965), pp. 62–63.
[98] Intelligence Summary, Palestine and Transjordan, by Wing Commander Ritchie, 2 December 1938, CO 732/81/10, TNA; Schechtman, *The Mufti and the Fuehrer*, pp. 62–63.
[99] From the Photographic Collection, Truman Institute Library, Hebrew University, Jerusalem.
[100] Summary of Intelligence, Palestine and Transjordan, 30 December 1938, by Wing Commander Ritchie [26/38], CO 732/81/10, TNA.

7.1 General O'Connor giving an address at the pro-Government Yatta
meeting, 18 December 1938
(from Roberta and Stanley Bogen Library, Truman Institute, Hebrew
University, Jerusalem)

attending the meeting and proclaimed their allegiance to Hajj Amin.[101]
Children in Jerusalem later stoned Khalil esh Sharif as punishment for
what he did.[102] The audience could not understand the classical Arabic
(that al-Sharif as a 'simple farmer' would have not been able to read
anyway) in which he gave the speech and peasants went back to their
villages wondering why they had attended.[103] For Keith-Roach, Yatta
was 'well organised as a show,' with Fakhri Nashashibi 'much in evidence,' but as he told General O'Connor afterwards, he heard Fakhri
Nashashibi,

giving asides to the people behind him and heard him say 'Clap'; as you were
coming nearer he said 'Not sufficient – clap louder,' and as you came nearer 'go

[101] CID Intelligence Summary 92/38, Jerusalem, 31 December 1938, pp. 4–6. S25/
22732, CZA.
[102] Ibid.
[103] Information re Mohd. Sherif and the Yatta Meeting, From Mohd Abu Sharar, son-in-
law of Mohd Sherif and Mustapha Issa Unis Dudein of Dura, from Mr Stewart (to
Charles), 25 January 1939, dated 26 January 1939, O'Connor Papers, 3/4/10, LHCMA.

on – more – more.' The letter that was read out, of course, was entirely incomprehensible to the majority of people there, and I noticed it did not appear to receive very warm support from those who were doubtless hearing it for the first time. When we walked round the crowds I did not notice any very warm welcoming smiles. Later in the day when I got back to Jerusalem an Englishman who was there told me he had overheard one of the men say to Fakhri – 'What about our money'?[104]

British soldiers and officials had little faith in the Nashashibis, supporting the argument made at the start of this chapter that peace bands were force multipliers of sorts but no more. O'Connor gave the Yatta audience a brisk address, reminding them of the need to obey the law.[105] Elliot, the British doctor working in Hebron, noted O'Connor's 'short soldierly speech' and the 'overpowering smell of fish that must surely have pervaded the whole gathering ... The visitors went home, the villagers dispersed, with or without their tongues in their cheeks.'[106] That Palestinians were weary of the disorder of the revolt was obvious: 'The safest thing to say is that it [the Yatta meeting] shewed [sic] that a section of the Arabs, long tired of the disorders, now feels sufficiently exasperated to voice an audible protest,' noted the High Commissioner.[107] The Yatta meeting provoked more violence: bombs and shootings directed at the Nashashibi family; guards in the Acre detention camp separated Nashashibi family members from other inmates for the former's protection.[108]

British civil and military officers oscillated in their views on and support for collaborators. Battershill's conclusion on Yatta was that there 'must be something behind it all. It is not good saying that they have all been bribed as there isn't enough money available from the sources which might have done the bribing. There is a movement amongst some of the fellahin to stop this banditry.'[109] The issue was how to encourage 'moderate fellahin' without releasing terror attacks by the Nashashibis against Hajj Amin that would plunge Palestine into a 'terrible vortex' of violence.[110] The Army was similarly ambivalent about events such as Yatta, one officer's marginalia on an intelligence report on Yatta recording simply: 'We know

[104] Keith-Roach to O'Connor, 25 January 1939, O'Connor Papers, 3/4/10, LHCMA.

[105] John Baynes, *The Forgotten Victor: General Sir Richard O'Connor* (London: Brassey's, 1989), p. 58.

[106] Diary, 18 December 1938, Foster Papers, GB165-0110, pp. 101–02, MEC.

[107] MacMichael (High Commissioner, Palestine) to MacDonald (Secretary of State for Colonies), 16 January 1939, Security Matters 1938–39, S25/22761, CZA.

[108] Letter, Burr to Parents, n.d. [December 1938–January 1939], 88/8/1, Burr Papers, IWMD.

[109] Diary, 26 December [1938], Battershill Papers, MSS. Brit. Emp. S. 467, Box 12, File 6, WL.

[110] Ibid.

about this. It signifies little.'[111] Similarly, with the police, a CID report of 21 December 1938 concluded: 'It is, of course, accepted in Arab circles that Government is responsible for all the activities of Fakhri Nashashibi and that this demonstration was fostered by the British.'[112] On the other hand, the intelligence summary of the West Yorkshire Regiment following the Yatta meeting was encouraging, noting that,

> There are a large number of Arabs in Palestine who secretly do not approve of the policy of terrorism at present existing and therefore are in opposition to HAJ AMIN. If FAKHRI NASHASHIBI can avoid being 'bumped off' in the next week or two, he will probably collect quite a large following and will constitute a definite menace to the absolute power hitherto enjoyed by the Mufti.[113]

The Army took note of the Yatta meeting in other ways. The Worcestershire Regiment – which had provided the guard of honour for the 'Loyal Address' at Yatta – behaved differently on operations afterwards: 'we went out every day, visiting some villages in our area. The type of visit has now changed; instead of going and searching them for arms we now went on back-slapping expeditions – telling them how good their village was and they would tell us how they like the troops, and so it would go on until we left them.'[114] Fakhri Nashashibi tried to hold other meetings like the Yatta one, in Jaffa, Gaza, Nablus, and Huleh, but he cancelled them after the Yatta meeting proved a failure, promoting little except more violence between the Nashashibis and Husaynis.[115]

The supreme military commander in Palestine in early 1939, General Sir Robert Haining, was sure – as were most British soldiers and administrators – that the Husayni faction was much stronger than the Nashashibis'. Irregular loyalist forces such as the peace bands pulled Haining in opposite directions, the authorities arming Palestinians just as British soldiers were working vigorously to disarm Palestinians, instituting draconian Emergency Regulations in which the ownership of even a single bullet was a capital offence. The Army, police, and colonial administration behaved differently towards the peace bands, some support coming at a grassroots level from Army officers at the same time as Chief Secretary Battershill was telling police and the District Commissioners that they should not issue arms and ammunition to

[111] Summary of Intelligence, Palestine and Transjordan, Wing-Commander Ritchie, 30 December 1938, CO 732/81/10, TNA.
[112] CID Intelligence Summary 90/38, Jerusalem, 21 December 1938, S25/22732, CZA.
[113] 2nd Battalion, West Yorkshire Regiment, Battalion Intelligence Summary No. 5, Ramallah, 17 November 1938, RYM.
[114] FIRM: Worcestershire Regiment Journal 11/1 (April 1939), p. 55.
[115] Palestine Police CID, Intelligence Summary 92/38, 31 December 1938, p. 4, S25/22732, CZA.

anti-rebel Palestinians, even for personal protection.[116] Haining raised a series of questions in a report on the peace bands that he sent to the War Office. Was 'Abd al-Hadi to be given official permission to carry arms? What guarantees did the British have that arms, licensed or otherwise, would only be used against the Mufti's men? How far could 'Abd al-Hadi be trusted? Haining then answered his own questions, giving an insight into the British military mind at the highest level:

> The attitude I took was that, while we could use these people as agents for information, any kind of official approval and collaboration was unthinkable. I was fully justified in this later as it was not long before ABDUL HADI was found to be reverting to his old habits and playing for both sides. The same situation occurred later in one or two other villages, and the individuals concerned mostly tended to be useful for a short time and then to lose their enthusiasm and pro-Government feelings.[117]

Despite these reservations, the British carried on with support for peace units into and beyond 1939, when the revolt had ended, there obviously being local military interest in pursuing such things and value in counter-gang operations. The British appointed five Army officers based in Acre in June 1939 to set up peace bands, although at that stage they were not yet giving out weapons.[118] In the same month, envoys from the Nashashibi party visited Tiberias and its hinterland to try to convince 'moderate' Arabs and to get into open action against the terrorists. They failed, as the Jewish intelligence chief in northern Palestine noted.[119] Such activities carried on into the 1940s, often wrapped up in disputes over Arab land sales to Jews, those who sold land throwing in their lot with the government. (Members of the Husayni family also sold land to Jews, an open secret in the family.[120]) The impact of cooperation between parts of the Palestinian community and the British lay less in how such things aided counter-insurgency operations as in how they added to the disorder that terrorised and demoralised (and so pacified) the peasantry and in how they made visible the internal divisions among Palestinians that damned the insurgency in the first place.

---

[116] Battershill, Chief Secretary, on behalf of the High Commissioner to District Commissioners and IG Police, 29 December 1938, S25/22761, p. 4, CZA.

[117] GOC Palestine (Haining) to War Office, Despatch on the Operations carried out by the British Forces in Palestine and Transjordan, 1 November 1938–31 March 1939, 24 April 1939, Evetts Papers, File 1, LHCMA; see also O'Connor Papers, 3/4/53, LHCMA.

[118] To Zaslani from 'M' in Haifa, 5 June 1939, files of Shiloah Zaslani, S25/22424, CZA.

[119] Letter, Feitelson (Tiberias, Intelligence Chief in North of Palestine) to Zaslani, 1 June 1939, S25/22424, p. 7, CZA.

[120] Ilan Pappe, *The Rise and Fall of a Palestinian Dynasty: The Husaynis, 1700–1948* (London: Saqi, 2010), p. 258; Palestine Police Force, Report from Tiberias Police on Nazareth District, c.1940, Nazareth Town, 17/4212/8, ISA.

Jewish Collaboration: Supernumerary and Special Police

The Jews in Palestine were keen to collaborate – or from their vantage point rather than collaborating they were fighting a patriotic liberation war – with the British from the outset of the revolt to defeat the existential Palestinian threat and to gain weapons and training. The most famous collaboration was the regionally limited (Galilee), time bounded (June–December 1938), and small (three platoons) British–Jewish Special Night Squads led by Orde Wingate, examined below. Of more interest for successful countrywide pacification was the mass-delivery, day-to-day, revolt-long auxiliary police collaboration between British forces and Jews delivered in the field and that ran counter to official policies of limiting help to the *Yishuv* for fear that such support would aggravate inter-communal violence. The avowed worries of the British military–civil high command about favouring one side did not stop senior officers such as GOC Wavell promoting units like the SNSs, even if Haining after him was less inclined to do so, while field officers through the revolt worked extensively with Jews. The High Commissioner on a trip to London in October 1938 told the Colonial Office that the short-term benefits of 'active military participation' with the Jews would achieve the 'immediate object' but would in the long-run leave the Jews in an 'unassailable and dominating position.'[121] Similarly, Wavell, when short of troops in late 1937, had told the War Office that he could employ more special police constables as the Jews 'would be only too delighted to offer help and to be armed and drilled' but his problem in equipping one community only was political.[122] The Army and civil authorities were stretched between the immediate benefits of arming thousands of Jews with the far-reaching implications of such a strategy as the Jews, in Wavell's view, had

a very large number of illegally armed settlers, and are longing to get them recognised and used against the Arabs. They have already made tentative suggestions in this direction … I should be in a difficult position if I was not strong enough to deal adequately with attacks on Jewish settlements and the Jews took the law into their own hands and attacked the Arabs, as they would be likely to do.[123]

---

[121] 1st Meeting at CO during High Commissioner visit to London, Delegates from CO, WO, Palestine Government, Secretary of State for Colonies in Chair, 7 October 1938, FO 371/21864, TNA.

[122] Wavell to Haining (DMO, WO), 23 October 1937, Palestine, 1937–38 Volume, Wavell Papers, POH.

[123] Wavell to Deverell (CIGS), 20 October 1937, Palestine, 1937–38 Volume, Wavell Papers, POH.

Jewish leaders such as Shertok and Ben-Zvi lobbied Battershill for Jews to take an 'active part' in suppressing the revolt with a joint British–Jewish 'pursuit force' and that Government-trained and armed Jewish supernumeraries should be offensive and not deployed defensively for settlement defence.[124] When Battershill resisted these demands, Shertok told him that Jewish patience was running out and how settlers would soon 'take the law into their own hands,' adding that Haganah would be alarmed if military courts tried any of its men for carrying arms, and how Battershill needed to authorise the Jews to negotiate with Raghib Nashashibi and Abdullah of Transjordan 'with regard to their co-operation in political matters.'[125] That Battershill refused these schemes perhaps proves that at the highest levels the Government tried to be balanced but the British clearly treated the two communities in Palestine very differently and supported the *Yishuv* militarily in ways that they did not with the Palestinians and the peace bands, especially among Army and police officers executing pacification.

Security forces readily helped Jewish semi-regular (or irregular) forces that they knew targeted Palestinians. When a Haganah weapons expert working in a basement room of the Hebrew University on tear gas and flame-thrower weapons needed to test a prototype mortar, he went with an accomplice to a British 'platoon police unit' to inspect, test, and measure a 3-inch mountain gun, and after several months the Jews were test firing their own light gun.[126] The Jews took the strain from security forces by paying for Jewish settlement guards called *ghaffirs*, one Jewish building contractor becoming the liaison officer between British forces and the *Yishuv*, and told by Shertok to improve the work of the *ghaffirs* working alongside the British.[127] The Jews asked for a British sergeant-major to train *ghaffirs*, to which the local Army colonel suggested that they train in British military camps for four- to six-week blocks, after which they would sit an exam set by the colonel and his officers; training also went on in Haifa.[128] The officer in charge in Nazareth deployed Jews on patrol with British troops, while Jews told their Haganah strike force *Palmach* men to wear uniforms and bear arms openly.[129] Jewish

---

[124] Letter, Battershill to Sir John Shuckburgh, 21 November 1937, Battershill Papers, MSS. Brit. Emp. S. 467, Box 10, File 3, WL.

[125] Ibid.

[126] Testimony, Eliyahu Sochever, 19 February 1950, 161.00020, pp. 1–2, HA.

[127] Testimony of Abraham Acar (or Icar), Testimonies of Haganah Officers Collected in the 1950s and 1960s, 141/33, p. 46, HA.

[128] Ibid., p. 50, HA.

[129] Ibid., pp. 54–56, HA.

notrim guards used their official roles as a cover to carry out operations, with training courses for such men in January 1937 conducted by more experienced Haganah men that made maximum use of 'legal opportunities.'[130] The authorities gave one Jewish neighbourhood *noter* guard a rifle and fifty rounds.[131] Jews hid masses of weapons and ammunition on their settlements in secret *slick* armouries, some of it supplied by the Government to officially sealed settlement armouries for local area protection or the Army passed on weaponry.[132] Policemen remembered how they supplied arms to Jewish settlements and taught them how to use them but how 'we didn't give the Arabs any arms.'[133] Wingate returned second-rate weapons sent to him for a Jewish sergeants' course, subsequently receiving good ones.[134] British troops did not treat the Jews as they did Palestinians. When a British officer caught a Haganah man with a grenade on a settlement, a senior Jewish official talked to the officer who then released the man and gave him back his grenade; in another incident, Haganah men launched a grenade attack on Arab 'gang' members in a coffee bar in west Jerusalem, with three Arabs killed and six injured, after which the Haganah officer and three privates remained on the scene until the police arrived.[135]

There was a great variety of 'special' paramilitary Jewish forces, with the Jewish Tel Aviv municipal authority asking the British in August 1938 if it could form 'so-called night squads': 'The Jewish population of the South will be as ready as that of the North to provide the requisite number of men of good quality to take part in the offensive operations of this kind.'[136] The budget for auxiliary operations came from Jewish funds but also from the Iraq Petroleum Company and the Palestine Electricity Corporation, so easing governmental budgets.[137] There were Jewish

---

[130] Testimony of Giyora (Shinan) Shinansky, Testimonies of Haganah Officers Collected in the 1950s and 1960s, 184/83, pp. 1–2, HA.

[131] Testimony of Chaim Franse, Testimonies of Haganah Officers Collected in the 1950s and 1960s, 182/46, pp. 1–2, HA.

[132] Interview with Moshe Brenner, 26 June 1990, Testimonies of Haganah Officers Collected in the 1950s and 1960s, 15/1/4, HA; *Ça Ira: The Journal of the West Yorkshire Regiment (The Prince of Wales's Own)* 8/2 (December 1936), p. 112.

[133] Kitson, 10688/6, IWMSA.

[134] Testimonies from SNS Fighters, Shlomo, S25/10685, p. 71, CZA.

[135] Testimony of Isaac Avrahami (Lt in Haganah), Testimonies of Haganah Officers Collected in the 1950s and 1960s, 94/29, pp. 8–9, HA.

[136] Statement of Jewish Agency views to Chief Secretary to the High Commissioner, 25 August 1938, given after interview with Chief Secretary on 24 August, in File 04/-165-B/622: The Riots: Negotiations with the Government, February 1936–June 1936 (August 1938), TAMA.

[137] Budget Figures, 15 August 1938, S25/8768, p. 78, CZA.

additional police, supernumeraries, *ghaffirs*, *notrim*, temporary additional constables, special constables, private police officers, an auxiliary port police force, temporary additional police, a special frontier protection unit, Jewish settlement police, Jewish supernumerary police (divided into four A–D categories), special auxiliary police, railway protection police, night watchmen, special policemen, an IPC TAPline protection force, Army special night and Q units, and Wingate's British–Jewish Special Night Squads. Some of these forces included Arab 'loyalist' recruits, but few and in fewer numbers. These labels were sometimes synonymous descriptors for the same force of men, but the plethora of names is telling: proof that the British could not find one phrase for all the auxiliary collaborating forces and of the officially supported (more or less) irregular para-military units with intimate knowledge of local human and physical terrain and which was a large force augmentation for the pacification of Palestine after 1936. Jewish and Palestinian auxiliaries also freed up regular British infantry from mundane protection and garrison duties for dynamic anti-rebel sweeps.

The numbers of variously labelled supernumerary security forces vary from 3,700[138] to 14,411[139] to 18,000[140] to 21,770.[141] Scrivenor noted the presence in Haifa alone of 700 'special constables' in January 1939.[142] The official *Survey of Palestine* detailed 978 active and 3,881 reserve Jewish settlement police enrolled in 1937.[143] By contrast the regular police force was 4,834 men by the end of 1938 (and 8,923 strong in 1947, of which 5,758 were British).[144] The collapse of the regular force as Arabs left and London sent out hastily recruited untrained replacement men, many of whom were former soldiers, made the employment of thousands of Jewish temporary policemen an attractive quick-fix. Payment for

---

[138] Martin Kolinsky, 'The Collapse and Restoration of Public Security,' in Michael J. Cohen and Martin Kolinsky (eds), *Britain and the Middle East in the 1930s: Security Problems, 1935–39* (London: Macmillan/King's, 1992), pp. 157–58.

[139] Lefen, *Ha-Shai*, pp. 40, 273.

[140] Yasin, *Al-Thawra al-'Arabiyya al-Kubra*, p. 41; J. L. Knight, 'Policing in British Palestine, 1917–1939' (Doctoral Thesis: University of Oxford, 2008), p. 2; 18,016 in John Knight, 'Securing Zion? Policing in British Palestine, 1917–39,' *European Review of History–Revue Européene d'Histoire* 18/4 (2011), p. 533.

[141] D. J. Clark, 'The Colonial Police and Anti-Terrorism: Bengal 1930–1936, Palestine 1937–1947, and Cyprus 1955–1959' (Doctoral Thesis: University of Oxford, 1978), pp. 148–50.

[142] Diary, 26 January 1939, Scrivenor Papers, MSS. Brit. Emp. S. 378, WL.

[143] *A Survey of Palestine, Prepared in December 1945 and January 1946 for the Information of the Anglo-American Committee of Inquiry* [1946] (Washington, DC: IPS, 1991), i, pp. 38–49.

[144] Clark, 'The Colonial Police and Anti-Terrorism,' pp. 148–50; Georgina Sinclair, *At the End of the Line: Colonial Policing and the Imperial Endgame, 1945–80* (Manchester: Manchester University Press, 2006), p. 22.

them came from different funds, but the Jewish Agency paid for half the cost of Jewish Settlement Police that the Jewish Settlement Defence Committee nominally supervised but was effectively under Haganah command.[145] Unpaid volunteers in Jewish settlement forces augmented officially recruited auxiliary police units, at no cost to the Government, or the Palestine Electricity Corporation or Iraq Petroleum Company paid for guards; British officers administered units such as the Railway Protection Police that was wholly manned by Jews.[146] Jewish corporals commanded Temporary Additional Constables in Jewish settlements that were responsible to a British sergeant.[147] The British weeded out communists among Jewish recruits for auxiliary forces, ever-convinced that the real threat came from Moscow and not Hajj Amin.[148] Jewish Agency budgetary proposals reflected the need to strengthen 'our position in the Palestine Police.'[149] Auxiliary forces could be well equipped. The 3,240 men graded A to C in the Jewish Supernumerary Police in January 1938 had uniforms and weapons, while 2,466 D-class men had only 372 rifles, a shortfall that the Jews looked to remedy.[150] Every A-class man received a basic pay of £P.6 per month, while B to D men were not paid so 'Negotiations are now in progress to increase the number of A class, i.e. of those paid by the Government, by another 260 men.'[151] Settlements and 'funds' supplemented the pay of these policemen, with training conducted by 'our own' (so Jewish) instructors with the approval of the local police officer in charge of supernumerary police.[152] One course passed out 222 men with further training

done by military instructors who visited each settlement in the evening hours to give lessons … In the late stages training has assumed the form of special camps adjacent to military camps in the country. There the trainees were under the constant supervision of their military instructors and under military discipline. These courses were passed by 188 men (24 of those received training in the Police School of the Palestine Police Force). The total of trained men amounts, thus, to 600. The duration of training being on an average of three and a half weeks. All trainees passed firing courses. Some of them, about 40%, as marksmen

---

[145] Clark, 'The Colonial Police and Anti-Terrorism,' pp. 148–50.
[146] Tom Bowden, *The Breakdown of Public Security: The Case of Ireland 1916–1921 and Palestine 1936–1939* (London and Beverly Hills, CA: Sage, 1977), pp. 159–61.
[147] Robert Martin, *Palestine Betrayed: A British Palestine Policeman's Memoir (1936–48)* (Ringwood: Seglawi, 2007), pp. 60–62.
[148] 16 August 1936, Shai Intelligence Reports: 8/GENERAL/40, p. 68, HA.
[149] Letter to Shertok and Caplan (in Jewish Agency), 9 December 1936, S25/8928-6, CZA.
[150] Jewish Supernumeraries, Joshua Gordon (Jerusalem) to B. Joseph, 5 January 1938, S25/8928-88, CZA.
[151] Ibid.
[152] Jewish Supernumeraries, Joshua Gordon (Jerusalem) to B. Joseph, 5 January 1938, S25/8928-89/90, CZA.

... Every settlement has a supernumerary Police Station which is at the same time the store for arms and uniforms.[153]

The men had cars for travel and they trained alongside 708 (or 704) railway supernumeraries finishing their month-long training course. A Jewish assessment in January 1938 of all classes of settlement defence policemen plus railway police totalled 5,567 men, on top of which there were fifty men for Government building protection, nine men to protect water supplies, and 108 employed by private firms and individuals, so 5,734 in sum.[154] Arabs provided 396 extra supernumeraries in the same report.[155] The British also 'unofficially recognised' Haganah FOSH field forces that were supernumerary to the supernumeraries.[156] The Jews offered Hebrew-language classes to policemen and gifted games and newspapers to Army regimental canteens.[157]

Jewish neighbourhoods took up the payment of local Jewish temporary policemen or *ghaffirs*, about seventy-five of them in Jerusalem – 'Every neighbour has to take care of payment of special policemen' – with the Government making up the balance.[158] Jewish advocates recommended fellow Jews for temporary police posts on proforma letter requests. Such demands for Jewish policemen came in from all around Haifa, payment again spread between the Government and the *Yishuv*.[159] Montgomery employed supernumerary police in March 1939 for patrolling Haifa, with the Jewish men armed, the Arab ones unarmed.[160] The Jewish auxiliary officers 'behaved improperly or foolishly' by firing over the heads of a Christian funeral procession and assaulting with a rifle the Arab driver of a refuse vehicle who did not show his pass, noted a Jewish official.[161] Jewish auxiliary police units filled death squads during the revolt in the south of Palestine according to civil officer Aubrey Lees who

---

[153] Ibid.
[154] Note on Supernumerary Constables, Jew and Arab, 12 January 1938, S25/8928-171, CZA.
[155] Ibid.
[156] Yigal Eyal, 'The Arab Revolt, 1936–1939: A Turning Point in the Struggle over Palestine,' in Mordechai Bar-On (ed.), *A Never-Ending Conflict: A Guide to Israeli Military History* (Westport, CT and London: Praeger, 2004), p. 29.
[157] M. Rogozak [?] to Sharett, 24 June 1937 and GOC Lincolnshire Regiment to Menorah Club (Jerusalem), 13 August 1936, S25/4390, CZA.
[158] In File 4: Riots, 1936–38, Box 4625, Jerusalem Municipality: Historical Archive, Department of Jewish Community, JMA.
[159] Letter, David Bar Ray Hay, Advocate, Haifa, also the Acting Chairman of the Jewish Community, 30 June 1936, File 1802/00089/20: Jewish Community of Haifa and the Commission of the Emergency, 1936, HMA.
[160] Interview with Maj-Gen B. L. Montgomery, 2 March 1939, by F. H. K., File 1836/00090/14: Commission of the Current Situation, 1939, HMA.
[161] Ibid.

encountered 'frantic' Palestinian women reporting Jewish police of some type 'shooting every man they could find'; a local Arab medical officer told Lees that such assassinations were daily occurrences.[162] As the District Commissioner Jerusalem at a British security conference much later in 1947 noted regarding the use of Jewish supernumerary police under the auspices of the Jewish Agency, 'this weapon had been turned eventually to political assassination.'[163] This did not stop officers in the field keen to crush the revolt training and equipping Jews. Colonel Farrar Morgan of the Border Regiment talked later in his life of his 'unofficial effort' to train Jews: 'I don't say that I ever made a Jewish army but shall we say I winked my eye at it being formed and I allowed them to have a certain amount of instruction ... The military high-ups wouldn't have liked to have been told that we were training them. They knew perfectly well. One of the fellows under me was Orde Wingate.'[164] Morgan then pointed to his own private army of '100 men and Wingate's was similar.'[165] Rank-and-file British soldiers trained kibbutzniks in military tactics.[166] The British militarised the *Yishuv* and the 'Jewish warrior – as a cultural and social model and as a fact of life – emerged during the Arab Rebellion.'[167] Jewish supernumerary police endured the military regimen, punished for not being shaved, having a dirty rifle, or being 'idle' on parade.[168] Wingate slapped and struck Jewish soldiers in his squads, who took this as a necessary part of their drill and called Wingate the 'insane one.'[169] British soldiers such as Corporal Howbrook serving with the SNSs saw the eccentric Wingate treat the Jews 'almost like dirt ... the rank and file he could do anything with them. He could push them around and order them about. And they'd almost run like kittens, little puppies.'[170] Close cooperation meant that kibbutzim had identifying building roof

---

[162] Extract from a Letter from an English Friend in Palestine, 11 January 1939, Lees Papers, 5/9, LHCMA; Memoir by Lees entitled Unbeaten Track: Some Vicissitudes in Two Years of a Public Servant's Life by el-Asi, Lees Papers, 5/13, pp. 3–4, LHCMA. Lees used the nom de plume, al-'Asi, the Arabic name of the River Orontes, also meaning a rebel.

[163] His Excellency's (Security) Conference (in Government House), 5 February 1947, Box 4, File 1, Sheet 30, GB165-0072, Cunningham Papers, MEC.

[164] Various Notes, p. 4, Lever Arch File 55, Thames TV Material on 'Palestine: Promises, Rebellion and Abdication' (1977–78), IWMFA.

[165] Ibid.

[166] Hutchinson-Brooks, 10148/5, IWMSA.

[167] Anita Shapira, *Land and Power: The Zionist Resort to Force, 1881–1948* (New York, NY: Oxford University Press, 1992), pp. 219ff.

[168] Defaulters Register for Jewish Supernumerary Police, 1937–40, Nazareth District, Palestine Police Force, 1936–40, M/5598/2, ISA.

[169] Testimonies of Special Night Squad fighters, made c. 1941–44, Tzvi, S25/10685, CZA.

[170] Fred Howbrook, 4619/03, p. 23, IWMSA. See also Trevor Royle, *Orde Wingate: Irregular Soldier* (London: Weidenfeld and Nicolson, 1995), p. 129.

markers for ground–air cooperation with the RAF.[171] The mingling of British and Jewish forces had nasty side-effects, such as Jewish sentries who when guarding Palestinians in cages were 'adept at starting a battle in the middle of the night.'[172] General Dill wondered about Jewish 'gangster methods' and how one day there was 'a possibility, amounting to a probability, that Jews may one day carry out a pretty useful massacre of Arabs as a retaliatory measure,' as would happen in 1948 at places such as Dayr Yasin.[173] Senior officers stressed the need to use Jewish auxiliary forces defensively and not offensively into Palestinian areas, an ideal outpaced by events on the ground.[174] Senior British commanders said one thing but did another. Wavell told Shertok in November 1937 that he had already 3,500 armed Jews and 'I should like to use more Jews for defence' such as railway protection and at Lydda airport 'so as to free soldiers and British police.'[175] Civil administrators who had to continue running the country when the soldiers had gone resisted extreme military measures and there were 'roars of protests' over the actions of the SNSs.[176] This acted as friction to the use of force, as discussed in earlier chapters. Nevertheless, the considerable official military sanction given to Jews emboldened their auxiliary forces who 'bitterly opposed' the laws on arms restrictions and wanted to expand.[177] The range and scope of Jewish auxiliary police-style units – many of which blended with Haganah formations – were immense and even accepting a conservative figure of 15,000 supernumeraries this equated to the numerical strength of an infantry division plus a brigade, a sizeable force addition of highly motivated, generally well-armed, reliable, and reasonably trained soldiers.

Jewish Collaboration: Special Night Squads

There is a good literature on the Special Night Squads led by Nazareth-based Army intelligence officer Captain Orde Wingate that fought in

---

[171] Minutes of the 20th Meeting of the Jewish Settlement Defence Committee held at Police HQ, 19 July 1939, Majors Brunskill and Wigham, O'Rorke and Joshua Gordon present, Minutes: Jewish Settlements Defence Committees, M/4259, ISA.
[172] Diary, 14 October 1938, Mullens Papers, LHCMA.
[173] Dill to Deverell (CIGS, London), 20 March 1937, Dill Papers, 2/9, LHCMA.
[174] Deverell (WO, London) to Dill, 19 February 1937, Dill Papers, 2/9, LHCMA.
[175] In Wavell to Haining (DMO, WO), 16 November 1937, Palestine, 1937–38 Volume, Wavell Papers, POH.
[176] John Bierman and Colin Smith, *Fire in the Night: Wingate of Burma, Ethiopia and Zion* (New York, NY: Random House, 1999), p. 125.
[177] Brig G. S. Brunskill, Typed Memoir, p. 9, Brunskill Papers, PP/MCR/136, IWMD.

Galilee in northern Palestine in 1938.[178] A dedicated (Christian) Zionist, Wingate died as a Major-General in an aeroplane crash in Burma in 1944 leading irregular forces against the Japanese. British commitment to the SNSs comprised three platoons of British–Jewish soldiers based around thirty-seven British soldiers stationed in Jewish settlements such as Hanita and Ein Harod, and commanded by three subalterns seconded from Brigadier Evetts' Haifa-based 16th Brigade: Lieutenants Mike Grove (Queen's Own Royal West Kent Regiment), Robert 'Rex' King-Clark (Manchester Regiment), and H. E. N. 'Bala' Bredin (Royal Ulster Rifles). Bredin later led irregular 'X' squads in Cyprus in the 1950s, known also as the 'Toads' with turned EOKA fighters.[179] The interest in the SNSs can overlook the fact they were never that large. Haining turned down Wingate's proposal to increase the force to 300 men; that said, the squads unofficially trained many Jewish fighter who were not on official manifests.[180] Their short six-month life from June to December 1938 proves four points: that the Army favoured the Jews with direct military support; that Wingate used British Army pacification methods to which he added extensive night operations and close Jewish intelligence cooperation; that irregular forces supercharged the embedded brutality of pacification; and that such brutality while achieving results in pacifying parts of Galilee sat badly with the Army's notions of controlled force. The SNSs were 'well-oiled killing machines,' in the words of Wingate's biographers, but so were the infantry regiments of the British Army.[181] The illegal and semi-legal terror used by Wingate's men grew from established population-centric methods but employed now by a maverick British officer removed from the usual chains-of-command and in charge of ideologically engaged, highly motivated auxiliary troops. The British knew the dangers of employing such auxiliary troops. King-Clark wrote how he was 'certain' that Jewish fighters with him would 'not let slip any opportunity of inflicting damage on persons or property that may arise.'[182] The blurred typology of Jewish auxiliary fighters was such

---

[178] Matthew Hughes, 'Terror in Galilee: British–Jewish Collaboration and the Special Night Squads in Palestine during the Arab Revolt, 1938–39,' *Journal of Imperial and Commonwealth History* 43/4 (December 2015), pp. 590–610; Simon Anglim, *Orde Wingate the Iron Wall and Counter-Terrorism in Palestine 1937–39* (Shrivenham: Joint Services Command and Staff College Occasional Paper 49, 2005); Anglim, *Orde Wingate and the British Army, 1922–44* (London: Pickering and Chatto, 2010).

[179] David French, *Fighting EOKA: The British Counter-Insurgency Campaign on Cyprus, 1955–1959* (Oxford: Oxford University Press, 2015), pp. 147–48.

[180] Bierman and Smith, *Fire in the Night*, p. 107.

[181] Ibid., p. 109.

[182] Special Night Squad, 1st Bn The Manchester Regiment, Personal Diary (with Training Notes by Wingate), 'Some Experiences in Palestine. Ex the Lorettonian,' 16 June 1938, King-Clark Papers, 83/10/1, p. 2, IWMD.

that King-Clark talked of taking *ghaffirs* into villages on operations.[183] Meanwhile Wingate mixed British troops with Jewish Supernumerary Police, including future Israeli soldier Moshe Dayan, and with men sent by the Jewish Agency.[184]

The sometimes lethal, usually brutal, and always exemplary action of the SNSs was standard military counter-insurgency practice for the British soldiers leading the squads, easily employed by them against local civilians and insurgents, now given added force by the irregular nature of the SNSs. SNS transformed 16th Brigade's exemplary force into 'counter-terror.'[185] The squads pacified parts of Galilee, in some measure through aggressive patrolling, night action, and use of intelligence, but also with levels of terror and assassination that forced the Army to close the unit at the end of 1938 and send Wingate home (after which the force had a half-life under Bredin in 1939). The force used was unjustifiable even by the draconian emergency laws in place at the time. Civil official Hugh Foot saw first-hand the effects of the SNSs as Wingate 'wiped out opposition gangs by killing them all. He was taking sides. It was a dirty war of assassination and counter-assassination. I don't think we should have got mixed up in that.'[186] The SNSs were 'just thuggery really,' in the view of another colonial administrator, and the people Wingate was 'bumping off, any odd Arabs who happened to go into the village at night, they weren't necessarily men who were blowing up the pipeline.'[187] The SNSs took British pacification methods of 'striking terror' into the hearts of the enemy by 'showing them that we can go one better,' in the words of King-Clark.[188] Irregular units changed the style of violence but the SNSs operated as some tougher infantry regiments did and were exceptional only in that their lethal behaviour was more permanent and less episodic, managed locally and not centrally, and carried out by engaged, armed Jewish settlers. Montgomery, who arrived in Palestine

---

[183] Special Night Squad, 1st Bn The Manchester Regiment, Personal Diary (with Training Notes by Wingate), 'Some Experiences in Palestine. Ex the Lorettonian,' 19 June 1938, King-Clark Papers, 83/10/1, p. 8, IWMD.

[184] Bredin, 4550/05, pp. 29, 36, IWMSA.

[185] Charles Townshend, 'In Aid of the Civil Power: Britain, Ireland and Palestine, 1916–1948,' in Daniel Marston and Carter Malkasian (eds), *Counterinsurgency in Modern Warfare* (Oxford: Osprey, 2008), p. 32.

[186] Interview with Lord Caradon (Hugh Foot), Lever Arch File 55, Wingate and SNS, p. 11, Thames TV Material on 'Palestine: Promises, Rebellion and Abdication' (1977–78), IWMFA.

[187] Charles Evans, Lever Arch File 55, Thames TV Material on 'Palestine: Promises, Rebellion and Abdication' (1977–78), IWMFA.

[188] Special Night Squad, 1st Bn The Manchester Regiment, Personal Diary (with Training Notes by Wingate), 'Some Experiences in Palestine. Ex the Lorettonian,' King-Clark Papers, 83/10/1, p. 1, IWMD.

towards the end of the life of the SNSs to command their divisional area
of operation, shared the unit's tough approach, leaving Anglican Bishop
of Jerusalem, the Rt. Rev. G. F. Graham-Brown (who had been a battalion adjutant of the King's Own Scottish Borderers in the Great War),
who was protesting about a Royal Ulster Rifles' 'regular' atrocity at the
village of al-Bassa, 'absolutely bewildered,' colonial officer Keith-Roach
noted. 'To every question, he said, Monty had but one reply: "I shall
shoot them." "The man is blood mad," the bishop moaned across my
office table.'[189]

Wingate and his men escalated standard Army counter-insurgency
collective punishment practices directed at Palestinian villagers
suspected of harbouring rebels, withholding information, or being near
insurgent attacks, such as blowing up the oil TAPline that ran across
Galilee to Haifa. Wingate told his men that they must strike hard in
'reprisal' attacks and on 11 June 1938 in one of the first operations,
Bredin and his men chased an Arab band into a village and threw
grenades into houses.[190] The SNSs in their short operational life carried
out outrages at Kfar Hittin (or Kafr Hattin), Hittin, Nin (or Nayn),
Kufur Masr (or Kafr Masr/Misr), Danna, Silat al-Dahr (pronounced
Silat ed-Daher), Beisan (Baysan, in Hebrew Beit She'an), and in and
around Daburiyya, alongside cumulative acts of extra-judicial brutality
in unnamed villages. These all occurred in lower Galilee in the Jezreel
Valley or near Tiberias, excepting Silat al-Dahr, located south-west
of Jenin on the West Bank that was an operational outlier. The names
of other villages where there were incidents when transliterated from
Arabic to Hebrew to English make no sense or are not even Arabic
sounding, such as Kokomble where the British threatened to force
oil-sodden soil into villagers' mouths.[191] Jewish fighters in the SNSs
learned from the British how to use violence, impressed by how British
soldiers exercised imperial control.[192] Bredin executed three prisoners
brought by Jews to him at Kfar Hittin, proclaiming, '"In the name of
the King of England, I find you guilty of murder and sentence you to
death" … He immediately ordered the English soldiers to carry out the
sentence, and they shot the Arabs on the spot. In this, Bridden [sic]

[189] Edward Keith-Roach (ed. Paul Eedle), *Pasha of Jerusalem: Memoirs of a District Commissioner under the British Mandate* (London: Radcliffe, 1994), pp. 194–95.
[190] Yehuda Slutsky (and Ben-Zion Dinur) (eds), *Sefer Toldot ha-Haganah* [*Book of the History of the Haganah*]. Volume 2, Part 2, *Me'Haganah le'ma'avak* [*From Defence to Struggle*] (Tel Aviv: Ma'arachot, 1963), pp. 919–20.
[191] Testimonies of Special Night Squad fighters, made c. 1941–44, Chaim Levkov, S25/10685, CZA.
[192] See testimonies of Special Night Squad fighters, made c. 1941–44, S25/10685, CZA.

was following in the practices of Wingate.'[193] This might be a reference to an incident on 20 October 1938 witnessed by Jewish Sergeant Yigal Allon (later a senior Israeli soldier and deputy prime minister) who had gone with Bredin to 'Hittin' where they shot a running Arab and also captured three suspects who 'on the way to the car' 'tried to escape and a squad shot them.'[194] Wingate told Corporal Howbrook and the men serving under King-Clark that the Arabs were terrorising villagers, so his squad was 'to terrorise the terrorists kind of thing and catch them and just wipe them out.'[195] Bredin stood out in his actions, as King-Clark remembered, proving that these were basic Army methods:

Bala took a very tough line with the villagers near the pipeline – he could be a very tough person, could Bala. In fact, some of the measures he took to prevent sabotage were far from orthodox. On one occasion, in particular, when he took truly Draconian action against a village which was harbouring gangsters, he very nearly came to grief – but the result of his action was so successful in terms of preventing subsequent sabotage, that his 'iron fist' method was conveniently filed away by higher authority.[196]

As the squads moved closer to Jewish settlers, they became embroiled in a murky war, 'the deeper Wingate's policy took us into the Jewish camp, the more outside the law we became,' as King-Clark put it.[197]

SNS terror was of classical proportions. One favoured method used by British and Jewish soldiers alike was that of the Roman legions – decimation, with variations on the proportion to be killed, and aimed at intelligence gathering, rifle confiscation or simply to instil fear into local villagers. Jewish forces executed every eighth male villager in Kufur Masr (or Kafr Misr) to get them to hand over illegally held rifles.[198] Bredin killed every fifteenth man, three in total, in a village that failed to produce rifles, as recalled by a former Jewish fighter called Jonathan in the 1940s.[199] Another group commanded by Bredin (Brodin in Hebrew) demanded seven rifles in fifteen minutes and Bredin told villagers he would kill every tenth man if they were not forthcoming with the rifles, and the next time every eighth man. Brigade Headquarters called Bredin

---

[193] Yosef Eshkol, *A Common Soldier: The Story of Zvi Brenner* (Tel Aviv: Ministry of Defence Books, 1993), p. 173.
[194] Letter, Yigal Allon to Jewish Supernumerary Police in Afule (Details of Operations, 20 October 1938) 26 October 1938, S25/8768, CZA.
[195] Fred Howbrook, 4619/03, p. 4, IWMSA.
[196] King-Clark, *Free for a Blast*, p. 187.
[197] Ibid., p. 177.
[198] Sonia Fathi el-Nimr, 'The Arab Revolt in Palestine: A Study Based on Oral Sources' (Doctoral Thesis: University of Exeter, 1990), p. 112.
[199] Testimonies of Special Night Squad fighters, made c. 1941–44, Jonathan, S25/10685, CZA.

in after this incident, after which he told his British and Jewish soldiers what to say in case of an official inquiry.[200] Wingate also decimated villages.[201] Palestinian villagers wrote a letter in English – composed by a lawyer, the Jews thought – complaining that Jewish supernumerary officers went into their village, lined up the men, and shot every eighth man after not getting rifles. The Jews then said that they would return and kill everyone. This seems to have been an SNS unit but the hazy mix of violence in Galilee with other British officers leading Jewish units and Jewish fighters acting unilaterally makes it difficult to decipher events.[202]

Jewish auxiliaries learned from their British experts and from officers such as Bredin, about whom jumbled but consistent stories emerge of executions and brutality.[203] After a massacre of nineteen Jewish civilians by rebels in Tiberias on 2 October 1938, the 'Jews also were in a mood for killing Arabs' and with British Servicemen present turned machine guns on the villagers of Daburiyya.[204] SNS men shot random Palestinians after the Tiberias massacre, as when an 'Englishman' shot at an Arab by the village of Lubiya (Lubya west of Tiberias) but as he was unable to hit him with his pistol he got a rifle from a Jew and shot the man dead.[205] In another account, after the Tiberias massacre, Bredin and his men

met an Arab riding his bicycle. Breeden [sic] shot him dead – this helped a bit in reviving the general atmosphere. When we arrived at Dabourria [sic] Breeden gave orders not to have mercy and not behave like gentlemen ... I remember that at the sight of a Jewish family, mother and children burnt in the Tiberias fire, tears ran down Breeden's cheeks and he said: 'Would I be allowed to take revenge, I would have eliminated all the Arabs.'[206]

Wingate attacked Daburiyya after the Tiberias massacre in what might have been the same attack detailed above, while Haganah intelligence later pinpointed Kfar Hittin as responsible for the Tiberias massacre prompting a punitive raid by Bredin.[207]

Squad soldiers provoked incidents, as when a Jewish soldier in the SNSs saw the force turn machine guns on Arabs who had come out to

---

[200] Note from 'A.A.,' 19–20 November 1938, S25/8768, CZA.

[201] Uri Ben-Eliezer, *The Making of Israeli Militarism* (Bloomington, IN: Indiana University Press, 1998), pp. 26–27.

[202] Note from 'A.A.', 19–20 November 1938, S25/8768, CZA.

[203] Testimonies of Special Night Squad fighters, made c. 1941–44, Arieh [Aryeh?], S25/10685, CZA.

[204] Ibid.

[205] Ibid.

[206] Untitled Reminiscence: Operations Tiberias and Tabor by Levacov [presumably Levkov], pp. 5–6, Alice Hay of Seaton Papers, JRL.

[207] Eshkol, *A Common Soldier*, pp. 169, 172.

extinguish a gasoline-induced fire started by the SNS, killing twenty. Jewish fighter Shlomo recalled how five soldiers, two Jews, two British, and a British officer, went to the village of Danna after a pipeline attack, possibly on 11 June 1938, in an undercover operation in civilian clothes on a rainy, muddy day, Shlomo remembering that the inclement weather annoyed the officer. The officer shot all running men at the village. He then gathered the surviving villagers and asked Shlomo how many lashes he thought that a man could take. Shlomo replied with the figure of twenty-five, to which the officer said that he would give each villager thirteen lashes. The British officer then whipped all the villagers except the *mukhtar* and a child. The officer also 'tortured' one Palestinian to obtain information on the gangs 'in a cruel manner … it was a horrible sight.'[208] As the officer whipped villagers, village women cried out and begged him to stop and kissed his feet. Another Jew remembered a lecture to Danna villagers from Arabic-speaking Wingate, and villagers being whipped as they ran away.[209] The officer angry at the muddy weather might have been Wingate but this ran counter to his well-known willingness to bear long marches and rough field conditions. The SNSs targeted villages for multiple raids, as at Danna. Zwi Brenner – another future Israeli military leader – watched as Wingate ordered the villagers of Danna 'to open their mouths and ordered the English soldiers to force into their mouths earth soaked in the oil which had poured from the pipeline. Here, too, Wingate made sure that those who carried this out were English soldiers – and not the Jews.'[210] Shlomo and the British also found two Arabs wounded and dying, and they conducted 'a field trial right there and killed them both.'[211] Mundane, non-lethal punishments were also commonplace as when Wingate humiliated local villagers by making the men run for miles in front of slowly moving Army vehicles.[212]

Howbrook was present at a TAPline rupture where no villager would talk, 'So Wingate said, "Right, we'll teach these so-and-so's a lesson." So we got all the men in the village. Oh, outside the … where the oil had been burnt there's a big pool of black oil burnt. And we got all the men by the side of this. And then we took an arm and a leg each and

[208] Testimonies of Special Night Squad fighters, made c. 1941–44, Shlomo, S25/10685, CZA.

[209] Testimonies of Special Night Squad fighters, made c. 1941–44, Chaim Levkov, S25/10685, CZA.

[210] Eshkol, *A Common Soldier*, p. 174.

[211] Testimonies of Special Night Squad fighters, made c. 1941–44, Shlomo, S25/10685, CZA.

[212] Meeting with Mr Tabori (Tavori) and Gershon Ritov, 27 March 1950, p. 8, Alice Hay of Seaton Papers, JRL.

flung them all into the middle of it.'[213] Wingate forced sand into villagers' mouths until they vomited.[214]

Wingate turned to one of the Jews and, pointing to the coughing and spluttering Arab, said 'shoot this man.' The Jew looked at him questioningly and hesitated. Wingate said, in a tense voice, 'Did you hear? Shoot him.' The Jew shot the Arab. The others stared for a moment, in stupefaction, at the dead body at their feet. The boys from Hanita were watching in silence. 'Now speak,' said Wingate. They spoke.[215]

Arabs who looked 'suspect' risked beatings and death if caught by the SNSs, as when a British SNS corporal captured a man at night near the village of Nin (or Nayn) who started begging as he had a weapon on him: 'killed on the spot' and his body taken to the police.[216] King-Clark felt that Bredin and his 'wild' behaviour helped force the closure of the SNSs after Wingate's departure:

Bala could be *very* tough and uncompromising, ably supported by his 'Wild Geese.' In fact, he got so tough with one village on the pipeline that he very nearly got into real trouble. But it stopped the conflagrations and this saved his bacon! (I'll tell you about it sometime.) When Wingate left (in Sep 38?) and Bala carried on, his squad got a bit Wild West and out of hand and I think that was one of the reasons the SNS closed down.[217]

The brutality and extra-judicial murders of the SNSs that supported pacification were not what the Army wanted or needed, while civil officials could not stomach such things.

Minorities and Collaboration: Druze, Christians, and Bedouin

Some non-Muslim or culturally distinct communities in Palestine actively cooperated with the British and the Jews. This was a small part of pacification but one that expanded the anti-rebel front from within the subject population, contributed intelligence, and hampered rebel recruitment and weapons smuggling. The Druze community in Palestine numbered only 9,148 in 1931 and some 12,000 by 1938 but some were effective collaborators, and while concentrated in parts of Galilee such

---

[213] Howbrook, 4619/03, p. 36, IWMSA.
[214] Leonard Mosley, *Gideon Goes to War* (London: Barker, 1955), pp. 44–45, 58; Eshkol, *A Common Soldier*, pp. 174–76.
[215] Mosley, *Gideon Goes to War*, pp. 44–45, 58.
[216] Operations of Patrols of Englishmen and Jews, 13 June 1938, 26/6: Reports on Fosh Actions, HA.
[217] Letter, King-Clark to Trevor Royle, 22 February 1993, MR4/17/307/1/4, TLSAC.

as Mount Carmel there were significant Druze communities in Syria and Lebanon whose participation limited rebel recruitment and gun-running abroad.[218] The British paid the Druze not to take part in the revolt but some collaboration went beyond receiving money to stand aside.[219] The British encouraged this, so when rebels raided Druze in the mixed village of Shafa 'Amr who would not join the revolt, the British retaliated by destroying Muslim houses in the village, so deepening rifts between Druze and Muslims.[220] Meanwhile, MacKereth in Damascus helped to fuse intra-Druze collaboration between Syrian (in the Jebel Druze area), Lebanese, and Palestinian Druze after rebel attacks on Druze in Galilee that angered all Druze communities.[221] The British and Jews combined forces for this operation. Jewish Agency northern Palestine agent Yosef (Joseph) Davidescu – a picaresque former British intelligence operative later assassinated, it seems, by the Stern Gang for working with CID – had good links to the British secret service (or was working for them) and he liaised with the Druze of Mount Carmel who had clashed with rebel bands such as Abu Durra's over deadly rebel raids on Druze villagers that also desecrated holy books, compounded by intra-band disputes over a prostitute.[222] Two Druze (Labib Abu Rukun and 'Fais,' the latter a peculiar name) came down from their villages to a Jewish settlement following a rebel attack, after which more Druze came and they all offered to work for the intelligence service, whether Jewish or British is not clear, as a local Jew remembered: 'some for money, some for other reasons … Therefore the High Command decided to give them weapons.'[223] The Jews seconded a Druze armed unit to a Jewish unit, ten Druze and ten Jews, akin to the mixed SNS format; meanwhile, security forces came and took Druze to Balad al-Shaykh in an armoured car where they pointed out people for the British to arrest.[224] That the British saw the Druze as a warrior people helped cooperation: 'one of the most martial and courageous people in the world,' in the words of

---

[218] E. Mills, *Census of Palestine 1931* (London: HMSO, 1933), i, pp. 83, 85; *Statistical Abstract of Palestine, 1939* (Jerusalem: Office of Statistics, 1939), p. 11; *A Survey of Palestine*, i, pp. 140–41.

[219] Druze Activities, S25/22793, pp. 215ff, CZA.

[220] Majid al-Haj, *Social Change and Family Process: Arab Communities in Shefar-A'm* (Boulder, CO and London: Westview, 1987), pp. 55–56; Swedenburg, *Memories of Revolt*, pp. 90ff.

[221] MacKereth (Damascus) to Jerusalem (repeated to FO), 15 December 1938, FO 371/21869, p. 105, TNA; Political Report Syria No. 6, Damascus, 28 December 1938, FO 371/23276, p. 150, TNA.

[222] Testimony of Tuvia Omani, 18 February 1971, 95/23, p. 14, HA.

[223] Ibid.

[224] Ibid.

policeman Douglas Duff.[225] The British also perceived them as racially superior and not Arab, a view supported by pseudo-scientific phreno-logical studies: 'on the measurements of the heads of fifty-nine adult male Druzes, ... not one single fell, as regards his cephalic index, within the range of the real Arab.'[226]

The Palestine Labour League (discussed in Chapter 3) further helped collaboration by building links between the Jews and the Druze, including those in Lebanon and Syria. *Histadrut*-sponsored Jewish agents went on secret missions abroad to Beirut and Damascus.[227] Jewish missions to negotiate with Lebanese–Syrian Druze started a 'de facto alliance' between the two sides.[228] Jews from the Haifa Labour Council travelled across the border near Metullah on 29 October 1937 to the village of Druze notable Tawfiq Hamadi where village elders told them that they opposed rebel agitation for local youths to enlist in the revolt for pay of between £P.4 and £P.4.500 per month pay (higher ranks would get £P.15–20 per month).[229] There was the possi-bility for Jews to have 'good relations' to stop enlistment to the gangs and to receive information from village elders about movements across the border.[230] After this useful Druze offer, the Haifa Labour Council delegation went to Damascus and then to Jebel Druze to a warm reception and a meeting with the brother of the Druze 'Sultan' where they 'spoke business.'[231] The author of the report on the trip requested to receive 'regular and thorough reports on all activities in Jebel Druze and Damascus concerning the Palestinian cause.'[232] The brother of the Sultan should use 'all his influence' on the notables of the mountain to 'prevent any intervention in Palestinian issues and in preventing enlist-ment into the gangs in Palestine ... he should influence the Sultan and his family ... to forge an alliance and treaty of friendship with the Jews in Palestine.'[233] Successful Jewish–Druze liaison blocked rebel recruitment and secured intelligence.[234] The Druze asked for favours

---

[225] Douglas Duff, *Bailing with a Teaspoon* (London: John Long, 1953), p. 168.

[226] Mills, *Census of Palestine 1931*, i, p. 83. The study was by an anthropologist from the University of Berlin.

[227] Zachary Lockman, *Comrades and Enemies: Arab and Jewish Workers in Palestine, 1906–1948* (Berkeley, CA: University of California Press, 1996), p. 251.

[228] Ibid.

[229] Report attached to Letter from Haifa Labour Council sent to Shertok, 1 November 1937, S25/5570-158/159 CZA.

[230] Ibid.

[231] Ibid.

[232] Ibid.

[233] Ibid.

[234] Report attached to Letter from Haifa Labour Council sent to Shertok, 1 November 1937, S25/5570-160 CZA.

in return: agricultural experts, water engineers, and Jewish influence to get bank loans, and in exchange the Druze would 'openly proclaim their friendship with the Jews.'[235] Jews needed, in their view, to look at the wider Arab Druze nation that had much in common with the *Yishuv*.[236] The Jewish–Druze connection kept Druze from southern Lebanon and Jebel Druze out of the revolt, and the two groups established a common bond early on in the revolt.[237] Arabic source material – parts of which are hard to decipher – even suggests that Druze worked with the British and Jews to help plant bombs in Haifa 'made by the government.'[238]

The Army took note of the Druze and British forces pitched in and promoted Jewish–Druze links. One of Montgomery's divisional orders emphasised that soldier must 'endeavour' to support 'loyal minorities such as the DRUSES' while Berkshire Regiment intelligence officer Tony Simonds recorded that the Druze had 'always been friendly to the Jews.'[239] Simonds was in touch with *Shai* agent Reuven Zaslani as early as 1934.[240] Druze told civil officer Blackburne in August 1938 that they had no intention of 'giving active support to the Muslim gangsters,' and that some Druze from outside Palestine were involved in the revolt but only as gun smugglers for 'mercenary reasons,' the implication being that they were not ideologically attached to insurrection.[241] Druze in Palestine wrote to those in Syria who were in favour of the revolt telling them to stay out of Palestine.[242] British intelligence noted Druze emissaries sent to their villages in Palestine and Lebanon to urge inhabitants to take no part in the disturbances.[243] While the Jews and British squeezed from one side, MacKereth maintained anti-rebel pressure from Syria, as the

---

[235] Ibid.
[236] Report entitled To Increase Our Relations with the Druze Nation, 5 November 1937, S25/3639-11/12, File: Letters from Syria, 1937–38 and 1946, CZA.
[237] Gelber, *Jewish–Transjordanian Relations*, p. 85.
[238] A Letter from the Fighter Arrested, Subhi al-Khadra, 20 September 1938 in Akram Zu'aytir, *Watha'iq al-Haraka al-Wataniyya al-Filastiniyya, 1918–39: Min Awraq Akram Zu'aytir* [*Documents of the Palestinian National Movement, 1918–39: From the Papers of Akram Zu'aytir*] (Beirut: IPS, 1979), p. 506.
[239] 8th Division Operation Instruction No. 10, by Montgomery, 21 January 1939, Queen's Royal West Surrey Regiment, 3/6/7, SHC; Typed Memoir, Pieces of War, p. 81, Simonds Papers, 08/46/1, IWMD.
[240] Eshed, *Reuven Shiloah*, p. 27.
[241] Monthly Administrative Report for August 1938, Galilee and Acre District, 2 September 1938, by Acting DC K. W. Blackburne, Blackburne Papers, MSS. Brit. Emp. S. 460, Box 3, File 2, WL.
[242] Summary of Intelligence, Palestine and Transjordan, 22 April 1938, by Wing Commander Ritchie at GHQ [8/38], CO 732/81/9, TNA.
[243] Summary of Intelligence, Palestine and Transjordan, 11 March 1938, by Wing Commander Ritchie at GHQ [5/38], CO 732/81/9, TNA.

Jews noted.[244] The leader of Syria's Druze sent MacKereth a message in December 1938 after Abu Durra's attacks on Druze villages that he was ready to send an armed party of Druze

to wipe out shameful attack by Abu Doreh's gang on Isfiya and Daliah ['Isfiya and Daliyat al-Carmil] and take bloody revenge for Druses there killed. He asked whether facilities could be arranged for such a party. I replied that British author-ities could not countenance private vendetta, but thanked him for his desire to help British authorities ... and I urged him to bring the weight of his counsel to bear on Palestinian agitators who were trying to keep disturbances going for their personal gain ... I have also received three deputations of Syrian Druses to convey thanks for the prompt intervention of the British forces which prevented more Druses being pressed into service with the gangs.[245]

Sixty-five Palestinian Druze elders wrote to the British Haifa commander in March 1939 to express their 'deep gratitude' to the Government 'which has done much to preserve the safety in the village by handing over 19 rifles to the local guards.'[246] Soldiers on patrol noted the rapprochement. The Hampshire Regiment journal wrote of 'friendly' Druze and how relations 'with them have been most cordial.'[247] Essex Regiment soldiers took pictures of themselves with Druze, adding captions such as: 'Lieutenant-Colonel Read and Mr Higson with friendly Druses villagers.'[248]

Christian Palestinians were less overt and committed collaborators but their more-or-less passivity removed around 11 per cent of the non-Jewish population from open revolt; 'indifferent or hostile' to the rebels in one British intelligence report.[249] Christians of Bethlehem gave information to the police.[250] Christians who had escaped to Syria tried to make links with Jews to forestall future dangers.[251] Urban Christians wanted to open their stores counter to rebels strike demands or they opened shops on Fridays, and they refused to wear rebel peasant 'national' headdress.[252]

---

[244] Discussion between Moshe Shertok, 'RZ' and British Consul in Damascus, 4 April 1938, S25/3639-22, File: Letters from Syria, 1937–38 and 1946, CZA.

[245] MacKereth (Damascus) to Jerusalem (repeated FO), 15 December 1938, FO 371/21869, p. 105, TNA.

[246] al-Haj, *Social Change and Family Process*, p. 56.

[247] *The Hampshire Regimental Journal* 34/2 (February 1939), p. 31.

[248] 'Extracts from the CO's Quarterly Letter to 31 December 1937,' *The Essex Regiment Gazette* 6/46 (March 1938), p. 281.

[249] *Statistical Abstract of Palestine, 1939*, p. 11; *Survey of Palestine*, i, pp. 140–41; Summary of Intelligence, Palestine and Transjordan, 6 May 1938, by Wing Commander Ritchie at GHQ [9/38], CO 732/81/9, TNA.

[250] Martin, *Palestine Betrayed*, pp. 85–87.

[251] Haganah Report, 24 August 1936, Shai Intelligence Reports: 8/GENERAL/40, p. 114, HA.

[252] Daily Intelligence, 27 April 1936, Arab Office and Intelligence: 8/GENERAL/35, HA; Summary of Intelligence, Palestine and Transjordan, 16 December 1938, by Wing Commander Ritchie at GHQ [25/38], CO 732/81/10, TNA.

There was no solely Christian rebel band, even in the more pluralist early phase of the revolt.[253] The authorities fined the Christians of Nazareth and destroyed houses in 1939 after a rebel raid, despite the local Christian clergy protesting their loyalty to the government. 'The terrorists will be glad that the fine has been imposed. Notices were said to have been left in the streets calling the people of Nazareth traitors,' noted local Anglican clergy.[254] Police files noted little trouble in Christian Nazareth, with one Army officer adding: 'I don't think so. I don't think they did, no. I can't remember that we ever had any trouble round Nazareth where there were quite a number of Christian Arabs.'[255] Army officer Gratton made similar comments about how Christians 'were pro-Western, very much pro-Western. They wouldn't have been, I don't think, involved in any shooting at the British soldiers.'[256] 'Peaceful Christian Arabs' in another soldier's view.[257] The Army knew which villages were Christian and left off searching them.[258] Christians also supplied the Army with intelligence officers, as with one Nicola Fares (whom rebels tried to kill), a former police sergeant attached to 16th Infantry Brigade headquarters (see Figure 7.2).[259] Rebels retaliated by marching into Christian Bir Zayt village chanting 'we are going to kill the Christians' instead of the more usual 'we are going to kill the British.'[260] References to Bedouin support for security forces are fleeting.[261] Jews were in touch with Bedouin from near Lake Tiberias who stayed in Israel and fought for it in 1948.[262] A British civil official felt that Bedouin apathy to the revolt was because they 'weren't politically minded at all.'[263] There were some 47,981 Negev Bedouin in southern Palestine in 1931 (out of a total 'nomad' population of 66,553) and the British secured the frontiers of their empire by incorporating them into a police camel section where they were 'very reliable chaps'; the British also paid subsidies of up to £10,000 to Transjordan

---

[253] Arnon-Ohanna, *Falahim ba-Mered*, p. 45.
[254] Bishop's Visit to Nazareth, 4 May 1939, J&EM Papers, GB165-0161, Box 62, File 1, MEC.
[255] Nazareth Town, Political, Agitators, Gang Leaders and Terrorists, Palestine Police Force, Report from Tiberias, M/4212/8, ISA; Dove, 4463/03, p. 30, IWMSA.
[256] Gratton, 4506/03, pp. 25–26, IWMSA.
[257] Letter, Bufton to Parents, 3 November 1938, Tufton Beamish (later Baron Chelwood), Beamish Papers, 1/6/9, ESRO.
[258] *The Hampshire Regimental Journal* 33/2 (February 1938), p. 51.
[259] '2 Christian Arabs Abducted by Gang,' *Palestine Post* (24 March 1938) in Scrapbook of Articles about the American Colony, Palestine, People and Events and Loose Enclosures 1938, ACHA.
[260] School Year Diary, 1938–39, Wilson Papers, GB165-0302, p. 7, MEC.
[261] *Survey of Palestine*, i, pp. 140, 159, ii, p. 925.
[262] Testimony of David Kna'ani, 12 July 1952, 68/6, HA.
[263] Bell, 10256/6, IWMSA.

7.2 Newspaper account of a Palestinian Christian working as an intelligence officer with the Army, one Nicola Fares, a former police sergeant (from American Colony Hotel Archive)

Bedouin to stay out of the revolt, while Britain's ally Abdullah exerted 'himself to prevent trouble spreading to Trans-Jordan, a danger he personally dreads.'[264]

Intelligence

The Army and RAF after April 1936 boosted pre-existing police CID and SSO intelligence networks, and without an Intelligence Corps (disbanded after the Great War and only re-formed in 1940) an expanded Jerusalem-based Combined Force Staff headquarters collated and disseminated information to soldiers on operations. The Army also heavily co-opted Jewish intelligence networks, alongside securing information from the Nashashibis that came both directly to the British and via the Jews. Intelligence came from CID, Jewish sources, the Nashashibis and their allies, Army battalion and area brigade-divisional military intelligence officers, Palestine civil officers, diplomats in neighbouring countries like MacKereth, RAF-led SSO political officers in place before the revolt, and MI5 Defence Security Officers who from 1938 were formed into Security Intelligence Middle East.[265] (MI5 directly covered Palestine as an imperial 'domestic' possession rather than SIS/MI6, although some soldiers talked of MI6 running operations in Lebanon, Syria, Transjordan, and Palestine at this time.[266]) The disorganised rebel front stood little chance in this information war. Experienced SSOs conducted much of the intelligence work and were based at the start of the revolt in Jerusalem, Haifa, Maan, and Amman; after April 1936, the military set up new SSO positions in Jaffa, Nablus, Nazareth, and the Jordan Valley.[267] There was also an SSO house in Jewish Nathanya (Netanya) north of Tel Aviv, and now a city of 200,000 people.[268] The Army relied extensively on Jews to supply information, as we will see. The network used informers, official reports, some sigint, interrogations, and captured documents for the information necessary to inform operations.

---

[264] Martin, 13518/6, IWMSA; Mansour Nasasra, 'Memories from Beersheba: The Bedouin Palestine Police and the Frontiers of the Empire,' *Bulletin of the Council for British Research in the Levant* 9 (2014), pp. 32–38; H. V. Muhsam, *Beduin of the Negev* (Jerusalem: Academic Press, 1966), p. 12; *Survey of Palestine*, i, pp. 140, 159, ii, p. 925; Letter, Wauchope to Secretary of State for Colonies, 7 June 1936, S25/22725, CZA.

[265] Calder Walton, *Empire of Secrets: British Intelligence, the Cold War and the Twilight of Empire* (London: Harper, 2013), p. 25.

[266] Walton, *Empire of Secrets*, p. 16; Typed Memoir, Pieces of War, p. 132, Simonds Papers, 08/46/1, IWMD.

[267] Bowden, *The Breakdown of Public Security*, p. 156.

[268] Appendix to Summary of Intelligence, Palestine and Transjordan, 18 November 1938, by Wing Commander Ritchie at GHQ [23/38], CO 732/81/10, TNA.

GOC Haining complained in November 1938 that there was 'too much organised intelligence' in Palestine, especially with Foreign Office-run information coming in from consuls in neighbouring countries, but at the start of the revolt the problem was the shortfall not the surfeit of good intelligence.[269] This problem stemmed from the Palestine police not having a Special Branch or any suitable alternative intelligence system. It relied instead on CID that while it had a Political D 'Special Branch' sub-unit (of nine men) did not function properly.[270] Poor police intelligence prompted the creation of a military-run intelligence state. The 'crucial weakness' for CID was its intelligence-gathering network that increased the number of police agents but not the quality or processing of information.[271] SSOs and the Army made almost 'no connection' to the police, thinking the force inadequate to the job.[272] CID was 'caught napping' in policeman Ted Horne's view, or as 'one wag at headquarters put it at the time. "There was no one to read the tea leaves properly".'[273] Police had focused on chasing communists before the revolt rather than rebel militants.[274] The British had expanded CID intelligence after the 1929 riots to a force of fifty-one officers by 1935 but it still achieved very little as it relied on Arab officers who during the revolt were either unreliable or were assassinated. Those not assassinated 'sat upon information' until it was of no use.[275] With little public assistance and denied the opportunity to use 'oriental methods' the police could not get information, in Lord Peel's view, notwithstanding the many charges of police 'inquisition methods' at the time.[276] Police Inspector General Roy Spicer spent the five years before the revolt building the force and trying to establish an effective CID to cover political matters but it was not ready in 1936. The lack of useful information meant that the British were unable to forestall insurgent actions such as the Qassamite assassination of Andrews in September 1937 or catch the culprits, as Battershill lamented:

Our C.I.D. can tell us very little and that branch of the police wants strengthening badly and as soon as possible. I have written privately to Sir John Shuckburgh [of the Colonial Office] asking him to consider two proposals viz. to send us

---

[269] Letter, Haining to O'Connor, 6 November 1938, O'Connor Papers, 3/2/1, LHCMA.

[270] *The Palestine Police: Annual Administrative Report, 1934* (Jerusalem: Government Printing Press, 1934), pp. 32–33.

[271] Thomas, *Empires of Intelligence*, pp. 240–41.

[272] Gelber, *Shorshey ha-Havatzelet*, p. 150.

[273] Edward Horne, *A Job Well Done (Being a History of the Palestine Police Force, 1920–1948)* (Tiptree: Anchor Press, 1982), pp. 206, 208–09.

[274] Thomas, *Empires of Intelligence*, p. 240.

[275] Bowden, *The Breakdown of Public Security*, p. 157.

[276] Cmd. 5479 *Report of the Palestine Royal Commission (Peel)* (London: HMSO, 1937), p. 186; Anon., 'British Methods in Palestine,' *Yorkshire Post* (23 November 1938).

someone with Egyptian and C.I.D. experience to be attached to the C.I.D. here to take charge of hunting down terrorists; and whether it might not be possible to send a super sleuth under some appropriate 'cover' to Haifa and to Damascus to try to get some information worth having. I regard this of great importance … as long as we employ present local C.I.D. methods we shall make no progress.[277]

When Indian police adviser Sir Charles Tegart came to Palestine in late 1937 to improve policing, Wavell saw the value of his mission and of the need for more military intelligence as police intelligence was the 'weak point at present.'[278] Haining as military commander after Wavell refused to work with Tegart amidst chaotic scenes of policemen openly fighting in Jerusalem.[279]

It was within the context of failing police CID that the SSOs and the Army latched on to effective, well-established Jewish intelligence networks run by Haganah–*Shai* and supported by the Jewish Agency. Jews knew from the start that their 'most important asset' in relations with the British was that their 'knowledge of the situation in the region was deeper and much more extensive than that of the British authorities.'[280] Ezra Danin was one key operative who worked for the Army, and who from his base at Hadera north of Tel Aviv had a network of informers that fed *Shai* and then the Army information through other agents such as Reuven Zaslani.[281] The Jewish Agency managed to 'sell' Danin to RAF intelligence based in Nablus:

The 'sale' was pushed through by Yehoshua [Joshua] Gordon of the Political Department, and from that time on, until 1948, all the information I gathered was passed on to the British Army. Most of the information on the gangs that we passed on was exact, and that enhanced our credibility in the eyes of the British army and police. All of this material came to Reuven Zaslany's desk first, and it was his job to make a deal on it with the British in return for various demands we made on them.[282]

Jewish counter-demands amounted to more supernumerary Jewish police and guards, and Army help for the Haganah, thus reinforcing the argument made above on military support for Jewish auxiliary forces. The interface between the two sides came through military intelligence and not CID. Both sides were keen to work with the other. Joshua

[277] Letter, Battershill to Wauchope, 12 October 1937, Battershill Papers, MSS. Brit. Emp. S. 467, Box 10, File 4, WL.
[278] Wavell to Haining (WO, DMO), 23 October 1937, Palestine, 1937–38 Volume, Wavell Papers, POH.
[279] Letter, O'Connor to Wife, n.d., O'Connor Papers, 3/1/20, LHCMA.
[280] Eshed, *Reuven Shiloah*, p. 30.
[281] Ibid., p. 34.
[282] Ibid.

Gordon was the head of the security division within the Jewish Agency's political department, under whom was ex-Army officer Frederick Kisch with Zaslani as his assistant; Zaslani worked closely with Sasson whose missions to Syria are discussed above. The Jews pro-actively sought new relationships with the Army, CID, and the British administration.[283] In the Jews' view, the Army was suspicious of the colonial administration and wanted to work outside 'the framework of usual police activities' and they could support soldiers operating without civil support with *Shai*-supplied information and guides; the Army also handed over captured documents for translation, so bypassing the Government and police.[284] Linked SSO–Jewish networks of operatives guided troops and translated documents.[285] The Jews had good intelligence across the piece, including on rebel activities in Damascus such as weapons smuggling, with files talking of 'our sources' in the rebel movement.[286] The violence of the revolt forced the Jews to look for new Palestinian humint sources as while 'faithful friends,' in one case, still visited a hut close to Tirat Zvi settlement south of Beisan to give information, this was getting harder due to rebel counter-measures.[287] Two Jewish communists penetrated the rebel camp of 'Halti Hit' (the literal transliteration from Hebrew) pretending to be Arabs.[288] *Mizrahi* Jews infiltrated the rebel camp as British soldiers could not, echoing British officer Robert Nairac's murder in 1977 in Northern Ireland while pretending to be an Irish Republican. Palestinian villagers had long taken their grievances to trusted Jewish elders or *shomrin* (watchers or guards). One such man was Yosef Teitelbaum, known to Palestinians as Abu Ismain (properly Isma'il): 'They flocked to his house for his judgements on disputes and had the greatest faith in the justice of his pronouncements.'[289] Of course, Teitelbaum passed all this information to the Haganah, while Jewish civil servants did the same in towns. Jewish *mukhtars* gathered information for Haganah intelligence.[290] Jews had eyes on the Palestinians at all levels. When Palestinian delegates including Hajj Amin met in the Palace Hotel after a trip to Amman to see Abdullah, the Hebrew report on proceedings is in the first person: Jews had an agent there

---

283 Ibid., p. 30.
284 Slutsky, *Sefer Toldot ha-Haganah*. Volume 2, Part 2, *Me'Haganah le'ma'avak*, p. 991.
285 Gelber, *Shorshey ha-Havatzelet*, pp. 149–50.
286 See material in S25/3639, File: Letters from Syria, 1937–38 and 1946, CZA.
287 Report, Settlement Tirat Zvi, 41/90, HA.
288 Headed Top Secret, File 04/-163-A/621: Riots, April 1936 [but actually June–September 1938] [one bundle of papers], TAMA.
289 Dekel, *Shai*, p. 181.
290 Abigail Jacobson and Moshe Naor, *Oriental Neighbors: Middle Eastern Jews and Arabs in Mandatory Palestine* (Waltham, MA: Brandeis University Press, 2016), p. 71.

talking personally to the Mufti.[291] The Jews had operatives everywhere, including a correspondent at the newspaper *al-Difa'* who for a payment gave them 'information and documents concerning the plans of Arab officials and Committee members. His position as a journalist on a "national" newspaper brought him into close contact with the members of the Arab Higher Committee and his sources were thus many and important.'[292] *Shai* had an agent who was a *muezzin* calling the prayers at a mosque and it had informers among Jaffa's stevedores and customs officials.[293] Hajj Amin's counter-terror against traitors forced Jews to recruit new agents paid by the 'piece' or for a 'regular monthly fee' among Palestinians, many of whom were short of money or unemployed following the rebel call to strike.[294] *Shai* operatives may not have liked these informers but they valued their information and met them among sand dunes or in the no-man's land between the two communities in places such as Tel Aviv–Jaffa.

The military instinctively attached itself to the Jewish intelligence superstructure and coordinated this activity through Army and RAF officers. Some of these men were Arabic speakers, some were based within RAF intelligence units, some were (or later became) MI5 or MI6 officers, while some were Army regimental intelligence officers. Many transferred from Iraq to Palestine during the revolt; some came from Sudan and Egypt. Wing Commander A. P. Ritchie as chief RAF intelligence officer in Combined Force Headquarters Staff in Jerusalem led this select, effective team that included Flight-Lieutenant R. F. J. Strange, Major John Teague, Flight-Lieutenant J. P. Domvile (sometimes spelt Domville), and Flight-Lieutenant C. M. Windsor, the last listed in the July 1936 *Air Force List* as in Iraq on language training and in the *Air Force List* for October 1937 as serving in Palestine alongside Domvile and Strange on the headquarters staff. Jews mentioned a Captain Fitzpatrick of the 9th Royal Hussars (a non-existent regiment) that may refer to a Captain T. D. Fitzpatrick of the Welch Regiment. Jews talked of dealing with an officer called A. Hackett-Fine on intelligence matters that must be a reference to Andrew U. H. Hacket Pain (sometimes Hacket-Pain) listed in the September 1938 *Army List* as a Captain in the Queen's Royal Regiment (West Surrey) that served around Tulkarm. Hacket Pain, the son of (Ulster Unionist) Brigadier-General Sir George W. Hacket

[291] Invitation from Abdullah, August 1936, Shai Intelligence Reports: 8/GENERAL/40, p. 260, HA.
[292] Dekel, *Shai,* p. 188.
[293] Ibid., p. 190.
[294] Ibid., pp. 194–95.

Pain, was ex-Sudan Defence Force and so was surely an Arabic speaker. Flying-Officer Norman Lash worked with the peace gangs and went on to command in Transjordan's Arab Legion. There was a Squadron-Leader Dawson (possibly Frank Philip Dawson who was a Flying-Officer in 1938) working on RAF intelligence in Palestine at start of revolt, while AOC Peirse in 1936 brought in for his intelligence unit fluent Arabic-speaker Group-Captain C. K. Buss.[295] Ritchie commanded I Branch that included these officers and others such as Squadron-Leader R. R. Greenlaw, Squadron-Leader G. S. Reed, Flight-Lieutenant V. J. Sofiano, Flight-Lieutenant A. C. Cuming, Flight-Lieutenant D. H. Marsack, and Flying-Officer A. M. N de Lavison.[296] The ranks confirm the central role of the RAF in intelligence work. I Branch produced daily and periodic intelligence summaries, as did lower-level field units. Army regimental intelligence officers such as Tony Simonds respected the SSOs and worked alongside them and I Branch.[297] These men built an intelligence architecture for the emergency security state, helped by Jewish and Palestinian collaborators. The SSOs were pivotal to operations as they were the 'sole military personnel authorized to run agents on their own initiative, and used regular inspection tours to keep their information system in place.'[298] They had cars with wireless transmitters. Meanwhile, geographical survey teams mapped Palestine to aid operations and produced between April and November 1936 some 23,000 maps for security forces.[299] Coordination won the day. As Ritchie instructed in May 1938 it was 'essential for the successful working of the scheme' for the occupation of Galilee and Samaria districts 'that all information shall be pooled,' to which end the British formed intelligence centres at each Army area base.[300] They coordinated as best they could with the police. CID detached an NCO for each centre, the whole team to work in a 'common office' on a 'common pool' of information to create a 'common intelligence service based on the coordination of all available information.'[301] Relations between the police and Army were strained but CID improved and increased from sixty-five personnel in 1936 to 473 officers by end of 1938, of which 237 were British, while every district had a CID

---

[295] Eldad Harouvi, *Palestine Investigated: The Story of the CID of the Palestine Police Force, 1920–48* (Sussex: Academic Press 2016), p. 143.

[296] From *Air Force List*, 1935–40.

[297] Thomas, *Empires of Intelligence*, pp. 245–49.

[298] Ibid., p. 245.

[299] Ibid., p. 247.

[300] Force Intelligence Instruction No. 1, A. R. Ritchie, Wing Commander, General Staff, British Forces in Palestine and Transjordan, Jerusalem, 20 May 1938, Captured and Translated Arabic Material with Commentary, Wingate Papers, Microfilm M2313, BL.

[301] Ibid.

section under a police assistant superintendent with direct contact to Jerusalem headquarters and Army area commands.[302]

Cordial relations between military and Jewish intelligence officers aided joint operations. Gordon was the Jewish Agency's liaison person with RAF intelligence in Nablus, led by Captain (so presumably Flight-Lieutenant) Windsor, known to the Jews as 'the Duke.'[303] Windsor later set up a meeting between Danin and Captain Fitzpatrick, intelligence officer for the non-existent 9th Royal Hussars. Lash replaced Windsor, codenamed 'the Lion' by the Jews.[304] Meanwhile, Zaslani was Domvile's interpreter and they were friends well into the 1940s. The Jewish polit-ical leader David Ben-Gurion met with Domvile; earlier, in 1934, Jewish agent 'Hos' had characterised Domvile as the country's 'best Zionist informer on the English.'[305] There was another SSO officer, much used by the Jews, referred to as A. Hackett-Fine (a phonetic transliteration from Hebrew, so surely Hacket Pain above), codenamed 'Khamis' and an MI5 or MI6 agent, who replaced Lash and with whom Danin was 'tight.'[306] Danin acted as arbiter between the police and Army on the value of captured intelligence; he decoded and translated Arabic documents; and the British allowed him to interrogate captured rebels.[307] Meanwhile, Wingate as initially an intelligence officer in Palestine from 1936 had established excellent relations with *Shai* and talking to one of Wingate's biographers many years later, King-Clark remembered that his superior officer had a 'secure intelligence network through the Jewish Agency.'[308] Mike Grove noted Wingate's contacts with the Jews, too, 'from the top downwards,' including the future Israeli President, Chaim Weizmann, 'to the heads of all the settlements. They all knew Wingate.'[309] Simonds made the same point.[310] Wingate's Palestine papers in the British Library prove that he was exchanging masses of secret documents with the Jews. Jews dressed in Army uniforms on operations with the British, and

---

[302] Harouvi, *Palestine Investigated*, pp. 142–46; Knight, 'Securing Zion?,' p. 532.
[303] Danin, *Tsiyoni be-kol Tnay*, pp. 135–36.
[304] Ibid., pp. 135–36; Lefen, *Ha-Shai*, p. 44. The Jews also gave Lash the codename 'Lesh' it seems, the Arabic for 'why': Gershon Rivlin and Aliza Rivlin, *Zar Lo Yavin: Kinuye-Seter Ba-Yishuv Ha-Yehudi Be-Erets-Yisra'el* [*The Stranger Cannot Understand: Code-names in the Jewish Underground in Palestine*] (Tel Aviv: Ministry of Defence, 1988), p. 262 (information courtesy of Dr Steven Wagner).
[305] Tuvia Friling, *Arrows in the Dark: David Ben-Gurion, the Yishuv Leadership and Rescue Attempts during the Holocaust* (Madison, WI: University of Wisconsin Press, 2005), i, pp. 279–80.
[306] Lefen, *Ha-Shai*, p. 44; Danin, *Tsiyoni be-Kol Tnay*, pp. 135–36, 163.
[307] Gelber, *Shorshey ha-Havatzelet*, p. 164.
[308] R. King-Clark to Trevor Royle, 22 February 1993, MR4/17/307/1/4, TLSAC.
[309] Grove, 4510/03, p. 23, IWMSA.
[310] Typed Memoir, Pieces of War, p. 4, Simonds Papers, 08/46/1, IWMD.

British soldiers dressed as Jews in civilian clothes.[311] The Jews and the British also encouraged Palestinian–Arab anti-rebel forces. Thus, Danin noted many years later that Pinhas Meital, a Jewish officer from Hadera, possibly in the police, mediated with the British for the return of loyalist Arabs to Palestine in 1938.[312] Meanwhile, Jews such as David Hacohen of Haifa paid Arab loyalists.[313] The Jews also supplied the Nashashibis with weapons that may well have come from the Army.[314] Zaslani presented information to British security services and persuaded them of its use; he opened his regional network of agents to the SSOs, who reciprocated with funding.[315] The Army sent Jewish agents on missions to Lebanon and Syria, 'financed by the British secret services, and usually involved coordination with local British representatives, such as Gilbert MacKereth, the British Consul-General in Damascus.'[316] The 'flamboyant, fascinating and controversial' Domvile had a deep part in this secret work and his 'involvement in these matters was much more extensive than was previously known and practically nothing has been written about him.'[317] Domvile was closely connected with the Nashashibis, too, bringing the British, Jews, and Nashashibis together in a common intelligence front.[318] Meanwhile, Zaslani used *Shai* information to broaden his contacts with the British and the two groups met with peace bands and 'helped them and their men with funds and intelligence on the Mufti's gangs.'[319] The British 'promised pardons' and gave help to participating Palestinians.[320] The peak of combined British–Jewish operations was in late 1938 and 1939 when information from men like Danin grew in scale and quality to guide both Haganah and Army units, with jointly agreed code numbers given to villagers and rebel band members.[321]

Informers and agents needed paying: 'you've got to pay for your information if you want it,' in the words of policeman Geoffrey Morton.[322]

---

[311] Dekel, *Shai*, pp. 202–03; Slutsky, *Sefer Toldot ha'Haganah*. Volume 2, Part 2, *Me'Haganah le'ma'avak*, pp. 919–20.

[312] Danin, *Tsiyoni be-Kol Tnay*, p. 141.

[313] CID Intelligence Summary 92/38, Jerusalem, 31 December 1938, S25/22732, CZA.

[314] Cohen, *Army of Shadows, passim*; Eliyahu Elyashar, *Li-Hyot im Falastinim [To Live with Palestinians]* (Jerusalem: Sephardic Community Committee, 1975), pp. 65–70.

[315] Gelber, 'Reuven Shiloah's Contribution' and Harouvi, 'Reuven Zaslany' in Carmel, *Intelligence for Peace*, p. 18.

[316] Ibid.

[317] Eshed, *Reuven Shiloah*, pp. 23–24.

[318] Ibid., p. 24.

[319] Ibid., p. 33.

[320] Ibid.

[321] Gelber, *Shorshey ha-Havatzelet*, p. 164.

[322] Morton, 12960/6, IWMSA.

The Shaw Commission in 1930 had noted the lack of funds available for intelligence work and during the revolt more money was made available.[323] SSOs generally arranged this, one allotted £P.50 per month for the task. He met his agents 'at the dead of night in some far-off olive grove.'[324] Such agents were the source of the nebulous 'acting on information' comment in so many British operational files. RAF Middle East C-in-C Robert Brooke-Popham in Cairo authorised in July 1936 £5,000 for AOC Peirse in Palestine 'in order to bribe people to get certain essential information,' adding how even £10,000 'spent in this way will be an economy in finance alone if it shortens the trouble by a month.'[325] Simonds recalled that the RAF gave their SSOs 'bags of gold.'[326] British intelligence insisted that the 'Government should not be mean' as the

results obtained may save lives and, in the long run, expenditure many times greater than the outlay in s.s. [secret service] funds will be avoided. Persons entrusted with these funds must be exempted from the submission of accounts supported by receipts or even list of persons to whom the money has been paid as it is an elementary principle in such matters that the informer's name should not be revealed ... Everything possible should be done to organise this service independently of any other services whether police or military. DCs and others should of course show the information which they acquire with the police and military authorities but the informant should be known only to his immediate employer. *Such informants should on no account be called upon to give evidence before the Courts or even the police.*[327]

The money made available went to military officers and SSOs, leaving one civil officer with just £P.5 per month to obtain information.[328] An informer 'managed to coax' £P.3 from ADC civil officer Brian Gibbs based in Safad in a 'clandestine meeting on the road.'[329] A spy captured by rebels admitted that a Palestinian police corporal paid him £P.7 for each piece of information supplied, a considerable sum of money.[330] The Jewish Agency gave Danin money for information but the sums were relatively small for its key operative, £P.45 per month in 1939.[331] With

---

[323] Cmd. 3530, *Report of the Commission on the Palestine Disturbances of August 1929* (London: HMSO, 1930), p. 148.

[324] Letter, Street to Father, 29 May 1938, Street Papers, File: Letters Home, LHCMA.

[325] Letter, Brooke-Popham (HQ, RAF, Cairo) to ACM Ellington (London), 4 July 1936, Brooke-Popham Papers, 4/3/40, LHCMA.

[326] Typed Memoir, Pieces of War, p. 6, Simonds Papers, 08/46/1, IWMD.

[327] Report 'A.C.S.' marked Secret, S25/22740, CZA.

[328] Ibid.

[329] Letter, Gibbs to Fiancée, 25 May 1938, Gibbs Papers, GB165-0117, 1/2, MEC.

[330] Confessions of a Spy. Mahmad Mifleh el Ghurayeb of El Masaid was Arrested by the Fighters on 23.10.38 and Gave the Following Declaration, Captured and Translated Arabic Material with Commentary, pp. 97–99, Wingate Papers, Microfilm M2313, BL.

[331] Lefen, *Ha-Shai*, pp. 42–43.

this in mind, the British financed part of Danin's payments to informers and the two parties established a 'reciprocal relationship.'[332] Danin's informers helped with information for the Army on rebel bands and carried out 'identification during closure operations in villages.'[333] Danin passed this information back to the Jewish Agency, including that from interrogations that the military allowed him to conduct on captured rebels.[334]

The British used other recruitment methods for agents (or 'stooges') with code names such as 'the otter' and 'Albert.'[335] Brigadier Evetts in Haifa engineered the escape of Yousef Hamdan, Abu Durra's second-in-command, captured by the Army and then handed over to Wingate. The plan failed as the captured rebel refused then to turn in his comrades.[336] Other agents were more forthcoming. 'Said ez-Zreikeh' (possibly Sa'id al-Zurayq) had fallen out of favour with rebel commanders and the British used him to find arms caches and as a concealed spotter to pick out suspects on village searches.[337] An informer gave the exact house location for a gang rendezvous north of Jenin, the British noting that 'present orders to the gangs are to concentrate on informers and Jews and to leave Military and police alone.'[338] The Army dressed informers in military uniforms and took such men as guides with them on operations, as when 14th Brigade headquarters sent the RUR an informer-guide whose information prompted an early morning sweep to surround a village. The guide for whatever reason sent the riflemen up the wrong hill so 'the village of BAQA [possibly Baqa al-Sharqiyya near Tulkarm[339]] was not surrounded before first light, as would have been the case,' and after finding nothing of note there the soldiers dropped off the informer at Qalqilya.[340] Unarmed Arabs accompanied the Army as guides for three days a week on other occasions, unless they worked alone when soldiers gave them a weapon.[341] The Army made heavy use of informers behind gauze screens in military vehicles to pick out suspected villagers

[332] Gelber, *Shorshey ha-Havatzelet*, p. 164.
[333] Ibid.
[334] Ibid.
[335] Christopher Sykes, *Orde Wingate* (London: Collins, 1959), p. 168; Geoffrey Morton, *Just the Job: Some Experiences of a Colonial Policeman* (London: Hodder and Stoughton, 1957), pp. 94ff.
[336] Morton, *Just the Job*, pp. 84–85.
[337] Ibid., p. 80.
[338] Letter to W. S. Moffat (Jenin) copied to Pollock, 5 April 1938, Scrivenor Papers, MSS. Brit. Emp. S. 377, p. 150, WL.
[339] There are other Baqa villages east of Hadera, east of Hebron and one west of Nablus.
[340] CO 2nd RUR (Nathanya) to 16th Inf Bde, 23 March 1938, December 1937–March 1939 File, Palestine Box, RUR.
[341] Feitelson to Zaslani, 30 May 1939, S25/22424, p. 11, CZA.

who would be graded as oranges, lemons, and grapefruits, after which the police took them away for interrogation, or as blood oranges 'badly wanted' by the police in another operation.[342] Rebels noted that the head of the Opposition in Gaza and friend of Fakhri Nashashibi, Haj Adel (Hajj Adil, possibly Gaza's deputy mayor 'Adil al-Shawwa, some of the family supporting the Husaynis), went in an Army vehicle to Sarafand prison to identify arrested men and that 'he was not ashamed to enter an armoured car.'[343] Palestinians tried to escape screening by a slight change of their names but spotters made this difficult.[344] The Border Regiment hunting Abu Durra set up a radio in the house of one informer who had a list of villages and then a simple signal to send to say which village was the one to raid to capture the rebel leader. The regiment captured Abu Durra's baggage, sword, and papers this way, but not the man himself; rebels later shot the radio traitor.[345] Abu Durra's captured documents listed gang members alongside the make of their rifles, correspondence between rebel leaders and headquarters, letters to Abu Durra asking for cases to be tried by rebel courts, and a war diary. Once translated at Nablus, the documents enabled 14th Brigade to 'make a surprise raid on eleven villages north of NABLUS. Twenty-five gangsters, whose names were on the lists among Abu Dorrah's documents, were arrested.'[346] Haining noted the 'increasing willingness' by April 1939 of Palestinians to supply information on arms dumps and rebel personnel, partly due in his view to the way such disclosure paid off 'personal or family feuds'; he concluded that the 'stream of information cannot be said to flow freely as yet, but there was a decided improvement since the Autumn, and up to the start of the London Conference.'[347] Local villagers passed information on rebels to police in Beisan that was sent to the Transjordan Frontier Force stationed close by the town for actioning.[348]

The Nashashibis and their allies were another element to the expanding portfolio of security force intelligence. They not only supplied

---

[342] Hose, p. 5, 4501/03, IWMSA; Parrot, p. 25, 4514/04, IWMSA; War Diary, 16–30 April 1939, 2nd Bn Queen's Royal West Surrey Regiment, 3/6/6, p. 1, SHC.

[343] Appendix: Explanatory Notes, Captured and Translated Arabic Material with Commentary, p. 154, Wingate Papers, Microfilm M2313, BL.

[344] Appendix: Explanatory Notes, Captured and Translated Arabic Material with Commentary, pp. 102–04, Wingate Papers, Microfilm M2313, BL.

[345] Morton, 12960/6, IWMSA.

[346] Summary of Intelligence, Palestine and Transjordan, 12 August 1938, by Wing Commander Ritchie at GHQ [16/38], CO 732/81/9, TNA.

[347] Despatch on the Operations carried out by the British Forces in Palestine and Transjordan, 1 November 1938–31 March 1939, GOC Palestine to WO London, 24 April 1939, Evetts Papers, File 1, LHCMA.

[348] Lawson, 17330/38, IWMSA.

information and informers to the British and Jews, but their collaboration disorientated the Palestinians as to who was friend and who was
foe. Fakhri Nashashibi had been giving CID chief Harry Rice details
of meetings of Arab heads prior to the declaration to end the general
strike in October 1936.[349] The flow of information in the later stages of
the revolt increased as Hajj Amin's supporters attacked the Opposition.
Under threat from 'gangs,' the Fahoums of Nazareth who were connected
to the Nashashibis assisted the police: 'They had no choice; they could
not protect themselves, but the Government could protect them so they
became supporters of the Government.'[350] *Shai* operatives encouraged
the Nashashibi–British–Jewish coalition.[351] Fakhri Nashashibi worked
closely with Simonds and met him 'clandestinely, after dark' at his residence in Shaykh Jarrah, the Nashashibi quarter in Jerusalem: 'Fakhri
provided me with a lot of useful information, contacts and agents.'[352] As
the Army chased rebel band leader 'Arif 'Abd al-Raziq out of Palestine in
April 1939, GOC Haining looked to Fakhri Nashashibi so 'we may get
a bit more information.'[353] Haining's divisional commander, O'Connor,
similarly wrote how 'such information as is available' came 'to a great
extent' from the Nashashibi National Defence Party.[354] Simonds took
with him Defence Party people on village screening operations. He
hid them inside Army lorries and they triaged suspects into goats and
sheep rather than types of fruit by nudging them through the vehicle's
canvas cover.[355] Information is power; the insurgency was doomed.
Hamula family disputes and the Nashashibi–Husayni clash deflected
rebel counter-terror campaigns against collaborators but the fundamental challenge was the power of the front arrayed against insurrection: willing collaborators within the Palestinian community, mobilised
Jewish operatives, and a British-led intelligence front built on imperial
traditions and combined, centralised, multi-layered, multi-sourced,
military-led intelligence-gathering systems that extracted the information to enable pacification.

[349] Harouvi, *Palestine Investigated*, pp. 61–62.
[350] Nazareth Town, Political, Agitators, Gang Leaders and Terrorists, Palestine Police
Force, Report from Tiberias, M/4212/8, ISA.
[351] Eshed, *Reuven Shiloah*, p. 34.
[352] Typed Memoir, Pieces of War, p. 55, Simonds Papers, 08/46/1, IWMD.
[353] Letter, Haining to O'Connor, 14 April 1939, O'Connor Papers, 3/2/20, LHCMA.
[354] Letter, O'Connor to Keith-Roach, 30 January 1939, O'Connor Papers, 3/4/10,
LHCMA.
[355] Typed Memoir, Pieces of War, p. 136, Simonds Papers, 08/46/1, IWMD.

8   Dirty Wars and Extra-judicial Violence

Law and Morality

The Israeli–Palestinian author Sayed Kashua includes in the fictional book *Dancing Arabs* his grandmother's memory of how British soldiers during a punitive search of her house during the Arab revolt destroyed everything and then 'peed right in front of her. Grandma says one of them sat on a big container of olives and took a shit right into it. They poured everything out afterward, and saw the Englishman's shit, big chunks.'[1] This outrage raises pertinent legal-moral questions regarding judicial force during the revolt. While defecating as such was not the primary intention of British lawmakers, destruction and fouling of household effects were perfectly legal and widely used collective punishments under Emergency Regulations. Soldiers usually poured household olive oil over everything. Soldiers did not steal the olives. Theft was patently extra-judicial, for which the Army sanctioned its men, as were certain other acts such as rape. Otherwise, the colonial emergency state legally empowered mass violence that readily extended to non-binary, supra-judicial outrages. This explains why the state prosecuted so few security force personnel for extra-judicial abuse, as to do so would betray the 'judicial' parts of the system. The problem is partly measurement – it is not clear when, say, lawful and accepted punishments like canings and beatings became the extra-judicial violence of torture – but the central issue is that law in Palestine after April 1936 was not the formal restraint of power but concerned its practical execution. Civil and military emergency laws during insurrection redefined power and made all violence against all Palestinians bar offences like stealing judicial in the context of an emergency state that permitted abuse that would be extra-judicial in a non-colonial, non-emergency setting. (Indeed, the state stole from Palestinians legally through fining and confiscation of livestock and crops.) Shooting cordon-curfew breakers became assassinations, legal

---

[1] Sayed Kashua, *Dancing Arabs* (New York, NY: Grove, 2004), p. 32.

brutality and interrogation-detention led to torture centres, searching villages extended to leaving men to die of thirst in the sun, reprisals meant massacres, and all within the context of shared guilt and concomitant punishment. Military law sanctioned reprisals, with the most recent 1929 edition of the *Manual of Military Law* detailing 'retribution' upon 'innocent individuals' as an 'indispensable' measure.[2] This translated to Army reprisals against the nearest village for rebel combat actions such as roadside bombs. These reprisals encompassed 'legal' fines, detention, and destruction but might include 'illegal' torture and executions depending on the circumstances, the regiment concerned, and the men's 'mood,' the last a function of unit dynamics as readers will see below with the Manchester Regiment's 'gauntlet' torture. The Royal Ulster Rifles talked indirectly of 'severe reprisals' following the death of a soldier in a landmine attack on the 'Yirka track'[3] in February 1939 and whose form we can only imagine.[4] There was no need for punitive action or reprisals if Palestinians were purely passive, but they had to be wholly so as the joint venture rule discussed in Chapter 2 meant that any Palestinians reasonably proximate to any incident were liable for punishment for any action by any other Palestinians anywhere else. Only if the entire population was quiescent was judicial violence illegal (or extra-judicial) as without any state of insurrection there would be no emergency laws in force, just the latent threat of their (re)enforcement under Orders in Council.

As the judicial world of colonial pacification made systematic violence systemic, so it was the normative worlds of Servicemen and civil officials and how they interpreted the law that guided and restrained them – not what was extra-judicial but what security forces thought was right or wrong and so intra- or extra-legal. It is the lies that people tell and their justifications that betray this moral space, one that is fairly constant over time and across cultures, and one that makes violence less than absolute.[5] This explains the sole prosecution in Palestine (that this author has uncovered) of four policemen for executing in broad daylight in Jaffa in front of the public a prisoner whom they had previously tortured: public assassination on a main urban street could only be justified by prosecution and the lie that it was an aberration to the rule of

[2] *Manual of Military Law, 1929* (London: HMSO, 1940), pp. 103, 331ff, 343; *War Office, By Command of the Army Council, Notes on Imperial Policing, 1934* (London: War Office, 30 January 1934), pp. 12, 39–41.
[3] Yarka, a Druze village about six miles south-east of Acre.
[4] *Quis Separabit: The Regimental Journal of the Royal Ulster Rifles* 10/1 (May 1939), p. 28.
[5] See Michael Waltzer, *Just and Unjust Wars* (London: Allen Lane, 1978), *passim*.

law.[6] The policemen knew that their actions were extra-judicial as they tried to make the prisoner run (he refused, obviously knowing what would happen) so that they could then legally (and justifiably) shoot him 'trying to escape'; similar things had happened before in Ireland.[7] One policeman delivered the *coup de grâce* to the man after the initial rifle volley only left him writhing in agony and not dead, again showing personal moral sense, for which the policeman concerned received the longest sentence for manslaughter; the policemen also called for a lorry to take away the body. Location and visibility affected moral judgement: had a single murder like this happened in a distant village there would have been no repercussions, no need to pretend that a prisoner was trying to make a run for it, and no need to dispose of the corpse. Rather than use the courts, the Government deported back to the UK twelve policemen whose manifest 'wild rampage' it could not justify.[8] Torture centres fell into the same category of actions that were obviously wrong and unjusti-fiable, so the police hid them away. When police searched and beat Jews, they knew that their actions were wrong and that they could get caught, and so removed their uniform numbers; similarly, in Ireland in the early 1920s soldiers had dressed up as policemen and vice versa to disguise their shooting civilians or they blackened their faces.[9] Oblique language betrayed the normative world of pacification. Policemen noted the 'pre-vious cruel Turkish system,' while an Army company commander talked of the soldier having to work with 'one hand tied behind his back' so his men turned 'the blind eye' to supra-judicial actions that were norma-tively extra-judicial: 'We in Palestine certainly turned the blind eye!'[10] Policemen expressed their morality when they talked euphemistically of applying 'gentle persuasion' and 'third degree methods.'[11]

---

[6] Matthew Hughes, 'A British "Foreign Legion"? The British Police in Mandate Palestine,' *Middle Eastern Studies* 49/5 (2013), pp. 696–711; Letter, Burr (Depot Mt Scopus) to Mother and Father, n.d. [late 1937], Burr Papers, 88/8/1, IWMD.

[7] F. S. L. Lyons, 'The War of Independence,' in W. E. Vaughan (ed.), *A New History of Ireland. Volume 6, Ireland under the Union, 1870–1921* (Oxford: Clarendon, 1996), p. 250; Brig-Gen F. P. Crozier, *Ireland for Ever* (London: Jonathan Cape, 1932), p. 122.

[8] Letter, Burr (Depot Mt Scopus) to Mother and Father, n.d. [late 1937], Burr Papers, 88/8/1, IWMD.

[9] Letter, Mordechai Segali [phonetic translation] of Mount Carmel Residents' Association to Jewish Community of Haifa, 20 July 1938, File 5588/00282/2: The Commission of the Current Situation/Security, Jewish Community, 1938–1939, HMA; Crozier, *Ireland for Ever*, pp. 183–84; Richard Bennett, *The Black and Tans* (Severn: Severn House, 1976), p. 111.

[10] Jack Binsley, *Palestine Police Service* (Montreux: Minerva, 1996), p. 39; Brig J. V. Faviell, Typed Memoir, Fifty Days with a Company in Palestine, p. 1, Faviell Papers, 82/24/1, IWMD.

[11] Letter, Burr (Central Police Billet Box 523 Haifa) to Mother and Father, n.d. [c. May–June 1937], Burr Papers, 88/8/1, IWMD.

Self-generated moral restraint within security forces is the true measurement of 'extra-judicial' violence: what those carrying out pacification thought was immoral and beyond the law as they understood such things, not what was illegal in statute. For example, why did the soldiers in Kashua's account above only foul personal effects and not sexually assault or kill his grandmother as would have happened in many other pacification campaigns? Obviously, rape was illegal but so was stealing and soldiers stole things in the context of a military campaign that made theft possible and so permissible; abuse of civilians was intra vires so why not abuse women in the same way as menfolk? British soldiers behaved differently towards female Palestinians, partly as the Army ordered them to do so – itself an interesting institutional moral subject – but also as this was their personal proclivity, an issue discussed in Appendix C. Anthropology (or sociology) and not history is the better methodological tool here, alongside some understanding of national self-character and combat, as Anthony Beevor illustrates in his recent book on the battle of Arnhem.[12] Such moral boundaries – hard to quantify, subjective, and expressed differently by an ordinary soldier versus a long-standing Arabic-speaking District Commissioner – made systemic violence less than systematic, partly as many men were moral or regiments behaved properly but also because widely used visible legally empowered punishments made hidden abuse unnecessary. Nor did the Army want others to see it replicating the 'frightfulness' of the Germans in the Great War, as a British doctor in Hebron noted: 'Apparently the military authorities declare that they have issued strict instructions against "frightfulness." I don't know if this makes things better or worse.'[13] Such sentiments mitigated dirty wars run at a deeper level by elements within the security forces such as police CID whose 'G men' ran torture houses (eventually closed down after complaints from Palestinians and civil officials), by some Army units that massacred villagers as reprisals for lost comrades (divisional and brigade commanders had to protect regimental commanders from widespread protests that reduced the incidence and scale of such things), searches that led to numerous deaths (compensation was paid to villagers), and within some auxiliary units such as the Special Night Squads (disbanded, not least after protests from within the Army).[14] Those in charge measured extra-judicial incidents against

---

[12] Anthony Beevor, *Arnhem: The Battle for the Bridges* (New York, NY: Viking, 2018).

[13] Anon., *Frightfulness in Retreat* (London: Hodder and Stoughton, 1917); Diary, 14 May 1939, Forster Papers, GB 165-0109, pp. 119–20, MEC.

[14] Ogden (British Consulate Damascus) to L. Baggallay (FO), 8 September 1938, FO 371/21881, p. 235, TNA.

the location, the numbers killed, publicity, inevitability, and the cruelty used, accepting some while curtailing others. Palestinians protested such actions across the piece, as did the Anglican church mission in Jerusalem, some soldiers, Arab propaganda centres in London, the German and Italian press, British civil officials, and British residents of Palestine such as Frances Newton. When the Anglican Bishop of Jerusalem presented photographs of 'alleged incidents' by security forces, General O'Connor could only comment on how 'contemptible and disloyal this is, especially considering the Bishop's position.'[15]

Central military and political command structures never sanctioned or wanted dirty wars, at most tolerating supra-judicial violence that they measured normatively anyway. Civil officials knew that while military measures were 'most repressive' and 'distasteful,' nevertheless 'Repression of this kind – and it is drastic in the extreme – is most unpleasant work but it is essential if we are to make any headway.'[16] Senior military commanders were unambiguous on the value of violence but were equivocal on its limits when used as an aid to civil power, while civil officials like Scrivenor reined in tough divisional commanders such as Montgomery. General O'Connor leading 7th Division in Jerusalem expressed his ambivalence on levels of force to his wife when he wrote to her about police using '3rd degree methods' in prisoner interrogation but 'when you think of the various temptations that exist, and the brutal treatment the police have endured in the last few months, one can understand it not condone it,' adding that while there was 'definitely a certain degree of black and tan methods about the Police, as I have said they are a force at the moment without discipline. I have issued stringent orders against harshness and unnecessary violence on the part of our own soldiers and I am sure that will be obeyed apart from the odd few who there will always be.'[17] O'Connor singled out Brigadier Evetts in charge of 16th Brigade in Haifa in the north as someone who had 'always (between ourselves) encouraged his men to be brutal, as being in the end, more humane. I disagree with him over this,' but Montgomery and not O'Connor commanded Evetts as part of 8th Division that supported the SNSs and 'counter-terror.'[18] Subordinate regional brigade and area

---

[15] Letter, O'Connor to Haining, 17 December 1938, O'Connor Papers, 3/2/10, LHCMA.

[16] Letter, Battershill to Sir John Shuckburgh, 21 November 1937, Battershill Papers, MSS. Brit. Emp. S. 467, Box 10, File 3, WL.

[17] Letters, O'Connor to Wife, 22 October and 2–3 November 1938, O'Connor Papers, 3/1/16–18, LHCMA.

[18] Letters, O'Connor to Wife, 22 October and 2–3 November 1938, O'Connor Papers, 3/1/16–18, LHCMA; Charles Townshend, 'In Aid of the Civil Power: Britain, Ireland and Palestine, 1916–1948,' in Daniel Marston and Carter Malkasian (eds), *Counterinsurgency in Modern Warfare* (Oxford: Osprey, 2008), p. 32.

regimental commanders graded their use of force within command structures, so if one of the two divisional commanders (and then sub-divisional brigade commanders) in Palestine permitted more leeway then regimental character determined consequent levels of force. Company and platoon commanders might or might not follow suit, depending on small-unit internal dynamics. Palestinians and British Palestine policemen picked out Scottish regiments for the worst abuse: 'the damage and havoc they wrought in the villages,' 'they used the bayonet on the slightest excuse,' 'caught twelve Arabs sniping from a cul-de-sac in the grounds of the mosque of Omar and bayoneted them to a man,' 'if an Arab sees anybody in a kilt they run a mile,' and 'These savage actions are mostly committed by ROYAL SCOTCH REGIMENTS.'[19] Scotland's motto, *Nemo me impune lacessit* ('no one attacks me with impunity') was also the regimental one for the Black Watch, the Scots Guards, the Scots Fusiliers, and the Royal Scots, all of which served in Palestine. Regimental steadfastness continued after Palestine: Scots Guards were involved in the Batang Kali killings in Malaya in 1948, while Irish Republicans levelled charges of brutality and sectarianism against the Black Watch during the 'rape' of the Falls Road in 1970.[20] There is also the case of the Argyll and Sutherland Highlanders' tough actions in the Aden Crater in 1967. It only took a few men in a unit to prompt an extra-judicial incident, as it only took a handful of paratroopers (about four) in one company of one 800-strong battalion of the six-battalion Parachute Regiment to fire in ten minutes many of the fatal shots in Derry on 'Bloody Sunday' in 1972.[21] Focusing on harsh commanders and hard-charging regiments ignores myriad men within the sixty infantry battalions and armoured units that rotated through Palestine during the revolt whose behaviour was 'judicial' in that they considered and measured their legal and moral world.

Roy Baumeister talks of four 'roots of evil': evil as a means to an end, egotism and revenge, idealism, and the joy of hurting, or what a later British enquiry on Northern Ireland described as 'indifference' or

---

[19] Robert Martin, *Palestine Betrayed: A British Palestine Policeman's Memoir (1936–48)* (Ringwood: Seglawi, 2007), p. 72; Letter, Burr to Mother and Father, 27 May 1937 [date then crossed out], Burr Papers, 88/8/1, IWMD; Letter, Burr (British Police Depot Sick Bay Box 610) to Mother n.d. [late 1937], Burr Papers, 88/8/1, IWMD; Addressed to British Regiments in Palestine, Arab Revolutionary Council, Southern Syria, Palestine, Signed by Aref Abdul Razik ['Arif Abd al-Raziq], Commander in Chief of the Arab Forces in Palestine, 19 November 1938, Report on an Arab Commander, 41/94, HA.

[20] T. P. Coogan, *On the Blanket: The Inside Story of the IRA Prisoners' 'Dirty Protest'* [1980] (Houndmills: Palgrave, 2002), pp. 54–55.

[21] Douglas Murray, *Bloody Sunday: Truths, Lies and the Saville Inquiry* (London: Biteback, 2012), pp. 36, 151–52, 257, 262, 306.

'pleasure' in the victim's pain.[22] British soldiers never saw Palestinians as the 'half-human, ill-educated kaffir' whose remains could be left on display in company mess areas as white South Africans later did their black enemy: 'We did not think of the enemy as men.'[23] British soldiers' language may have been patronising and racist but it was not eliminationist. Commanders accepted rank-and-file revenge-brutality after deaths of soldiers but British soldiers were neither ideologically nor psychologically committed to evil in Palestine and they settled in the 'means to an end' category excepting when comrades were killed, when they temporarily wanted cruel revenge (what Christopher Browning calls 'battlefield frenzy') but even here regiments behaved differently.[24] There is undoubtedly a 'joy of hurting' in some of the accounts detailed here but soldiers had no 'skin in the game,' a point made to this author by rebel fighter Bahjat Abu Gharbiyya who remembered how while the Army mechanically destroyed villages it had no visceral attachment to the violence, unlike the police force and associated auxiliary units that tortured people 'in methods we would hear about in the Middle Ages.'[25] This mitigated both the scale and type of abuse. The same was true in Kenya in the 1950s during the Mau Mau insurgency where aux-iliary white settler and black loyalist police-reserve units and not the Army committed the foulest abuse. Security forces in Palestine never colluded to run semi-official dirty wars built on absolute violence; rather, sub-elements to the security apparatus – often those closest to the subject population and with the least regard for officially formed discipline such as police and settler-loyalist auxiliary units – instituted dirty wars whose temporary and partial character in the face of resist-ance from the entire system undercuts the claim for a systemic dirty war, unlike the one that, say, police chief Maurice Papon in France ran for the Algerian war.[26] Police CID in Palestine tortured suspects as it could not obtain, as the Army did, the necessary information without

---

[22] Roy F. Baumeister, *Evil: Inside Human Cruelty and Violence* (New York, NY: Freeman, 1997), chs 4–7; Compton Report (1971) quoted in John McGuffin, *The Guinea Pigs* (London: Penguin, 1974), p. 90.

[23] Anthony Feinstein, *In Conflict* (Windhoek: New Namibia, 1998), p. 70.

[24] Christopher Browning, *Ordinary Men: Reserve Police Battalion 101 and the Final Solution in Poland* (New York, NY: HarperCollins, 1993), pp. 160–61.

[25] The detail here is from Author interview, Bahjat Abu Gharbiyya, Amman, 21 June 2009 and subsequent elucidatory correspondence to Abu Gharbiyya via his son Sami Abu Gharbiyya, July–December 2009.

[26] Discussed in full in J. House and N. MacMaster, *Paris, 1961: Algerians, State Terror and Memory* (Oxford: Oxford University Press, 2006). See also Paul Aussaresses, *The Battle of the Casbah: Terrorism and Counter-Terrorism in Algeria, 1955–57* (New York, NY: Enigma, 2002), p. 122.

violence from paid informers and Jewish sources. Torture was a sign of weakness, disorder, and frustration – in short, systemic failure. This is not glibly to blame cruelty in Palestine on 'a few bad apples' – as one critic puts it in relation to the later 'Troubles' in Northern Ireland – and to ignore the racism and brutal history of empire but to ask comparative questions about dirty wars and how far abuse has to go to be systematised into a hidden sub-war.[27] Instead of an autonomous deep, dark regime of extra-ordinary, unregulated (or re-regulated), hard-edged torture and assassination, British military forces in Palestine preferred limited, managed, sustained punishments that were extensions to accepted operational methods and established rules. Extreme violence was reactive more than proactive. The Army massacred villages or carried 'mascots' after a rebel mine attack, soldiers killed villagers as they would not hand over rifles, and the police tortured Palestinians as they would not give information. The success of the Mandate emergency state's tight legal grip on Palestine alongside the Army's experience of pacification obviated the need for the extreme measures of less well-managed colonial administrations, and it meant that extra-judicial dirty wars in Palestine of deaths squads, assassinations, shooting of prisoners, massacres, and torture centres were not only incidental but localised, sporadic, personal, and unnecessary, unlike the necessary, visible, judicial, pacification regime of fining, curfews, demolition, and summary detention. This is not to diminish the grisly nature of the evidence presented here – echoing material throughout this book, all of which helped 'pacify' Palestinians – but violence came in many forms and focusing on sensational episodic brutality as detailed below detracts from the managed, official, and visible force that drove forward British pacification. The detail that follows moves from the systematic cruelty of police torture and Army reprisals to conclude with 'random' acts of violence that are harder to qualify, except to say that organised violence makes 'ordinary' men do extraordinary things.

Torture and Torture Centres

Police Special Branch across the British Empire usually led the fight against colonial insurgency. It poisoned insurgent food supplies and tampered with arms dumps; it drove forward interrogation, as in Rhodesia in the 1970s where 'Special Branch was brought in to assist' in beating suspects 'and we knew that they were real professionals at

---

[27] McGuffin, *The Guinea Pigs*, p. 136.

that kind of thing.'[28] Police CID fulfilled this role in Palestine and rebel fighter Bahjat Abu Gharbiyya in interview detailed torture by elements within CID.[29] British records support his claims. Abu Gharbiyya charged (phonetically) an Inspector 'Rex' or 'Ricks' with leading the abuse – probably a reference to Jerusalem-based CID Deputy Superintendent Alfred Riggs,[30] a point clarified in subsequent correspondence with Abu Gharbiyya.[31] (It should be noted here that a former Palestine policeman wrote to this author after seeing Abu Gharbiyya's allegations to say that it was 'hard to believe' that the 'amiable' Riggs was associated with torture.[32]) Abu Gharbiyya remembered that a Jewish police officer 'Sofer' took part in torturing suspects, a point supported by the written record in which two Britons, Biggs and Robinson,[33] and a Jew, Sofer,[34] were 'principal offenders.'[35] Robinson – of 'Greek' descent – once interrogated Abu Gharbiyya, who also recalled a 'notorious' Arab CID officer of (Christian) Lebanese origin, Munir Abu Fadil, who later became a member of Lebanon's parliament. Emile Ghoury in London wrote to William Ormsby-Gore, the Secretary of State for the Colonies, as early as September 1936 about the 'deplorable behaviour of the police in general, and of certain Police Officers, such as Messrs Sigrist, Schiff[36] and Langer' who 'worked towards the creation of violence.'[37] Abu Gharbiyya shot Assistant Police Superintendent Alan Sigrist by St Stephen's Gate

---

[28] Jake Harper-Ronald, *Sunday, Bloody Sunday: A Soldier's War in Northern Ireland, Rhodesia, Mozambique and Iraq* (Alberton: Galago, 2009), pp. 92, 186.

[29] Author interview, Bahjat Abu Gharbiyya, Amman, Jordan, 21 June 2009 (and subsequent correspondence).

[30] *Government of Palestine: Civil Service List 1937* (Jerusalem: Government Printing Press, 1937), p. 209.

[31] 'It does seem that Riggs is the person. Rex can be an Arabic mispronunciation of Riggs. "Inspector" in this context [the interview with the author on 21 June 2009] was used as a general term [by Bahjat Abu Gharbiyya] and not a precise rank.' Correspondence, Sami Abu Gharbiyya (son of Bahjat Abu Gharbiyya, present at the interview on 21 June 2009) to Author, 7 July 2009.

[32] Correspondence, Edward Horne to Author, 5 September 2009.

[33] Presumably CID Detective Inspector Robinson; the author has found no further reference to Biggs except that in translated Arabic material there is a note that Biggs 'left Palestine': Allegations of Ill-treatment of Arabs by British Crown Forces in Palestine (translated from the Arabic by F. Newton, 19 June 1939), J&EM Papers, GB165-0161, Box 65, File 5, p. 142, MEC.

[34] Presumably Solomon Soffer, who was a Detective Inspector in 1936 and a CID Acting Assistant Superintendent in 1938.

[35] Allegations of Ill-treatment of Arabs by British Crown Forces in Palestine (translated from the Arabic by F. Newton, 19 June 1939), J&EM Papers, GB165-0161, Box 65, File 5, p. 142, MEC.

[36] Presumably ASP Solomon Schieff, based in Jaffa in 1938.

[37] Letter, Emil Ghoury (London) to Ormsby-Gore (Secretary of State for Colonies), 8 September 1936, Arab Delegation to London: RG65: P3220/17, ISA.

in Jerusalem on 12 June 1936 in retaliation for his brutal behaviour, badly wounding him.[38] As a Palestinian girl remembered, Sigrist's name 'hissed down around every corner' as he struck 'out with his cane at the demonstrators, sometimes so ferociously as to break his arm. His aim, however, was to break the dignity and self-respect of the people.'[39]

Security forces conducted torture in dedicated police-run centres, especially (but not only) during a six-month stretch in late 1938 to 1939. As well as the central police headquarters at the Russian compound in west Jerusalem, CID had a separate, secret house at the Talavera military camp at the Allenby barracks in south Jerusalem, now covered by residential housing; another torture site was in Acre Citadel prison. According to Abu Gharbiyya, Arab suspects were 'lifted' from their homes and executed; others were tortured.[40] One CID officer told Abu Gharbiyya, who was working as a journalist at the time, 'You have not seen anything yet … we will use the same things against you as we did in Ireland.'[41] Abu Gharbiyya had friends who were abused a variety of ways. In addition to regular beatings in which guards knocked out suspects' teeth and which could leave victims 'almost unrecognizable,'[42] Abu Gharbiyya detailed a litany of torture, especially in the latter stages of the revolt:

- The simplest method – known, ironically, as 'playful' – involved tying a naked prisoner to a board with his legs raised and tied to a window. Jailers would then leave him there for several days during which time he would soil himself.
- Guards would treat prisoners as per the 'playful' method described above but they would also tie the prisoner's genitals, after which the guards would rub or beat the swollen organ. In at least one case, such torture led to the severing/tearing of the testicles, resulting in their having to be stitched. One British officer recalled a lighted cigarette applied to a Palestinian prisoner's testicles.[43]
- At the Talavera camp, police officers laid a 'religious man' on the ground, inserted a funnel into his mouth, and poured in water after which they stepped on the man's distended stomach.

[38] Matthew Hughes, 'A History of Violence: The Shooting of British Assistant Superintendent Alan Sigrist, 12 June 1936,' *Journal of Contemporary History* 45/4 (2010), pp. 725–43.

[39] Serene Husseini Shahid, *Jerusalem Memories* (Beirut: Naufal, 2000), pp. 91–92.

[40] Author interview, Bahjat Abu Gharbiyya, Amman, 21 June 2009 and subsequent elucidatory correspondence to Abu Gharbiyya via his son Sami Abu Gharbiyya, July–December 2009.

[41] Ibid.

[42] Prison Conditions in League for the Rights of Man, 28 December 1938, J&EM Papers, GB165-0161, Box 65, File 5, p. 116, MEC.

[43] David Smiley, *Irregular Regular* (Norwich: Michael Russell, 1994), p. 15.

- There was the 'crucifixion' torture in which guards laid the prisoner on a table with a 2 cm ridge running down the middle, along the prisoner's spine. They then tied sandbags to the prisoner's arms and legs.
- The police also used 'awful' local Arabs to rape (male) prisoners – employing a 'Castero/Kastero' in Jaffa and a 'Salih Alwalaji' in Jerusalem for this purpose, both later assassinated by the rebels but 'there were others' – to the extent that some handsome young Arab men would be detained for the purpose of sexual abuse.[44]

Jews made similar claims, although not specifically against the police, accusing the British of being like the 'Turks' in caning and flogging people.

As the barbarian Turks, the British flog the Jewish prisoners on their feet, smashing their genitals, days and night, till they pass out. As the Nazis in Dachau, British officer put his hands on a young Jewish lady's breasts, threatening her that she would be raped by soldiers ... We call to create a special committee to investigate all these cases and save the honour of Britain.[45]

The German newspaper *Deutsche Allgemeine Zeitung* spoke of how CID was 'Notorious and feared throughout the country' and detailed the 'inquisition methods of the Criminal Investigation Department against suspects from whom it wants to force a confession. In many cases prisoners were pumped full of water and then punched in the bloated stomach. Sanitary conditions in the concentration camp at Akko are unbelievable. The prison there contains a so-called flogging room where only British police are present.'[46] Similarly, the Arab Women's Committee in February 1938 wrote to the High Commissioner to direct his 'attention to the unheard-of methods of the Criminal Investigation Department.'[47]

CID-led violence by a stretched, collapsing police force is unsurprising. What is more surprising is how senior officers such as Sir Charles Tegart, the police officer brought in from India to give advice, countenanced torture centres known euphemistically as 'Arab Investigation Centres' where suspects got the 'third degree' until they 'spilled the beans'; the British only closed a major one in a Jewish quarter of west Jerusalem after colonial officials such as Edward Keith-Roach complained to the

[44] Author interview, Bahjat Abu Gharbiyya, Amman, 21 June 2009 and subsequent elucidatory correspondence to Abu Gharbiyya via his son Sami Abu Gharbiyya, July–December 2009.
[45] Notice entitled Jewish Youth, File 04/-163-B/621: Riots, April 1936 [but actually January 1939–February 1940] [one bundle of papers], TAMA.
[46] Quoted in anon., 'British Methods in Palestine,' *Yorkshire Post* (23 November 1938).
[47] Arab Women's Committee of Jerusalem to High Commissioner Palestine, 5 February 1938, FO 371/21875, p. 81, TNA.

High Commissioner.[48] The use of the phrase 'third degree' reappeared in Kenya, where the 'Arab' Investigation Centres were replaced with 'Mau Mau' ones.[49] Interrogators in Palestine used the 'water-boarding' torture at these centres.[50] Abu Gharbiyya stated that torture only ended in Jerusalem after questions were asked in Britain's Parliament, possibly a reference to a question to the Secretary of State for the Colonies in June 1939 about 'gross' charges against the Mandate authorities, 'foul and filthy ones.'[51] Keith-Roach, to his credit, raised the issue that the 'questionable practices' carried out by CID officers on suspects were counter-productive both in terms of the information gathered and the effect that they had on local people's confidence in the police.[52] References to the torture houses found their way back to London, with the High Commissioner having to reply to the Colonial Office about an 'allegation that a picked body of British police' were 'using "third degree" methods' in a house formerly occupied by police Inspector General Roy Spicer in Jerusalem.[53] Police had used this empty house to detain suspects after Andrews' assassination in September 1937. Spicer stepped down as Inspector General of Police in November 1937 and Colonel Alan Saunders, his replacement as police chief, told the High Commissioner that it was essential to hold such prisoners incommunicado but

no accommodation was available in any prison or lock-up which would have ensured complete segregation. Undoubtedly, and indeed inevitably, there were cases in which rough measures were employed ... but Saunders assures me that there is no foundation whatever for the allegation that various forms of torture were used and states that this was proved in a recent police and medical investigation. The house has not been used for many months for the detention and examination of prisoners and in fact is now occupied by Munro, the officer in charge of the police training school.[54]

---

[48] Edward Keith-Roach (ed. Paul Eedle), *Pasha of Jerusalem: Memoirs of a District Commissioner under the British Mandate* (London: Radcliffe, 1994), p. 191; Tinker, 4492, pp. 34–35, IWMSA; Charles Smith, 'Two Revolts in Palestine: An Examination of the British Response to Arab and Jewish Rebellion, 1936–48' (Doctoral Thesis: University of Cambridge, 1989), pp. 114–19; Anwar Nusseibeh, 28 March 1977, Lever Arch File: Nigel Maslin, Thames TV Material on 'Palestine: Promises, Rebellion and Abdication' (1977–78), IWMFA.

[49] Caroline Elkins, *Imperial Reckoning: The Untold Story of Britain's Gulag in Kenya* (New York, NY: Holt, 2005), pp. 63, 87.

[50] Tom Segev, *One Palestine, Complete: Jews and Arabs under the British Mandate* (New York, NY: Owl, 2001), pp. 416–17.

[51] Author interview, Abu Gharbiyya, Amman, 21 June 2009; Question by Mr Maxton to Secretary of State for Colonies in *Hansard*, HC Deb, 28 June 1939, vol. 349, cc401–02.

[52] Typed two-page document by Edward Keith-Roach, untitled or dated, at the end of which is added pencilled comment, Keith-Roach Papers, AL-KR.

[53] High Commissioner to Shuckburgh (CO), 20 October 1938, FO 371/21865, p. 197, TNA.

[54] Ibid.

It is not clear why a civilian house would give more security and segregation than a purpose-built prison unless the aim was to hide torture. Saunders supported his men. When police 'smartened' up a Jew
with rubber truncheons causing 'blood to spurt from his nose and ears'
in front of a British clergyman in the station to report his car stolen,
'Saunders took no action in the matter at all except to write and inform
the Revd. Gentleman that he had complete faith in his officers and their
actions.'[55] The police punished the clergyman by giving him a court date
for fake parking tickets: 'We'll fix him,' one noted.[56] Some policemen
appreciated Saunders as he was 'all for rougher methods and it helps a
lot when you know their [sic] is someone to back us up. Spicer was all
the brown brother business and people have actually been dismissed for
thrashing taxi drivers and shopkeepers when they have had the audacity
to ask for payment.'[57] Arab propaganda over abuse exercised London,
and the Foreign Office wrote to MacKereth in Damascus about the
High Commissioner's investigation into the use of Spicer's house and
any 'third-degree methods' and how 'if such things do take place, they
ought to be stopped at once.'[58] British Consulate officials in Damascus
took the matter of Spicer's house a step further, talking of a 'picked body
of men, all British, who are sworn to secrecy' using 'Third degree persuasion' and how the

victims are taken by night to a house outside Jerusalem which used to be the
house of Spicer, the former Inspector-General of the Palestine police. Here the
G-men, as I am told they are called, are permitted to inflict every kind of torture
they can think of. Beaumont, when in Jerusalem a week or two ago, was told
by a British policeman of some of the methods he himself had seen used. On
one occasion an Arab had been suspended upside down and a policeman had
urinated into his nostril. He was taken down just before he succumbed.'[59]

A representative from Britain's Beirut Consulate went to see High
Commissioner MacMichael in late September 1938 to express his
concerns, to which the High Commissioner admitted to some 'roughness,'
adding that allegations should be suppressed and how he would speak
to the Army GOC.[60] The timeline is significant: Qassamite gunmen shot
Andrews in September 1937 and a year later in September 1938 the

[55] Letter, Burr (Inlying Piquet Haifa) to Father, n.d. [last days of 1937?], Burr Papers, 88/
    8/1, IWMD.
[56] Ibid.
[57] Ibid.
[58] FO to MacKereth (Damascus), 14 November 1938, FO 371/21865, p. 199, TNA.
[59] Ogden (British Consulate Damascus) to Baggallay (FO), 8 September 1938, FO 371/
    21881, p. 235, TNA.
[60] Furlonge (Beirut Consulate) to Baggallay (FO), 27 September 1938, FO 371/21881,
    p. 243, TNA.

same torture house was still in operation; it then seems to have been closed down, at the moment after the Munich settlement when troops flooded in and pacified the country using standard, less draconian operational methods. Spicer's house resembles the building at al-Biar near Algiers where French paratroopers and legionnaires tortured suspects in the 1950s, but without the automatic post-torture execution common in Algeria.[61] The unofficial detention centre in Spicer's house may have been a temporary measure and eventually closed but it was not the only one; nor did torture only happen in dedicated torture centres.

There was the issue of whether torture left marks, some methods having an advantage here. Policeman Duff saw a 'great deal' of the 'beating and "third degree"' endured by 'hill villages near the scene' of a 'crime,' what he called 'bastinadoings.'[62] The problem was that such whippings left marks, unlike the 'Hoist,' or 'water-can' that left 'no traces for doctors to detect':

The victim was held down, flat on his back, while a thin-spouted coffee-pot poured a trickle of water up his nose, while his head was clamped immovably between cushions that left no marks of bruising. It is not pleasant to talk about and even unpleasanter to admit having witnessed. Usually, we British officers remained discreetly in the background, not wishing to have the skirts of our garments soiled, but we were ready to benefit by information wrung by our subordinates from the wretched suspects or criminals.[63]

The British absolved themselves by getting Jewish guards in prison to beat Arab suspects and vice versa, while a British officer working with loyalist Arab troops in the Transjordan Frontier Force remembered how they had to make villagers more frightened of the security forces than the rebels, so some of his Arab officers would sometimes say, '"Well, look, you look tired. Go and take your lunch the other side of the hill." And one under the circumstances wouldn't be quite certain what went on while you were away but the information might or might not be forthcoming.'[64] A tortured suspect after 'gentle persuasion' gave information to the police on arms hidden on a village threshing room, one policeman adding that he hoped that they were there 'for his sake. Most of the information we get is extracted by third degree methods, it is the only way with these people.'[65] Prisoners at other detention sites jumped to their

[61] Henri Alleg, *The Question* (New York, NY: Braziller, 1958), *passim*; Aussaresses, *The Battle of the Casbah*, pp. 117ff.
[62] Douglas Duff, *Bailing with a Teaspoon* (London: John Long, 1953), p. 168.
[63] Ibid.
[64] Prison Conditions in League for the Rights of Man, 28 December 1938, J&EM Papers, GB165-0161, Box 65, File 5, 116, MEC; Tinker, 4492/03, pp. 34–35, IWMSA.
[65] Letter, Burr (Central Police Billet Box 523 Haifa) to Mother and Father, n.d. [c. May–June 1937], Burr Papers, 88/8/1, IWMD.

deaths from high windows to escape their captors; they had their testicles tied with cord; they were tortured with strips of wood with nails in; they had wire tightened around their big toes; hair was torn from their faces and heads; special instruments were used to pull out fingernails; red hot skewers were used on detainees; prisoners were sodomised; boiling oil was used on prisoners as were intoxicants (morphine, cocaine, and heroin); there were electric shocks; water was funnelled into suspects' stomachs; and there were mock executions.[66] When commenting on reports of abuse by Frances Newton, MacKereth wrote to Battershill in May 1938 about whether she should be deported (she was, eventually), after which a handwritten note was added to one of Newton's London-based Arab Centre pamphlets entitled 'Punitive Measures in Palestine,' perhaps by a civil servant, which read: 'Not correct: one of them was kept under an ice cold spray till he gave away the names of his friends. He jumped out of a 4th storey window not off the roof and crashed naked onto the pavement below – missing a Jewess who was passing by only a few inches!'[67] This does not appear to be a note by Newton, not least as MacKereth commented in the same file: 'Obviously if we cannot keep our own people in order.'[68] Newton's view was that 'the police asked per-mission to use torture to the prisoners to extract information and that permission was granted from the Colonial Office. Several of the leading police officers in Jerusalem refused to countenance it. One of them has since left the country,' a measure of the friction within security forces that retarded absolute violence.[69] Arab propaganda from Damascus made similar points, reporting how a man was 'taken from his home by soldiers, his head covered with a piece of cloth. They took him to an unknown destination where they tied his sexual organs by a piece of string and pulled them in different directions and pressed him until he was nearly dead.'[70] Arab-based reports echoed some of the claims above made by Abu Gharbiyya and picked up on the sexualised content to abuse, usu-ally against male prisoners. Thus, the Army picked up a Mohamed Abdul

---

[66] Palestine Prisons for Howard League for Penal Reform, 6 April 1938, J&EM Papers, GB165-0161, Box 65, File 5, pp. 76ff, MEC; Allegations of Ill-treatment of Arabs by British Crown Forces in Palestine (translated from the Arabic by Frances Newton, 19 June 1939), J&EM Papers, GB165-0161, Box 65, File 5, pp. 141–43, MEC; Extract from Syrian Press ('Fata el-Arab'), 23 February 1938, CO 733/368/4, p. 80, TNA.

[67] Mackereth (Damascus) to Battershill (Palestine), 24 May 1938, FO 371/21877, p. 49, TNA.

[68] Ibid.

[69] The Alleged Ill-treatment of Prisoners by F. Newton (sent to the Howard League for Penal Reform), 15 April 1938, J&EM Papers, GB165-0161, Box 65, File 5, p. 94, MEC.

[70] Bulletin issued by Bureau Nationale, Damascus [summer 1938], Creech Jones Papers, MSS. Brit. Emp. S. 332, Box 30, File 2, WL.

Qader al-Yason (Muhammad 'Abd al-Qader al-Yasin), a thirty-year-old farmer found in a village not his own, after which at 'an unknown place' in Jerusalem 'soldiers came and tied ropes to his arm' and 'proceeded to hoist him from the ground' while another beat and interrogated him about rebel band leaders 'Arif 'Abd al-Raziq and 'Abd al-Rahim al-Hajj Muhammad.[71] The suspect said nothing (or had nothing to say), so guards took him down and wrapped his head in a blanket and took him to another 'unknown place' where soldiers and police stripped him: 'he was then laid out on his stomach and his hands tied behind his back, a soldier kneeling on them to hold him down, while his feet were pulled up backwards,' after which his guards whipped him with a cane whereupon he lost consciousness.[72] When he regained consciousness, guards

inserted the thick end of one of the canes in his anus and started working it to the right and the left, back and forth until he again fainted. On his coming to they took strong threads of hemp and tied his testicles with thread, each testicle with a different thread. Then each person took hold of the end of a thread and they began to jerk them in opposite directions until they felt that he was on the point of death, when they left off. Others then came and began to rub his testicles in the palms of their hands and finally to squeeze them violently. [An Israeli interrogator, a 'Captain George,' whose proper name was later revealed, allegedly sodomised a Lebanese suspect, Mustafa Dirani, in the same manner in the 1990s.][73]

The man's ordeal was not over. Guards continued to punch al-Yason, after which he was again wrapped in a blanket and taken to another secret location and kept there and tortured for three days, including by some men who 'visited him in this place bringing dogs which were set upon him and tearing his thighs,' and only after this attack did guards take him blindfolded to Acre prison.[74] The anal rape of male prisoners reappeared in Northern Ireland in the early 1970s: 'It was barbaric, they put him in overalls and cut out the crotch and dragged him over the concrete, so his testicles were practically raw, and then they got a brush shaft and stuck it up his anus.'[75] Joint police (often Special Branch)–military

---

[71] Bulletin No. 210, 4 September 1938, Arab National Bureau in Damascus, FO 371/21880, p. 211, TNA.

[72] Ibid.

[73] Ibid.; Yonah Jeremy Bob, 'Supreme Court: Lebanese Terrorist Can't Sue Israel for Interrogators' Alleged Rape,' *Jerusalem Post* (15 January 2015); Tomer Zarchin and Gili Cohen, 'Ex-IDF Investigator Accused of Abuse, Torture of Mustafa Dirani to Sue State,' *Haaretz* (23 January 2012); Revital Hovel, 'Gag Order Lifted,' *Haaretz* (30 December 2013).

[74] Bulletin No. 210, 4 September 1938, Arab National Bureau in Damascus, FO 371/21880, p. 211, TNA.

[75] Interview with Charles Morrison in Joanne O'Brien, *A Matter of Minutes: The Enduring Legacy of Bloody Sunday* (Dublin: Wolfhound, 2002), p. 24; Fathers Denis Faul and

torture centres after Palestine were located in Army bases: in Fort Morbut and Waterloo barracks (or Lines) in Aden in the 1960s, and Palace and Girdwood barracks in Northern Ireland in the early 1970s.[76]

Police violence smacked of frustration and loss of discipline. British Assistant District Commissioner Aubrey Lees (a former soldier) wrote of the police reaction to a raid by a rebel band on Hebron in August 1938, after which the police punished the inhabitants: 'the British police, no less valiant in "suppressing disorder," had set fire to three shops, utterly gutting them, and had then looted three general goods stores, stealing some £300 worth of goods and altogether doing damage later assessed by a C.I.D. Committee of Enquiry (which would presumably not err on the side of extravagance) at £3,000.'[77] The official phrase for such police operations was 'restoring order,' as Lees noted ironically.[78] Lees later wrote to the (new) Secretary of State for the Colonies, Malcolm MacDonald, about this rebel raid in 1938 and the 'the comparatively trivial matter of the two old men and two boys wantonly shot and permanently disabled by troops' and how he had reported this to Battershill, after which the High Commissioner 'authorized the payment of £250 to these persons. I have no knowledge of similar compensation ever been paid to the scores of similar victims in other places, and indeed if the action taken in Hebron had been taken everywhere it is doubtful whether the Treasury could have met it.'[79] Extra-legal police brutality could be crude and outside any hidden torture centres. Thus, a group of police raided the homes of poor Palestinian families in the Manshiya district on the border between Jaffa and Tel Aviv on 23–24 October 1938. It is not clear why police targeted this poor neighbourhood. The police made the

Raymond Murray, *British Army and Special Branch RUC Brutalities, December 1971– February 1972* (Cavan: Abbey, 1972), *passim*.

[76] Amnesty International (Peter Benenson), *Aden 1963–1966: A Report by Amnesty International* (London: Amnesty, 1966); Amnesty International (S. Rastgeldi), *Aden Report* (London: Amnesty, 1966); *Report by Roderic Bowen QC on Procedures for the Arrest, Interrogation and Detention of Suspected Terrorists in Aden, 14 November 1966* (London: HMSO, 1966); Aden reports in the (Scottish) *Sunday Mail* of 17 December 1978, 26 April 1981, 3 May 1981, and 10 May 1981; Fred Halliday, *Arabia without Sultans* (New York, NY: Vintage, 1975), pp. 215–19; Faul and Murray, *British Army and Special Branch RUC Brutalities, passim*; McGuffin, *The Guinea Pigs, passim*. See also David Cesarani, *Major Farran's Hat: Murder, Scandal and Britain's War against Jewish Terrorism, 1945–48* (London: Heinemann, 2009).

[77] Memoir by Lees, Unbeaten Track: Some Vicissitudes in Two Years of a Public Servant's Life by el-Asi, Lees Papers, 5/13, p. 2, LHCMA.

[78] Memoir by Lees, Unbeaten Track: Some Vicissitudes in Two Years of a Public Servant's Life by el-Asi, Lees Papers, 5/13, p. 3, LHCMA.

[79] Letter, Lees to MacDonald (Secretary of State for Colonies), 8 January 1939, Lees Papers, 5/8, LHCMA.

mistake of committing the outrage when Lees was in the area. Officers beat up local people, a two-year-old girl had her femur broken by a bullet as police opened fire on a woman trying to bar their entry (wounding the woman, too), houses were robbed, men cudgelled, windows broken, police broke chairs on people's heads, they beat Palestinians with pistol butts, police kicked men in the testicles so badly that the victims were hospitalised, police smashed up a local bakery, and they assaulted the bakery staff. Lees 'found the wrecked and blood-spattered rooms and the bullet holes, and I saw the less seriously injured victims. In one room I found an old man of evidently well over eighty years, lying on the floor on his blood-stained bedding, a blood-soaked bandage around his head, and his poor belongings lying in shreds and splinters around him.'[80] The police also humiliated women in Manshiya, lining them up, questioning them in Arabic, 'asking them their names and saying "How much to-day?" God knows what they meant. They then made indecent gestures with their revolvers and sticks.'[81]

Assassinations and Death Squads

Tacit official backing (or more exactly an unwillingness to sanction anyone) for the Manshiya operation was such that when Lees protested to the British Chief Magistrate and gave the name of one policeman involved nothing happened. More seriously, furious local Palestinians drew his attention to the scene of an assassination of an Arab suspect in the Manshiya neighbourhood on the morning of 24 October 1938, the day after Lees was dealing with the attack on Manshiya. On the spot, recording the assault on the residents of Manshiya, Lees discovered a public assassination by police nearby. Lees collated the statements from seventeen witnesses who saw four uniformed British policemen stop their Dodge saloon car in the street in Jaffa and force out of the vehicle a handcuffed Arab with them in the car, Muhammad Haddad, telling him to run. They tried this twice. Haddad refused to move, obviously aware that once he was some distance from the officers they would shoot him while escaping. When he refused the second time, the police shot him with a rifle from about two metres as he stood close to the officers, after which the man faltered, a volley of shots then left

<hr />

[80] Memoir by Lees, Unbeaten Track: Some Vicissitudes in Two Years of a Public Servant's Life by el-Asi, Lees Papers, 5/13, p. 4, LHCMA.

[81] The Manshia Exploits of the Three British Policemen in Mufti during the Night of 23–24 October, 1938, Exploit No. 1, Khalil Hamameh and Witness Statements, Forster Papers, GB165-0109, pp. 79ff, MEC.

Haddad writhing on the ground, at which point one of the officers, W. E. T. Wood, shot him with his pistol at close range. Haddad refused to die and, still writhing, he tried to raise himself on his elbow, 'whereupon one of the other policemen stooped down and struck him a blow on the side of his head with his fist. After this the Arab lay still and the four Policemen started smoking cigarettes and laughing.'[82] A police truck later came to the scene and picked up the body. An official report said that the dead man had been shot 'while attempting to escape.'[83] A policeman later the same day stopped at the local garage of Amin Andrawus (also spelt Andraus) – a local man who had seen the outrage – and spoke to the garage clerk about what had happened: '"Know all about that. The man was a gangster, and had to be killed," or words to that effect. The clerk remonstrated, saying that if he was a gangster he should be properly tried and convicted, to which the constable replied, "No, it's better to kill him like this," or words to that effect.'[84] Andrawus feared for his life as a material witness and fled to Beirut. His family and friends had urged him not to appear as a witness 'as it might cost him his life.'[85] In a plea to the Palestine High Commissioner, Andrawus wrote: 'I make this report in great fear of my own life and that of my wife and family. Murder by the police is not uncommon there are so many means available to them to carry it out. I ask Your Excellency's personal security for myself and my family be protected against police vengeance.'[86]

Lees, meanwhile, made an official report that helped to prompt a trial of the four policemen in December 1938. The policemen involved – T. Mansell, P. Crossley, W. E. T. Wood, and T. Crossley – received sentences in January 1939 ranging from being bound over (the two Crossleys) to one year in jail (Mansell) to three years for Wood (for manslaughter). The courts reduced Mansell's sentence on appeal.[87] Wood had had 'the comparative decency to administer the "coup de grace" to the poor wretch whose bowels were protruding from wounds in the back' and he paid the judicial price as it was his pistol that delivered

---

[82] The Manshia Exploits of the Three British Policemen in Mufti during the Night of 23–24 October, 1938, Incident of the Bumped off Gangster, GB165-0109, pp. 80ff, MEC. This material is also in J&EM Papers, GB165-0161, Box 66, File 2, MEC.

[83] The Manshia Exploits of the Three British Policemen in Mufti during the Night of 23–24 October, 1938, Incident of the Bumped off Gangster, GB165-0109, p. 82, MEC.

[84] Ibid.

[85] Statement of Mr Amin Andraus (Jaffa), 27 October 1938, J&EM Papers, GB165-0161, Box 66, File 5, MEC.

[86] Andraus (Jaffa) to High Commissioner (Palestine), 26 October 1938, J&EM Papers, GB165-0161, Box 66, File 5, MEC.

[87] 'Allegations of Irregular Conduct Denied in London,' *Palestine Post* (11 December 1938).

the final shot, leaving him accused of the most serious charge.[88] The colonial Government had neutered the Palestine judiciary following the Jaffa ruling by British Chief Justice McDonnell that had gone against the Government in 1936, as detailed in Chapter 5, and by 1938 the judiciary knew its place and returned (without a jury, as was the case in Palestine) the astonishing verdict of 'attempted manslaughter' on Wood. The Colonial Secretary made the most of this judgement, telling Parliament in London that abuse allegations were unfounded but if found the Government would not hesitate to prosecute offenders.[89] The Cabinet in London reported in December 1938 that 'the fact that we were determined to deal sternly with the case might mitigate to some extent the damage.'[90] Meanwhile, the High Commissioner sent the troublesome Lees home to the UK, a tale told in detail by an angry Lees in his private papers. Afterwards, police officers broke into Lees' home in Jaffa – Soviet secret police 'OGPU' methods as a friend of Lees pointed out.[91] British friends had told Lees before he left Palestine not to sit by un-curtained windows or be out of doors after dark lest he 'stop' a 'stray bullet' from the offended police.[92] S. O. Richardson of Jaffa, a British lawyer and local representative of the Federation of British Industries, wrote to the High Commissioner regarding the Manshiya assassination, concluding how if the High Commissioner were to take any action, 'I ask that you will if possible suppress my name. Even an Englishman of some prominence is in no small danger in these days if he offends the police.'[93] Such fears give a sense of the dirty war being run by the police in Palestine and it may be that being white and British did not guarantee protection from

[88] Memoir by Lees, Unbeaten Track: Some Vicissitudes in Two Years of a Public Servant's Life by el-Asi, Lees Papers, 5/13, pp. 6–7, LHCMA.

[89] Ibid.

[90] Extract from Cabinet Conclusions 58(38), 7 December 1938, FO 371/21868, p. 105, TNA.

[91] Lees to M. MacDonald, 8 January 1939, Lees Papers, 5/8, LHCMA; Lees to High Commissioner (Palestine), 31 October 1938, Lees Papers, 5/8, LHCMA; S. O. Richardson (Federation of British Industries, Jaffa) to High Commissioner (Palestine), 26 October 1938, J&EM Papers, GB165-0161, Box 66, File 5, MEC; Lees to Under Secretary of State (CO), n.d., Lees Papers, 5/8, LHCMA; Habib G. Homsi (Advocate Jaffa) to Lees, 3 June 1939, Lees Papers, 5/10, LHCMA; Richardson (Solicitor, Jaffa) to Lees, 29 July 1939, Lees Papers, 5/9, LHCMA; Lees (Assistant District Commissioner) to District Commissioner, Southern District, 25 October 1938, Forster Papers, GB165-0109, p. 77, MEC; Memoir by Lees, Unbeaten Track: Some Vicissitudes in Two Years of a Public Servant's Life by el-Asi, Lees Papers, 5/13, pp. 6–7, LHCMA; OGPU methods see Richardson to Lees, 9 June 1939, Lees Papers, 5/9, LHCMA.

[92] Memoir by Lees, Unbeaten Track: Some Vicissitudes in Two Years of a Public Servant's Life by el-Asi, Lees Papers, 5/13, p. 11, LHCMA.

[93] S. O. Richardson (Federation of British Industries, Jaffa) to High Commissioner (Palestine), 26 October 1938, J&EM Papers, GB165-0161, Box 66, File 5, MEC.

police depredations in Palestine (such as extra parking fines), but British police never tortured white British residents as a French Foreign Legion 'specialist' did Frenchman Henri Alleg in Algeria in the 1950s; indeed, French torturers in Algeria claimed that when they had a 'European' to work on they would 'look after him better than the "wogs".'[94]

Determining the details surrounding the murky business of police assassinations is problematic. Lees was sure that the police shooting of Haddad was 'by no means unique,' as he told the Secretary of State for the Colonies in January 1939, but was simply the only one made public and so the 'the conclusion is inescapable that the responsible officials of the Palestine Administration do not favour any revelation of acts of "counter-terrorism" and that both the High Commissioner and yourself are kept in the dark as to events which are known not only to the "man-in-the-street" in Palestine and neighbouring countries but to all foreign Powers who have consulates in Palestine.'[95] Partial names of those responsible emerge from the archives. The post-script to a letter from Richardson to Lees in 1939 about shame and men with a conscience mentioned the Miska village executions by police in May 1938 (as touched on in Chapter 5) and how those responsible 'would have fallen – as distinct from those actually involved of course – Fitzgerald, Miller and the Serg. (who committed suicide).'[96] Many Servicemen thought the extreme violence of field executions justified. One officer talked of the Miska affair as a battle in which the police killed six rebels but 'I heard afterwards from the police that three of them had surrendered to the police who then had them bumped off – can't say I blame them either.'[97] Writing to Lees about another incident, Richardson noted how the 'man who is really responsible for these murders was of course Collinge who has now joined the murdered,' adding that the 'victim is the son of the litigant Ibrahim Abu Kuheil whom you know, a youth of 21. As far as I can ascertain he was shot merely in mistake for an alleged terrorist.'[98] This refers to an assassination at Jaffa's Dajani hospital by police of an alleged terrorist – or a witness in a trial, it is not entirely clear – in which the assassins who had been 'ordered to bump off' the suspect shot the wrong man, 'the first wounded man they could find, in the hope of clicking for the King's

---

[94] Alleg, *The Question*, pp. 50, 109. The expression 'wogs' is translated from the French slang *troncs*: Henri Alleg, *La Question* (Paris: Minuit, 1958), p. 26.
[95] Letter, Lees to MacDonald (Secretary of State for Colonies), 8 January 1939, Lees Papers, 5/8, LHCMA.
[96] Post-script to Letter, Richardson (Solicitor, Jaffa) to Lees, 6 April 1939, Lees Papers, 5/9, LHCMA.
[97] Letter, Street to Father, 29 May 1938, Street Papers, File: Letters Home, LHCMA.
[98] S. O. Richardson (Solicitor, Jaffa) to Lees, 29 July 1939, Lees Papers, 5/9, LHCMA.

Police Medal which usually follows these episodes in Palestine.'[99] The incident that Richardson was referring to was at the private Dajani hospital on 15 June 1939 when a party of police in mixed uniform and mufti appeared. Some of them climbed over the wall, while others knocked at the door. When let in by the doorman, a group of four policemen went to a ward in which was one Ibrahim obn (or ibn) Khail (sic, presumably the son of the person as mentioned above, spelt Khalil Abu Khalil in another file, probably Ibrahim Ibn Khalil), suffering from a bullet wound in the shoulder inflicted by police four days earlier.[100] 'As the light was switched on, the man wakened from sleep and finding himself covered by revolvers sat up in bed with a scream. The police fired one shot through his head, blowing out his brains, and retired whence they came.'[101] One of the policemen present then remarked:

'we have carried out our orders.' Later a police officer arrived, ostensibly to take statements. He explained that the victim had tried to escape through the window … It should be noted that, 'Shot while trying to escape,' or, 'Shot while breaking the cordon' is a daily announcement in this country. Most, or many, of these incidents are 'bumpings-off' – nothing more or less.[102]

According to Lees, the target for the police was a man who was one of the principal witnesses against a British police sergeant and a Jewish advocate who were to be tried for conspiracy and the taking and giving of bribes to facilitate illegal Jewish immigration.[103] Police searched Dr Dajani's house after the incident and upset his family.[104] Rebels tried to obtain the names of the officers involved in the Dajani execution, while Dajani himself 'intimates his intention to return certain decorations bestowed on him by His Majesty as a protest against the shooting.'[105]

The Manshiya and the Dajani hospital incidents prove that there were forms of locally organised police death squads in Palestine, euphemistically called 'special squads.' When back in London, Lees met a former constable of the Palestine police who told him that Haddad, the prisoner shot in Jaffa, had first been tortured and then taken out to be killed: 'he

[99] Ibid.
[100] Statement by Dr Dajani of Jaffa from Arab National Bureau, Damascus, 6 July 1939, Attachment to CID Intelligence Summary, Jerusalem, No. 50/39, 20 July 1939, 47/89, HA.
[101] Note, Jerusalem, 25 June 1939, Lees Papers, 5/9, LHCMA.
[102] Ibid.
[103] Memoir by Lees, Unbeaten Track: Some Vicissitudes in Two Years of a Public Servant's Life by el-Asi, Lees Papers, 5/13, p. 14, LHCMA.
[104] Statement by Dr Dajani of Jaffa from Arab National Bureau, Damascus, 6 July 1939, Attachment to CID Intelligence Summary, Jerusalem, No. 50/39, 20 July 1939, 47/89, HA.
[105] CID Police Intelligence Jerusalem, Summary 50/39, 20 July 1939, 47/89, HA.

had actually heard the British C.I.D. Sergeant concerned give the order to his "Special Squad" to take the prisoner out and shoot him ("Take him for a ride" were the actual words), after repeated floggings had failed to elicit from him whatever information it was the Sergeant desired.'[106] Friends told Lees not to return to Palestine as his life was under threat.[107] This was not new. Such things were called 'assassination direction' in Ireland, after which the 'hidden hand' protected those involved in breaking the law.[108] The hidden world of terror extended to Jewish auxiliary forces, again witnessed and reported on by Lees who saw Jewish police in trucks enter the village of Sarafand al-Kharab near Jaffa:

They met the first year little boys from the village school who were just proceeding from school on their way home. A member of the police hurled a bomb at the little boys which exploded and killed three of them, two being aged six years each and one aged seven. The Jews continued their drive, and when passing near the Mosque one of them fired his rifle at a person *who was praying* and killed him. Another Jew fired one shot at a woman carrying her grandchild (aged under two years). The shot killed the grandmother, while the child was injured and taken to hospital.[109]

Jewish supernumerary police threatened Lees with a 'Tommy gun' and barred his way. Lees then heard gunfire:

more bursts of firing which were immediately followed by shrill wails of feminine anguish proceeding from the direction of the big Arab house. Not long afterwards two or three frantic Arab women from the house burst in upon us, incoherently explaining that the Jews were upon them and had shot, or were shooting, every man they could find ... we heard the sound of the lorry departing.[110]

Lees called for the (presumably British) police who arrived and took away two wounded Palestinians; the Jewish police had shot and carried away other men in their lorry. Lees visited the two Palestinians in hospital two days later and the 'Arab Medical Officer in charge, seeing that I was interested in this wanton attempted murder, mentioned that similar cases were admitted almost daily.'[111] Lees reported these cases

---

[106] Memoir by Lees, Unbeaten Track: Some Vicissitudes in Two Years of a Public Servant's Life by el-Asi, Lees Papers, 5/13, pp. 6–7, LHCMA.

[107] Ibid., p. 22, LHCMA.

[108] Brig-Gen F. P. Crozier, *Impressions and Recollections* (London: Werner Laurie, 1930), p. 258; Crozier, *Ireland for Ever*, pp. 107, 184; Robert Kee, *The Green Flag: A History of Irish Nationalism* (London: Weidenfeld and Nicolson, 1972), pp. 669, 672.

[109] Extract from a Letter from an English Friend in Palestine, 11 January 1939, Lees Papers, 5/9, LHCMA.

[110] Memoir by Lees, Unbeaten Track: Some Vicissitudes in Two Years of a Public Servant's Life by el-Asi, Lees Papers, 5/13, pp. 3–4, LHCMA.

[111] Ibid.

to the police and civil authorities, but nothing happened. British forces collaborated with Jewish settlers on other occasions, as when British police officer Jack Binsley saw British soldiers go with a Jewish police inspector to the Jewish settlement of Zichron Yaakov south of Haifa after an Arab attack. Binsley then came across the bodies of six bayonetted Arab men from a local village on a threshing room floor in a large grain store with 'Dreadful wounds in their chests and stomachs.' The settlers had primed the soldiers with food and drink, after which they 'rushed' a local village even though there was no evidence that any attack had come from there, and they selected six probable bandits for bayonetting. 'The real murderer was the inspector though he had used my countrymen to carry out his dirty work, knowing that the matter would be hushed up to avoid a scandal involving British troops,' wrote Binsley.[112] Palestine police picked up the dumped bodies of security force assassinations in the south of Palestine. Police officer Richard Catling saw 'remains' of what he thought were some special night units. When asked what he meant by this, he continued: 'I was still in Jaffa at the time. Certainly, on two occasions we picked up the bodies of dead Arabs that had been killed by these, this special unit … In the rural area surrounding Jaffa.'[113] After soldiers had murdered an Arab man by throttling him with signal wire, a police truck arrived to take away the body: 'I later learned that he would be dumped outside one of the villages and left there without a word to anyone,' a soldier recalled.[114]

Army Reprisals: al-Bassa

Army reprisals were deterrence and punishment; they also stretched the legal limits of violence. The most egregious reprisal that this author has uncovered in terms of the methods used and numbers of Palestinians killed was in September 1938 at al-Bassa in northern Palestine near the Lebanese border. British troops operating around the village claimed that they had been the victims of roadside bomb and mine attacks prior to September 1938. The commander of the local Army unit, the Royal Ulster Rifles, informed the *mukhtars* of the Palestinian villages along the Lebanese frontier zone that if any of his men hit a mine he would take punitive measures against the nearest village to the scene of the explosion. The commander's logic was that Arab insurgents when they laid a mine always informed the villages nearest to it so that they would not

[112] Binsley, *Palestine Police Service*, pp. 104–05.
[113] Catling, 10392/9/4, pp. 16–17, IWMSA.
[114] Arthur Lane, *Lesser Gods, Greater Devils* (Stockport: Lane, 1993), pp. 45–46.

blow up local Palestinians. It is not clear that this was the case. Rebel groups often came from outside Palestine and contained foreigners, so local villagers would have had patchy knowledge of their activities, one assumes. On the evening of 6 September 1938, an RUR armoured lorry hit a mine near the village of al-Bassa, killing four soldiers – Lieutenant John Anthony Law, Lance-Corporals J. Andrews and C. Kennedy, and Rifleman A. Coalter – two of whom (Andrews and Coalter) died on the 6th, with two dying from their wounds on the 7th (Kennedy) and the 9th (Law).[115] They are all buried in Ramleh CWGC military cemetery. One soldier switched trucks just before the incident and so escaped the blast.[116] The explosion also seriously wounded two men. An RUR officer, Desmond Woods, recalled in a later oral history interview what then happened:

Now I will never forget this incident … We were at al-Malikiyya, the other frontier base and word came through about 6 o'clock in the morning that one of our patrols had been blown up and Millie Law [Lieutenant John Anthony Law, the dead officer] had been killed. Now Gerald Whitfeld [Lieutenant-Colonel G. H. P. Whitfeld, the battalion commander] had told these *mukhtars* that if any of this sort of thing happened he would take punitive measures against the nearest village to the scene of the mine. Well the nearest village to the scene of the mine was a place called al-Bassa and our Company C were ordered to take part in punitive measures. And I will never forget arriving at al-Bassa and seeing the Rolls Royce armoured cars of the 11th Hussars peppering Bassa with machine gun fire and this went on for about 20 minutes and then we went in and I remembered we had lighted braziers and we set the houses on fire and we burnt the village to the ground. Now Monty [B. L. Montgomery] was our divisional commander at the time, with his headquarters at Haifa, and he happened to be out on his balcony of his headquarters, and he saw a lot of smoke rising in the hills and he called one of his staff officers and he said 'I wonder what this smoke is in the hills there' and one of them said 'I think that must be the Royal Ulster Rifles taking punitive measures against Bassa.' Well we all thought that this was going to be the end of our commanding officer Gerald Whitfeld, because you know certainly if it happened these days it would've been. Well anyway Monty had him up and he asked him all about it and Gerald Whitfeld explained to him. He said 'Sir, I have warned the *mukhtars* in these villages that if this happened to any of my officers or men, I would take punitive measures against them and I did this and I would've lost control of the frontier if I hadn't.' Monty said 'All right

[115] *Quis Separabit: The Regimental Journal of the Royal Ulster Rifles* (1939), pp. 117–19; *Palestine Post* (11 September 1938); *Filastin* [*Palestine*] (Jaffa) (15 September 1938); Harry Arrigonie, *British Colonialism: 30 Years Serving Democracy or Hypocrisy* (Bideford: Gaskell, 1998), pp. 35–36.

[116] Personal information from Pete Robinson to author as the RUR soldier involved was his father, Thomas Robinson.

but just go a wee bit easier in the future' [a curious claim as the *Army List* dates Montgomery's arrival in Palestine to 28 October 1938].[117]

This is not the full story. Before or after destroying the village (more likely the latter), RUR soldiers with some attached Royal Engineers collected around fifty men from al-Bassa and blew them up in a contrived explosion under a bus. Harry Arrigonie, a British Palestine policeman at al-Bassa at the time, recalled what happened in his memoirs, with the British 'herding' about twenty men from al-Bassa

onto a bus. Villagers who panicked and tried to escape were shot. The driver of the bus was forced to drive along the road, over a land mine buried by the soldiers. This second mine was much more powerful than the first [i.e., the rebels' mine] and it completely destroyed the bus, scattering the maimed and mutilated bodies of the men on board everywhere. The villagers were then forced to dig a pit, collect the bodies, and throw them unceremoniously into it.[118]

Arrigonie provides grisly photographs of the maimed bodies, taken by British Constable Ricke, present at the incident, and he claims that the officer involved had been 'severely reprimanded.'[119] Recalling the same incident, a senior British Palestine police officer, Raymond Cafferata, wrote to his wife: 'You remember reading of an Arab bus blown up on the fron-tier road just after Paddy [a slang term for the Irish, so the RUR] was killed. Well the Ulsters did it – a 42 seater full of Arabs and an RE [Royal Engineers] Sgt [Sergeant] blew the mine. Since that day not a single mine has been laid on that road.'[120]

A letter in Arabic of 8 September 1938 giving the Palestinian side of events compresses the timeline of the al-Bassa incident and extends the atrocity to include premeditated torture; the Lebanese and German press also reported the incident.[121] The letter dates the explosion to 22.30 hrs on 6 September, following which, on the morning of 7 September, soldiers came to al-Bassa. They shot four people in the streets, in cafes, and in the homes of the village, after which the soldiers searched and looted the village. Soldiers gathered and beat inhabitants with sticks and

---

[117] Woods, 23846, IWMSA.

[118] Arrigonie, *British Colonialism*, pp. 35–36.

[119] Ibid. Arrigonie collected the black and white photographs of the Palestinian dead in the book.

[120] Letter, Cafferata to Wife, 22 October 1938, Cafferata Papers, CP.

[121] Letter from Acre about the English Soldiers' Atrocities in the Village of al-Bassa, 8 September 1938 in Akram Zu'aytir, *Watha'iq al-Haraka al-Wataniyya al-Filastiniyya, 1918–39: Min Awraq Akram Zu'aytir* [*Documents of the Palestinian National Movement, 1918–39: From the Papers of Akram Zu'aytir*] (Beirut: IPS, 1979), pp. 503–04; *Al-Nahar* [*The Day*] (Beirut) (9 September 1938), p. 5; German press in anon., 'British Methods in Palestine,' *Yorkshire Post* (23 November 1938).

rifle butts. The British then took 100 villagers to a nearby military base – Camp Number One – where soldiers tortured four men (the letter lists their names) selected by the commander in front of the group. Soldiers made the four men undress and forced them to kneel barefoot on cacti and thorns, specially prepared for the occasion. Eight soldiers then told off the four men and two per Arab detainee set about beating them 'without pity' in front of the group. Pieces of flesh 'flew from their bodies' and the victims fainted; an Army doctor came and checked their pulses.[122] Harshly whipping villagers was not new. The British had done the same to fellahin during the Egyptian revolt in 1919 and photographed the effects.[123] Interestingly, when the British tried lashing Jewish insurgents who were in jail on robbery charges in 1946, they met with articulate resistance. Jewish fighters replied by kidnapping and lashing four British officers; the British then pragmatically stopped using this method of punishment. Meanwhile, at al-Bassa, after the beatings, the Army took the group of villagers to another base – Camp Number Two – while soldiers destroyed the village of al-Bassa. All of this happened on the morning of 7 September, with the Army withdrawing at 13.00 hrs on the same day.[124] While this letter does not mention the villagers blown up on the bus, another letter of 20 September 1938 refers to British and Jewish police blowing up arrested suspects in this fashion along the Lebanese border, the British sending back to the villages the mangled bits of bodies or quickly burying them.[125] The difference in dates suggests that the Army destroyed the village on the 7 September and then returned some days later with engineers and police officers to kill more villagers in one or more mine explosions under vehicles filled with local Arabs.

An 11th Hussars NCO at al-Bassa remembered how he and his men had 'flattened' the village – 'blew the lot' – before referring to a similar incident near Nablus where the 11th Hussars after suffering casualties destroyed another village.[126] There are other obscure comments in the archives from British officers to villages being destroyed and burnt but the vague references to what happened and the reticence of British officers fully to record what they were doing hamper further research. The Rt. Rev. W. H. Stewart, the Anglican Archdeacon of Jerusalem (and from

---

[122] Letter from Acre about the English Soldiers' Atrocities in the Village of al-Bassa, 8 September 1938 in Zu'aytir, *Watha'iq al-Haraka*, pp. 503–04.

[123] See the files and photographs in FO 3715–3722, TNA.

[124] Letter from Acre about the English Soldiers' Atrocities in the Village of al-Bassa, 8 September 1938 in Zu'aytir, *Watha'iq al-Haraka*, pp. 503–04.

[125] A Letter from the Fighter Arrested, Subhi al-Khadra, 20 September 1938 in Zu'aytir, *Watha'iq al-Haraka*, pp. 505–06.

[126] Tinson, 15255, IWMSA.

1938 Honorary Chaplain to the Palestine Police), wrote of dark deeds in rural areas of Palestine but concluded that while his evidence was 'absolutely trustworthy, is second hand and not such that I can produce.'[127] Intelligence officer Tony Simonds in his memoir wrote of 'Lt. Col. Ley of the Borderers' arresting all the armed Arab officers after the assassination of Walter Moffatt in August 1938 and how he 'hanged each one of them on every lamp-post down the main street. He also hanged two known terrorists and murderers,' for which Ley 'was reprimanded and sent away from his Regiment.'[128] After five military casualties in an engagement near 'Atil north-east of Tulkarm in December 1938, Arabic sources recorded how soldiers burnt houses, attacked mosques, and killed people in the village, including women, children, and the elderly.[129] Similarly, after a mine exploded in Acre district killing nine soldiers and an officer, tracker dogs took the Army to Sha'ab village in Galilee where soldiers destroyed or damaged 150 houses but stopped short of killing people, it seems.[130] This was to deter rebel attacks, as the Army saw it. The Irish Guards like the RUR threatened villagers with being put in vehicles and driven along mined roads: 'They knew we'd do this.'[131] Foreign news wires reported in November 1938 on how British troops 'shot on the spot' twenty men at Irtah village south-west of Tulkarm.[132] There were police reprisals, too, which also had deterrence value, as when rebels wounded two 'wog' police officers in Haifa, after which British policemen went into town smashing up cafes,

lads hitting out left right and centre. All tables were broken and the floor was covered in blood. One Arab took a flying dive through the window when he saw a BC [British constable] coming for him swinging his rifle by the muzzle. Next day over 40 people attended the hospital and two have died. The purpose of this thrashing was to show the denizens of the sook what will happen if a Britisher is fired upon.[133]

Reprisals were deterrence.

[127] Letter, Stewart to J. G. Matthew, 9 June 1936, J&EM Papers, GB165-0161, Box 61, File 1, MEC.
[128] Typed Memoir, Pieces of War, pp. 54–55, Simonds Papers, 08/46/1, IWMD. This is a curious claim as neither the King's Own Scottish Borderers nor the South Wales Borderers served in Palestine in 1938.
[129] A Notice of the Office of the Arab Revolt about the Tragedy of 'Atil, 11 December 1938 in Zu'aytir, *Watha'iq al-Haraka*, p. 529.
[130] A Notice of the Revolt Commander in the North about the British forces bursting into the Village of Shab, 1938–39 in Zu'aytir, *Watha'iq al-Haraka*, p. 545.
[131] Watton, 14750/3, IWMSA.
[132] Sir M. Paterson (Baghdad) to FO, 17 November 1938, FO 371/21884, TNA.
[133] Letter, Burr to Mother and Father, n.d. [March–April 1938?], Burr Papers, 88/8/1, IWMD.

The Manchester Regiment's 'Gauntlet'

Reprisals took many forms. Arthur Lane, a soldier with the Manchester Regiment, was in a clash with rebels in which four to five British soldiers had died and he gives a graphic account detailing what happened to the Arab prisoners captured after the firefight and taken back to the military camp where soldiers tied them to a post:

they were in a state and they were really knocked about ... whoever had done it when they got them on the wagons to bring them back to camp the lads had beat them up, set about them ... [the interviewer asks him with what] ... Anything. Anything they could find. Rifle butts, bayonets, scabbard bayonets, fists, boots, whatever. There was one poor sod there he was I would imagine my age actually and I'd heard people say in the past that you could take your eye out and have it cleaned and put it back and I always believed it but it's not so because this lad's eye was hanging down on his lip, on his cheek. The whole eye had been knocked out and it was hanging down and there was blood dripping on his face.[134]

When asked why the soldiers had done this, Lane replied simply,

Same as any soldier. I don't care whether he's English, German, Japanese or what. He's the victor he's the boss and you accept the treatment that he gives you. I don't care what you say. That was repeated to me later [the Japanese took Lane prisoner in 1942]. But it's even today. There's a beast in every man I don't care who he is. You can say the biggest queen or queer that you come across but there's a beast in him somewhere and in a situation like that it comes out.[135]

Lane then described how the men destroyed their own tents, an act that the commanding officer allowed so that his men could let off steam. In this trashing of their own camp, the soldiers left untouched the Arab detainees. The events give a sense of the 'mood' of the men and how officers managed charged situations. One sergeant – described by Lane as deranged – led the Arab captives to the armoury to show them all the weapons there and spoke to them in English, which the Arabs did not seem to understand. He was on the point of letting the Arabs go free through the gates of the camp when an officer stopped him. Then before the Army sent the Arabs to Acre jail, the soldiers took them

around the back and any lads who were doing nothing at the time we all gathered round and stood and formed two lines of men with pick axes, pick axe helves, some with bayonets, scabbards you know with a bayonet inside, some with rifles, whatever was there, tent mallets, tent pegs. And the rebels were sent one at a time through this what do you call it? Gauntlet and they were belted and bashed until

---

[134] Lane, 10295, pp. 23ff, IWMSA.
[135] Ibid.

they got to the other end. Now any that could run when they got to the other end went straight into the police meat wagon and they were sent down to Acre. Any that died they went into the other meat wagon and they were dumped at one of the villages on the outside.[136]

The men were deflated after a battle in which they had lost friends. Here was the 'joy of hurting.' The captured rebels meanwhile 'must have realized that they were as good as dead anyhow, and that the troops were just playing cat and mouse with them,' with soldiers staking the prisoners to the ground

to await their fate. The next morning the men took matters into their own hands. As was usual when prisoners were taken, a message was sent to the Palestine police HQ, and it was the job of these police to take charge of them until they could be tried by the courts. This particular morning the officer conveniently disappeared and the prisoners were dragged out of the tents and told in a smattering of Arabic and English that they would be required to run the gauntlet, anyone refusing would be shot immediately … I only watched once and the sickening noise and screams from the unfortunate victims was enough for me. I looked around for officers but there were not to be seen. Later when we were leaving for Singapore I asked one of the junior officers why no one had stopped the men from such things and I was told that 'It bloods the youngsters' … Of the seven Arabs we captured two went for trial, were found guilty and hanged in the square at Acre town. The bodies of the others were taken and dumped outside one of the villages in the early hours.[137]

Lane includes a photograph of a 'gauntlet' from Palestine in the book version of his military memoir, with about five soldiers on either side of the gauntlet swinging rifles at a hooded running man who was presumably one of the Arab prisoners. This was obviously an Army tradition as the Parachute Regiment used the same gauntlet method in 1972 against Republican detainees, if with less lethal force employed: 'there were two lines of seven or eight Paras on each side with batons, hose pipes and rifles. We were invited to run for it. I took quite a few blows and was glad of the heavy coat I was wearing.'[138]

The idea of 'blooding' young soldiers reappeared with the North Staffordshire Regiment in battle in December 1937 at Wadi 'Amud on the north-west shore of Lake Tiberias: 'The going was bad – the hills steep, boulder strewn and covered with thick undergrowth,' with fighting at twenty-five yards, during which the British killed three Arabs: 'Five more, all armed, and who had escaped the covering fire owing to the excellence of their cover, were shot out of hand, thereby blooding a lot of

---

[136] Ibid.
[137] Lane, *Lesser Gods*, pp. 50–52.
[138] Quoted in O'Brien, *A Matter of Minutes*, p. 104.

B and C companies.'[139] On another occasion, men from the Royal Ulster and West Kent regiments caught about sixty Arabs near Jenin 'as they walked out with their arms up' and 'mowed them down with machine guns. I inspected them afterwards and most of them were boys between 16 and 20 from Syria ... No news of course is given to the newspapers, so what you read in the papers is just enough to allay public uneasiness in England.'[140] Simonds with an English county regiment witnessed how near Nablus 'suspected guerrillas were mown down in cold blood; without them firing in reply. They were hastily buried in some shallow trenches; and some of them were found to be wounded and buried alive, to die.'[141] Fawzi al-Qawuqji talked of British commanders using local villagers as a human shield, with villagers placed between the British soldiers and Palestinian fighters.[142] Policemen also executed prisoners in the field. An Arab lawyer from Haifa wrote in March 1939 of how police Assistant Superintendent (ASP) Geoffrey Morton went to a village and searched the menfolk, asking for names and nicknames. He then picked out two men and said: 'Bid this man farewell because he will be brought to you tomorrow morning in the coffin and a few minutes after taking those two young men away the villagers heard several shots but it was night time.'[143] The next day at midday an armoured car brought the corpses of the two young men: 'The motive presumed is that it had been reported to the said A.S.P. that the two said young men were intending to murder him.'[144]

Searching as Torture: Halhul

Another egregious single incident to rank alongside al-Bassa was at the village of Halhul in May 1939. Located on the road between Hebron and Bethlehem, the British believed that the villagers of Halhul were sympathetic to the rebels. The Scottish-based Black Watch Regiment surrounded and took over the village in May 1939. What followed was an attempt to get the villagers to hand over rifles – a recurring British demand during village searches – by setting up two wired cages. One

---

[139] *China Dragon: Regimental Magazine of the North Staffordshire Regiment* 23/2 (April 1938), pp. 48, 51.

[140] Letter, Burr to Parents, March 1938 [date pencilled in], Burr Papers, 88/8/1, IWMD.

[141] Typed Memoir, Pieces of War, p. 155, Simonds Papers, 08/46/1, IWMD.

[142] Khayriyya Qasimiyya (ed.), *Filastin fi-Mudhakkirat al-Qawuqji* [*Palestine in the Memories of Fawzi al-Qawuqji*] (Beirut: PLO Research Centre and Jerusalem Publishing House, 1975), ii, p. 34.

[143] Letter, Atalla Bey (Advocate Haifa) to Tannous, 1 March 1939, Activity of the British Army, RG65: P361/5, ISA.

[144] Ibid.

was a 'good' cage in which there was plenty of water, food, and shelter from the sun, and one was a 'bad' cage in which men were left in the open in the intense heat with between half and one pint of water per day. In an interview with a BBC 'Timewatch' team working on a 1991 programme on the Arab revolt – what it called 'the first intifada' – the commanding officer of the Black Watch emphasised the voluntary nature of the action; villagers could escape the heat simply by handing over a rifle, after which soldiers moved them to the 'good' cage. The officer in charge did not make clear what the villagers were to do if they did not have a rifle.[145] Bahjat Abu Gharbiyya in his memoirs talks of the Army's use of 'cages' but does not make specific reference to Halhul, suggesting that this was not an isolated incident, and there are many references to 'cages' throughout the archival record.[146]

Again, closer examination of the primary sources paints a darker picture of the events at Halhul. Keith-Roach, in a private letter, wrote that soldiers only distributed a half pint of water and he does not refer to a 'good' cage. Instead, after the military high command had given the commander of the Black Watch permission, soldiers rounded up all the men of the village,

instructed that they be kept there [in an open cage] and he gave them half a pint of water per diem. I saw the original order. The weather was very hot for it was summer. According to Indian Army Medical standards, four pints of water a day is the minimum that a man can live upon exposed to hot weather. After 48 hours treatment most of the men were very ill and eleven old and enfeebled ones died. I was instructed that no civil inquest should be held. Finally, the High Commissioner, MacMichael, decided compensation should be paid, and my Assistant and I assessed the damage at the highest rate allowed by the law, and paid out over three thousand pounds to the bereft families.[147]

A British doctor based in Hebron's St Luke's Hospital, Elliot Forster, talked of two cages, one for the men and one for the women, and he does not mention any way to escape the cages. They were there just for punishment. 'We may yet teach Hitler something new about the conduct of concentration camps' was Forster's conclusion.[148] An Arab whose father died at Halhul claimed that between eleven and fourteen men died after

---

[145] 'Palestine: The First Intifada' (BBC: Timewatch, 27 March 1991). The Black Watch commanding officer claimed that his men distributed one pint of water per person per diem.

[146] Bahjat Abu Gharbiyya, *Fi Khidamm al-nidal al-'arabi al-filastini: Mudhakkirat al-munadil Bahjat Abu Gharbiyya* [*In the Midst of the Struggle for the Arab Palestinian Cause: The Memoirs of Freedom-Fighter Bahjat Abu Gharbiyya*] (Beirut: IPS, 1993), p. 60.

[147] Typed two-page document by Edward Keith-Roach, untitled or dated, at the end of which is added pencilled comment, Keith-Roach Papers, AL-KR.

[148] Diary, 13 May 1939, Forster Papers, GB165-0109, 119, MEC.

two weeks in the sun with no food and water, one at a village well where 'soldiers kept pushing him and he was killed.'[149] The same man recalled electric generators (or floodlights/heaters) running all night to increase the detainees' privations, some being so hungry that they ate dirt. A woman from Halhul noted that ten men died, two at the village well, the British only releasing the men after the villagers produced forty old Turkish rifles. This was after eight days' captivity. The same woman also recalled the night-time lights and that the soldiers beat them and threw away food that the women brought for their captive menfolk. 'Without guns those men will never be released,' one British officer/official ('local British ruler') told her.[150] Other Arab accounts talk of the use of 'cages' for three days 'at least' in military operations in other villages.[151]

In correspondence held in the Imperial War Museum Film Archive surrounding a Thames TV programme on Palestine in the 1970s,[152] both Morton (formerly of the Palestine police) and Sir Thomas Scrivenor (a former Assistant District Commissioner in Palestine) challenged the idea that villagers were denied water in village searches, with Morton questioning the 'senile old' peasant that Thames TV had 'dragged in' to recount his tale. It is not clear if these relate to Halhul or are more general comments, but Thames TV's reply is interesting:

The problems of the oral tradition (confusing hearsay with personal experience) made us doubt it, too, and the sequence was cut when our Zionist adviser told us that these stories originated as black propaganda in Nazi Germany. One of my colleagues, however, undertook a personal search in the Public Record Office [Kew, London] and found the original papers. As soon as this incident took place, Government House informed the Secretary of State that people had died during an arms search. The Secretary of State asked for full details because of the danger of Nazi propaganda, and payments of £2,000 were made to the bereaved families.[153]

The reference to compensation suggests that this could be a reference to the Halhul incident of May 1939. One of the survivors of the cages at Halhul recounted to Forster, the Hebron doctor, the events of May 1939:

---

[149] Account Translated from Arabic of Hassan el-Qader, Thames TV Papers, GB165-0282, Box 2, File 5, MEC. This is a jumbled file and there is ambiguity about whether this witness is from Halhul.

[150] Account Translated from Arabic of Woman Resident of Halhul, Thames TV Papers, GB165-0282, Box 2, File 5, pp. 16–18, MEC.

[151] Account Translated from Arabic of Unnamed Arab Villager, Thames TV Papers, GB165-0282, Box 2, File 4, p. 12, MEC.

[152] 'Palestine: Promises and Rebellion' (London: Thames TV, three parts, 1977–78).

[153] Letter, Nigel Maslin to Sir Thomas Scrivenor, 29 August 1978, Lever Arch File: British Letters S–T, Thames TV Material on 'Palestine: Promises, Rebellion and Abdication' (1977–78), IWMFA.

On my return this morning I found a man had been admitted suffering from the effects of his internment at Halhul. He is a Hebron man who had the misfortune to be caught in the round up. He has not suffered permanently and is not seriously ill. The point is that he strikes me as being a quiet and reliable witness. He denies the lurid stories that were set forth in the two [Arab] petitions you showed me this morning, and says that apart from one man who was drowned in a well only the ten men we know of died from exposure. The death of this man in the well was bad enough, but again he says the horrible story told in the petition is not true. The man was suffering badly from thirst and in order to get a drink he told a false story of a rifle hidden in a well. He was let down into the well and drank his fill, but on being hauled up empty handed he was struck with the butts of rifles. He had a knife and managed to cut the cord on which he depended, fell back into the well and was drowned. My patient said the first few days were terrible, and the allowance of water was pitifully small. He says that he and others did in fact drink their own urine. During the latter part of his internment – he was there twelve days in all – things were somewhat better. As is usual with the oriental petitioner, these folk seem to spoil their case with exaggeration and falsehood. In this present case surely the unvarnished truth was terrible enough.[154]

The Black Watch knew that its actions were excessive and wrong – a standard operating procedure pushed to such a limit as to be non-standard, hence the compensation and the need to hide the outrage. For instance, the Black Watch B Company commander at Halhul, Captain Neville Blair, later told O'Connor's biographer how when brigade headquarters summoned him, the

Brigadier himself gave me the orders. I was expressly forbidden to take any notes, nor, I was told, would I get any written confirmatory orders. It was to be a completely secret operation, with nothing put down in writing. I presume the Brigade Major was present, but there was no one else present from my Battalion, not even my Commanding Officer. I forget now if I was authorized to tell him the details, but I believe that he was simply warned, perhaps by me, that the next day my company was to surround and search Halhul.[155]

The operation was punitive and arranged locally at brigade level. The Army completed the search in one day, but Blair's superiors ordered him to keep the detained men in the sun for several more days. Blair complained to his commanding officer about the inhumane treatment but 'was told that these were the orders of the local brigadier, and if he did not like them he had better send in his resignation,' although after the incident the Army

---

[154] Forster [unsigned] to Anglican Bishop in Jerusalem (Graham Brown), Confidential, Not to be Quoted or Referred to in Public, 25 May 1939, J&EM Papers, GB165-0161, Box 62, File 1, MEC.

[155] John Baynes, *The Forgotten Victor: General Sir Richard O'Connor* (London: Brassey's, 1989), pp. 61–62.

convened a court of inquiry that looked to blame Blair until O'Connor intervened to take responsibility between himself and the local brigadier.[156] There are other references to excesses comparable to al-Bassa and Halhul in the primary sources. Forster mentions a 'worse' atrocity at the village of Bayt Rima south-west of Nablus, another example of the tangential comments made to other atrocities: 'Ballard [a military officer in Hebron] says a man at Beit [Bayt] Rima died after a beating by an officer. "He's a known sadist" is the explanation.'[157] The Anglican Bishop in Jerusalem wrote of 'serious charges' against soldiers in operations at Bayt Rima and Michmash (Mukhmas) north-east of Jerusalem, following which the Bishop protested to senior officers.[158] The Anglican Mission in Jerusalem listed twenty-two villages and towns in which occurred single or multiple outrages, sometimes over a period of many months.[159] In 1977, a local man, Qasim al-Rimawi (likely a rebel and later 'Abd al-Qadir Husayni's secretary and a Jordanian cabinet minister), claimed that soldiers tortured to death three villagers at Bayt Rima during a thirteen-day search involving 2,000 troops.[160] In November 1938, the Army also set up fake executions for villagers in Halhul in the hope of getting them to hand over weapons, as a major recalled with 'enormous pride' in a conversation with Forster.[161] 'The Royal Ulster Rifles treated the Arabs very firmly indeed but by Jove it paid dividends but of course you can't do those sorts of things today' was how one RUR officer put it.[162] After a comrade was blown up by a mine near the village of Kafr Yasif north-east of Acre in February 1939, soldiers burnt down seventy houses, blew up forty more and, reportedly, told nine villagers from the neighbouring village of Kuwaykat to run after which the soldiers gunned them down.[163] 'I do not think the circumstances differ from those with which we are familiar' noted a local Anglican Chaplain.[164] Under pressure

---

[156] Ibid.

[157] Diary, 14 May 1939, Forster Papers, GB165-0109, pp. 119–20, MEC.

[158] Anglican Bishop in Jerusalem to Miss Trevelyan, 29 May 1939, J&EM Papers, GB165-0161, Box 62, File 1, MEC.

[159] J&EM Papers, GB165-0161, Box 66, Files 1–2, MEC.

[160] Qasim al-Rimawi (Amman), 19 September 1977, Lever Arch File: Nigel Maslin, Thames TV Material on 'Palestine: Promises, Rebellion and Abdication' (1977–78), IWMFA.

[161] Diary, 5 November 1938, Forster Papers, GB165-0109, p. 93, MEC.

[162] Woods, 23846, IWMSA.

[163] Anglican Chaplain [signature illegible], Haifa, to Bishop (Graham Brown), 28 February 1939, J&EM Papers, GB165-0161, Box 62, File 1, MEC; Ted Swedenburg, *Memories of Revolt: The 1936–1939 Rebellion and the Palestinian National Past* (Minneapolis, MN: University of Minnesota Press, 1995), p. 108.

[164] Anglican Chaplain [signature illegible], Haifa, to Bishop (Graham Brown), 28 February 1939, J&EM Papers, GB165-0161, Box 62, File 1, MEC.

from the Anglican clergy, the Army provided some relief to the homeless villagers, the Anglican Chaplain in Haifa concluding:

On the whole I cannot help wondering at the way the Arabs trust us and believe us and believe that in the end we will try and do what is right. Some of the villages which have recently been hardly [sic] hit seem to go as far as possible in making allowances. Sometimes they appear to accept the severest treatment as the inevitable result of acts of violence by the gangs, even though they themselves are not responsible. And they do not hold the government responsible for actions taken by the military authorities, though we know that the government can't disclaim responsibility. The people at Kafr Yasif were very eager to point out that the troops who destroyed their houses were not English but Irish.[165]

Following the reprisal action against Kafr Yasif, local Palestinians gathered outside the German Consulate shouting 'We want Hitler – We want Mussolini.'[166] The British targeted Muslim homes in this operation.[167]

'Mascots' and 'Shot Trying to Escape'

Another 'means to an end' act of cruelty was the carrying of what the Army called 'mascots' on convoys to deter rebel mine attacks. Such group preventative actions prompted casual acts of personal evil by soldiers. It was common Army practice to make local Palestinians ride with military convoys to prevent mine attacks. Soldiers often carried them on or tied them to the bonnets of lorries, or they put the hostages on small flatbeds on the front of trains, all to prevent mining or sniping attacks. 'The naughty boys who we had in the cages in these camps' were put in vehicles in front of the convoy for the 'deterrent effect,' as one British officer put it.[168] The Army told the Arabs that they would shoot any of them who tried to run away.[169] Some soldier drivers in the lorries would brake hard at the end of a journey and then casually run over the Palestinian who had tumbled from the bonnet, killing or maiming him, as Lane, the Manchester Regiment private candidly recalled:

when you'd finished your duty you would come away nothing had happened no bombs or anything and the driver would switch his wheel back and to make the truck waver and the poor wog on the front would roll off into the deck. Well if he was lucky he'd get away with a broken leg but if he was unlucky the truck behind coming up behind would hit him. But nobody bothered to pick up the bits they

---

[165] Ibid.
[166] Ibid.
[167] Swedenburg, *Memories of Revolt*, p. 109.
[168] Shepperd, 4597, p. 64, IWMSA; Woods, 23846, IWMSA.
[169] Woods, 23846, IWMSA.

were left. You know we were there we were the masters we were the bosses and whatever we did was right ... Well you know you don't want him anymore. He's fulfilled his job. And that's when Bill Usher [the commanding officer] said that it had to stop because before long they'd be running out of bloody rebels to sit on the bonnet.[170]

In another account Lane added that if a rebel fell from the bonnet then 'one of the lads would put a hole in him. In either case he would be lucky to escape.'[171] A Jewish chauffeur driving for the British made the same point about the mayor of Nablus who was 'forcibly taken, tied well, and seated on the roof of my truck. I left as usual from the Nablus Gate without the convoy, but this time with my bright lights on in order to attract the attention of the gangs to the truck.'[172] Such hostage taking was less of a moral issue for the British and even divisional commander O'Connor summoned local 'Arab leaders' to ride on trolley cars along the Jaffa–Jerusalem railway.[173] The British had done the same in the 1920s in Ireland, with IRA hostages used on high-risk patrols.[174]

'Shot trying to escape' covered executions by security forces, including the alleged assassin of Moffatt in August 1938 who was a blond hunchback 'Mohammed' with the nickname 'gazelle.'[175] Moffatt's assassin shot him six times and then walked out into the lobby of Moffatt's office building where up to thirty Arabs were waiting, reloaded, went back into the office and shot him again, passing two Palestinian policemen on the way. 'He later tried to escape from the Military Camp and was shot at and died later.'[176] Men were shot on the way to interrogation if security forces were angry, or after interrogation once their value for information was gone.[177] Frustration led to executions, as when security forces missed catching a rebel band so the senior police officer present let the men 'beat up a village where they stayed the night.'[178] The perceived

---

[170] Lane, 10295, p. 18, IWMSA. Lane repeated this charge in Lane, *Lesser Gods*, p. 45.

[171] Lane, *Lesser Gods*, p. 45.

[172] Benjamin 'Adin (Edelman), *Adventures at the Wheel: Memoirs of a Native-born Jerusalemite* (Jerusalem: Alfa, 1965), p. 84.

[173] Baynes, *The Forgotten Victor*, pp. 56–57.

[174] Tony Geraghty, *The Irish War: The Hidden Conflict between the IRA and British Intelligence* (Baltimore, MD and London: Johns Hopkins University Press, 2000), p. 340.

[175] Telegram to Secretary of State, n.d., S25/22762, CZA; *Haaretz* (26 August 1936); Akram Zu'aytir, *Al-Haraka al-Wataniya al-Filastiniyya, 1935–39: Yawmiyyat Akram Zu'aytir* [*The Palestinian National Movement, 1935–39: Diaries of Akram Zu'aytir*] [1980] (Beirut: IPS, 1992), p. 438.

[176] Summary of Intelligence, Palestine and Transjordan, 26 August 1938, by Wing Commander Ritchie at GHQ [17/38], CO 732/81/9, TNA.

[177] Letter, Burr (Depot Mt Scopus) to Mother and Father, n.d. [late 1937], Burr Papers, 88/8/1, IWMD.

[178] Letter, Burr to Mother and Father, 19 December 1937, Burr Papers, 88/8/1, IWMD.

leniency of military courts and the need for 'evidence to convict' meant summary executions: 'So any Johnny Arab who is caught by us in suspicious circumstances is shot out of hand.'[179] 'Another man whom we knew had participated in the murder but against whom we had no evidence was shot while trying to escape.'[180]

The abuse detailed here was in some sense 'personal.' No one forced the men concerned to inflict suffering on others. British personnel knew what was normatively wrong and what could get them in trouble. Such brutality pacified Palestinians but it is not clear that soldiers acted as they did for this reason. Insurgency and counter-insurgency prompted casual, random acts of violence. Soldiers in lorries pushed out their rifle butts when passing on the road Palestinian peasants on donkeys, smashing in the heads of men and women alike: 'I felt the bump as one of the men brought his rifle crashing down against an unsuspecting Arab's head … It was all over in a very short time and the trucks resumed their normal speed. No one spoke for the remainder of the journey.'[181] Local traditions of violent justice exacerbated the latent brutality of pacification. Thus, an Army officer working with Palestine police in the 1940s caught three Palestinians suspected of murder:

> The first man was seized by two Arab policemen and held upside down while his feet were placed between a rifle and its sling. He was then kept in this position while policemen took turns to beat the soles of his feet with a leather belt, with short pauses for questioning. After a time he agreed to talk, and the beating ceased. The second man talked after the application of a lighted cigarette to his testicles, but the third seemed to be the leader and more truculent. In a flash the Arab sergeant flew at him and hit him in the face until both his eyes were closed, blood was flowing and a number of teeth were spewed on the floor. He then agreed to talk … I was shocked by all of this and said to the police officer in charge: 'The sort of thing savours of the Gestapo.' He seemed amused by my reactions and replied: 'These men have confessed to helping the murderers and now they've told us where they are.' These methods of extracting information, he said, were justified. I expressed some doubts. He added that force was the only language these Arabs understood. Under Turkish rule they had been brought up to respect such methods. 'Where do you think we would get,' he asked me 'if we questioned them like a London bobby? I'll tell you; the police methods would be laughed at, we should get no results, and our methods would be regarded as a sign of weakness.'[182]

As American helicopter gunners 'hunting Viets' in Vietnam shot down peasants in fields as they flew over, a Palestine policeman helping the

---

[179] Ibid.
[180] Letter, Burr to Mother and Father, n.d. [March–April 1938?], Burr Papers, 88/8/1, IWMD.
[181] Lane, *Lesser Gods*, p. 46.
[182] Smiley, *Irregular Regular*, pp. 15–16.

Army on a Lewis machine gun in a battle near Jenin 'had a spot of practice' on a peasant 'on a donkey. I don't know whether he was one of the
gang, but if he wasn't he was just unlucky.'[183] This was in early 1938 when
security forces lacked manpower, as shown by the same policeman's
comment apropos another incident when he and 'the others came all
right at the enquiry over the shot informer. We all thought we would get
the boat but they are badly in need of men now.'[184]

The extreme violence detailed in this chapter was another tool to
pacification. The emergency conditions of colonial insurrection enabled
such extra-ordinary violence, most of which the perpetrators knew was
wrong, if not legally then normatively. Some of the police torture became
systemic, as did much of the Army reprisal measures against villages.
Reprisal measures were constant over the course of the revolt, getting
worse in late 1936 and late 1938 simply because more Army battalions
arrived in Palestine and executed more pacification using similar methods.
Measures such as punishing villages were a central, accepted part of pacification and so it was the way in which security forces managed the punitive regime that decided the move from judicial to extra-judicial violence.
Brigade command enabled levels of force that area battalions mediated,
at which point regiments acted differently at the margins of violence and
many units bounded their reprisals to non-lethal methods that they did
not have to make invisible. Others did not. British soldiers fought in an
'army of tribes' and regiments behaved differently.[185] This did not stop
shocking incidents of personal cruelty, some wilful, some casual, some
reactive, that cannot be explained by operational necessity. The pacification of Palestine was a history of violence.

[183] Daniella Gioseffi (ed.), *Women on War: An International Anthology of Women's Writing
from Antiquity to the Present* (New York, NY: Feminist Press, CUNY, 2003), p. 114;
Letter, Burr (Inlying Piquet Haifa) to Mother and Father, n.d. [January–February
1938?], Burr Papers, 88/8/1, IWMD.

[184] Letter, Burr (Inlying Piquet Haifa) to Mother and Father, n.d. [January–February
1938?], Burr Papers, 88/8/1, IWMD.

[185] See the broader discussion in Edward Burke, *Army of Tribes: British Army Cohesion,
Deviancy and Murder in Northern Ireland* (Liverpool: Liverpool University Press, 2018),
passim.

Afterword
Policy, Violence, and the Arab Revolt

Palestine's three communities all used force after April 1936 to realise policy objectives. In their own ways, the Palestinians, Jews, and British did so successfully, but only the Jews secured their long-term political ends. The case of the Palestinians and the British is peculiar. A Palestinian diplomatic track to transform shock action into political gains paralleled the uprising against the British state and Jewish settlers. 'Paralleled' does not fairly describe Palestinians' actions; a better assessment is that there were military and diplomatic tracks in operation, both avowedly designed to change British policy, neither of which properly worked with the other. War was not the Clausewitzian continuation of policy by other means but was a popular eruption of anger that Palestinian leaders were unable or unwilling to make purposeful, while neighbouring Arab leaders directed the violence for their own political ends. Thus, alongside the insurrection, there appeared a discrete diplomatic channel, notably by rulers in Transjordan, Iraq, Saudi Arabia, and Yemen, to which the Palestinian Arab Higher Committee attached itself, or not as the case may be as Hajj Amin, for one, was suspicious of Abdullah of Transjordan. These rulers at various times and in diverse ways worked with the British to end the violence. This is well known and does not bear repeating here, except to say that violence without good political leadership is destined to fail, as it did for Germany in 1945. The willingness of the Higher Committee to rely on outside Arab rulers did not help the Palestinian cause, nor did the inclination of some such as the Nashashibis (and Abdullah) to call for an end to violence as soon as it had started, but what was fatal was the unwillingness (or inability) of Palestinian leaders to commit to protracted struggle. Just as Fawzi al-Qawuqji was starting forms of disciplined insurgency from late August 1936, the Higher Committee and Arab leaders such as Abdullah and Nuri al-Sa'id of Iraq brokered the 12 October 1936 ceasefire. The Palestinians had achieved their goal of getting London to re-assess its Palestine policy. The Palestinians rejected the Peel Commission decision the following summer to partition Palestine and violence resumed in September 1937, again successfully, bringing with the Woodhead Commission in late 1938 the scrapping of the Peel partition plan and then in May 1939 after the London Conference of February–March 1939 a White Paper that committed Britain to ending Jewish immigration to Palestine. Before the conflagration of the Second World War and the Holocaust had invalidated the White Paper, Palestinian leaders had already rejected it. Palestinian peasants through their endurance of a punishing British pacification campaign had succeeded in making Britain commit to a new policy that favoured the majority community. If Palestinian political leaders did not want partition and they did not want an end to Jewish immigration then they needed the force to forge the third way: Britain's withdrawal from Palestine, leaving the Palestinians to settle the Jewish community in the country as they saw fit. (Or, as happened in 1948, the British left and the Jews settled the Palestinians as they saw fit.) This was Quixotic, to say the least. With Britain's need to control the Middle East for the war looming in Europe, the May 1939 White Paper was the best deal available, better than the UN partition plan of November 1947 or what the Palestinians got after war with Israel in May 1948 when they lost the whole country excepting Gaza and the West Bank. It was just such a compromise deal that Irish nationalists acknowledged in 1922 after their similarly successful insurrection against Britain, 1919–21: an Irish Free State but one that was a British imperial Dominion, fealty to the British Crown, Royal Navy access to Irish ports, and the loss of the north of the country to Protestant settlers. Michael Collins and the new Irish Government crushed dissenters in the civil war that followed the Anglo-Irish Treaty of December 1921, but *after* the insurgency not during it. Similarly, the intra-Jewish *Altalena* battle between Haganah (now the Israeli Defence Forces) and *Etzel* occurred in June 1948 a month after Israeli independence. The Vietminh compromised at the Geneva conference in 1954 following their stunning victory over the French at the battle of Dien Bien Phu and accepted the partition of the country and the loss of hard-won territory south of the 17th parallel to a US-backed regime in Saigon. The insurgents only gained power in the north. The Franco-Syrian Treaty granting independence and territorial unity ended the Syrian insurgent-strike of 1936 but also committed the country to an alliance with and granted military bases to France. EOKA after its insurgency in Cyprus dropped its demand for the union of the island with Greece on independence in 1960 and it recognised local British military bases. In the same way, the IRA accepted the political compromise of the Good Friday (Belfast) Agreement in 1998 that ended the Republican insurgency in Ulster but without a united Ireland. Without the power to force a military solution, a political compromise is inevitable if insurgents want any political gains, ones that can be a springboard for more advantage, as the Irish proved in 1937 when they transitioned to a republic, and the North Vietnamese demonstrated in 1975 when they seized all of Vietnam. The Palestinians preferred nothing to something that was not everything. There is not the space in this military history to detail the diplomacy of the Arab revolt but the negotiations in late 1936 and with the Peel Commission, and in late 1938 and early 1939 before the White Paper could have made all the suffering and violence worthwhile. The British pacification campaign was a model of controlled violence but at its heart the failure of the Arab revolt lay with weak, maladroit Palestinian political leadership. The insurgency exploded and then imploded. The Palestinians at the sharp end of the reprisals, fining, curfews, demolition, beatings, and detention of pacification deserved better. The Palestinian insurgency never bridged the gap between urbanite leaders and the peasantry, a point that Frantz Fanon made more broadly in 1961 in his classic critique of colonialism, *The Wretched of the Earth*. Moreover, the punishment of Palestine in the 1930s shattered the Palestinian community for the existential war of 1948 with Israel. The British Army had inadvertently done the Jews' work for them, defeating one of the main enemy forces that the Arabs could array against Israel in 1948, and before the war had even started. This helps to explain the weakness of Palestinian resistance in 1948 and their reliance on the neighbouring, self-aggrandising armies of Egypt, Iraq, Syria, and Transjordan.

The British Army did everything that London asked of it. It reduced the country in 1936 and with the threat of martial law and added military force helped to effect a ceasefire in October 1936 that the Colonial Office and the Palestine High Commissioner needed to open the diplomatic track leading to the Peel Commission. Military action in lieu of a functioning police force made possible the link between force and politics. The Army wanted to carry on the fighting in 1936, expecting a recrudescence of insurrection. This came in September 1937 with Andrews' assassination[1] by Qassamite gunmen, but it was not until September 1938 and the Munich settlement that the Army could flood Palestine with the requisite infantry battalions needed to screw down the population and shatter rebel bands. It was a question of numbers. As GOC Haining put it, before October 1938 'there had not been sufficient

---

[1] For a contrasting periodisation of the revolt see Matthew Kelly, *The Crime of Nationalism: Britain, Palestine, and Nation-Building on the Fringe of Empire* (Berkeley, CA: University of California Press, 2017), pp. 107ff, 180.

troops in the country to hold the main centres and communications and also to take active measures against the rebels.'[2] The Army then crushed the insurrection in about six months using considerable, managed, and often excessive but not boundless violence. This made possible the London Conference of February–March 1939. Military defeat of the revolt enabled political concessions and the May 1939 White Paper. Wider political forces at work during and after the Second World War scuppered the Army's success in the late 1930s in Palestine. British imperial weakness after the Second World War combined with the Jewish insurrection after 1945 to reshape the geopolitical landscape and to push Britain out of Palestine in 1948, but for the duration of the war London had Palestine as a vital base area in the fight against Italy and Germany. The considerable military power used in 1936 proves that force was at the root of the British operational method against insurrection. The marriage of military power with the colonial state's legal-administrative structures made pacification devastatingly effective. The management of pacification through well-established emergency laws and military traditions contained soldiers' violence, reining in excessive violence, at least in relative terms to similar population-centric counter-insurgency campaigns by other colonial or neo-imperial powers. This is certainly how British troops saw themselves: 'if Hitler had the Palestine mandate how long would these troubles have lasted!' in the words of one officer.[3] Or as Parachute Regiment battalion commander Colonel Derek Wilford unhelpfully put it much later when talking about counter-insurgency in Northern Ireland: that his paratroopers did not kill more than thirteen demonstrators in Derry on 'Bloody Sunday' in 1972 proved the limits to the use of force.[4] This is some measure of British exceptionalism, as is the fact that the Parachute Regiment and the violence of 30 January 1972 were exceptional.

The Jews played the minor part during the revolt, participating with auxiliary forces alongside British troops and providing intelligence to the Army, but their community benefitted the most politically and militarily from the fighting. Links with British military intelligence boosted the *Yishuv*'s information-gathering system while military training in the Special Night Squads and in auxiliary police formations toughened the

---

[2] Despatch on Operations by British Forces in Palestine and Transjordan, 1 November 1938–31 March 1939, Force HQ Jerusalem, dated 24 April, sent to WO London, Haining Papers, Despatches, GB165-0131, MEC.

[3] Diary, 24 January 1939, Tufton Beamish (later Baron Chelwood), Beamish Papers, 1/6/11, ESRO.

[4] Douglas Murray, *Bloody Sunday: Truths, Lies and the Saville Inquiry* (London: Biteback, 2012), p. 123. There were eventually fourteen deaths.

community for the next war with the Palestinians and Arabs in 1948. The British Army's crushing of the Palestinians was of greatest benefit to the Jews. Not only did the Army scatter rebel bands but it left the rural populace impoverished by the counter-insurgency and without the strength for another round of fighting in 1948. The British led the way in colonial occupation and after the war of 1948 both the Arabs and Israelis utilised British legal measures to control the Palestinians, notably the 1945 Emergency Regulations used originally against Jewish insurgents but also the 1937 Order in Council.[5] Israel, like Britain, attached great importance to law and propriety.[6] The British revoked the 1945 regulations just before they left Palestine in May 1948 but the newly formed Israeli state claimed that as this decision had not been published in the *Palestine Gazette* such laws were still valid; Egypt and Jordan similarly kept British laws as they were so useful for repression in Gaza and the West Bank.[7] The Israelis layered on their own laws such as the 'Israeli Law and Administration Ordinance of 1948' to British legislation.[8] Instead of the High Commissioner having the right to enact any necessary laws, the Israeli Prime Minister now had the power to make Emergency Regulations 'as may be expedient in the interests of the defence of the state, public security and the maintenance of supplies and essential services' – phrasing that could be lifted straight from the detail in Chapter 2 of this book.[9] Similarly, the Jordanians employed the 1945 British regulations to control the West Bank after 1948, laws that Israel took over in 1967 after the Six Day War and to which it then added new security legislation.[10] British imperial systems of pacification were still being used decades later.[11] *Plus ça change.*

---

[5] 1945 Defence (Emergency) Regulations (in *Official Gazette of Palestine Supplement 2* (No. 1442) 855), 27 September 1945 in *Ordinances, Regulations, Rules, Orders and Notices. Government of Palestine. Annual Volume for 1945. Volumes 2 and 3* (Jerusalem: Government Printing Press, 1946), pp. 1055–95 (on microfilm in BL at SPR Mic. P1); Baruch Bracha, 'Restriction of Personal Freedom without Due Process of Law According to the Defence (Emergency) Regulations, 1945,' in Y. Dinstein and F. Domb (eds), *Israel Yearbook on Human Rights. Volume 8* (Tel Aviv: Intersdar, 1978), pp. 297–300.

[6] Lisa Hajjar, *Courting Conflict: The Israeli Military System in the West Bank and Gaza* (London: University of California Press, 2005), p. 49.

[7] Ibid., p. 60.

[8] Bracha, 'Restriction of Personal Freedom,' pp. 297–300.

[9] Raja Shehadeh, *Occupier's Law: Israel and the West Bank* (Washington, DC: IPS, 1985), p. 65.

[10] Arie Pach, 'Human Rights in West Bank Military Courts,' in Y. Dinstein and F. Domb (eds), *Israel Yearbook on Human Rights. Volume 7* (Tel Aviv: Israel, 1977), pp. 224–45.

[11] Bracha, 'Restriction of Personal Freedom,' pp. 322–23.

Appendix A
Order of Battle

THE ARABS–PALESTINIANS

Introduction

The lack of record keeping and extant files for the rebels means that combat figures for Arab and Palestinian forces are neither as fulsome nor as exact as those for British soldiers. Figures for rebel numbers and leaders usually derive from British and Jewish sources, or from captured documents. As with Jews, many fighters were part-timers, further complicating the calculation of numbers. Palestinian villages also supplemented rebel forces with tens or hundreds of armed men, temporarily inflating combat figures. Rebel forces were loosely organised, never ascending to regular force structures of even battalion or regimental strength in the style of Mao Zedong's guerrillas in China in the same period. Fawzi al-Qawuqji's four company-sized units deployed from August to October 1936 were the largest formed rebel units deployed, and each of these companies was effectively a reinforced platoon. The Palestinian units were organised as bands called *fasa'il* that would match in conventional military terms a platoon of some fifty men but at times to a strength up to 200 men that would be a company in a regular army.

Numbers

Subhi Yasin gives a figure for the rebels at their zenith of their power at 9,000–10,000 rebels comprising 3,000 full-time members, 1,000 urban rebels and 6,000 part-time villagers, some of whom would have been called out via rebel *faz'a* calls for help from local villagers.[1] When al-Qawuqji left Palestine in October 1936, a local call to arms to help him

---

[1] Subhi Yasin, *Al-Thawra al-'Arabiyya al-Kubra (fi Filastin) 1936–1939* [*The Great Arab Revolt in Palestine, 1936–1939*] (Damascus: Shafa 'Amr Haifa, 1959), pp. 41–42.

raised 5,000 armed villagers, including women and children.[2] The High Commissioner assessed full-time rebel numbers in December 1938 at 2,000.[3] A British General Staff report detailed the 'active insurgents' as never exceeding 1,500.[4] Al-Qawuqji's unit of some 200 men deployed in September–October 1936 was the largest single band. More permanent and larger bands of fifty to seventy full-time insurgents fought all through the revolt and began appearing in the summer of 1936, whose members devoted all their time and energy to the insurgency, and most discrete full-time rebel bands did not exceed this figure and numbers diminished to single figures or a score of men by the end of the revolt. British Army accounts rarely talk of fighting rebel bands in single encounters of more than fifty men, but the rough terrain made for incomplete British assessments as soldiers could not count enemy numbers and they usually exaggerated them. British Palestine GOC Haining in April 1939 assessed that rebel bands of more than a dozen were by then a 'rarity.'[5]

Field Commanders

(1) Fawzi al-Qawuqji: arrived on 22 August 1936 with about 200 Iraqi, Transjordanian and Syrian volunteers, promoted originally by the head of an Iraqi delegation, Sa'id Thabit, and he fought in Samaria, the northern part of the West Bank. The Syrians included about thirty Druze. Al-Qawuqji left Palestine with his force for Iraq via Transjordan in late October 1936, arriving there in early November. Al-Qawuqji deployed four companies with commanders as follows: Iraqis (Jasim al-Karadi), Syrians (Muhammad al-Ashmar), Druze (Hamad Sa'ab), and Palestinians (Fakhri 'Abd al-Hadi).

Qassamites (2–6 below) of the *Ikhwan al-Qassam* (Brethren of al-Qassam), Porath recording that these commanders were the most nationalistic and were 'important and devout organisers and commanders' of rebel units, with alternative names given in parentheses:

---

[2] Akram Zu'aytir, *Al-Haraka al-Wataniya al-Filastiniyya, 1935–39: Yawmiyyat Akram Zu'aytir* [*The Palestinian National Movement, 1935–39: Diaries of Akram Zu'aytir*] [1980] (Beirut: IPS, 1992), pp. 221ff.

[3] Yehoshua Porath, *The Palestinian Arab National Movement: From Riots to Rebellion. Volume 2, 1929–1939* (London: Cass, 1977), p. 248.

[4] A. R. B. Linderman, *Rediscovering Irregular Warfare: Colin Gubbins and the Origins of Britain's Special Operations Executive* (Norman, OK: University of Oklahoma Press, 2016), p. 77.

[5] Despatch on the Operations carried out by the British Forces in Palestine and Transjordan, 1 November 1938–31 March 1939, GOC Palestine to WO London, 24 April 1939, Evetts Papers, File 1, LHCMA.

(2) Khalil Muhammad 'Isa (Khalil al-'Issa, Abu Ibrahim al-Kabir) (see 14 below).

(3) Yusuf Sa'id Abu Durra (hanged, see 13 below).

(4) Shaykh Farhan al-Sa'di (betrayed to the British 22 November 1937 and hanged five days later).

(5) Shaykh 'Atiyya Muhammad 'Awad (killed in battle March 1938).

(6) Muhammad al-Salih (Abu Khalid) (of Silat al-Dahr) (killed 13 September 1938 in an RAF-led attack at Dayr Ghassanah during a rebel meeting).[6]

Nationalist activists (7–15 below), some described by the British and by Jewish authors as criminals and fugitives, often fighting in the area close to their homes, including two Qassamites listed above, and one of al-Qawuqji's subordinates:

(7) 'Abd al-Qadir al-Husayni, Jerusalem area (wounded and captured in 1936, wounded again in either 1938 or 1939, probably November 1938, killed fighting the Jews in April 1948). The Cameronians recorded capturing him on 7 October 1936, after which at some point the British must have released him in the ceasefire period, killing in the same firefight 'one of the six most important leaders in Palestine' 'SAID EL A'ASI.'[7]

(8) Fakhri 'Abd al-Hadi of 'Arraba, Sha'rawiyya area, north of Tulkarm up to Jenin, also Jezreel valley (killed in 1943, possibly because of his collaboration with the British during the revolt).

(9) 'Isa al-Battat, Hebron sub-district (killed May 1938), succeeded by 'Abd al-Halim al-Jawlani (colloquially Julani also known as Abu Zaydan, Shalaf, Abu Shalaf or Abu Mansur) in the Hebron area. Policeman Briance's comment on the death of 'Easa Battat' was that police caught him and he was 'promptly shot on the spot.'[8]

(10) Hasan Salama (Abu 'Ali) of Qulah, Jaffa-Lydda-Ramleh area (possibly collaborated with the Jews in 1936, died fighting the Israelis in June 1948).[9]

(11) 'Arif 'Abd al-Raziq (Abu Faysal) of Tayiba, Bani Sa'b area (south of Tulkarm) (surrendered to the French April 1939).

---

[6] Porath, *The Palestinian Arab National Movement*, p. 183.

[7] Entry, 7 October 1936, 2nd Bn Cameronians, War Diary Palestine, September–December 1936, South Lanarkshire Council, Hamilton.

[8] Letter, Briance to Mother, 14 May 1938, Unnamed Loose Folder of Letters from Briance, Briance Papers, BP.

[9] Hillel Cohen, *Army of Shadows: Palestinian Collaboration with Zionism, 1917–1948* (Berkeley, CA: University of California Press, 2008), p. 255.

(12) 'Abd al-Rahim al-Hajj Muhammad (Abu Kamal) of Dhanaba, Wadi al-Sha'ir area (the valley extending from Tulkarm to Nablus) (killed March 1939, peace bands helping to track him down).[10]

(13) Yusuf Sa'id Abu Durra of Silat al-Harithiyyah in northern Samaria, Haifa and the Jezreel valley (captured in the summer of 1939 and hanged in late 1939 or, more likely, early 1940, at one stage 'chased down' by joint Haganah-Druze unit).[11]

(14) Khalil Muhammad 'Isa (Abu Ibrahim al-Kabir) of Shafa 'Amr in the northern district.[12]

(15) 'Abdallah al-As'ad – northern front commander (killed in battle March 1938).

Commissars (16–18 below): rebel HQ in Syria established a new band of better-educated political commissar-style deputy commanders in December 1938:

(16) Wasif Kamal and Mamduh al-Sukhn from Nablus, deputies for 'Abd al-Rahim al-Hajj Muhammad.

(17) Farid Ya'ish of Nablus (arrested a week after starting in post) and Mustafa Tahir from Jaffa (both teachers), deputies for 'Arif 'Abd al-Raziq.

(18) al-Hajj Khalid al-Farid (a journalist) from Jaffa and Amin al-Sharqawi of Haifa, deputies for Yusuf Sa'id Abu Durra.[13]

(19) Jewish files noted that Damascus appointed Abu Bakr of Silat al-Dahr (Silat ed-Daher south of Jenin) to replace 'Abd al-Rahim al-Hajj Muhammad after his death, 'previously a teacher and a student, tried to stamp out the anarchy which various gang commanders had introduced into the country' but he 'did not succeed' as monetary gain and opportunities for power outweighed Abu Bakr's instructions from Damascus that had 'no fist.'[14]

(20) Palestinian–Israeli author Mustafa Kabha adds to this list Tawfiq al-Ibrahim (Abu Ibrahim al-Saghir) of lower Galilee, and Fawzi Rashid, 'Abdallah al-Sha'ir and 'Abdallah al-Asbah of Safad.[15]

---

[10] Ibid., p. 152.
[11] Ibid., p. 167.
[12] Porath, *The Palestinian Arab National Movement*, p. 185.
[13] Ibid., p. 258.
[14] Appendix: Explanatory Notes, Captured and Translated Arabic Material with Commentary, p. 130, Wingate Papers, Microfilm M2313, BL.
[15] Mustafa Khaba, *The Palestinian People: Seeking Sovereignty and State* (Boulder, CO and London: Lynne Rienner, 2014), p. 13.

Central Organisation

The French held Hajj Amin in internal exile in Lebanon after his arrival from Palestine in October 1937. Thus, 'Izzat Darwaza was a central figure in the 'Central Committee of the Jihad (Holy War)' in Damascus, arriving there in December 1937. The membership of this higher Central Committee command was not stable and included Akram Zu'aytir, Mu'in al-Madi, Muhammad 'Izzat Darwaza, Khalil Muhammad 'Isa, and Jamal al-Husayni, some of whom were members of the AHC.[16] Hajj Amin directed this Committee remotely. The Central Committee tried relentlessly to organise the rebels and it offered the command of the rebel bands to a Syrian. He declined. In early 1938, Hajj Amin offered field command to al-Qawuqji and two others, all of whom said no, the refusal stemming from internal Syrian causes. The Central Committee operated in the background from the autumn of 1937 to the end of the revolt. British and Jewish agents put pressure on veterans of the 1925 Syrian revolt against the French not to go to Palestine. Meanwhile, rebels in Palestine in 1937–38 opposed al-Qawuqji becoming their commander, remembering the problems of late 1936 when they clashed with his command in Samaria. Overall, the rebels' internal power structures in the field developed 'without any regard' for the Central Committee and so all through the revolt local bands organised themselves organically.[17] This caused a raft of problems and the failure of the Central Committee to appoint a commander-in-chief meant that it formed in the autumn of 1938 a 'Bureau of the Arab Revolt in Palestine' of regional commanders, comprised of 'Abd al-Rahim al-Hajj Muhammad (Abu Kamal), 'Arif 'Abd al-Raziq (Abu Faysal), Yusuf Sa'id Abu Durra, Hasan Salama (Abu 'Ali) and 'Abd al-Fattah al-Hassan (the last not a band commander and charged with logistics, and killed it seems in January 1939 by British-backed Nashashibi forces).[18] The Bureau was 'stillborn from the outset,' not least as the Jerusalem–Hebron bands were not represented, and 'Abd al-Qadir al-Husayni (as in 1936) resisted his subordination to peasant commanders.[19] 'At best the Bureau served as a limited coordination body,' says Porath.[20] The head of the Bureau should have changed in

---

[16] Porath, *The Palestinian Arab National Movement*, pp. 242–43.
[17] Ibid., p. 244; Joseph Nevo, 'Palestinian–Arab Violent Activity during the 1930s,' in Michael J. Cohen and Martin Kolinsky (eds), *Britain and the Middle East in the 1930s: Security Problems, 1935–39* (London: Macmillan/King's, 1992), pp. 180–82.
[18] Death mentioned is of Abdul Fattah in 2nd Battalion West Yorkshire Regiment, Battalion Intelligence Summary No. 16, Ramallah, 2 February 1939, RYM.
[19] Porath, *The Palestinian Arab National Movement*, pp. 244–45.
[20] Ibid.

rotation but, in reality, two commanders competed for the role: 'Abd al-Rahim al-Hajj Muhammad and 'Arif 'Abd al-Raziq. 'Abd al-Rahim al-Hajj Muhammad wanted to establish a rebel General Council, an idea supported by Yusuf Sa'id Abu Durra, to confirm him as 'Commander-in-Chief' of the revolt (a title he had assumed in the spring of 1938). 'Arif 'Abd al-Raziq opposed this and called himself 'Commander-in-Chief of the Rebels in Southern Syria,' while 'Abd al-Rahim al-Hajj Muhammad, as just mentioned, called himself 'Commander-in-Chief of the Arab Rebels in Palestine.' Muhammad al-Salih, the Qassamite, tried to mediate between the two and called rebels to a meeting on 13 September 1938 at Dayr Ghassanah but the RAF attacked this gathering and killed al-Salih. In February 1939, the Central Committee insisted on the return of 'Abd al-Rahim al-Hajj Muhammad to Palestine (he was out of the country then) but he said that he would only return if the Central Committee recognised him as Commander-in-Chief and it did this as he was one of its best field commanders. A few days after his return, in March 1939, the Army surrounded his force and killed him. The revolt was fading by this stage and the Central Command appointed a former schoolteacher to command in Palestine, Ahmad Muhammad Hasan.

Local Organisation

The bands in the field were organised locally in the following structures:

- 'Abd al-Rahim al-Hajj Muhammad organised sub-*fasa'il*, each one representing a village or cluster of villages and each with a leader who deferred to him.
- 'Arif 'Abd al-Raziq had a similar hierarchy with eight subordinate commanders at the head of eight bands under his general command.
- Fakhri 'Abd al-Hadi organised his followers into one larger band of 100 men.
- The Jerusalem area had one big band of several hundred members, many former members of the youth troops of the Palestine Arab Party and 'Abd al-Qadir al-Husayni joined this band which was based in Ramallah district.

Local coordination from the outset of the revolt was poor, so when in 1936 initial 'steps were taken to form a unified framework for the rebels, neither 'Abd al-Qadir al-Husayni nor other commanders from the Southern regions participated.'[21] At the end of July 1936, the rebels made their first attempts to coordinate bands; they held a second meeting

[21] Ibid., p. 186.

to arrange coordination on 7 August 1936, where Fakhri 'Abd al-Hadi was regarded as Commander-in-Chief of all bands in the Jenin–Tulkarm area. In the summer of 1936, 'Abd al-Hadi and not 'Abd al-Qadir al-Husayni was the central figure in the revolt. The arrival of full-time fighters made provision of supplies and arms difficult, with the AHC and the National Committees bearing the cost. Al-Qawuqji's arrival in late August 1936 should have improved local-level organisation but he never asserted full control over local Palestinian units. Al-Qawuqji issued *bayanat* published by the 'General Command of the Arab Revolt in Southern Syria (Palestine)' and he signed these as the 'Commander-in-Chief of the Revolt in Southern Syria.' On 2 September 1936, al-Qawuqji met six commanders of local bands – Fakhri 'Abd al-Hadi, 'Abd al-Rahim al-Hajj Muhammad, 'Arif 'Abd al-Raziq, Shaykh Farhan al-Sa'di, Shaykh 'Atiyya Muhammad 'Awad, and Muhammad al-Salih (the last three were Qassamites) – and they gave him a written assurance of his position as overall commander.[22] Al-Qawuqji organised his force into four companies of Iraqis (Jasim al-Karadi), Syrians (Muhammad al-Ashmar), Druze (Hamad Sa'ab), and Palestinians ('Abd al-Hadi), with an attached intelligence unit (Munir al-Ra'is, it seems).[23] The British first clashed with al-Qawuqji's forces on 3 September 1936, when the rebels shot down at least one RAF aeroplane. Even before this battle, rumours spread that al-Qawuqji was a British spy sent by the British commander in Transjordan, John Bagot Glubb 'Pasha,' or that he had a link to RAF intelligence in Iraq.[24] The departure of al-Qawuqji in late October 1936 meant the collapse of rebel hierarchical military structures. The second stage of the revolt began when Qassamites who were active in lower Galilee under Muhammad al-Salih killed British official Lewis Andrews in Nazareth on 26 September 1937. Stockpiling of weapons from 1936 supported the second phase of the revolt and during this stage of fighting the Qassamites enlisted volunteers and gave villagers weapons training.

THE BRITISH

Introduction

Two infantry battalions based in Jerusalem and Haifa from the Loyal (North Lancashire) and the (Queen's Own) Cameron Highlanders regiments garrisoned Palestine in April 1936, with an attached RAF

---

[22] Ibid., p. 189.
[23] Ibid.
[24] Ibid., p. 191; Laila Parsons, *The Commander: Fawzi al-Qawuqji and the Fight for Arab Independence* (New York, NY: Hill and Wang, 2016), p. 117.

bomber squadron and one armoured car squadron less a section of cars, all under overall RAF command and with headquarters in Jerusalem.[25] The British could also call on the British-led Transjordan Frontier Force (TJFF) of over 1,000 men with a base near Beisan, and the TJFF served in Palestine against the rebels during the revolt. After the start of the revolt, there was a reinforcement of a new battalion of infantry from Egypt in early May 1936, after which British troops surged into Palestine in two waves: one in June–July and a second echelon in September– October 1936. There was a full infantry division in Palestine by late July 1936 – a division typically had twelve infantry battalions in three brigades equalling some 12,000 men with support troops – and by October 1936 the British had over twenty battalions of infantry in or on their way to Palestine. They organised these into two divisions based in Jerusalem (1st Division) and in Haifa (5th Division), each subdivided into brigades and then battalion areas of operation further broken down into picquets and posts that sent out mobile 'flying' columns, up to 25,000 soldiers in total. The movement of troops to Palestine in September 1936 was 'the biggest movement of a large body' of troops since the First World War, in the words of a contemporary in-house military journal.[26] The schedule below establishes that the deployment of troops to Palestine to pacify the country was immense and much more extensive than is allowed for in accounts of the revolt: twenty-four infantry battalions in 1936 and twenty- eight by 1938–39, leaving aside extensive cavalry-armour and support troops. In the second phase of the revolt, notably after September 1938 with the resolution of the Munich crisis, the British sent out to Palestine two infantry divisions (7th in Jerusalem under O'Connor and 8th in Haifa under Montgomery) plus an extra infantry brigade, up to 30,000 soldiers. Support troops, cavalry units with tanks and armoured cars, RAF warplanes, and attached Royal Navy units augmented the infantry core to the force in Palestine, including Royal Engineers and the Royal Army Ordnance Corps whose men demolished houses and defused rebel mines. The Army in the inter-war years had a strength of about 180,000, a third of which was in India, so at least a quarter of the remainder was in Palestine.[27] In October 1938 before the troop surge following the Munich settlement, the infantry deployment was as follows:

---

[25] See M. Roubicek, *Echo of the Bugle: Extinct Military and Constabulary Forces in Palestine and Transjordan, 1915–1967* (Jerusalem: Franciscan, 1975), pp. 29ff.

[26] Anon., 'Service Problems in Palestine: From a Correspondent in Jerusalem,' *Journal of the Royal United Service Institution* 81 (November 1936), p. 806.

[27] Anthony Clayton, '"Deceptive Might": Imperial Defence and Security, 1900–1968,' in Judith M. Brown and Wm. Roger Louis (eds), *The Oxford History of the British Empire. Volume 4, The Twentieth Century* (Oxford: Oxford University Press, 1999), p. 283.

7th Division (HQ Jerusalem, General O'Connor):
   18th Brigade (Jerusalem, 3 infantry battalions)
   19th Brigade (Jaffa, 3 infantry battalions)
8th Division (HQ Haifa, General Montgomery):
   14th Brigade (Nablus, 4 infantry battalions)
   16th Brigade (Haifa, 5 infantry battalions)
GHQ reserve:
   20th Brigade (2 infantry battalions)

The schedule below lists the tour dates and areas of deployment for battalions and units. The names and dates in parentheses after the units list the men who died during the revolt and are buried in Ramleh British war cemetery in Israel, with month of death and multiples if there was more than one death that month. They help to confirm deployments and give an idea of when fighting was most intense. The schedule omits deaths noted on headstones as accidental and deaths from December 1936 to August 1937. Some of the deaths during periods of fighting will have been non-combat related but this is not always discernible from the headstones, only some of which record 'killed in action,' 'killed on active duty,' 'on duty' or 'in service' or 'died of injuries.' Some give the location of a battle with rebels, others mark an 'accidental death.'

Commanders (AOCs and GOCs) in Palestine:

Air-Vice Marshal Richard Peirse: 30 September 1933–8/15 September 1936[28]

Lieutenant-General Sir John Dill: 8/15 September 1936–21 July/19 August 1937[29]

Lieutenant-General Archibald Wavell: 21 July/19 August 1937–26 March/9 April 1938[30]

Lieutenant-General Sir Robert Haining: 26 March/9 April 1938–14 July 1939

Lieutenant-General Michael Barker: 14 July/3 August 1939 onwards

---

[28] The *Air Force List* for October 1936 gives a date of 15 September 1936 for the change in command; the *Army List* for December 1936 gives a date of 9 September for the start of Dill's command.

[29] The *Army List* for December 1937 gives a date of 19 August 1937 for the start of Wavell's command.

[30] The *Army List* for June 1938 gives a date of 26 March 1938 for the start of Haining's command.

Organisation

1936

Infantry

(1) **2nd Bn, Bedfordshire and Hertfordshire Regiment**[31]

Dates: combat period of 2 June to 2 October 1936, sailed for the UK on 29 November 1936

Deployment: based in Jaffa for some of this period assisting in the destruction of the old town, based in the south of the country with Southern Brigade, also at Qalqilya, deployed in Samaria in late October 1936 tracking al-Qawuqji's band

Deaths: Ramleh June 1936, August 1936, September 1936, October 1936, November 1936

(2) **2nd Bn, Berkshire Regiment**[32]

Dates: This battalion had been in Palestine in 1934 and was ordered to Palestine again in May 1936 when it was based in Egypt but the order was then cancelled, although a detachment of some sort from the regiment did go to Haifa in May 1936 it appears, with one history talking of a 'brief emergency return' when the unit was based in Egypt in 1936–37, and Berkshire Regiment officer Tony Simonds was in Palestine during the revolt as a regimental intelligence officer[33]

(3) **2nd Bn, The Buffs (Royal East Kent Regiment)**

Dates: arrived in Palestine in October 1936

Deployment: in Acre in November 1936

(4) **2nd Bn, (Queen's Own) Cameron Highlanders**

Dates: in Palestine from November 1935 to October 1936, stationed in Egypt by early 1937

Deployment: on operations with the Dorsetshire Regiment in Latrun area in June 1936

Deaths: Ramleh May 1936, September 1936 x2

---

[31] Royal Anglian Regiment, *The Story of the Bedfordshire and Hertfordshire Regiment (The 16th Regiment of Foot). Volume 2, 1914–1958* (Regimental History Committee, 1986), p. 421; 2nd Battalion, Bedfordshire and Hertfordshire Regiment, War Diary, X550/3/9, BLARS; *The Wasp: The Journal of the 16th Foot* [Bedfordshire Regiment] 8/5 (1936) pp. 269ff.

[32] Gordon Blight, *The History of the Royal Berkshire Regiment* (London: Staples, 1953), pp. 123ff. The Rifles Berkshire and Wiltshire Museum has no record of the Berkshires serving in Palestine.

[33] F. Myatt, *The Royal Berkshire Regiment* (London: Hamish Hamilton, 1968), p. 108; Typed Memoir, Pieces of War, Simonds Papers, 08/46/1, IWMD.

(5) **2nd Bn, The Cameronians (Scottish Rifles)**[34]

Dates: in Palestine, from 16 September 1936 to 21 December 1936

Deployment: in the south around Bethlehem and Hebron

(6) **2nd Bn, Cheshire Regiment**[35]

Dates: arrived 8/9 June 1936 and stayed to 8 December 1936

Deployment: based at Tulkarm, detachment served in Gaza and Jaffa

Deaths: Ramleh June 1936, August 1936, September 1936 x3, October 1936

(7) **3rd Bn, Coldstream Guards**

Dates: Late September 1936 left the UK and landed in Haifa on 1 October 1936, sailed for home with the Scots Guards in December 1936 to arrive back in the UK on 29 December 1936

Deployment: one company in Nablus in November 1936

(8) **2nd Bn, Dorsetshire Regiment**[36]

Dates: arrived 10 June 1936 in Palestine and left from Haifa on 20 December 1936 (CO was Col C. H. Woodhouse)

Deployment: stationed in and around Jerusalem, units in Hebron, and units deployed up to Nablus, in September 1936 deployed north to Nablus–Tulkarm–Jenin area and based in Jenin, deployed in Samaria in late October 1936 tracking al-Qawuqji's band

Deaths: Ramleh October 1936

(9) **2nd Bn, East Yorkshire Regiment** (some reservists from the (Queen's Own) Royal West Kent Regiment served with the East Yorkshire Regiment in August 1936)[37]

Dates: arrived at the end of the first phase of the revolt and involved in fighting in October 1936, left in November 1937 or January 1938

---

[34] War Diary, 2nd Battalion, The Cameronians, Cameronians (Scottish Rifles) Regimental Archive, South Lanarkshire Council, Hamilton.

[35] 2nd Battalion in *The Oak Tree: The Cheshire Regiment* (July–September 1936), p. 284 and (spring 1937), p. 52.

[36] C. T. Atkinson, *The Dorsetshire Regiment. Volume 2* (Oxford: Oxford University Press, 1947), pp. 182–87; Regimental War Diaries, Dorsetshire Regiment, 2nd Battalion Palestine 1937, Shelf C4, Box 3, KMM. The death in October 1936 was from a motor accident; the regiment won two Military Medals in Palestine, one of which is in the Keep Military Museum, Dorchester.

[37] *The Snapper: The Monthly Journal of the East Yorkshire Regiment (The Duke of York's Own)* 31–33 (1936–38).

(10) **1st Bn, Essex Regiment**[38]

> Dates: in Palestine from 31 October 1936 to 14 January 1938, and then 11 July 1938 until 27 September 1938 when sent back to Egypt, arriving there on 1 October 1938
>
> Deployment: stationed in the north of the country on the first tour, eventually in 16th Brigade with RUR and Hampshire regiments; second tour based again in the north in Galilee and Nazareth

(11) **2nd Bn, Hampshire Regiment**[39]

> Dates: arrived in Palestine on 1 October 1936, left on 15 January 1938
>
> Deployment: based in the north of the country in Nazareth and Jezreel (Esdraelon) valley in December 1937

(12) **1st Bn, King's Own Scottish Borderers**

> Dates: arrived 30 August 1936 and stayed in Palestine to 11 December 1936, some accounts say to early 1937
>
> Deployment: based in Galilee with HQ in Nazareth
>
> Deaths: Ramleh September 1936

(13) **2nd Bn, King's Royal Rifle Corps**

> Dates: arrived 29 September 1936 to 29 November 1937, sailed for UK, relieved by 1st Bn, Border Regiment
>
> Deployment: based at Sarafand, less one company at Wilhelma

(14) **2nd Bn, Lincolnshire Regiment**[40]

> Dates: arrived July 1936 from Malta, left Palestine on 11 December 1936, with war diaries noting active service between 19 July and 29 November 1936, deployed in Samaria in late October 1936 tracking al-Qawuqji's band (CO was Col Cooke)
>
> Deployment: based at Tulkarm with detachments elsewhere such as at Qalqilya
>
> Deaths: Ramleh, July 1936, September 1936

(15) **1st Bn, Loyal Regiment (North Lancashire)**[41]

> Dates: in Palestine from 24 February 1936 to 13 March 1937, dates confirmed by the regimental archive
>
> Deployment: based at Haifa with a small detachment at Nablus – including the future Field Marshal Sir Gerald Templer, then

---

[38] T. A. Martin, *The Essex Regiment, 1929–1950* (Essex: Regiment Association, 1952), p. 8.

[39] Entries in *Hampshire Regimental Journal* 32–33 (1937–38).

[40] Regimental War Diaries in Lincolnshire Regiment, LAL.

[41] Files in 1 Loyals 1914–38, Box 4, QLRM and further correspondence from the regimental museum, Fulwood Barracks, Preston.

a Brevet Major – that was withdrawn, and units sent to Metullah, Rosh Pinna, Safad, Jenin, and Nazareth, among other places deployed to in Galilee and northern Samaria

Deaths: Ramleh September 1936, October 1936

(16) **2nd Bn, North Staffordshire Regiment**[42]

Dates: arrived in September 1936 according to the regimental journal and left in January 1938 when relieved by the Royal Scots (Royal Regiment) (CO was Col Robb)

Deployment: initially posted to Jaffa and Qalqilya, and in December 1936 to Jerusalem and then late in 1936 two companies sent up to the Syrian border and served near Lake Tiberias

(17) **1st Bn, Royal Irish Fusiliers**[43]

Dates: arrived in Haifa on 24 September 1936 and left Palestine just before Christmas 1936

Deployment: served in Nablus and Ramallah

(18) **2nd Bn, Royal Northumberland Fusiliers**

Dates: left UK 12 September 1936 for Palestine, stayed to 31 December 1936

Deployment: relieved elements of the Dorsetshire Regiment around Jerusalem

Deaths: Ramleh November 1936

(19) **1st Bn, Royal Scots Fusiliers**

Dates: arrived June 1936

Deployment: operated in Lydda area August 1936, deployed in Samaria in late October 1936 tracking al-Qawuqji's band

Deaths: Ramleh September 1936

(20) **2nd Bn, Scots Guards**[44]

Dates: arrived in Haifa on 30 September 1936 and departed Palestine in December to arrive back in the UK on 29 December 1936

Deployment: based in Jerusalem

---

[42] *China Dragon: Regimental Magazine of the North Staffordshire Regiment* 22/2 (December 1936), p. 65; H. Cook, *History of the North Staffordshire Regiment* (London: Leo Cooper, 1970), p. 103.

[43] From M. Cunliffe, *The Royal Irish Fusiliers 1793–1950* (London: Oxford University Press, 1952), p. 375; correspondence from the regimental museum, Armagh, Northern Ireland.

[44] There was a possible deployment of the 1st Battalion, Scots Guards to Palestine in 1938 but there are no details in the standard regimental history: David Erskine, *The Scots Guards, 1919–1955* (London: Clowes, 1956).

(21) **1st Bn, Seaforth Highlanders**
Dates: arrived May/June 1936 and stayed in Palestine until at
least October 1936
Deployment: stationed for some or all the period at Nablus
Deaths: Ramleh June 1936 x2, July 1936, August 1936 x3

(22) **2nd Bn, South Wales Borderers**
Dates: served in Palestine during the 1929 disturbances,
arrived on 14–18 July 1936 and stayed in Palestine to 11
December 1936
Deployment: based in Jaffa and Rehovot
Deaths: Ramleh August 1936

(23) **2nd Bn, West Yorkshire Regiment (Prince of Wales's Own)**
Dates: in Palestine, 1 October to 19 December 1936
Deployment: deployed in Samaria in late October 1936
tracking al-Qawuqji's band
Deaths: Ramleh October 1936 x2

(24) **1st Bn, York and Lancaster Regiment**[45]
Dates: arrived from Egypt on 8 June 1936 and in Palestine to
29 November 1936
Deployment: based at Nazareth, Safad, Afule, Rosh Pinna
and Beisan
Deaths: Ramleh July 1936, August 1936 x4, September
1936 x3

Cavalry and Armour

(1) **11th Hussars**[46]
Dates: based in Egypt and moved to Palestine and started
operations on 11 July 1936, stayed to October 1936 when
returned to Egypt
Deployment: based at Sarafand, served near Jenin August
1936, deployed in Samaria in late October 1936 tracking
al-Qawuqji's band

(2) **8th (King's Royal Irish) Hussars**
Dates: based in Egypt and deployed to Palestine by road on 26
June 1936, returning to Egypt on 14–15 November 1936
Deployment: outskirts of Jerusalem but units went on to
Gaza, Nablus, Beersheba, and Jericho

---

[45] O. F. Sheffield, *The York and Lancaster Regiment, 1919–1953* (Aldershot: Gale and Polden, 1956), pp. 2–8; *The Tiger and Rose: A Monthly Journal of the York and Lancaster Regiment* 9/16 (June 1936).
[46] Dudley Clark, *The Eleventh at War* (London: Michael Joseph, 1952), p. 44.

(3) **6th Bn, Royal Tank Regiment/Corps**[47]
  Dates: May–3 November 1936
  Deployment: C Company of the battalion went to Palestine
  from its base in Egypt, deployed in Samaria in late October
  1936 tracking al-Qawuqji's band
  Deaths: Ramleh October 1936

RAF and Support Units

RAF (Ramleh August 1936, September 1936 x3)
Royal Army Service Corps and Royal Signals
Royal Army Ordnance Corps (Ramleh July 1936 but also
  marked as with Cheshire Regiment, November 1936)
Royal Artillery (Ramleh August 1936)
Royal Engineers (Ramleh September 1936, November 1936 x2)
One company of armoured cars (Ramleh July 1936, from RAF)
Royal Navy and Royal Marine detachments

1937

Infantry

(1) **2nd Bn, Black Watch**
  Dates: arrived and relieved the Royal Sussex Regiment in
  September 1937
  Deployment: based in Jerusalem in November 1937
  Deaths: Ramleh October 1937, November 1937 x2
(2) **1st Bn, Border Regiment**[48]
  Dates: arrived on 29 November 1937 and stationed in
  Palestine to April–May 1939, arriving back in UK on 7
  May 1939
  Deployment: in the south of the country in Ramleh area, and
  then with HQ in Jenin and to Samaria (Ya'bad and Umm
  al-Fahm)
  Deaths: Ramleh December 1937
(3) **2nd Bn, East Yorkshire Regiment**
  Dates: arrived at the end of the first phase of the revolt and
  involved in fighting in October 1936, left in November
  1937 or January 1938

---

[47] The Tank Museum at Bovingdon confirmed to the author that C Coy from the 6th
  Battalion, Royal Tank Regiment went to Palestine from Egypt in 1936.
[48] 1st Battalion, Border Regiment, Regimental Diary 1937–39, KORRM; *The Border
  Regiment Regimental Association Newsletter* 2/7 (June 1939), p. 6, KORRM.

(4) **1st Bn, Essex Regiment**

   Dates: in Palestine from 31 October 1936 to 14 January 1938, and then second tour of duty from 11 July 1938 until 27 September 1938 when sent back to Egypt, arriving there on 1 October 1938

   Deployment: stationed in the north of the country on the first tour, eventually in 16th Brigade with RUR and Hampshire regiments; second tour based again in the north in Galilee and Nazareth

   Deaths: Ramleh September 1937

(5) **2nd Bn, Hampshire Regiment**

   Dates: arrived in Palestine on 1 October 1936, left on 15 January 1938

   Deployment: based in the north of the country in Nazareth and Jezreel (Esdraelon) valley in December 1937

   Deaths: Ramleh October 1937

(6) **2nd Bn, North Staffordshire Regiment**

   Dates: arrived in September 1936 according to the regimental journal and left in January 1938 when relieved by the Royal Scots (Royal Regiment) (CO was Col Robb)

   Deployment: initially posted to Jaffa and Qalqilya, and in December 1936 to Jerusalem and in December 1937 units went north to the Haifa–Safad road where they fought a battle with rebels at Wadi 'Amud, losing a Private Creasy (spelt Creasey in Ramleh cemetery)[49]

   Deaths: Ramleh December 1937

(7) **1st Bn, Royal Sussex Regiment**[50]

   Dates: arrived December 1936 – 'towards the end of 1936' says the official history[51] – and left Palestine by November 1937, possibly in September 1937, relieved by the 2nd Bn, Black Watch

   Deployment: based in Jerusalem

(8) **2nd Bn, Wiltshire Regiment**

   Dates: sailed for Palestine in September 1936 and returned in September 1937

   Deployment: to Sarafand

[49] *China Dragon: Regimental Magazine of the North Staffordshire Regiment* 23/2 (April 1938), pp. 48–51.

[50] Gen Wavell mentioned (in his papers held by his grandson Owen Humphrys) that he wanted to retain the Sussex Regiment in September 1937; the Sussex Regiment left Palestine in October 1937 according to Wavell; the regimental association confirmed that the 1st Battalion left Palestine in September 1937.

[51] G. D. Martineau, *A History of the Royal Sussex Regiment, 1701–1953* (Chichester: Moore, 1955), p. 210.

1938–39

Infantry

(1) **1st Bn Argyll and Sutherland Highlanders**[52]

Dates: advance party arrived in Jenin 17 April 1939, the main body arriving in Haifa on 2 May 1939, left Palestine between 4 and 8 September 1940, or June 1940 in some accounts

Deployed: with 16th Brigade in the north of Palestine in Galilee, in Jenin in September 1939

Deaths: Ramleh June 1939

(2) **1st Bn, Bedfordshire and Hertfordshire Regiment**[53]

Dates: arrived in Palestine from India on 11 October 1938, left 18 July 1939 for Egypt

Deployment: based in the south of the country around Ramleh and Qibya

Deaths: Ramleh January 1939, April 1939 x4

(3) **2nd Bn, Black Watch** (with a reinforcement of 200 men from the 1st Bn, Black Watch)

Dates: arrived in September 1937 to Jerusalem and in spring of 1938 went to Nablus

Deployment: Based in Jerusalem in September 1939

Deaths: Ramleh June 1938, July 1938, August 1938 x2, May 1939, June 1939 x2, November 1939

(4) **1st Bn, Border Regiment**

Dates: arrived on 29 November 1937 and stationed in Palestine to April–May 1939

Deployment: in south of country in Ramleh area, and then with HQ in Jenin and to Samaria (Ya'bad and Umm al-Fahm)

Deaths: Ramleh March 1938, October 1938

(5) **1st Bn, The Buffs (Royal East Kent Regiment)**[54]

Dates: arrived in October 1938 and stayed to 1939, leaving for Egypt, in May 1939

Deaths: Ramleh November 1938, January 1939, June 1939 x4

---

[52] P. J. R. Mileham. *Fighting Highlanders! A History of the Argyll and Sutherland Highlanders* (London: Arms and Armour, 1993), p. 109.

[53] 1st Battalion, Bedfordshire and Hertfordshire Regiment, Digest of Service, 1938–39, X5500/2/2, BLARS.

[54] Gregory Blaxland, *The Buffs (Royal East Kent Regiment) (The 3rd Regiment of Foot)* (London: Leo Cooper, 1972), p. 92.

(6) **3rd Bn, Coldstream Guards**[55]

> Dates: arrived from Egypt in October 1938, and left in April 1939 to go back to Egypt
>
> Deployment: October 1938 in Jerusalem for the capture of the old city, where the battalion fought as Monck's Regiment to preserve secrecy, then deployed in the south to Gaza, Jericho, and Bethlehem, and subsequently to Jaffa, Haifa, Acre, Lydda, Tulkarm Abu Dis, and Sarafand
>
> Deaths: Ramleh October 1938, November 1938, December 1938[56]

(7) **1st Bn, Essex Regiment**

> Dates: in Palestine from 31 October 1936 to 14 January 1938, and then second tour of duty from 11 July 1938 until 27 September 1938 when sent back to Egypt, arriving there on 1 October 1938
>
> Deployment: stationed in the north of the country on the first tour, eventually in 16th Brigade with RUR and Hampshire regiments; second tour based again in the north in Galilee and Nazareth
>
> Deaths: Ramleh July 1938, August 1938

(8) **1st Bn, Green Howards**[57]

> Dates: the regiment served in Palestine in 1929 during the riots, arrived again in October 1938 and left Palestine in April 1939 for the UK
>
> Deployment: covering the road from Jerusalem to Haifa via Nablus
>
> Deaths: Ramleh December 1938, March 1939 x3[58]

(9) **1st Bn, Hampshire Regiment**

> Dates: served in Palestine between 9/10 October 1938 to July 1939
>
> Deployment: served near Acre
>
> Deaths: Ramleh January 1939

---

[55] Michael Howard and John Sparrow, *The Coldstream Guards, 1920–1946* (London: Oxford University Press, 1951), pp. 10–11.

[56] Guardsman Patfield died in the taking of Jerusalem's old city in October 1938: Julian Paget, *Second to None: The Coldstream Guards, 1650–2000* (London: Leo Cooper, 2000), p. 83.

[57] G. and J. Powell, *The History of the Green Howards: Three Hundred Years of Service* (London: Leo Cooper, 2002), pp. 181–82.

[58] These three dead were non-combat related, the result of a vehicle fuel tank exploding: Powell, *The History of the Green Howards*, p. 182.

(10) **2nd Bn, Highland Light Infantry**
Dates: arrived in Palestine in 1938, possibly in June 1938, and still in combat in September 1939
Deaths: Ramleh January 1939, June 1939, July 1939 x2, September 1939 x3

(11) **1st Bn, Irish Guards**
Dates: July–September 1938
Deployment: Nablus
Deaths: Ramleh August 1938 x2, September 1938

(12) **2nd Bn, King's Own Royal Regiment (Lancaster)**[59]
Dates: deployed to Palestine, arriving Haifa 19 September 1938 to June 1940 when it left for Egypt (CO was Col Neil Ritchie)
Deployment: based in Gaza and Ein Karem, in Hebron in September 1939
Deaths: Ramleh September 1938, October 1938 x2, November 1938 x2, May 1939 x2, November 1939, December 1939

(13) **2nd Bn, Leicestershire Regiment**
Dates: in Palestine October 1938–September 1939
Deployment: in Acre district
Deaths: Ramleh October 1938 x3, November 1938, December 1938, February 1939 x2, March 1939, May 1939, August 1939, December 1939

(14) **1st Bn, Manchester Regiment**[60]
Dates: arrived January 1938 and in Palestine to 25 September 1938
Deployment: served in the north of Palestine near Acre – some sources say Tiberias – and in Galilee, supplied men for the Special Night Squads
Deaths: Ramleh March 1938, August 1938 x4

(15) **2nd Bn, Middlesex Regiment**
Dates: served around Tiberias in January 1938
Deaths: Ramleh October 1938

(16) **2nd Bn, (Queen's Own) Royal West Kent Regiment** (some reservists from this regiment served with the East Yorkshire Regiment in August 1936 in Palestine)[61]

---

[59] Letters from Lt H. J. Darlington to his Wife, September 1938–December 1939, Darlington Papers, KO 1333/01, KORRM.

[60] The Wavell Papers (held by Owen Humphrys) note this regiment coming out in November 1937 to replace the Green Howards.

[61] For dates see the account by the unit CO Col W. V. Palmer in H. D. Chaplin, *The Queen's Own Royal West Kent Regiment* (London: Michael Joseph, 1954), pp. 73, 107, confirmed

Dates: arrived on 14 January 1938 and left Palestine on 22
March 1939 (CO was Col W. V. Palmer)

Deployment: served in Haifa area, supplied men for the
Special Night Squads

Deaths: Ramleh April 1938 x2, May 1938, July 1938,
October 1938 x2, November 1938 x2, December 1938 x2,
April 1939

(17) **2nd Bn, Queen's Royal Regiment (West Surrey)**[62]

Dates: arrived in Palestine on 10 January 1939 having
embarked from the UK on 31 December 1938, relieved the
Royal Scots (Royal Regiment), stayed to 7 September 1940
when it left for Egypt

Deployment: based around Tulkarm

Deaths: Ramleh January 1939, May 1939, June 1939,
December 1939

(18) **2nd Bn, Rifle Brigade**[63]

Dates: deployment to Palestine in 1939, arriving in June 1939
from India and leaving for Egypt in January 1940

Deployment: Nablus

Deaths: Ramleh June 1939, October 1939 x2, November 1939

(19) **2nd Bn, Royal Irish Fusiliers**

Dates: in Palestine from 15 October 1938 to 30 March 1939

Deployment: based at Haifa and Safad

Deaths: Ramleh November 1938 x3, January 1939 x2

(20) **1st Bn, Royal Northumberland Fusiliers**

Dates: in action retaking the old city of Jerusalem in
October 1938

Deaths: Ramleh October 1938, December 1938, February
1939 x2

(21) **1st Bn, Royal Scots (Royal Regiment)**[64]

Dates: arrived in Palestine in 13 January 1938 and left
Palestine on 11 January 1939 (sailing from Egypt on 13

by correspondence from Queen's Own Royal West Kent Regiment Museum, Maidstone.
The dead soldier in Ramleh cemetery from April 1939 (L/Cpl George Sprankling) is
from the 'Queen's Own Royal' Regiment (so presumably the West Kents) and is marked
as having 'died at Haifa on service' on 8 April 1939 and so must have died of wounds or
illness after his regiment had left Palestine.

[62] R. Foster, *The History of the Second Queen's Royal Regiment. Volume 8, 1924–1948*
(Aldershot: Gale and Polden, 1953), pp. 30–35, 112–14; correspondence from the
Princess of Wales's Royal Regiment and Queen's Regiment Museum, Dover and from
Surrey History Centre, Woking.

[63] Basil Harvey, *The Rifle Brigade* (London: Leo Cooper, 1975), p. 85.

[64] Trevor Royle, *The Royal Scots: A Concise History* (Edinburgh: Mainstream, 2006),
p. 156; A. Michael Brander, *The Royal Scots (The Royal Regiment)* (London: Leo

January 1939), took over from the 2nd Battalion North
Staffordshire Regiment and relieved by the Queen's Royal
Regiment (West Surrey), leaving the March 1939 death as
an outlier

Deployment: stationed at Sarafand with detachment at Lydda,
moved to West Bank on operations (Tulkarm and Nablus)

Deaths: Ramleh February 1938, March 1938 x2, July 1938 x2,
August 1938, September 1938, October 1938, November
1938 x5, December 1938, January 1939, March 1939 (regimental sources confirm that fifteen men died in Palestine;
the figures from Ramleh cemetery totals sixteen)

(22) **2nd Bn, Royal Ulster Rifles**

Dates: arrived in Palestine on 27 November 1937, stayed in
Palestine to 22 March 1939

Deployment: in Galilee with 16th Brigade, including along
Lebanese border, supplied men for the Special Night Squads

Deaths: Ramleh January 1938 x2, July 1938, September 1938
x4, February 1939

(23) **1st Bn, Sherwood Foresters**

Dates: in Palestine in 1939, confirmed by dead in Ramleh
war cemetery, and the battalion was still in Palestine in
September 1939

Deployment: in Haifa

Deaths: Ramleh May 1939, August 1939

(24) **1st Bn, South Staffordshire Regiment**[65]

Dates: arrived in September 1938 to September 1939 with a
regimental history noting that the battalion had no fatalities
in Palestine, despite the one dead from October 1938[66]

Deployment: based in Tiberias–Nazareth area

Deaths: Ramleh October 1938

(25) **1st Bn, Welch Regiment**[67]

Dates: arrived 3 May 1939 to 15 October 1939

Cooper, 1976), p. 80; Robert Paterson, *Pontius Pilate's Bodyguard: A History of the First
or the Royal Regiment of Foot, The Royal Scots (The Royal Regiment). Volume 2, 1919–2000*
(Edinburgh: The Royal Scots History Committee, 2001), pp. 52–59; correspondence
from the Royal Regiment of Scotland, The Castle, Edinburgh.

[65] Summary of Intelligence, Palestine and Transjordan, 18 November 1938, by Wing
Commander Ritchie at GHQ [23/38], CO 732/81/10, TNA notes the deployment of
2nd Battalion of the South Staffordshire Regiment on operations near Nazareth in
September–October 1938. Other sources state that it was the 1st Battalion of the South
Staffordshire Regiment that was present, such as W. L. Vale, *The History of the South
Staffordshire Regiment* (Aldershot: Gale and Polden, 1969), p. 398.

[66] Vale, *History of the South Staffordshire Regiment*, p. 399.

[67] 1st Battalion News in *Men of Harlech: Welch Regiment* (1939), pp. 86–90.

Deployment: based in Haifa in the north of Palestine, deployed to Lebanese border, and to Safad

Deaths: Ramleh July 1939, October 1939

(26) **2nd Bn, West Yorkshire Regiment (Prince of Wales's Own)**[68]

Dates: deployed from 14 October 1938 to 3 September 1939, or to 16 December 1939 as noted in the unit war diaries in the regimental archive in York

Deployment: based at Ramallah to July 1939, then Sarafand to October 1939, then Tiberias to December 1939

Deaths: Ramleh October 1938, December 1938, January 1939, June 1939

(27) **1st Bn, Worcestershire Regiment**[69]

Dates: arrived in Palestine 26 September 1938 and served to August 1939, so the one death in September 1939 could have been a soldier who died of wounds or illness

Deployment: based in the south of the country, in Hebron, Yatta and Bethlehem

Deaths: Ramleh October 1938 x2, November 1938, December 1938, July 1939, August 1939, September 1939

Cavalry and Armour

(1) **11th Hussars**

Dates: squadrons of the 11th Hussars in Palestine July 1938 to March 1939, but after October 1938 not all the regiment was in Palestine as some squadrons returned to Egypt

Deaths: Ramleh July 1938

(2) **1st The Royal Dragoons**

Dates: went to Palestine in the autumn of 1938 and seems to have been there when the Second World War started in September 1939

Deployment: Gedera

Deaths: Ramleh March 1939 x2, December 1939

(3) **4th/7th Royal Dragoon Guards**[70]

Dates: Motorised squadron sent to reinforce the Royal Scots Greys, sailing from UK on 4 October 1938 and stayed to August 1939

[68] The regimental archive gave the author the date of 3 September 1939.
[69] Lord Birdwood, *The Worcestershire Regiment, 1922–1950* (Aldershot: Gale and Polden, 1952), pp. 15–16.
[70] J. M. Brereton, *A History of the 4th/7th Royal Dragoon Guards* (Catterick: Published by the Regiment, 1982), p. 361.

(4) **5th Royal Inniskilling Dragoon Guards**
    Dates: squadron sent to Palestine in late 1938 to reinforce 1st
    Royal Dragoons
(5) **Royal Scots Greys**[71]
    Dates: on 30 September 1938 the regiment sailed for Palestine
    and on 5 November 1938 it moved to Rehovot; stayed in
    Palestine to May 1940
    Deployment: in Rehovot
    Deaths: Ramleh October 1938, May 1939, July 1939

RAF and Support Units

RAF (Ramleh February 1938 x3, April 1938 x2, August 1938
x6, October 1938, November 1938 x2, February 1939 x4 but
one of these deaths was at Amman, May 1939, June 1939 x4,
July 1939, August 1939, September 1939)
Arab Legion (Ramleh March 1939)
Military Police (Ramleh January 1938)
Royal Army Medical Corps (Ramleh July 1939)
Royal Army Service Corps (Ramleh October 1938, November
1938, March 1939, April 1939, May 1939)
Royal Artillery (Ramleh June 1939)
Royal Engineers (Ramleh January 1938, July 1938, August
1938, November 1938, April 1939, September 1939)
Royal Marines (from HMS *Malaya*) (Ramleh September 1938)

British Regimental Battle Honours
The following regiments have 'Palestine' or 'Mufti's Revolt in Palestine'
as a campaign or battle honour:

West Yorkshire Regiment (1936, 1938)
11th Hussars (1936, 1938–39)
The Cameronians (1936)
(Queen's Own) Royal West Kent Regiment (1938)[72]

The Army awarded soldiers who served in Palestine between 19 April
1936 and 3 September 1939 the campaign clasp (or bar) 'Palestine' to
the medal ribbon for the General Service Medal (1918).

---

[71] R. M. P. Carver, *Second to None: The Royal Scots Greys, 1919 to 1945* (Glasgow: Caxton, 1954), pp. 34–35.
[72] Campaign honours are from Arthur Swinson (ed.), *A Register of the Regiments and Corps of the British Army* (London: Archive Press, 1972).

Senior Police Officer Ranks and Numbers[73]

Inspector General of Police and Prisons
Deputy Inspector General (x2)
District Superintendent (x6)
Superintendent of Prisons (x1)
Deputy Superintendent (x10)
Ranks above All British
Assistant Superintendent (x22)
Rank above a Mix of British, Palestinian and Jewish
Acting Assistant Superintendent (x10)
Rank above a Mix of British, Palestinian and Jewish

Eldad Harouvi notes 3,216 policemen at the end of 1936 including the prison service staff, the Arab complement at 1,894 men.[74] A police history gives numbers for 1936 as 61 British officers, 693 British other ranks, 102 Palestinian officers and 2,027 Palestinian other ranks, so 2,883 in total.[75] The regular police force was 4,834 by the end of 1938 in another assessment.[76] These totals exclude supernumerary police as detailed in Chapter 7.

[73] *Palestine Civil Service List 1937* (Jerusalem: Government Printing Press, 1937), pp. 186ff.
[74] Eldad Harouvi, *Palestine Investigated: The Story of the CID of the Palestine Police Force, 1920–48* (Sussex: Academic Press 2016), p. 63.
[75] Charles Jeffries, *The Colonial Police* (London: Parrish, 1952), pp. 153–56.
[76] D. J. Clark, 'The Colonial Police and Anti-Terrorism: Bengal 1930–1936, Palestine 1937–1947, and Cyprus 1955–1959' (Doctoral Thesis: University of Oxford, 1978), pp. 148–50.

Appendix B
Casualties

British: Overall Numbers

The tally of British dead as discussed in Chapter 3 from the revolt was 244 soldiers and fifty-four police officers over the period of the revolt, April 1936–December 1939, omitting the months December 1936–August 1937. These figures derive from the headstones at Ramleh military, Haifa civil and military, and Jerusalem civil cemeteries.[1] (That the British neatly grouped their Service dead make this addition possible in a way that is impracticable for Jewish and Palestinian dead.) The rebels never killed any military personnel above the rank of Army major, two killed, plus two RAF squadron-leader equivalent rank, and three of these deaths may have been non-combat related. Casualties spiked between August and October 1936, with twenty-eight mostly combat dead, and in late 1938, corresponding to peaks of military operations. The Army and police figures here exclude headstones obviously marking deaths from accidents or illness as some do, recording, say, death by drowning or accidental death but as some are worded ambiguously it is certain that some of the 298 deaths (244 plus 54) are from non-combat causes, as is usual with any deployment of soldiers. If half this number were combat deaths, this gives a total figure of 122 military combat dead, added to which there are twenty-seven police combat deaths (half of fifty-four) totalling 149 Service combat deaths. As a comparator, in the US Army accidents caused over half of all deaths in active-duty male soldiers between 1990 and 1998.[2] The well-researched Thames TV 'Palestine: Promises, Rebellion and Abdication' programme (1977–78) gives a total of 153 British lives lost, so similar to the total presented

---

[1] Ramleh CWGC cemetery; Haifa Khayat Beach war cemetery and adjoining Haifa (Sharon) British civil cemetery; Haifa Jaffa Road cemetery; Jerusalem Protestant cemetery (Mount Zion, via Jerusalem University College); Jerusalem Latin (Catholic) cemetery (Mount Zion).

[2] Lisa Lewandowski-Romps et al., 'Risk Factors for Accident Death in the U.S. Army, 2004–2009,' *American Journal of Preventive Medicine* 47/6 (2014), pp. 745–53.

here; the less well-researched Wikipedia webpage for the Arab revolt has
a figure of 262 security force dead, derived from partial primary material
in a secondary source that when totalled equals 265 not 262 dead.[3]
As some sixty infantry battalions and armoured units rotated through
Palestine, excluding extensive support corps deployment, airmen, and
land-based naval units, the figure of 244 military dead is tiny, just
0.49 per cent of troop numbers assuming conservatively a total troop
throughput of 50,000, or 0.24 per cent combat fatalities if we assume
that half the number were non-combat deaths. In thirty-six months of
active operations, April 1936–December 1939, excluding December
1936–August 1937, seven soldiers per month died on average, many from
non-combat causes.[4] Charles Jeffries details sixty-two British policemen
killed from 1936 to 1945.[5] The Palestine Police Association's roll of
honour for officers killed during the revolt records twenty-two killed on
duty or from wounds (so close to the twenty-seven total above), eleven
killed in accidents or from natural causes, one missing believed dead,
and one who died in the UK in October 1939 from injuries sustained
in Palestine.[6] The breakdown of police fatalities based on burial records,
omitting those obviously marked as accidental, is as follows, totalling
fifty-four, so many must have been accidental or natural deaths:

British: Police Deaths

1936

Deaths, Ramleh: May 1936, October 1936
Deaths, Haifa (Jaffa Road): September 1936 x5, November 1936
Deaths, Jerusalem (Protestant): May 1936, July 1936

1937

Deaths, Haifa (Jaffa Road): September 1937, November 1937
Deaths, Jerusalem (Protestant): September 1937, October 1937
Deaths, Jerusalem (Latin): October 1937

---

[3] Wikipedia's data come from Haim Levenberg, *Military Preparations of the Arab Community in Palestine, 1945–48* (London: Cass, 1993), pp. 74–76, derived from figures given out by the High Commissioner.
[4] The Tegart Papers have detailed breakdowns of casualties: GB165-0281, Box 1, File 2, MEC.
[5] Charles Jeffries, *The Colonial Police* (London: Parrish, 1952), p. 161.
[6] *Palestine Police Old Comrades' Association Newsletter* 100 (September 1975).

1938–39

Deaths, Ramleh: May 1938 x2, June 1938, September 1938, February 1939 x2, July 1939

Deaths, Haifa (Khayat Beach): December 1938, January 1939, March 1939, May 1939 x2, August 1939 x2, September 1939 x3

Deaths, Haifa (Jaffa Road): March 1938 x2, April 1938 x4, May 1938 x2, August 1938 x2, October 1938

Deaths, Jerusalem (Protestant): July 1938, September 1938, April 1939 x2, June 1939, August 1939 x2, October 1939 x2

Deaths, Jerusalem (Latin): September 1938, April 1939

Rebels assassinated two British civil officials, Lewis Andrews and Walter Moffatt, and shot dead the archaeologist James Starkey in what might have been a bungled roadside robbery. Casualty evacuation for British wounded in rough field conditions was arduous, so one can only imagine the suffering of Arab wounded. It took thirteen hours to get one British officer with a gunshot wound to military hospital at Sarafand: stretchered off the hill, a lorry to camp, a normal passenger train to Sarafand, an ambulance to the hospital, and eventually a journey to Egypt and a ship to the UK.[7]

Rebels and Palestinians: Official and Unofficial Deaths

Security forces killed more than 2,000 Arabs in combat according to official British figures and they hanged 112 (sometimes 108 or 110), two of whom were Jews (a policeman who shot a Palestinian comrade and an *Etzel* fighter), while 961 died because of 'gang and terrorist activities.'[8] Walid Khalidi built on the British statistics to present figures of 19,792 casualties for the Arabs, comprising 14,760 wounded and 5,032 dead, broken down into 3,832 killed by the British and 1,200 in intra-communal 'terrorism,' using a rough three-to-one ratio of wounded to dead.[9] A more recent British secondary source gives a figure of 2,150

---

[7] Brig J. V Faviell, Typed Memoir, Fifty Days with a Company in Palestine, p. 17, Faviell Papers, 82/24/1, IWMD.

[8] From *A Survey of Palestine. Prepared in December 1945 and December 1946 for the Information of the Anglo-American Committee of Inquiry* [1946–47] (Washington, DC: IPS, 1991), i, ch. 2 and cited in Walid Khalidi (ed.), *From Haven to Conquest* (Beirut: IPS, 1971), pp. 846–49.

[9] Khalidi, *From Haven to Conquest*, pp. 846–49; Ted Swedenburg, *Memories of Revolt: The 1936–1939 Rebellion and the Palestinian National Past* (Minneapolis, MN: University

rebels killed and 108 hanged between 1936 and 1938.[10] Hebrew-language studies built on Arabic material record between 900 and 4,500 Palestinian deaths from intra-communal violence, with Hillel Cohen's recent work making the case for the lower figure, while Yuval Arnon-Ohanna's earlier work pushed the higher figure.[11] Cohen argues that Yuval Arnon-Ohanna based his higher figure of 3,000–4,500 on a weak methodology and he revises the number down to 900–1,000, roughly in line with Khalidi's figure of 1,200.[12] Another Israeli author estimates that 6,000 Arabs died over the course of the revolt and as the British and Jews only killed 1,500, then 4,500 died in acts of internal terror, so repeating Arnon-Ohanna's assessment.[13] One of the Nashashibi family writing much later returned to the idea that many Palestinians died at the hands of compatriots: 'It was ironical that in the three years of the 1936 rebellion the greatest number of casualties were Arabs, and that about a quarter of the Arabs who lost their lives were murdered by their own people.'[14] The figure for intra-communal killings is significant as it speaks to the story of Palestinian disunity, with critics pushing the higher figure while those sympathetic to the Palestinians emphasised the lower one. The police force included many Palestinian (Arab) officers and Charles Jeffries in his police history details 107 Arab policemen killed from 1936 to 1945.[15] The methodology of halving deaths to accommodate accidents and illness as considered above with British security forces applies equally to rebel forces, reducing combat versus non-combat deaths.

The figures of deaths for rebels and Palestinian civilians caught up in fighting are less granulated. Many deaths went unreported while Emergency Regulations curtailed coroners' courts. One British civil officer noted how 'casualties seem to have been suppressed from the death registrations department. No death certificates were given, all

---

of Minnesota Press, 1995), p. xxi; Walid Khalidi and Yasin Suweyd, *Al-Qadiyya al-Filastiniyya wa al-Khatar al-Sahyuni* [*The Palestinian Problem and the Zionist Danger*] (Beirut: IPS, Lebanese General Staff Fifth Branch and Ministry of Defence, 1973), pp. 239–40.

[10] Norman Rose, *A Senseless, Squalid War* (London: Bodley Head, 2009), p. 45.

[11] Yuval Arnon-Ohanna, *Herev mi-Bayit: ha-Ma'avak ha-Pnimi ba-tnu'a ha-le'umit ha-falastinit, 1929–39* [*The Internal Struggle within the Palestinian Movement, 1929–39*] (Tel Aviv: Hadar, 1989), pp. 286–87; Hillel Cohen, *Tzva ha-Tzlalim: Mashtapim Falestinim be-Sherut ha-Ziyonut, 1917–48* [*An Army of Shadows: Palestinian Collaborators in the Service of Zionism, 1917–48*] (Jerusalem: 'Ivrit, 2004), pp. 142–45.

[12] Cohen, *Tzva ha-Tzlalim*, pp. 142–45.

[13] Haggai Eshed, *Reuven Shiloah: The Man behind the Mossad* (London: Cass, 1997), p. 31.

[14] Nasser Eddin Nashashibi, *Jerusalem's Other Voice: Ragheb Nashashibi and Moderation in Palestinian Politics, 1920–1948* (Exeter: Ithaca, 1990), p. 73.

[15] Jeffries, *The Colonial Police*, p. 161.

presumably to keep the incident quiet.'[16] Policeman Burr wrote home of troops machine-gunning sixty surrendering rebels in one battle near Jenin and it being kept from the press.[17] Policeman Harry Arrigonie tells comparable stories in his memoir.[18] Official reports noted 'very heavy' casualties of '60–80 dead and many wounded' in one firefight.[19] The balance in rebel battle dead between Palestinians and foreign fighters is unknown but the British noted that many rebel dead included Jordanians, Iraqis, and, especially, Syrians, the last possibly a catch-all term for any rebel not obviously a local Palestinian. That British soldiers left wounded fighters to die on the battlefield further muddles the computation of numbers, one noting after they took an Arab who had been accidentally shot to a hospital: 'He's about the only one that did get to a hospital. We never used to bother with them.'[20] A military hospital refused to admit another wounded gunman, so soldiers took him to a civil hospital where he died.[21] Jewish troops fighting with the British executed two wounded Arabs after a field court martial, while the officer in another incident administered the *coup de grâce* to a wounded insurgent.[22] When Jews found an Arab hiding after a battle they beat him, before a British soldier arrived, removed his 'bayonet from his rifle and began making a salad of the Arab,' the commanding officer (Orde Wingate) only complaining that they should have interrogated him first.[23] What happened to the bodies of such men is unclear. One official report noted that thirteen of thirty dead 'were picked up next day' and fifty-two of eighty-four bodies 'recovered' elsewhere.[24] When soldiers accidentally shot an old Palestinian man, they left his body in a ditch.[25] Soldiers had no personal investment in carrying heavy bodies off the battlefield for burial, once they had removed personal

[16] Extract from a Letter from an English Friend in Palestine, Addressed Dear Miss Newton [possibly from S. O. Richardson, Lawyer, Jaffa], 11 January 1939, Lees Papers, 5/9, LHCMA.

[17] Letter, Burr to Parents, March 1938 [date pencilled in], Burr Papers, 88/8/1, IWMD.

[18] Harry Arrigonie, *British Colonialism: 30 Years Serving Democracy or Hypocrisy* (Bideford: Gaskell, 1998).

[19] Summary of Intelligence, Palestine and Transjordan [26/38], 30 December 1938, by Wing Commander Ritchie, CO 732/81/10, p. 6, TNA.

[20] Howbrook, p. 35, 4619/03, IWMSA.

[21] Diary, 6 March 1939, Scrivenor Papers, MSS. Brit. Emp. S. 378, WL.

[22] Testimonies from SNS Fighters, Shlomo and Yosef Assa, S25/10685, pp. 76, 112–13, CZA.

[23] Testimonies from SNS Fighters, made c. 1941–44, Chaim Levkov, S25/10685, ZA.

[24] Summary of Intelligence, Palestine and Transjordan [26/38], 30 December 1938, by Wing Commander Ritchie, CO 732/81/10, p. 6, TNA; Summary of Intelligence, Palestine and Transjordan [24/38], 2 December 1938, by Wing Commander Ritchie, CO 732/81/10, p. 12, TNA.

[25] King-Clark, p. 57, 448607, IWMSA.

effects for intelligence or as souvenirs. Legionnaires in Algeria cut off the heads of dead insurgents to take back for identification while Royal Marines did the same in Malaya in the 1950s, also cutting off hands for fingerprinting.[26] There is no evidence of dismembering in Palestine but soldiers knocked gold teeth out of the jaws of dead Arabs.[27] Police brought a truck to take away the body of a prisoner that policemen in a 'special squad' had executed in broad daylight in Jaffa, but only because it was an urban residential street.[28] The police torched the body of an Arab after one battle.[29] Dumping bodies in rural areas was one method of disposal.[30] When soldiers caught an Arab entangled in their camp wire, an officer told the men to shut him up, so they noosed him with signal wire, pulled tight and almost decapitated him, after which they called for the police as they had a body for 'disposal': 'I later learned that he would be dumped outside one of the villages and left there without a word to anyone.'[31]

Arab–Palestinian deaths are also a matter of combatant versus non-combatant deaths, with the more plentiful and easily targeted villagers enduring the brunt of official violence. The numbers of villagers shot breaking cordon are unknown but cases of soldiers firing on running people fill military records, after which there is no record of what happened to the bodies so presumably villagers buried any fallen. Set against this, Army reports of firefights with armed rebels are usually of distant battles with few casualties and soldiers rarely found enemy dead, concluding that the rebels must have removed their dead, prob- ably because in truth the Army did not kill as many rebels at long dis- tance as it thought. But in thirty-six months of active operations, April 1936 to December 1939, omitting the ceasefire period, Khalidi's figure above of 3,832 is low. It equals 106 deaths per month, less than twice the number that Burr recounts as soldiers having killed in one action. Put differently, as around sixty infantry and armoured units rotated through Palestine during the revolt, it would mean that each unit killed 64 people

[26] Simon Murray, *Legionnaire: An Englishman in the French Foreign Legion* (London: Sidgwick and Jackson, 1982), p. 101; Simon Harrison, *Dark Trophies: Hunting and the Enemy Body in Modern War* (New York, NY: Berghahn, 2012), p. 158.

[27] Arthur Lane, *Lesser Gods, Greater Devils* (Stockport: Lane, 1993), pp. 50–52. Lane also left an oral history in the IWMSA.

[28] Matthew Hughes, 'A British "Foreign Legion"? The British Police in Mandate Palestine,' *Middle Eastern Studies* 49/5 (2013), p. 702.

[29] Testimony of Giyora (Shinan) Shinansky (18 July 1938), Testimonies of Haganah Officers Collected in the 1950s and 1960s, 184/83, p. 2, HA. The police 'torch the body' is the exact transliteration.

[30] Catling, 10392/9/4, pp. 16–17, IWMSA.

[31] Lane, *Lesser Gods*, pp. 45–46.

on average while on deployments from a few months to two years, but this omits the RAF and support troops, engineers and the like, naval forces, and the police. This author would increase the figure of 3,832 dead by at least a half to 5,748 to reflect the cumulative effects of soldiers shooting escaping villagers, of poor rebel medical services, of soldiers leaving wounded Arabs to die, of one-off battles in which larger numbers of rebels died, of RAF strafing runs of fleeing bands in remote locales, of prisoners 'promptly shot on the spot,'[32] and of death squad and torture camp actions, while respecting the sporadic nature of battles, their long-range, relatively small numbers in rebel bands, and the fact that soldiers claimed large numbers of enemy dead after battles but often never found the bodies. The figure of 5,748 also acknowledges official orders to shoot those who failed to halt when challenged and the qualitative accounts in Chapter 6 of how soldiers readily shot 'anything that moved' and used Palestinians for 'target practice.'[33] British fortnightly secret intelligence reports noted 101 Arabs 'definitely killed' in battle against 'armed bands' in a two-week period in December 1938 (and twenty-eight 'known' wounded) that if multiplied by seventy-two (thirty-six months doubled) equals 7,272 *official* battle dead but this figure excludes villagers and unofficial killings.[34] Other fortnightly reports in the same TNA file have figures of sixty-one and eighty-four dead Arabs, or of seventy 'approximately' killed per fortnight. There are photographs in soldiers' papers of rows of bloodied corpses, suggestive of heavy Arab casualties after certain battles, in this case at Kfar Kana (Kafr Kanna near Nazareth).[35] Murky killings by security forces as detailed in Chapter 8 complicate definitive quantitative analysis and they could push the final figure above 5,748 (or 7,272) Palestinian and Arab dead as while many regiments behaved properly soldiers' 'wild' behaviour in other units 'got a bit Wild West and out of hand.'[36] Soldiers in lorries would casually smash in the heads of Palestinians on donkeys with their rifle butts as they passed them on the road, killing or wounding them we will never know – 'Behind I could see two more trucks bearing down and on either side of the road wounded and lifeless bodies of Arabs, not only men, the women on donkeys got the same treatment' – but a fellah with a smashed skull had poor access

---

[32] Letter, Briance to Mother, 14 May 1938, Unnamed Loose Folder of Letters from Briance, Briance Papers, BP.

[33] Packer, 4493/02, pp. 9, 17, IWMSA; Letter, Burr (Bury Billet Haifa) to Mother and Father, 9 September 1938, Burr Papers, 88/8/1, IWMD.

[34] Summary of Intelligence, Palestine and Transjordan [25/38], 16 December 1938, by Wing Commander Ritchie, CO 732/81/10, p. 9, TNA.

[35] Memoir, Short Back and Sides, pp. 92–93, Passfield Papers, ERMC.

[36] Letter, King-Clark to Trevor Royle, 22 February 1993, MR4/17/307/1/4, TLSAC.

to good medical services.[37] Set against this is the fact that soldiers limited group killing of civilians in terms of numbers killed on each occasion, as argued in Chapter 5. The figure of 5,748 excludes the 1,000 intra-communal killings that when added together boost the number to 6,748 dead, but the accounts in Chapter 4 of systematic gang attacks on the peasantry would, as with the security forces, support a higher figure for intra-communal violence, perhaps half again to 1,500, so a joint total of 7,248 (5,748 + 1,500). If one accepts the extrapolated figure above from the intelligence reports the figure would be 8,772 (7,272 + 1,500).

Rebels and Palestinians: Wounded

We can never tell the full story of Palestinians and Arab volunteers wounded and maimed in fighting and the calculation of overall casualty numbers is imprecise. Khalidi's estimate of wounded is 14,760, as detailed above. There are five issues here, from which we can determine alternative, higher casualty figures, if still inexact:

- those who died of wounds that would not have been fatal had there been functioning rebel medical services;
- typical ratios of killed to wounded in battle;
- the definition of a 'casualty' in the context of an insurgency in which security forces beat and brutalised but did not shoot many suspects, an officer hitting one man so hard that he broke his hand, so a casualty on both sides;[38]
- the British left Palestinian wounded untended in a sub-war conflict without the usual rules of combat;
- the rough terrain that hampered transport of wounded for first aid.

The key variable was supporting rebel medical services for victims of high-velocity gunshots, artillery fire or RAF machine-gun strafing and bombing runs that were immediately life-threatening. One estimate for the 1916 battle of the Somme is that a third of the dead on the first day of fighting died of wounds that would not have been fatal had they made it to a first-aid station.[39] Over 99 percent of the British soldiers in the 1982 Falklands War who made it to first-line surgical teams survived. Considering Palestinian rebels' exiguous medical services and rural Palestine's basic

---

[37] Lane, *Lesser Gods*, p. 46.
[38] Lt-Col R. King-Clark, Special Night Squad, Personal Diary with Training Notes by Wingate on Some Experiences in Palestine. Ex the Lorettonian, 23 June 1938, p. 13, King-Clark Papers, 83/10/1, IWMD.
[39] John Keegan, *Face of Battle* [1976] (London: Penguin, 1987), p. 274.

health network of Government-run clinics in a country that had no state
health system before 1918, wounded Palestinians (rebels or civilians)
were more likely to die from untreated gunshot-trauma wounds than
would necessarily be the case, unless a wounded villager or fighter
lived near a city and could get to a civil (often private) hospital, where
that person might then be arrested or executed in his bed by police as
happened at Jaffa's Dajani hospital.[40] Security forces discouraged good
Samaritans who succoured the wounded by demolishing their homes.
That Palestinians went to more numerous Jewish doctors in peaceful
times further hampered access to medical services in times of mass civil
unrest.[41] This means that typical combat ratios of wounded to dead of
three or four to one need revising to perhaps two to one, there being
very few seriously wounded who survived combat as they expired on the
battlefield or very soon thereafter.[42] This supports the higher total above
of 5,748 dead, while the non-lethal casualties of broken bones, whip cuts,
cracked skulls, cactus-hedge wounds, and smashed teeth that went with
searching-detention lift the number of wounded above Khalidi's 14,760,
perhaps to three times the higher number of deaths (7,248) to 21,744.
This is a conservative assessment considering widespread non-lethal
wounding by security forces. To give 'non-lethal' injuries human substance, consider the following account of a rifle-butt beating delivered
by a British policeman to a Palestinian in the 1920s, as remembered by
a fellow officer:

When one of the Nablus detachment produced an old cigarette tin containing
the brains of a man whose skull he had splintered with his rifle butt ... I felt physically sick ... the sight of that grog-blossomed face of the gendarme with his can
half-full of human brains proudly brandishing his smashed rifle-butt as proof of
his prowess, altered something inside of me.[43]

Rebel-gang-criminal violence short of murder further boosts the
numbers of wounded, as would any consideration of psychological
trauma if such an evaluation were possible. The final figures for Arab
and Palestinian casualties presented here are as follows. The wounded
total includes gunshot or significant non-lethal injuries but excludes
rough treatment or beatings that did not leave permanent marks, with
the higher figures in the range deriving from the extrapolated fortnightly
intelligence reports:

---

[40] Hughes, 'A British "Foreign Legion",' p. 703.
[41] *A Survey of Palestine*, ii, p. 614.
[42] Christopher A. Lawrence, *War by Numbers: Understanding Conventional Combat* (Lincoln,
NE: University of Nebraska Press, 2017), ch. 15.
[43] Douglas V. Duff, *Bailing with a Teaspoon* (London: John Lang, 1953), p. 46.

Killed by security forces: 5,748–7,272
Killed in internecine fighting: at least 1,500
Seriously wounded: 21,744–26,316
Total: 28,992–35,088

Jews

Police CID assessed that from April to October 1936 eighty Jews died.[44] The *Survey for Palestine* records that rebels had killed 255 Jews by the end of 1938 and ninety-four Jews in 1939; so for the three years this gives a figure of 429 dead but possibly excluding 1937.[45] Martin Kolinsky's assessment is that the rebels killed 547 Jews.[46] Another author gives a total of 495 Jewish fatalities, 1936–38.[47] Meanwhile, Charles Jeffries details seventy-eight Jewish policemen killed from 1936 to 1945 who may or may not be included in the aforementioned data.[48]

---

[44] The Political History of Palestine under British Administration, p. 20, Creech Jones Papers, MSS. Brit. Emp. S. 332, Box 32, File 4, WL; CID, Jerusalem, Periodical Appreciation Summaries 15/36 and 16/36, 1 and 28 September 1936, L/PS/12/3343: Political Situation – Police Summaries, IOR.

[45] *A Survey of Palestine*, i, pp. 38–49.

[46] Martin Kolinsky, 'The Collapse and Restoration of Public Security,' in Michael J. Cohen and Martin Kolinsky (eds), *Britain and the Middle East in the 1930s: Security Problems, 1935–39* (London: Macmillan-King's, 1992), p. 162.

[47] Rose, *A Senseless, Squalid War*, p. 45.

[48] Jeffries, *The Colonial Police*, p. 161.

Appendix C
Women and Violence

From house destruction to beatings, shootings, and sexual violence, Palestinian women were caught up in the violence of pacification. Myriad village women joined *faz'a* calls for help for rebels from local villagers, as when al-Qawuqji escaped closing Army pincers in October 1936, and they protected their villages and resisted Army searches, and were beaten up and, occasionally, shot for their troubles. Sexual violence (or the fear of it) against Palestinian women increased the population-centric terror to British operations; rebels' use of women (also mosques) to avoid security force searches helped the national struggle; women supporting their menfolk or as warriors themselves added to rebel fighting power; there were also incidences of men dressing up as women to avoid capture or carry out assassinations. That said, sexual violence was muted (probably because it was indeed rare), the British shot limited numbers of women, there were few named female fighters, and rebels did not utilise women to, say, plant bombs, as the *Front de Libération Nationale* did in Algeria in the 1950s. As intelligence officer Tony Simonds noted, during the revolt, 'female terrorists were almost unknown.'[1] Palestinians made some allegations of sexual assault, but the charges rarely have the specificity and never the amplification of accusations about general brutality, which is not to say that such things never happened, but deep archival mining reveals scant material on sexual assault by British troops. As one British resident of Palestine put it in the context of tens of thousands of troops in-country, 'Rape is rare. There have been a few cases however and one is pending now at Tulkarm or Kalkilieh [Qalqilya] I forget which.'[2] The author has anonymised the victims of the sexual assault in what follows but not those who allegedly committed rape as naming suspects throws light on the systemisation of sexual violence. Non-British

[1] Typed Memoir, Pieces of War, p. 136, Simonds Papers, 08/46/1, IWMD.
[2] Extract from a Letter from an English Friend in Palestine, Addressed Dear Miss Newton [possibly from S. O. Richardson, Lawyer, Jaffa], 11 January 1939, Lees Papers, 5/9, LHCMA.

personnel committed some of the alleged sexual assaults, a useful fact that can only be discerned by naming the alleged perpetrators.

As Victims: Sexual Violence

Accounts of sexual assault in the form of molestation rather than penetrative rape appear sporadically in the archives and might have been the result of clumsy attempts by soldiers to search frightened village women. The claim was often that soldiers touched women's breasts: 'the wife of [AA] of Bir Zeit while on her way to the village spring for water was stopped by a soldier who proceeded to search her and feel her breasts ... On the same day, July 6th, 5 women of Bir Zeit were fetching water from the spring to the north of the village. The troops rushed, searched them and shamelessly handled their breasts and bodies in spite of their cries and protests.'[3] Again, 'In another case the soldiers went in and found an unmarried girl in bed they forcibly took off her vest played with her breasts and tried to assault her but her shrieks attracted the neighbours and this was prevented.'[4] Soldiers made women line up in front of them in a search at Tulkarm and bare their breasts to prove that they were not men.[5] Accounts of rape are hard to find. A semi-autobiographical novel in Arabic in 1939 written by an insurgent recounts British soldiers arriving in the village of the book's hero, a Doctor Sabri, and raping his sister during a punishment raid: the 'English bequeathed an irreparable stigma ... stole her virginity.'[6] There is an archival record of an assault by troops who 'attempted to attack the honour of the wife of [BB] but she refused and yelled for help and consequently was rescued from the claws of the civilised troops by her village women neighbours.'[7] Another accusation of the rape of a girl was directed at British troops: '[CC] aged 12, raped by the army. She received a dangerous wound on her head which

---

[3] Points 7–8 in President of Bir Zeit Council, J&EM Papers, GB165-0161, Box 66, File 1, MEC.

[4] Report by Frances Newton dated 27 June 1938 on Search in Balad esh Sheikh of 24 June 1938, J&EM Papers, GB165-0161, Box 65, File 3, MEC.

[5] Tom Segev, *One Palestine, Complete: Jews and Arabs under the British Mandate* (New York, NY: Owl, 2001), p. 421.

[6] Muhammad Mustafa Ghandur, *Tha'r al-Dam* [*Blood Revenge: A Story from the Core of the Events of the Palestinian Revolt by the Pen of the Fighter Muhammad Mustafa Ghandur*] (Syria: n.p., 1939), n.p.

[7] S.O.S. From Halhool, The Martyr Village (stamped 22 May 1939), J&EM Papers, GB165-0161, Box 66, File 1, MEC. See also rape allegations (including of children) in Abdullah Abu Limun (Attil) to Abu Kamal, n.d., Captured and Translated Arabic Material with Commentary, pp. 99–100, Wingate Papers, Microfilm M2313, BL.

broke the skull.'[8] A soldier who 'spoke a little broken Arabic' and 'seemed to understand' a young girl during a house search 'tried to pat her head, but she shrank away in terror. He shrugged and turned to leave, virtually colliding' with the girl's panicked mother, assuming the worst of the soldier who was simply searching the building.[9] The Anglican mission in Jerusalem dealt with a gang rape allegation but against three Arab policemen, not British soldiers: 'They beat me with their rifle butts – laid me on the ground. One sat on my chest and kept my mouth shut, etc., while another assaulted me – then the men changed places; all three had me in turn.'[10]

Rebels threatened to attack British women in retaliation, but never actually killed or sexually assaulted anyone, only wounding a Miss Newman travelling in a car with RAF Squadron-Leader R. E. Alderson in an ambush in February 1938. (The wounding of a British woman aggravated security force punishments delivered to local villages after the attack.) In December 1938, rebel leader 'Abd al-Rahim al-Hajj Muhammad 'issued a warning to the effect that if British troops in Palestine kill, assault, or in any way maltreat any Arab woman, reprisals will be taken against English women. This policy has been opposed by some of the rebels and no agreement has yet been reached.'[11] Rough handling by troops of village women during search operations might have translated into accusations of sexual assault that were non-sexual in that the intent of the assault was punitive, such as removing chattel or evacuating villagers from buildings to be demolished, which local women resisted. This might explain incidents such as the one that the national propaganda bureau in Syria claimed in July 1938 when 'unknown persons' destroyed a kilometre of the Tegart fence along the Lebanese border, after which troops came to neighbouring villages and 'gathered the men of the villages and took them to the place of cut wire and kept them to be tortured for two days while the soldiers carried on search [sic] in these villages. The soldiers not only beat women and children, but indecently assaulted women who violently resisted them. Four women were seriously injured and one miscarriage took place.'[12] An Army lieutenant, meanwhile, noted the rape of

[8] Allegations of Ill-treatment of Arabs by British Crown Forces in Palestine (translated from the Arabic by Frances Newton, 19 June 1939), J&EM Papers, GB165-0161, Box 65, File 5, p. 144, MEC.

[9] Ghada Karmi, In Search of Fatima (London: Verso, 2009), pp. 12–13.

[10] Report on Visit to Azzun, 12 May 1938 and Azzun, 16 May 1938 (account of assault on DD, wife of EE, aged about 16–18) both in J&EM Papers, GB165-0161, Box 66, File 1, MEC (quotation from 16 May report, p. 1).

[11] Political Report Syria No. 6, Damascus, 28 December 1938, FO371/23276, p. 150, TNA.

[12] Bulletin issued by Bureau Nationale Damascus (28 July 1938) in Creech Jones Papers, MSS. Brit. Emp. S. 332, box 30, file 2, WL.

Jewish women in a rebel raid on a kibbutz, while other files noted rebels raping women of the Irsheid family: 'violated the honour of the women and did other unpleasant things.'[13] Jewish files on insurgents noted the 'social tenseness obtaining over this matter in the Arab village public' and how had 'the gangsters tried to touch the women, there would have been an uproar.'[14]

Elements within British security forces, possibly in CID, outsourced some sexual abuse to local Arab proxy forces, prison guards telling one naked female detainee in Bethlehem's Ladies' prison whom they had previously tortured, 'If you won't speak, we'll bring a nigger [meaning an Arab] to rape you,' although the victim recalled that 'it seems that they had an order not to rape me.' Guards did, however, molest her.[15] This threat was repeated to a Jewish female prisoner, Jews alleged, the guards like those in Dachau touching a 'young Jewish lady's breasts, threatening her that she would be raped by soldiers ... We call to create a special committee to investigate all these cases and save the honour of Britain.'[16] In interview with this author, the rebel fighter Bahjat Abu Gharbiyya claimed the rape of male prisoners by non-British security force personnel. The police used 'awful' local Arabs to rape male prisoners, employing a 'Castero/Kastero' in Jaffa and a 'Saleh Alwalaji' in Jerusalem, both subsequently assassinated by rebels, but 'there were others' who detained handsome young Arab men to be sexually abused.[17] Similarly, the British in Kenya in the 1950s used local Kenyan askaris to sodomise prisoners, Caroline Elkins claims.[18] There are echoes here of Tal Nitzan's 2006 thesis that Israeli troops do not sexually assault Palestinian women for racist reasons, not wanting to sleep with Arab women.[19]

The British strenuously challenged charges of sexual impropriety, pointing to Palestinian hyper-sensitivities on any male interactions with

[13] Magill-Cuerden, 004485/05, p. 26, IWMSA; Abd el Rahim el Haj Mahmad, Captured and Translated Arabic Material with Commentary, p. 33, Wingate Papers, Microfilm M2313, BL.
[14] Appendix: Explanatory Notes, Captured and Translated Arabic Material with Commentary, p. 119, Wingate Papers, Microfilm M2313, BL.
[15] Case of RL, Arrested 15 May 1936, J&EM Papers, GB165-0161, Box 65, File 5, pp. 7–8, but pp. 122–23 in overall file pagination, MEC. The prison building still exists, now part of Bethlehem University.
[16] Notice entitled Jewish Youth, File 04/-163-B/621: Riots, April 1936 [but actually January 1939–February 1940] [one bundle of papers], TAMA.
[17] Author interview, Bahjat Abu Gharbiyya, Amman, 21 June 2009.
[18] Caroline Elkins, *Imperial Reckoning: The Untold Story of Britain's Gulag in Kenya* (New York, NY: Holt, 2005), pp. 136, 157, 208.
[19] Tal Nitzan, 'Controlled Occupation: The Rarity of Military Rape in the Israeli–Palestinian Conflict' (Master's Thesis: Tel Aviv University, 2006).

women. In September 1936, the Gaza town crier went up and down the main street warning women not to leave their houses, alleging that British soldiers had been visiting homes. The commanding officer of the local unit, the King's Royal Irish Hussars, wrote to his brigade headquarters, annoyed at accusations of 'meditated rape,' pointing out that beyond some accusation of stealing oranges, there had been no 'serious misbehaviour by the troops. A few of them, newly arrived from Jerusalem, went for a walk in the town and may or may not have looked at some women. I have since put the town "Out of Bounds".'[20] As a British policeman told Army officer David Smiley on operation in Palestine in 1940, after they had watched fellow Arab police officers beat and hold lighted cigarettes to the testicles of three village men accused of murder, 'It was a golden rule, he added, that women were never questioned or touched.'[21] In a punitive raid during the revolt, an Army officer, after having candidly described smashing up villages on punitive operations, detailed how he came across a woman, supposedly in labour, so he left: 'but I daresay she probably had a couple of rifles hidden under the bed or somewhere. But you know one just didn't molest the women at all. You couldn't touch the women. One just didn't nor did the soldiers. And if she had got stuff hidden there, grenades or anything else, she got away with it. Lucky for her.'[22] Ellen Fleischmann also points to the reluctance of British to search women, some of whom hid weapons behind the shield of children and babies.[23] Similarly, when Spanish secret police came to search George Orwell's hotel room during the Spanish Civil War, his wife Eileen was in bed:

Yet all this time they *never searched the bed*. My wife was lying in bed all the while; obviously there might have been half a dozen sub-machine-guns under the mattress … Yet the detectives made no move to touch the bed, never even looked underneath it … they were also Spaniards, and to turn a woman out of bed was a little too much for them … making the whole search meaningless.[24]

GOC Haining emphasised the official view that women 'are not molested in any way. They are only searched on occasions when the services of a Police woman searcher are available … Women searchers are occasionally employed as a deterrent against rebels disguising themselves as women,

[20] Col Thornton (CO 8th KRI Hussars, Gaza) to HQ 2nd Inf Bde (Jaffa), 30 September 1936, Lees Papers, 5/6/5, LHCMA.
[21] David Smiley, *Irregular Regular* (Norwich: Michael Russell, 1994), pp. 15–16.
[22] Gratton, 4506/03, pp. 14–15, IWMSA.
[23] Ellen Fleischmann, *The Nation and Its 'New' Women: The Palestinian Women's Movement, 1920–1948* (Berkeley, CA: University of California Press, 2003), p. 127.
[24] George Orwell, *Homage to Catalonia* (London: Secker and Warburg, 1986), p. 179.

as has happened on several occasions.'[25] Such British witnesses could be lying but they all tell the same story and they are usually frank about general brutality directed at Palestinians. British Servicemen may have been reticent on talking about sex but as readers will see below, some delighted in telling tales about visits to brothels. British personnel saw local women differently, too, looking to date Jewish women, for which two Jewish men beat up police officer Sydney Burr; on another occasion, when Jews beat up a policeman for dating a Jewish woman, they also told her that 'she'd have her hair cut off.'[26] The British also viewed non-Muslim Palestinians differently, as when Burr had a meal in a Druze village:

All the lads were hoping to get a glimpse of some of their women who are remarkable for their beauty. We saw one little beaut[y] who fell over before she could dart into her house. She had practically yellow hair and what is seldom seen in England very dark blue eyes. Whereas the Arab women wear all black these girls are dressed in white, with a black velvet band round their foreheads.[27]

'Nordic in appearance' noted another policeman of the Druze, descendants of the crusaders and 'courageous and brave in war.'[28]

As Colonial Subjects: Searching Women

Emergency Regulations during the revolt never altered the 1924 Arrest of Offenders and Searches Ordinance that decreed that only women could search female suspects.[29] When it came to searching local women, female 'wardresses' attached to British units were deployed to search women villagers down to their 'private parts.'[30] On another occasion, an Army officer complained of police 'mismanagement' in failing to bring along a female 'searcher' on an operation, suggesting that female searchers were used in the field.[31] There were, however, very few female searchers for the whole of Palestine, so outside the major towns women should not have been searched unless a woman searcher was present, impracticable in fast-moving search-and-sweep operations. This was a

---

[25] Report by Gen Haining on 'Hostile Propaganda in Palestine,' 1 December 1938, FO 371/21869, p. 169, TNA.
[26] Edwards, 10317/5, p. 7, IWMSA.
[27] Letter, Burr (Bury Billet Haifa) to Mother and Father, 9 September 1938, Burr Papers, 88/8/1, IWMD; Letter, Burr (Inlying Piquet) to Mother and Father, 24 February 1938, Burr Papers, 88/8/1, IWMD.
[28] Douglas Duff, *A Sword for Hire* (London: Murray, 1934), p. 130.
[29] Moses Doukhan (ed.), *Laws of Palestine, 1918–1925* (Tel Aviv: Rotenberg, 1933), i, p. 43.
[30] Report by Frances Newton dated 27 June 1938 on Search in Balad esh Sheikh of 24 June 1938, J&EM Papers, GB165-0161, Box 65, File 3, MEC.
[31] Diary, 19 October 1937, Major White, Relating to Service in Palestine, 1974-04-24-8, NAM.

boon for rebels who could hide weapons with women, as an Army in-house journal recognised: 'The only real difficulty is when women are stated to be ill in bed, as the bed probably also contains whoever one is looking for. Official female searchers are practically never obtainable in any country.'[32] Wealthy Palestinian women hid explosives and guns under their car seats 'which the British did not dare to search because of their respect for the "sanctity" of Muslim women.'[33] The British used Jewish and Armenian women as searchers – 'no British woman would lower herself to do it' – but, for example, in October 1938 in Jerusalem they had just two Arab women for this task, one at the Jaffa Gate and one at the Damascus Gate.[34] There are pictures of female Jewish searchers and 'Russian Christian police women' in the American Colony Hotel Archive, the police women dressed in mufti, with the caption 'New Police Regulations, February 1938.'[35] In June 1936, when the British wanted to search women escaping the destruction of old Jaffa, they sent seven women from the prison service in Jerusalem down to Jaffa for the job, commandeering a local building especially for the purpose.[36] The British police claimed that the Arab rebels hid their 'stuff' with Palestinian women, Palestinians countering that hidden goods were simply valuables or money that they did not want stolen by Servicemen.[37] Similarly, Jewish women (or *slickeriyot* from the Hebrew slang verb to hide *lehaslick*) hid weapons under their clothes. Roger Courtney remembered that women 'were never searched, except in towns such as Jerusalem, where there were women searchers, nor were the mosques. Both the women and the religion of Islam were inviolate.'[38] One trick used by the British to uncover men hiding among women as deployed in India so 'not to offend purdah' was to ask to see everyone's hands.[39] Hajj Amin escaped the *Haram al-Sharif* in 1937 dressed as a woman, in the view of British police.[40] Earlier, during riots in 1920, Governor Ronald Storrs used Indian Muslim troops to search women – a curious claim as the key issue was gender not religion – and 'many of the women were found to be carrying all

[32] Capt E. P. A. Des Graz, 'Military Control of Disturbed Areas,' *Journal of the Royal United Service Institution* 81 (November 1936), p. 813.
[33] Fleischmann, *The Nation and Its 'New'Women*, p. 131.
[34] J. M. Thompson (Government Welfare Inspector) to Archdeacon, 23 October 1938, J&EM Papers, GB165-0161, Box 61, File 4, MEC.
[35] Arab Revolt in Palestine Photograph Album 1938, ACHA.
[36] al-Difa' [*The Defence*] (Jaffa) (18–19 June 1936).
[37] Diary, Wilson Papers, GB165-0302, MEC, pp. 12–13.
[38] Roger Courtney, *Palestine Policeman* (London: Herbert Jenkins, 1939), p. 88.
[39] William Slim, *Unofficial History* (New York, NY: David McKay, 1959), p. 97.
[40] Edward Horne, *A Job Well Done (Being a History of the Palestine Police Force, 1920–1948)* (Tiptree: Anchor Press, 1982), p. 223.

sorts of weapons. Storrs sent the collection to England, where it remains on display at the police museum in Chichester.[41] (There was no police museum in Chichester before the 1950s, so this is possibly a reference to the Sussex Regiment barracks in the town that the Royal Military Police subsequently moved into and where it located its museum prior to moving it to Southwick Park in 2007; much of the material from the Chichester police museum is now in West Sussex Records Office, but nothing relating to Palestine.[42])

As Resistors: Women as Warriors

Fatma Ghazzal was killed in battle at Wadi Azzoun in 1936, the only named Palestinian woman that this author can find who died as a female combatant.[43] In an ambush, an Essex Regiment soldier wrote of two dead Arabs, 'one of whom was a woman.'[44] Yet, peasant women's mass involvement was physical and direct, not least as it was 'their communities that were coming under physical attack' from the Army and bandit gangs.[45] Village women sacrificed more than urban women and were arrested for being members of the Black Hand band, for writing threatening letters to the police, for hiding wounded rebel fighters, and they kept secrets.[46] Urban women collected money, took part in demonstrations, sent protests to the government, and formed women's committees.[47] There were schoolgirl strikes; security forces arrested women for curfew violations.[48] Women raised money, sometimes reaching £P.100; they also sold their jewellery.[49] In June 1936, a demonstration of women in Bethlehem left two British constables and several Arab women injured; four arrests were made.[50] In August 1936, a rebel band up to eighty strong, among which were women, attacked the Jewish settlement of

[41] Ilan Pappé, *The Rise and Fall of a Palestinian Dynasty: The Husaynis, 1700–1948* (London: Saqi, 2010), p. 198.
[42] E-mail communication, Royal Military Police Museum to author, 21 August 2017; e-mail communication, Chichester District Council to author, 21 August 2017; e-mail communication, Malcolm Barrett (curator, police museum) to author, 22 August 2017. The Chichester barracks is now a housing estate. There was also a Philosophical and Literary Society in Chichester until 1924, after which it closed and sold off its collection.
[43] Fleischmann, *The Nation and Its 'New' Women*, p. 126.
[44] Typed Memoir, L/Cpl F. C. Metson, Metson Papers, 13691/13696, p. 4, ERMC.
[45] Fleischmann, *The Nation and Its 'New' Women*, p. 125.
[46] Ibid., p. 128.
[47] Ibid., p. 129.
[48] Ibid., pp. 129–31.
[49] Ibid., p. 133.
[50] Disturbances of 1936, 30 May–5 June, US Consul General Palestine to State Department, 6 June 1936, 867N.00/310 [Reel M#1037/1], NARA II.

Gesher.[51] The British arrested women demonstrating near DC Thomas Scrivenor's office in Haifa and 'the three ring leaders were removed in a prison van and released at a sufficiently great distance from Haifa to keep them busily occupied for some time walking back.'[52] Across Palestine women protested. Police shot dead a girl who was stoning them during a village search.[53] In the same (or another incident), women atop houses stoned the police, 'one British constable being badly injured and were obliged to open fire aiming over the heads of the women. The High Commissioner deeply regrets to announce that an Arab girl was hit by a stray bullet and mortally wounded.'[54] Police shot a girl during a stoning of forces in 1938 in Kafr Kenna (Kafr Kanna near Nazareth), alongside interning the village Imam for preaching 'jihad.'[55] When the British put 2,000 women into a 'pen' soldiers noted their relief when they released detainees because they made so much noise.[56] Widows of dead fighters also took up arms and led by example, the 'moral' being 'that in Jenin women are fighting while in Acre even the men are reluctant to carry a rifle,' in the words of colonial official Kenneth Blackburne.[57] At 'Ara village south-east of Haifa, women encouraged their 'menfolk to go to the assistance of the gang, but this, it is thought, they refused to do.'[58] In the north the Royal Ulster Rifles noted that a 'considerable number' of women from the 'truculent' village of Sasa had 'stirred up' the local population and so the Army 'evacuated them in lorries.'[59] During al-Qawuqji's escape, a *Faz'a* call for help drew out local villagers and 'many times the women were seen running behind their husbands ululating as they are want [sic] to do thereby exciting their men to action.'[60] The British

---

[51] Haganah Report, 30 August 1936, Shai Intelligence Reports: 8/GENERAL/40, p. 135, HA.

[52] Diary, 23 April 1938, Scrivenor Papers, MSS. Brit. Emp. S. 378, WL.

[53] Village of Kafrkenna, Political Activities, Punitive Measures, Palestine Police Force: Report from Tiberias: M/4212/8, ISA.

[54] Telegram, High Commissioner Palestine to Secretary of State for Colonies, 25 May 1936, L/PS/12/3344–45: Palestine Situation, IOR. See also C. G. T. Dean, *The Loyal Regiment (North Lancashire) 1919–53* (Preston, 1955), p. 66.

[55] Kafrkenna, Villages Collective Punishment and Punitive Reports, Police Station Diary, Nazareth, M/4212/8, ISA.

[56] *FIRM: The Worcestershire Regiment (29th Foot)* 11/1 (April 1939), pp. 54–55.

[57] Monthly Administrative report for August 1938, Galilee and Acre District, 2 September 1938, by Acting DC K. W. Blackburne, Blackburne Papers, MSS. Brit. Emp. S. 460, Box 3, File 2, WL. The reference here to Yusuf Sa'id Abu Durra makes little sense as he died in 1939.

[58] Daily Police Report, 9 April 1938, Scrivenor Papers, MSS. Brit. Emp. S. 377, p. 160, WL.

[59] 2nd RUR (Safad) Report on Operations to 16th Inf Bde, 6 July 1938, Report on Occupation Northern Area, 4–5 July, December 1937–March 1939 File, Palestine Box, RUR.

[60] Captured and Translated Arabic Material with Commentary, p. 15, Wingate Papers, Microfilm M2313, BL.

arrested the wife of the editor of *al-Karmil* (*The Carmel*) in March 1939 for organising demonstrations and they sent her to Bethlehem Women's Prison on renewable three-month detention orders to February 1940.[61]

Rebels dressed as women to escape security checks and effect assassinations. A patrol of the TJFF encountered a 'bandit who was disguised as a woman and threw off his clothing and attempted to escape was shot dead.'[62] On another occasion, an assassin 'dressed in women's clothing' shot dead a temporary Arab police constable near Hebron police station, while CID reported on rebels dressed as women in December 1938.[63] One man broke an Army village cordon and 'escaped dressed as a woman. A sentry pulled his veil off and saw it was a man, he bolted, and though the sentry fired after him, he missed him in the half light.'[64] Cross dressing for men ran in both directions with rebels arresting and detaining (down a well) an armed man dressed as a peasant woman, 'Suspected, he was caught. He was found armed and perhaps with evil intentions.'[65] A Jewish intelligence file gives a useful summary of Palestinian women's lives during the revolt, and of how the *Yishuv* saw such things:

> The duties of the women were generally transport of water, cooking, washing and sewing of gangsters' clothes. Sometimes they carried messages and hid men in their abodes. The playing of a special part in the rebellion cannot be claimed by the Arab woman. Some welfare women in towns, mostly Christian, imitated men in lectures, meetings, demonstrations and speeches. A great service was rendered by women who hid arms and men disguised as women. The British took great care not to touch a woman. This was taken advantage of by the rebels. Later the authorities appointed women police who helped by carrying out searches … Generally the Yishuv did very little to penetrate into the Arab woman's circle of life. This neglect was a pity, because there could have been profit in enquiry into this sphere.[66]

Finally, as mentioned above, soldiers and police did discuss sexual matters. Policeman Jack Binsley saw prostitutes in Gaza, alongside sleeping with Yemeni Jewish women as they were 'not so strict' as other

[61] Fleischmann, *The Nation and Its 'New' Women*, p. 132.

[62] 'Bandit dressed as Woman,' *Palestine Post* (16 May 1939), p. 2.

[63] Summary of Intelligence, Palestine and Transjordan, 4 November 1938, by Wing Commander Ritchie at GHQ [22/38], CO 732/81/10, TNA; CID Haifa to DIG CID, 19 December 1938, S25/22793: Druze Activities, p. 44, CZA.

[64] Capt Cummins, Report by OC TARCOL of Operations, 19 September 1938, December 1937–March 1939 File, Palestine Box, RUR.

[65] Diary, 29 October 1938, in Thomas Ricks (ed.), *Turbulent Times in Palestine: The Diaries of Khalil Totah, 1886–1955* (Jerusalem: IPS and Passia, 2009), p. 239.

[66] Appendix: Explanatory Notes, Captured and Translated Arabic Material with Commentary, p. 119, Wingate Papers, Microfilm M2313, BL.

Jews.[67] In Gaza, Binsley wrote how, 'Pimps and prostitutes were there, with others I sampled an unsatisfying interlude in a cactus grove with a prostitute whose forty piaster charge was arranged by our mess boy, aged fifteen years, who spoke some English.'[68] In the early 1920s in Haifa many 'Englishmen lived openly with native women, some were foolish enough to marry them, whilst prostitutes and loose women could be seen coming and going from the billets.'[69] The Army's need to keep soldiers healthy meant that they monitored brothels and ensured that such establishments had condom machines in each room; one soldier recalled staying away from the Saturday-evening visit to the brothel because of his fear of disease.[70]

---

[67] Jack Binsley, *Palestine Police Service* (Montreux: Minerva, 1996), pp. 31, 35, 40.
[68] Ibid., p. 31.
[69] Douglas Duff, *A Sword for Hire* (London: Murray, 1934), p. 123.
[70] Typed Memoir, Maj B. A. Pond, Pond Papers, 78/27/1, IWMD; Proctor, 16801/5, IWMSA.

Appendix D
Sartorial Wars

Clothing signified rebellion as well as social class, rurally based rebels wearing the traditional turban-style *kufiyya* headdress (or variations thereof with the *hatta* and *iqal*) and demanding the same of townsfolk who might otherwise wear European dress with a red *tarbush* headdress (called also a fez), with the added advantage that rebels could then blend with the urban populace, up to a point as rural attire still looked different. Bahjat Abu Gharbiyya hid the Beretta pistol that he used to shoot Assistant Police Inspector Alan Sigrist in June 1936 under his *tarbush*, at a time earlier in the revolt when *kufiyyat* were not de rigueur.[1] The British recognised the significance of this sartorial resistance and General Montgomery in Haifa wanted to ban the *kufiyya* (he also issued an order 'that persons going about with their hands in their pockets will be viewed with suspicion'), one of his civil officials, Thomas Scrivenor, telling him that banning *kufiyyat* was unenforceable.[2] Undeterred, Montgomery 'repeated that he did not want any prosecutions and that, if people disregarded the order, the head-dress should simply be removed from their heads by patrols and that if they insisted they would be put in the cage for a day or two to cool off.'[3] In January 1939, Scrivenor noted that 'the General's proposals for the abolition of the kefieh and agal had been turned down by the Government. The Order was apparently considered to be legal by the Attorney General but the High Commissioner had introduced his veto.'[4] The pro-Government Nashashibis also asked villagers to wear the *tarbush* and not the *kufiyya*.[5] That said, it is questionable that any villager, even the most pro-Nashashibi, would have

---

[1] Matthew Hughes, 'A History of Violence: The Shooting of British Assistant Superintendent Alan Sigrist, 12 June 1936,' *Journal of Contemporary History* 45/4 (2010), p. 729.
[2] Note on Conversation with Montgomery by Scrivenor, [12] January 1939, Scrivenor Papers, MSS. Brit. Emp. S. 377, pp. 298–304, WL.
[3] Ibid.
[4] Diary, 13 January 1939, Scrivenor Papers, MSS. Brit. Emp. S. 378, WL.
[5] Yusuf Rajab, *Thawrat 1936–1939 fi-Filastin: Dirasa Askariyya* [*Revolt of 1936–1939 in Palestine: A Military Study*] (Beirut: Institute of Arab Research, 1982), p. 100.

followed this order as the *tarbush* was for all villagers a symbol of the decadence and arrogance of townsfolk.

With their leaders dead or in prison, a measure of authority for insurgents came with orders telling men to wear the *kufiyya* and for women to adopt the veil. Urban women were veiled for complex reasons and not just because of rebel pressure, including showing that they were Arabs and not Jews, but 'the mainstream nationalist leadership also called upon (urban) women to dress modestly like their "sisters the warriors of the village",' although rural women were much less likely to be veiled.[6] As was noted at the time: 'another edict forbade all Arab Christian ladies from wearing hats and the Moslem ladies were ordered to don the more conservative form of veiling.'[7] Ellen Fleischmann notes the fear among women because of internecine violence, 'particularly among those women with Nashashibi ties.'[8] A popular ditty connecting women's dress, chastity, and honour reflected the revolt's conservative tones, and was recited by boys who harassed women in the street who wore Western hats:

> *Umm al-bunya, al-raqqasa*
> *Biddha bumba wa rasasa*
>
> [The woman who wears a hat, the dancer
> Deserves a bomb and a bullet]

'Dancer' here meant a 'loose' woman, 'a virtual prostitute,' while *umm al-bunya*, the woman who wears a hat, was likely to be a Christian woman, although elite Muslim women also donned hats instead of veils, while some wore Western dresses and carried handbags but wore veils.[9] Well-to-do city Christian women were often at the forefront of demonstrations alongside their politically active husbands; the first women's demonstration in 1929 processed in cars through Jerusalem, a luxury item that village women would not have owned.[10]

---

[6] Ted Swedenburg quoted in Ellen Fleischmann, *The Nation and Its 'New' Women: The Palestinian Women's Movement, 1920–1948* (Berkeley, CA: University of California Press, 2003), pp. 133–34.

[7] Arab Revolt in Palestine Photograph Album 1938, ACHA.

[8] Fleischmann, *The Nation and Its 'New' Women*, pp. 133–34.

[9] Ibid.; Walid Khalidi (ed.), *Before Their Diaspora: A Photographic History of the Palestinians, 1876–1948* (Washington, DC: IPS, 2004), p. 101; the 2016 French–Israeli film 'In Between' nicely dissects class and social issues among Palestinian women in a contemporary context.

[10] Yuval Arnon-Ohanna, *Herev mi-Bayit: ha-Ma'avak ha-Pnimi ba-tnu'a ha-le'umit ha-falastinit, 1929–39* [*The Internal Struggle within the Palestinian Movement, 1929–39*] (Tel Aviv: Hadar, 1989), pp. 214–16.

A rebel leadership general order on 27 August 1938 decreed that all Palestinians should wear the *kufiyya*, and within a week everyone was doing so, reports Subhi Yasin.[11] British intelligence noted the same rebel order, posted up in Jerusalem telling everyone to wear the *kufiyya* and *iqal* by 29 August 1938, 'until European dress is also abolished and until some curb is put on the imagination of the town dandy who now parades the street with a halo of glory as little like the peasant's black rope agal as the discarded tarbush.'[12] As rebels lost the military war, they pushed the symbolic one, with another order dated 7 May 1939 proclaiming:

In the name of Almighty God. The Higher Leadership of the Arab Revolt in Palestine … To the Generous Arab people. Some of you are saying that the revolt has been disregarded and it has been ended. The traitors are flocking to the Towns inciting the people against the revolt, and to disobey the word of the nation. They are doing this for sums of money. The revolt is still flourishing, and it will not end till the Government grants our full demands. The traitors who are inciting the nation will be killed by bullets, whenever they are found. You should comply with the order of the nation. The Government have planned to forbid the wearing of the Kaffieh and agal and this scheme is meaningless. You must know that the headwear of today is the Kaffieh and agal, and anyone who wears the tarbush, and incites the people to obey the orders of the Government, will be shot dead. For the leadership (no signature).[13]

A British policeman recalled 'gangs of youths' who 'took it upon themselves to enforce this edict and they would tear a fez from the head of anyone wearing one … the poor offender had to walk bareheaded to the nearest store and buy a headdress.'[14] The rush to look like rebels led to a 'general scramble to exchange tarbooshes for hattas and agals, shopkeepers are doing a roaring trade in this article, which represents the latest in Arab nationalist fashion,' reported the local press.[15] So much extra cloth was needed for *kufiyyat* that the price rose and merchants went abroad to find cloth.[16]

As British forces triumphed over rebel bands by late 1938, they won the sartorial war, helped by Christian merchants in Jerusalem who held a meeting to decide that they would open their shops on Fridays, an act

[11] Subhi Yasin, *Al-Thawra al-'Arabiyya al-Kubra (fi Filastin) 1936–1939* [*The Great Arab Revolt in Palestine, 1936–1939*] (Damascus: Shafa 'Amr Haifa, 1959), p. 47.

[12] Summary of Intelligence, Palestine and Transjordan, 9 September 1938, by Wing Commander Ritchie at GHQ [18/38], CO 732/81/9, TNA.

[13] Attachment to Police CID Jerusalem, Intelligence Summary 33/39, 11 May 1939, 47/82, HA.

[14] Robert Martin, *Palestine Betrayed: A British Palestine Policeman's Memoir (1936–48)* (Ringwood: Seglawi, 2007), p. 43.

[15] 'Arab Townsmen in New Headgear,' *Palestine Post* (2 September 1938), p. 2.

[16] Arnon-Ohanna, *Herev mi-Bayit*, p. 282.

forbidden by rebels, 'and that they would no longer wear the Kaffiyah and Agal.'[17] The rebels put one Armenian Christian before a revolutionary court 'for refusing to wear the Arab headdress. The rebels had ordered that non-Arab Christians do so, a demand that was understandably resisted by the Armenians and Greeks.'[18] By May 1939 the local press was reporting how the *tarbush* was returning to towns as the most popular form of headdress.[19] Police CID noted the same, reporting how the

tarbush and takieh [a close-fitting cap that can be worn under a *tarbush* and that was sometimes worn by the urban proletariat instead of a *tarbush*] are slowly reappearing in the place of the hatta and agel. In Jenin the townspeople were requested by the District Administration to revert to wearing the tarbush. Public response was encouraging following the example set by Government servants, and there were no untoward incidents. In Haifa notices were posted in the Suk threatening with death any person who wears a tarbush or incites the public to obey the orders of the Government.[20]

Palestinians had an added incentive to discard *kufiyyat* as soldiers were less likely to fire on them. One police order earlier in the revolt instructed Palestinian *ghaffir* village guards to wear a crowned *kalpack*[21] police cap and not a *kufiyya* 'in order that the army will not fire on them.'[22] Police officer Geoffrey Morton noted the change in mood by the spring of 1939, with shops open and notables agreeing once again to wear the *tarbush*.[23] Similarly, the Gaza District Commissioner in March 1939 reported to the Chief Secretary that the 'tense period' when the rebels were in control had passed and how 'the kafia and agaal head-dress is gradually being discarded by those who did not normally wear it.'[24]

[17] Summary of Intelligence, Palestine and Transjordan, 16 December 1938, by Wing Commander Ritchie at GHQ [25/38], CO 732/81/10, TNA.
[18] Itamar Radai, 'The Rise and Fall of the Palestinian–Arab Middle Class under the British Mandate, 1920–39,' *Journal of Contemporary History* 51/3 (July 2016), p. 503.
[19] 'Terrorist Threat Warning,' *Palestine Post* (2 May 1939), p. 3.
[20] Police CID Jerusalem, Intelligence Summary 33/39, 11 May 1939, p. 1, 47/82, HA.
[21] A (typically) high-crowned thicker cap of Turkish origin made of felt or fur and worn by Palestine policemen.
[22] Police/DIS Report, 23 July 1936, Arab Office and Intelligence: 8/GENERAL/39, HA.
[23] Geoffrey Morton, *Just the Job: Some Experiences of a Colonial Policeman* (London: Hodder and Stoughton, 1957), p. 98.
[24] Letter, C. E. Buxton (DC, Gaza-Beersheba) to Chief Secretary, 16 March 1939, Buxton Papers, MSS. Brit. Emp. S. 390, Box 1, Palestine File, WL.

Appendix E
Dramatis Personae and Membership of the Arab Higher Committee

Arabs and Palestinians

'Abd al-Hadi, Fakhri (died 1943): from the village of 'Arraba near Jenin; Arab rebel band leader in 1936; collaborated with the British and Nashashibis as a peace band leader in 1938–39; murdered in 1943 at his son's wedding in 'Arraba, whether because of a family dispute or because of his collaboration is not clear.[1] Muhammad 'Izzat Darwaza wrote that his attacks on family members in the late 1930s led to another family member shooting him, while Hillel Cohen notes that rebels publicly passed a death sentence on 'Abd al-Hadi for his collaboration activities.[2] The police officer who signed for 'Abd al-Hadi's gun licence told this author that 'Abd al-Hadi was murdered in the course of a blood feud while attending a wedding, 8 April 1943.[3] Jewish intelligence officer Ezra Danin's assessment was that 'Abd al-Hadi's reasons for joining peace bands were 'only a little' ideological and mostly personal, that he drank, was involved in love affairs, and was murdered in 1943 in Palestine.[4]

'Abd al-Raziq, 'Arif (Abu Faysal): rebel band leader of Tayiba area, operated south of Tulkarm; left Palestine on 13 April 1939 and surrendered to the French in Syria 'in a state of

[1] Ezra Danin, *Te'udot u-Dmuyot me-Ginzey ha-Knufiyot ha-Arviyot, 1936–39* [Documents and Portraits from the Arab Gangs Archives in the Arab Revolt in Palestine, 1936–39] (Jerusalem: Magnes, 1981), p. 24; Yehoshua Porath, *The Palestinian Arab National Movement: From Riots to Rebellion. Volume 2, 1929–1939* (London: Cass, 1977), p. 258.
[2] Entry, 21 May 1938, Muhammad 'Izzat Darwaza, *Mudhakkirat Muhammad 'Izzat Darwaza: Sab'a wa tis'una 'aman fil-haya* [*The Diaries of Muhammad 'Izzat Darwaza: 97 Years in a Life*] (Beirut: Dar al Gharb al Islami, 1993), iii, pp. 392–93; Hillel Cohen, *Army of Shadows: Palestinian Collaboration with Zionism, 1917–1948* (Berkeley, CA: University of California Press, 2008), p. 133.
[3] Letter, Ted Horne to Author, 23 April 2013.
[4] Danin, *Te'udot u-Dmuyot*, p. 24, ft. 56.

complete physical collapse' and was detained.[5] Described in Haganah files as a bully, cruel and a thief, and forever fighting against fellow rebel leader 'Abd al-Rahim al-Hajj Muhammad, with both men attacking each other's villages.[6] British CID files from May 1939 noted that many Arabs thought him a traitor escaping the vengeance of his Arab victims, and bribed by the British to the sum of £P.10,000 to leave Palestine.[7]

Abu Durra, Yusuf Sa'id (Abu Abed) (1900–39): leading rebel band commander, former Qassamite; captured in Transjordan in July 1939 by British forces after losing his entire arsenal in Palestine to a British raid in Samaria; extradited to Palestine and hanged by the British in September 1939 or early 1940 in some accounts.[8]

Abu Gharbiyya, Bahjat (1916–2012): Palestinian fighter against the British in Jerusalem in 1936, including shooting British police officer Alan Sigrist in June 1936; fought Israel as a guerrilla leader in 1948; interviewed by the author in 2009.

al-'Alami, Musa (1897–1984): worked for the Palestine civil service until 1937 as private secretary to the High Commissioner, 1932–33 then as Government Advocate; expelled for his association with the revolt in 1937, after which lived in exile in Lebanon and Iraq as an adviser to Hajj Amin; after 1948 established an experimental agricultural project for refugee youths near Jericho and settled down there until his death; following the 1967 war had connections with many Israelis, including Moshe Dayan.

Darwaza, Muhammad 'Izzat (1887–1984): born in Nablus, member of *Istiqlal* party; served on the AHC in the 1940s; central figure in rebel headquarters (the Central Committee of the Holy War) in Damascus during the second stage of the revolt after 1937; close assistant of Hajj Amin.

al-Hajj (sometimes Haji in British files) Amin al-Husayni (the Mufti) (Mohammed Amin al-Husayni) (1895–1974): Muslim religious leader or 'Mufti' of Jerusalem and Chairman of the Supreme Muslim Council, leader of the Arab revolt 1936–39;

---

[5] Porath, *The Palestinian Arab National Movement*, p. 259.
[6] Court Houses of the Revolt, Internal Document from the PM's Office from the Class of Stateworkers who deal with Minorities, Documents from Arab Gangs, 1936–39, Report dated 4 September 1938, Printed in Jerusalem in 1958, Letters and Files Relating to Ezra Danin, 80/58P/14, p. 21, HA.
[7] Police CID Jerusalem, Intelligence Summary 33/39, 11 May 1939, p. 1, 47/82, HA.
[8] Porath, *The Palestinian Arab National Movement*, p. 260.

head of the Arab Higher Committee, 1936–37; went into exile in Lebanon in October 1937, pursued by British forces, after which he went to Iraq, Iran, Nazi Germany, France, Egypt, and back to Lebanon where he died in 1974. Fawzi al-Qawuqji summarised Hajj Amin as follows, which whether true or not gives a sense of the poor relations between two key Arab revolt leaders:

He is a coward. He has never fought on the battlefield of any country. He lays claim to leadership whenever he feels that his life is threatened; then he steals the money and retreats in defeat. He is an ignorant man. He is not a graduate of either a religious school or a secular one. He claims absolute knowledge and authority. He restricts all work in all fields to his person alone, and he exerts every effort to destroy any name that starts to shine among the Arabs. He is a conceited man. He believes that each individual must be at his disposal, and if it happens that he disagrees with him, he accuses him of betrayal. His motto is: Either you agree with me or you will play the role of hypocrite and traitor. He is a devious man. Whenever he hears that an influential name has surfaced, he is gripped by a fit of rage and desperation, so he gives his orders to destroy him or assassinate him.[9]

al-Hajj Muhammad, 'Abd al-Rahim (Abu Kamal) (1892–1939): rebel band leader in the Jenin 'triangle of terror' area; killed by British forces on 26 (sometimes 23rd) March 1939 in Sanur village in Samaria; peace bands helped to track him down.

al-Husayni, 'Abd al-Qadir (1907–48): commander of the rebel 'holy war' force *al-jihad al-muqaddas* in the 1930s; Palestinian rebel band leader in the Jerusalem area in the Arab revolt; nephew of Hajj Amin; seriously wounded by British forces in an attack on his band in Bani Na'im village near Hebron in November 1938;[10] killed fighting Jewish forces in April 1948.

Mufti (of Jerusalem): see Hajj Amin.

Nashashibi, Fakhri (1899–1941): nephew of Raghib Nashashibi and 'fierce opponent'[11] of Hajj Amin; formed with British and Jewish help anti-rebel peace bands in Palestine in 1938; assassinated in Baghdad in November 1941 by gunmen probably

---

[9] Quoted in Laila Parsons, *The Commander: Fawzi al-Qawuqji and the Fight for Arab Independence* (New York, NY: Hill and Wang, 2016), p. 200.

[10] Date from Porath, *The Palestinian Arab National Movement*, p. 257. Cohen notes al-Qadir being wounded and captured in a skirmish near Bethlehem in the summer of 1936 and a big battle at Bani Na'im with al-Qadir and the British in late 1938: Cohen, *Army of Shadows*, pp. 111, 148. Al-Qadir's Passia biographical entry notes that he was wounded twice during the revolt, in 1936 and 1939: www.passia.org (accessed 5 September 2016).

[11] From his biographical entry on the Passia website at www.passia.org (accessed 2 September 2016).

acting on orders from Hajj Amin but it was 'Abd al-Qadir al-Husayni who was arrested for plotting the assassination.

Nashashibi, Raghib (Bey) (1881/82–1951): Jerusalemite notable, former mayor of the city (1920–34), leader of the National Defence Party; uncle of Fakhri Nashashibi; served on AHC but abdicated in 1937 and was thus not expelled by the British; opponent of Hajj Amin and the Husayni family during latter stages of the Arab revolt; later served as a West Bank Governor under Jordanian rule.

al-Qassam, Shaykh 'Izz al-Din (1881/82/83–1935): born in Jabla in modern-day Syria; Muslim cleric and rebel band leader in Palestine, associated with the rebel Black Hand group after 1933; his death at the hands of British police near the village of Ya'bad on 20 November 1935 helped to trigger the Arab revolt the following year; buried outside the Israeli town of Nesher in the Muslim cemetery alongside two fellow fighters killed on 20 November 1935. The tombstone has been vandalised and repaired with a statement saying that someone has died and his life had been good with firm conviction (*husn yaqin*), and then the epitaph (in the form of a classical Arabic poem in two rhyming parts):

Here (lies) the martyr [*shaheed*], the most noble Aalim [learned person in Islam and a religious authority], who was a trustworthy guide. He is our Shaykh, al-Qassam, he who was the first among us to rise with us the flag of Jihad for the victory of Islam. He died as a martyr in a pure act of grace during the Ya'bad battle – in the [Muslim] month of Shaaban; therefore Allah awarded him with his finest favour – pleasing him with the paradise virgins. And if you wish to describe his sepulchre in history, say: 'In the highest place of heaven 'Izz al-Din al-Qassam (lies).'

On the fallen (vandalised) older headstone behind the main memorial there is inscribed from the Quran: 'And never think of those who have been killed in the cause of Allah as dead. Rather, they are alive with their Lord, receiving provision.'

al-Qawuqji, Fawzi (Fawz al-Din) (sometimes Fauzi or Fawzi in British files) (1890–1977): officer in the Ottoman Army; fought in the Syrian revolt (1925) and then in Palestine from late August to late October 1936 (28 August–20 October 1936 in Jewish files[12]) against the British; seen by the British as an

---

[12] Internal Document from the PM's Office from the Class of Stateworkers who deal with Minorities, Documents from Arab Gangs, 1936–39, report dated 4 September 1938, Printed in Jerusalem in 1958, 80/58P/14, pp. 14–15, HA.

effective commander, not least as he organised the rebels into formal military units; went on to fight in Iraq in 1941 against the British and in 1948 against Israel. He appears to have gone to Jerusalem in 1935 to meet British intelligence, one of them a prominent person, and this officer informed him that the British 'care' about him, after which Qawuqji said that he 'kept in touch' with the British officer, all prior to the revolt.[13] There were suggestions that he was working for the British in 1936 and when he left Palestine in October–November 1936 Jewish files from a clerk on the TAPline at the H3 pumping station in Transjordan record that al-Qawuqji and his party arrived with an (Arab) TJFF officer (so in British pay and service) on 4 November 1936, after which an RAF aeroplane landed on 5 November and 'payments' were made to al-Qawuqji.[14] British warplanes machine gunned al-Qawuqji near Palmyra in 1941 during Rashid Ali's revolt, leaving a bullet lodged in al-Qawuqji's head, forcing him to wear a hat indoors in cold weather as the metal of the bullet easily cooled down.

al-Rahim: see al-Hajj.

al-Sa'di, Shaykh Farhan (died 1937): Qassamite rebel leader in Samaria, served with al-Qassam in November 1935; later fought in the Arab revolt; turned in to British authorities on 22 November 1937 by relatives of a local man that Farhan's men had murdered;[15] tried on 24 November and hanged on 27 November 1937. Hugh Foot recalled capturing Shaykh Farhan al-Sa'di in a planned village search following an informer's tip off, after which he pleaded with the High Commissioner for the old man's life, to no avail, and the rebel leader 'was tried and hanged in Acre Prison within the week.'[16] Hanged after a military trial despite being eighty years old, noted an Arab source.[17] When he was with al-Qassam and being chased by the British in November 1935, Shaykh Farhan

[13] Khayriyya Qasimiyya (ed.), *Filastin fi-Mudhakkirat al-Qawuqji* [*Palestine in the Memories of Fawzi al-Qawuqji*] (Beirut: PLO Research Centre and Jerusalem Publishing House, 1975), ii, p. 30.

[14] From a diary of a clerk at H3, 1936 November, 4–5 November 1936, S25/3033-124, CZA. Porath, *The Palestinian Arab National Movement*, p. 191 made the original claim based on this file.

[15] Cohen, *Army of Shadows*, p. 135.

[16] Hugh Foot, *A Start in Freedom* (London: Hodder and Stoughton, 1964), p. 51. See also Cohen, *Army of Shadows*, p. 135.

[17] Izzat Tanus, *Al-Falastiniyun* [The Palestinians] (Beirut: PLO Research Centre, 1982), p. 194.

resisted battle, saying that it would compromise the rebels as they were not properly organised and that any action would draw attention to them but al-Qassam insisted on fighting the British, so Shaykh Farhan al-Sa'di dissented and went back to his village.[18] The Royal Ulster Rifles logged al-Sa'di's capture as a 'carefully prepared' trap by the East Yorkshire Regiment and 'done with the aid of informers.'[19]

al-Sakakini, Khalil (1878–1953): born in Jerusalem; Palestinian writer and educator; worked in the Palestine education department; left extensive diaries, translated partially into Hebrew; influenced many of the young generation of his time.

Tannous, 'Izzat (1896–1969): born in Nablus; medical doctor; served in the Arab Office in London during the revolt and was on the Arab Higher Committee; politically pro-*Majlis*.

Zu'aytir, Akram (1909–96): born in Nablus; founding member of the *Istiqlal* party; served on the Nablus National Committee during the revolt; imprisoned by the British; went into exile in 1937 and worked in Damascus with the rebel Central Committee of the Holy War in the second stage of the revolt after September 1937.

British

Andrews, Lewis (1896–1937): District Commissioner for Northern District in Palestine; assassinated by Qassamite Arab gunmen in Nazareth on 26 September 1937; buried in Jerusalem's Protestant cemetery on Mount Zion with the epitaph 'gave his life for this land.' A Palestinian who witnessed the assassination of Andrews described him as the 'top British officer whose mission was the Judaization of Galilee.'[20]

Battershill, William (1896–1959): Chief Secretary to the Palestine Government, March/April 1937–39, succeeding John Hathorn Hall (who was Chief Secretary, 4 August 1933–29 April 1937).

[18] Samih Hammudah, *al-Wa'y wa-al-thawrah: dirasah fi-hayah wa-jihad al-Shaykh 'Izz al-Din al-Qassam 1882–1935* [*Awareness and Revolution: A Study in the Life and Struggle of Shaykh 'Izz al-Din al-Qassam 1882–1935* (Jerusalem: Arab Studies Association, 1986), pp. 72–73.
[19] Searching for Suspects after an Outrage, Functions of the British in Palestine, Palestine Box, RUR.
[20] 'Khaled al-Fahoum Yatadhakkar' ['Khaled al-Fahoum Remembers'], *al-Quds* (2 September 1998), p. 17.

Blackburne, Kenneth (1907–80): Assistant District Commissioner in Nazareth in 1935 and then Acting District Commissioner, Galilee District, May–September 1938; later Governor of Jamaica.

Bredin, Major-General Humphrey E. N. 'Bala' (1916–2005): subaltern with the Royal Ulster Rifles in Palestine during the revolt, earning the MC and Bar in 1938; led one of the Special Night Squads; earned the nickname 'Bala' while in India and not from the Bal'a battle of September 1936; went on to fight in counter-insurgencies after 1945 in Palestine and Cyprus.

Brooke-Popham, Air Chief Marshal Sir (Henry) Robert (1878–1953): RAF Commander-in-Chief, Middle East, based in Cairo, 1935–36.

Brown, Right Reverend George Francis Graham (1891–1942): Anglican Bishop of Jerusalem, 1932–42, with a jurisdiction covering Palestine, Transjordan, Syria, Lebanon, Cyprus, and Iraq, as well as parts of Turkey; based at St George's Cathedral in east Jerusalem; killed in his car when hit by a train at a level crossing on the Palestine–Lebanon border, there being no lights on the train or level crossing and the car lights dimmed as it was wartime.

Buss, Group-Captain K. C. (1887–1961): RAF intelligence officer; the *Air Force List* for August 1936 notes that Buss was in Cairo with the Air Staff; subsequent *Air Force Lists* detail that from 15 September 1936 he was seconded to British Forces in Palestine and Transjordan; from 26 July 1937 he was with the Air Ministry in London in the Department of the Chief of the Air Staff as the Deputy Director of the Deputy Directorate of Intelligence; retired as an Air Commodore.

Dill, Lieutenant-General Sir John (1881–1944): commander (GOC) of British forces in Palestine and Transjordan, 8 September 1936–21 July 1937; later CIGS and Field Marshal.[21]

Domvile (or Domville), Flight-Lieutenant John Patrick (born 1900): RAF intelligence officer in Palestine from 1930 to late 1937 when he re-deployed to Iraq; supposed to have met al-Qawuqji in Iraq in the summer of 1936.[22] Laila Parsons

---

[21] The *Army List* for December 1936 gives the date of 8 September 1936 for the start of his command in Palestine. Dill seems to have arrived in Haifa on 13 September.

[22] The *Air Force List* for December 1937 details Domvile as posted to Iraq from 9 September 1937.

concludes that al-Qawuqji was never a British spy managed by Domvile but instead a victim of the machinations and lies of Hajj Amin: 'Scholars writing about the Mufti have shown that accusing people of treachery was part of his standard repertoire and served as one of the many weapons he used to silence his opponents. There is no evidence in any of the hundreds of original sources used for this book to indicate that Qawuqji was a spy for the British.'[23] Spelt Domvile in the index to the *Air Force List* while in the main text entry the spelling is Domville or Domvile, but if related to the pro-Nazi Admiral Barry Domvile (as is certainly the case) then the latter spelling is correct. 'Patrick Domville was a flamboyant, fascinating and controversial man who played an important role in the Jewish Agency's political struggle with the British authorities, particularly on issues relating to security. His involvement in these matters was much more extensive than was previously known and practically nothing has been written about him.'[24] Ended his life in poverty according to the same source.

Evetts, Brigadier John (1891–1988): commander of 16th Brigade in northern Palestine (Haifa and Galilee District, later Galilee and Acre District), 1936–39; ended his career as a Lieutenant-General.

Foot, Hugh (later Lord Caradon) (1907–90): Arabic speaker; posted by the Colonial Office to Palestine in 1929; stayed to 1938 as an Assistant District Commissioner in Nablus and Galilee; Assistant British Resident in Transjordan (1939); Governor of Jamaica (1951) and Cyprus (1957) where he tried to control the Army's excessive methods against EOKA.

Hacket Pain (sometimes Hacket-Pain), Major Andrew Uniacke Hereford (1904–87): intelligence officer with the Queen's Royal Regiment (West Surrey); in Palestine in 1939; formerly with the Sudan Defence Force; undoubtedly an Arabic speaker; later Consul for Jordan.[25]

---

[23] Parsons, *The Commander*, pp. 117, 173.

[24] Haggai Eshed, *Reuven Shiloah: The Man behind the Mossad* (London: Cass, 1997), pp. 23–24.

[25] See the September 1938 *Army List*. The Queen's Royal Regiment (West Surrey) served from January 1939 around Tulkarm. Hacket Pain is listed as 'attached' to the Sudan Defence Force in late 1938 and then listed as back with his Regiment in the February 1939 *Army List*, suggesting that he was transferred from the Sudan Defence Force (where he was in late 1938) back to the regiment as it was deploying to Palestine.

Haining, Lieutenant-General Sir Robert (1882–1959): commander (GOC) of all British forces in Palestine and Transjordan, 26 March 1938–14 July 1939.[26]

Hall, John Hathorn (1894–1979): (see Battershill).

Keith-Roach, Edward (1885–1954): District Commissioner for Northern District (1931–37) and then Jerusalem District (1937–43); chairman of the Palestine Central Censorship Board for Films and Plays.

Kirkbride, Alec Seath (1897–1978): replaced the assassinated Lewis Andrews as District Commissioner for Galilee and Acre District from 8 October 1937 to 1939; British Resident and Minister in Transjordan after 1939.

Lash, Brigadier Norman (1908–60): intelligence officer with a chequered career, serving with the Palestine police as a constable and as an officer, with the RAF as an officer, and then Transjordan's Arab Legion as a brigadier while seconded from the Palestine police. A Flying Officer N. O. Lash appears in the *Air Force List* for November 1938 serving with Middle East Command, effective from September of that year, presumably as an intelligence officer. Lash had before this been in the Palestine police as a constable and after the Arab revolt he served as a brigadier in Transjordan's Arab Legion, fighting in the 1948 war with Israel, having joined the force on 1 May 1939 from a substantive post of superintendent (or deputy superintendent) in the Palestine police. Major-General James Lunt who fought with the Arab Legion provides a more detailed timeline for Lash's service: Lash joined the Palestine police in 1932 (presumably as a constable); on 26 November 1934 his term of contract expired and he transferred to the Arab Legion; on 1 September 1938 Lash resigned from the Legion to join the RAF (one assumes on service in Palestine as an intelligence officer, corroborated by the *Air Force List*); on 17 April 1939 the Air Ministry released him for service back in Transjordan; on 1 May 1939 Lash was appointed deputy superintendent in the Palestine police but seconded to Transjordan; on 15 August 1943 Lash was promoted to superintendent and seconded permanently to the Arab Legion with the rank of *Kaymakam* (an Ottoman rank according to state

---

[26] The *Army List* for June 1938 gives a date of 26 March 1938 for the start of Haining's command; the *Army List* for October 1939 notes the start of the command of his successor in Palestine, Barker, to 14 July 1939.

official or governor). As a brigadier, Lash then fought in the 1948 war with Israel but was replaced during the fighting and he ended his life as a schoolteacher back in the UK, having read History at university in the 1920s. 'He was, as I said, really an intellectual type,' remembered a fellow officer.[27]

Lees, Aubrey (1899–1969): Assistant District Commissioner southern district Palestine based in Gaza, removed from colonial service for criticisms of pacification methods in 1939; involved in the British fascist movement during the war and interned.

McDonnell, Sir Michael (1882–1956): Chief Justice of Palestine, 2 May 1927–28 January 1937; dismissed for his critical anti-Government ruling on the Jaffa demolitions of June 1936; replaced by Sir Harry Trusted on 28 January 1937; worked for the Ministry of Information in 1940.

MacKereth, Colonel Gilbert (1893–1962): British Consul in Damascus, 1933–39, involved in intelligence work during the revolt and liaised with Palestine police to fight rebels; Consul-General in Addis Ababa in 1940 and Counsellor in the Legation in Beirut, 1943.

MacMichael, Sir Harold (1882–1969): Arabic speaker; served in the Sudan as a colonial official for some three decades; Governor of Tanganyika in 1934; High Commissioner for Palestine, 1 March 1938–September 1944; Jewish insurgents tried to assassinate him in the 1940s; went on to serve in Malaya and Malta.

Moffatt, Walter (1893–1938): Acting Assistant District Commissioner in Jenin; shot dead in his office in Jenin, 24 August 1938; buried in Haifa's Jaffa Road cemetery with the epitaph 'gave his life for this land.'

Montgomery, Major-General Bernard (1887–1976): served in the Irish War of Independence; commander of 8th Division in northern Palestine, the *Army List* notes his period in the country from 28 October 1938–July 1939; later Field Marshal and Viscount; oversaw as the head of the Army the final withdrawal of British troops from Palestine nine years later in 1948.

O'Connor, Major-General Richard (1889–1981): commander of 7th Division in southern Palestine and Military Governor of Jerusalem from 29 September 1938 (16 October in some accounts) to 1939 and so able to issue orders directly to the

---

[27] Letter, Glubb to Lunt, 24 August 1980, Lunt Papers, 2009-08-51-89, NAM.

city's police and civil officials; knighted 1941; commanded in north Africa and France in the Second World War; General in 1945.

Ormsby-Gore, William (1885–1964): Conservative politician Fourth Baron Harlech; Secretary of State for the Colonies, 1936–38; resigned the post when he succeeded to peerage in 1938, partly over the question of partition of Palestine, to which Ormsby-Gore felt committed, despite the Government moving away from partition as it looked to appease the Arabs in the face of a worsening world crisis.

Peirse, Air Vice Marshal Richard (1892–1970): Air Officer commanding all forces in Palestine and Transjordan, 1933–36; replaced by General Dill in September 1936; back in the UK as Director of operations and intelligence and Deputy Chief of the Air Staff, January 1937. Appointed KCB 1940.

Ritchie, Wing-Commander Alan P. (1899–1961): intelligence officer attached from HQ RAF Middle East as the chief RAF officer with the Combined Force Headquarters Staff in Palestine; based in Jerusalem; organised three intelligence centres in Palestine – in Haifa, Nablus, and Jerusalem – and put Wingate in charge of the Nazareth one.[28] Retired as an Air Vice Marshal.

Saunders, Colonel Alan (1886–1964): Entered Palestine with the British Army in 1917; joined police force in Palestine in 1920; February 1936 went to command police in Nigeria; returned to Palestine as Inspector General of Police and Prisons Palestine in November 1937, stayed to August 1943; retired from the colonial service and became a police adviser to Allied forces in Greece, 1944.

Scrivenor, Thomas (1908–98): Assistant District Commissioner in northern Palestine, 1937–43; returned to Palestine as Principal Assistant Secretary in 1946; served in British African colonies, 1948–60.

Spicer, Roy (1889–1946): commanded Kenya police; Inspector General of Police and Prisons Palestine, 16 July 1931–24 November 1937 (to 1938 in his *Who's Who* entry); survived attempted assassination, June 1937; Chief Constable of the Isle of Wight, 1938–45.[29]

---

[28] From the October 1937 *Air Force List*, with Domvile, Strange, and Windsor listed as subordinate officers.

[29] *Who Was Who* lists 1938 as the date for Spicer's departure.

Strange, Flight-Lieutenant Royle Frederick John (1896–?): intelligence officer, listed (with Domvile) in the *Air Force List* for July 1936 with the Air Staff with British Forces in Palestine and Transjordan alongside Major J. Teague as an attached military liaison duties officer; detailed as political officer for northern Palestine, Haifa district in the Alice Hay of Seaton Papers; had served previously in Iraq in 1928 on the intelligence staff.

Teague, Colonel John (1896–1983): intelligence officer; following First World War Army service went to General Staff Intelligence in Iraq; language student in Persia, 1933; liaison officer with RAF in Palestine during the Arab revolt based in Jerusalem; served with SIME and MI6 (SIS), and the Foreign Office.

Tegart, Sir Charles (1881–1946): formerly Indian police; the Colonial Office wanted him to be Inspector-General of the Palestine police in 1937 but Tegart refused; sent to Palestine on an advisory mission, December 1937–January 1938 with Sir David Petrie of the Indian intelligence bureau (Petrie later became Director General of MI5); in Palestine intermittently to May 1939 (in London, August–September 1938); established the 'Tegart wall' fence along Palestine's northern border to exclude rebels, built spring of 1938 to August 1938, and the 'Tegart forts,' many still extant; survived a rebel ambush on 31 December 1938.

Wauchope, General Sir Arthur (1874–1947): formerly of the Black Watch Regiment and wounded in the legs in the Boer War; wounded in the chest in the First World War; promoted Major-General in 1923 (and full General in 1936); High Commissioner for Palestine, 1931–February 1938 (formally to 1 March 1938). Subordinates found Wauchope difficult, his Chief Secretary, William Battershill, in thinly veiled code in his diary, described him as, 'the very head of a totalitarian state in many respects. A very Hitler if only he knew something of administration … His methods of doing public business would make saints weep … He was a hustler.'[30] Being High Commissioner meant pleasing no one. The Army viewed him with disfavour for supposedly being too lenient towards the rebels, while the Palestinian, Akram Zu'aytir, wrote on

---

[30] Diary, 14 August 1937, Battershill Papers, MSS. Brit. Emp. S. 467, Box 12, File 6, WL; Diary, 1 January 1939, Battershill Papers, MSS. Brit. Emp. S. 467, Box 12, File 6, WL.

Wauchope's departure how 'we are waving him goodbye with insults and damnation despite his kindness and faking being equal ... Palestine witnessed the worst measures. Jewish immigration came en masse to Palestine ... It doesn't matter how bad MacMichael will be; he can't be worse than Wauchope.'[31] The Zionist leader, Chaim Weizmann, meanwhile, observed that Wauchope was too lenient to the rebels as he did not understand 'Arab psychology.'[32] An earlier Chief Secretary remembered how the 'Jews played on him like a piano.'[33] Wauchope took no further part in public life after retiring from Palestine except becoming Colonel of the Black Watch.

Wavell, Lieutenant-General Archibald (1883–1950): fought in Palestine with General Allenby in the First World War; commander (GOC) of all British forces in Palestine and Transjordan, 19 August 1937–26 March 1938; his 'conventional exterior masked a complex personality with much sympathy for the unorthodox,' and someone who 'cast a protecting mantle over Wingate';[34] commanded in the Second World War in north Africa; later Viceroy of India, Field Marshal and Earl.

Windsor, Flight-Lieutenant Charles M. (1911–41): intelligence officer; listed in the July 1936 *Air Force List* in Iraq on language training and in the *Air Force List* for October 1937 as serving in Palestine alongside Domvile and Strange on the HQ of Combined Force Staff. Died in a training accident in 1941.

Wingate, Captain (later Major-General) Orde (1903–44): British Army intelligence officer in Palestine, 1936–38; fervent (Christian, Plymouth Brethren) Zionist; commander of the irregular British–Jewish Special Night Squads in Galilee in 1938 and removed later in the year and sent back to the UK; died in an air crash while leading Chindit forces against the Japanese in Burma in 1944.

---

[31] Akram Zuʻaytir, *Al-Haraka al-Wataniya al-Filastiniyya, 1935–39: Yawmiyyat Akram Zuʻaytir* [*The Palestinian National Movement, 1935–39: Diaries of Akram Zuʻaytir*] [1980] (Beirut: IPS, 1992), p. 338.

[32] Record of Conversation (Weizmann and Ben Gurion) with the Secretary of State, 31 August 1936, FO 371/20024, TNA.

[33] Notes of Interviews, Hathorn Hall (London), n.d., Palestine Research Lever Arch File, Thames TV Material on 'Palestine: Promises, Rebellion and Abdication' (Thames TV, 1977–78), IWMFA.

[34] Wavell in C. G. Matthew and Brian Harrison, *Revised Oxford Dictionary of National Biography* (Oxford: Oxford University Press, 2004). The *Army List* for December 1937 gives a date of 19 August 1937 for the start of his command in Palestine; the *Army List* for June 1938 gives a date of 26 March 1938 for the start of Haining's command.

Jewish

Danin, Ezra (1903–85): Jewish intelligence officer at Hadera, operated intelligence network for Haganah and the British, 1936–39; Arabic speaker, born in Jaffa; headed up Arab section of *Shai*.

Epstein (later Eilat), Eliyahu (1903–90): Born in Russia; emigrated to Palestine in 1924; Arabic speaker; worked for the Jewish Agency's political department in the 1930s.

Palmon, Yehoshua (Josh) (1913–94): worked in the Sodom potash plant (1935–39) and then with Jewish intelligence and the *Shai* Arab section as a senior operative; in April 1948, Palmon negotiated with al-Qawuqji who was then fighting for the Palestinians against Jewish forces.

Sasson, Elias (later Eliyahu) (1902–78): Born in Damascus; educated in Arab schools and Arabic speaker; worked as an Arabist (as Director of the Arab Division) for the Jewish Agency's Political Department.

Shertok (later Sharett), Moshe (1894–1965): born in Russia, came to Palestine in 1906/08; Arabic speaker; fought with the Ottoman Army in the Great War; head of the political department of the Jewish Agency during the Arab revolt. Later, Israel's Foreign Minister and Prime Minister.

Shiloah, Reuven: see Zaslani.

Zaslani (or Zaslany) (born Zaslanski), Reuven (underground codename of Reuven Shiloah, later adopted as his last name) (1909–59): Haganah intelligence officer; born in Ottoman Jerusalem; Arabic speaker; worked with Jewish Agency's political department in intelligence in late 1930s, liaising with British intelligence officers in the RAF for whom he was a secretary-translator; later became director of Israeli Mossad intelligence agency. The British said of Zaslani, noting that he was born in 1906: 'Head of intelligence section of the Hagana and liaises on behalf of the Hagana with the Political Department and the Recruiting Office of the Jewish Agency. Travels frequently to Syria and Egypt ... An unpleasant personality.'[35]

---

[35] Who's Who of Palestine Jewish Politicians and Personalities, Jerusalem 1944, CID HQ Political Reference Library, Catling Papers, MSS. Medit. S. 20, File 4, WL.

Membership of the Arab Higher Committee, Formed 25–26 April 1936

Hajj Amin of the Palestine Arab Party was President (1). Heads of the six major parties joined as follows, leaving aside the Palestine Communist Party: Raghib Nashashibi (2) of the National Defence Party; Jamal al-Husayni (3) of the Palestine Arab Party; Ya'qub al-Ghusayn (4) of the Congress of Youth Party; 'Abd al-Latif al-Salah (5) of the National Bloc; and Husayn al-Khalidi (6) of the Reform Party. 'Awni 'Abd al-Hadi (7) leader of the *Istiqlal* Party was appointed General Secretary and Ahmad Hilmi 'Abd al-Baqi (8), also from *Istiqlal*, was made Treasurer. Alfred Rok (9), a Greek Catholic and active member of the Palestine Arab Party, represented Christians, together with Ya'qub Farraj (10), a Greek Orthodox with the Nashashibi bloc. Thus, the Husayni bloc had three members (Hajj Amin, Jamal al-Husayni, Alfred Rok), the Nashashibis (Raghib Nashashibi, Ya'qub Farraj) and *Istiqlalists* ('Awni 'Abd al-Hadi, Ahmad Hilmi 'Abd al-Baqi) two apiece, and the three remaining parties one member each, totalling ten members of the AHC.[36] The British outlawed the AHC and National Committees on 1 October 1937 and deported AHC members to the Seychelles, Hajj Amin evading the net by hiding up in the *Haram al-Sharif* before escaping to Lebanon, the British possibly conniving in his escape.[37] Jamal al-Husayni also escaped the British but was later captured in Iran and deported to Rhodesia. On 16 October 1937, the British appointed a commission to administer the *awqaf* in place of the Supreme Muslim Council. The literature often omits *Istiqlal* from the list of Palestinian political parties ('remained aloof'), reducing the number to five.[38] Weldon Matthews usefully argues that the British and Palestinian notables combined to rescue the elite politics by forming the Arab nationalist political parties detailed above to counter *Istiqlal*'s claim to represent a new 'element of politically aware Palestinian Arabs that consciously strove to create a public that made claims on the government in the name of the nation.'[39]

---

[36] From Porath, *Palestinian Arab National Movement*, p. 165.
[37] A Quarter of My Century by Dudley Clarke, p. 551, Clarke Papers, 99/2/1–3: DW/8, IWMD; Typed Memoir, Pieces of War, p. 44 [deleted sections of text], Simonds Papers, 08/46/1, IWMD.
[38] *A Survey of Palestine, Prepared in December 1945 and January 1946 for the Information of the Anglo-American Committee of Inquiry* (Jerusalem: Government Printer, 1946), i, p. 33.
[39] Weldon C. Matthews, *Confronting an Empire, Constructing a Nation: Arab Nationalists and Popular Politics in Mandate Palestine* (London: Tauris, 2006), pp. 233–34.

Appendix F
Currency and Wages

The Colonial Office set up the London-based Palestine Currency Board in 1926 to launch a new currency for Palestine to replace the Egyptian currency of 100 piastres to the Egyptian pound in use in the country since 1917. The new currency of the Palestine pound broken down into mils coins went into circulation in November 1927. The change was not immediate and payments during the period of the Arab revolt were sometimes still recorded in piastres. The removal of Egyptian coin cut out the Egyptian Government and the National Bank of Egypt, so enabling the Palestine Government to profit financially from its own currency and helping to promote economic activity such as citrus fruit exports.[1] The new Palestine pound was equivalent to a pound UK Sterling ($£$), the UK currency broken down at the time into 20 shillings of 12 pence per shilling, so 240 pence to the pound. The British marked the new Palestine currency as $£$P.1 or (derived from Latin for pound weight, *libra pondo*) LP.1 for, say, one Palestine pound, broken down into 1,000 mils per pound, with notes starting at 500 mils through $£$P.1, $£$P.5, $£$P.10 and $£$P.50 to $£$P.100. The bank notes had depictions on their face of Rachel's Tomb (500 mils), the Dome of the Rock ($£$P.1), and the White Tower (Mosque) of Ramleh ($£$P.5–100), avoiding offence to Jews and Muslims with any graven images, with the Jerusalem Citadel on the reverse of all notes. Christians complained that nothing represented their faith on the bank notes, although the Currency Board report of 1928 described the White Tower as the Crusaders' Tower so perhaps it thought that this was a Christian image.[2] Bank note designs drafted after 1933 included new images of Absalom's Tomb (500 mils), the Church of the Holy Sepulchre ($£$P.5–10), and al-Jazzar Mosque ($£$P.50–100) but none went

---

[1] *Report of the Palestine Currency Board for the Period Ending 31 March 1928* (London: Waterlow, 1928); Raphael Dabbah, *Currency Notes of the Palestine Currency Board* (Jerusalem: Israel Numismatic Society, 2005); Howard M. Berlin, *The Coins and Banknotes of Palestine under the British Mandate, 1927–47* (Jefferson, NC: McFarland, 2001).

[2] *Report of the Palestine Currency Board*, p. 3.

into circulation. The UK-based company Thomas de La Rue printed the new Palestine bank notes with English, Arabic and Hebrew inscriptions, the last antagonising Palestinians, as did the poor aesthetics of the Arabic text. The Royal Mint in London struck the coins: the 50 and 100 mils coins in silver, with 1, 2, 5, 10 and 20 mils coins in nickel-bronze or bronze. Dates were in the Christian calendar. Finding neutral symbols for the coins and space for the trilingual legends needed was problematic. The British settled on an olive sprig or wreath for the reverse of the coins. The Palestine Currency Board authorised Barclay's Bank just outside Jerusalem's old city walls as its currency agent and distribution centre; later, the British opened currency distribution centres in Haifa and Amman. The British broke down the Palestine Pound in common usage into shillings, 20 per pound, 12 pence per shilling, with government fines, for instance, occasionally expressed as LP.200.00, like UK currency with pounds, shillings, and pence. The granulation of currency was more usually in the form of, say, £P.3.100, so a sum of three pounds and 100 mils. To map decimal mils coinage to the non-decimal British system, the British set the 100 mils coin as equivalent in value to a tenth of a pound that matched a Florin of two shillings, so ten shillings equalled 500 mils, while a shilling was worth 50 mils. How the British mapped the 12 pence of a shilling to 50 mils is unclear, presumably 25 mils equalled six pence. The American Consul in Jerusalem matched 20 mils to ten US cents. Jews and Palestinians also called the Palestine pound the dinar. Hebrew-language files in the 1930s sometimes referred to the Palestine pound as the lira, as in the 'pound' of the Land of Israel, *lira Eretz-Yisraelit*. That rebels in the revolt did not appear to have forged currency is curious as forgers, notably in Egypt, produced counterfeit 50 and 100 mils coins during the Mandate period. Nazi Germany later counterfeited £P.5 notes to pay its agents in the Middle East. Virtually all known counterfeit bank notes were £P.1 and £P.5 denominations, not least as larger notes attracted scrutiny as they had so much purchasing power.

Triangulation of pacification measures such as fining or paying informers demands a measure of the value of money in Palestine in 1936. The Chief Secretary's salary was £P.1,600 per annum plus £P.400 allowances; a District Commissioner earned £P.1,200 plus £P.350 expenses; an Arab District Office £P.550–700 per year.[3] A British constable's salary was between £P.11–18 per month including board, while Fakhri 'Abd al-Hadi paid his peace band men £P.6 per month as opposed to the insurgents' typical pay of 30 shillings (so £P.1.500

---

[3] *Palestine Civil Service Lists 1935–39* (Jerusalem: Government Printing Press, 1935–39).

mils) to £P.4.[4] Rebels offered Lebanese Druze £P.4–4.500 per month to join armed bands and commanders £P.20.[5] The estimated average yearly wage of a Palestinian rural peasant family was £P.25–30.[6] Jewish intelligence noted that the ordinary village wage was 80 mils per diem for a 'slaving' working day up to fourteen hours while £P.3–4 per month was considered a large sum.[7] One specialist text estimates that a £P.100 note was worth $486 and 'represented more than 40 months' wages for the average skilled worker. Even a single £P10 note was "a lot of money" then.'[8] Wounded rebels were paid £P.5 a month while convalescing and £P.10 on re-joining.[9] The Jewish-owned *Nesher* cement company paid Jewish *Histadrut* factory workers 448 mils per day in 1935, skilled ones up to 750 mils; Arab workers with *Nesher* received 100–125 mils per diem for a longer working day.[10] Experienced stevedores in Haifa port earned up to £P.13.500 per month (500–550 mils per day), although this assumed daily work; Jewish labourers earned between £P.3 and £P.7.500 per month, a more realistic measure of wages.[11] A gun with ammunition cost £P.8–9.

[4] *The Palestine Police: Annual Administrative Report 1934* (Jerusalem: Government Printing Press, 1934), p. 10.
[5] Report attached to Letter from Haifa Labour Council sent to Shertok, 1 November 1937, S25/5570-160 CZA.
[6] Rosemary Sayigh, *The Palestinians: From Peasants to Revolutionaries* (London: Zed, 2007), p. 25.
[7] Appendix: Explanatory Notes, Captured and Translated Arabic Material with Commentary, p. 158, Wingate Papers, Microfilm M2313, BL.
[8] Berlin, *The Coins and Banknotes of Palestine*, p. 103.
[9] CID, Jerusalem, Periodical Appreciation Summary 73/38, 18 October 1938, L/PS/12/3343: Political Situation – Police Summaries, IOR.
[10] Deborah Bernstein, *Constructing Boundaries: Jewish and Arab Workers in Mandatory Palestine* (Albany, NY: SUNY Press, 2000), p. 122.
[11] Bernstein, *Constructing Boundaries*, p. 154; Lilach Rosenberg-Friedman, *Birthrate Politics in Zion: Judaism, Nationalism, and Modernity under the British Mandate* (Bloomington, IN: Indiana University Press, 2017), p. 106. An illegal abortion cost about £P.6.

Appendix G
The Escapes of al-Qawuqji and Hajj Amin

Fawzi al-Qawuqji's escape from Palestine in late October 1936 is interesting as multiple sources confirm that the British cleared a path for his removal from the country. The story of his departure adds to our understanding of his place in Palestinian life, his military acumen, and how the British linked diplomacy to military action. Following the cease-fire on 12 October 1936, British military high command told its soldiers who had been hunting al-Qawuqji to halt operations. As policeman Ted Horne later wrote, 'There did come a time when Fawzi was surrounded by soldiers so that he could have been captured and put on trial' but then 'sealed orders came from Jerusalem that he be allowed to escape. It is reported that the army was furious. Years later the army was able to say in 1941, "We told you so" [Al-Qawuqji returned to fight Britain in Iraq in 1941, the British severely wounding him in an air strike].'[1] When Arab potentates had pushed for a ceasefire in 1936, al-Qawuqji had argued that his fighters were in a strong position and that if the British attacked them after any ceasefire, he and his men would resume the war a fortiori. With the 12 October 1936 ceasefire, al-Qawuqji issued orders to his men to stop fighting and not to make any 'spark' that would affect negoti-ations.[2] When British troops visited Bayt Iba village on 17–18 October 1936, the *mukhtar* told them that he had read a notice in Jerusalem from al-Qawuqji that 'if any Arab fired at a British soldier he would be liable to suffer a severe penalty, the nature of which would be decided by FAWZI. If this is true it would appear that the gangs are hoping that they will

---

[1] Notes by Ted Horne, This Is the Story of Fawzi Kauwakji, Lodged with MEC in 2016. See also Laila Parsons, *The Commander: Fawzi al-Qawuqji and the Fight for Arab Independence* (New York, NY: Hill and Wang, 2016), pp. 165–67 and Eyal, Yigal, 'The Arab Revolt, 1936–1939: A Turning Point in the Struggle over Palestine,' in Mordechai Bar-On (ed.), *A Never-Ending Conflict: A Guide to Israeli Military History* (Westport, CT and London: Praeger, 2004), p. 26.

[2] Muhammad 'Izzat Darwaza, *Mudhakkirat Muhammad 'Izzat Darwaza: Sab'a wa tis'una 'aman fil-haya* [*The Diaries of Muhammad 'Izzat Darwaza: 97 Years in a Life*] (Beirut: Dar al Gharb al Islami, 1993), ii, pp. 237–45.

be granted a general pardon if they remain quiet and well behaved.'[3] Al-Qawuqji left behind a group of key figures – akin to village notables in the transliteration – to be responsible for the safety and preservation of mujahideen arms, keeping them 'ready' 'as and when' they would be needed again, adding that 'command' would keep a list of weapons.[4] Al-Qawuqji was ready to resume the fight and added on 22 October 1936 that the enemy would never have accepted the calls for ceasefire but for the recent Palestinian victories. He was proud of his achievements and how 'we brought the country to the point where the kings and leaders of the Arab world can take this to negotiations,' adding that 'we will stop the fighting to support the negotiations and we will be back to fighting if the British do not give the Palestinians their rights.'[5] A day later, Hajj Amin wrote to al-Qawuqji, the latter noting: 'I received this from the Mufti ... I am keen that you come out of the current engagement, that you successfully and safely engaged in, so the nation can enjoy your skills and capabilities in the new era.'[6] Al-Qawuqji in Palestine was a threat to Hajj Amin and to the British and so they needed to extract him and his men. Al-Qawuqji was preparing to withdraw by 20 October and on the 24th someone told him that the road was open. On 25 October, villagers came with guns to help him escape and on the 26th al-Qawuqji and his men crossed the River Jordan.[7] As al-Qawuqji crossed the river into Transjordan, up to 5,000 villagers mobilised to help him.[8] Al-Qawuqji talks in his Beirut papers about the road and Jordan River crossing points being clear, and how he and his men crossed the night of 24–25 October 1936, with al-Qawuqji sending someone ahead to check whether it was safe or not: 'The enemy knew of our intentions and the date of

[3] Dorsetshire Regiment, Situation Report 20 by BIO, 16th Inf Bde, Nablus, 17–18 October 1936, 88/353, Shelf C4, Box 3, KMM.

[4] Memorandum No. 17, 20 October 1936, by General Command of Arab Revolt in South Syria and Palestine, addressing the Palestinian people after the strike has stopped and waiting for the outcome of the negotiation and waiting also for the organisation of the revolutionary regions in Khayriyya Qasimiyya (ed.), *Mudhakkirat Fawzi al-Qawuqji* [*Memories of Fawzi al-Qawuqji*] (Damascus: Dar al-Namir, 1996), pp. 578–79.

[5] Memorandum No. 18, 22 October 1936 that Fawzi issued in response to Arab kings' call for ending the strike and revolt ['after stopping the fighting' in another header] in Qasimiyya, *Mudhakkirat Fawzi al-Qawuqji*, p. 580.

[6] Qasimiyya, *Mudhakkirat Fawzi al-Qawuqji*, pp. 582–83.

[7] Khayriyya Qasimiyya (ed.), *Filastin fi-Mudhakkirat al-Qawuqji* [*Palestine in the Memories of Fawzi al-Qawuqji*] (Beirut: PLO Research Centre and Jerusalem Publishing House, 1975), ii, pp. 56–59.

[8] Akram Zu'aytir, *Al-Haraka al-Wataniya al-Filastiniyya, 1935–39: Yawmiyyat Akram Zu'aytir* [*The Palestinian National Movement, 1935–39: Diaries of Akram Zu'aytir*] [1980] (Beirut: IPS, 1992), pp. 221ff.

our march.'⁹ The Dorsetshire Regiment recorded at the same time how 'Confirmation has been received from several sources that FAWZI crossed the Jordan on the night 25/26 [October]. The general impression amongst the Arabs is that the troops were withdrawn in order to allow him to pass,' adding that local villagers fired off shots to celebrate al-Qawuqji's safe departure.¹⁰ West Yorkshire Regiment soldiers covering the ford where al-Qawuqji was to cross then received orders to vacate the area 'for political reasons.'¹¹ Army officer A. J. H. Dove recalled how he 'tried to catch him but we had to call off the operation and for political reasons he was allowed to go back to Iraq.'¹² An RAF officer in Iraq told US diplomats there how 'the British knew of Fawzi's intended departure from Palestine and planned to capture him as he crossed the border into Transjordan. They received orders from London, however, to allow him to proceed without molestation.'¹³ A CID file attests to a convoy of vehicles taking al-Qawuqji out of Palestine and these can only have been British ones, possibly of the British-led Transjordan Frontier Force (TJFF):

the country was full of rumour that Fawzi had been surrounded at Raba. Many villagers over a wide area prepared to turn out to assist him ... Had Fawzi been surrounded there is little doubt that a large number of Palestinians would have gone to his aid ... they [al-Qawuqji's band] were encouraged to move off towards their own country, and accordingly during the night 3rd/4th November some 12 to 20 vehicles passed Mufrak, a station on the pipeline, conveying the remains of Fawzi's party, said to be some 200 men, their arms and baggage.¹⁴

Jewish files recorded the RAF flying in financial payments to al-Qawuqji in Transjordan. They also noted the presence of at least one TJFF officer with al-Qawuqji. This information came from a Jewish agent, possibly an Arab clerk working at the one of the TAPline pumping stations in Transjordan, who recorded how al-Qawuqji was at the H3 pumping station on 4–5 November 1936: '4th of November ... Fawzi Kavukchi [sic] and

---

⁹ Photocopied handwritten notebook/journal (pp. 90–171) [almost certainly by al-Qawuqji and now a bundle of sheets of paper], n.d. [but 1936], pp. 133ff, al-Qawuqji Papers, IPS, Beirut.

¹⁰ Dorsetshire Regiment, Situation Report 29 by BIO, 16th Infantry Brigade, Nablus, 27 October 1936, 88/353, Shelf C4, Box 3, KMM.

¹¹ *Ça Ira: The Journal of the West Yorkshire Regiment (The Prince of Wales's Own)* 8/2 (December 1936), pp. 109, 112.

¹² Dove, 4463/03, p. 29, IWMSA; Joseph Nevo, *King Abdallah and Palestine: A Territorial Ambition* (Houndmills: Macmillan, 1996), p. 34.

¹³ Minister Resident and US Consul General Iraq to State Department, 18 November 1936, 867N.00/422 [Reel M#1037/2], NARA II.

¹⁴ CID, Jerusalem, Periodical Appreciation Summary 18/36, 7 November 1936, L/PS/12/3343: Political Situation – Police Summaries, IOR.

his party accompanied by Transjordan Frontier Force Officer Ad'd Bey Sukhon[15] (?) arrived H3 at 2015 GMT night.'There follows a short entry for 5 November noting that an RAF plane landed and 'payments' made, for what purpose is unclear.[16] A Jewish commentary on captured Arabic material noted that al-Qawuqji escaped with £12,000 transferred to a bank in Syria, accrued nefariously while in Palestine.[17] Laila Parsons has suggested to this author that the H3 payment might have been from Ibn Saud – who worked strongly behind the scenes in the ceasefire talks – or maybe from the Iraqi Government through Nuri al-Sa'id.[18] The second edition of al-Qawuqji's memoirs records that on 3 November 1936 an adviser came from King Abdullah and 'I knew from him that the English can pay any cost for me to leave Jordan, even if I ask for British army vehicles to transfer me to Iraq.'[19] Worried that the withdrawal might be a British plot, al-Qawuqji made a condition that the Emir's adviser and his secretary 'be with me during the withdrawal, and not to appear on our journey any English plane or armoured vehicle. Otherwise, I will destroy the pipelines ... and the Prince accepted so I asked immediately for vehicles to transfer the Iraqi units and some soldiers from the Palestinian units and Druze units ... Palestinians to Palestine, Syrians [literally Levant] to Damascus,' concluding how in the morning his sixty-vehicle convoy headed east to pumping station H5 where they 'took a rest there in the view of the English soldiers. Then we continued the journey with the groups,' arriving in Iraq on 6 November 1936.[20] An Army officer recalled how al-Qawuqji 'had actually been captured by the Transjordan Frontier Force and released because he wasn't really ... you know they didn't want to be bothered with having to court martial him.'[21] The Army was sure that politics muddled operations: 'I don't think they wanted to get him.'[22] Troops were ready to block al-Qawuqji's escape but the AHC came to the rescue on 24 October and 'announced that the strike would begin all over again on the 26th unless the military operations in the hills were stopped. The armistice, it claimed was being broken' in the words of

---

[15] There is no officer with such a name in the TJFF section of the *Palestine Civil Service List 1937* (Jerusalem: Government Printing Press, 1937), p. 258. Possibly Ahmad Bey Sukhn.

[16] From a diary of a clerk at H3, 4–5 November 1936, S25/3033-124, CZA; Yoav Gelber, *Jewish–Transjordanian Relations, 1921–48* (London: Cass, 1997), p. 99.

[17] Captured and Translated Arabic Material with Commentary, pp. 15–16, Wingate Paper, Microfilm M2313, BL.

[18] Correspondence, Laila Parsons to Author, 26 June 2016.

[19] Qasimiyya (ed.), *Mudhakkirat Fawzi al-Qawuqji*, pp. 253–54.

[20] Ibid.

[21] Gratton, 4506/03, pp. 29–30, IWMSA.

[22] Thomas, 4545/04, p. 32, IWMSA.

Colonel H. J. Simson.[23] 'Open the chain of soldiers' to let him escape, in the words of a Hebrew-language source as there was 'an agreement' with the AHC.[24] The Government had either to let al-Qawuqji go or postpone the Peel Commission and see a renewal of the strike, so it facilitated his escape. The evidence of high-level directives to achieve this end is overwhelming.

Security force personnel were sceptical regarding Hajj Amin's escape in October 1937, too, blaming it on politics and London's desire to keep Hajj Amin as its negotiating partner out of jail. Hajj Amin hid in the *Haram al-Sharif* after the British banned the AHC and as High Commissioner Wauchope had earlier complained, 'we can't "eliminate" the Haram area!'[25] Similarly, GOC Wavell's comment on Hajj Amin was that Palestine would 'never have peace till we get to the source of all the trouble. But to winkle him out of his lair is not easy, and an unsuccessful attempt might be disastrous.'[26] The Chief Secretary's observation to Wauchope was that if Hajj Amin made 'a determined effort in disguise I think his attempt is bound to be successful. It is not possible to keep police at all exits from the Haram and from the Old City ... the Mufti could get out by hidden exits which almost certainly exist.'[27] When Hajj Amin did flee by ship to Lebanon, the Army was sure that the civil authorities had a hand in his escape, senior intelligence operative Dudley Clarke recording how, 'It was said that there was some collusion in high places, for the Palestine Police made no effort to stop his flight, whereas the Lebanese authorities had ample warning to welcome him when he arrived by sea off Beirut.'[28] Berkshire Regiment intelligence officer Tony Simonds thought the same, aided by police corruption:

I had the job of carrying out his arrest with a small group of my Intelligence men. I went down the street to the Mufti's house in time to see a Palestine Police car

---

[23] Col H. J. Simson, *British Rule and Rebellion* (Edinburgh and London: Blackwood, 1937), pp. 294–96.

[24] Yuval Arnon-Ohanna, *Falahim ba-Mered ha-'Aravi be-eretz Yisrael, 1936–39* [*Fellahin during the Arab Revolt in the Land of Israel*] (Tel Aviv: Shiloh Institute, Tel Aviv University, 1978), pp. 75ff; Captured and Translated Arabic Material with Commentary, p. 17, Wingate Paper, Microfilm M2313, BL.

[25] Letter, Wauchope to Battershill, 26 September [1937], Battershill Papers, MSS. Brit. Emp. S. 467, Box 10, File 4, WL.

[26] Appreciation, 14–15 October 1937, Wavell to Haining (DMO, London), Palestine, 1937–38 Volume, Wavell Papers, POH.

[27] Letter, Battershill to Wauchope, 10 October 1937, Battershill Papers, MSS. Brit. Emp. S. 467, Box 10, File 4, WL. Such (now gated) exits are still visible in the city's curtain walls.

[28] Brig Evetts quoted in A Quarter of My Century by Dudley Clarke, p. 551, Clarke Papers, 99/2/1–3: DW/8, IWMD.

drive away. It subsequently turned out that the Mufti was in it. [The following section is struck out but legible.] The car belonged to the D.I.G./Palestine Police, a man called Kingsley-Heath,[29] and the rumour was that he/someone took a £1,000 bribe to do it [the struck-out section ends]. Anyway, the Mufti was driven down to Jaffa in a Palestine Police car and taken off in a launch to a tramp steamer, which then took him to Beirut.[30]

---

[29] Deputy Inspector General A. J. Kingsley-Heath of the Palestine police.
[30] Typed Memoir, Pieces of War, p. 44, Simonds Papers, 08/46/1, IWMD.

Bibliography

PRIMARY SOURCES (UNPUBLISHED)

ISRAEL

American Colony Hotel, Jerusalem

American Colony Archive Jerusalem
  Captioned Photograph Albums (1936–39)
  Papers of Bertha Spafford Vester
  Scrapbooks of Articles about the American Colony and Palestine

Avraham Harman Institute of Contemporary Jewry, Oral History Division, Hebrew University, Jerusalem
Meir Levin: Interviews, 26 March 1971 and 31 December 1973 (57/8–9)

Central Zionist Archives, Jerusalem
Financial Department: S1
Political Department: S25

Haganah Archive, Tel Aviv
Arab Office and Intelligence: 8/GENERAL/35, 36, 37, 38, 39
Yitzhak (Isaac) Ben-Zvi Personal Archive and Reports, 1937–38: 80/153P/7,
  80/153/9, 80/153P/11 [also listed as file 80/153/11]
British Intelligence CID Files: 47/82, 47/89
Diary of Events: 73/77/1
Intelligence on Arab Leaders: 41/104
Intelligence Reports: 8/GENERAL/2
Journals, March 1939: 41/6
Letters and Files Relating to Ezra Danin: 80/58P/14
Position of the Troops, Extracts from Emergency Legislation, 1936: 115/97
Report on an Arab Commander: 41/94
Report on Settlement Tirat Zvi: 41/90
Reports from 1937 on Abdullah – National Commission, January–July
  1936: 80/153P/9
Reports on Fosh Actions: 26/6
Shai Intelligence Reports: 8/GENERAL/40
Testimonies of Haganah Officers:

Avraham Acor: 141/33
Isaac Avrahami: 94/29
Chaim Barkay: 227/13
Moshe Brenner: 15/1/4
Efrain Devinsky: 155/24
Chaim Franse: 182/46
David Kna'ani: 68/6
Tuvia Omani: 95/23
Giyora (Shinan) Shinansky: 184/83
Eliyahu Sochever: 161/20
Yiga'el Yadin: 143/12

Haifa Municipal Archive, Gottlieb Schumacher Street, Haifa
The Commission of the Current Situation/Security, Jewish Community, 1938–39: File 5588/00282/2
Commission of the Current Situation, 1939: File 1836/00090/14
Jewish Community of Haifa and the Commission of the Emergency, 1936: File 1802/00089/20

Israel State Archive, Jerusalem
Activity of the British Army: RG65: P361/5
Arab Delegation to London: RG65: P3220/17
Arab Higher Committee Minutes: RG65: P3221/18 and P410/3781 (latter is the old accession)
Arab Office in London: RG65: P351/37
Chief Secretary's Office: RG2
Galilee District Commissioner's Office: RG27
Gaza District Commissioner's Office: RG26
Haifa District Commissioner's Office: RG25
Jerusalem District Commissioner: RG23
Lydda-Tel Aviv District Officer: RG24
Mandate (M) files within the major records groups
Map Collection: 138
Palestine Police Force, written in the 1940s: Report from Tiberias: ISA17/4212/8
Police Force: RG17
Private Papers:
  Bernard Joseph (Dov Yosef): 69.3
  Moshe Sharett: 72.35
Public Information Office: 137.2
Public Works: RG12
al-Sakakini material: P378/2646
Samaria District Commissioner's Office: RG112

Jerusalem Municipal Archive, Safra Square, Jerusalem
Jerusalem Municipality, Historical Archive, Department of Jewish Community
  Box 4625 Arab Revolt and Prisons Files
  Box 848 Security

Roberta and Stanley Bogen Library, Truman Institute, Hebrew University, Jerusalem
Photographs Collection

Tel Aviv Municipal Archive, City Hall, Tel Aviv
Files on 1936–39 Disturbances: 04-161, 162, 163 and 165

LEBANON

American University in Beirut
Special File on Palestine

Institute for Palestine Studies, Beirut
Fawzi al-Qawuqji:
  File: Letters and Documents on al-Qawuqji in 1926, 1927 and 1936 in
    Palestine
  File: Various Documents about al-Qawuqji's Activities in Palestine
  Miscellaneous Photocopied Journal Notebooks

UNITED KINGDOM

British Library, London, Manuscript Collections
Maj-Gen Orde Wingate: Microfilm Reel M2313

British Postal Museum and Archive, London
Palestine and Middle East: POST 33
Palestine Telegram Service: POST 121

East Sussex Record Office, Lewes (now in Brighton)
Tufton Beamish (later Baron Chelwood) (officer, British Army)

Essex Regiment Museum, Chelmsford
L/Cpl F. C. Metson
Len Passfield (signals section)

Imperial War Museum, London, Department of Documents
H. Atkins (NCO, Queen's Royal Regiment)
Brig John Barraclough
Maj-Gen H. E. N. Bredin
Brig G. S. Brunskill
Sydney Burr (policeman)
Brig Dudley Clarke
Brig J. V. Faviell
Lt-Col Rex (Robert) King-Clark
G. J. Morton (police officer)
Capt C. P. Norman (Royal Navy)
L. A. Passfield (soldier, Essex Regiment)

Group-Capt J. E. Pelly-Fry
Col S. K. Pembroke
Maj B. A. Pond
Brig J. M. Rymer-Jones
Lt-Col A. C. Simonds

Imperial War Museum, London, Department of Film
Correspondence and primary source material collected for the three-part TV
series: 'Palestine: Promises and Rebellion' (London: Thames, 1977–78) in
variously named lever arch files
Film Reels with Sound PAL 64: Sir Hugh Foot (later Lord Caradon) (civil
official)
Film Reels with Sound PAL 104: Maj-Gen H. E. N. Bredin
Film Reels with Sound PAL 130: Gen Sir John Hackett

Imperial War Museum, London, Sound Archive
Pvt Thomas Atkinson
Sir Gawain Bell (civil official)
Pvt James Bellows
Maj-Gen H. E. N. Bredin
Sir Richard Catling (police officer)
Napier Crookenden (officer, Cheshire Regiment)
Maj-Gen A. J. H. Dove
Ernest Edlmann (officer, Royal East Kent Regiment)
Frederick Edwards (policeman)
Capt J. S. Elliot
Lt-Gen Sir John Evetts
Col Henry Fuare-Walker
Frederick Gardner (policeman)
Lt-Gen Sir John Bagot Glubb
Col J. S. S. Gratton
Lt-Col M. R. L. Grove
Gen Sir John Hackett
Brig J. D. Haigh
ACM Sir Arthur Harris
Col H. C. R. Hose
Cpl Fred Howbrook
Maj R. Hutchinson-Brooks
Pvt Tom Jagger
Colin Kerr (police special constable, attached to Cameron Highlanders)
Lt-Col Rex (Robert) King-Clark
Reuben Kitson (policeman)
Arthur Lane (soldier, Manchester Regiment)
Col John Charles Lawson (TJFF)
John Leggart (policemen)
Eric Linsell (policeman)
ACM Sir William MacDonald
Lt-Col V. Magill-Cuerden

Robin Martin (policeman)
Geoffrey Morton (police officer)
Sgt Percy Munn
Thomas Newman (policeman)
Capt C. P. Norman (Royal Navy)
Gen Sir Richard O'Connor
Bandsman Charles Packer
Maj W. Parrott
Capt F. J. Powell
Pvt Frank Proctor
Ian Proud (policeman)
Dan Ram (Jewish soldier, SNS)
Maj-Gen J. Scott Elliot
Walter Sendell (policeman)
Lt-Col G. A. Shepperd
Brig C. J. C. Sherman
Pvt Matthew Alfred Smith
James Tait (policeman)
Alexander Ternent (policeman)
Lt-Col I. G. Thomas
Brig E. H. Tinker
Charles Tinson (NCO, 11th Hussars)
William Watton (soldier, Irish Guards)
Sgt Howard Wharton
Pvt Ernest Whitewick
Lt-Col Desmond Woods
Maj David Wilkinson
Gen Sir Brian Wyldbore-Smith

India Office Records and Private Papers Library (Asian and African Library), British Library
Disturbances 1936: L/PS/12/3344–45
Disturbances and Anti-Jewish Riots; Reactions in Foreign Countries: L/PS/12/3346
Palestine – Police Summaries: L/PS/10/1315
Political and Secret Annual Files: L/PS/11/179
Political Situation – Police Summaries 1934–38: L/PS/12/3343
Reinforcements for Palestine: L/MIL/7/10827
Sir Charles Tegart: Mss Eur C.235, Mss Eur F118/85/12–18, Mss Eur F161/247

John Rylands Library, Manchester
Alice Ivy Hay of Seaton (Wingate's mother-in-law)
Maj P. W. Mead: OW/1/17 in the Wingate Papers

King's Own Royal Regiment, Lancaster
Lt H. J. Darlington
Gen Sir N. M. Ritchie

Liddell Hart Centre for Military Archives, King's College London
Air Commodore Douglas Amlot
Brig Sir Richard Hamilton Anstruther-Gough-Calthorpe
ACM Sir (Henry) Robert Brooke-Popham
Lt-Gen Laurence Carr
FM Sir John Dill (Palestine GOC)
Lt-Gen Sir John Evetts
ADC Aubrey T. O. Lees
Sir Basil Liddell Hart
Brig Guy John de Wette Mullens
Gen Sir Richard O'Connor
Brig John Stone
Maj-Gen Vivian Street
Maj-Gen T. N. S. Wheeler

National Archives, Kew, London
Air Ministry files
Colonial Office files
Declassified files: FO 492, FO 464, FO 1073, FO 1103
Foreign Office files
War Office files

National Army Museum, London
Maj-Gen James Lunt
Maj A. D. F. White

Parliamentary Archives, Houses of Parliament
Foreign Jurisdiction, 1890. Order in Council, dated 26 September, 1936, entitled The Palestine Martial Law (Defence) Order in Council 1936. Presented to the House of Commons in Pursuance of Section 11 of the Act. Privy Council Office, 20 November 1936

Regimental Archives and Records, UK
Bedfordshire and Hertfordshire Regiment, Bedfordshire and Luton Archives and Records Service, Bedford
Border and King's Own Royal Border Regiment, Regimental Museum, Carlisle
Cameronians (Scottish Rifles), South Lanarkshire Council, Hamilton
Cheshire Regiment, Regimental Museum, Chester
Dorsetshire Regiment, The Keep Military Museum, Dorchester, Dorset
East Yorkshire Regiment, Prince of Wales's Own Regiment of Yorkshire Museum, York
Essex Regiment, Regimental Museum, Chelmsford
Hampshire Regiment Archive, Serle's House, Winchester
King's Own Royal Regiment, Regimental Museum, Lancaster
King's Own Scottish Borderers, Regimental Museum, Berwick upon Tweed
Leicestershire Regiment, Record Office for Leicestershire, Leicester and Rutland, Leicester

Lincolnshire Regiment, Lincolnshire Archives, Lincoln
The Loyal Regiment (North Lancashire), Museum of the Queen's Lancashire
    Regiment (now Lancashire Infantry Museum), Fulwood Barracks, Preston
Manchester Regiment, Regimental Museum and Tameside Local Studies and
    Archive Centre, Ashton-under-Lyne, Greater Manchester
Queen's Royal West Surrey Regiment, Surrey History Centre, Woking
Royal Green Jackets Regimental Archive, Hampshire Record Office, Winchester
Royal Irish Fusiliers, Regimental Museum, Armagh
Royal Ulster Rifles Regimental Museum, Waring Street, Belfast
South Wales Borderers, Regimental Museum of the Royal Welsh, Brecon
Welch Regiment, Regimental Museum, Cardiff
West Yorkshire Regiment, Prince of Wales's Own Regiment of Yorkshire
    Museum, York
Worcestershire Regiment, Museum Trust, Worcester

Royal Air Force Museum, Hendon, London
ACM Sir Arthur Harris
ACM Sir R. E. C. Peirse (Palestine AOC)

St Antony's College, Middle East Centre, Oxford
'Arif al-'Arif (civil official, Arab nationalist)
Estelle Blyth (daughter of Bishop in Jerusalem)
H. E. Bowman (civil official, Director of Education)
Col Raymond Cafferata (police officer)
Percy Cleaver (policeman)
James De Lacy (policeman)
Stephen Edwards (policeman)
John Faraday (police officer)
Elliot Forster (doctor, Hebron)
Brian Gibbs (civil official)
Lt-Gen Sir John Bagot Glubb (Arab Legion)
Gen Sir Robert Haining (Palestine GOC)
Jerusalem and the East Mission (Anglican church mission)
John Loxton (civil official)
Sir Donald MacGillivray (personal secretary to High Commissioner)
Sir Harold MacMichael (High Commissioner)
Brig-Gen Angus McNeil
Palestine Police Old Comrades' Association
Palestine Police Oral History interviews (on disc)
Ivan Lloyd Phillips (civil official)
DIG Col Harold Rice (police officer, CID)
Lt-Col Frederick Salmon (civil official, lands)
DIG Col Alan Saunders (police officer)
Rupert F. Scrivener (civil official, railways)
Heather Teague (wife of SIS officer John Teague)
Sir Charles Tegart (police officer)
Thames Television material (from 'Palestine: Promises, Rebellion and
    Abdication,' 1977–78)

Abdul-Latif Tibawi (Palestinian educationalist)
Hilda Wilson (school teacher)

Tameside Local Studies and Archive Centre, Ashton-under-Lyne, Greater Manchester
Lt-Col Rex (Robert) King-Clark

Weiner Library, Institute of Contemporary History, London
British Union of Fascists pamphlets

Weston Library, Oxford (Charles Wendell David Room)
Sir William Battershill (civil official)
Sir Kenneth William Blackburne (civil official)
A/DC Clarence Edward Buxton (civil official)
Sir Richard Catling (police officer)
Arthur Creech Jones (Colonial Office)
Col John Patrick I. Fforde
Ronald Fraser (police officer)
Sir Harold MacMichael (High Commissioner)
Robin Martin (police officer)
Charles Ross (judge)
Sir Thomas Scrivenor (civil official)
Cpl Hugh Tulloch

Worcestershire Regiment, Museum Trust, Worcester
Capt P. H. Graves-Morris

Privately Held Papers
John Briance (police officer, CID) in possession of Prunella Briance
Raymond Cafferata (police officer) in possession of John Robertson when
  consulted, papers now stored in the Middle East Centre, St Antony's
  College, Oxford
Edward Keith-Roach (civil official) in possession of Christobel Ames-Lewis and
  Philip Keith-Roach
FM Sir Archibald Wavell, 1st Earl (GOC Palestine) in joint custody of Owen
  Humphrys

UNITED STATES

Library of Congress, Washington DC
Papers of John D. Whiting (visual materials)

National Archives and Records Administration, College Park, Maryland
Records of the Department of State Relating to the Internal Affairs of Palestine,
  1930–44: Reports from the US Consulate General in Jerusalem to the State
  Department: 867N.00/77–330 [Reel M#1037/1]

Records of the Department of State Relating to the Internal Affairs of Palestine, 1930–44: 867N.00/331–576 [Reel M#1037/2]
Records of the Department of State Relating to the Internal Affairs of Palestine, 1930–44: 867N.01/606–740 [Reel M#1037/4]
Records of the Department of State Relating to the Internal Affairs of Palestine, 1930–44: 867N.12/4-867N.402/1 [Reel M#1037/12]
Stills Picture Research Room: Palestine: *New York Times* Paris Bureau: RG 306NT, Box 1181

FIELDTRIPS (ISRAEL, 2010)

Haifa: Jaffa Road British Commonwealth War Graves cemetery
Haifa: Khayat Beach British Commonwealth War Graves cemetery and adjoining Haifa (Sharon) British civil cemetery
Jerusalem: Protestant Mount Zion cemetery and adjacent Latin (Catholic) cemetery
Nesher: Muslim cemetery
Ramleh: British Commonwealth War Graves cemetery
Tel Aviv: Trumpeldor Old Jewish cemetery

INTERVIEWS AND CORRESPONDENCE

Bahjat Abu Gharbiyya, Amman, Jordan, 21 June 2009 (and subsequent correspondence)
Edward Horne, Barton-on-Sea, UK, 9 September 2006 and 26 February 2013 (and subsequent correspondence and telephone conversations)
Sabri Jiyris, Haifa, Israel, 29 June 2006
Gen Sir Frank Kitson, UK, correspondence, June 2013
Anat Stern, Jerusalem, Israel, 12 July 2006

PRIMARY SOURCES (PRINTED, ARABIC)

al-Kayyali, 'Abd al-Wahhab, *Watha'iq al-Muqawama al-Filastiniyya al 'Arabiyya dida al-Ihtilal al-Baritani wa al-Sahyuniyya* [Documents of the Palestinian Arab Resistance against British Occupation and Zionism] (Beirut: IPS and Association of Palestinian Fund in Baghdad, 1968)
Zu'aytir, Akram, *Watha'iq al-Haraka al-Wataniyya al-Filastiniyya, 1918–39: Min Awraq Akram Zu'aytir* [Documents of the Palestinian National Movement, 1918–39: From the Papers of Akram Zu'aytir] (Beirut: IPS, 1979)

PRIMARY SOURCES (PRINTED, ENGLISH)

A Survey of Palestine, Prepared in December 1945 and January 1946 for the Information of the Anglo-American Committee of Inquiry (two vols) (Jerusalem: Government Printer, 1946 and Washington, DC: IPS, 1991)
Air Force List, 1928–40
Amnesty International (Peter Benenson), *Aden 1963–1966: A Report by Amnesty International* (London: Amnesty, 1966)
(S. Rastgeldi), *Aden Report* (London: Amnesty, 1966)

Anon., *Frightfulness in Retreat* (London: Hodder and Stoughton, 1917)

Army List, 1930–40

Bentwich, Norman (see *Legislation of Palestine*)

Callwell, C. E., *Small Wars: Their Principles and Practices* [1896] (London: HMSO, 1906)

Civil Service List (see *Government of Palestine*)

Cmd. 3530 Report of the Commission on the Palestine Disturbances of August 1929 (London: HMSO, 1930)

Cmd. 5479 Report of the Palestine Royal Commission (Peel) (London: HMSO, 1937)

Cmd. 5854 Report of the Palestine Partition Commission (Woodhead) (London: HMSO, 1938)

Cmd. 6019 Statement of Policy by His Majesty's Government (The 1939 White Paper) (London: HMSO, 1939)

Cohen, Israel, *Palestine and the British Tax Payer* (London: Jewish Agency, 1929)

Colonial Audit Department, *Annual Report of the Director of Audit on the Accounts of the Government of Palestine and the Palestine Railways' and Ports and Operated Lines for the Financial Year 1946–7* (Jerusalem: Government Printer, 1948)

Cosmos' Palestinian Colloquial Arabic: Specially Prepared for the British Police and Members of H. M. Forces in Palestine (Jerusalem: Cosmos, 1939)

Dill, Gen Sir John (see *War Office*)

Doukhan, Moses (ed.), *Laws of Palestine 1918–25* (two vols) (Tel Aviv: Rotenberg, 1933)

  Laws of Palestine 1926–31 (four vols) (Tel Aviv: Rotenberg, 1932–33)

  Laws of Palestine, 1932 (Tel Aviv: Rotenberg, 1933)

  Laws of Palestine 1934–35 (Tel Aviv: Rotenberg, 1936)

Drayton, Robert H., *The Laws of Palestine in Force on 31 December 1933* (three vols) (London: Waterlow, 1934)

Duties in the Aid of the Civil Power (see *War Office*)

Field Service Regulations 1909. Part I, Operations (London: HMSO, 1912)

Friedland, Jane (ed.), *Records of Jerusalem. 1917–71: Volume 3 and Volume 4* (Oxford: Archive Editions, 2002)

Fry, Michael and Itamar Rabinovich, *Despatches from Damascus: Gilbert MacKereth and British Policy in the Levant, 1933–39* (Tel Aviv: Dayan Center, 1985)

Goadby, F., *Commentary on Egyptian Criminal Law and the Related Criminal Law of Palestine, Cyprus and Iraq* (three vols) (Cairo: Government Press, 1924)

Government of Palestine: Civil Service List (Jerusalem: Government Printing Press, 1936–39)

Government of Palestine. Ordinances. Annual Volume for 1934 (Jerusalem, Government of Palestine: Greek Convent Press, 1935)

Government of Palestine. Ordinances. Annual Volume for 1935 (Jerusalem, Government of Palestine: Greek Convent Press, 1936)

Gwynn, Maj-Gen Sir Charles, *Imperial Policing* (London: Macmillan, 1934)

Hansard (1938–39)

Henderson, Lt-Col David, *Field Intelligence: Its Principles and Practices* (London: HMSO, 1904)

Hooper, C. A., *The Civil Law of Palestine and Trans-Jordan* (London: Sweet and Maxwell, 1934)

Indian Army Forces Form D.908, *Instructions to Officers Acting in Aid of the Civil Power for Dispersal of Unlawful Assembly*

Jenkin-Jones, C. M., *Report on the Traffic Organisation, Facilities and Rates of the Palestine Railways 1935* (London: Crown Agents, 1935)

King's Regulations for the Army and the Army Reserve, 1935 (London: HMSO, 1935)

Laws of Palestine (see Doukhan and Drayton)

League of Nations (see *Report by His Majesty's Government*)

Legislation of Palestine, 1918–25, Including the Orders-in-Council etc. (two vols, compiled by Norman Bentwich) (Alexandria: Whitehead Morris, 1926)

Lenin, V. I., 'On Guerrilla Warfare' [1906] in *Lenin Collected Works. Volume 11* (Moscow: Progress Publishers, 1965) (accessed via www.marxists.org/archive/lenin/works/1906/gw/index.htm on 28 August 2016)

Manual of Military Law 1884, 1899, 1907, 1914, 1929 (London: HMSO, 1884–1940)

Mao Tse-tung [Mao Zedong] (trans. Samuel B. Griffith), *On Guerrilla Warfare* [1937 in Chinese] [1961] (New York, NY: Doubleday Books, 1982)

    Strategic Problems in the Anti-Japanese Guerrilla War [1938 in Chinese] (Peking: Foreign Language Press, 1954)

Mills, E., *Census of Palestine 1931* (two vols) (London: HMSO, 1933)

Naval Intelligence Division, *Palestine and Transjordan* (Oxford: Naval Intelligence Division, December 1943)

Notes on Imperial Policing (see *War Office*)

Ordinances, Regulations, Rules, Orders and Notices. Government of Palestine. Annual Volume for 1936 (three vols) (Jerusalem: Government Printing Press, 1937)

Ordinances, Regulations, Rules, Orders and Notices. Government of Palestine. Annual Volume for 1937 (three vols) (Jerusalem: Government Printing Press, 1938)

Palestine Civil Service Lists (see *Government of Palestine*)

Palestine Index Gazetteer (Cairo: Survey Directorate, 1945)

The Palestine Police Force. Annual Administrative Report, 1934, 1935, 1936, 1938 (Jerusalem: Government Printing Press, 1934–36, 1938)

Palestine Royal Commission: Memoranda Prepared by the Government of Palestine (London: HMSO, 1937)

Palestine. Statement of Policy by His Majesty's Government in the United Kingdom (London: HMSO, 1930)

Peel Commission (see Cmd.)

Pittaway, Jonathan (ed.), *Selous Scouts: The Men Speak* (Durban: Dandy Agencies, 2013)

Proclamations, Regulations, Rules, Orders and Notices: Annual Volumes for 1928, 1932, 1935 (Jerusalem, Government of Palestine: Greek Convent Press, 1928–35)

Report by His Majesty's Government in the United Kingdom of Great Britain and Northern Ireland to the Council of the League of Nations on the Administration of Palestine and Transjordan for the Year 1936 (London: HMSO, 1937)

Report by His Majesty's Government in the United Kingdom of Great Britain and Northern Ireland to the Council of the League of Nations on the Administration of Palestine and Transjordan for the Year 1937 (London: HMSO, 1938)

Report by Roderic Bowen QC on Procedures for the Arrest, Interrogation and Detention of Suspected Terrorists in Aden, 14 November 1966 (London: HMSO, 1966)

Report of the Palestine Currency Board for the Period Ending 31 March 1928 (London: Waterlow, 1928)

Roberts, Adam and Richard Guelff (eds), *Documents on the Laws of War* (Oxford: Oxford University Press, 2000)

Rotenberg, L. M. (see Doukhan)

Sachar, Howard (ed.), *The Rise of Israel: A Documentary Record from the Nineteenth Century to 1948. Volume 20, The Intensification of Violence, 1929–1936* (New York, NY and London: Garland, 1987)

Simson, Col H. J., *British Rule and Rebellion* (Edinburgh and London: Blackwood, 1937)

Skeen, Gen Sir Andrew, *Passing It On: Short Talks on Tribal Fighting on the North-West Frontier of India* [1932] (Aldershot: Gale and Polden, 1943) republished as *Lessons in Imperial Rule: Instructions for British Infantrymen on the Indian Frontier* (London: Frontline, 2008)

Statistical Abstract of Palestine, 1936, 1937–38, 1939, 1940 (Jerusalem: Office of Statistics, 1936–40)

War Office, *By Command of the Army Council, Notes on Imperial Policing, 1934* (London: War Office, 30 January 1934)

Notes on the Tactical Lessons of the Palestine Rebellion 1936 (London: War Office, 1937 by Gen Sir John Dill)

By Command of the Army Council, 5 August 1937, Duties in the Aid of the Civil Power (London: War Office, 1937)

Woodhead Commission (see Cmd.)

PRIMARY SOURCES (PRINTED, ENGLISH, ON MICROFILM AT BRITISH LIBRARY)

Ordinances, Regulations, Rules, Orders and Notices. Government of Palestine. Annual Volume for 1938. Volumes 2 and 3 (Jerusalem: Government Printing Press, 1939) (at SPR Mic. P1)

Ordinances, Regulations, Rules, Orders and Notices. Government of Palestine. Annual Volume for 1939. Volumes 2 and 3 (Jerusalem: Government Printing Press, 1940) (at SPR Mic. P1)

Ordinances, Regulations, Rules, Orders and Notices. Government of Palestine. Annual Volume for 1945. Volumes 2 and 3 (Jerusalem: Government Printing Press, 1946) (at SPR Mic. P1)

PRIMARY SOURCES (PRINTED, HEBREW)

Danin, Ezra, *Te'udot u-Dmuyot me-Ginzey ha-Knufiyot ha-Arviyot, 1936–39* [*Documents and Portraits from the Arab Gangs Archives in the Arab Revolt in Palestine, 1936–39*] [1944] (Jerusalem: Magnes, 1981)

Gershon, Rivlin and Aliza Rivlin, *Zar Lo Yavin: Kinuye-Seter Ba-Yishuv Ha-Yehudi Be-Erets-Yisra'el* [*The Stranger Cannot Understand: Code-names in the Jewish Underground in Palestine*] (Tel Aviv: Ministry of Defence, 1988)

DIARIES AND MEMOIRS (ARABIC)

Abu Gharbiyya, Bahjat, *Fi Khidamm al-nidal al-'arabi al-filastini: Mudhakkirat al-munadil Bahjat Abu Gharbiyya* [*In the Midst of the Struggle for the Arab Palestinian Cause: The Memoirs of Freedom-Fighter Bahjat Abu Gharbiyya* (Beirut: IPS, 1993)

Darwaza, Muhammad 'Izzat, *Mudhakkirat Muhammad 'Izzat Darwaza: Sab'a wa tis'una 'aman fil-haya* [*The Diaries of Muhammad 'Izzat Darwaza: 97 Years in a Life*] (six vols) (Beirut: Dar al Gharb al Islami, 1993)

Ghandur, Muhammad Mustafa, *Tha'r al-Dam* [*Blood Revenge: A Story from the Core of the Events of the Palestinian Revolt by the Pen of the Fighter Muhammad Mustafa Ghandur*] (Syria: n.p., 1939)

al-Kabir, Abu Ibrahim (Khalil Muhammad 'Isa 'Ajak) (ed. Nazih Abu Nidal), *Mudhakkirat Abu Ibrahim al-Kabir: al-Qa'id al-qassami li-thawrat 36–39* [*Memoirs of Abu Ibrahim al-Kabir: The Qassamite Commander of the 1936–39 Revolt*] (Ramallah: PLO Supreme Council of Culture, 2010)

Nashashibi, Fakhri, *Sawt Min Qubur Filastin al-'Arabiyya* [*A Voice from the Graves of Arab Palestine*] (Jerusalem: n.p., 1938)

Qasimiyya, Khayriyya (ed.), *Filastin fi-Mudhakkirat Fawzi al-Qawuqji* [*Palestine in the Memories of Fawzi al-Qawuqji*] (two vols) (Beirut: PLO Research Centre and Jerusalem Publishing House, 1975)

(ed.), *Mudhakkirat Fawzi al-Qawuqji* [*Memories of Fawzi al-Qawuqji*] [amended 1995] (Damascus: Dar al-Namir, 1996)

al-Sakakini, Khalil (ed. Hala al-Sakakini), *Kadha Ana Ya Duniya* [*Such Am I, Oh World!*] [1955] (Beirut: al-Ittihad, 1982)

(ed. A. Mussalam), *Yawmiyyat Khalil al-Sakakini: Yawmiyyat, Rasa'il, ta'amulat* [*Diaries of Khalil al-Sakakini: Diaries, Letters and Meditations*] (eight vols) (Jerusalem: Institute of Jerusalem Studies, 2003–10)

Sayih, Shaykh Abdul Hamid, *Filastin; la Sala Tahta al-Hirab: Mudhakkirat al-Shaykh 'Abd al-Hamid al-Sa'ih* [*Palestine; No Prayer Under Bayonets: The Memoirs of Shaykh Abdul Hamid Sayih*] (Beirut: IPS, 1994)

Zu'aytir, Akram, *Al-Haraka al-Wataniya al-Filastiniyya, 1935–39: Yawmiyyat Akram Zu'aytir* [*The Palestinian National Movement, 1935–39: Diaries of Akram Zu'aytir*] [1980] (Beirut: IPS, 1992)

DIARIES AND MEMOIRS (ENGLISH)

Aburish, Said K., *Children of Bethany: The Story of a Palestinian Family* (Bloomington, IL: Indiana University Press, 1988)

'Adin (Edelman), Benjamin, *Adventures at the Wheel: Memoirs of a Native-born Jerusalemite* (Jerusalem: Alfa, 1965)

Alleg, Henri, *The Question* (New York, NY: Braziller, 1958)

Arrigonie, Harry, *British Colonialism: 30 Years Serving Democracy or Hypocrisy* (Bideford: Gaskell, 1998)

Aussaresses, Paul, *The Battle of the Casbah: Terrorism and Counter-Terrorism in Algeria, 1955–57* (New York, NY: Enigma, 2002)

Bentwich, N., *England in Palestine* (London: Kegan Paul, 1932)
Mandate Memories, 1918–48 (London: Hogarth, 1965)

Binsley, Jack, *Palestine Police Service* (Montreux: Minerva, 1996)

Courtney, Roger, *Palestine Policeman* (London: Herbert Jenkins, 1939)

Crozier, Brig-Gen Frank Percy, *Impressions and Recollections* (London: Werner Laurie, 1930)

Ireland for Ever (London: Jonathan Cape, 1932)

The Men I Killed (New York, NY: Doubleday, 1938)

Dayan, Moshe, *Story of My Life* (London: Weidenfeld and Nicolson, 1976)

Duff, Douglas V., *A Sword for Hire* (London: Murray, 1934)

Palestine Unveiled (London: Blackie, 1938)

Bailing with a Teaspoon (London: John Long, 1953)

Feinstein, Anthony, *In Conflict* (Windhoek: New Namibia, 1998)

Fergusson, Bernard, *The Trumpet in the Hall, 1930–58* (London: Collins, 1970)

Foot, Sir Hugh (Lord Caradon), *A Start in Freedom* (London: Hodder and Stoughton, 1964)

Haldane, Lt-Gen Sir Aylmer, *The Insurrection in Mesopotamia, 1920* [1922] (Nashville, TN: Battery Press, 2005)

Harper-Ronald, Jake, *Sunday, Bloody Sunday: A Soldier's War in Northern Ireland, Rhodesia, Mozambique and Iraq* (Alberton: Galago, 2009)

Hodgkin, E. C. (ed.), *Thomas Hodgkin: Letters from Palestine, 1932–36* (London: Quartet, 1986)

Imray, Colin, *Policeman in Palestine* (Devon: Gaskell, 1995)

Jabra, Ibrahim Jabra (trans. Issa J. Boullata), *The First Well: A Bethlehem Boyhood* (Fayetville, AR: University of Arkansas Press, 1995)

Jordan, Ruth, *Daughter of the Waves: Memories of Growing up in Pre-War Palestine* (New York, NY: Taplinger, 1983)

Karmi, Ghada, *In Search of Fatima* [2002] (London: Verso, 2009)

Keith-Roach, Edward (ed. Paul Eedle), *Pasha of Jerusalem: Memoirs of a District Commissioner under the British Mandate* (London: Radcliffe, 1994)

King-Clark, Rex (Robert), *Free for a Blast* (London: Grenville, 1988)

Kisch, F. H., *Palestine Diary* (London: Gollancz, 1938)

Kluk, Ephraim, *A Special Constable in Palestine* (Johannesburg: Kluk, 1939)

Lane, Arthur, *Lesser Gods, Greater Devils* (Stockport: Lane, 1993)

Lang, Michael, *One Man in His Time: The Diary of a Palestine Policeman* (Sussex: Book Guild, 1997)

Levi, Carlo, *Christ Stopped at Eboli* (London: Farrar, 1947)

Lowe, Eric, *Forgotten Conscripts: Prelude to Palestine's Struggle for Survival* (Victoria: Trafford, 2007)

Martin, Robert, *Palestine Betrayed: A British Palestine Policeman's Memoir (1936–48)* (Ringwood: Seglawi, 2007)

Morton, Geoffrey, *Just the Job: Some Experiences of a Colonial Policeman* (London: Hodder and Stoughton, 1957)

Murray, Simon, *Legionnaire: An Englishman in the French Foreign Legion* (London: Sidgwick and Jackson, 1982)

Newton, Frances, *Fifty Years in Palestine* (London: Coldharbour, 1948)

Phillips, Norman, *Guns, Drugs and Deserters* (London: Werner Laurie, 1954)

Pritzke, Herbert (trans. Richard Graves), *Bedouin Doctor: The Adventures of a German in the Middle East* (London: Weidenfeld and Nicolson, 1957)

Quickfall, Dennis, *Shadows over Scopus: Reflections of an Ex-Palestine Policeman* (Manchester: Cromwell, 1999)

Ricks, Thomas (ed.), *Turbulent Times in Palestine: The Diaries of Khalil Totah, 1886–1955* (Jerusalem: IPS and Passia, 2009)

Shahid, Serene Husseini, *Jerusalem Memories* (Beirut: Naufal, 2000)

Slim, William, *Unofficial History* (New York, NY: David McKay, 1959)

Smiley, David, *Irregular Regular* (Norwich: Michael Russell, 1994)

Thompson, Sir Robert, *Make for the Hills: Memories of Far Eastern Wars* (London: Leo Cooper, 1989)

Vester, Bertha Stafford, *Our Jerusalem: An American Family in the Holy City, 1881–1949* (Lebanon: Middle East Export, 1950)

DIARIES AND MEMOIRS (FRENCH)

Alleg, Henri, *La Question* (Paris: Minuit, 1958)

Aussaresses, Paul, *Service Spéciaux: Algérie, 1955–57* (Paris: Perrin, 2001)

DIARIES AND MEMOIRS (HEBREW)

Danin, Ezra, *Tsiyoni be-kol Tnay* [*Zionist under Any Condition*] (Jerusalem: Kidum, 1987)

NEWSPAPERS

ARABIC

al-Difaʿ [*The Defence*] (Jaffa)
Filastin [*Palestine*] (Jaffa)
al-Jamiʿa al-Islamiyya [*The Islamic Community*] (Jaffa)
al-Karmil [*The Carmel*] (Haifa)
al-Liwaʾ [*The Province*] (Jerusalem)
al-Nahar [*The Day*] (Beirut)
al-Sirat al-Mustaqim [*The Right Path*] (Jaffa)

ENGLISH

Daily Telegraph (London)
Haaretz [English edition] (Tel Aviv)
Palestine Gazette (Official Gazette of the Government of Palestine) (Jerusalem)
Palestine Post (Jerusalem)
Sunday Mail (Glasgow)
The Times (London)
Yorkshire Post (Leeds)

FRENCH

L'Orient [*The Orient*] (Beirut)

HEBREW

Davar [*Issue*] (Tel Aviv)
Haaretz [*The Land*] (Tel Aviv)

REGIMENTAL JOURNALS

Borderers' Chronicle: King's Own Scottish Borderers
The Border Regiment Regimental Association Newsletter
Ça Ira: The Journal of the West Yorkshire Regiment (The Prince of Wales's Own)
China Dragon: The Chronicle of the Royal Berkshire Regiment
China Dragon: The Regimental Magazine of the North Staffordshire Regiment
The Essex Regiment Gazette
FIRM: The Worcestershire Regiment (29th Foot)
Green Tiger: The Records of the Leicestershire Regiment
The Hampshire Regimental Journal
The Lancashire Lad: Journal of the Loyal Regiment (North Lancashire)
Lincolnshire Regiment: Monthly Newsletter
Men of Harlech: Welch Regiment
The Oak Tree: The Cheshire Regiment
Quis Separabit: The Regimental Journal of the Royal Ulster Rifles
The Snapper: The Monthly Journal of the East Yorkshire Regiment (The Duke of York's Own)
The Tiger and Rose: A Monthly Journal of the York and Lancaster Regiment
The Wasp: The Journal of the 16th Foot (Bedfordshire Regiment)

REGIMENTAL HISTORIES

Atkinson, C. T., *The Dorsetshire Regiment. Volume 2* (Oxford: Oxford University Press, 1947)

Barclay, C. N., *The History of the Cameronians (Scottish Rifles). Volume 3* (London: Praed, 1947)

Bell, A. C., *History of the Manchester Regiment: First and Second Battalions, 1922–1948* (Altrincham: Sherratt, 1954)

Birdwood, Lord, *The Worcestershire Regiment, 1922–1950* (Aldershot: Gale and Polden, 1952)

Blaxland, Gregory, *The Buffs (Royal East Kent Regiment) (The 3rd Regiment of Foot)* (London: Leo Cooper, 1972)

Blight, Gordon, *The History of the Royal Berkshire Regiment* (London: Staples, 1953)

Brander, A. Michael, *The Royal Scots (The Royal Regiment)* (London: Leo Cooper, 1976)

Brereton, J. M., *A History of the 4th/7th Royal Dragoon Guards* (Catterick: Regimental Publication, 1982)

Carver, R. M. P., *Second to None: The Royal Scots Greys, 1919 to 1945* (Glasgow: Caxton, 1954)

Chaplin, H. D., *The Queen's Own Royal West Kent Regiment* (London: Michael Joseph, 1954)

Clarke, Dudley, *The Eleventh at War* (London: Michael Joseph, 1952)

Cook, H., *History of the North Staffordshire Regiment* (London: Leo Cooper, 1970)

Corbally, M.J.P.M., *The Royal Ulster Rifles, 1793–1960* (London: Paramount, 1960)

Cunliffe, Marcus *The Royal Irish Fusiliers 1793–1950* (London: Oxford University Press, 1952)

Daniell, D. S., *The Royal Hampshire Regiment. Volume 3* (Aldershot: Gale and Polden, 1955)

Dean, C. G. T., *The Loyal Regiment (North Lancashire) 1919–1955* (Preston: Mayflower, 1955)

Erskine, David, *The Scots Guards, 1919–1955* (London: Clowes, 1956)

Foster, R. C. G., *The History of the Second Queen's Royal Regiment. Volume 8, 1924–1948* (Aldershot: Gale and Polden, 1953)

Graves, Charles, *The Royal Ulster Rifles. Volume 3* (Mexborough: Times, 1950)

Harvey, Basil, *The Rifle Brigade* (London: Leo Cooper, 1975)

Holloway, Roger, *The Queen's Own Royal West Kent Regiment: The Dirty Half-Hundred* (London: Leo Cooper, 1973)

Howard, Michael and John Sparrow, *The Coldstream Guards, 1920–1946* (London: Oxford University Press, 1951)

Linklater, Eric and Andro, *The Black Watch* (London: Barrie and Jenkins, 1977)

Martin, T. A., *The Essex Regiment, 1929–50* (Essex: Regiment Association, 1952)

Martineau, G. D., *A History of the Royal Sussex Regiment, 1701–1953* (Chichester: Moore, 1955)

Mileham, P. J. R., *Fighting Highlanders! A History of the Argyll and Sutherland Highlanders* (London: Arms and Armour, 1993)

Myatt, F., *The Royal Berkshire Regiment* (London: Hamish Hamilton, 1968)

Paget, Julian, *Second to None: The Coldstream Guards, 1650–2000* (London: Leo Cooper, 2000)

Paterson, Robert, *Pontius Pilate's Bodyguard: A History of the First or the Royal Regiment of Foot, The Royal Scots (The Royal Regiment). Volume 2, 1919–2000* (Edinburgh: The Royal Scots History Committee, 2001)

Powell, Geoffrey and John, *The History of the Green Howards: Three Hundred Years of Service* (London: Leo Cooper, 2002)

Royal Anglian Regiment, *The Story of the Bedfordshire and Hertfordshire Regiment (The 16th Regiment of Foot). Volume 2, 1914–1958* (Regimental History Committee, 1986)

Royle, Trevor, *The Royal Scots: A Concise History* (Edinburgh: Mainstream, 2006)

Sheffield, O. F., *The York and Lancaster Regiment, 1919–1953* (Aldershot: Gale and Polden, 1956)

Vale, W. L., *The History of the South Staffordshire Regiment* (Aldershot: Gale and Polden, 1969)

Woollcombe, Robert, *All the Blue Bonnets: The History of the King's Own Scottish Borderers* (London: Arms and Armour, 1980)

POLICE HISTORIES AND JOURNALS

Horne, Edward, *A Job Well Done (Being a History of the Palestine Police Force, 1920–1948)* (Tiptree: Anchor Press, 1982)

Jeffries, Charles, *The Colonial Police* (London: Max Parrish, 1952)
Mosse, George, *Police Forces in History* (London: Sage, 1975)
Palestine Police Magazine
Palestine Police Old Comrades' Association Newsletter
Police Journal

LEGAL AND REFERENCE TEXTS

Abu-Sitta, Salman H., *Atlas of Palestine 1948* (London: Palestine Land Society, 2004)
   Atlas of Palestine, 1917–1966 (London: Palestine Land Society, 2010)
Bagehot, Walter, *The English Constitution* [1867] (Cambridge: Cambridge University Press, 2001)
Banning, S. T., *Military Law (Made Easy)* (Aldershot: Gale and Polden, 1932)
Berlin, Howard M., *The Coins and Banknotes of Palestine under the British Mandate, 1927–47* (Jefferson, NC: McFarland, 2001)
Cotterell, P., *Railways of Palestine and Israel* (Abingdon: Tourret, 1984)
Dabbah, Raphael, *Currency Notes of the Palestine Currency Board* (Jerusalem: Israel Numismatic Society, 2005)
Dicey, A. V., *Introduction to the Study of the Law of the Constitution* (London: Macmillan, 1902)
Eisenman, Robert H., *Islamic Law in Palestine and Israel* (Leiden: Brill, 1978)
Fiddes, Sir George, *The Dominions and Colonial Offices* (London: Putnam's, 1926)
Finlason, W. F., *The History of the Jamaica Case* (London: Chapman, 1869)
Friedman, Leon (ed.), *The Law of War: A Documentary History. Volume 1* (New York, NY: Random House, 1972)
Hobman, J. B. (ed.), *Palestine's Economic Future* (London: Percy Lund, 1946)
Holdsworth, Sir William, *A History of English Law* [1903] (sixteen vols) (London: Methuen, 1982)
Kantrovitch, Henry, *The Law of Criminal Procedure in Palestine* (Tel Aviv: Mizpah, 1938)
Khalidi, Walid (ed.), *All That Remains: The Palestinian Villages Occupied and Depopulated by Israel in 1948* (Washington, DC: IPS, 1992)
   (ed.), *Before Their Diaspora: A Photographic History of the Palestinians, 1876–1948* (Washington, DC: IPS, 2004)
Laserson, Max M. (ed.), *On the Mandate: Documents, Statements, Laws and Judgements Relating to and Arising from the Mandate for Palestine* (Tel Aviv: Igereth, 1937)
Liebesny, Herbert J., *The Law of the Near and Middle East: Readings, Cases and Materials* (Albany, NY: SUNY Press, 1975)
Matthew, H. C. G. and Brian Harrison, *Revised Oxford Dictionary of National Biography* (Oxford: Oxford University Press, 2004)
Napier, Maj-Gen Sir Charles, *Remarks on Military Law and the Punishment of Flogging* (London: Boone, 1837)
New Oxford Dictionary for Writers and Editors (Oxford: Oxford University Press, 2005)
Peters, Rudolph, *Jihad in Classical and Modern Islam: A Reader* (Princeton, NJ: Wiener, 2005)
Roberts, Adam and Richard Guelff (eds), *Documents on the Laws of War* (Oxford: Oxford University Press, 2000)

Roubicek, M., *Echo of the Bugle: Extinct Military and Constabulary Forces in Palestine and Transjordan, 1915–67* (Jerusalem: Franciscan, 1975)

Salant, E., *Criminal Procedure and Practice in Palestine* (Tel Aviv: Bursi, 1947)

Shems, A. A., *A Manual of the Magistrates' Law in Palestine* (Tel Aviv: Magistrate, 1934)

Skyrme, Sir Thomas, *The Changing Image of the Magistracy* (London: Macmillan, 1979)

History of the Justices of the Peace (London: Barry Rose, 1994)

Slapper, Gary and David Kelly, *The English Legal System, 2014–15* (London: Routledge, 2014)

Swinson, Arthur (ed.), *A Register of the Regiments and Corps of the British Army* (London: Archive Press, 1972)

Wilding, Norman and Philip Laundy, *An Encyclopaedia of Parliament* (New York, NY: St Martin's, 1971)

BOOKS (ARABIC)

'Allush, Naji, *Al-Muqawama al-'Arabiyya fi Filastin, 1917–48* [*The Arab Resistance in Palestine, 1917–1948*] (Beirut: Attaliya, 1969)

Hammudah, Samih, *al-Wa'i wa-al-thawra: dirasa fi-haya wa-jihad al-Shaykh 'Izz al-Din al-Qassam 1882–1935* [*Awareness and Revolution: A Study in the Life and Struggle of Shaykh 'Izz al-Din al-Qassam 1882–1935* (Jerusalem: Arab Studies Association, 1986)

Kabha, Mustafa, *Thawrat 1936 al-Kubra* [*The Great Revolt of 1936*] (Nazareth: Maktabat al-Kabs, 1988)

Khalidi, Walid and Yasin Suweyd, *Al-Qadiyya al-Filastiniyya wa al-Khatar al-Sahyuni* [*The Palestinian Problem and the Zionist Danger*] (Beirut: IPS, Lebanese General Staff Fifth Branch and Ministry of Defence, 1973)

Rajab, Yusuf, *Thawrat 1936–1939 fi-Filastin: Dirasa Askariyya* [*Revolt of 1936–1939 in Palestine: A Military Study*] (Beirut: Institute of Arab Research, 1982)

Shurrab, Muhammad Muhammad Hasan, *'Izz ad-Din al-Qassam: Shaykh al-Mujahidin fi Filastin* [*Izz ad-Din al-Qassam: Sheikh of the Holy Fighters in Palestine*] (Damascus: Dar al-Qalam, 2000)

Tanus, Izzat, *Al-Filastiniyun* [*The Palestinians*] (Beirut: PLO Research Centre, 1982)

Yasin, Subhi, *Al-Thawra al-'Arabiyya al-Kubra (fi Filastin) 1936–1939* [*The Great Arab Revolt in Palestine, 1936–1939*] (Damascus: Shafa 'Amr Haifa, 1959)

Zu'aytir, Akram, *Al-Qaddiya al-Filistiniyya* [*The Palestinian Problem*] (Cairo: Information Press, 1955)

BOOKS (ENGLISH AND FRENCH)

Abu-Lughod, Ibrahim (ed.), *The Transformation of Palestine: Essays on the Origin and Development of the Arab-Israeli Conflict* (Evanston, IL: Northwestern University Press, 1971)

Ackroyd, Carol et al., *The Technology of Political Control* (London: Pluto, 1980)

Anderson, David, *Histories of the Hanged: Britain's Dirty War in Kenya and the End of Empire* (London: Weidenfeld and Nicolson, 2005)

Anderson, David and David Killingray (eds), *Policing and Decolonisation: Politics, Nationalism and the Police, 1917–65* (Manchester: Manchester University Press, 1991)

Andrew, Christopher, *The Defence of the Realm: The Authorized History of MI5* (London: Penguin, 2009)

Anglim, Simon, *Orde Wingate the Iron Wall and Counter-Terrorism in Palestine 1937–39* (Shrivenham: Joint Services Command and Staff College Occasional Paper 49, 2005)

Orde Wingate and the British Army, 1922–44 (London: Pickering and Chatto, 2010)

Applebaum, Anne, *GULAG: A History of the Soviet Camps* (London: Allen Lane, 2003)

Arendt, Hannah, *Eichmann in Jerusalem: A Report on the Banality of Evil* (New York, NY: Viking, 1963)

On Violence (New York, NY: Harcourt Brace, 1970)

Arielli, Nir, *Fascist Italy and the Middle East, 1933–40* (Houndmills: Palgrave, 2010)

Assaf, M., *The Arab Movement in Palestine* (New York, NY: Masada Youth, 1937)

Bartlett, T. and K. Jeffery (eds), *A Military History of Ireland* (Cambridge: Cambridge University Press, 1996)

Baumeister, Roy F., *Evil: Inside Human Cruelty and Violence* (New York, NY: Freeman, 1997)

Baynes, John, *The Forgotten Victor: General Sir Richard O'Connor* (London: Brassey's, 1989)

Beckett, Ian F. W. (ed.), *The Roots of Counter-Insurgency: Armies and Guerrilla Warfare 1900–1945* (London: Blandford, 1988)

Modern Insurgencies and Counter-Insurgencies: Guerrillas and Their Opponents since 1750 (London and New York, NY: Routledge, 2001)

Ben-Eliezer, Uri, *The Making of Israeli Militarism* (Bloomington, IN: Indiana University Press, 1998)

Ben-Yehuda, Nachman, *Political Assassinations by Jews: A Rhetorical Device for Justice* (New York, NY: SUNY Press, 1993)

Bennett, Huw, *Fighting the Mau Mau: The British Army and Counter-Insurgency in the Kenya Emergency* (Cambridge: Cambridge University Press, 2013)

Bennett, Richard, *The Black and Tans* [1959] (Severn: Severn House, 1976)

Bernstein, Deborah, *Constructing Boundaries: Jewish and Arab Workers in Mandatory Palestine* (Albany, NY: SUNY Press, 2000)

Bethell, Nicholas, *The Palestine Triangle* (London: Futura, 1980)

Bierman, John and Colin Smith, *Fire in the Night: Wingate of Burma, Ethiopia and Zion* (New York, NY: Random House, 1999)

Bowden, Tom, *The Breakdown of Public Security: The Case of Ireland 1916–1921 and Palestine 1936–1939* (London and Beverly Hills, CA: Sage, 1977)

Bowyer Bell J., *Terror out of Zion: Irgun Zvai Leumi, Lehi and the Palestine Underground, 1929–49* (New York, NY: Discus, 1977)

Browning, Christopher, *Ordinary Men: Reserve Police Battalion 101 and the Final Solution in Poland* (New York, NY: HarperCollins, 1993)

Burke, E. and I. Lapidus (eds), *Islam, Politics and Social Movements* (Berkeley, CA: University of California Press, 1988)

Burke, Edmund and David Yaghoubian (eds), *Struggle and Survival in the Modern Middle East* (Berkeley, CA: University of California Press, 2006)

Burke, Edward, *Army of Tribes: British Army Cohesion, Deviancy and Murder in Northern Ireland* (Liverpool: Liverpool University Press, 2018)

Callwell, C. E., *Small Wars: Their Principles and Practices* [1896] (London: HMSO, 1906)

Campbell, Bruce B. and Arthur D. Brenner (eds), *Death Squads in Global Perspective: Murder with Deniability* (New York, NY: St Martin's, 2000)

Carmel, Hesi (ed.), *Intelligence for Peace: The Role of Intelligence in Times of Peace* (London: Cass, 1999)

Cesarani, David, *Major Farran's Hat: Murder, Scandal and Britain's War against Jewish Terrorism, 1945–48* (London: Heinemann, 2009)

Charters, David A., *The British Army and Jewish Insurgency in Palestine, 1945–47* (London: Macmillan-King's, 1989)

Clark, Alan, *The Donkeys* (London: Random House, 1961)

Clayton, Anthony, *Counter-Insurgency in Kenya: A Study of Military Operations against Mau Mau* (Nairobi: Transafrica Historical Papers 4, 1978)

Cohen, Hillel, *Army of Shadows: Palestinian Collaboration with Zionism, 1917–1948* (Berkeley, CA: University of California Press, 2008)

Year Zero of the Arab-Israeli Conflict 1929 (Waltham, MA: Brandeis University Press, 2015)

Cohen, Michael, *Palestine, Retreat from the Mandate: The Making of British Policy, 1936–1945* (London: Elek, 1978)

and Martin Kolinsky (eds), *Britain and the Middle East in the 1930s: Security Problems, 1935–39* (London: Macmillan-King's, 1992)

Collett, Nigel, *The Butcher of Amritsar: General Reginald Dyer* (London: Hambledon, 2005)

Connell, J., *Wavell: Scholar and Soldier* (London: Collins, 1964)

Conrad, Joseph, *Nostromo: A Tale of the Seaboard* (London: Harper, 1904)

Coogan, T. P., *On the Blanket: The Inside Story of the IRA Prisoners' 'Dirty Protest'* [1980] (Houndmills: Palgrave, 2002)

Cormac, Rory, *Confronting the Colonies: British Intelligence and Counterinsurgency* (London: Hurst, 2013)

Coss, Peter (ed.), *The Moral World of the Law* (Cambridge: Cambridge University Press, 2000)

Crozier, Brian, *The Rebels: A Study of Post-War Insurrections* (London: Chatto and Windus, 1960)

Dekel, Efraim, *Shai: The Exploits of Haganah Intelligence* (New York, NY: Yoseloff, 1959)

Dickens, Peter, *SAS: The Jungle Frontier. 22 Special Air Service Regiment in the Borneo Campaign, 1963–66* (London: Fontana, 1984)

Downing, Taylor, *Palestine on Film* (London: Council for Advancement of Arab-British Understanding, 1979)

el-Eini, Roza I. M., *Mandated Landscapes: British Imperial Rule in Palestine, 1929–1948* (London and New York, NY: Routledge, 2006)

Elkins, Caroline, *Britain's Gulag: The Brutal End of Empire in Kenya* (London: Jonathan Cape, 2005) published in the US as *Imperial Reckoning: The Untold Story of Britain's Gulag in Kenya* (New York, NY: Holt, 2005)

Elliott, Maj-Gen J. G., *The Frontier, 1839–1947: The Story of the North-West Frontier of India* (London: Cassell, 1968)

Ellis, John, *From the Barrel of a Gun: A History of Guerrilla, Revolutionary and Counter-Insurgency Warfare, from the Romans to the Present* (London: Greenhill, 1995)

Eshed, Haggai, *Reuven Shiloah: The Man behind the Mossad* (London: Cass, 1997)

Eshkol, Yosef, *A Common Soldier: The Story of Zwi Brenner* (Tel Aviv: Ministry of Defence, 1993)

Fairburn, Geoffrey, *Revolutionary Guerrilla Warfare* (London: Penguin, 1974)

Fanon, Frantz, *Black Skin, White Masks* [1952 in French] (London: Pluto, 1986)

Farwell, Byron, *The Great Anglo-Boer War* (New York, NY: Norton, 1976)

Faul, Fathers Denis and Raymond Murray, *British Army and Special Branch RUC Brutalities, December 1971–February 1972* (Cavan: Abbey, 1972)

Fein, Helen, *Imperial Crime and Punishment: The Massacre at Jallianwala Bagh and British Judgment, 1919–1920* (Honolulu, HI: University of Hawaii Press, 1977)

Fiddes, George V., *The Dominion and Colonial Offices* (London and New York, NY: Putnam, 1926)

Figes, Orlando, *Peasant Russia, Civil War: The Volga Countryside in Revolution* (Oxford: Clarendon, 1989)

Fiore, Massimiliano, *Anglo-Italian Relations in the Middle East, 1922–1940* (Farnham: Ashgate, 2010)

Firro, Kais M., *A History of the Druze* (Leiden: Brill, 1992)

Fishman, W. J., *The Insurrectionists* (London: Methuen, 1970)

Fitzpatrick, Peter, *The Mythology of Modern Law* (London: Routledge 1992)

Fleischmann, Ellen, *The Nation and Its 'New' Women: The Palestinian Women's Movement, 1920–1948* (Berkeley, CA: University of California Press, 2003)

Fortescue, J. W., *A History of the British Army. First Part. Volume 2* (London: Macmillan, 1899)

French, David, *The British Way in Counter-Insurgency, 1945–67* (Oxford: Oxford University Press, 2011)

  Fighting EOKA: The British Counter-Insurgency Campaign on Cyprus, 1955–1959 (Oxford: Oxford University Press, 2015)

Friling, Tuvia, *Arrows in the Dark: David Ben-Gurion, the Yishuv Leadership and Rescue Attempts during the Holocaust* (two vols) (Madison, WI: University of Wisconsin Press, 2005)

Frisch, Hillel, *The Palestinian Military: Between Militias and Armies* (London: Routledge, 2008)

Galula, David, *Counterinsurgency Warfare: Theory and Practice* [1964] (Westport, CT: Praeger, 2006)

Gelber, Yoav, *Jewish–Transjordanian Relations, 1921–48* (London: Cass, 1997)

Geraghty, Tony, *The Irish War: The Hidden Conflict between the IRA and British Intelligence* (Baltimore, MD and London: Johns Hopkins Press, 2000)

Ginzburg, Carlo, *Clues, Myths and the Historical Method* (Baltimore, MD: Johns Hopkins University Press, 1990)

Gudgin, Peter, *Military Intelligence: The British Story* (London: Arms and Armour, 1989)

al-Haj, Majid, *Social Change and Family Process: Arab Communities in Shefar-A'm* (Boulder, CO: Westview, 1987)

Hajjar, Lisa, *Courting Conflict: The Israeli Military System in the West Bank and Gaza* (Berkeley, CA and London: University of California Press, 2005)

Halliday, Fred, *Arabia without Sultans* (New York, NY: Vintage, 1975)

Hamilton, Nigel, *Monty: The Making of a General, 1887–1942* (London: Hamish Hamilton, 1981)

Hanna, Paul L., *British Policy in Palestine* (Washington, DC: American Council on Public Affairs, 1942)

Haritos-Fatouros, Mika, *The Psychological Origins of Institutionalized Torture* (London: Routledge, 2003)

Harouvi, Eldad, *Palestine Investigated: The Story of the CID of the Palestine Police Force, 1920–48* (Sussex: Academic Press, 2016)

Harrison, Simon, *Dark Trophies: Hunting and the Enemy Body in Modern War* (New York, NY: Berghahn, 2012)

Haswell, J, *British Military Intelligence* (London: Weidenfeld and Nicolson, 1973)

Heller, Tzila, *Behind Prison Walls: A Jewish Woman Freedom Fighter for Israel's Independence* (Hoboken, NJ: KTAV, 1999)

Hennessey, Thomas, *The Evolution of the Troubles, 1970–72* (Dublin: Irish Academic Press, 2007)

Hobsbawm, Eric, *Primitive Rebels: Studies in Archaic Forms of Social Movement in the 19th and 20th Centuries* (Manchester: Manchester University Press, 1959)
Bandits (London: Weidenfeld and Nicolson, 1969)

Hoffman, Bruce, *Anonymous Soldiers: The Struggle for Israel 1917–47* (New York, NY: Knopf, 2015)

Hopkinson, Michael, *The Irish War of Independence* (Montreal and Kingston: McGill-Queen's University Press, 2002)

Horne, Alistair, *Savage War of Peace: Algeria, 1954–62* (London: Pan, 2002)

Hourani, Albert et al. (eds), *The Modern Middle East: A Reader* (London: I. B. Tauris, 2004)

House, J. and N. MacMaster, *Paris, 1961: Algerians, State Terror and Memory* (Oxford: Oxford University Press, 2006)

Hughes, Matthew (ed.), *British Ways of Counter-insurgency: A Historical Perspective* (Oxford: Routledge, 2013)

Hull, Isabel, *Absolute Destruction: Military Culture and the Practices of War in Imperial Germany* (Ithaca, NY: Cornell University Press, 2006)

Hull, Roger H., *The Irish Triangle: Conflict in Northern Ireland* (Princeton, NJ: Princeton University Press, 1976)

Hussain, Nasser, *The Jurisprudence of Emergency: Colonialism and the Rule of Law* (Ann Arbor, MI: University of Michigan Press, 2003)

Innes-Robbins, Simon, *Dirty Wars: A Century of Counterinsurgency* (Stroud: History Press, 2016)

Jacobson, Abigail and Moshe Naor, *Oriental Neighbors: Middle Eastern Jews and Arabs in Mandatory Palestine* (Waltham, MA: Brandeis University Press, 2016)

Jameelah, Maryam, *Shaikh Izz-ud-Din Al-Qassam Shaheed: A Great Palestinian Mujahid (1882–1935). His Life and Work* (Lahore: Mohammad Yusuf Khan, 1990)

Jeffery, Keith, *MI6: The History of the Secret Intelligence Service* (London: Bloomsbury, 2010)

Jenkins, Richard, *Black Magic and Bogeymen: Fear, Rumour and Popular Belief in the North of Ireland 1972–74* (Cork: Cork University Press, 2014)

Joes, Anthony James, *Guerrilla Warfare: A Historical, Biographical, and Bibliographical Sourcebook* (Westport, CT: Greenwood, 1996)

Jones, Howard, *My Lai,Vietnam, 1968, and the Descent into Darkness* (New York, NY: Oxford University Press, 2017)

Judd, Denis and Keith Surridge, *The Boer War* (Houndmills: Palgrave, 2003)

Kabha, Mustafa, *The Palestinian Press as Shaper of Public Opinion: Writing Up a Storm* (London: Vallentine Mitchell, 2006)

The Palestinian People: Seeking Sovereignty and State (Boulder, CO and London: Lynne Rienner, 2014)

Kanaaneh, Rhoda, *Surrounded: Palestinian Soldiers in the Israeli Military* (Stanford, CA: Stanford University Press, 2008)

Kanafani, Ghassan, *Palestine: The 1936–1939 Revolt* (London: Tricontinental, c. 1982)

Karlinsky, Nahum, *California Dreaming: Ideology, Society, and Technology in the Citrus Industry of Palestine, 1890–1939* (Albany, NY: SUNY Press, 2005)

Kashua, Sayed, *Dancing Arabs* (New York, NY: Grove, 2004)

Kayyali, A. W., *Palestine: A Modern History* (London: Third World Centre, 1981)

Kee, Robert, *The Green Flag: A History of Irish Nationalism* (London: Weidenfeld and Nicolson, 1972)

Keegan, John, *Face of Battle* [1976] (London: Penguin, 1987)

A History of Warfare (London: Pimlico, 1993)

Kelly, Matthew, *The Crime of Nationalism: Britain, Palestine, and Nation-Building on the Fringe of Empire* (Berkeley, CA: University of California Press, 2017)

Khalaf, Issa, *Politics in Palestine: Arab Factionalism and Social Disintegration, 1939–1948* (Albany, NY: SUNY Press, 1991)

Khalidi, Rashid, *The Iron Cage: The Story of the Palestinian Struggle for Statehood* (Oxford: Oneworld, 2007)

Palestinian Identity: The Construction of Modern National Consciousness [1997] (New York, NY: Columbia University Press, 2010)

Khalidi, Walid, *From Haven to Conquest* (Beirut: IPS, 1971)

Khalili, Laleh, *Time in the Shadows: Confinement in Counterinsurgencies* (Stanford, CA: Stanford University Press, 2012)

el-Khazen, Ghassan, *La Grande Révolte Arabe de 1936 en Palestine* (Beirut: Éditions Dar An-Nahar, 2005)

Kilcullen, David, *Counterinsurgency* (London: Hurst, 2010)

Kimmerling, Baruch and Joel S. Migdal, *The Palestinian People: A History* (Cambridge, MA: Harvard University Press, 2003)

Kirk-Greene, Anthony, *On Crown Service: A History of HM Colonial Service and Overseas Civil Services 1837–1997* (London: I. B. Tauris, 1999)

Kitson, Frank, *Gangs and Counter-Gangs* (London: Barrie and Rockliff, 1960)

Low Intensity Operations: Subversion, Insurgency, and Peace-Keeping (Harrisburg, PA: Stackpole, 1971)

Bunch of Five (London: Faber and Faber, 1977)

Kolinsky, Martin, *Law, Order and Riots in Mandatory Palestine, 1928–35* (London: St Martin's, 1993)

Kostal, R. W., *A Jurisprudence of Power: Victorian Empire and the Rule of Law* (Oxford: Oxford University Press, 2005)

Kushner, T. and K. Lunn (eds), *Traditions of Intolerance: Historical Perspectives on Fascism and Race Discourse in Britain* (Manchester: Manchester University Press, 1979)

Lapping, Brian, *End of Empire* (New York, NY: St Martin's, 1985)

Lawrence, Christopher A., *War by Numbers: Understanding Conventional Combat* (Lincoln, NE: University of Nebraska Press, 2017)

Ledwidge, Frank, *Losing Small Wars: British Failure in Iraq and Afghanistan* (New Haven, CT and London: Yale University Press, 2011)

Lesch, Ann Mosely, *Arab Politics in Palestine: The Frustration of a Nationalist Movement* (Ithaca, NY and London: Cornell University Press, 1979)

Levenberg, Haim, *Military Preparations of the Arab Community in Palestine, 1945–48* (London: Cass, 1993)

Likhovski, Assaf, *Law and Identity in Mandate Palestine* (Chapel Hill, NC: University of North Carolina Press, 2006)

Linderman, A. R. B., *Rediscovering Irregular Warfare: Colin Gubbins and the Origins of Britain's Special Operations Executive* (Norman, OK: University of Oklahoma Press, 2016)

Littlejohn, Gary et al. (eds), *Power and the State* (London: Croom Helm, 1978)

Lloyd, Christopher, *Collaboration and Resistance in Occupied France: Representing Treason and Sacrifice* (Houndmills: Palgrave, 2003)

Lockman, Zachary, *Comrades and Enemies: Arab and Jewish Workers in Palestine, 1906–1948* (Berkeley, CA: University of California Press, 1996)

Ma'oz, Moshe (ed.), *Palestinian Arab Politics* (Jerusalem: Hebrew University, 1975)

Marlowe, John, *Rebellion in Palestine* (London: Cresset, 1946)

Matthews, Weldon, *Confronting an Empire, Constructing a Nation: Arab Nationalists and Popular Politics in Mandate Palestine* (London: I. B. Tauris, 2006)

McCuen, John, *The Art of Counter-Revolutionary Warfare* (London: Faber and Faber, 1966)

McGuffin, John, *The Guinea Pigs* (London: Penguin, 1974)

Merom, Gil, *How Democracies Lose Small Wars* (Cambridge: Cambridge University Press, 2003)

Migdal, Joel S. (ed.), *Palestinian Society and Politics* (Princeton, NJ: Princeton University Press, 1980)

Milgram, Stanley, *Obedience to Authority* [1974] (London: Pinter and Martin, 1997)

Miller, Rory, *Divided against Zion: Anti-Zionist Opposition in Britain to a Jewish State in Palestine, 1945–49* (London: Cass, 2000)

Miller, Ylana N., *Government and Society in Rural Palestine, 1920–48* (Austin, TX: University of Texas Press, 1985)

Millett, Kate, *The Politics of Cruelty: An Essay on the Literature of Political Imprisonment* (New York, NY: Norton, 1994)

Mockaitis, Thomas, *British Counterinsurgency, 1919–1960* (New York, NY: St Martin's, 1990)

Mogannam, Matiel, *The Arab Woman and the Palestine Problem* (London: Herbert Joseph, 1937)

Moreman, T. R., *The Army in India and the Development of Frontier Warfare, 1849–1947* (Houndmills: Macmillan, 1998)

Mosley, Leonard, *Gideon Goes to War* (London: Barker, 1955)

Moyer, Mark, *Triumph Forsaken: The Vietnam War, 1954–1965* (New York, NY: Cambridge University Press, 2006)

Muhsam, H. V., *Beduin of the Negev* (Jerusalem: Academic Press, 1966)

Murray, Douglas, *Bloody Sunday: Truths, Lies and the Saville Inquiry* (London: Biteback, 2012)

Muslih, Muhammad Y., *The Origins of Palestinian Nationalism* (New York, NY: Columbia University Press, 1988)

Nagl, John A., *Learning to Eat Soup with a Knife: Counterinsurgency Lessons from Malaya and Vietnam* (Chicago, IL: University of Chicago Press, 2005)

Nashashibi, Nasser Eddin, *Jerusalem's Other Voice: Ragheb Nashashibi and Moderation in Palestinian Politics, 1920–1948* (Exeter: Ithaca, 1990)

Nasson, Bill, *The South African War, 1899–1902* (London: Arnold, 1999)

Nevo, Joseph, *King Abdallah and Palestine: A Territorial Ambition* (Houndmills: Macmillan, 1996)

Newsinger, John, *British Counterinsurgency from Palestine to Northern Ireland* (Houndmills: Palgrave, 2002)

The Blood Never Dried: A People's History of the British Empire (London: Bookmarks, 2006)

Nolan, Victoria, *Military Leadership and Counterinsurgency: The British Army and Small Wars Strategy since World War II* (London and New York, NY: I. B. Tauris, 2012)

Norris, Jacob, *Land of Promise: Palestine in the Age of Colonial Development, 1905–1948* (Oxford: Oxford University Press, 2013)

O'Brien, Joanne, *A Matter of Minutes: The Enduring Legacy of Bloody Sunday* (Dublin: Wolfhound, 2002)

Omissi, David, *Air Power and Colonial Control: The Royal Air Force, 1919–39* (Manchester: Manchester University Press, 1990)

Orwell, George, *Homage to Catalonia* (London: Secker and Warburg, 1986)

Oulds, Robert, *Montgomery and the First War on Terror: What a British Military Hero Can Teach Those Fighting Today's War on Terror* (Epsom: Bretwalda, 2012)

Paget, Julian, *Counter-Insurgency Operations: Techniques of Guerrilla Warfare* (New York, NY: Walker, 1967)

The Last Post: Aden, 1964–1967 (London: Faber and Faber, 1969)

Pakenham, Thomas, *The Boer War* (New York, NY: Random House, 1979)

Pappe, Ilan, *The Rise and Fall of a Palestinian Dynasty: The Husaynis, 1700–1948* (London: Saqi, 2010)

Parsons, Laila, *The Commander: Fawzi al-Qawuqji and the Fight for Arab Independence* (New York, NY: Hill and Wang, 2016)

Pearlman, M., *Mufti of Jerusalem: The Story of Haj Amin El Husseini* (London: Gollancz, 1947)

Penkower, M. N., *Palestine in Turmoil, 1933–39* (New York, NY: Touro, 2014)

Peters, Rudolph, *Islam and Colonialism: The Doctrine of Jihad in Modern History* (The Hague: Mouton, 1979)

Phillips, Joshua, *None of Us Were Like This Before: American Soldiers and Torture* (London: Verso, 2012)

Pitzer, Andrea, *One Long Night: A Global History of Concentration Camps* (London: Little, Brown, 2017)

Pollack, Kenneth, *Arabs at War: Military Effectiveness 1948–1991* (Lincoln, NE: University of Nebraska Press 2002)

Porath, Yehoshua, *The Palestinian Arab National Movement: From Riots to Rebellion. Volume 2, 1929–1939* (London: Cass, 1977)

Porch, Douglas, *Counterinsurgency: Exposing the Myths of the New Way of War* (Cambridge: Cambridge University Press, 2013)

Pringle, Peter and Philip Jacobson, *Those Are Real Bullets: Bloody Sunday, Derry, 1972* (New York, NY: Grove Press, 2000)

Probert, Henry, *Bomber Harris: His Life and Times* (London: Greenhill, 2001)

Quandt, William et al. (eds), *The Politics of Palestinian Nationalism* (Berkeley CA: University of California Press, 1973)

Radai, Itamar, *Palestinians in Two Cities, 1948* (London: Routledge, 2015)

Raviv, Dan and Yossi Melman, *Every Spy a Prince: The Complete History of Israel's Intelligence Community* (Boston, MA: Houghton Mifflin, 1990)

Reid, Donald, *Lawyers and Politics in the Arab World, 1880–1960* (Minneapolis, MN: Bibliotheca Islamica, 1981)

Reid-Daly, R. F., *Pamwe Chete: The Legend of the Selous Scouts* (Weltevreden: Covos, 1999)

Rejali, Darius, *Torture and Democracy* (Princeton, NJ: Princeton University Press, 1997)

Robinson, Shira, *Citizen Strangers: Palestinians and the Birth of Israel's Liberal Settler State* (Stanford, CA: Stanford University Press, 2013)

Robson, Brian, *Crisis on the Frontier: The Third Afghan War and the Campaign in Waziristan, 1919–20* (Staplehurst: Spellmount, 2004)

Robson, Laura, *Colonialism and Christianity in Mandate Palestine* (Austin, TX: University of Texas Press, 2012)

Rose, Norman, *A Senseless, Squalid War* (London: Bodley Head, 2009)

Rosenberg-Friedman, Lilach, *Birthrate Politics in Zion: Judaism, Nationalism, and Modernity under the British Mandate* (Bloomington, IN: Indiana University Press, 2017)

Rossiter, C. L., *Constitutional Dictatorship: Crisis Government in the Modern Democracies* (Princeton, NJ: Princeton University Press, 1948)

Royle, Trevor, *Orde Wingate: Irregular Soldier* (London: Weidenfeld and Nicolson, 1995)

Saward, Douglas, *Bomber Harris* (New York, NY: Doubleday, 1985)

Sayigh, Rosemary, *The Palestinians: From Peasants to Revolutionaries* [1979] (London: Zed, 2007)

Schechtman, Joseph B., *The Mufti and the Fuehrer: The Rise and Fall of Haj Amin el-Husseini* (New York, NY: Yoseloff, 1965)

Schmitt, Carl, *Theory of the Partisan* (New York, NY: Telos, 2007)

Segev, Tom, *One Palestine, Complete: Jews and Arabs under the British Mandate* (New York, NY: Owl, 2001)

Shamir, Ronen, *The Colonies of Law: Colonialism, Zionism and Law in Early Mandate Palestine* (Cambridge: Cambridge University Press, 2000)

Shapira, Anita, *Land and Power: The Zionist Resort to Force, 1881–1948* (New York, NY: Oxford University Press, 1992)

Sheehan, Neil, *A Bright Shining Lie* (London: Pan, 1990)

Shehadeh, Raja, *Occupier's Law: Israel and the West Bank* (Washington, DC: IPS, 1985)

Simpson, A. W. B., *In the Highest Degree Odious: Detention without Trial in Wartime Britain* (Oxford: Clarendon, 1992)

Sinclair, Georgina, *At the End of the Line: Colonial Policing and the Imperial Endgame, 1945–80* (Manchester: Manchester University Press, 2006)

Slater, Robert, *Warrior Statesman: The Life of Moshe Dayan* (London: Robson, 1992)

Sluka, Jeffrey (ed.), *Death Squad: The Anthropology of State Terror* (Philadelphia, PA: University of Pennsylvania Press, 2000)

Smith, M. L. R. and D. Jones, *The Political Impossibility of Modern Counterinsurgency* (Columbia, NY: Columbia University Press, 2015)

Staniland, Paul, *Networks of Rebellion: Explaining Insurgent Cohesion and Collapse* (Ithaca, NY and London: Cornell University Press, 2014)

Strachan, Hew, *The Politics of the British Army* (Oxford: Clarendon, 1997)

Sunday Times Insight Team, *Israel and Torture* (London: Arab Dawn, 1977)

Swedenburg, Ted, *Memories of Revolt: The 1936–1939 Rebellion and the Palestinian National Past* (Minneapolis, MN: University of Minnesota Press, 1995)

Swinson, Arthur, *Six Minutes to Sunset: The Story of General Dyer and the Amritsar Affair* (London: Peter Davies, 1964)

Sykes, Christopher, *Orde Wingate* (London: Collins, 1959)

Taber, Robert, *War of the Flea* [1965] (Washington, DC: Brassey's, 2002)

Taggar, Yehuda, *The Mufti of Jerusalem and Palestine Arab Politics, 1930–37* (New York, NY and London: Garland, 1986)

Taslitt, Israel, *Soldier of Israel: The Story of General Moshe Dayan* (New York, NY: Funk and Wagnalls, 1969)

Teveth, Shabtai, *Ben-Gurion: The Burning Ground, 1886–1948* (London: Hale, 1987)

Moshe Dayan (London: Weidenfeld and Nicolson, 1992)

Thomas, Martin, *Empires of Intelligence: Security Services and Colonial Disorders after 1914* (Berkeley, CA: University of California Press, 2008)

Violence and Colonial Order: Police, Workers and Protest in the European Colonial Empire, 1918–1940 (Cambridge: Cambridge University Press, 2012)

Thompson, Sir Robert, *Defeating Communist Insurgency: The Lessons of Malaya and Vietnam* (New York, NY: Praeger, 1966)

Townshend, Charles, *The British Campaign in Ireland, 1919–1921: The Development of Political and Military Policies* (Oxford: Oxford University Press, 1975)

Britain's Civil Wars: Counterinsurgency in the Twentieth Century (London: Faber and Faber, 1986)

Desert Hell: The British Invasion of Mesopotamia (Cambridge, MA: Harvard University Press, 2010)

Vaughan, W. E. (ed.), *A New History of Ireland. Volume 6, Ireland under the Union, 1870–1921* (Oxford: Clarendon, 1996)

Vittori, Jean-Pierre, *Confessions d'un professionnel de la torture: La Guerre d'Algérie* (Paris: Ramsay, 1980)

Wagner, Steven, *Statecraft by Stealth: How Britain Ruled Palestine 1917–40* (Ithaca, NY: Cornell University Press, 2018)

Walsh, Dermot P. J., *Bloody Sunday and the Rule of Law in Northern Ireland* (Houndmills: Palgrave, 2000)

Walton, Calder, *Empire of Secrets: British Intelligence, the Cold War and the Twilight of Empire* (London: Harper, 2013)

Waltzer, Michael, *Just and Unjust Wars* (London: Allen Lane, 1978)

Wassserstein, Bernard, *The British in Palestine: The Mandatory Government and the Arab–Israeli Conflict, 1917–29* [1978] (Oxford: Blackwell, 1991)

Weigley, Russell, *The American Way of War: A History of United States Military Strategy and Policy* (Bloomington, IN: Indiana University Press, 1977)

Wilson, Mary, *King Abdullah, Britain and the Making of Jordan* (Cambridge: Cambridge University Press, 1987)

Yapp, M. E., *The Near East since the First World War* (London: Longman, 1991)

Ziegler, Philip, *Soldiers: Fighting Men's Lives* (New York, NY: Knopf, 2002)

Zimbardo, Philip, *The Lucifer Effect: Understanding How Good People Turn Evil* (New York, NY: Random, 2007)

BOOKS (HEBREW)

Arnon-Ohanna, Yuval, *Falahim ba-Mered ha-'Aravi be-eretz Yisrael, 1936–39* [*Felahin during the Arab Revolt in the Land of Israel*] (Tel Aviv: Shiloh Institute, Tel Aviv University, 1978)

    Herev mi-Bayit: ha-Ma'avak ha-Pnimi ba-tnu'a ha-le'umit ha-falastinit, 1929–39 [*The Internal Struggle within the Palestinian Movement, 1929–39*] (Tel Aviv: Hadar, 1989)

Cohen, Hillel, *Tzva ha-Tzlalim: Mashtapim Falestinim be-Sherut ha-Ziyonut, 1917–48* [*An Army of Shadows: Palestinian Collaborators in the Service of Zionism, 1917–48*] (Jerusalem: 'Ivrit, 2004)

Elyashar, Eliyahu, *Li-Hyot 'im Falastinim* [*To Live with Palestinians*] (Jerusalem: Sephardic Community Committee, 1975)

Eyal, Yigal, *Ha-Intifada ha-Rishona: Dikuy ha-Mered ha-Aravi al yedey ha-Tzava ha-Briti be-Eretz Yisrael, 1936–39* [*The First Intifada: The Suppression of the Arab Revolt by the British Army, 1936–39*] (Tel Aviv: Ma'arachot, 1998)

Gelber, Yoav, *Shorshey ha-Havatzelet: ha-Modi'in ba-Yishuv, 1918–1947* [*A Budding Fleur-de-Lis: The Intelligence Services of the Jewish Yishuv (in Palestine), 1918–47*] (Tel Aviv: Ministry of Defence, 1992)

Lefen, Asa, *Ha-Shai: Shorasheha Shel Kehilat ha-Modi'in ha-Yisraelit* [*The Roots of the Israeli Intelligence Community*] (Tel Aviv: Ministry of Defence, 1997)

Slutsky, Yehuda (and Ben-Zion Dinur) (eds), *Sefer Toldot ha-Haganah* [*Book of the History of the Haganah*]. Volume 2, Part 2, *Me'Haganah le'ma'avak* [*From Defence to Struggle*] (Tel Aviv: Ma'arachot, 1963)

    Sefer Toldot ha-Haganah [*Book of the History of the Haganah*]. Volume 3, Part 1, *Me'ma'avak le'Milhama* [*From Struggle to War*] (Tel Aviv: 'Am Oved, 1972)

JOURNAL AND NEWSPAPER ARTICLES (ARABIC)

Anon., 'Khalid al-Fahum Yatadhakkar' ['Khalid al-Fahum Remembers'], *al-Quds* (2 September 1998), p. 17

Kanafani, Ghassan, 'Thawrat 1936–1939 fi Filastin: Khalfiyyat, tafasil wa tahlil' ['The 1936–1939 Revolt in Palestine: Background, Details and Analysis'], *Shu'un Filastinyya* [*Palestinian Matters*] 6 (January 1972), pp. 45–77

JOURNAL AND NEWSPAPER ARTICLES (ENGLISH)

Abboushi, W. F., 'The Road to Rebellion: Arab Palestine in the 1930s,' *Journal of Palestine Studies* 6/3 (Spring 1977), pp. 23–46

Anon., 'Service Problems in Palestine: From a Correspondent in Jerusalem,' *Journal of the Royal United Service Institution* 81 (November 1936), pp. 805–10

Anon., 'Arab Leader and Former Mufti Accused of "Diverting Noble Revolt",' *Yorkshire Post* (24 October 1938)

Anon., '"Sub-War" in Palestine,' *Yorkshire Post* (24 October 1938)

Anon., 'Troops in Control at Jerusalem,' *Yorkshire Post* (24 October 1938)

Anon., 'British Methods in Palestine,' *Yorkshire Post* (23 November 1938)

Arielli, Nir, 'Italian Involvement in the Arab Revolt in Palestine, 1936–39,' *British Journal of Middle Eastern Studies* 35/2 (2008), pp. 187–204

Arnon-Ohanna, Yuval, 'The Bands in the Palestinian Arab Revolt, 1936–39: Structure and Organization,' *Asian and African Studies* 15/2 (1981), pp. 229–47

Beaumont, Roger, 'Thinking the Unspeakable: On Cruelty in Small Wars,' *Small Wars and Insurgencies* 1/1 (April 1990), pp. 54–73

Beckett, Ian, 'The Study of Counter-Insurgency: A British Perspective,' *Small Wars and Insurgencies* 1/1 (April 1990), pp. 47–53

Ben-Gurion, David, 'Our Friend: What Wingate Did for Us,' *Jewish Observer and Middle East Review* (27 September 1963), pp. 15–16

Bennett, Huw, 'The Other Side of the COIN: Minimum and Exemplary Force in British Army Counterinsurgency in Kenya,' *Small Wars and Insurgencies* 18/4 (2007), pp. 638–64

'"A Very Salutary Effect": The Counter-Terror Strategy in Early Malayan Emergency, June 1948 to December 1949,' *Journal of Strategic Studies* 32/3 (June 2009), pp. 415–44

Bowden, Tom, 'Politics of the Arab Rebellion in Palestine, 1936–39,' *Middle Eastern Studies* 11/2 (December 1975), pp. 147–74

Cahill, R. A., '"Going Beserk [sic]": "Black and Tans" in Palestine,' *Jerusalem Quarterly* 38 (2009), pp. 59–68

Clarence-Smith, W. G., 'Class Structure and Class Struggles in Angola in the 1970s,' *Journal of Southern African Studies* 7/1 (1980), pp. 109–26

Cohen, Gili, 'Bedouin and Christian Arabs, the Israeli Army Wants You,' *Haaretz* (2 January 2017)

Cohen, Michael, 'British Strategy and the Palestine Question, 1936–39,' *Journal of Contemporary History* 7/3 (April 1972), pp. 157–83

'Sir Arthur Wauchope, the Army and the Rebellion in Palestine,' *Middle Eastern Studies* 9/1 (January 1973), pp. 19–34

'Direction of Policy in Palestine, 1936–39,' *Middle Eastern Studies* 11/3 (October 1975), pp. 237–61

'Secret Diplomacy and Rebellion in Palestine, 1936–39,' *International Journal of Middle East Studies* 8/3 (July 1977), pp. 379–404

Connolly, Kevin, 'Charles Tegart and the Forts That Tower over Israel,' *BBC News* (10 September 2012)

Dixon, Paul, '"Hearts and Minds"? British Counter-Insurgency from Malaya to Iraq,' *Journal of Strategic Studies* 32/3 (June 2009), pp. 353–81

Dove, Captain A. J. H., 'House Demolitions in Palestine,' *Royal Engineers Journal* 50 (December 1936), pp. 515–19

Elpeleg, Zvi, 'The 1936–1939 Disturbances: Riot or Rebellion?,' *Weiner Library Bulletin* 31/45–46 (1978), pp. 40–51

Faure-Walker, H. W., 'Operations in the Old City of Jerusalem, October 1938,' *The Guards Magazine* (Autumn 1979), pp. 99–102

Gershoni, Israel, 'The Muslim Brothers and the Arab Revolt in Palestine, 1936–39,' *Middle Eastern Studies* 22/3 (1986), pp. 367–97

Goodman, Giora, 'British Press Control in Palestine during the Arab Revolt, 1936–39,' *Journal of Imperial and Commonwealth History* 43/4 (December 2015), pp. 699–720

Goodwin, Gavin and Gerry Burke, 'I Accuse the Argylls,' (Scottish) *Sunday Mail* (26 April 1981), pp. 1–2

Goren, Tamir, 'Developing Jaffa's Port, 1920–1936,' *Israel Affairs* 22/1 (2016), pp. 172–88

Graz, Captain E. P. A. Des, 'Military Control of Disturbed Areas,' *Journal of the Royal United Service Institution* 81 (November 1936), pp. 811–16

Gregory, Adrian, 'Peculiarities of the English? War, Violence and Politics, 1900–1939,' *Journal of Modern European History* 1/1 (2003), pp. 44–59

Haim, Y., 'Zionist Policies and Attitudes towards the Arabs on the Eve of the Arab Revolt, 1936,' *Middle Eastern Studies* 14/2 (1978), pp. 211–31

Hoffman, B., 'The Palestine Police Force and the Challenges of Gathering Counterterrorism Intelligence, 1939–1947,' *Small Wars and Insurgencies* 24/4 (2103), pp. 609–47

Hughes, Geraint and Christian Tripodi, 'Anatomy of a Surrogate: Historical Precedents and Implications for Contemporary Counter-Insurgency and Counter-Terrorism,' *Small Wars and Insurgencies* 20/1 (2009), pp. 1–35

Hughes, Matthew, 'The Banality of Brutality: British Armed Forces and the Repression of the Arab Revolt in Palestine, 1936–39,' *English Historical Review* 124/507 (April 2009), pp. 313–54

'The Practice and Theory of British Counter-Insurgency: The Histories of the Atrocities at the Palestinian Villages of al-Bassa and Halhul, 1938–39,' *Small Wars and Insurgencies* 20/3–4 (September–December 2009), pp. 528–50

'A History of Violence: The Shooting of British Assistant Superintendent Alan Sigrist, 12 June 1936,' *Journal of Contemporary History* 45/4 (2010), pp. 725–43

'A British "Foreign Legion"? The British Police in Mandate Palestine,' *Middle Eastern Studies* 49/5 (2013), pp. 696–711

'Terror in Galilee: British-Jewish Collaboration and the Special Night Squads in Palestine during the Arab Revolt, 1938–39,' *Journal of Imperial and Commonwealth History* 43/4 (December 2015), pp. 590–610

'Palestinian Collaboration with the British: The Peace Bands and the Arab Revolt in Palestine, 1936–39,' *Journal of Contemporary History* 51/2 (April 2016*)*, pp. 291–315

Jankowski, James, 'The Palestinian Arab Revolt of 1936–1939,' *Muslim World* 63/3 (1973), pp. 220–33

Johnson, Robert, 'Command of the Army, Charles Gwynn and Imperial Policing: The British Doctrinal Approach to Internal Security in Palestine 1919–29,' *Journal of Imperial and Commonwealth History* 43/4 (December 2015), pp. 570–89

Kedourie, Elie, 'The Bludan Congress on Palestine, September 1937,' *Middle Eastern Studies* 17/1 (January 1981), pp. 107–25

Kelly, Matthew, 'The Revolt of 1936: A Revision,' *Journal of Palestine Studies* 44/2 (Winter 2015), pp. 28–42

Kingsley Heath, A. J., 'The Palestine Police Force under the Mandate,' *The Police Journal* 1/1 (1928), pp. 78–88

Knight, John, 'Securing Zion? Policing in British Palestine, 1917–39,' *European Review of History-Revue Européene d'Histoire* 18/4 (2011), pp. 523–43

Kochavi, Arieh, 'The Struggle against Jewish Immigration to Palestine,' *Middle Eastern Studies* 34/3 (1998), pp. 146–67

Kolinsky, Martin, 'Reorganization of the Palestine Police after the Riots of 1929,' *Studies in Zionism* 10/2 (1989), pp. 155–73

Krozier, Gad, 'From Dowbiggin to Tegart: Revolutionary Change in the Colonial Police in Palestine during the 1930s,' *Journal of Imperial and Commonwealth History* 32/2 (2004), pp. 115–33

Lawrence, Jon, 'Forging a Peaceable Kingdom: War, Violence, and Fear of Brutalization in Post-First World War Britain,' *Journal of Modern History* 75/3 (2003), pp. 557–89

Lewandowski-Romps, Lisa et al., 'Risk Factors for Accident Death in the U.S. Army, 2004–2009,' *American Journal of Preventive Medicine* 47/6 (2014), pp. 745–53

MacDonald, A. Callon, 'Radio Bari: Italian Wireless Propaganda in the Middle East and British Countermeasures, 1934–38,' *Middle Eastern Studies* 13/2 (May 1977), pp. 195–207

Mason, T. David and Dale A. Crane, 'The Political Economy of Death Squads: Towards a Theory of the Impact of State-Sanctioned Terror,' *International Studies Quarterly* 33/2 (1989), pp. 175–98

Mayer, Thomas, 'Egypt and the 1936 Arab Revolt in Palestine,' *Journal of Contemporary History* 19/2 (1984), pp. 275–87

Mockaitis, Thomas, 'The Origins of British Counter-Insurgency,' *Small Wars and Insurgencies* 1/3 (December 1990), pp, 209–25

Myers, Capt E. C. W., 'An Arab "Mouse Trap" and Other Booby Traps, Palestine 1936,' *Royal Engineers Journal* (December 1937), pp. 546–55

Nasasra, Mansour, 'Memories from Beersheba: The Bedouin Palestine Police and the Frontiers of the Empire,' *Bulletin of the Council for British Research in the Levant* 9 (2014), pp. 32–38

Neocleous, Mark et al. (eds), 'On Pacification,' *Socialist Studies/Études Socialistes* (Special Issue, Winter 2013), pp. 1–198

Norris, Jacob, 'Repression and Rebellion: Britain's Response to the Arab Revolt in Palestine of 1936–39,' *Journal of Imperial and Commonwealth History* 36/1 (March 2008), pp. 25–45

Parry, Marc, 'A Reckoning: Colonial Atrocities and Academic Reputations on Trial in British Courtroom,' *Chronicle of Higher Education* (1 June 2016)

Parsons, Laila, 'Soldiering for Arab Nationalism: Fawzi al-Qawuqji in Palestine,' *Journal of Palestine Studies* 36/4 (Summer 2007), pp. 33–48

Popplewell, Richard, '"Lacking Intelligence": Some Reflections on Recent Approaches to British Counter-Insurgency, 1900–1960,' *Intelligence and National Security* 10/1 (1995), pp. 336–52

Radai, Itamar, 'The Rise and Fall of the Palestinian–Arab Middle Class under the British Mandate, 1920–39,' *Journal of Contemporary History* 51/3 (July 2016), pp. 487–506

Rose, Norman, 'The Arab Rulers and Palestine, 1936: The British Reaction,' *Journal of Modern History* 44/2 (June 1972), pp. 213–31

Sanagan, Mark, 'Teacher, Preacher, Soldier, Martyr: Rethinking 'Izz al-Din al-Qassam,' *Welt des Islams* 53/3–4 (2013), pp. 315–52

Schleifer, S. Abdullah, 'The Life and Thought of 'Izz-id-Din al-Qassam,' *Islamic Quarterly* 2 (1979), pp. 61–81

Sheffer, Gabriel, 'Appeasement and the Problem of Palestine,' *International Journal of Middle East Studies* 11/3 (1980), pp. 377–99

Shoul, Simeon, 'Soldiers, Riot Control and Aid to the Civil Power in India, Egypt and Palestine, 1919–39,' *Journal of the Society for Army Historical Research* 36/346 (Summer 2008), pp. 120–39

Sinclair, Georgina, '"Get into a Crack Force and Earn £20 a Month All Found …": The Influence of the Palestine Police upon Colonial Policing 1922–1948,' *European Review of History* 13/1 (2006), pp. 49–65

Stein, Kenneth, 'Palestine's Rural Economy, 1917–1939,' *Studies in Zionism* 8/1 (1987), pp. 25–49

Swedenburg, Ted, 'The Palestinian Peasant as National Signifier,' *Anthropological Quarterly* 63/1 (1990), pp. 18–30

Thornton, Rod, '"Minimum Force": A Reply to Huw Bennett,' *Small Wars and Insurgencies* 20/1 (2001), pp. 215–26

'The British Army and the Origins of Its Minimum Force Philosophy,' *Small Wars and Insurgencies* 15/1 (2004), pp. 83–106

Townshend, Charles, 'Martial Law: Legal and Administrative Problems of Civil Emergency in Britain and the Empire, 1800–1940,' *The Historical Journal* 25/1 (1982), pp. 167–95

'The Defence of Palestine: Insurrection and Public Security, 1936–39,' *English Historical Review* 103/409 (1988), pp. 917–49

Wagner, Kim, 'Savage Warfare: Violence and the Rule of Colonial Difference in Early British Counterinsurgency,' *History Workshop Journal* (3 January 2018) (online first at doi.org/10.1093/hwj/dbx053)

Wasserstein, Bernard, 'Clipping the Claws of the Colonisers: Arab Officials in the Government of Palestine, 1917–48,' *Middle Eastern Studies* 13/2 (May 1977), pp. 171–94

Yazbak, Mahmoud, 'From Poverty to Revolt: Economic Factors in the Outbreak of the 1936 Rebellion in Palestine,' *Middle Eastern Studies* 36/3 (2000), pp. 93–113

JOURNAL ARTICLES (HEBREW)

Gavish, Dov, 'Mivz'a Yafo: Shipur Koloniali Shel Pnei ha-'Ir' ['The Old City of Jaffa: A Colonial Urban Renewal Project'], *Eretz Israel: Mehkarim be-Yedi'at ha-Aretz ve-Atikoteha* [*Eretz Israel: Archaeology, Historical and Geographical Studies*] 17 (1983), pp. 66–73

BOOK CHAPTERS (ENGLISH)

Allon, Yigal, 'The Making of Israel's Army: The Development of Military Conceptions of Liberation and Defence,' in Michael Howard (ed.), *The Theory and Practice of War* (London: Cassell, 1965)

Anglim, Simon, 'Orde Wingate and the Special Night Squads: A Feasible Policy for Counter-Terrorism?,' in Tim Benbow and Rod Thornton (eds), *Dimensions of Counter-Insurgency: Applying Experience to Practice* (London: Routledge, 2014)

Asprey, Robert, 'Guerrilla Warfare' in 'The Theory and Conduct of War,' *Encyclopaedia Britannica: Macropaedia* (Fifteenth Edition, 1997)

Bowden, Tom, 'Policing Palestine 1920–36: Some Problems of Public Security under the Mandate,' in George Mosse (ed.), *Police Forces in History* (London: Sage, 1975)

Bracha, Baruch, 'Restriction of Personal Freedom without Due Process of Law According to the Defence (Emergency) Regulations, 1945,' in Y. Dinstein and F. Domb (eds), *Israel Yearbook on Human Rights. Volume 8* (Tel Aviv: Intersdar, 1978)

Clayton, Anthony, '"Deceptive Might": Imperial Defence and Security, 1900–1968,' in Judith M. Brown and Wm. Roger Louis (eds), *The Oxford History of the British Empire. Volume 4, The Twentieth Century* (Oxford: Oxford University Press, 1999)

Eyal, Yigal, 'The Arab Revolt, 1936–1939: A Turning Point in the Struggle over Palestine,' in Mordechai Bar-On (ed.), *A Never-Ending Conflict: A Guide to Israeli Military History* (Westport, CT and London: Praeger, 2004)

Gelber, Yoav, 'Reuven Shiloah's Contribution to the Development of Israeli Intelligence,' in Hesi Carmel (ed.), *Intelligence for Peace: The Role of Intelligence in Times of Peace* (London: Cass, 1999)

Hack, Karl, 'Screwing Down the People: The Malayan Emergency, Decolonisation and Ethnicity,' in Hans Antlöv and Stein Tønnesson (eds), *Imperial Policy and Southeast Asian Nationalism* (Richmond: Curzon, 1995)

Harouvi, Eldad, 'Reuven Zaslany (Shiloah) and the Covert Cooperation with British Intelligence during the Second World War,' in Hesi Carmel (ed.), *Intelligence for Peace: The Role of Intelligence in Times of Peace* (London: Cass, 1999)

Harries, Patrick, 'The Battle of Algiers: Between Fiction, Memory and History,' in Vivian Bickford-Smith and Richard Mendelsohn (eds), *Black and White in Colour: African History on Screen* (Oxford: Currey, 2007)

Hughes, Matthew, 'Lawlessness Was the Law: British Armed Forces, the Legal System and the Repression of the Arab Revolt in Palestine, 1936–39,' in Rory Miller (ed.), *Palestine, Britain and Empire, c. 1841–1948* (Aldershot: Ashgate, 2010)

Kabha, Mustafa, 'The Palestinian Exile: Drama Shapes Memory,' in A. Sela and A. Kadish (eds), *The War of 1948: Representations of Israeli and Palestinian Memories and Narratives* (Bloomington, IN: Indiana University Press, 2016)

Khalidi, Rashid, 'The Palestinians and 1948: The Underlying Causes of Failure,' in E. Rogan and A. Shlaim (eds), *The War for Palestine* (Cambridge: Cambridge University Press, 2007)

Kolinsky, Martin, 'The Collapse and Restoration of Public Security,' in Michael J. Cohen and Martin Kolinsky (eds), *Britain and the Middle East in the 1930s: Security Problems, 1935–39* (London: Macmillan-King's, 1992)

Kostiner, Joseph, 'Britain and the Challenge of the Axis Powers in Arabia: The Decline of British–Saudi Cooperation in the 1930s,' in Michael J. Cohen and Martin Kolinsky (eds), *Britain and the Middle East in the 1930s: Security Problems, 1935–39* (London: Macmillan-King's, 1992)

Lachman, Shai, 'Arab Rebellion and Terrorism in Palestine, 1929–39: The Case of Sheikh Izz al-Din al-Qassam and His Movement,' in E. Kedourie and S. Haim (eds), *Zionism and Arabism in Palestine and Israel* (London: Cass, 1982)

Moore, Robin J., 'Imperial India, 1858–1914,' in Andrew Porter (ed.), *Oxford History of the British Empire. Volume 3, The Nineteenth Century* (Oxford: Oxford University Press, 1999)

Nevo, Joseph, 'Palestinian–Arab Violent Activity during the 1930s,' in Michael J. Cohen and Martin Kolinsky (eds), *Britain and the Middle East in the 1930s: Security Problems, 1935–39* (London: Macmillan-King's, 1992)

Pach, Arie, 'Human Rights in West Bank Military Courts,' in Y. Dinstein and F. Domb (eds), *Israel Yearbook on Human Rights. Volume 7* (Tel Aviv: Tel Aviv University, 1977)

Palmer, Col W. V., 'The Second Battalion in Palestine,' in H. D. Chaplin (ed.), *The Queen's Own Royal West Kent Regiment* (London: Michael Joseph, 1954)

Parsons, Laila, 'Rebels without Borders: Southern Syria and Palestine, 1919–36,' in C. Shayegh and A. Arsan (eds), *The Routledge Handbook of the History of the Middle East Mandates* (London: Routledge, 2015)

Pimlott, John, 'The British Experience,' in Ian F. W. Beckett (ed.), *The Roots of Counter-Insurgency: Armies and Guerrilla Warfare 1900–1945* (London: Blandford, 1988)

Porath, Y., 'The Political Organisation of the Palestinian Arabs under the British Mandate,' in Moshe Ma'oz (ed.), *Palestinian Arab Politics* (Jerusalem: Hebrew University of Jerusalem, Truman Institute Studies, 1975)

Sheffield, G. D., 'Introduction: Command, Leadership and the Anglo-American Experience,' in G. D. Sheffield (ed.), *Leadership and Command: The Anglo-American Experience since 1861* (London: Brassey's, 2002)

Shy, John and Thomas Collier, 'Revolutionary War,' in Peter Paret (ed.), *Makers of Modern Strategy: From Machiavelli to the Nuclear Age* [1986] (Oxford: Clarendon, 2000)

Tauber, Eliezer, 'The Army of Sacred Jihad: An Army or Bands?,' in Efraim Karsh and Rory Miller (eds), *Israel at Sixty: Rethinking the Birth of the Jewish State* (London: Routledge, 2009)

Townshend, Charles, 'In Aid of the Civil Power: Britain, Ireland and Palestine, 1916–1948,' in Daniel Marston and Carter Malkasian (eds), *Counterinsurgency in Modern Warfare* (Oxford: Osprey, 2008)

THESES (ENGLISH)

Bartels, Elizabeth, 'Policing Politics: Crime and Conflict in British Mandate Palestine (1920–1948)' (Doctoral Thesis: City University of New York, 2004)

Black, Ian, 'Zionism and the Arabs, 1936–1939' (Doctoral Thesis: University of London, 1978)

Byrne, Eileen, 'Palestine as a News-Story: Axis Initiatives and the British Response, 1936–39' (MLitt Thesis: Oxford University, 1985)

Caspi, Joshua, 'Policing the Holy Land, 1918–57: The Transition from a Colonial to a National Model of Policing and Changing Conceptions of Police Accountability' (Doctoral Thesis: City University of New York, 1991)

Clark, D. J., 'The Colonial Police and Anti-Terrorism: Bengal 1930–1936, Palestine 1937–1947, and Cyprus 1955–1959' (Doctoral Thesis: Oxford University, 1978)

Knight, J. L., 'Policing in British Palestine, 1917–1939' (Doctoral Thesis: Oxford University, 2008)

Mockaitis, Thomas, 'The British Experience in Counterinsurgency, 1919–1960' (Doctoral Thesis: University of Wisconsin-Madison, 1988)

el-Nimr, Sonia Fathi, 'The Arab Revolt in Palestine: A Study Based on Oral Sources' (Doctoral Thesis: University of Exeter, 1990)

Nitzan, Tal, 'Controlled Occupation: The Rarity of Military Rape in the Israeli–Palestinian Conflict' (Master's Thesis: Tel Aviv University, 2006)

Rahman, Abdel Wahab Ahmed Abdel, 'British Policy towards the Arab Revolt in Palestine, 1936–1939' (Doctoral Thesis: University of London, 1971)

Rossetto, Luigi, 'Maj-Gen Orde Charles Wingate and the Development of Long-Range Penetration' (Doctoral Thesis: Kansas State University, 1982)

Sanagan, Mark, 'Lightning through the Clouds: Islam, Community, and Anti-colonial Rebellion in the Life and Death of 'Izz al-Din al-Qassam, 1883–1935' (Doctoral Thesis: McGill University, 2016)

Seikaly, Sherene, 'Meatless Days: Consumption and Capitalism in Wartime Palestine, 1939–1948' (Doctoral Thesis: New York University, 2007)

Sheffer, Gabriel, 'Policy Making and British Policies towards Palestine, 1929–39' (Doctoral Thesis: Oxford University, 1970)

Shoul, Simeon, 'Soldiers, Riots, and Aid to the Civil Power in India, Egypt and Palestine, 1919–39' (Doctoral Thesis: University of London, 2006)

Smith, Charles, 'Two Revolts in Palestine: An Examination of the British Response to Arab and Jewish Rebellion, 1936–1948' (Doctoral Thesis: University of Cambridge, 1989)

Wagner, Steven, 'British Intelligence and Policy in the Palestine Mandate, 1919–39' (Doctoral Thesis: Oxford University, 2014)

Whittingham, Daniel, 'The Military Thought and Professional Career of Charles E. Callwell (1859–1928)' (Doctoral Thesis: University of London, 2013)

WEBSITES

Biographies, Palestinian Academic Society for the Study of International Affairs (Passia) at www.passia.org

Murder in Aden at http://blackwatchforums.co.uk/showthread.
   php?11583-The-%91Pitchfork-Murders%92
Oxford English Dictionary at www.oed.com
Ramleh Cemetery, Commonwealth War Graves Commission at www.cwgc.org
The Palestinian Revolution at http://learnpalestine.politics.ox.ac.uk/

FILMS

'Al-Taghriba al-Filastiniyya' ['The Palestinian Exile'] (Syria, 2004)
'Bethlehem' (Yuval Adler, 2013)
'Palestine: Promises, Rebellion and Abdication' (Thames TV, three parts,
   1977–78)
'Palestine: The First Intifada' (BBC Timewatch, 27 March 1991)
'The Gatekeepers' (Dror Moreh, 2012)
'The Law in These Parts' (Ra'anan Alexandrowicz, 2012)

Index

Made in United States
North Haven, CT
11 April 2023

35326254R00280